DIA

D0349852

J.F. Bosher
Ottawa
2007

From Telegrapher to Titan

From Telegrapher to Titan

The Life of
William C. Van Horne

VALERIE KNOWLES

THE DUNDURN GROUP
TORONTO

Copy-Editor: Andrea Pruss
Design: Jennifer Scott
Printer: Transcontinental

National Library of Canada Cataloguing in Publication Data

Knowles, Valerie
    From telegrapher to Titan : the life of William C. Van Horne/Valerie Knowles.

Includes bibliographical references and index.
ISBN 1-55002-488-4

1. Van Horne, William Cornelius, Sir, 1843-1915. 2. Canadian Pacific Railway — Presidents —
Biography. 3. Capitalists and financiers — Canada — Biography. 4. Art — Collectors and collecting
— Canada — Biography. I. Title.

HE2808.2.V3K58 2004   971.05'092   C2003-907196-0

1   2   3   4   5   08   07   06   05   04

Conseil des Arts   Canada Council   Canadä   ONTARIO ARTS COUNCIL
du Canada   for the Arts   CONSEIL DES ARTS DE L'ONTARIO

We acknowledge the support of the **Canada Council for the Arts** and the **Ontario Arts Council** for
our publishing program. We also acknowledge the financial support of the **Government of Canada**
through the **Book Publishing Industry Development Program** and **The Association for the Export
of Canadian Books,** and the **Government of Ontario** through the **Ontario Book Publishers Tax
Credit** program, and the **Ontario Media Development Corporation's Ontario Book Initiative.**

Printed and bound in Canada.⊕
Printed on recycled paper.
www.dundurn.com

Dundurn Press
8 Market Street
Suite 200
Toronto, Ontario, Canada
M5E 1M6

Dundurn Press
2250 Military Road
Tonawanda NY
U.S.A. 14150

From Telegrapher to Titan

Table of Contents

Preface

The idea for this book originated years ago with my husband, David's, observation that no adult-length biography of Sir William Van Horne had been published since 1920. This work, entitled *The Life and Work of Sir William Van Horne*, was written by Walter Vaughan, who had known Van Horne for twenty-five years and who had worked for the Canadian Pacific Railway's legal department for seven years.

The very idea of an autobiography or a biography was anathema to Sir William, who responded positively only to requests that he write a history of his beloved Canadian Pacific Railway. To this end, he arranged in the summer of 1914 for Katherine Hughes, a freelance writer who had served as the provincial archivist of Alberta, to collaborate with him in such a work. Unfortunately, the First World War intervened, and in September 1915 Van Horne died without having made a start on the projected history. Their father's death persuaded Bennie Van Horne and his sister, Addie, to continue the arrangement that Sir William had made with Katherine Hughes, but with one significant difference: she would write a biography of their father, not a history of the CPR.

Katherine Hughes collected material and produced the first draft of a book-length biography. In the summer of 1919, however, Bennie Van Horne approached Walter Vaughan with the rough, unpublished manuscript and asked him if he would write a biography of Sir William. Vaughan undertook the task, basing his work largely on the contents of Hughes's manuscript. The result is a work that captures Van Horne's larger than life personality but that is undocumented and provides virtually no details about his courtship or his relationship with family members. Since the book has long been out of print, Michael Bliss, the well-known Canadian historian, observed years ago that "a new Van Horne biography was badly needed."[1]

My husband's remark and Bliss's observation goaded me into launching this project. I was also nudged by longstanding questions I had entertained about Van Horne and his family. Sir William had been a friend of my great-grandfather, Senator Robert Mackay, and yet I knew next to nothing about the man as an individual or about his many achievements. One of these was the assembling of a magnificent art collection housed in his huge Sherbrooke Street mansion, which I often trudged past when living in Montreal. In taking on a biography of Van Horne I would find the answers to many of my questions. In embarking on such an undertaking, however, I knew that I faced daunting challenges. Not the least of these was the challenge of making my portrait of Van Horne eminently believable. He had so many talents and attracted so many accolades during his lifetime that he invites a hagiography. I only hope that I have avoided this. I also hope that I have succeeded in bringing to life the vivid personality and amazing accomplishments of a colourful and complex individual whose role in helping to knit this country together by a ribbon of steel and in promoting Canadian nationalism should be more widely known.

Valerie Knowles
Ottawa, Ontario, September 6, 2003

Acknowledgements

A s with every undertaking of this nature, this one required the help of
many people. I am especially grateful to Dr. Duncan McDowall of
Carleton University, who read every chapter and provided invaluable criticism and suggestions for improving content. I am also indebted to Dr.
Thomas White, curator of the James Jerome Hill papers, who not only
authorized the granting of a James Jerome Hill Reference Library research
grant but also provided another "set of eyes" for one of my draft chapters.
Dr. Charles Hill, curator of Canadian art at the National Gallery of
Canada, and his colleague Michael Pantazzi, curator of European art,
kindly reviewed chapters for me.

Archivists and librarians, of course, proved indispensable. I am grateful
to National Archives of Canada archivist Stephen Salmon and to several of
his colleagues for their assistance, as well as to librarians at the National
Library of Canada who helped me to find my way through the labyrinth of
research. I also owe a debt of thanks to Roger Gambrel of the Joliet Public
Library, Katie Schrimpf, reference librarian at Hayner Public Library
District in Alton, Illinois, Gregory Ames of the A.C. Kalmbach Memorial
Library, National Model Railroad Association, Rochelle Hartman of the
Bloomington Public Library, and Jason D. Stratman of the Missouri
Historical Society. Thanks also to Victor Dohar who produced the maps.

From Barrington, Illinois, researcher and author Gene V. Glendinning
furnished information about the Chicago and Alton Railroad and later
sent me a copy of his newly published history of the railway. From
Fredericton, Janet MacLellan Toole, oral history archivist, supplied information about Minister's Island and the Canadian Sardine Company.
Closer to home, architect Michael Fish made himself available for a long
interview in which he furnished particulars about the campaign to save the

11

Van Horne mansion in Montreal. In Ottawa, psychiatrist Dr. A.M. Sokolowska graciously gave of her time to help me understand Van Horne the man, while Drs. Rebecca McDermot and Eve Tomiak reviewed my descriptions of Van Horne's health problems.

Finally, I would like to thank the following: the Ontario Arts Council, which provided a welcome grant; Judith Turnbull, who edited some draft chapters; editor and author Penny Williams, who furnished valuable suggestions for organizing the second half of the manuscript; and Andrea Pruss of Dundurn Press, who copy-edited the entire manuscript and piloted it through its final stages. Patrick Macfadden, to my eternal gratitude, proofread the page proofs. A vote of thanks also goes to Wade Veinotte, who took me on a guided tour of Covenhoven, and to Henry Yates, who has championed this project from the beginning and provided whatever help he could. And last, but far from least, I would like to thank my husband, David, for suggesting the idea of a Van Horne biography and for dealing with all the computer problems associated with it. If I have missed anyone, I only hope that my gratitude is expressed adequately by means of endnotes in the book and by thanks over the phone or in correspondence.

Prologue

In the summer of 1910, as he had for so many past summers, Sir William Van Horne retired to Covenhoven, the magnificent estate in New Brunswick that he had named after his father, Cornelius, and his Dutch forebears. As was his custom, the American-born multi-millionaire, railroading genius, and Renaissance man — the "Hill and Harriman of Canada"[2] — would while away the coming months in the company of his close-knit family. That summer, Lady Van Horne (Lucy Adaline, commonly known as Addie), their unmarried daughter, Adaline (Addie), their son, Richard Benedict (Bennie), and his family preceded him in late June. Not until July 7 did the local paper, the *Beacon*, announce the arrival of the gregarious Sir William, reporting that he would be "spending a few quiet weeks with brush and canvas" at his summer home.

Like so many other prominent fixtures in Van Horne's life, Covenhoven was an extension of his own forceful personality. Given his prodigious energy, wide-ranging talents, and countless interests it could not have been otherwise. This, after all, was the man whom his CPR colleague J.H.E. Secretan, the well-known locating engineer, described as the "most versatile man" that he had ever met.[3] As it turned out, Van Horne could have found no better place than Minister's Island to showcase some of these many interests and talents.

Minister's Island, the site of Covenhoven, is in Passamaquoddy Bay, around a point of land not far from the New Brunswick town of St. Andrews. Twice a day, when the famous Fundy tide is out, the five-hundred-acre island can be approached by foot or car; visitors merely walk or drive over an exposed gravel bar, an extension of the Bar Road, which descends a long hill from Highway 127. A notice at the foot of the road states when it is safe to make the crossing to the island and the now unoc-cupied estate, which today is owned by the New Brunswick government.

Van Horne was president of the Canadian Pacific Railway when he first saw the island in the late 1880s. After his purchase of a large chunk of it, he would boast that "his island" was only one of three in the world that could be reached by a gravel bar when the tide is out. While the location of Minister's Island made Covenhoven an ideal retreat, the gregarious Sir William could not shun the outside world for long. Playing poker and swap-ping yarns with this continent's leading industrialists, statesmen, and artists had become such a large and irresistible part of his life that lengthy periods of seclusion were unthinkable. It should come as no surprise, then, that this remarkable man took great pride in showing people around Covenhoven and that he made a practice of inviting friends to the island each summer. At Van Horne's summer retreat, they would see striking evidence of their host's talents and interest in art, architecture, and stockbreeding.

In the summer of 1910, Van Horne had more time than usual to paint and to receive and entertain guests. Hitherto he had made it a practice to punctuate his sojourns at Covenhoven with trips to Montreal, New York, and Cuba to pursue his myriad business interests. But this summer was different. This summer he was determined to shed responsibilities and cur-tail his travelling. Away from the muttering noise of Montreal and the grandeur of his Montreal home, he would devote as much time as he could to painting nearby vistas, immersing himself in the details of raising stock, and enjoying the company of his family in the bracing seaside air.

This drawing back was foreshadowed by Van Horne's retirement in April from the chairmanship of the Canadian Pacific Railway, a position that he had held since 1899, when he had given up the CPR presidency. He had reached the age of sixty-seven, and his bushy moustache and well-trimmed beard were mostly white, his hair had receded to the back of his gleaming pate, and his massive body was beginning to testify to the strain that had been placed on it both by working too hard under too much pressure and by indulging himself with life's pleasures — princi-pally good food and plump Havana cigars. Only his piercing ice blue eyes, finely chiselled nose, and deep shoulders remained unaltered by time. As he reported that July to a correspondent who had invited him to participate in a new business undertaking, "I am getting too old for new ventures and am now devoting myself entirely to getting out of most of the things I am already in."[4]

Van Horne was divesting himself of directorships and turning down invitations to participate in new business schemes, but he was not giving up the presidency of the Cuba Company, the privately held company that he had established in 1900 to build the Cuba Railroad and pioneer the development of eastern Cuba. Although the railway's main line had been opened in December 1902, Sir William was still adding branch lines to it in 1910. In fact, he had just returned from an unscheduled trip to Cuba, and now, in July, he was "in a state of intense anxiety" because the Cuban Congress had failed to pass a subsidy bill that would have eased the railway's financial problems.[5]

Business worries weighed heavily on Van Horne during the months of June, July, and August, nerve-wracking weeks when he was preoccupied with finding "money to skin along with and avoid trouble."[6] Anxiety about finances, his diminishing vitality, and the approach of old age no doubt turned Van Horne's thoughts increasingly toward his family, which had always figured prominently in his life. The straight-talking financier and railroading man had a great love for all his family, but he was especially fond of his only grandson, William Cornelius Covenhoven Van Horne, the lone child of Bennie, Van Horne's only surviving son, and Bennie's wife, Edith Van Horne, née Molson. William lived with his parents in the Van Horne mansion on Montreal's Sherbrooke Street, and there, as at Covenhoven, his grandfather spoiled him beyond reason.

The summer of 1910 was no exception, and that July the doting grandfather demonstrated his love in a remarkable way. Heaving his large frame onto a stepladder in the nursery specially built for William, Van Horne painted a delightful frieze of romping Dutch children attired in traditional costume. Beside it he added the inscription, "Painted for Master William Cornelius Covenhoven Van Horne in commemoration of his third birthday, 29th July 1910, by his loving grandfather, Sir William Van Horne."

A project such as this served like no other to hold pressing Cuban concerns at bay and to conjure up for Van Horne the time when he was a young child growing up in frontier Illinois. Money had been scarce during his childhood, particularly after the death of his lawyer father, but he had been able to take comfort in the knowledge that he came from a long line of illustrious Dutch ancestors. Now, as he applied paint to the nursery wall with drumstick-sized brushes, an oversized cigar clenched between his teeth, he probably reminded himself that he was fortunate to have such a heritage. From his forebears he had inherited an abundance of energy and determination, two qualities that had served him well in his countless undertakings over the years.

Chapter One
Growing Up in Frontier Illinois

Van Horne was never indifferent to his family tree, but it was not until the final years of his exceptionally crowded life that he found time to study his lineage, and then he did so with the abundant enthusiasm that he brought to all his undertakings. Still, his plunge into genealogy did not always yield the desired results. In fact, his limited success at tracking down his ancestors led him to confess to Lady Nicholson of Stanstead Abbotts in Hertfordshire, a distant relative and one of several parties who queried him about his ancestry, that he had no accurate knowledge of any forebears who had lived prior to the eighteenth century.[7]

If family lore had it right, his branch of the Van Horne family was descended from Jan Cornelissen Van Horne, "a citizen of Amsterdam" who probably came originally from Hoorn in northern Holland.[8] A true pioneer, he had left Amsterdam for America in 1635 and had helped to found New Amsterdam (now New York City) on Manhattan Island, which the Dutch West India Company had purchased from Native chiefs in 1626. To Lady Nicholson, Van Horne jocularly reported that little was known of this adventurous ancestor other than the fact that he frequently wrote home for money. In other words, he was what Van Horne labelled a "remittance man," albeit a remittance man of some substance, as he possessed the means to purchase land and houses.

Far more was known about those ancestors who had lived in the late seventeenth century. By 1664 the English had taken possession of New Netherland, and Jan Cornelissen Van Horne's grandson, Abram, was assiduously ensuring the ascent of his family in the colony's social and economic hierarchy. As the owner of a residence on Wall Street and mills and storehouses nearby, Abram was one of the leading citizens of New York, a vibrant, pluralistic community described by one observer in 1692 as "too great a mixture of nations and English the least part."[9] Abram's already lofty status was further enhanced when he acquired a fifteen-thousand-acre land grant in the Mohawk Valley and married a daughter off to William Burnet, the English governor, whose subsequent popularity would be ascribed to his alliance with one of the colony's leading Dutch families. The Wall Street merchant's wealth was so substantial that one of his eleven children, his namesake, Abram, was able to acquire a three-thousand-acre estate just west of New York, in Hunterdown County, New Jersey. There, in 1752, the younger Abram erected a large, steep-gabled residence, known as the White House, from which the present town of Whitehouse, New Jersey, takes its name. To this country home he brought his wife, Antia Covenhoven, a member of a prominent Dutch-American family descended from Wolfert Gerritson Covenhoven, who had emigrated from Holland to New Amsterdam in 1630.[10]

Van Horne was most knowledgeable about his paternal grandfather, Abram the fourth, a clergyman who died in 1840, three years before his grandson's birth. Grandfather Abram had served as a youth in George Washington's army and had then gone on to graduate in theology from Columbia College in New York. Emulating the example of his own grandfather, Abram the second, and other Van Horne males, he too married into the Covenhoven family. In 1785 he wed Anna, daughter of wealthy Cornelius Van Covenhoven of Corroway, Keyport, New Jersey.

Grandfather Abram began his ministry at Esopus, New York, on the Hudson River, but within a few years the Dutch Reformed Church called him to Caughnawaga (now Fonda), New York. Since he was the only preacher in a large circuit, he was required to perform pastoral duties throughout a wide area in central New York State. Nevertheless, during his ministry in Caughnawaga, Abram succeeded in organizing many churches throughout the United States as well as two in Canada.[11] In the thirty-eight years that he served in Caughnawaga he was noted not only for his energy but also for his great ability, his extensive knowledge, and his private philanthropy.

Although his ministry covered a large area and his salary and fees were lamentably small, "the Dominie," as he was affectionately called (in his later years he was known as "the old Dominie"), managed to maintain himself, his wife, and their nine children in comfort thanks to substantial legacies that both he and his wife had received from their respective fathers. With this generous assistance, the family was able to support as many as twenty slaves and to continue the Van Horne and Covenhoven clans' tradition of abundant hospitality. Nobody contributed more to this tradition than Abram, who became renowned throughout the state as a raconteur and a delightful host and companion.

It was into this highly regarded, socially prominent family that Van Horne's father, Cornelius Covenhoven, was born in 1794. Cornelius grew up in Caughnawaga and then attended Union College, a liberal arts college for men in Schenectady, New York. At Union he was known for his indomitable will, his quick intelligence, and his jokes. The Dominie had entertained high hopes that of his four sons, all of whom attended Union College, Cornelius would be the one to enter the ministry, but the high-spirited lad had other plans. In 1813, when he was only nineteen, Cornelius married Elizabeth Vedder, a daughter of Colonel John Vedder of Schenectady, and the following year, after graduating from Union, he embarked on law studies.

About the time that he began his law practice, Cornelius became active in the Democratic Party of New York State, lending his support to Martin Van Buren, a fellow lawyer of Dutch descent and an eminently skilful politician known as "The Little Magician," who would become the eighth president of the United States at the beginning of the financial panic of 1837. Cornelius's successful law practice and his close friendship with the non-annexationist Van Buren augured well for his professional and political prospects on the eastern seaboard. In 1832, however, like thousands of other restless Yankees in that same decade, the intrepid young man turned his back on the sophisticated community that he had known and the relative security that it offered and struck out for the American Midwest. In search of fortune and hoping to find the freedom of a less restrictive society, he abandoned many of the fixtures that had figured in his earlier life.

With the blessing of his father, Cornelius uprooted his family and took them by covered wagon to the frontier state of Illinois, destined to become the fastest-growing territory in the world in the middle of the nineteenth century.[12] After undergoing the usual vicissitudes of the trail, the family chose a spot in the north of the state, in what would become known as New Lenox Township. There, they cleared land and constructed a cabin, but two years later they moved to nearby Frankfort Township, an area that consisted for the most part of rolling prairie. The family settled beside Hickory Creek, about a mile west of the town of Frankfort, identified on William Cornelius Van Horne's tombstone as his birthplace. Their new home was carved out of the wilderness, on land that would be surveyed for the town of Chelsea in 1848–49. Chelsea does not appear on a present-day map of Illinois because its inhabitants abandoned it for Frankfort, which can be found on today's maps, after that settlement acquired a new railway line in the 1850s. Now a town of some seven thousand people, it nestles in the southwest suburbs of sprawling Chicago. Back in the 1830s, however, it was a mere hamlet in a part of Illinois so sparsely populated that the nearest centre of any size, Chicago, was only a village almost lost in a sea of mud.

In this thinly settled part of what would become Will County, Cornelius Van Horne became a respected community leader noted for his great force of character, his shrewdness, and his "bold, outspoken way of giving vent to his honest convictions."[13] This bluntness, a trait inherited by his son, William, so impressed contemporaries that a nineteenth-century history of Will County includes a lengthy and colourful story about Cornelius. Evidently, an elderly man who was passing through the area on foot in 1840 was discovered in an old blacksmith shop suffering from a "fit." After being taken to the house of "one McLaughlin," he recovered sufficiently to resume his journey to Pennsylvania, his home state. Some days later he was found in another fit, this time near "Skunk's Grove." On this occasion his mutterings indicated that he had been robbed, and, indeed, a search of his person revealed that a considerable sum of money that he had been carrying earlier was gone. The McLaughlins immediately became the prime suspects, and Cornelius did not hesitate to label them guilty. Before their guilt or innocence could be proven, however, the transient died.

The case was taken before a grand jury, and McLaughlin's son was charged. He was released on bail before his court appearance, but when the time came for him to make that appearance he failed to show up. Cornelius Van Horne claimed that the son had run away to avoid the trial, while the McLaughlins asserted that members of the Van Horne family had robbed the old man and then killed young McLaughlin to prevent his case from coming to trial and the truth being revealed. Tensions rose steadily in the community as McLaughlin senior and some sympathetic neighbours searched for the ostensibly lost son. In due course a search party found a wagon track running from "one of the Van Hornes" (Cornelius had two brothers who lived nearby) to a millpond. The pond was dragged, and the body of a man in an advanced state of decay, minus some teeth, was discovered. Despite glaring discrepancies in the evidence, a coroner's jury found the body to be that of young McLaughlin, and while no charge was brought against anyone, McLaughlin senior swore out a warrant and had Van Horne arrested. In the heat and excitement of the day many were ready to hang Cornelius without the benefit of a proper trial. Eventually, however, it occurred to somebody that the transient's grave should be searched. This was done and the coffin found to be empty. Meanwhile, incoming mail at the post office was being carefully monitored, and when an envelope addressed to McLaughlin senior was opened it was found to contain a letter from his son. The tide of public opinion had begun to swing in Van Horne's favour when the empty grave came to light; with this latest development, those who had been so eager to hang Cornelius were now even more eager to hang McLaughlin and his wife.[14] Had the grave not been revealed as tenantless, Cornelius might not have lived to raise another family and continue his good work in the community.

Before these dramatic events unfolded, the young lawyer had served as the first schoolteacher in the area, conducting classes in the winter of 1832–33 in a log cabin beside Hickory Creek. He had also become Will County's first postmaster and justice of the peace. However, Cornelius's early years in Illinois were also scarred by tragedy. A daughter, Margaret Catherine, died in infancy, and in 1838 his wife, Elizabeth, passed away, leaving him with four young children who were sent to live with relatives or friends. To add to his burden, in the winter of 1839–40, while he was on business in the state capital, Springfield, some 150 miles away, the family home was "consumed by fire."[15]

After the blaze, which claimed his homestead, barns, books, and other personal effects, Cornelius Van Horne set about rebuilding a home. In this he was aided by his brother Matthew, a prosperous farmer who had settled nearby in 1833 with another brother, William. It was to this log house that he brought his second wife, Mary Minier Richards, in 1842.[16] The woman who would become chatelaine of his new home and the revered mother of William Van Horne was the daughter of a Pennsylvanian of French origin, Margaret Minier, and an American of German descent who had emigrated to the colonies as a young man and settled in Philadelphia.

William Cornelius Van Horne was born on February 3, 1843, the first child of this second marriage. Over an eight-year period he would be joined by four siblings: Augustus Charles in 1844, Elizabeth in 1846, Theodore in 1848, and Mary in 1852. Interestingly, both of William's brothers would also take up a railway career, but neither would rise to such lofty heights as the eldest son, who, as first-born, would come to exhibit many of the characteristics that psychologists associate with the oldest child in a family, namely, natural leadership, reliability, conscientiousness, and a striving for perfection.

For a person whose destiny would be linked with railways, the 1840s was an exciting and significant period in which to be born. This was the decade that witnessed a boom in railway construction, the perfection of the technology of railway transportation, and the tentative beginnings of the railway's metamorphosis into what noted American business historian Alfred Chandler, Jr. has called "the first modern business."[17] In the enormity of their impact on American business and society, these developments would perhaps compare favourably with the all-pervasive influence of the Internet on present-day North American business and society.

The railway construction boom got underway in the late 1840s, when William Cornelius Van Horne was still a young boy, and continued until the severe economic depression of the 1870s. During this orgy of railway building, particularly in the pre–Civil War years, small towns everywhere frantically sought a railway, believing that its arrival would ensure them life and prosperity.[18] Determined to guarantee their town's salvation, some local citizenry all but sold their souls to raise the money necessary to build a bridge or finance the construction of a line so that a train would come through their community.

In the first explosion of railway construction, the fewer than three thousand miles of track that existed in 1840 had more than tripled to approximately nine thousand miles by 1850. Railway construction fever continued to grip the nation in the 1850s; in that decade, work gangs built another twenty-one thousand miles of track and provided the country east of the Mississippi River with its basic overland transportation network. In an equally dramatic and almost simultaneous development, moves were made to complete the great intersectional trunk lines connecting East and West (the Baltimore and Ohio, the Erie, and the New York Central) and to lay down a new transportation network in the old Northwest.[19]

As track was laid across the continent, the technology of railway transportation improved rapidly. When Van Horne was still a mere tyke, railway technology ushered in such notable advances as the development of uniform methods of construction, tunnelling, grading, and bridging as well as the widespread adoption of the iron "T" rail. By the close of the 1840s, the locomotive had acquired such familiar features as the sandbox, leading swivel trucks, and equalized drivers; passenger cars, moreover, had become "long cars" capable of transporting sixty people.[20]

All these developments culminated in a form of fast, all-weather transportation, but to ensure that they could operate successfully, railways had to become trailblazers with respect to organization and management. To move sizeable numbers of people and goods safely, efficiently, and reliably over large distances, and to maintain the structures necessary to do this, railways developed a large internal organizational structure with carefully defined lines of authority, responsibility, and communication between the central office, departmental headquarters, and field units. Salaried managers were employed in the central office to supervise functional activities over an extensive geographical area. Their work in turn was supervised, evaluated, and coordinated by an administrative cadre of middle and top managers who reported to a board of directors.[21] By the time the Civil War erupted, salaried middle and top railway managers — the nation's first modern managerial class — had developed organizational and accounting methods that enabled their enterprises to coordinate and monitor a high volume of freight and passenger traffic that moved at a speed, and with a regularity, hitherto unknown.

The demands of railway building led inevitably to fundamental changes in the nation's financial and construction sectors. Because railway construction required far larger quantities of capital than canal construction, railway companies in the United States became the first private business enterprises to obtain capital from outside their own regions. Hitherto, funds for railway construction had been raised from farmers, manufacturers, and merchants living alongside the road, or from European money markets, but with the explosion in railway building, funds-seekers journeyed with increasing frequency to New York City to obtain the necessary capital. The rapid spread of railways across the continent thus contributed in no small way to the centralization of the capital market in New York. Likewise, the railways helped to transform the construction trade by directing jobs into the hands of large contractors that could handle all aspects of construction and supply, including the provision of such necessary equipment as locomotives and rolling stock.

The period at the time of Van Horne's birth also saw the emergence of another marvel of communication that was destined to influence his life. In 1843, Congress voted to pay Samuel Morse to build the first telegraph line in the United States, from Baltimore to Washington. The following year Morse sent the first message on this line. Soon the telegraph was sending instantaneous messages along copper wires that ran alongside the railway lines, which would shortly span the American continent. Like the railway, the telegraph would help to shrink distance and create a new sense of community. It would also help to further the careers of those who became proficient in its technology, people like the young boy who grew up in Chelsea and Joliet, Illinois.

Before the Van Horne family moved to Joliet, some fourteen miles away, young William's world was defined by the family homestead and its immediate surroundings in Chelsea. His home, a spacious log house sheltered by trees, was built on the brow of a hill overlooking a valley and the Sauk Trail, along which the wagons of immigrants crawled westward to the famed Oregon Trail, a popular route to the Pacific coast. In the woods, not far from the house, was a stable and other log outbuildings, while nestled in the valley, beside Hickory Creek, was a largely inactive sawmill. It saw little use because Cornelius did not cultivate his lands extensively. Trained as a lawyer, not as a farmer, he eked out a living by dabbling in milling and farming while he waited for a clientele to develop. Occasionally he would ride to the courthouse at Springfield to settle claims and land titles. There, he might engage in animated political discussion with fellow lawyers Abraham Lincoln, who had been practising law in Springfield since ending his single term in Congress, and Stephen Douglas, the leading Democrat in Illinois and Lincoln's political rival.

When he was six years of age, young William Van Horne began attending school. Weather permitting, he would trudge off to the small schoolhouse, located a mile or two from his home, hoping fervently that he would not encounter one of the wolves that shared the woods with a handful of humans. Wolves loomed large in his fecund, childish imagination. Indeed, his fear of the beasts was so great that he began consuming large quantities of pepper after hearing his father say that "the Mexicans used so much pepper that the wolves wouldn't eat them."[22]

It was while exploring the nearby woods and fields that Van Horne developed his remarkable curiosity and powers of observation. These rambles sowed the seeds for two hobbies that would become lifelong passions — paleontology and art. Lacking toys for amusement, the youngster took to collecting pebbles from the rivulet that flowed at the base of the hill on which the family home stood. One day, when he was still very young, he discovered, among some little nests of pebbles in that stream, a small, thin piece of shiny black stone. He eagerly picked up this promising new addition to his stockpile of treasures, but to his great chagrin the stone became a lacklustre grey while drying in his hand. Nevertheless, he carried it home to his mother, hoping that she could restore its former colour for him. While this resourceful and sympathetic woman could not do that, she could do something better.[23]

Mary Van Horne, in fact, opened up a whole new world for her son when she demonstrated that his stone, a piece of slate, could be used to make marks on another piece of slate. Henceforth the excited youngster scratched on slate at every opportunity. His first attempts at reproducing likenesses were unsuccessful, but soon he was able to execute crude drawings of children, dogs, and horses. When the soft slate wore out and he could not find any more to replace it, he resorted to drawing on the whitewashed walls of the family home, encouraged by his mother. Mary Van

Horne had a gift for art and was evidently prepared to sanction deface-
ment of the homestead's walls in the interests of her son's artistic development. The boy's father aided and abetted the cause by bringing chalks and
pencils from Joliet, and before long young William had covered every wall
in the house, as high as his small arm could reach, with drawings.[24]
Without realizing it, he had taken the first steps on the road to becoming
a proficient amateur artist.

Van Horne's first glimpse of the exciting and mysterious world that lay
outside his valley occurred when, at the age of seven, he was taken to Joliet,
the small town that straddled both banks of the Des Plaines River, some thir-
ty-seven miles southwest of Chicago. On this trip, his first to the seat of Will
County, the awestruck child saw more houses than he could possibly have
imagined, two-storey dwellings so impressive to him that he would retain
vivid recollections of them late in life. Such a tantalizing glimpse of a more
sophisticated society and a less constricted lifestyle must have made him
long for the exciting life offered by an urban centre. If such was the case, the
remedy was not long in coming. The following year, 1851, Cornelius Van
Horne, repudiating his marginal existence in Chelsea and no doubt hoping
to obtain better schooling for his children, moved his family to Joliet. With
this move, young William's horizons expanded dramatically.

A flourishing town of some two thousand inhabitants, situated in a
rich agricultural area that also boasted large coal and limestone deposits,
Joliet was fast attracting settlers and cultivating an air of prosperity. It not
only had a school, a church, a courthouse, and shops, but it also boasted
the National Hotel, a Bluff Street landmark. This unique hotel had fresh
spring water in its basement kitchen as well as a bell system consisting of
wires that ran from the rooms to the office, where they were attached to
bells on springs.[25] After the nearby Illinois-Michigan canal opened in
1848, the hotel provided accommodation for the thousands of passengers
carried by the boats that plied the canal's waters. Then, when the Chicago,
Rock Island and Pacific Railroad entered Joliet in 1852, the hostelry began
shuttling train passengers from its front door to the station, using a bright
yellow bus drawn by a team of grey horses.

As soon as Van Horne's father had resumed his law practice and settled his family into their new home on the open prairie at the southeast
corner of Sherman Street and Third Avenue, he began to involve himself
in community affairs.[26] For the public-spirited and well-educated
Cornelius it was an exciting time to take the plunge into municipal politics. Joliet was then entering a significant period in its development, a
highlight being its incorporation as a city. In June 1852, the Illinois gen-

eral assembly passed the enabling act to establish the city of Joliet, and the following month local voters approved the new city charter. In the city's first election, two councilmen were chosen from each of the five wards and Cornelius Van Horne was elected mayor.[27] With his new status, it seemed that the better life he had hoped for was fast becoming a reality.

While his father carried out his mayoral duties, served as justice of the peace for Joliet and Will County (a position that he assumed by virtue of holding the office of mayor), and practised law, young William eagerly explored Joliet and its park-like environs on the banks of the Des Plaines River. The boy revelled in the new opportunities presented for collecting rocks, for, like so many other Victorians, he had become a zealous naturalist, bent on collecting and describing things from nature. One day, after noting some unusual markings on a chunk of rock, he chipped away at the surface with a stone. After removing the surrounding edges, he discovered a well-defined and symmetrical figure beneath, which he labelled "a worm-in-the-rock." This became his first treasure, and, as might be expected of such a cherished possession, it invested him with a sense of increased importance both in his own mind and in the minds of those schoolmates to whom he showed it. Henceforth he searched for new specimens with even more zeal.

Nothing would shake Van Horne's later conviction that every boy should take up a hobby that involved a collection of some sort. He observed to a friend, perhaps when contemplating the role that collecting can play in preparing the mind for complex management:

> The best thing a boy can do is to begin to collect. Let him collect something — I don't care what it is — and you will find he begins to notice, and from noticing he begins to classify and arrange. Interest develops, and wherever he goes there is nothing connected with his collection about which he is not keenly interested. The real education for a boy is simply a matter of impressions. These cannot be selected for him, but they colour the whole of his life.[28]

If the new school that Van Horne attended in Joliet was typical of its time, he would have been drilled in the venerated "3 Rs," but little more. Despite the school's most likely stultifying routine and cold, inflexible system of punishment, the young boy succeeded in mastering the basics. He also became an avid reader. In fact, by ten years of age he was reading every book that he could lay his hands on, soaking up knowledge like a sponge.[29] His love of books even dictated even his choice of Sunday school. He and his brother

Augustus had at first gone to Sunday school at St. John's Universalist Church, which their mother attended. Van Horne, however, deserted the Universalist Sunday school for its Methodist counterpart when he discovered that the Methodist Sunday school had "the better books." It was thus partly because of his voracious appetite for reading that Van Horne was exposed to the teachings of Methodism, whose demand for self-denial, personal holiness, and careful stewardship helped to inspire the lives of well-known capitalists, such as Sir Joseph Flavelle, one of early twentieth century Canada's most respected businessmen and philanthropists.[30] If Methodism's teachings helped Flavelle in his meteoric rise from humble origins to celebrated businessman and financier, they most probably exerted some influence on young Van Horne, even though he would never express an interest in organized religion and, in fact, would shun church attendance as an adult.

In July 1854, when he was only eleven, Van Horne's world was shattered by his father's sudden death from cholera, then sweeping the state. Although sorrow comes to all of us, it comes, as Abraham Lincoln expressed it, "with bitterest agony" to the young, "because it takes them unawares."[31] Van Horne has left no description of how his father's death affected him personally, but we can speculate that his sense of loss was profound and that on a deeper level it may have been partly responsible for the bouts of melancholy that would afflict him in the years just before his marriage.

Cornelius Van Horne left a good name, and, in his son's words, "a lot of accounts payable and some bad accounts receivable." In an undated draft letter to his beloved grandson, William, Van Horne penned some poignant recollections of his beloved father:

> He was a lawyer who seldom took fees. I can remember him refusing payment for services not once but many times, when I felt sure that he had not a penny in his pocket. I could not understand it then, and I am not quite sure that I do now, but this occurred in a newly settled country where all were poor alike, and my father, perhaps, felt himself richer than the others because of having a mortgaged roof, while most of the others had hardly any roof at all.[32]

The death of the family's principal provider was a devastating blow, especially as William, the oldest of the five children, was still of school age. William's resourceful and courageous mother, however, managed to keep "bread," usually hominy, on the table by taking in sewing and by selling produce from her garden. As an economy measure, Augustus, the elder of Van Horne's two brothers, was sent to live with the family of kindly "Uncle William Gouger," who had been Cornelius's first neighbour in Illinois. Notwithstanding such measures, the family was still forced to move from their comfortable home with spacious grounds to a small cottage. With his father's untimely death, young Van Horne had driven home to him the lesson that life is a struggle and his progress through it would depend to a considerable extent on his own efforts.

In an attempt to rescue the family income from subsistence levels, young William contributed small sums of money that he earned out of school hours. Some of these earnings came from delivering telegraph messages for Joliet's telegraph operators. While waiting for the messages he would sit in the telegraph office, listening to the tapping instrument and watching the tape slowly unwind as it spelled out a message in dots and dashes. Although the youngster could not have predicted it at the time, the knowledge of telegraphy that he picked up in this desultory fashion would pay big dividends when he was older. So would some of the other things that he was exposed to in the telegraph office: little gems of wisdom, the practice of yarn-swapping, and the game of poker, which he would later define as "not a game but an education." Late in life he would remark in reference to his telegraph work, "I was put on the station service and as I was very young, the men didn't mind my asking questions, and what is more, they answered them and told me things."[33] In this account Van Horne makes no mention of the role that telegraphy itself played in broadening his horizons, but there is little doubt that this new technology subtly, but effectively, gave the youngster a sense of the world beyond Joliet and opened up new vistas for him.

Chopping wood also brought in some sorely needed money. Van Horne, with his later penchant for hyperbole, would claim that he had never worked since he had split logs at the age of ten. In the intervening years he had "only enjoyed."[34] Certainly he brought a boyish enthusiasm and a conspicuous facility to nearly everything that he undertook, but can it be said that he always enjoyed his work? The answer has to be no. Still, it is interesting to note that he regarded woodcutting as the only "real" work that he had ever done because it was a task that he detested.

When he was thirteen, Van Horne parlayed his artistic skills into a profitable business. Inspired by illustrations in back issues of *Harper's Magazine*, he produced an impressive panorama of London's famous exhibition hall, the Crystal Palace, which was then showcasing the latest marvels produced by industry, technology, and science in an age of dramatic technological progress. The panorama, which showed London's spires and towers in the background, was painted on the back of a large roll of wallpaper that was then mounted on rollers. William exhibited the finished product in a tent on a street corner "under the auspices of W.C. Van Horne, Proprietor; H.C. Knowlton, Secretary and Treasurer; Henry E. Lowe, Business Manager." While his assistants slowly unrolled the panorama by means of a crank, Van Horne delivered a travelogue that he had written himself. The performance was so impressive that it attracted many adults, thereby allowing the young entrepreneur and his fellow syndicate members to increase the admission fee.[35]

Van Horne's formal education continued until his fourteenth year. Like so many of today's so-called underachievers, he had a lively intelligence and a retentive memory but was easily bored in the classroom. Certain subjects held little interest for him and so, in their study, he rarely exerted himself. By contrast, he loved reading and making caricatures of his teachers and comrades. Brawling in the schoolyard was another favourite pursuit. Extremely pugnacious, he would take on all comers and usually win. On one of the few occasions when he lost it was to a youngster from out of town. That sound thrashing seriously tarnished his reputation for toughness, but Van Horne quickly re-established his dominance by fighting every boy who volunteered for combat. Schoolyard brawls came to an end for Van Horne only after he was caught caricaturing the school principal. The ensuing punishment was so severe that, though he was just thirteen, he chose never to return to the classroom. By then, however, he had acquired quite a good education by the minimal standards of the day. He could read, write, and reason deftly; but even more important, he had an innate intelligence and a love of learning.

The abrupt end of his formal schooling did not spell an end to Van Horne's education. To satisfy his hunger for information, he continued to read voraciously. One day, while visiting the home of a playmate, Augustus Howk, he found an illustrated history of Jefferson County, New York, lying on the parlour table.[36] While flipping through it, he was amazed to discover a rendition of his own precious fossil in a chapter on geology. Van Horne could not contain his excitement as he eagerly devoured the chapter. All thought of going fishing evaporated instantly and the boys instead set off for a nearby quarry to search for fossils. Henceforth Van Horne, accompanied by Howk, spent Sundays tramping every quarry, creek, and riverbed in the neighbourhood in search of new finds. One day a state geologist who was visiting Joliet inquired if there were any interesting fossils to be found in the area. He was told about two boys who were forever collecting rocks, though nobody knew why. Intrigued, the geologist sought out Van Horne and his friend. So impressed was he with their rock collections that he told an uncle of Howk's about the boys' enterprise and industry. The uncle thereupon sent his nephew a copy of Hitchcock's book on geology.[37]

For young William, the now impassioned rock collector, this book became the most desired object in his life. In later years he would recall, "I never envied anyone as I envied that boy. I would have sold all my chances in life and thrown in my soul too to have had it. Sometimes I was allowed to peep at it if I had washed my hands."[38] Finally, fortune came to his aid. When he learned that the Howk family was planning a visit to New York, Van Horne persuaded his young friend to lend him the book for the duration of the family's absence from Joliet. In return, Van Horne would surrender all the duplicate fossils in his collection.

With the book in his possession, Van Horne avoided the Howks before their departure, not wanting to run the risk of having the newly cemented deal revoked. On the first night that he had the book, and for many successive nights, after his day's work he pored over the volume, hoping to commit it to memory. When this seemed too impossible a task, he conceived the idea of reproducing the book and thereby making it his own. In the past he had always turned over all his earnings from carrying telegraph messages to his mother. He now decided to use a twenty-five-cent tip from a grateful telegram recipient to purchase the foolscap necessary to copy the book. Armed with a ream of paper, he spent hours each night hunched over the volume in the small, candle-lit attic that served as his bedroom. The job of copying Hitchcock's *Elements of Geology* proceeded over five weeks, Van Horne often working through most of the night to reproduce with great care the index and every page, illustration, and note. Referring to this Herculean effort, he would later say, "The copying of that book did great things for me. It taught me how much could be accomplished by application; it improved my handwriting; it taught me the construction of English sentences; and it helped my drawing materially. And I never had to refer to the book again."[39]

At first glance it would appear that Van Horne's all-consuming thirst for knowledge lay behind his determination to copy this book. His motivation, however, probably had more to do with his irrepressibly competitive personality than with anything else. Even at this young age he could not resist the temptation to demonstrate his prowess and to confound others, two traits that would accompany him throughout life.

The youngster was now seriously studying telegraphy at the city office, for he realized that with his school days behind him he had to master a trade that would provide him with full-time employment. He perhaps also realized that mastery of this new and exciting technology could open career doors for him. In any event, when Abraham Lincoln was campaigning in the 1856 presidential contest, young William had developed his telegraph operator skills to the point where he could help to send a message describing Lincoln's reception in Joliet.

Practically no correspondence remains from this period in Van Horne's life, but one letter that has survived is both revealing and prophetic. Written by a railroading man who had obviously recognized the precocious teenager's great potential and who believed in self-help rhetoric, it reads:

> My dear young friend, yours of a few days since came duly to hand and we were glad to hear from you and that you are doing so well ... You are young now [Van Horne was thirteen at the time of writing] and by proper conduct can grow up to be a good man if not a great one. Your destiny mostly lies in your own hands. What you will at your age by perseverance and determination you can greatly accomplish. So aim high. What is this life without accomplishing some great good which altho you do not directly see it extends far and wide. Have some grand and glorious object in view and not live as some live to eat drink and sleep. If you can, earn enough by telegraphing to give you a good schooling. I noticed while in Joliet you had a great tast [sic] for reading and study and I think it a pity you should not have a chance of improving it. ...[40]

Van Horne was only fourteen when the Joliet telegraph operator found employment for him as a telegrapher with the celebrated Illinois Central Railroad Company, a line destined to play a remarkable role in converting much of unoccupied Illinois into a prosperous, settled area. Chartered by the state, this north-south line ran the length of Illinois and was shaped much like a thin wishbone, with one section running south from Chicago and a second extending south from Dunleith, the two lines converging at Centralia and continuing down to Cairo at the confluence of the Mississippi and Ohio Rivers. Although still in its infancy when Van Horne joined it, the company had already chalked up two distinctions: it was the first railway company to receive a federal land grant — 2,595,133 acres of unused, unoccupied, potentially productive federal lands in Illinois — and in 1856, five years after its founding, it had completed 700 miles of track to make it the single longest railway in the world.[41]

The teenager enjoyed the work assigned to him in the mechanical superintendent's office, located in the railway's Weldon shops in Chicago. Nevertheless, his new telegrapher's job did not claim his undivided attention. Whether it was to get himself noticed by the adults around him or to one-up his colleagues, or perhaps both, Van Horne resorted to playing practical jokes. On one occasion he ran a ground wire from the storage battery to a steel plate in the rail yard. Then he amused himself by watching the contortions of those men unfortunate enough to step on it. The joke miscarried when S.J. Hayes, the superintendent, came along the cinder path. Before Van Horne recognized him and could turn off the "juice," Hayes received a shock. Unlike the yardsmen, this railwayman had sufficient knowledge of the principles of electricity to realize what was up. In no time at all, Hayes was in the perpetrator's office, where Van Horne promptly, if somewhat reluctantly, confessed that he was the culprit. The irate superintendent fired him on the spot.[42] With this abrupt dismissal, the frightened prankster returned to Joliet, a chastened and more mature young man.

That autumn, through the good offices of his young friend Henry Knowlton, Van Horne obtained employment as a messenger and freight-checker on the "Cut-Off," a line forty-five miles long that ran from Joliet to Lake Junction, Indiana, where it connected with the Michigan Central. Built by the Joliet and Northern Indiana, the Cut-Off had been opened to traffic in May 1855, at which time it was leased to the Michigan Central, thereby becoming the Joliet division of that railway. It was popularly known as the Cut-Off because it bypassed Chicago.[43]

The recent entry of the Chicago, Rock Island and Pacific Railroad and the Michigan Central Railroad into Joliet had done much to boost the city's economic fortunes and make it a thriving centre. As a result, the Cut-Off was a busy line, and Van Horne was kept well occupied checking freight shipments and doing errands for the superintendent. In the course of these duties he frequently came into contact with local businessmen, whom he invariably impressed with his industriousness and shrewd intelligence. A Captain Ellwood met Van Horne in these early years and remarked in 1916, "I remember him in 1854, a thoughtful little fellow, so frail I thought he would never be strong. But when I came back from the military academy in France a few years later he astonished me. He looked stronger — healthy even, and he was already being talked about in Joliet as an unusual young fellow."[44] By the time he was fourteen Van Horne was starting to make a name for himself.

After holding his new position for only a few months, Van Horne convinced the assistant superintendent, Henry Knowlton's father, that the Cut-Off should have an independent telegraph line and that he should be allowed to operate it. The line duly installed, the teenager immersed himself in his new duties as telegrapher. Of all the messages that he received and relayed during this period probably none made more of an impression on him than an account, in 1858, of one of the debates between Lincoln and Douglas, adversaries in a bitterly fought Senate race. Lincoln's attempt in this legendary series of debates to identify his opponent with a pro-slavery conspiracy and Douglas's branding of Lincoln as a Black Republican whose abolitionist doctrines would destroy the Union and flood Illinois with "degenerate" black people stirred not only people in Illinois but also Americans across the country.

Now that he had continuous access to the telegraph, Van Horne was able to perfect his skills to the point where he could discard the use of the tape and decipher incoming messages by merely listening to the instrument's clicks and clacks. According to his biographer, Walter Vaughan, he was the first operator in his particular district and among the first in the country to master this feat.[45] And while he was chalking up these distinctions the new technology was enabling him to acquire a world view.

Van Horne's duties as a telegrapher did not claim all his attention. Hitherto he had been familiar with the storehouse, but now he began to familiarize himself with other operations on the Cut-Off. Slipping into the draughtsman's office at lunch hour and at night, he began to make drawings of illustrations in the draughtsman's books. This attracted the admiration of the draughtsman, who was especially impressed with the young man's skill in reproducing lettering. The inquisitive and indefatigable youngster also began to understudy the duties of the accountant, the cashier, the time-keeper, and the other men around him, all managers with clearly defined responsibilities, for the railway had to be managed as no other business before had been. He did all this while deliberately cultivating his already remarkable memory. Whenever he could spare the time he would challenge those around him to memory contests in which the contestants would attempt to memorize the numbers on the cars of long trains that passed through the yards. Van Horne was usually the victor.

Up to this point Van Horne's boundless energy and ambition had been largely unfocused; he had just wanted to acquire as many railroading skills as he could. When he was eighteen, however, this lack of direction quickly gave way to a clearly defined ambition. The trigger was a visit paid by the Michigan Central's general superintendent, the railway's chief executive, to the Cut-Off. It had not been the practice of the company's general officers to visit the Cut-Off, so when the general superintendent arrived everybody from the assistant superintendent down was on hand to greet him. Van Horne watched transfixed as a portly gentleman in a closely buttoned linen duster swung down from his private car and came forward to meet the lesser mortals waiting to receive him. When the visitor was taken to look over the buildings and machinery, the teenager seized the opportunity to walk around the private car. Peering in, he saw luxurious easy chairs and a dining room table covered with gleaming white linen and decorated with flowers.[46] This opulent spectacle and the ceremony surrounding the arrival of the general superintendent crystallized Van Horne's career goal. As he reported many years later to his beloved grandson, "I found myself wondering if even I might not somehow become a General Superintendent and travel in a private car. The glories of it, the pride of it, the salary pertaining to it, and all that moved me deeply, and I made up my mind then and there that I would reach it."[47]

Having made himself this promise, that he would manage a railway system rather than create one, Van Horne set out with single-minded determination to meet his objective, convinced that "he who makes an ambitious time-table is likely to try to run by it."[48] In the belief that a general superintendent must know everything about a railway, the young man jettisoned any holiday time owed him and worked nights and Sundays to inform himself about the details of every department. Without neglecting his own tasks, he haunted the repair shops in order to become familiar with tools, machinery, and methods. He learned about locomotives and cars, and badgered the roadmaster for details about line repairs and so forth. Any bit of knowledge that would bring him closer to his goal he eagerly devoured.

With the rapid expansion of the nation's rail network, these were certainly exciting years in which to be launching a career in railroading. The United States, boasting nine thousand miles of rail in 1850, had led the world, but this accomplishment paled in comparison to the twenty-one thousand miles that were laid between 1850 and 1860 and that provided the country in 1860 with a larger rail network than all existing networks in the rest of the world combined.[49] The growth rate of construction across the nation was uneven, however. In New England, because promoters had overextended themselves in the 1840s, the rate of increase was under 50 percent. By contrast, the mid-Atlantic saw a doubling of railway mileage and the South more than a quadrupling. The most spectacular growth occurred in Van Horne's part of the world, the old Northwest, where railway mileage increased about eightfold during the decade.

Railway growth was so dramatic in Illinois that by 1860 that state was surpassed only by Ohio in railway mileage.[50] The resulting transformation of the countryside and the wonders wrought by this new form of transportation excited the imagination of many an aspiring entrepreneur. Van Horne's future brother-in-law, young Tyrus Hurd, was so struck by what he was witnessing that he wrote in 1857, "Even now may be heard the strokes of the artesans hammers or the shrill whistle of the ponderous engine as it whirrs along over the iron belts that connect the distant parts of that great state."[51]

While the railway revolution was making itself felt, the telegraph, that other invention to which Van Horne's life was closely tied, was shrinking the world with its form of fast, regular, and dependable communication. Both of these marvels would profoundly alter American life, but none more so than the railway.

Belching smoke from their large funnel-shaped smoke stacks and showering sparks, steam locomotives roared through the countryside, knitting towns and cities closer together, opening up wilderness areas, and providing the fast, regular, and dependable transportation so essential to high-volume production and distribution. In the process, society was radically changed. Before 1840, country towns were quiet, uneventful places. Most, if not all, of them were inhabited by a class of staid, solid men — men of property but few ideas. By the end of the decade this hereditary class of men had given way to a new class of businessmen who would direct things during the second half of the century. The railways, more than anything else, helped to bring this class, the managerial class, into being.

With the expansion of the American network in the 1850s came an increase in investment in the industry, from $300 million to $1.15 billion by 1860.[52] In 1850, only two American railroads were capitalized at over $10 million, while by the middle of the decade at least ten had a greater capitalization. Five, in fact, had issued over $19 million worth of bonds and stock. Likewise, the number of employees and the volume of passengers and freight carried increased dramatically.

In response to these developments, the railways began to pioneer new methods of corporate management. Railroaders were innovators not necessarily because they were more imaginative, perceptive, or energetic but simply because they were the first managers to face the challenge of having to handle large numbers of employees and sizeable amounts of materials and money within a single business unit.[53] As a result, modern business administration first appeared in the United States between 1849 and 1855.

While Illinois and the rest of the country were undergoing this great transformation, Van Horne was immersing himself in his career, but as dedicated to the job as he was, he still found time to pursue his interest in paleontology, an area of study that, like railway management, makes extensive use of categorization. In addition to reading widely on the subject, Van Horne tramped the countryside around Joliet in search of new specimens. After the possibilities in this fossil-rich area had been exhausted, he and some like-minded companions headed further afield, to the Kankakee River, where they discovered new fossils. Van Horne's collection would eventually boast nine previously unclassified specimens; these would be named after him and would bear the descriptive suffix "Van Hornei" in paleontological encyclopedias.[54]

Inspired by the establishment of the Illinois Natural History Society at Bloomington, Illinois, Van Horne and his comrades founded the Agassiz Club of Joliet in the winter of 1859. They installed the club's quarters on the top floor of a bank and then set out to erect a permanent exhibition composed of contributions from every member. With a public museum their goal, the budding geologists asked a Joliet lumber merchant if he would donate wood for shelving. Regrettably, their targeted benefactor refused to contribute anything toward the advancement of "a pretended science which aimed to refute the Biblical history of the world."[55]

The club was no frivolous venture. Club members carried out weekend trips to centres as far distant as Wilmington and Mason Creek, some twenty-five miles away. When not scavenging the countryside for new fossils, Van Horne and his friends carried out an extensive correspondence with geology authorities and arranged their collections, carefully observing the Smithsonian Institute's directions for the care and preservation of specimens. With Van Horne's move away from Joliet, however, the club dissolved, and along with it his dream of establishing a local museum. Decades later, his own fossil collection, enlarged and classified, would be given to the University of Chicago.

Chapter Two
Early Career

Van Horne was working as a telegrapher in the dingy Cut-Off office when the American Civil War broke out in the spring of 1861. Before it ended in 1865, this bitter conflict would devastate a third of the country and turn all of it, North and South, into "one vast central hospital," as Walt Whitman, America's renowned poet, so picturesquely described the war's impact.[56] When hostilities began, few, if any, observers could have predicted that they would claim over six hundred thousand lives and hopelessly maim thousands of other participants in body or mind. In 1861, such a gruesome and tragic outcome would never have occurred to most Americans, including Van Horne, who, like most young people, was stirred by tales of battle. Most of us outgrow this romantic concept of war, but not combative Van Horne. Even late in life he would contend that universal peace was not "possible or desirable" and that "all the manliness of the civilized world is due to wars or the need of being prepared for wars."[57]

This belief in the desirability of conflict was only reinforced in 1861 by the groundswell of patriotic fervour that gripped the free states when the Confederate stars and bars were raised over Fort Sumter on April 14. Reading the *Joliet Republican* and conversing with his colleagues in the Cut-Off office, the young telegrapher learned that citizens everywhere, in city and village alike, were cheering the Union flag and vowing to wreak vengeance on traitors. And no doubt he was taken aback by the ferocity of people's reactions. Certainly an elderly Harvard professor was. He was moved to declare: "The heather is on fire. I never knew what a popular excitement can be ...The whole population, men, women, and children, seem to be in the streets with Union favors and flags." From Ohio and the West rose "one great Eagle-scream" for the flag. "The people have gone stark mad."[58]

The news of the bombardment of Fort Sumter galvanized Lincoln's and Van Horne's state, where there was little sympathy for the efforts of pro-slavery men to dissolve the Union. In Joliet, the news of the fort's surrender shocked and outraged the residents, many of whom crowded into the courthouse on April 17 to learn more about the crisis and to spearhead the raising of a military company. An old fairground was quickly converted into a camp, and by mid-May it boasted a full regiment, including two companies from Will County. As the 20th Regiment Illinois Infantry, it would be mustered into military service on June 13, 1861.[59] A total of 3,696 men from Will County volunteered for service in the war, and of these over 500 would die in battle, from wounds or disease, or during internment in prison camp.[60]

Elsewhere across Illinois calls went up for the citizenry to avenge the insult to the flag, the *Chicago Journal* proclaiming that the South had "outraged the Constitution, set at defiance all law, and trampled under foot that flag which had been the glorious and consecrated symbol of American liberty."[61] The Democratic leader, Stephen Douglas, who would die in June 1861, urged his followers to uphold the federal government. "This rebellion is a prodigious crime," the Little Giant told the Illinois state legislature, "and the shortest way to peace is the most unanimous and stupendous preparation for war."[62] Responding to this aroused nationalism, leaders from both parties came together to organize the recruitment of troops and the raising of money and supplies for the conflict, the war for which the country was less prepared than for any other war in its history.

If he was like most Unionists, eighteen-year-old Van Horne looked upon the upstart rebellion in South Carolina with disbelief. Perhaps he, too, predicted that the whole affair would blow over in no time at all. At any rate, one morning, without consulting anyone in the Cut-Off office, he enlisted for service in the federal army. As soon as word of his actions reached his place of work, however, the assistant superintendent interceded to have the enlistment cancelled. He was adamant that Van Horne remain on the job because not only was he the principal support of his widowed mother, he was also an exceptionally capable telegrapher whose services had become indispensable to the Cut-Off office, the Cut-Off itself having become the junction for troop trains being rushed south, east, and west. When the war started the *American Railroad Journal* had rashly declared that most railways would be unaffected by the conflict. Its prediction proved to be way off the mark, for soon both Union and Confederate railways were crowded with trains transporting troops and supplies to the front.[63]

In the early months of the war, Van Horne could take great comfort in the knowledge that his superiors considered his services indispensable. Nevertheless, he took alarm when rumours began to circulate through the Cut-Off office and the yards that declining traffic and earnings caused by the war would force the Michigan Central to lay off staff. When its regular traffic was disrupted by the war the railway began operating at a loss, and with the passage of each day the threat of layoffs increased. Nobody was more disturbed by the prospect of being laid off than Van Horne. The thought of dismissal, with all that it signalled — a loss of income for his family and the derailment of his career plans — plunged him into the depths of despair. Decades later he would vividly recall the war's opening months, a time when disorganization reigned supreme in America, railway staffs were reduced, railways ran at a loss, and he himself feared for his job:

> All the men on our part of the line knew they might be dismissed; no one could be sure of keeping his situation from one day to another. There were nine of us working together and I felt I would be one of the first to go, for one man was a nephew of one of the Directors of the line and another was a grandson of the Superintendent. At last the dreaded telegram came, and as I was a telegraph clerk I took it down and handed it to our chief. He read it and said nothing, but I made up my mind I must go.[64]

Van Horne's fears never materialized. His boss, realizing that the office was fast becoming an important centre for troop transportation and that Van Horne's exceptional talent as a telegrapher would prove indispensable, decided to keep him on. The young man's relief at being spared was so great that when the assistant superintendent asked him how much work he could do Van Horne promptly replied that he thought that he could do it all. He immediately set out to prove himself, drawing on his ample store of energy, initiative, and knowledge of the office, the shops, and the yards to carve out a role for himself as the assistant superintendent's right-hand man.

His new responsibilities should have kept him more than fully occupied. Nevertheless, the inveterate prankster still found time to indulge his penchant for practical jokes. As outlets for his surfeit of energy and inventiveness these pranks had no equal when he was in the early stages of his career. Unfortunately, some of them demonstrated bad taste as well, a conspicuous example being one that involved duping the war-weary residents of Joliet. Central to this prank was a bogus, but authentic-sounding, telegram announcing a great Union victory on the field of battle. On hearing the news the excited townspeople hastened to run up flags and celebrate. The festivities ended abruptly, however, with the arrival of the Chicago newspapers and the discovery that they contained no account of such a victory. When they realized that they had been deceived a party of irate citizens went in search of Van Horne at the Cut-Off office, only to find that he had prudently headed for home.

Word of Van Horne's capabilities spread to the Chicago and Alton Railroad, and in 1862, he was offered the position of telegraph operator and ticket agent at Joliet with a substantial increase in salary. The raise was a reflection of just how demanding the position's duties and responsibilities were. This was especially true of the telegrapher's job, which required an even-tempered individual with superior organizational skills and the ability to cooperate and work effectively with people.

Van Horne accepted the offer, and for the next decade he tied his career fortunes to a line that linked the fertile agricultural region around Springfield, Illinois, with the Mississippi River port of Alton, located on the river's east bank.[65] The increase in responsibilities and pay would, of course, have elated him. But, as ambitious as he was, Van Horne must have entertained not a few reservations about his new employer, a worn-out road that dated from 1847 but had the distinction of being the first railway to acquire Pullman sleeping cars — two of its own coaches, which had been remodelled in 1858 by a young George Pullman, who had hired Leonard Seibert, a German immigrant and craftsman in the railway's Bloomington shops, to help him.[66] As the Chicago and Mississippi, the railway had eked out a very precarious existence in the 1850s and had then sunk into bankruptcy before the state of Illinois intervened and appointed a commission to reorganize it on a firm basis. Reorganized and bearing a new name, the Chicago and Alton was embarking on a six-year rehabilitation program when it approached Van Horne. Joliet's location on the Chicago and Alton's main line from St. Louis to Chicago, and the realization that the position would bring him into contact with headquarters officials, probably persuaded the young man to accept the offer.

As the Chicago and Alton's telegrapher and ticket agent at Joliet, Van Horne was quick to demonstrate his initiative and resourcefulness. In at least one instance these reaped benefits for both the railway and the farmers who used it. After noting that butter deteriorated when left in a warm freight shed while awaiting shipment, Van Horne arranged for it to be stored in a primitive cold-storage chamber of his own design. He reasoned that if cold temperatures preserved the quality of the butter, farmers would obtain higher prices for their product and ship more of it by the Chicago and Alton, thereby increasing the road's earnings.[67] His prescience and resourcefulness paid off. The practice worked so well that the railway soon introduced it at other freight sheds on the line.

Van Horne's career received another boost in the autumn of 1864, when he was promoted to train dispatcher at Bloomington, a Chicago and Alton divisional point located in a rich agricultural area in central Illinois, some ninety miles southwest of Joliet and sixty-five miles northeast of Springfield. Since this new position was several notches higher and much better paying than the one that he had occupied at Joliet, it represented a sizeable step up the railway ladder. If we are to believe a letter that he wrote in January 1865, however, Van Horne had not anticipated such a promotion, at least not as early as 1864.[68] Still, it should have come as no surprise, since his reputation for brains, industry, and trustworthiness was travelling fast from one end of the Chicago and Alton to the other. Moreover, he was a pioneer with no superior in the fast-developing field of telegraphy, then regarded as an invaluable tool in ensuring the efficient and safe operation of trains.

When Van Horne was promoted to train dispatcher at Bloomington, the Civil War was still raging and trains were busily hauling troops, food-stuffs, horses, forage, ordinance, lumber, equipment, and supplies south-ward and returning soldiers and prisoners northward. In his new position, Van Horne had his hands full helping to direct the flow of people and supplies from Chicago to St. Louis on the one main line then operated by the Chicago and Alton.[69] Some twenty years later, during the Northwest Rebellion of 1885, he would have occasion to exploit the valuable expert-ise that he had acquired during this earlier wartime period.

Before telegraphy made its debut on the railway scene in the 1850s, train orders were communicated verbally and then committed to memory by train crews. The system worked reasonably well except when a train could not keep to its assigned schedule because of such untoward developments as mechanical failure, the depletion of fuel, or track damage. When its sched-ule was disrupted, only those operating the train knew exactly where they were on the run. With the widespread introduction of the telegraph as a communication tool in the 1860s, however, it became possible for a dis-patcher to establish the location of any train in his jurisdiction at all times. Skilled telegraphers like Van Horne were therefore much in demand.

Van Horne's diligent study of telegraphy had equipped him well for moving up the railway hierarchy. In this respect he could be compared to the modern-day youngster who acquires a college degree and advanced computer skills with a view to landing a good job. When looking back over the years and reflecting on the role that his telegraphy expertise had played in his career, Van Horne would constantly advise young men considering a railroading career to "learn telegraphy," for he was thoroughly convinced that the easiest and surest way up the railway hierarchy was via the dispatcher's office.[70] But Van Horne's telegraphy skills alone, of course, did not account for the steady advancement of his career. His formidable intelligence, his insatiable curiosity, and his ambition, which had been nurtured and sharpened by poverty, also played an important role, as did, if we are to believe Walter Licht's research, a nebulous something that used to be known as "good breeding."

Van Horne's abilities resulted in his superiors assigning him to the night shift, the shift normally worked by only the most competent dispatchers. On this shift he worked from 6:30 p.m. to 5:00 a.m., watching and directing the movement of up to twenty trains at any one time on almost three hundred miles of track. When all the trains were "on time" there was little, if any, work to do, but when one or more of them fell behind schedule he had to plot new locations and times for trains running at different speeds, or in opposite directions, or both. It was exacting, complicated work that this avid chess player likened to playing a game of chess, but, as he ruefully admitted, it was not nearly so fascinating. On the other hand, he was quick to note that a single error in dispatching could pose a serious threat to life, property, or both and result in an abrupt end to a dispatcher's career.[71]

When not holding down his train dispatcher's job, Van Horne found time, as he had in his other positions, to become knowledgeable about operations outside his immediate areas of responsibility. Of special interest was the work carried out in the shops and yards, as in Joliet he had never seen anything to compare with the much better equipped Chicago and Alton works in Bloomington, which boasted engine-servicing facilities, car shops, a foundry, and a powerhouse. Circumstances permitting, he would have taken additional lessons in telegraphy, but in early 1865, at any rate, such instruction had to be postponed indefinitely.

Van Horne's already impressive expertise in telegraphy and train dispatching, coupled with his wide knowledge of the workings of other departments, enabled him to acquire a certain authority among his Chicago and Alton colleagues. This, together with his personal magnetism and wit, helped to make him a recognized leader whose opinion was eagerly sought whenever disputes involving the interpretation of train rules and related matters arose.

All this contributed to a growing self-confidence. This, along with his increasing familiarity with railway officials, dampened the awe that he had once held for general superintendents and emboldened him one day to intervene when he saw the Chicago and Alton's visiting general superintendent devising a new train schedule. In those days the drawing up of such a schedule required that the responsible official arrange threads and pins on charts to designate where trains should run and cross. As he watched the general superintendent laboriously plot the pins and threads Van Horne could not contain his impatience. Finally he quietly muttered, "That's a hell of a way to make a time-sheet." Getting to his feet, the superintendent replied, "If you can do it better, take the job." Van Horne immediately took over and with such good results that the arrangement of train schedules was assigned to him for the remainder of his time in Bloomington.[72]

When he took up residence in Bloomington it was a mere prairie town, noted for its railway shops and its corn, but not for its civic amenities. For Van Horne, who relished visits to Chicago museums and art galleries, and who delighted in attractive surroundings, this unlovely place of blue-collar labour, smoke-belching powerhouse, and grime seemed to be "outside the limits of civilization." At no time was this more true than in the late fall and early spring, when the town's wooden sidewalks and dusty, rutted streets were deep in mud. In mud season despondency would sometimes overtake him and he would bemoan the fact that he lived in a town where good lectures and art exhibitions were rare and where, initially at any rate, he had no acquaintances other than his railway colleagues.

Perhaps even more distressful, his home in Bloomington was not an inviting place of refuge. A rented room, located in a working-class section of town designated "the western deport" by the "up town folks," it lacked the most basic of amenities for that time, a fireplace. He was thus denied the luxury of being able to warm himself beside a crackling fire on cool evenings. If he wanted to read or write he had to repair to the office, where he was usually interrupted by loafers accustomed to congregating there like moths around a light. At best these living arrangements were tolerable, but even when it was warm enough he was not tempted to use his room for anything but sleep as the din from the nearby railway shops was not conducive to reading, writing, or reflective thinking.[73]

If there was no lively arts scene to patronize during his leisure hours Van Horne could at least do some watercolour painting and indulge his interest in science. The demands of the job were such that he did not have much time for fossil-hunting, although occasionally he fitted in a thirty-five-mile trek in search of new specimens. He did, however, find time to cultivate a friendship with John Wesley Powell, who had served in the Union Army throughout the Civil War and had then become a professor of geology and curator of the museum at Illinois Wesleyan University in Bloomington. The multitalented Powell, who would become celebrated both for his pioneering classification of Native American languages and for his survey of the Rocky Mountain region, was probably the party responsible for putting Van Horne in touch with (Jean) Louis Agassiz, the famous Swiss-American naturalist, geologist, and teacher. Advised that Agassiz would be passing through Bloomington on a certain train, Van Horne met the train, introduced himself, and travelled with the celebrity for some distance.[74] The meeting proved to be fruitful, for their conversation culminated in a correspondence that continued until Agassiz's death in 1873, but which unfortunately did not survive until the present day.

Geology was not the only science that claimed Van Horne's attention. He also pursued an interest in chemistry and botany, sometimes setting aside a Sunday to "reviewing his chemistry lessons."[75] Astronomy was another field that intrigued him. Elaborate charts in his papers indicate that he closely followed the progress of a comet that was sighted in Bloomington, Lexington, Odell, and Wilmington on the morning of April 16, 1868.[76]

In Bloomington, as elsewhere, Van Horne would dash off caricatures and sketches. While working for the Michigan Central he had written an account of an unpopular official and then illustrated it with humorous drawings that elicited widespread amusement when the manuscript was circulated along the line. In the employ of the Chicago and Alton, he continued to amuse his colleagues with deftly executed caricatures and drawings. Sometimes he would adorn posted reprimands from headquarters with ludicrous caricatures of the officials who had sent them. Similar treatment was given to executive warnings of accidents, which he illustrated with whimsical or terrifying pictures of the accidents that might arise should the grave warnings not be taken seriously.

Since life in Bloomington offered few distractions and his home was a rented room, Van Horne was able to devote a sizable portion of his salary to providing for his mother and his two sisters, Elizabeth and Mary, in Joliet. Fortunately his oldest brother, Augustus, had already begun to make his own way in the world, having landed a job as a carpenter with a bridge-building crew in 1861 when he was only seventeen. A year later he became a fireman on the Michigan Central, and in 1864 he obtained similar work on the Chicago and Alton.[77] When he was old enough, Theodore, the younger brother, would follow in Van Horne's footsteps by securing work as a telegraph operator for the Chicago and Alton in Bloomington. Mary, the youngest sister, would also venture into the workforce. After obtaining a teacher's certificate in the late 1870s she would take on a teaching position in La Crosse, Wisconsin.

Van Horne was still based in Joliet when he met the young woman who would become his devoted wife. She was Lucy Adaline Hurd (Adaline is frequently and incorrectly written as Adeline), the daughter of Anna and Erastus Hurd. Hurd was a civil engineer who had been appointed chief engineer of the Fort Wayne Western Railroad before his untimely death in 1857. The family, which also included a son, Tyrus (known as Ty), was originally from the Arlington area of Vermont. From there, Erastus's career had taken them to Galesburg, Illinois, a budding railway centre and college community slated to play an important role in the abolition movement. Just as Van Horne's father's death had plunged his family into penury, so did the death of Addie's father. To satisfy creditors and make ends meet, real estate was sold and Adda, or Addie, as she was affectionately known by family and friends, went to work as a music teacher at St. Joseph Female College in St. Joseph, Missouri. From there, she remitted money to her widowed mother in Galesburg. For his part, her younger brother, Ty, struck out in 1860 for southern Kansas, taking a horse, some cattle, his surveying instruments, and camping equipment with a view to acquiring a quarter-section and erecting a home for himself, his mother, and his beloved sister.[78] Ty did put down roots in that frontier state, but his mother and sister did not join him there. Instead, they eventually settled in Joliet, where Anna had a civil engineer cousin, Samuel Benedict Reed, a Vermont native who would rise to prominence as construction engineer of the Union Pacific, the first transcontinental railway. When Van Horne first met Addie in Joliet, Reed was spanning the western high country for the Union Pacific as a division engineer.

At their first meeting it was probably Addie's refined beauty that made the most forceful impression on Van Horne. A portrait photograph taken in this period shows a young woman with a broad forehead and short, black, gently waving hair. With her head angled slightly, she stares ahead with a pensive expression and no trace of a smile. It would have been difficult, of course, for her to force a smile for five minutes while the photographic plate was exposed to her image, but even if this had not been the case, Addie's fear of the camera and maybe some degree of apprehension about the future would have prevented her from smiling.

Later, Van Horne would describe Addie as tall and slender with softly waving black hair, hazel eyes, and an apple-blossom complexion.[79] If he considered her beautiful he was not alone. His friends, it appears, were bowled over by her looks. A future cleric, the Reverend E.P. Savage, confessed that when he and some other friends heard that Van Horne was to marry Miss Hurd "it just took our breath away. All the rest of the boys in the Agassiz Club liked parties and girls except Will. And here he was engaged to the most beautiful girl we knew."[80] Van Horne was probably also captivated by her quiet dignity and reserve. These were two qualities that would later be remarked on by contemporary observers, including the well-known British journalist and obsessive diarist Henry Beckles Willson, who described her as "a quiet, intelligent woman, of simple manners and entirely devoted to her husband and family."[81]

The woman who would become his great love and who would provide the tranquility and solace that Van Horne so desperately needed in his packed, stressful life was born on September 19, 1837, in Galesburg,[82] to a middle-class family that revered education and placed ideals before material possessions. In this respect it was not the quintessential American bourgeois family, for whom nourishing the soul ranked behind satisfying a voracious appetite for material things. Before her marriage, Addie conducted Sunday school classes in the Universalist Church, studied and taught music in Missouri and Chicago, and cultivated an interest in literature. Her brother was cast in the family mould. Tyrus, after serving in the Union forces in the Civil War, became a teacher, for whom appreciation of his work more than compensated for the small salary that he received.[83]

In addition to beauty, highly respectable middle-class origins, and cultured tastes, Addie had a college degree, an asset that was extremely rare among women of her day. Her alma mater was Lombard College, a liberal institution founded in 1851 by members of the Universalist Church of America, a church that preached the salvation of all souls and that would unite with the American Unitarian Association over a century later, in 1961. Located in Galesburg, Lombard was one of the first colleges in the United States to admit women as students on the same terms as men, allowing them to graduate in the same classes with equal honours. Addie Hurd was one of six graduates of the college's first graduating class in 1856. One of two women in the class, she graduated with a Master of Arts, which was conferred upon every Bachelor of Arts of three years' standing with "a good moral character."[84] Since she was nineteen years old when she graduated, and Van Horne was only thirteen at the time of her graduation, Addie Hurd was several years older than her future husband, a fact that she undoubtedly took some pains to hide as only one Canadian source can be found for her age, the 1901 Canadian census, and the age that it assigns to her is patently incorrect.

In recognition of her beauty and talents, this striking young woman was chosen by the Republican ladies of Galesburg to present a magnificent banner to Abraham Lincoln when he visited their town on October 7, 1858. The occasion, a historic outdoor debate between Lincoln and Douglas, would long be remembered by those who were among the twenty to thirty thousand people from all walks of life who ignored the heavy rains of the previous day and the fierce, gusting winds on the morning of October 7 to travel by foot, wagon, or horseback to Galesburg to watch the two hard-hitting speakers debate the future of slavery and the Union. The enthralled audience included a Mr. and Mrs. Standish, who years later recalled that "Miss Adda Hurd" arrived on a hay rack attended by a dozen or more young, costumed ladies and presented Lincoln with a "citizen's banner." Another observer claimed that "Miss Hurd, who is of queenly appearance, rode up at the head of a troop of equestrians and receiving the banner from the attendant presented it in a very neat and well spoken address."[85]

Interestingly, Addie Hurd's prominent role in the proceedings would be disputed fifty years later by a professor, who claimed in a newspaper article that another party, not Addie, had presented the Lombard College banner to Lincoln.[86] When replying to a friend's letter reporting this, Addie hastened to set the record straight. "There were several ladies & gentlemen who rode that day — myself included among the number — to meet the late President Lincoln. I had a brief address to make & I so well remember that I kept repeating it to myself fearing I might forget some of it in the presence of one so distinguished."[87]

Addie Hurd was thus a woman of some distinction when she first met her future husband, at that time the Chicago and Alton's ticket agent at Joliet. According to Walter Vaughan, this encounter took place in 1864, when Van Horne was twenty-one.[88] Whether this is correct or whether we are to infer from a letter of Van Horne's that they knew each other as early as 1863, the story of their first meeting is the stuff of which family legend is made. This lore has it that the couple met quite by chance in Joliet when Addie, returning by a late train from Chicago, where she had been taking vocal and instrumental music lessons, was stranded at the train station without a ride home. Although he was normally overcome with shyness when in the presence of women, Van Horne gallantly offered to escort her to her home. They set off, but not before the young man shoved the pipe that he had been smoking into his jacket pocket. As he walked on, absorbed in conversation, Van Horne suddenly detected the odour of burning wool. He then remembered that his pipe was still alight and with great haste he quietly smothered the embers as best he could.

By the fall of 1864, when the South was being pummelled by Union forces, the couple were exchanging letters. Van Horne composed his missives, in still legible handwriting, from Bloomington, where he had recently taken up his new position with the Chicago and Alton. From Joliet, or Chicago, where she studied and taught music, or wherever her frequent visits to relatives took her, Addie dispatched letters written in a fine, loopy hand that at times defies deciphering. On October 12, 1864, when visiting a professor cousin in Galesburg, she wrote to her "dear friend Mr. Vanhorn" to express her "grateful appreciation" for an unnamed courtesy that he had extended to her. She remarked on the profusion of books, shells, and dahlias scattered on the table before her, but in this, as in other letters, Addie did not confine herself to domestic and family trivia. A cultivated woman of broader interests, she also commented on the world around her, in this case the political climate in Galesburg, where everyone, she discovered, was a staunch Republican and most Republicans were abolitionists, "who cannot too strongly condemn the Democratic party or rather such of them who are termed Copperheads."[89] Galesburg, it seems, differed in this respect from Joliet, where there was widespread opposition to the war policy of the president and Congress, especially among the Copperheads (the faction of the northern Democratic party that denounced the transformation of the Civil War into a total war — a war to crush the old South instead of to restore the Union).

Writing to his "dear friend" in March 1865, Van Horne wanted to know if she liked Washington Irving's novel *Bracebridge Hall.* But instead of awaiting her reply, he immediately anticipated her answer: "I need not have asked that question — of course you do — How can you help it. There is nothing like such a book for dispelling the gloom of such a day as this ... How much better such a book than a lugubrious one like 'Jane Eyre'! But wait this may be premature: I have not yet finished the book some of my new friends may 'fall from grace.' I hope not."[90]

If this and other early letters to Addie are any indication, Van Horne frequently sought relief from worries and spells of monotony at work in uplifting works by contemporary giants of both American and British literature. By his own admission, he was often bored while on the job. Indeed, he once conceded that when he had nothing to do but sit in the office all day, he "could almost consider a 'smash-up' on the road as a godsend" as it would give him something to do and make the time pass quickly.[91] Did he have in mind something like the horrendous train wreck that occurred on July 17, 1856, when a North Pennsylvania Railroad (now the Reading) excursion train collided head-on at Camp Hill near Philadelphia, killing sixty-six people? As bored as he was, he probably did not wish to see such a gruesome horror occur on his line. Nevertheless, if not during his first stint with the Chicago and Alton, Van Horne was probably involved with at least one accident in his American railroading career, because relative safety in American railroading came to an abrupt end in 1853. Starting in that year, when a series of major railway accidents killed 234 passengers, calamities occurred with striking frequency throughout the remainder of the century. Largely because of cheap and poor construction, engines derailed and exploded, boilers burst, bridges collapsed, and, when trains collided, primitive passenger car stoves ignited the debris of splintered coaches.[92]

Long, weary hours of night duty and slow days might have invited boredom, but it was grey, sombre skies and chilly temperatures that rekindled longstanding feelings of melancholy and self-doubt. In a revealing letter to his beloved in the spring of 1866, Van Horne observed:

> This has been a cold, dismal day, without a ray of sunlight to brighten it; and were it not for sweet recollections of the hours spent with you Sunday I should have had one of my old-fashioned fits of melancholy or "blues" as they are more expressively termed. O, how I used to suffer from these! — a little cloudy, chilly weather was sure to bring on a general attack; sometimes, however, it did not require the presence of unpleasant weather to induce an attack. You know from whence came the predisposition, and how a short visit to the country effected a perfect cure. Wonderful, isn't it? But can you imagine how I suffered from these attacks? You certainly cannot unless you have experienced similar ones. But now my fits of melancholy have given way to happiness.[93]

By 1866 the friendship had blossomed into a passionate love affair that saw Van Horne shuttling back and forth by either passenger or freight train between Bloomington and Joliet. When apart from his beloved, he seized every opportunity to write to her, frequently punctuating his letters with gallant solicitousness. Regarding a projected trip to New England, he advised:

You must be very careful, dearest, and not in any way endanger your health; I fear you are not sufficiently cautious in that respect ... And in travelling you must not hesitate to call upon the conductors for any information or assistance that may be conducive to your safety and comfort. The best plan in travelling is to think all you meet rascals and act accordingly. Such a supposition, at the present time particularly, is justifiable and in the majority of cases I think will prove true. Rascals of all descriptions are infesting the great thoroughfares in unusual numbers, and you must look out for them. Trust no one with your baggage checks, at Troy, unless you <u>know</u> the party to be a responsible one ...[94]

In his assiduous courtship of Addie, Van Horne did not find undiluted joy and peace of mind. When they were apart, which was most of the time, he was overcome by apprehension and anxiety. Just contemplating the perils and fatigue that Addie would experience on a two-thousand-mile train journey to Vermont was enough to make him utterly miserable. "I cannot get over this anxiety when I am away from you and am never happy unless I can see your dear face. I know it's wicked to wish away time but I can't help it. Never did I look forward to anything anxiously and impatiently as I do to the coming autumn," he wrote in April 1866 in apparent reference to a fall marriage date.[95] In the months ahead his anxiety would be assuaged only by visits with Addie and by the almost sure knowledge that they would be marrying in the autumn. So overpowering was his love for Addie that it dwarfed everything else in his life and led to the conviction that only marriage to the one he loved would put a permanent end to the "aimless, cold, <u>loveless</u> and mechanical existence" that was his life without her.[96] Of all the hyperbolical statements uttered by Van Horne this has to be one of the most exaggerated given the fact that Mary Van Horne, his mother, was devoted to him, although she may not have expressed her motherly love in a demonstrative way.

For some unexplained reason the marriage did not take place that autumn. Clearly Addie was in love with the taciturn young man who was subject to spells of melancholy, but who seemed headed for great things. "I thought of you constantly & was only happy in closing my eyes & transporting myself to the time when I could again be with you & relive the only true pleasure which your presence alone can give," she informed him in the summer of 1866.[97] This same letter makes it obvious, however, that Addie, despite her love for Van Horne, was apprehensive about marriage. It appears that her "insecure health," as she rather ambiguously expresses it, had a lot to do with this. Although she loved Van Horne deeply, Addie entertained qualms about marriage, fearing that this ambitious, talented man would jeopardize a promising future by marrying a woman of delicate health. "Dont you know others would likewise pity you? You may think why did I write the above: for the reason that you will not permit anyone to advise you & I should at least be <u>just</u>," she wrote with great poignancy. Ironically, Addie Hurd would live to an advanced age, but when she was young frequent illnesses or periods of poor health may have led her to question her stamina and her fitness to marry and have children. If nothing else, she probably feared the physical pain and danger associated with childbearing in the nineteenth century. Contemporary ideology taught women to expect fulfillment through marriage and motherhood, but all too often there was a yawning disparity between ideology and reality. As a devout Christian, Addie knew that she had to expect and be prepared to deal with both blessings and trials in life, but it is quite likely that her health did not give her the confidence to face the anticipated demands of marriage, at least not in 1866.

Certainly her mother's views on marriage did nothing to bolster Addie's confidence in taking the momentous leap out of spinsterhood. A self-centred, fearful woman who dreaded the thought of losing her "baby child" to somebody else, Mrs. Hurd did not flinch at painting the institution of marriage in less than flattering colours. "My darling child the imorality I see in men & womin too of this day makes me shudder when I think of your being united to one, it is like a lotery and God only knows if your are to draw a prise," she told her daughter. Moreover, by her own admission, Anna Hurd frequently predicted that Addie would never get married.[98] Nevertheless, in December 1866, Addie was able to inform Van Horne, "At last I have been able to see Mamma long enough to discuss the affair with her. She leaves it entirely to me although I know she thinks I am not qualified to make an efficient wife for your worthy self."[99]

Because she worked outside the home, Addie Hurd may have also harboured some reservations about relinquishing her independence. Van Horne must have suspected or known as much because at one juncture he claimed that he would sooner kill his love and himself with it than ask Addie to sacrifice her independence for poverty. "No, Addie, God bless you, I love you too well to bring you to want and hardship; my greatest happiness shall be in soothing your way and making you happy. None of the objections you have yet urged or the burdens you imagine I am taking upon myself have the weight of a feather and <u>if</u>

<u>they had</u> weight there is <u>love</u> to bear them," declared the lovesick young man in an undated letter.[100]

Suspense and anxiety would dog Van Horne until the late winter of 1866–67, by which time Addie finally made up her mind to marry him, despite the host of doubts that she entertained about her ability to take on "the duties of a wife." On March 6, 1867, she explained, "The delays that have been occasioned were unavoidable and not employed as 'pretexts' for postponements. It is true I dread entering a relation that involves happiness most complete or wretchedness most appalling ... I was not always so stoical as I at times seem ... I have made life so dark for you ... As your dear wife I shall try to make amends."[101]

Van Horne's fondest wish was finally realized in the last week of what had been a cold, wet March. On the twenty-sixth of that month, when most of the attention of Joliet's citizenry was focused on "exorbitant taxes" and "gross official corruption," the two were quietly married by the Reverend Charles A. Gilbert, rector of Joliet's Christ Church.[102] The marriage took place when Mrs. Hurd was visiting in Vermont and on the day after twenty-four-year-old Van Horne had obtained a marriage licence. Decades later, his failing memory would lead him to record an incorrect marriage date (March 17 instead of March 26) when he was compiling genealogical charts.

The couple did not have long together before Van Horne had to leave Addie in Joliet and return to Bloomington. There, a number of his friends at the depot greeted him with congratulations and wishes for much joy, while looking around for Addie. For his part, the newly minted husband feigned surprise and asked who had "been making April Fools of them." They hadn't considered this possibility, and after weighing the question they stared blankly at one another, reported Van Horne to Addie in a letter the next day: "'Are you not married,' they asked. 'Really,' I replied, 'I have never been absent for three or four days but that you had me married.'" This was followed by another blank stare and then each man went his way. "The last suspicion that might have been lurking in their minds vanished when, at supper at the 'Hotel de G,' I took my accustomed place at the table; and now I think no one but my friends here in the office really believes that I am married," Van Horne concluded in his summary of the incident.[103]

The day after they were parted Addie wrote a teasing letter to her husband in which she speculated that his "troubled, suspicious heart" must finally be at rest now that "the coveted possession" was at long last his.[104] In the months to come, however, Van Horne's heart would not be completely at rest as Addie was determined to cling to some shred of independence. Much to her husband's chagrin, she would embark on trips that he did not sanction, prompting expressions of great pain and martyr-like forbearance. "I hope you will have your visit out and will enjoy it, so that when you return home you will be able to content yourself a short time. But I do wish you could know what pain and sorrow a broken promise sometimes causes ... If the object of your prolonged stay is to visit Chicago I object most decidedly to your going there and hope you will regard my wishes in this case," he wrote in an aggrieved fashion in the summer of 1867.[105]

Van Horne was not left to his own devices for long because shortly after his marriage his mother, Mary, his sister Mary, and his mother-in-law, Anna, moved to Bloomington to share the rented home at 506 North Mason Street that he had had repapered, whitewashed, and painted. It was a highly unusual arrangement, even for Victorian times, but since the women got on well together it boded well for the future. With these three compatible women to minister to his domestic needs, Van Horne could look forward to enjoying a warm, serene home environment, something that he craved. From time to time it would be buffeted by sickness and bereavement, but nevertheless he always knew that he could look to it for comfort and solace from the pressures of a job with irregular hours and frequent changes of residence. This would prove extremely important to him as he continued his steady progress up the railway hierarchy.

Meanwhile, there were friendships and leisure pursuits to cultivate in Bloomington itself, a far more appealing place now that he had been able to acquire his own home there and settle his family in it. As a member of the Natural History Society of Illinois, Van Horne came to know fellow member W.H. Sennett, who practised medicine "for pay" in Bloomington before leaving the town in 1867 and going on to become auditor of expenditures for the Chicago and Northwestern Railway and the Chicago, St. Paul, Minneapolis & Omaha Railway. Another friend was Captain J.H. Burnham, long-time editor of the *Pantograph* and a Civil War captain. Given his passion for natural history and his interest in chemistry, it is not surprising that Van Horne also came to know Dr. J.A. Sewall, a professor of natural history, chemistry, and botany. Then there was Aaron Ockley, a locomotive engineer and assistant master mechanic for the Chicago and Alton at Bloomington, and W.A. Gardener, who, like Van Horne, rose to meteoric heights in the railroading world. When Van Horne knew him, Gardener was a telegraph operator in Bloomington; in 1912, he was president of the Chicago and Northwestern Railway and the St. Paul, Minneapolis & Omaha Railway. Another friend from his Bloomington days who also made a name for himself was Peter Whitman, a lumber dealer who became a large manufacturer and finally a bank president.[106] All these individuals would play a role in Van Horne's life when he was in Bloomington — but not for long because the up-and-coming railroader would soon be on the move again, this time to Alton, Illinois, to take up a new job with the Chicago and Alton.

By the time that he left Bloomington, Van Horne had established a solid foundation in his chosen career, rising in a cutting-edge industry strategically situated in the American economy and in the Midwest. To his career credentials, Van Horne could also add those of bourgeois respectability. Not only was he the son of a middle-class professional father, he was also a married man with a family, two attributes that could not help but favour his advancement up the railway ladder, if a study done of nineteenth-century Illinois Central Railroad employees is any indicator of factors favouring advancement in the railroading industry. This study reveals that an employee's father's occupation and marital status were important factors in the speed of promotion. Fast risers, like Van Horne, tended to be sons of businessmen, professionals, and skilled workers. Conversely, farmers' sons, unskilled labourers, and, what is most surprising, sons of railwaymen climbed more slowly up the ladder. Married men also tended to advance more quickly than single men.[107] Van Horne's obvious assets, such as intelligence and interest in hard work, would figure prominently in his advancement up the railroading hierarchy, but other, less conspicuous factors would also stand him in good stead — factors such as his family origins, marital status, and the solid foundation that he had been building in Joliet and Bloomington.

Chapter Three
Rapid Advancement

Van Horne's dream of becoming general superintendent of a railway came closer to becoming a reality when he was made superintendent of the Chicago and Alton's entire telegraph system on May 1, 1868.[108] As an assistant superintendent of the railway (he was one of two assistant superintendents), he came into frequent contact with the company's leading officials, who, not surprisingly, were impressed by both his force of character and his bearing. Already aware of Van Horne's reputation for initiative and efficiency, these Chicago and Alton officials soon offered him a new job with even greater authority, that of superintendent of the newly created southern division of the railway, the appointment to take effect February 9, 1869.[109] Van Horne promptly accepted, and in 1869 he moved his entire family to Alton, Illinois. Like the modern-day diplomat's or serviceman's family that finds itself on the move every two to three years, the Van Hornes soon learned that they had to be prepared to pack and move on short notice.

It must have been with some reluctance that the family bid farewell to Bloomington. Not only were they taking leave of good friends they had made there, they were also saying goodbye to the birthplace of Van Horne's and Addie's first child, daughter Adaline. "Little Addie," as she came to be called by the family, had been born June 7, 1868, weighing about six pounds.[110] As the years rolled by, this devoted daughter would grow to over six feet and would come to resemble her father in girth as well as in her excellent head for business, her love of art, and her interest in collecting things.

Little Addie was a mere infant when the Van Hornes moved to Alton, a hilly river town that sits on limestone bluffs overlooking the meandering Mississippi River, some twenty-five miles north of St. Louis, Missouri. The town, which then boasted a population of over eight thousand, had a decidedly upbeat air when Van Horne and his family moved to it, but its future had not always looked rosy. Alton had grown rapidly in the 1830s thanks to a growing steamboat trade with St. Louis and New Orleans, but between then and the Van Hornes' arrival in 1869, various setbacks had interrupted its progress. In the same year that the town was incorporated, 1837, pro-slavery sympathizers murdered Elijah Lovejoy, an abolitionist minister, editor of the Alton *Observer*, and soon to be Alton's most celebrated martyr. The murder tarnished the town's reputation, and its outlook was further blighted by the demise of the steamboat era, which dampened economic growth. But Alton bounced back as a commercial centre, and by the 1850s it was able to open its first railway station. When the Van Hornes took up residence in Alton the town had stately homes on lovely, wide, tree-shaded streets and was quickly attracting heavy industry because of its excellent railway facilities and Mississippi River location.[111]

Van Horne waxed ecstatic when describing the residence that had formerly belonged to Mayor Beall and that would soon be the Van Horne home.[112] The ten-room brick dwelling, he informed Addie, was "most delightfully situated" on a "pretty street" that overlooked Alton's business district and commanded a view of the city and of the river for many miles to the south and west of it. Among the home's many selling points were the brick walks that surrounded it, a brick washroom, a summer kitchen, a cow stable with attached cistern, and a spacious backyard with arbours, trellises, and fruit trees.[113] He conceded that the house itself was a little larger than the family required, but nevertheless he was sure that it would please Addie. Whether it did or not is open to question, but no doubt it suited Van Horne admirably. He was developing a taste for large residences, and indeed, in later life he would profess that he liked his homes "fat and bulgy like myself."

In his new job Van Horne was responsible for the safe day-to-day movement of all passengers and freight over the southern division, the discipline and conduct of the employees involved in these operations, the hiring of agents, and the maintenance of the division's structures and equipment. Such an array of duties represented a formidable responsibility for a young man who had just turned twenty-six when he assumed the position. But even if he had not anticipated being promoted so swiftly to this position he would certainly have coveted it because, in addition to broadening his railway experience, it placed him on the direct line of authority from Timothy Blackstone, the company's president. As one of the railway's two assistant superintendents, Van Horne reported directly to the superintendent, who in turn reported to Blackstone, the Chicago and Alton having adopted the decentralized divisional structure now found in many American railways. Timothy Blackstone, after whom the turn-of-the-century luxury hotel the Blackstone, a Chicago landmark, was named, was an engineer who had been brought into the Chicago and Alton via the leased Joliet and Chicago. A sound and honest businessman who paid careful attention to detail, he became a director of the ailing railway in 1864 and, within three months of his appointment, its president. With his elevation to the presidency, the company's prospects began to improve. Blackstone was not entirely responsible for the upward turn of the railway's fortunes, but in the months and years ahead his managerial expertise would pave the way for the Chicago and Alton to become one of the most profitable American railways. He would occupy the office of chief executive officer for thirty-five years, "the longest continuous tenure of any railroad president."[114]

Managerial expertise can express itself in many ways, one being an ability to spot hard-working, talented subordinates and encourage their advancement. Fortunately for the ambitious Van Horne, he would come to the notice of Timothy Blackstone. Closer to home, in Alton, he would come under the direct observation of a Chicago and Alton director who resided in the river port, John Mitchell, a prominent western railroading man who would be identified with the Chicago and Alton for the next thirty years. The interest that these two men came to take in Van Horne would play no small role in advancing his career.

That Blackstone and Mitchell were impressed by Van Horne's enthusiasm, administrative skills, and industry is evident in his promotion in 1870 to the railway's headquarters in Chicago, where he was placed in charge of the movement of passengers and freight over the entire Alton system.[115] In his new job, as assistant superintendent in charge of transportation, he made efficiency his watchword as he strove to eliminate the competition by making operations as streamlined as possible. His vigilance was such that he often visited the train dispatcher's office in the early hours of the morning to check on how the trains were running.

Van Horne was no doubt delighted to be based once again in vibrant Chicago, a lake port with a population of some three hundred thousand people and railway links to both coasts. More than any other American city, brash, raw-boned Chicago in these years embodied the United States' continuing transformation from a rural society into an urban industrial nation. Situated at the mouth of the Chicago River at the southwest corner of Lake Michigan, it had grown from its humble beginnings in 1830 into a vital transhipment centre for the grain, livestock, and lumber produced in the Midwest. When Van Horne returned to Chicago in 1870, it boasted more than 1,100 factories, 17 grain elevators, wholesale houses, commercial exchanges (for example, the Board of Trade), private libraries, the Chicago Academy of Design, and a city within a city, the Union Stock Yards.[116]

Chicago was a city with an enviable future, but the port also had its less commendable features. Like so many other frontier towns, it was awash in gambling establishments, saloons, and houses of prostitution. And worse, it was crowded with wooden structures. Two-thirds of its buildings, in fact, were made of wood, and many of these were cheaply built with no view to safety. The city's wooden buildings, wooden side-walks, some fifty-seven miles of wood-paved streets, and wooden bridges all created the ideal conditions for a major fire.

This was Chicago in early October 1871, when Van Horne found himself catapulted into one of the great dramas of the century. On the evening of Saturday, October 8, in an autumn following an exceptionally dry summer, a fire of unknown origin broke out in the city. It was contained, but the following night another fire erupted about one and a half miles southwest of the downtown, either in or very near the celebrated O'Leary barn. A cow, it came to be widely believed, had knocked over a lamp while being milked. Whatever its origin, this conflagration quickly spread to neighbouring buildings. Lashed by a strong southwest wind, it ripped through dry wooden shanties and then crossed the Chicago River to the city's south side. From there it tore like a tornado through the business district to the northeast, demolishing everything in its path. On the south side, the fire was finally checked with the use of gunpowder; in the north, it had almost reached the open prairie before an early morning rainfall brought it to an end after some twenty-seven hours of destruction. All told, the flames razed an area approximately four miles long and three-quarters of a mile wide, destroying some eighteen thousand buildings, leaving some ninety thousand people homeless, and killing at least three hundred other people.

When the second fire began around 9:00 p.m. on Sunday, October 9, Addie Van Horne was recovering after delivering the couple's second child, William, born twenty-four hours earlier. Van Horne was at home rejoicing at the arrival of the newborn and fretting about his wife's condition when he learned that the fire was rapidly approaching Chicago's business district and the Union Depot. Despite concerns about the fate of his family, he immediately made plans to rescue what Chicago and Alton equipment he could. Once he had left the family home at 153 Green Street, in the city's South Division, the first thing he did was he hasten to the top of a tall building so that he could see for himself the advancing wall of flame.

Thoroughly alarmed, he hurried to the freight depot, located on Van Buren Street in the West Division.[117]

There, Van Horne arranged with the few employees still around to clear the company's freight sheds. Most of the company's rolling stock had already been removed for safety reasons, but he obtained a Chicago, Milwaukee and St. Paul shunting engine and several flat cars to transport any remaining freight that could be rescued. He then circulated among the crowds of people on the Jackson Street Bridge, offering five dollars an hour to any man who would help him to load freight onto the flat cars. Many took up the offer, but before long they would leave the station to watch the progress of the fire. Between trying to keep his recruits at work and rushing out to way-lay more help, Van Horne was almost beside himself. He eventually succeeded, however, in having the freight moved to a safe location five miles away, but when he set out to pay those workers who had stayed on the job he could not find them. They had disappeared, never to return for their money. Satisfied that there was nothing more that he could do to protect the Chicago and Alton's property, Van Horne set off for home.

Van Horne would never forget that trip back to his family. The whole city appeared to be an inferno of blazing buildings and sidewalks. Smoke and sparks, flying pieces of burnt lumber, shingles, and roofing were everywhere. So were fear-crazed humans and beasts. Beating his way back to Green Street, Van Horne navigated through throngs of people, their faces blackened and blood-stained, who were trying to escape with the few precious possessions they had managed to save. The streets were an obstacle course of squealing rats smoked from their holes and desperate horses that had broken away from drivers or escaped from city stables and were now stampeding through the city, neighing in panic.[118]

When he arrived home Van Horne was blackened from head to foot, but he was safe. Addie and the rest of the family had also been spared. Having assured himself of this, he removed from the house any bedding and clothes that could be spared and, assisted by his mother, loaded them onto a commandeered grocer's wagon for delivery to shivering refugees camped in a nearby park.[119]

About a year before the Chicago fire, Van Horne had been asked if he would be interested in taking on the superintendency of an unnamed three-hundred-mile-long line. He had not accepted the invitation, but neither had he rejected it outright. Instead he had mulled it over, confessing his indecision to Addie and going so far as to speculate that he might get "along faster by going slower."[120] After the fire, he accepted an offer from the Chicago and Alton to manage one of its smaller roads, the St. Louis, Kansas City and Northern Railway. He became general superintendent of this road on July 15, 1872, at an annual salary of $5,000.[121] At the young age of twenty-nine, he had realized his dream of becoming a railway superintendent. Moreover, he could congratulate himself on becoming, most probably, the youngest railway superintendent in the world.

The 581-mile-long railway line that Van Horne had been chosen to manage and develop was another road headed by Timothy Blackstone. Blackstone, John Mitchell, and some other associates in St. Louis and the East had recently purchased the ailing Northern Missouri Railway, which in 1868 had completed a line from Moberly, Missouri, to Harlem, across the Missouri River from Kansas City. The associates planned to reorganize the line, bring it up to Chicago and Alton standards, and then make it a link in the Chicago and Alton's growing system. As such, it would represent the first acquisition in their long-range scheme to control a transcontinental line. Meanwhile, the road was to be reorganized as a nominally independent line, the St. Louis, Kansas City and Northern Railroad, with Van Horne as its first superintendent.

St. Louis, Missouri, Chicago's arch-rival in the Midwest, would be the family home for the next two years. A cosmopolitan community and a commercial metropolis, it had been the leading city in the Midwest before the Civil War erupted. With the advent of hostilities and the cessation of Mississippi River traffic from the South, however, it had lost ground to Chicago, only to resume its progress after 1865. In the decade leading up to 1870, the city's population almost doubled, reaching 310,640. When Van Horne took up residence in St. Louis, in the summer of 1872, the city was expanding rapidly in all directions and savouring the fruits of a golden age that would last until the turn of the century.

In what had become established practice when a move was planned, Van Horne preceded the family to the new location and scouted out a home for them. This time he was able to lease an elegant new house on St. Louis's Olive Street, some "2 1/2 miles out." With its ten rooms, two storeys, mansard roof, finely finished stone front, and location in a "very good neighbourhood," it was judged to be "as good as any in the city."[122]

House hunting, of course, was just a diversion. Most of the time he was preoccupied with settling into the new job. Writing to Addie on July 10, 1872, he reported that he has been busy all day with his new duties. He continued: "I leave early tomorrow morning by special train for a trip over the line with the genl frt. agent, chief engineer & asst. genl supt. Mr

Blackstone will go part way with us & Mr Mitchell will join us tomorrow somewhere on the line. My advent at the North Mo. office caused something of a sensation among the <u>fossils</u>. Everything promises well."[123] Evidently, the young superintendent's innovative methods and no-nonsense approach to doing things were beginning to make waves.

Late that same summer, Van Horne became the central figure in a little drama whose outcome would further embellish his growing reputation. He was on an inspection trip when four seedy-looking young toughs boarded the train and settled directly across the aisle from him. As the train rumbled across Missouri, they began to indulge in loud, boisterous conversation. This upset an invalid black child, who began to cry. Irritated by the infant's plaintive wailing, one of the ruffians grabbed and slapped the child, shouting, "Shut up." The mother, who knew that she could not stand up to these men, looked for some escape. Van Horne had been watching the altercation with mounting fury and at this point he leapt out of his seat, grabbed the assailant by the collar, and pulled him into the aisle.

"Leave that child alone," he barked.

"Who the hell are you?" snarled the unrepentant man.

"Never mind," replied Van Horne. "Be careful how you conduct yourself or I shall throw you off the train."

Van Horne was outnumbered, but his voice and the ferocity of his gaze so intimidated the bully that he shrugged and sat down. By the time they pulled into the station, however, this unsavoury character had regained his nerve, at which point he advanced threateningly toward Van Horne. As he did so, his companions intervened and hurriedly dragged him off the train. The conductor, who had been mysteriously absent all the while, suddenly appeared. He dashed over to Van Horne and told him to duck down. "Don't you know who those men are?" he whispered. "That's Jesse and Frank James and the Young brothers. Stay where you are or they may decide to aim a shot or two at you as the train leaves." Although somewhat shaken, Van Horne pretended that nothing out of the ordinary had occurred.[124]

Once installed in his new job, Van Horne energetically set about improving the efficiency of the road's equipment. With this goal in mind, he badgered the road's owners to purchase steel rails, which were far more durable and had a much higher load capacity than the standard iron ones. He also exhorted his employees to take money-saving measures whenever possible and to perform to the best of their ability.

Saving money and getting the best performance possible out of his employees would be crucial to the road's rehabilitation, for in the fall of 1873 an economic crisis struck, igniting one of the worst depressions ever experienced by the United States. In early September, banks collapsed after lending money to a couple of defaulting railways. Then, on September 18, much to Wall Street's astonishment, the illustrious Jay Cooke & Co. failed. Ironically, Cooke, who had been the leading financier of the Union cause during the Civil War, was ruined by a railway — the mighty Northern Pacific, chartered by Congress in 1864 to run from the westernmost arm of the Great Lakes to the Pacific Northwest. Misfortune dogged the NP. It started with a huge grant of land that sprawled across the "northern tier" of the American West, but the parcels did not sell. When Cooke entered the picture in 1869, he agreed to underwrite $100 million of Northern Pacific bonds. However, this was just before the Franco-Prussian War erupted, curtailing European investment. After its tracks reached Bismarck, North Dakota, the NP defaulted. Cooke tried to rescue it with short-term loans, but in September 1873, hopelessly overextended, he could no longer meet his own obligations and went bankrupt.

Cooke's fall precipitated the panic of 1873. Investors panicked, and stock prices plummeted. Investment houses toppled, and on September 20 the New York Stock Exchange closed for the first time in its history. The exchange reopened after ten days, but nevertheless the economy skidded into a crippling six-year decline that would be known until the 1930s as the Great Depression. Its impact on the railway industry was staggering. Construction plunged from 7,500 miles in 1872 to 1,600 in 1875. By the following year over half of the country's roads had gone bankrupt.[125] In those railways that did survive, managers attempted to stabilize their markets, meet fixed costs, and economize wherever possible.

As strict a disciplinarian and as hard a taskmaster as he was, however, Van Horne was no martinet. He never demanded that an employee put in as many hours of service as he put in himself. Moreover, he sympathized with the plight of those railroading men who had to spend long periods of time away from their families. To provide for their comfort when they were on the road he established clubs and reading rooms at divisional points. But while he appreciated the drawbacks of the railroader's life, he had no sympathy for an inebriated employee. In fact, he could be ruthless when confronted by drunkenness, one of railroading's cardinal sins (regulations prohibited the use of alcohol by engineers, trainmen, and others when on duty). When this or any other misbehaviour occurred he would "cuss out" the offender with great energy and effectiveness. After a St. Louis, Kansas City and Northern engineer was dismissed for being drunk on the job, Van Horne experienced his first railway strike as a manager. The engineer was replaced by an efficient substitute, whom the

Brotherhood of Engineers promptly labelled a strikebreaker and a scab. Despite the uproar Van Horne refused to discharge him or to reinstate his predecessor, bluntly informing the union delegates who interviewed him, "The Chicago and Alton have had their nose brought down to the grind-stone too often, and they are not going to do it this time if I can help it."[126]

In the long and bitter struggle that followed, the strikers indulged in often ruthless sabotage, but Van Horne, who always relished a good fight, refused to back down. For weeks on end, he worked inhuman hours, astounding staff by his ability to function with so little sleep. He was always there to see the first train of the day leave and the last one pull in. And when no firemen were available, he recruited volunteers from his own office staff to man the locomotives. Danger was ever-present since there was always the possibility that furious strikers would place objects on the track or throw switches the wrong way.

Fortunately for Van Horne, the strike ended in complete victory for him and the company. Nevertheless, peace brought no slackening of discipline. "A railway," he reminded the men, "was no reform school." This point was driven home when a conductor was dismissed for disobeying a train order and another employee was let go for a slight impertinence to a passenger.[127] On more than one occasion, the general superintendent learned of employee misbehaviour by listening to the tapping of a telegraph machine when he was visiting a small station. He was able to decipher the incoming dots and dashes so accurately and administer punishment so swiftly that he quickly earned a reputation for uncanny powers. Years later, when stopping by the Canadian Pacific Railway's New York telegraph office, he demonstrated these celebrated powers by deciphering an incoming communication that was addressed to him. "Here is your message, Sir William," said the clerk. "Yes, and here is my answer," Van Horne immediately replied. He had been composing his answer as the message came in.[128]

When working for the St. Louis, Kansas City and Northern Railway, Van Horne looked much as he would for the rest of his life. Although not handsome, he was a striking man with fine features and alert blue eyes that appeared lidless when they bore right through you. His nose was small and finely chiselled, and his short, immaculately trimmed beard suggested a rock-hard jaw beneath. His hair had already receded back from his high forehead to the middle of his pate, which would become completely bald in later years. A contemporary described Van Horne as "rather heavy set." With the passage of time he would become decidedly corpulent, but never would his bulk suggest softness. Van Horne, no matter how old, would always radiate strength and power.

Despite his grave manner, Van Horne would also retain an impish sense of humour and love of pranks. When the family lived in Bloomington, he had put his artistic talents to work transforming figures in the illustrations of one of his mother's fashion journals into a collection of freaks. In St. Louis, he took liberties with some of the artwork reproduced in copies of *Harper's Magazine* that he intercepted before they reached Mrs. Van Horne. He once altered a series of portrait sketches of American authors by Canadian artist Wyatt Eaton in such a way that they appeared to be pictures of cowboys and bandits. The transformation of the sketches was so convincing that his mother and mother-in-law were thoroughly deceived, protesting that it was scandalous that the magazine's editors had allowed the ridicule of such illustrious writers as Longfellow and Emerson. When somebody showed him the distorted illustrations years later, without explanation, Wyatt Eaton himself was deceived.

While the family was living in St. Louis, Addie came down with smallpox, then one of the most deadly and loathsome of scourges. An extremely contagious viral disease, it was characterized by a flu-like illness and a rash that spread over the body and eventually developed into pus-filled, encrusted blisters. In the nineteenth century, it was customary to isolate smallpox patients in a so-called pesthouse, but Van Horne would have none of this for his beloved Addie. Putting an end to all discussion, he prepared to care for her himself in the attic-study where he kept his fossil collection.[129] As long as the illness lasted, he whiled away his days in this sanctuary, devotedly nursing his wife and amusing himself with his fossil collection. With the coming of night he would change his clothing, thoroughly disinfect himself, and then set off for his deserted office to attend to the day's work. This done, he would return to the study in the early hours of the morning to snatch some sleep or to resume nursing Addie. It was a punishing regimen, but Van Horne had the satisfaction of seeing his wife make a splendid recovery with few, if any, disfiguring scars. Moreover, because of the precautions that he adopted, nobody else in the house contracted the disease.

The St. Louis, Kansas City and Northern had been under his resourceful and energetic management for almost two years when Van Horne decided to leave the railway. On June 28, 1874, he advised Addie that he intended to submit his resignation the following day because railway developments had finally culminated very much as he had anticipated they would. "The bitter feeling towards the Chicago & Alton & everyone who was ever connected with it is the principal cause," he reported. "This together with the ill feeling of those interested in this company who were also interested in some of the 'side shows' — branch lines etc and whose toes have been trodden upon has made my position here since the election very unpleasant."[130]

After labouring under what a railway contracting agent for the St. Louis, Kansas City and Northern referred to as "many difficulties" (these were not spelled out) for almost two years,[131] Van Horne decided that he had had enough. It was thus with some relief that he submitted his resignation. No sooner had he done so than the company's board of directors met and unanimously recorded "their high appreciation of his faithful and industrious administration of the duties of his office." They then proceeded to authorize the railway's president to grant him a month's salary as severance pay.[132]

To at least one observer Van Horne's resignation came as a great surprise. J.P. Hall, of the Missouri River, Fort Scott & Gulf Railway Company, was struck "dumb & speechless." He recovered sufficiently, however, to write: "I am very sorry, from my standpoint, that you found it to be in your best interest to resign & leave the improvements in every branch of the management that had been made & grown up under your care & guidance."[133] A Roman Catholic priest who ministered to the spiritual needs of the railway's employees wrote: "In parting from you my good friend I have only to thank you from the bottom of my heart for the many courtesies received at your hands. You have been the means of bringing a joy that is not of this earth, to the poor men who labored under your charge, because it would have been impossible for me to attend to their many wants had it not been for the favors you so kindly and generously bestowed ..."[134]

In the over fifteen years that he had been gainfully employed, the hard-driving, thirty-one-year-old railroading man had never been without a job. The inevitable result was a bout of self-questioning and despondency, which only the company of Addie and the children could assuage. That summer, when his wife and children were away visiting in Bloomington and Joliet, Van Horne found the family home in St. Louis so desolate and cheerless that he was moved to observe, "Whatever misfortunes may come in a business way I cannot be unhappy while my dear treasures are left to me. You cannot imagine how lonely I feel without you here. Sometimes I feel as if I could _fly_ to you."[135] During these trying and unstructured months of relative inactivity, when most days seemed like "a lot of Sundays strung together," the hitherto self-confident railway executive even began to question whether his future lay in railroading. To Addie, he admitted, "I am more and more inclined to go into business & let railroads alone hereafter. It may not pay as well for a time but it certainly will in the end."[136]

At some juncture in this angst-ridden summer, Van Horne gave serious thought to going into business with John Mitchell in either Salt Lake City or St. Louis.[137] Like Van Horne, Mitchell no longer had any association with the St. Louis, Kansas City and Northern. When differences had arisen with their fellow directors prior to Van Horne's departure, he and Blackstone had sold their interest in the road. The two men continued, however, to keep a benevolent eye on their promising young protegé. In fact, it is quite possible that it was Mitchell who approached Van Horne about the possibility of their establishing a business together. Whether or not he initiated the idea, nothing came of it, probably because Mitchell became aware of a small, financially weak railway that somebody with Van Horne's management skills and railroading expertise might be able to save. The railway was the Southern Minnesota Railway, an unfinished road that ran from the Wisconsin-Minnesota boundary opposite La Crosse, Wisconsin, westward through some 167 miles of sparsely settled southern Minnesota to Winnebago City. When John Mitchell learned through the road's New York bondholders that the Southern Minnesota was in receivership, the Chicago and Alton director persuaded these eastern capitalists that Van Horne was just the person to build the line up and transform it into a profitable enterprise. Mitchell then prevailed upon Van Horne to leave St. Louis and become general manager of the Southern Minnesota, whose offices were located in La Crosse, a Mississippi River town that owed much of its prosperity to the lumbering industry.

From his office in La Crosse, Van Horne could look out over bluffs and coulees to the river that had been the boundary of his boyhood world. His new railway lay beyond the Mississippi, to the west, and as he contemplated it, he must have felt both exhilaration and apprehension: exhilaration because if he performed brilliantly as the railway's new general manager he could further enhance his growing reputation in railway circles; apprehension because as a general manager he had the power to make or break towns, to build them up by bestowing his favour on them, or to "make the grass grow on their streets" by withholding it.

But if he was presented with an exceptional opportunity, Van Horne was also confronted with intimidating challenges. The Southern Minnesota Railroad was an all too typical "streak of rust" with all the problems posed by such an operation. Like so many others of its ilk, it had been constructed during a period of extravagant development following the Civil War, its builders more interested in reckless speculation than in sound railway operation. Typical of their breed, they had tapped into the hotly debated railroad land grants program, a series of federal and state acts designed to encourage the construction of the transcontinental railway and telegraph systems and the settlement of the West. Enacted between 1850 and 1871, these acts offered 170 million acres of public land to railway companies to facilitate the realization of these lofty public goals. Prior to 1862, the grants were made via state governments, but with the advent of interstate transcontinental railways in 1862 the federal government began to award grants directly to railway corporations. Eventually, some 131 million acres of land would be employed in the construction of 18,738 miles of railway, chiefly on the frontier and beyond.[138]

As a condition of receiving a grant, a railway would agree to construct a road within a specified period of time, furnish railway service in perpetuity, and haul military and postal freight at a reduced rate. Once in receipt of a grant, the company would sell the land to settlers and use the funds so obtained to pay for the construction of the road and a telegraph line. In Minnesota, railways could avail themselves of an 1857 federal act that provided for generous grants via the territorial government and its successor, the state government. This legislation stipulated that the lands awarded to a railway could be sold only in batches of sections as the building of the line progressed and all lands not sold for the purposes of the act within ten years had to revert to the United States.[139]

As with most of the federal government's public lands disposal schemes, the railway lands grants program was riddled with pork barrel politics and fraud. Whether from a lack of capital, engineering problems, building ahead of demand, rough terrain, or repeated bankruptcies, fraud, and outright corruption, numerous railways that received land grants were not built as planned. This led to many of the land grants being forfeited, a process that began even before they were all distributed and that continued for some seventy-five years.

Van Horne launched his career with the Southern Minnesota at a time when American roads were embarking on consolidation or system building. Prior to the 1870s, most roads were small, local operations that were financed by small, local capitalists and had independent managers. Lacking substantial capital, these lines were barely more than stubs that radiated short distances outward from small cities. Connecting links were rare and interchange of rolling stock was almost non-existent. When freight moved past a road's end point it was unloaded and then transferred to the cars of a connecting railway. Likewise, when passengers and their luggage reached the end of the line they too were transferred to the next carrier. In 1869, however, Cornelius Vanderbilt blazed the way for a new modus operandi when he seized control of the Lake Shore and Michigan Southern, combined it with his New York Central and Hudson River (itself the product of four merged independent lines), and created the New York Central, the first continuous line between New York City and Chicago.

Vanderbilt's bold move was soon emulated by other visionary railroading entrepreneurs. One of these was the professional engineer who built and then managed the Pennsylvania Central, J. Edgar Thomson. Determined to create a self-contained system, he initiated a process that saw his road quickly gobble up a host of smaller parallel, connecting, and end-to-end railways by purchase or lease. From a line of 491 miles of track, the Pennsylvania grew in five years to one of just under 6,000 miles. By 1874, the total mileage that it directly administered equalled that of Prussia's railway network. Only France and Great Britain boasted more miles of railway than the Pennsylvania system.[140]

System building was probably far from what Van Horne had in mind when he took over the management of the reorganized Southern Minnesota on October 1, 1874.[141] The railway, after all, was then controlled by the United States Circuit Court through a receiver. From its opening in 1870, the road had led a precarious existence, and when Van Horne swooped down on it, it was about to be foreclosed for the second time. Its taxes were in arrears, its workforce had not seen the pay car in months, and parts of its roadbed were in such a state of disrepair as to be almost unusable.[142]

To its new general manager fell the daunting challenge of increasing the road's earnings so that they not only met expenses and interest charges but also paid off old debts and freed the railway's right-of-way of all claims. He faced the additional challenge of making the road a paying property at a time when the country was in the midst of the crippling six-year depression that had been brought on by the 1873 failure of banker Jay Cooke.

With his characteristic gusto, Van Horne set out to rescue the decrepit property from its financial miasma. He would take about three years to accomplish these goals, years of frustration, setbacks, and triumph. The highlights of this period are recorded in three Southern Minnesota letterbooks, regrettably the only letterbooks that survive from his American railroading days. As a window on this stage of his career and his operating methods these books are invaluable, but they are interesting for another reason as well: they testify forcefully to the vital role that correspondence played in an age when the telephone had yet to link major centres. When not on the road, the general manager often penned daily letters to his reporting superior, Cornelius Gold, head of the Southern Minnesota's executive committee and later the railway's president. When major developments were breaking, he often dispatched two letters a day to this New York-based official. And, of course, in addition to this correspondence, Van Horne would fire off missives to other railroading officials and colleagues, invariably in his own hand as opposed to a secretary's.

In what would become customary practice for him when taking over the management of a new road, Van Horne launched his stint at the Southern Minnesota by replacing some of his predecessor's staff with men who had worked with him before and in whom he had confidence. With a revamped staff in place, he instituted stringent economies and embarked on settling all outstanding claims for right-of-way by dealing directly with the owners. So much headway was made in achieving these goals that by August of 1876 he was able to predict a surplus for September, October, and November that would make "a big hole" in the claims against the road.[143]

Looking to the future, Van Horne had new snow fences built (in February 1875, he observed that they had saved the company a lot of money by keeping protected cuts clear of snow[144]) and prepared for a heavy spring traffic in wheat by improving the railway's rolling stock and roadbed. The following year, he spent lavishly on what he labelled "renewals and improvements," that is, repairs to track, bridges, and roadbed, and the construction of new buildings. This was all carried out against a background of periodic rate wars, designed to grab business from competing divisions of rival railways.

The erection of new stations competed for attention in 1877. To his superior, Gold, Van Horne dispatched a plan for a new passenger depot at Albert Lea, declaring that such a building was urgently needed. "We must erect one there without delay or lose all of the through travel as the present depot isn't fit for cattle and the new roads are putting up a fine one," he observed. As a sweetener, he pointed out that the plan contained rooms where an agent could live. "The advantage of having the agent (or operator) within reach at all hours is very great and we can take enough from his wages (as operator) to cover interest on the extra cost. Room should be provided over all our depots as far as practicable."[145]

Van Horne's efforts to rehabilitate the line soon began to pay off. Gross earnings for the first year of his management were the highest in the railway's history. Moreover, operating expenses had slid from 72 to 56 per cent of earnings, and there was a respectable sum in the railway's coffers.[146] These encouraging results were enthusiastically greeted by the road's bondholders, some of whom resided in the Norwich, Connecticut, area, which Van Horne labelled, with typical hyperbole, "the greatest center of wealth in New England outside of Boston."

In response to an invitation from these capitalists, Van Horne attended a January 1876 meeting in Norwich. Writing from his pied-à-terre in New York, the Fifth Avenue Hotel, he informed Addie just days before the meeting, "Our bondholders are more than happy over the past year's results and are profuse in their expressions of satisfaction and confidence. In fact, I can't discover that I was wanted here for much aside from congratulations."[147] Even if the get-together produced nothing but fulsome praise for the general manager, the trip to Norwich was not a waste of time as it enabled Van Horne to meet some of the railway's principal investors. Chief among them were Charles Johnson, George P. Bissell, Cornelius Gold, and Peter M. Myers, a Wall Street broker who had become the road's vice-president and secretary. Without question, these were the men to impress, for they could help or hinder the advancement of Van Horne's career. In any event, their hearty endorsement of his managerial expertise no doubt buoyed up his spirits and persuaded him that he was achieving the right mix of cost-cutting and property renewal.

The pilgrimage east allowed Van Horne to take in some live theatre in New York City. He attended a "splendidly produced" production of Julius Caesar at Booth's Theater and the melodrama *Pique*, in the company of Jason Easton, a Minnesota banker friend and investment crony, at New York's fashionable Fifth Avenue Theater. He was well advised to take time off to relax because back in La Crosse he would face a host of problems, some the result of a ferocious storm that struck later in the winter.

The storm that swept through the Midwest in the first week of March played havoc with rail traffic in southern Minnesota. All roads operating in the area were affected, and none more so than the Southern Minnesota, whose track and bridges were severely damaged by a freshet on March 5. "The track was broken in about a dozen places between here and Spring Valley — 4 of the breaks were bad ones. On Monday the water was higher than ever known before. It stood 1 foot deep on the shop floors at Hokah and one foot over the <u>tops of flat cars</u> on Mount Prairie side track," recounted Van Horne in one of the countless letters that he dispatched to Cornelius Gold in this period.[148] The freshet was followed by even more damaging floods later in the month, resulting in the suspension of traffic for weeks on end and heavy losses for the railway. As a result, not even the normally optimistic Van Horne entertained much hope that the road would meet its July interest payment without a delay of a month or two. He pronounced it "still possible but not probable" in a letter to Gold on

March 19. It must have come as a welcome surprise, then, that he could report three months later that the road's earnings were about $45,660.00 ahead of the first five months of 1875.[149]

Unfortunately for the young general manager the damage occurred before there existed properly equipped and trained wrecking crews to construct or repair bridges, abutments, track, embankments, and the like. For repairs he could call upon a few experts from the shops, but most of the work had to be performed by gangs of workmen recruited from among the scattered settlers, and they were expected to remain on the scene until the work had been completed. In the absence of skilled labour, Van Horne spent a good deal of time in the field supervising repairs. He saw to it that the workers were generously supplied with good food and strong black coffee to keep them awake. On one occasion nervous fatigue brought on by the pressure of work and copious quantities of strong coffee led some workmen to grumble. This prompted a foreman to remark, "Damn you! It's a good thing to have a man like Van Horne come around here once in a while with such grub to take the wrinkles out of your bellies!"[150]

Van Horne believed fervently that tasty, well-prepared food was a powerful inducement to good performance on the job. While working for the Southern Minnesota he made it clear that no eating house along the line would be patronized unless it provided the best possible meals. He himself carried out frequent taste tests of the available fare. Nor did he ignore his own needs. While on the road he frequently placed a telegraphed order at the next eating stop for two roast chicken dinners and then devoured both upon his arrival. But if his appetite was prodigious so was his energy. His vitality at this time, as later in his career, earned him the reputation of being a "human dynamo of high voltage." A glutton for work, he toiled away in his office from nine-thirty or ten in the morning until eleven or twelve at night, taking time off only for dinner. The last meal of the day and breakfast were the only two repasts that he permitted himself.

In the spring of 1876, Van Horne took a small stab at system building when he added the management of a thirty-eight-mile-long railway, the Central Railroad, to his burgeoning array of challenges. The road, which the Southern Minnesota leased for $42,000 annually, was in bad shape. When he took charge of the line, at the end of May, the wages of all its employees were in arrears and numerous claims were on the books. Never one to beat around the bush, the general manager wrote immediately to Cornelius Gold, insisting that outstanding claims be paid at once and adding for good measure, "There can be no debts in the East half as pressing. These interfere with the business of the road — those in the East do not."[151] Despite his continuing unease about "the Central matter," as he dubbed it, Van Horne championed the road's retention, since it enabled the Southern Minnesota to hold onto profitable through freight and passenger business that might otherwise have been lost. The loss of the Central Railroad "would knock the bottom out of our west end profits," he told Peter Myers when lobbying for continued control of the road.[152] To the everlasting benefit of the Southern Minnesota, it succeeded in keeping its new acquisition and preventing the road from falling into the clutches of the Sioux City Railroad, its arch-rival.

With the arrival of summer, the Southern Minnesota faced another calamity of nature's making. A devastating plague of Rocky Mountain locusts (commonly known as grasshoppers) wreaked havoc on northern Minnesota before moving into the southern part of the state. In August, black clouds of the small, olive brown insects, their progress closely followed by Van Horne, moved from west to east above the Southern Minnesota line, dropping from time to time to the surrounding fields to deposit eggs just below the surface and then to munch their way through huge swaths of wheat and other grains. As one field of grain after another was reduced to stubble, Van Horne became increasingly anxious, knowing full well that depleted wheat crops spelled smaller freight loads for the Southern Minnesota and that deposited eggs would invariably hatch the following spring to unleash new destruction.

Both farmers and railroading men dreaded and feared a grasshopper plague, but whereas farm families often took to offering up public prayers for the banishment of this "terrible engine of destruction,"[153] Van Horne decried such a practice. "It's all very well your turning to prayers," he declared, "but I don't believe it will move the grasshoppers. What you have got to do is take off your coats and hustle."[154] And hustle he did, using his ingenuity to devise an effective "hopperdozer" to destroy the pests. This invention, consisting of a piece of sheet iron or stretched canvas thickly smeared with coal tar, was dragged through an infected field by a horse. Disturbed by the horse, the grasshoppers would fly upwards and become entangled in the tar. According to Walter Vaughan, farmers eagerly adopted Van Horne's hopperdozer. The state supplied free tar, and the Southern Minnesota cooperated by carrying both the iron and the tar free of charge. Soon Van Horne had the satisfaction of seeing black heaps of dead hoppers dotting the prairie. Finally, one day, the survivors flew away in a huge cloud, but only after leaving deposits of eggs that would hatch in the spring of 1877, releasing new hoppers to "take the wheat."[155]

The improvements and renewals that Van Horne instituted in 1876 paid further dividends in 1877, when operating expenses dropped significantly. That year, he allocated even more money to upgrading, particularly track and bridges, many of which had been deteriorating rapidly. As a result, he could report net earnings of $296,266.15 for 1877, and this despite the reduction in freight traffic caused by the failure of the 1876 wheat crop and the 1877 grasshopper invasion that swept through most of the territory served by the road.[156] Such a significant improvement in the road's fortunes prompted him to boast to Gold in January 1878 that "the condition of the entire property will now compare favorably with that of any other road of its class in the northwest."[157]

Getting the property into top condition required Herculean effort and ingenuity, but this was made easier by the esprit de corps that Van Horne developed on the railway. As part of a program to involve every employee in the Southern Minnesota's regeneration, the general manager introduced contests in many areas of the railway's operations, from track repairing to engine driving. A prize, along with a personal letter from Van Horne, was awarded to every man whose job performance met the advertised goal of the best work at the least cost. Many a recipient, it seems, attached more value to Van Horne's letter than to the prize itself. The Southern Minnesota's auditor, Hauman Haugan, a veteran railway official in Minnesota and Illinois, recalled that "Van Horne created on that old Minnesota Road an esprit de corps rarely equalled. It went through the entire working body. Just as poor as crows we were. We had to look twice at every cent. But we all enjoyed working on that road. Van Horne was full of ways to get around difficulties, and as full of ideas for improving every branch of the work."[158]

The parlous state of the railway's finances was not reflected in the large salary that its general manager received, making for an anomaly that could have given him a few misgivings. It appears, though, that Van Horne had no qualms about this, at least during the first years of his stint with the Southern Minnesota. His conscience began to niggle him only when he realized that the Southern Minnesota's highly respected vice-president, Peter Myers, might leave the line because of inadequate pay. Reflecting on the possible repercussions of this potential defection as well as on the railway's not-so-attractive pay scale, Van Horne resolved to change things. After discussing the situation at length with his friend and confidant, James Easton, on one of their periodic trips to New York, the general manager decided that he would make more money available for salary increases by taking a cut in his own paycheque. Writing to Myers, who had become a friend, he said, "I don't know how it can be arranged so as to satisfy Mr Gold, give you a fair salary and keep within the figures the situation of the road would justify. I have thought it all over and made up my mind to reduce my own salary materially on January 1st [1878], no matter what action the board takes in regard to the others."[159] Van Horne spelled out why he was embarking on this course. "First, although I think I earn what I get, it doesn't look well for a road like this to pay as large a salary. Second, the wear and tear will not be as great in the future as in the past."[160] Certainly his first observation is correct, and probably the second one is also. In any event, through his actions and this letter Van Horne clearly revealed himself to be a chief executive who could be sensitive to how the public might perceive the spectacle of a senior officer pulling in a huge salary when his company was in straitened circumstances. In this respect, he differs markedly from some of his present-day counterparts operating under similar conditions.

The hard-working manager pursued solutions to challenges as assiduously as he had once hunted down fossils. Because wheat was the principal commodity carried by his road, he sought to corner every possible bushel by offering inducements for the erection of flour mills and suitable grain elevators along the line. His efforts evidently bore fruit because in his first annual report he noted that six "first-class" elevators had been built within the past six months and three large mills were in the process of being constructed.[161]

In order to restrain competition and further increase the Southern Minnesota's earnings, Van Horne arranged with rival lines to divide, in accordance with pre-established terms, either the traffic or the earnings realized from the traffic of the participating roads. One such pool arrangement involved the St. Paul and Sioux City Railroad, with which the Southern Minnesota would later be engaged in a bitter fight over railway legislation.

Van Horne considered it imperative that his road seize every available opportunity to maximize its earnings. In 1876, he mounted a tireless campaign to have the Southern Minnesota extend its line westward from Winnebago City, Minnesota, to just beyond the South Dakota border. To investors and members of the executive committee alike he pitched his arguments:

> Now, there is an average profit to the present road of over
> $30.00 in every car of wheat or flour hauled from
> Winnebago City to La Crosse. If, therefore, the 45 miles of
> road from Winnebago to Jackson should only contribute 4
> cars per day to the present road, our profits would amount

to <u>over $37,000</u> per annum or more than enough to pay
the additional interest, saying nothing of the profits from
the increased passenger traffic and west-bound freight. If
the business of this 45 miles of road is only equal to the
western 22 1/2 miles of our present road there will be a
profit left for the present road, after paying the additional
interest and operating expenses, and this profit will rapidly increase as the country develops.[162]

By way of additional bait, the general manager noted that company-
owned land in Martin and Jackson counties, south of the proposed line,
would increase in value if an extension were built. Keeping in mind the
interests of both shareholders and upper management, he averred, "It <u>is</u>
possible to build a railroad honestly in this region and I hope for an opportunity to prove it — and also to prove that there is a <u>good sound profit</u> in
the extension scheme for the parties furnishing the money to build it, as
well as for the present road."[163]

Van Horne did not hanker after the additional responsibilities and
cares that such a project would entail; he was already shouldering an
extremely heavy workload. Nevertheless, he continued to press month
after month for the building of the extension, believing that strategic
expansion was essential if his road was to keep one jump ahead of its competitors. His frustration at the executive committee's failure to act swiftly
enough on the matter mounted steadily when it was driven home to him
that "settlers — mostly well to do Englishmen" were pouring into the
country west of the Southern Minnesota and that if his road did not push
a line through to this part of the state another company would.[164]

To goad the executive committee into quick action, he declared, "We
are in a position to do something now and we ought to be moving. It
would rain Hell with our future prospects to have some one slip in a road
ahead of us."[165] Then to downplay the financial risks involved, he opined
that the extension could pay its way from the first year of operation.
Moreover, if the line could be financed by the proceeds from a small bond
issue and "without addition to the contemplated stock debt" it would
greatly increase the value and safety of the Southern Minnesota's bonds
and stock.[166] As much as he wanted to see the extension built, however,
cost-conscious Van Horne was not prepared to see it constructed on just
any terms. If the extension could not be constructed with lightly bonded
debt and aid voted by the towns it would serve, it was preferable, he contended, that it not be built at all.

In 1876 and 1877, the general manager devoted much of his time and energy to championing the construction of his proposed extension and to discussing the most suitable vehicle for making it a reality. His efforts eventually persuaded the powers-that-be to extend the line westward by means of a separate company organized for this purpose. The *St. Paul Dispatch* confirmed the outcome of the long, drawn-out battle on January 21, 1878, informing its readers that a new railway company, the Southern Minnesota Extension Company, had been organized at Lanesboro on January 17 for the purpose of extending the Southern Minnesota Railway westward during the coming season. It listed Van Horne's friend and occasional business associate Jason C. Easton as president of the company and Van Horne as its vice-president.[167] According to Van Horne, construction of the extension would begin on February 11 at the Blue Earth River bridge after appropriate ceremonies had taken place at St. Paul. Drinking, he emphasized, would not be allowed near the line.[168]

By this time extensive route surveys had been carried out. These had been closely scrutinized by Van Horne, who was keenly interested in the locating and naming of stations. So interested was he, in fact, that wherever a Native association still persisted he incorporated it in the name. One such place was Pipestone, where Native Americans, observing an ancient custom, still assembled once a year to collect red stone for making peace pipes.[169]

The building of an extension involved Van Horne in much more than promoting its construction. He also had to organize a company to build it, chase funds for its construction (he himself pledged $2,000 for the stretch between Winnebago and Fairmont[170]), and lobby for a charter and for the transfer of the Southern Minnesota's lapsed land grant to the new company. It would have been far easier to hire a lawyer or a legislator to act as a lobbyist for the company (railways were among the first firms to hire full-time lobbyists, a practice that they began adopting in the 1850s), but to spare expense the general manager decided to take on the role himself. Boning up on railway law and sharpening his powers of persuasion, he plunged into what had hitherto been a completely foreign world to him, that of state politics. When legislation of interest to the Southern Minnesota was under debate in the legislature, he would make frequent trips to the state capital, St. Paul, a booming city located at the head of navigation on the mighty Mississippi. In times of perceived crisis, the legislature building — the rather austere-looking, Italianate edifice that preceded Gilbert Cass's monumental, soaring structure — became his second home. Here, in cigar smoke-filled committee rooms and crowded corridors, he would seek out key politicians who might support his railway's cause and attempt to enlighten them about the Minnesota's needs and aspirations.

In long letters to Cornelius Gold and other company officials, Van Horne summarized proceedings in the House and the Senate that had a bearing on his company's fortunes. He informed Peter Myers on March 6, 1876, that "a resolution requesting Minn delegation to Congress to use their influence to secure extension of our land grant for 5 years passed the Senate at St. Paul almost unanimously last week. It was amended, however, requiring the completion of the road to a junction with the SC & SP road [St. Paul and Sioux City Railroad] before the end of the year 1877."[171] The proposed amendment was eventually defeated, but not before igniting a lively "squabble" between two parties appearing before the House railway committee. "Both," reported Van Horne to Gold, "became excited and Handran delivered an address on the 'Depravity of Man' that would have pleased you. Horn nearly choked with rage."[172]

The planned extension involved Van Horne in still another round of strenuous politicking, this time in the early months of 1878. That January, he began lobbying vigorously to have the Minnesota legislature turn over the Southern Minnesota's lapsed land grant to the newly formed extension company.[173] The ensuing struggle, waged against a background of competing railway interests, proved lively. "Hulley and Dunn are at S Paul working hard but so far as I can see they have no support in either house. They are telling mighty lies about our connection with the Martin Co RR Co etc but unless Drake comes out openly and fights us they can't do anything," reported a combative Van Horne on February 10.[174] By the following month, the struggle had become open warfare. Reported Van Horne on March 8:

> We have had a bitter fight with the SP & SC party in S
> Paul. They opened fire on us a week ago Tuesday — a few
> days after the Southwestern party gave up the fight. They
> at first attempted to amend our bill do as to give the SP
> & SC Co the lands west of their grant on condition that
> they should construct a branch line through Pipestone
> Co. this year. Failing in that they tried to amend our bill
> so as to compel us to build west from their line this year
> — a condition with which we could not comply — and
> in case of our default the lands to go to the SP & SC Co
> should they build the branch line. They made a desper-
> ate fight and by means of a powerful lobby ... of votes

developed great strength and came near to beating us. The fight was made in the Senate Committee of the whole ... our bill went through the next day with only a few dissenting votes.[175]

To quash opposition to the Southern Minnesota bill, Van Horne had recourse to some vigorous arm-twisting. When it produced the desired outcome, he was elated. At the juncture of one extremely bitter fight, he announced triumphantly, "His constituents had instructed him to support the other scheme but we got a large number of them down here last week and converted them; so we have now no opposition except from Winnebago and Blue Earth City."[176] In late February and early March, when debate on the bill became particularly heated and the opposition to it especially fierce, the general manager devoted himself exclusively to politicking at the Capitol.[177] "The Southern Minnesota Question," as the *St. Paul Dispatch* referred to it, was finally settled in the first week of March when both houses of the legislature passed legislation providing for the transfer of all the lands and privileges vested earlier (1866) in the Southern Minnesota Railroad to the Southern Minnesota Railway Extension Company. As a condition of this, the company would be required to complete and put into operation a line between Winnebago and the west line of Minnesota before the end of 1880.

When visiting the Minnesota state capital the general manager hobnobbed with fellow lobbyists and prominent railwaymen of the West. These legislature denizens would later describe the Southern Minnesota general manager as a "man of commanding intellect and energy, who knew what he knew for certain," but who could combine persuasion with diplomacy and tact.[178]

Undoubtedly one of the railwaymen whom Van Horne met in the corridors of the Capitol at this time and who formed strong opinions of him was James Jerome Hill, the transplanted Canadian who was on his way to achieving fame and fortune as the builder of the Great Northern Railroad. In fact, the hard-driving, wily Hill would figure prominently in the general manager's later career, and decades later would report that he first met Van Horne when he was managing the operations of the Southern Minnesota.[179]

Although he was able to chalk up quite a few political successes, Van Horne was not enamoured of the game of politics, and to the end of his life he harboured a distaste for it and for encounters with its practitioners. In this respect, he probably resembled John S. Kennedy, Hill's financial adviser and friend, whose jaundiced view of politics prompted some acid comments. Early in 1885, Kennedy wrote in relation to state legislators,

"The majority are men who are ignorant, stupid, and full of prejudice who do not desire to know the truth and the more you try to enlighten them the more stubborn and unreasonable they become."[180]

If the political game was vexing for Van Horne, even more so was his road's failure in the early months of 1878 to attract immigrants' freight. The previous year's bumper crops had combined with a good market for grains to create an extraordinary demand for Minnesota's cheap and productive lands. As a result, the spring of 1878 saw a flood of settlers and land-hunters pour into the southwestern part of the state. The Southern Minnesota should have profited from this land rush, but only rarely was it able to tap into the market provided by the settlers' traffic. Van Horne blamed the unrealistic prices that his road charged for its land in Martin and Jackson counties (they were far in excess of those asked by rival roads for land in neighbouring counties). He also hastened to inform Cornelius Gold that the steep prices of some railway lands had invited a lot of unfavourable comment during the last session of the legislature. Then he confessed, "It is humiliating, to say the least, to see hundreds of settlers going west every day and be unable to stop one in a thousand of them." The general manager recommended that land prices be significantly reduced, adding for good measure, "Six or seven parties here want about 3000 acres which they will break at once if they can get the lands on favourable terms. They had contemplated taking lands on the NP RR or SP & Pacific but they will wait a week or so to see what we can offer ... Please telegraph me this week if something of this kind can be done."[181]

Van Horne was shrewd enough to realize that settlers cultivating the soil and creating traffic for the railway were far more important to the road than the dollar figures realized by land sales. Consequently, his first priority was good settlers, and on at least one occasion, in 1877, he even urged the waiving of the Southern Minnesota's claims to some of its lands if certain settlement conditions could be met. In this particular case, his target was the "good class of people" then being settled on the Minnesota prairie by a noted prelate, whom Van Horne had greatly impressed during one brief meeting on the plains. This was the idealistic John Ireland, coadjutor bishop of St. Paul, who had founded the Catholic Colonization Bureau of St. Paul as a successor to the old Irish Emigration Society and who would successfully establish ten rural villages and farming communities between 1876 and 1881.[182]

The general manager fought hard for competitive prices and worked diligently to attract settlers to his railway's lands. As work on the extension progressed he devised a scheme whereby settlers received credits for breaking and seeding their land within a specified period of time. Credits acquired in this way could be applied to the first payment due on a piece of land. In the spring of 1878, Van Horne jubilantly reported the disposition of 4,480 acres of extension lands at $7.00 an acre, less credits for breaking and seeding, and gleefully predicted, "There will be lively times on the prairie when we get our land matters in proper shape."[183] How right he was. The scheme proved to be such a powerful sales tool that land sales alongside the extension multiplied rapidly and soon newly sprouted settlements were generating traffic for the Southern Minnesota.

That spring and summer Van Horne was preoccupied with more than just the day-to-day operations of the Southern Minnesota. He was also spending a good deal of time pondering his future. By now he was known widely as one of the ablest railway operators in the country and, in the words of one railroading man, one who was "bigger than his job."[184] But if his credentials augured well for a brilliant future in the railroading industry, it was imperative that the ambitious general manager make the right moves to ensure that future. That would not be easy, especially when competing job offers tested his loyalty. Such was the case in early 1878, when the Chicago and Alton tried to lure him away from the Southern Minnesota and the latter strove valiantly to keep him. The exercise of evaluating the merits of the railroads' respective proposals plunged Van Horne into agonies of indecision and fretting.

As usual, when weighing questions of mighty import, he turned for comfort and advice to Addie. In March, he told her that it would be decidedly in his best interest to accept the Chicago and Alton offer. On the other hand, his present employer was so eager to retain his services that it had proposed he fill both the office of general manager and that of president. To tempt him further, the Southern Minnesota had offered an annual salary of $12,000, a figure that Van Horne felt was outrageously high given the road's circumstances. He also felt strongly that he could not afford to accept it "as it would injure [him] in the end."[185] Addie, of course, sympathized with his predicament and wished that she could help him. But ultimately, she said, nobody but Van Horne could make the decision.[186]

He resolved his quandary, at least temporarily, by agreeing to stay with the Southern Minnesota and to take on the additional office of president later in the year. The offer of the railway's presidency may have entered into this decision, although he would claim that "the office of President [had] nothing whatsoever" to do with his remaining with the Southern Minnesota.[187] His decision notwithstanding, Van Horne would find it increasingly difficult to contemplate a future with such a small, obscure railway.

There was also the not-so-small question of Addie's health. It had been failing for a year or more, no doubt because of the loss of their second-born child, Willie, who died at five years of age. The sudden death of this "bright and lovely little sunbeam" on May 17, 1876, was a terrible blow, one from which Van Horne thought his wife might never recover.[188] Both parents would find it exceedingly difficult to adjust to the terrible absence of this beloved child, even with the arrival of a second son, Richard Benedict (Bennie), the following May. In any event, Van Horne was convinced that his wife's deteriorating health would only improve if the family moved to a more salubrious climate. Probably more than any other factor, this led him to conclude that nothing would now stand in the way of his leaving the Southern Minnesota. The die was evidently cast late that summer when he resolved to consider any attractive job opportunity that came his way rather than dismiss it and perhaps later be obliged to accept a less enviable position elsewhere. As it happened, a desirable opportunity did present itself. It took the form of an invitation to become general superintendent of the Chicago and Alton. Van Horne accepted the offer, and the family, with the exception of his sister Mary, who was to remain at teachers' college in La Crosse, once again prepared to uproot itself and relocate, this time to Chicago.

Before taking up his new position, Van Horne was able to combine business and pleasure while on a late summer visit to New York City. Accompanied by Jason Easton, he set off on a September afternoon for Manhattan Beach, then regarded by the upper and middle classes as one of the more civilized parts of Coney Island because it had not been overrun by corrupt politicians (like Boss Tweed), big-time gamblers, and their girlfriends.[189] The two friends arrived at five o'clock, in time for a daytime "bath in the surf," which probably involved nothing more than striding resolutely and briskly into the water until it was waist-high. Following their dip in the ocean they had supper and then "rode to and from" Brighton Beach, another tony section of the five-mile-long popular seaside resort. Van Horne was absolutely enchanted by the nighttime landscape. Barely able to contain his enthusiasm, he wrote Addie, "The whole coastline was brilliantly illuminated with electric lights which had a fine effect. There were also tens of thousands of colored lights. The hotels — immense affairs — were very light and handsome as were the baths, houses, pavilions etc. The whole after dark was like a fairy scene."[190]

Van Horne was so struck by Coney Island, which in those days was truly an island, that he decided to return the following evening with his friend, Mr.

Dumont, and spend the night there. The trip to and from New York City, after all, could be made in an hour by the New York and Manhattan Beach Railway. No mention is made of where they put up for the night, but it was probably at Manhattan Beach or nearby. If they weren't stinting on overnight accommodation, they could have stayed at the recently opened eight-hundred-foot-long Manhattan Beach Hotel, in those days the most elegant and fashionable hotel in the United States.[191] As much as he enjoyed and appreciated elegance and fine appointments, however, it is difficult to imagine Van Horne shelling out money for such luxurious accommodation at this stage of his career. No doubt he and his friend contented themselves with a more modest, but nevertheless comfortable, hostelry with a seaside view.

Van Horne's imminent departure from the Southern Minnesota was announced by the press in late September, prompting a barrage of laudatory letters from railroading colleagues and acquaintances. One of the most notable of these was from the Office of the State Railroad Commission's William Marshall, who wrote, "I regard your removal from Minnesota as a public loss. You have so ably managed an important railroad of the state promoting both the interests of the owners and creditors of the road and adding to the public facilities and political economies of the state."[192]

Although Van Horne was leaving the Southern Minnesota for the Chicago and Alton, and La Crosse for Chicago, he was not severing his connection with the Minnesota road entirely, as he would retain the offices of president and director. Such an arrangement would allow him to continue directing the progress of the extension, which would eventually terminate at Flandreau, South Dakota. The decision to leave La Crosse and Minnesota was a more final one, and Van Horne would find the move difficult for he loved the state and its people. Addie was equally reluctant to leave, but, as her husband pointed out, she probably "would not survive another winter" there.

Upon departing from Minnesota, Van Horne closed the most significant chapter in his American railroading career. As a stepping stone to career advancement, it would prove invaluable because thanks to his newly acquired friends Jason Easton and Peter Myers, he had learned a great deal more about railway financing. He had also broadened his knowledge of other fields and acquired some exposure to a completely new one, politics, all this while yanking a down-at-heels railway out of bankruptcy and making it into a paying property. As a result of this major achievement, and his turnaround of the St. Louis, Kansas City and Northern Railroad, he now enjoyed an excellent reputation among his colleagues in the railroading industry. It was a reputation to be proud of and one that would stand him in good stead when he took on the new challenges that awaited him.

Chapter Four
New Challenges and Hobbies

Van Horne was thirty-five years old, a seasoned railroader, and an experienced professional manager in a cutting-edge industry when he was lured back to the Chicago and Alton in October 1878. When he had first joined the road over fifteen years earlier, it had been as a telegraph operator and ticket agent. With this most recent appointment, he became the general superintendent of an important, well-established railway that during the Timothy Blackstone era (1864 to 1899) never failed to pay a dividend of 6 percent a year and took pride in its claim of being the best sectional road in the West.[193]

Because of his reputation as an iconoclast in railway operations, news of his appointment struck fear in the hearts of many men at the Chicago and Alton. Once he had taken up his new post, however, conscientious employees quickly found that they had no reason to be alarmed. As one railroading man later summed up the situation, "Everybody thought Van Horne would tear things. Everybody looked for lightning to strike. Even the general manager was disturbed over his appointment. But Van Horne went his gait in a characteristic go-ahead style, invariably hitting it right."[194]

The railway that Van Horne was now associated with was a prosperous, well-run road that boasted 840 miles of first mainline and hauled more coal into Chicago than any other road. It was also a prime mover of corn, wheat, and livestock from its Kansas City terminal.[195] But to achieve and maintain this position it waged a ceaseless war with other roads for traffic that had decreased during the depression of the mid-seventies. Ironically, one of these competing railways was Van Horne's old employer, the St. Louis, Kansas City and Northern Railway. Against it the Chicago and Alton competed furiously for Kansas City traffic. Van Horne, with his combative temperament, energy, and abundance of initiative was, of course, well suited to this type of conflict. So he plunged joyously into the struggle, waging such a successful battle for business that he attracted the attention of the heads of other, more important railways.

In his campaign to attract additional traffic, Van Horne introduced an innovation designed to capture passengers through their stomachs. Departing from common practice, he arranged for the railway to own and operate its own dining cars rather than use dining cars supplied by the Pullman Car Company, which had provided the railway with the first dining car used on any road, the *Delmonico*.[196] Once the cars arrived, Van Horne instructed the Alton dining car staff to serve more generous portions than those served by their Pullman counterparts.[197] As general manager of the Canadian Pacific Railway, he would again refuse to lease from the Pullman Company and would instead purchase all CPR sleeping, dining, and parlour cars at the outset.

Van Horne also put his fertile mind to work in another area — car construction. On his frequent visits to the company's car shops he often passed on new ideas to the car builders. If they could not readily grasp what he had in mind, he illustrated his concepts with sketches. When new mail cars were required, he dispatched the Chicago and Alton's master car builder to Washington to learn from the general superintendent of the United States mail service how best to equip a mail car. In the car shops, in fact in all departments, Van Horne revealed himself as a manager obsessed with detail and quality. Fortunately, he was lavish in his praise of good work. On the other hand, he could be scathing in his denunciation of inferior results and performance. Confronted by work or performance that did not meet his quality test, he would go to great pains to see that it soon measured up to his expectations.[198]

Although this young dynamo appeared virtually invincible to fellow railroaders, Van Horne did not succeed in overcoming all the railroading challenges that came his way. On one notable occasion he was soundly defeated by a rival road. The occasion in question involved the travel plans of United States President Rutherford B. Hayes. In 1878, when he was returning from a tour of the West, Hayes decided that he wanted to travel from Kansas City to his hometown of Fremont, Ohio, via Illinois. To accommodate the president's wishes, the official in charge of the president's itinerary asked the Chicago and Alton to furnish a special train for the journey. The railway, only too happy to oblige, immediately entrusted the necessary arrangements to Van Horne, who quickly made up a train of the finest cars that he could lay his hands on and engaged a celebrated Chicago restaurant to provide meals. All seemed in order when the general superintendent and his New York City stockbroker friend George B. Hopkins left Chicago for Kansas City, where the president and his party were to board the special train. It became evident the next day, however, that Van Horne's painstaking plans were not unfolding as anticipated.

At about five o'clock that morning, as the special train stood in the Kansas City terminal yards, the general superintendent rose, dressed, and went outside for a stroll. Passing the telegraph office, he heard telegraph keys tapping out his name. Intrigued, he stopped to listen, and as he stood transfixed his anger quickly mounted. He had good reason to be furious, because the deciphered message revealed that a rival railway official had asked his general manager to make up a special train to take the president's party across Illinois. The elated sender, delirious with joy at the thought of having snared the president's entourage for his road, closed his message with the accurate prediction, "Van Horne will be as mad as hell."

He was as mad as hell, but there was next to nothing that he could do but watch the president arrive at Kansas City and then leave for his hometown on the rival railway's special train. Van Horne returned to the Chicago and Alton's train, stung to the quick and mortified beyond belief. But as upset as he was, he did not explode with rage in front of his friend. In a remarkable demonstration of self-control, Van Horne merely mentioned the rival road's coup and held back from venting his true feelings. The two men then sat back in luxury as the Chicago and Alton special, carrying only the two friends and the train crew, made its way from Kansas City to Chicago, "unlocking" the stretch of line from Kansas City to the Mississippi River that had been "locked" to facilitate the scheduled passage of Hayes's party over the Chicago and Alton road.

As the special hurtled along, the two men spotted crowds of people who had assembled at small western stations to cheer the president. When he realized how eager the waiting spectators were to catch a glimpse of Hayes, Van Horne summoned up his usual resourcefulness. Rather than see the crowds disappointed, he prevailed upon Hopkins, who had donned a frock coat for the occasion, to stand in for Hayes. Accordingly, the handsome, suitably attired Hopkins stood on the train's rear platform and graciously greeted the waiting throngs of people, who were just as impressed by him as they would have been by the president whom he impersonated.

If Van Horne found one redeeming aspect to the depressing journey it would have been the abundance of fine food at the two friends' disposal. They sat down to a $10,000 dinner, with twenty-five waiters in attendance and a chef and five assistants at their beck and call. Given his state of mind, however, it is unlikely that the general superintendent devoured the sumptuous meal with his customary enthusiasm for gourmet fare.

The climax of the day's events occurred when the Chicago and Alton special met the rival road's special at an Illinois junction. Here, Van Horne encountered General William Tecumseh Sherman, one of the Civil War's most able, if controversial, generals, who in 1878 was commanding general of the U.S. Army. Sherman, who was then travelling with the president's entourage, entered Van Horne's car to beg for a Scotch and soda, complaining that he had travelled with the president for four days without so much as one drink. He invited Van Horne to go with him to see Hayes, but the abject general superintendent turned him down. Finally Sherman made his way back to his train, only to return with the president, who said how much he regretted the contretemps. News of the incident circulated widely in railroading circles, where rival railroaders crowed over the humbling of the hitherto invincible Van Horne. Van Horne, of course, felt his defeat keenly, but soon he came to regard it as a great joke.[199]

Although his new position at the Chicago and Alton was demanding, Van Horne still found time to add to his fossil collection and to snatch an hour here and there to discuss fossils with a fellow collector who may have travelled miles to sell him a branchiopod or trilobite. His passion for fossils had become widely known and all along the railway lines men kept an eye out for finds that might interest him. Trilobites, the ancient ancestors of today's spiders, insects, centipedes, crabs, and lobsters, held a special fascination for him, as they do for many present-day paleontologists and collectors, who pay huge prices for top-notch specimens of these bizarre prehistoric bugs. One of his collection's most eagerly sought specimens dated from the time that he was based at Alton, where he had been tantalized for weeks on end by the sight of a magnificent trilobite embedded in one of the town's streets. Finally he could resist the temptation no longer. One morning, he returned to the site with his hammer, deliberately smashed the pavement, and triumphantly carried the slab containing the trilobite away.[200] When he lived in La Crosse, he had the good fortune to be within easy reach of Hokah, which then boasted a limestone quarry rich in fossils. Whenever the men working at this site uncovered a new stratum they would telegraph him, and Van Horne would head to the quarry as soon as he could to hack out specimens.

In Chicago, Van Horne also devoted leisure hours to another favourite pursuit, gardening. He had taken up this hobby in La Crosse, determined to produce larger and more luxurious blooms than his neighbours. In his quest for the perfect bloom, he dug his own beds, took up the study of fertilizers, carefully tended each and every plant himself, and walked long distances on the Bluffs to obtain leaf mould for his roses. A special favourite was the castor oil bean plant, which he clumped together in sizeable masses and coaxed to an impressive height. He experimented with the *datura metel cornucopia* (Devil's Trumpet), an exotic, usually double-flowered, trumpet-shaped plant. According to biographer Walter Vaughan, Van Horne succeeded in producing a "triple trumpet flower" at a time when only the double flower was known, at least in his locality.[201] But gardening also had its lighter, more frivolous side. As if to demonstrate this, Van Horne one day showed that he was still an incurable prankster by planting a malodorous skunk cabbage bed close to the fence that separated his Chicago property from that of his nearest neighbour, a clergyman.

He cultivated tulips and hyacinths in the attic and cellars of the large brick house that the family occupied at 48 Park Avenue, Chicago. Warm and well-lit areas were employed to promote growth and cool, dark ones to delay it. He was exceedingly pleased with the blooms produced under these conditions, so much so that in later years he would heap scorn on the best results achieved by his skilled Montreal gardener, who enjoyed the twin advantages of a conservatory and more modern cultivation techniques.

The family's spacious, rambling Chicago home may have been to Van Horne's liking, but it did not endear itself to Addie, who shuddered when contemplating its profusion of halls and predicted that it would be difficult to keep clean. "I wish I were back in our house [in La Crosse] a thousand times," she wrote plaintively to her sister-in-law Mary in October 1878, shortly after moving into 48 Park Avenue. "We have an immense house without convenience where needed," she explained. Having noted that her mother was better and that her mother-in-law was "unusually well," Addie declared that she was sure that she loved everybody in La Crosse.[202]

This second Chicago interlude would be a trying one for Addie in other ways as well. She was still recovering from the death of her beloved Willie, whose sudden passing had precipitated a long bout of ill health. The brother who had been born after his death, Bennie, was two years old in June 1879, when Addie unburdened herself in a letter to Aunty Kee, her father's sister. This sad litany of trial and tribulation reveals that although Bennie looked very much like "little Willie," he could not, of course, take his place. Moreover, since he was only two years old, the youngest Van Horne required the "constant care" of his mother, who, as a consequence, was housebound most of the time. Chicago's changeable climate, with its abundance of cool, windy weather, was another irritant. Apparently, it did not agree with family members, who appear to have been sick more than usual since their arrival in the Midwestern city. To further complicate matters, Will, as Addie called her husband, was gone much of the time.[203]

Most of Van Horne's time away from Chicago was taken up with visits to La Crosse, where in his continuing role as president of the Southern Minnesota he oversaw the completion of the railway's extension, then being carried out by his friend, and divisional superintendent, John M. Egan. In addition to attending to railway business in La Crosse, Van Horne seized the opportunity to check on some recently acquired investment properties, one of which boasted a farm. These parcels of land had been purchased in Minnesota's Freeborn and Faribault counties in 1877 and 1878,[204] undoubtedly with the aid of funds borrowed from his banker friend Jason Easton. On June 15, 1877, Van Horne owed Easton the large sum of $1,000, which he promised to pay in full in sixty days' time with interest at 10 percent.[205]

The Chicago and Alton had been under his management for only a year when Van Horne accepted an offer to become general superintendent of the Chicago, Milwaukee and St. Paul Railroad, a rapidly expanding railway with extensive mileage in Wisconsin, Illinois, Iowa, the Dakotas, Minnesota, and Missouri. His remarkable success in resurrecting the Southern Minnesota and the tenacity and resourcefulness with which he waged the Chicago and Alton's ferocious battles for traffic had caught the attention of the Milwaukee management. Van Horne's particular type of genius, they were convinced, was just what was needed to consolidate the numerous roads that the St. Paul was acquiring and blend them into a harmonious, effective system. Accordingly, the St. Paul people offered him the titular position of general superintendent, intending to vest him with the duties and powers of a general manager.

A Midwestern road, the Chicago, Milwaukee and St. Paul traced its origins back to 1847, when it was chartered as the Milwaukee & Waukesha Rail Road. Over the years, various reorganizations and acquisitions had resulted in its becoming the Milwaukee and St. Paul in 1863, and then, with the 1873 completion of a line from Milwaukee south to Chicago, the Chicago, Milwaukee and St. Paul in 1874. The railway continued to expand through construction and acquisition during the remainder of the 1870s, inspired by the vision of its president, Alexander Mitchell, a local Milwaukeean who wanted to create a strong, unified rail system to serve the people of Wisconsin and meet the needs of that state's growing agricultural, mining, and lumber industries.[206] Beginning in 1878, the expansion program accelerated under the guidance of the road's general manager, Shelburne S. Merrill, who defined and pushed through such an aggressive policy of expansion that the aggrieved president of the Northwestern Railroad declared that the St. Paul seemed "to be building, buying and negotiating for almost every Road in the market."[207] When congratulating Van Horne on his new appointment, S.A. Miller, a Cincinnati attorney and fellow fossil collector, would echo this rueful observation. Wrote Miller, "I am rejoiced to hear of your good fortune and to learn that the smiles of that eagle which ornaments the American dollar are now being showered into your purse while the extended wings are used to draw all the Railroads of the North West under your control."[208]

Van Horne accepted the plum appointment because, in his blunt phraseology, it was "a question of dollars and future" for him. Nevertheless, his correspondence suggests that he might have turned down the offer had he believed that the Southern Minnesota was still in danger and that a move to the Chicago, Milwaukee and St. Paul would be considered disloyal and improper by his Southern Minnesota colleagues.[209] For ease of mind, Van Horne could take comfort in the fact that the Minnesota road was now under the able management of Peter Myers and John Egan and was in respectable shape. His imminent departure from the Chicago and Alton would not prick his conscience either. Indeed, he could feel sanguine, if not positively jubilant, about the condition in which he was leaving that railway. As he reported to his friend Cornelius Gold in late October 1879:

> Our increase for the year — for the last 8 months of the year — will reach $1,000,000 and that isn't a "spurt." There is more business in sight than ever before — more freight offering than we can possibly move and the immense corn crop is yet to be shipped. We are refusing enough business to support one or two ordinary railroads ... The Kansas City extension is doing splendidly. You will remember that Mr Mitchell and I made a higher estimate of its business than anybody else but it is going to turn out better than even we expected. We have been victorious in our fight, our position is established and nobody wants to step on our coat tails. The Alton has demonstrated its ability to make money in a fight that would ruin any of its competitors ... I think it safe to say we made more money during the 5 months of the fight than in any consecutive 5 months in 7 years before ...[210]

On this soaring note, Van Horne made preparations to leave Chicago for Milwaukee, where he was to take up his new appointment on January 1, 1880.[211] Once again he faced the prospect of uprooting himself from a city in which he had had barely time to settle. Before his departure, however, he had to deal with a host of chores related to the pending move. One of these involved selling the large family home that had so dismayed Addie. It appears that he planned to unload it for $4,500, about $2,000 less than it had cost him with improvements. He also had to line up accommodation in Milwaukee, but this time he intended to lease, not purchase.[212]

New Year's day dawned with the family still in Chicago and Van Horne in Milwaukee, trying to learn the ropes and yearning for the family's arrival. A rank newcomer, he looked forward eagerly to seeing the sights of Wisconsin's largest city, then known as the "Cream City," perhaps an allusion to the light-coloured brick employed in its commercial and residential buildings.[213] Great was his chagrin, therefore, when Shelburne Merrill's sleigh arrived to whisk him off "for a New Years call." To his way of thinking, the much preferred option would have been a tour of the bustling port city and beer-brewing capital, whose extensive gardens, broad, smooth streets, and "general air of elegance and prosperity" would captivate at least one guidebook writer.[214] Summing up the outing for Addie, Van Horne wrote, "Mrs Merrill and a number of other ladies were receiving in fine style. Fortunately business suits are the thing here for a New Years call so I was all right in that respect. I stayed but a few minutes. Mrs M is a very pleasant lady and their house is very fine and has splendid grounds around it."[215]

Rumours had led Van Horne to expect a rather frigid reception from the men at the Chicago, Milwaukee and St. Paul. It was with welcome relief, then, that he was able to inform Addie, "I have been very cordially received here — more cordially than I could have expected in view of the harsh colours in which I have been pictured to the employees. From what I have heard some of them looked for a regular ogre with fangs and fiery breath."[216] As promising as this initial assessment of the situation was, not all was smooth sailing. Although his qualifications for the job could not be disputed, several important officials objected strenuously to a new man being placed over their heads and did not hesitate to express their antagonism. They even encouraged insubordination on the part of younger men. Although outwardly indifferent to the hostile atmosphere that surrounded him, Van Horne was, in fact, very sensitive to it. And since he was a man who believed in not beating around the bush, he decided on one occasion to confront the situation head-on. "Why are you prejudiced against me?" he asked Frederick D. Underwood, a young clerk who would become president of the Erie Railroad in 1899 and would be remembered for rebuilding it. "I am not prejudiced; and now that I come to think of it, I have no reason to be against you at all," replied Underwood.[217] It would be several months before Van Horne could feel that he had the full support of his fellow officers. By 1881, however, his expertise, inexhaustible patience in thrashing out details and business plans, natural buoyancy of spirit, and irresistible personality had won over all the disaffected.

During the first year that Van Horne was with the Milwaukee road it acquired still more small roads and added another Mississippi bridge at Sabula, Iowa. As a result of two of these acquisitions, in 1880 the railway boasted 3,775 miles of track and owned 425 locomotives, 13,000 freight cars, and 319 passenger cars.[218] The task of integrating the road's different branches, such as the Chicago and Pacific, and welding them into one well-coordinated system represented a major challenge for the new general superintendent. But he faced an even more intimidating one: pruning the Milwaukee's costs of operation. Ruthless rate wars between rival roads, especially those in competitive regions, had led to a steady reduction in freight rates. Where formerly a profit could be made on an average rate of one and a half or two cents per pound of freight, now it was almost impossible to meet interest charges and retain dividends on an average rate of a cent or less a pound.[219] One solution to the problem, and the one adopted by Van Horne, was to institute more economical methods of operation.

For this he was eminently qualified, having, of course, successfully implemented stringent economies at the Southern Minnesota when he served as its general manager. Installed at the Chicago, Milwaukee and St. Paul, he immediately set about slashing costs and introducing efficiencies in its operations. He implemented cost-cutting measures in every area, singling out the freight department for special attention. In freight transportation, his goal was to reduce costs as much as possible by increasing the train load and lowering the ton-mile cost. According to Walter Vaughan, men not familiar with Van Horne's past history were astonished by the liberties he took in making up a train, while men who knew his reputation applauded his resourcefulness and ingenuity. An unidentified railroader reported that Van Horne started a revolution in the operation of railroads and the cost of operating, and railway presidents of today continue to practise the methods introduced by him. He taught the railway world how to load cars to their fullest capacity. In fact, it might be said that he created cars on the Milwaukee by making eight hundred do the work of a thousand. He applied similar strictures to engines and, indeed, to all the equipment.[220]

This assessment of Van Horne's contribution to railway operations is supported by Frank Underwood, who gained Van Horne's confidence during the time they worked together on the Chicago, Milwaukee and St. Paul. "Most of the present, up-to-date methods of transportation were thought out by him. Some of them have been enlarged and improved. The original suggestions, however, were his," Underwood informed Katherine Hughes.[221]

As might be expected, not everybody lauded Van Horne's revolutionary methods for optimizing the performance of railway equipment. The Milwaukee's locomotive engineers were aghast when they learned how he wanted their beloved locomotives to be treated. In the eyes of these pioneer engineers the locomotive was a sentient being. As such, it should be spared unnecessary strain and be driven by only one person. The engineers therefore protested loudly when Van Horne ordered that a locomotive be driven to its fullest capacity and that it be operated by whichever qualified engineer was available for the job. Their protests were in vain.

As part of his campaign to streamline operations and reduce costs, Van Horne instituted a comprehensive store and accounting system. This was preceded by the appointment of a three-member committee to study and report on the systems adopted by other large railways. One of the committee members was Van Horne's young clerk, Thomas George Shaughnessy, destined to become a protegé of Van Horne's and to play a major role in the CPR. Shaughnessy returned with an excellent report and recommendations, and in short order his boss set about implementing a "complete and coordinated system of railway stores and accounting."[222] The new system, which went into effect January 1, 1881, was managed by Shaughnessy, who took charge of all materials for the locomotive and car departments and kept accounts for them.

Among Van Horne's many responsibilities at the Chicago, Milwaukee and St. Paul was the erection of new stations and buildings. It was a challenge that he welcomed, for it provided him with an opportunity to marry function with art and to express himself in the creation of new structures. Hitherto, railways had been content to erect merely cost-saving, functional buildings. Van Horne, however, set out to design structures that not only met the requirements of function and economy but also harmonized with their surroundings and appealed to the eye. Some of the plans that he produced for the Milwaukee were used during his stint with the road, while others were filed away, to be resurrected between 1906 and 1909 when the western extension was built. At that time the road's architects pronounced them more up-to-date and in tune with current railway conditions than any other available plans.[223]

No sooner had Van Horne become general superintendent of the Chicago, Milwaukee and St. Paul than it managed to snare his old road, the Southern Minnesota, a road in which it owned a majority of the common stock. The purchase was made in the spring of 1880, years after a prescient Van Horne told Cornelius Gold, "The CM & St. P want the S.M. road badly."[224] As much as it coveted the Southern Minnesota, however, the Milwaukee road waited five years before gaining full control of it. The takeover proceeded without reported incident. But such was not the case when the Chicago, Milwaukee and St. Paul set out to secure possession of a small, obscure road called the Chicago, Rockford and Northern.

The smaller road was in receivership when the Milwaukee attempted to secure possession of it in the winter of 1880–81. Since the Milwaukee road was engaged in a continuing dispute with the road's receiver, Van Horne had recourse to what can only be described as rough-and-tumble tactics. One day he summoned A.J. Earling, a divisional superintendent, to his office and thrust a large bundle of documents and correspondence at him with the order to go out and take possession of the Chicago, Rockford and Northern. Earling did as instructed, taking with him two engines and twenty men. After reaching the crossing of the two roads, he had the engines moved onto the smaller road's line. And there they sat.

When the receiver attempted to oust the trespassers and recover possession, he found himself confronted by Earling with his mountain of documents and phalanx of men. Dismissing the documents as inconsequential and unable to move Earling by persuasion, the receiver hastened back to Chicago for reinforcements of his own. The divisional superintendent suspected what he was up to and telegraphed Van Horne for more men. Both sides proceeded to raise the stakes until Earling eventually had eight hundred men supporting him on the spot. Five or six times a day he consulted with his chief by telegraph and at the end of each parley Van Horne reiterated by wire, "Be sure to have plenty of good provisions for your men. As long as you keep their bellies full, they will remain loyal." Fortified by good food, the Milwaukee squad emerged from a week of enforced idleness and threats with flying colours. Van Horne's road remained in possession of the Chicago, Rockford and Northern and subsequently the courts decided that the two claimants should have joint use of the disputed road.[225]

Van Horne had been with the Chicago, Milwaukee and St. Paul for just a little over a year and a half when he was invited to become general manager of the infant and faltering Canadian Pacific Railway, then embarking on the construction of Canada's first transcontinental railway. He was now thirty-eight years of age, nearing the prime of his life. He had resurrected one bankrupt railway, the Southern Minnesota, left another, the Chicago and Alton, in admirable shape, and had recently completed the consolidation of the Chicago, Milwaukee and St. Paul's jumbled network. Now he was looking to expand the rich and powerful Milwaukee road into the Red River Valley, where his friend James Jerome Hill was attempting to cement the hold of his St. Paul, Minneapolis and Manitoba Railroad.

Van Horne's plans to build a branch from Ortonville in Dakota Territory to tap into Canadian business to the north did not, of course, sit well with Hill. The prospect of this shrewd, aggressive general superintendent pushing his road into what Hill considered to be his private preserve was not just unsettling, it was positively alarming. Hill could have fended off his potential rival by persuading him to throw in his lot with the Manitoba. Instead, he resorted to another solution, one that was prompted by his association with the CPR. As a member of the CPR's executive committee, the transplanted Canadian was acutely aware of its myriad problems and of its need for a strong, able general manager. He therefore talked his rival into taking on the Canadian road. For Van Horne, this latest job offer would prove to be the opportunity of a lifetime.

Chapter Five
New Horizons

Van Horne was earning his laurels as general superintendent of the Chicago, Milwaukee and St. Paul when fate intervened in the form of Hill's unexpected job proposition. The actual offer was made by the president of the fledgling Canadian Pacific Railway Company, George Stephen, who asked Van Horne if he would take on the position of general manager of the CPR, then embarking on the most daunting railway construction project ever undertaken.

More ambitious than even the celebrated Union Pacific in the United States, this undertaking aimed to link eastern Canada with British Columbia by a ribbon of steel, thereby fulfilling an essential condition of the agreement by which that province had entered Confederation in 1871. Dr. J.S. Helmcken, a leading member of British Columbia's Legislative Council in 1870, had declared bluntly in relation to the railway question, "We should be better off without Canada if we have no Railway."[226] Now, an increasingly impatient British Columbia was waiting for the promised railway to become a reality.

At the time the offer was made to Van Horne, in the early autumn of 1881, the company was in the early stages of constructing railway links between Callander (near Lake Nipissing) and Port Arthur (now Thunder Bay), Ontario, as well as between Winnipeg and Savona's Ferry, on Lake Kamloops in British Columbia. Government contractors were laying track between Port Arthur and Winnipeg and between Port Moody, British Columbia, and Savona's Ferry. To complete the monumental task assigned to it the CPR would have to build 650 miles across mostly intractable terrain in wild, remote northern Ontario, 850 miles across undulating prairie, and approximately 500 miles in mountainous British Columbia. It would also have to take over the operation of the government-built segments once they were completed and operate the entire transcontinental line in an efficient manner. To the new general manager would fall the awesome responsibility of determining a significant portion of the CPR's main line, pushing through its construction, organizing all the company's departments, selecting the men who would preside over them, and supervising day-to-day operations. It was a challenge well calculated to intimidate any top railroading man of the day, even Van Horne.

The Milwaukee general superintendent was more than secure in his job. It counted for a lot that Alexander Mitchell and Shelburne Merrill were extremely pleased with his performance and would be loath to lose him. For a young man of Van Horne's towering ambition and energy, however, the challenge of building an epic transcontinental railway in Canada and the far-reaching nature of its general manager's responsibilities were tempting beyond words. Equally enticing was the dazzling prospect of adventure and of making things happen, of seeing bustling communities spring up alongside newly laid railway track.

Irresistible as these considerations appeared, though, Van Horne was not prepared to accept the offer without first travelling north of the border and making a reconnaissance of the CPR's operations. Only after he had seen first-hand Winnipeg and the rugged wilderness of the Canadian Shield did he signal his intention to throw in his lot with the CPR's big gamble. In doing so, he perhaps sensed that his acceptance would mark a turning point in his career and his life.

Although the Canadian Pacific Railway Company was incorporated on February 16, 1881, the issue of a transcontinental road had been stirring the passions of Canadians ever since Confederation. Indeed, as far back as 1867, many observers believed that the embryonic country might not survive without such a railway to tie the fragile union together. One such observer was Sir John A. Macdonald, Canada's first prime minister. He realized that such a railway was essential if Canada was to strengthen the extremely tenuous control that it had over the country west of Ontario, confirm Canada's ownership of the West, and bring British Columbia into the union. When British Columbia did enter Confederation in 1871, with the federal government's promise to begin construction of a railway to the Pacific in two years and complete it within ten, the building of such a road became both imperative and urgent.

An undertaking of this magnitude, however, posed a huge challenge: not only was Canada a vast, sprawling country with a population of less than four million people but it also had a chronic shortage of capital and a federal government with slender resources. Moreover, building a railway line across the rocky, barren Canadian Shield and through vast, mountainous British Columbiaa would pose horrendous construction problems and involve huge expense.

After considering various possibilities, Macdonald's Conservative government decided to have a private company build and operate the railway, but with some government assistance, just as there had been for earlier railways and canals. In this case, the company that obtained the contract would be awarded a grant of $30,000,000 and 50,000,000 acres of land. Two companies immediately competed for the contract: the Interoceanic Company, an all-Canadian concern headed by Senator David L. Macpherson, and the Canadian Pacific Railway Company, which included both Canadian and American interests and which was led by Sir Hugh Allan, the powerful Canadian steamship entrepreneur. The prime minister tried to persuade the two companies to join forces, but when negotiations broke down he chose Allan, the experienced financier with an international reputation. Macdonald then issued a charter to set up the Canadian Pacific Railway Company with directors from the membership of each group.

The whole enterprise collapsed in 1873, however, after the eruption of the "Pacific Scandal" and the revelation that Allan, a cohort of Jay Cooke, the American railway magnate, had contributed large sums of money to the Conservative party in the federal election of August 1872. The sordid details of the Pacific Scandal shook the Conservatives, and a sharply critical speech in the House by Conservative member Donald A. Smith (later Lord Strathcona) delivered the final blow to the beleaguered government. On November 5, 1873, convinced that he would be defeated on a division, a haggard Macdonald handed in his resignation. Later, on January 22, 1874, he went down to a crushing defeat in a general election that saw the redoubtable Independent Donald Smith stand for his Selkirk seat and support Liberal leader Alexander Mackenzie.

When Alexander Mackenzie's fundamentally unprepared Liberal government took office in November 1873, not a mile of the CPR had been built, although significant progress had been made in conducting surveys for the proposed transcontinental line. These had been led by the visionary and persistent Sandford Fleming (later Sir Sandford), who had been appointed chief engineer of the Canadian Pacific Railway in April 1871. Fleming, who would become deeply involved in the railway's planning, launched his survey parties in the newly created province of British Columbia and then followed up the work there with a survey of the Prairies.

Fairly soon in the undertaking the engineer concluded that the Yellowhead Pass in the Rockies offered the best route for a railway, and in April 1872 his choice was officially approved by an order-in-council. The decision to adopt the Yellowhead Pass essentially dictated the route westward from the Red River, which Fleming decided to bridge at Selkirk instead of at Winnipeg twenty miles to the south. From Selkirk the line was to head northwest, cross the fertile valley of the North Saskatchewan River by way of Battleford and Edmonton, and then run southwest to the Yellowhead Pass. From there it would continue down the valleys of the Thompson and Fraser Rivers to Burrard Inlet on the Pacific. In the East, the line would run across rugged, desolate terrain from Lake Nipissing to Fort William.

In one of life's ironies, frugal, Scottish-born Alexander Mackenzie took on the thankless Ministry of Public Works portfolio, which required that he supervise the building of a railway that he and other Liberals had been attacking and denouncing for years. A former stonemason, Mackenzie shared to some extent Macdonald's vision of a Canada that stretched from ocean to ocean, and honourable man that he was he realized that his government could not ignore the pledge made to British Columbia, no matter how irresponsible he might think it. Nevertheless, the prime minister did not see how it was economically feasible to complete a railway in the near future given the advent of the Great Depression, dwindling government funds, and his own frugal, mid-nineteenth-century laissez-faire beliefs. He certainly wanted to see a transcontinental railway built, but he was troubled and baffled by the means of achieving such an ambitious goal.

Mackenzie soon let it be known that the railway could not be completed by 1881 and that the agreement with British Columbia would have to be modified. He also announced that his government would attempt to interest a private company in constructing the line, and to this end he shoved through the Canadian Pacific Railway Act of 1874, offering $12,000 cash and 20,000 acres of land per mile of main-line track to the capitalist with the most suitable bid. However, with the depression in full force and memories of the Pacific Scandal still fresh, there were no takers. Confronted by this situation, Mackenzie and the Liberals adopted a cautious strategy involving the piecemeal building of the most urgently required sections. In line with this thinking a plan was devised that called for the government to construct a few short lines and to link them up to steamboats (on "the watery stretches") and to existing railways. It was hoped that such incremental construction would be enough to satisfy the demands of the West and prevent British Columbia's withdrawal from Canada without enraging the cost-conscious electorate or Mackenzie's divided caucus.

Accordingly, work was begun on the so-called Pembina branch, which was to connect St. Boniface, across the Red River from Winnipeg, with St. Vincent, Minnesota, on the international border. (Macdonald charged that a bill proposing the lease of this branch to an American railway company was intended as a reward to Donald Smith for the "servile support" he had given the Liberals.)[227] A telegraph line from British Columbia to Winnipeg was placed under contract in 1874, and the following year provision was made for its extension to Lake Superior. In the East, the Canada Central Railway, a road that would furnish an invaluable link in extending the future CPR eastward to Montreal, was awarded a subsidy to extend its line from near Pembroke, north of Ottawa, to Lake Nipissing. A bill providing for construction of a railway from Esquimalt to Nanaimo on Vancouver Island was defeated in the Senate, however, leaving restless British Columbia with nothing to show for the railway clause in the union agreement.

Notwithstanding the depression and shortage of funds, Mackenzie's government spent 25 percent of its budget on surveys and construction in one year alone. All told, it managed to construct some 700 miles of line before it was tossed out of office. This mileage included the Pembina branch, which, in 1878, connected at the border with the St. Paul & Pacific, later the St. Paul, Minneapolis & Manitoba Railroad (now the Great Northern Railway).

In the federal election of September 17, 1878, which followed an exceptionally rancorous session, Mackenzie's government was soundly defeated by Macdonald and his Conservatives, who rode back into power on the strength of their National Policy and its system of protective tariffs. Returned to the position of prime minister, Macdonald postponed a decision on the railway for two years while he preoccupied himself with other matters. Only when British Columbia threatened to secede and it became patently evident that the resurrected Northern Pacific or some other American railway near the international border might build spurs northward into Canada and siphon off commerce from the Northwest did he decide to act on the railway question.

Fortunately the depression of the seventies was lifting by then and various parties had begun to express an interest in building and operating a transcontinental railway. One of these businessmen was Duncan McIntyre, who controlled the Canada Central Railway, but behind him were the directors of the St. Paul, Minneapolis and Manitoba Railway, notably the impressive figure of George Stephen, whom Van Horne would come to know well. To Stephen and other members of this remarkable group of men, Donald Smith, R.B. Angus, and Van Horne's friend James J. Hill, would eventually fall the task of building the CPR.

Van Horne was busy transforming the bankrupt Southern Minnesota Railroad into a paying property when Donald A. Smith, George Stephen, and James Hill began pursuing a common interest in transportation in the Red River valley in Minnesota and Manitoba. Stephen and Smith were strangers to Van Horne when the CPR syndicate approached him with its job offer. James J. Hill, of course, was not.

Since their first meeting in 1876, Hill had become Van Horne's mentor and friend, which is not surprising. Both of them were driven, gifted, practical railroading men with amazing stamina, inquiring minds, a strong aesthetic streak, and a passion for art. They even bore a striking physical resemblance to each other — stocky, bald, and barrel-chested. Once Van Horne began to make his influence felt in the CPR, however, the two railroading men started down the path toward arch-rivalry and bitter antagonism. The result was a feud that lasted the duration of Van Horne's service with the CPR and that is all too often singled out for special attention by observers who ignore or downplay other aspects of their relationship. This is indeed unfortunate, because the Van Horne–Hill relationship, was, as Hill biographer Abro Martin rightly points out, essentially a very creative one.[228]

Ontario-born James Jerome Hill, the celebrated "Empire Builder" who pushed the Great Northern Railway west to the Pacific coast, started his career as an independent businessman. His base of operations, St. Paul, Minnesota, at the head of navigation on the Mississippi, was the embarkation point for both Canadians and Americans headed northward to the Canadian Prairies, since Canada north of the Great Lakes was too rugged and lake-strewn to afford easy access from the east. Hill was seventeen years old when he strode into St. Paul in mid-summer 1856, an ambitious youth of tireless energy and foresight who dreamed of building a fleet of steam-

Courtesy of the National Archives of Canada, C6654.

James J. Hill, empire builder of the American Northwest and Van Horne's friend and arch railroading rival.

boats on exotic rivers in the Orient. St. Paul, he hoped, would be the first leg of a journey westward to the fabled lands of the Far East and the making of his destiny.[229] It was in this raw frontier city, the transportation hub for the American West, however, that shrewd young James made his home and launched his outstanding, multifaceted career. Eventually this career would rank him among the leading organizers and managers of the American West.

Hill first found employment as a shipping clerk for a firm that served as local agents for the Dubuque and St. Paul Company's fleet of Mississippi steamboats. He worked for several employers over the next several years and then, as might be expected of an extremely intelligent, highly motivated, highly acquisitive individual, he went into business for himself. By the 1860s, this hard-driving entrepreneur had his own forwarding and transportation agency as well as a thriving fuel business, which would become one of the cornerstones of his fortune.

At first Hill was primarily interested in the Mississippi trade, but as time went on he began to cast his eye north to the lusciously fertile Red River valley, which he expected would soon attract a steady stream of immigrants, provided suitable transportation was available. As it was, Red River ox carts furnished the only freight transportation in this period. Cumbersome, two-wheeled vehicles, made entirely of wood and bound with leather, they lumbered along with their shrieking wooden axles emitting an almost deafening sound. On the five-hundred-mile, approximately thirty-day trip between St. Paul and the Red River valley, the carts carried provisions and groceries for valley trappers and pioneer wheat farmers; inbound to St. Paul, they bore buffalo hides and beaver, otter, and muskrat pelts.[230] Looking to the future, James Hill realized that a water transportation business located in St. Paul was ideally situated to serve not only the valley itself but also the huge expanse of Canadian prairie that lay beyond. And so the young man began scheming to gain control of the river traffic between St. Paul and Fort Garry, in Winnipeg. Before making his first, exploratory moves into the Red River trade, though, he joined forces with another Canadian-born entrepreneur, tough, courtly Norman Kittson.

Kittson, who was almost twenty-five years Hill's senior, had entered the employ of John Jacob Astor's American Fur Company when only sixteen years old. After roaming around Lower and Upper Canada in pursuit of furs, he had headed off in the 1830s to northern Minnesota, where he spent years near the international border competing with the posts and traders of the Hudson's Bay Company. Finally, in 1854, he settled in St. Paul, where he served as mayor in 1858 and 1859 and where he established what would become a flourishing general supply house. By the time that Hill arrived on the scene, Kittson was already a venerable pioneer with the distinction of having completed several terms in the Minnesota legislature as a member from the Pembina district. He was also one of St. Paul's leading businessmen and wealthiest citizens, having amassed a small fortune as a forwarding agent for the Hudson's Bay Company in St. Paul and as a successful investor in real estate.

Kittson came into contact with Hill though their mutual interest in operating barges and steamers on the Red River. The two men became good friends, and when the Hudson's Bay Company looked askance at Kittson's dealing with independent traders. Kittson arranged to turn over this business to Hill as a casual partner. When it came to commercial ventures Hill and Kittson usually collaborated with each other, but not always. Sometimes collaboration gave way to ruthless competition. Such was the case after regular steamboat service was established on the Red River in 1871 to carry immigrants, their belongings, and supplies from St. Paul to Winnipeg in the newly established province of Manitoba. A steamboat operated by Hill's firm, Hill, Griggs and Company, competed head-to-head with a vessel operated by Kittson for the fast-growing river trade. The ruthless competition continued until Jim Hill quietly abandoned his aggressive tactics and arranged for his company to merge with the Kittson operation. The result was the formation, in 1872, of the Red River Transportation Company, which soon gained a monopoly over transportation on the Red River and went on to earn its two partners a great deal of money even in the depths of the international depression.

Although he had been interested in Red River and Canadian trade for several years, Hill did not venture down the river and into Manitoba until March 1870. From a weather standpoint, the timing of the journey could not have been less propitious as winter still had a firm grip on the land north of St. Paul. Hill, however, was eager to size up the situation in Fort Garry, where Métis rebels, under the leadership of fiery Louis Riel, had been stoutly resisting Ottawa's attempts to impose its authority on the newly created province of Manitoba. The absence of a telegraphic link between Ottawa and Fort Garry and the immense obstacles to travel between eastern and western Canada meant that nobody in the nation's capital knew what was going on in the Manitoba outpost. Hill, the transplanted Canadian, who had been closely following developments in the emerging dominion, suggested to the federal government that he find out first-hand what was happening there. Besides, he wanted to sniff out potential trading opportunities in the Red River country, as trade between Fort Garry and St. Paul had been growing rapidly since the end of the

Civil War. When his offer was gratefully accepted by Joseph Howe, Secretary of State for the Provinces, the intrepid adventurer embarked on a gruelling, stamina-testing trip to Fort Garry, travelling by the St. Paul and Pacific Railroad, stagecoach, dog team, and even river raft.

As his dog sled was pushing across the remaining miles of frozen wilderness to Fort Garry, Hill spotted a party coming from the fort. One of its members was Donald Alexander Smith, who was en route to Ottawa from Fort Garry, where he had been acting as Macdonald's personal emissary in his dealings with the rebels. The two snow-encrusted travellers had first met on Christmas Day in 1869, when the enterprising, shrewd Smith had paused briefly in St. Paul on his trip to the fort.[231] At that time, the two adventurers had talked about the need for improved transportation on the north-south axis. Now, on the snow-driven prairie near the American frontier hamlet of Pembina, they broached the topic once again after discussing the Métis revolt and the need for the government at Ottawa to move quickly to assert its authority. Before taking leave of each other, the two travellers came to the conclusion that the Red River country had a bright future, if only its problems of transportation and politics could be resolved. It was a topic that would preoccupy them in 1873 and 1874 when Smith, making his annual spring pilgrimage to the opening of Parliament, stayed with the Hills in St. Paul.

Donald Alexander Smith, a man of vision and dogged determination who shared Hill's consuming interest in transportation, was born in Scotland in 1820. As a penniless youth of eighteen he sailed for Canada, where he entered the employ of the Hudson's Bay Company. He served at posts on the lower St. Lawrence River before spending twenty years in remote, bleak Labrador, which he left in 1869 to take charge of the Hudson's Bay Company's Montreal district. Later he spent a great deal of time in the future province of Manitoba, which he came to know well. After being sent by Sir John A. Macdonald to Manitoba in 1870 to defuse the crisis at Fort Garry, he would go on to become chief commissioner of the HBC in 1871, a member of the Manitoba legislature, and a member of Parliament, to which he was elected also in 1871.

As a result of his March 1870 and subsequent visits to Manitoba, Hill became impressed by the fertility of the Red River valley, and so with his partners he moved energetically into the steamboating and forwarding trade. Yet as he did so the young man realized that the days of this commerce were numbered, because once railways, which provided all-weather service, reached the Red River they would soon eliminate river traffic altogether. Moreover, when one of these railways extended its line to the international boundary to connect there with a Canadian road, Fort Garry would be linked to St. Paul in an all-weather route. People and freight arriving in St. Paul by rail would no longer have to be transferred to Red River carts or dog sleds and hauled to a landing stage on the Red River for a barge trip north to Fort Garry. The resulting savings and convenience would be incalculable. Jim Hill therefore began to follow the fortunes of the St. Paul and Pacific Railroad, the road widely expected to extend a branch line north to the border. In fact, the plight of this much-abused railway became his favourite topic, for Hill knew that whoever controlled this road would control the transportation corridor between his home city and Winnipeg.[232] And Hill was determined to have a large stake in the new order.

Created by the reorganization of the bankrupt Minnesota and Pacific Railroad in 1862, the St. Paul and Pacific struggled for years, under-financed and controlled by different groups until 1870, when it was acquired by the Northern Pacific, which was guided by Jay Cooke, the principal financier of the Union cause in the Civil War. When the NP became bankrupt in 1873, one of the St. Paul and Pacific's two sections, the revenue-producing First Division, was placed in bankruptcy. With the railway thrust into limbo, Jim Hill was poised to gain control of the road. In fact, he had devoted years to preparing for just such an opportunity by acquiring a wide knowledge of all the practical aspects of railroading and by mastering the many intricacies of the St. Paul and Pacific's financial and legal history.

What particularly interested Hill about the railway was its so-called St. Vincent Extension, which, when completed, would continue its main line from Breckenridge, just north of St. Paul, to the international boundary. The railway and its potential also interested Donald Smith. Smith, who was often required to make the long, difficult journey from Montreal to Winnipeg on Hudson's Bay Company business, dreamt of improved communications between eastern Canada and the Northwest, communications that would link Manitoba with the outside world and open the Northwest to settlement. The Hudson's Bay official therefore seized the opportunity of a stopover at St. Paul in October 1873 to discuss the languishing St. Paul and Pacific with Hill and Kittson. In this and subsequent meetings were sown the seeds of a five-year battle for control of a railway plum that was ripe for plucking.

Initially just Hill, Smith, and Kittson were involved in the scheme to seize control of the road. However, when it became imperative that substantial sums of money be raised to buy the railway's bonds from its Dutch bondholders, Smith enlisted the help of his first cousin George Stephen (later Lord Mount Stephen), with whom he had discussed at length his dreams of rail connections between eastern Canada and the Northwest. Smith realized that it would probably be the distant future before any transcontinental Canadian railway linked eastern Canada with the settlements on the Red and Saskatchewan Rivers. After all, the stupendous Canadian Pacific Railway project had already been postponed twice, first by the Pacific Scandal and then by the Great Depression. Nevertheless, the Hudson's Bay Company officer questioned whether the Canadian West should have to wait indefinitely for the advent of more favourable circumstances and the revival of the scheme. A visionary, he was convinced that it was possible to provide a simpler, more provisional system of communication to bridge the distance between eastern Canada and the Northwest. Indeed, it was more than just possible, since the components for such a system were already in place, or soon would be. Mackenzie's government was building a branch of the future Canadian Pacific Railway south to Pembina, and the St. Paul and Pacific was creeping, albeit with great difficulty, northwards toward Canada. When they got together in Montreal to discuss "anything and everything of importance," Smith told his cousin that if the Hill-Kittson-Smith group could gain control of the railway at a bargain price and persuade the Canadian government to lease running rights over the Winnipeg-Pembina branch to the St. Paul and Pacific, railway communication could be completed between eastern and western Canada.

For his part, Stephen could not summon up much enthusiasm for the St. Paul and Pacific lines and the possible role that they could play in securing railway connection between eastern Canada and the Northwest. Donald Smith would later explain that his cousin "thought of Minnesota, as many others did, that it was at the North Pole somewhere."[233] It was not until May 1877, when Smith and Hill met with Stephen in Montreal, that the Montreal financier showed a glimmer of interest in the associates' scheme to gain control of the St. Paul and Pacific and push it all the way to the Canadian border. After Jim Hill had spun his rhetorical web, the three men arrived at several tentative agreements, one of which would see Stephen attempt to obtain British funding when he was on a planned trip to London in the autumn. In September, following a trial run over the lines of the St. Paul and Pacific, Smith's cousin decided to become a full-fledged member of the enterprise.

George Stephen, a tall, sartorially elegant man with soulful eyes, was a former draper's assistant and, like Smith, an immigrant from Scotland. After settling in Montreal, he had become a pillar of the Scottish business community and one of Canada's leading businessmen. By the time that Hill first met him, in the spring of 1877, Stephen had parlayed the small fortune that he had made in dry goods into a much larger one encompassing the Paton Woollen Mills of Sherbrooke, a rolling mill that made iron rails for railways, and a company that produced railway cars and locomotives. After being elected in 1871 a director of the Bank of Montreal, then Canada's most important financial institution, he had gone on to become its president in 1876. In short, he was a man of enterprise, courage, and determination. He was also a businessman who combined prudence with original and daring thinking.

Fortunately for the success of the venture, Hill and Stephen hit it off well on their first meeting, as would Stephen and Van Horne when they first met. Because he had gotten on well with Hill and had the courage to take gambles, Stephen decided to take a chance on the project. He agreed then and there that when he visited England in the fall he would attempt to raise a major share of the $5.5 million required to purchase the railway's bonds and to foreclose on and complete the road. The worldwide depression throttled his attempts to raise investment funds in England's financial markets. Nevertheless the new associate demonstrated his mettle by summoning his colleagues to Montreal in December 1877 and devising an alternate plan to finance the railway's takeover.

By then two other financiers had become involved in the project: Richard B. Angus, who would later be closely involved with Van Horne in the CPR, and John S. Kennedy. Angus, who was destined to play a major role in the St. Paul and Pacific enterprise and later the CPR, was an affable Scot whose faculty was cultivating business and social contacts and negotiating railway takeovers. In 1869, his business acumen and diplomatic skills had vaulted him into the general manager's chair at the Bank of Montreal. His soon-to-be associate John Kennedy was a shrewd, hardworking Scottish immigrant who had come to the United States in 1857 at the age of twenty-seven.[234] After earning a partnership in the respected financial house of Morris K. Krupp, he had left to launch his own firm, J.S. Kennedy & Company, which specialized in funnelling investment capital into the risky arena of western railways. In 1874, when the hapless Dutch investors sought to have a receiver appointed to the St. Paul and Pacific, they chose Kennedy's firm to represent their interests in the United States. Largely because of Kennedy's influence, aging, avaricious Jesse P. Farley, of Dubuque, Iowa, whom Van Horne would describe as "a stinker,"[235] was appointed the receiver in charge of managing the railway's bankrupt First Division and any construction that it undertook.

Farley's appointment played directly into the hands of the associates, who took advantage of his receivership and management to further their plans to seize control of the railway. Aided by Kennedy, who joined Stephen in raising capital, and by Farley, who worked closely with Hill and Kittson to persuade the Dutch that the railway was a loser, the associates forged ahead with their scheme. By February 1878, Hill, Smith, Kittson, Stephen, and Kennedy, who would form a lifelong friendship with Hill, had succeeded in convincing the Dutch consortium to accept the associates' offer for all classes of bonds. The four original partners then proceeded to obtain a line of credit from the Bank of Montreal and pay off the Dutch bondholders, who possessed the only real equity in the railway. The following month, March, the associates were in control of the road. With proceeds from the sale of special debentures and land grants in Minnesota, they pressed ahead with completion of the through line from St. Paul to Emerson. After it became operational in November, it was extended over the international border to Emerson, Manitoba, where it linked up with the recently completed Pembina branch of the CPR. Manitoba was at last linked to the outside world, much to Hill's and Smith's delight. For Hill now saw himself controlling rail traffic to and from the Red River valley, while Smith saw himself presiding over the brisk sale of Hudson's Bay Company lands.

The next stage in the takeover saga occurred in January 1879, when Stephen negotiated the purchase of the First Division's stock, thereby enabling the partners to foreclose on the railway's properties. Once full control of the road had been gained, Hill wasted little time in sending Jesse Farley packing. It was a move fraught with consequences, as was Hill's contemptuous dismissal of certain demands by the receiver, who insisted that he be rewarded for his services.

The four original associates called their new corporate entity the St. Paul, Minneapolis and Manitoba Railway Company. Stephen was made president and Kittson vice-president. Hill undertook its management, assisted by R.B. Angus. In no time at all the associates were making money from both the railway's operations and the sale of lands awarded by the Minnesota legislature. Their various machinations and ferocious hard work had paid off, but even more important, the fruit of their labours, the Manitoba, would, under expert management, increase its value dramatically and earn exceedingly handsome profits for its partners and shareholders. Still later, it would metamorphose into the Great Northern and earn the distinction of being the only transcontinental American road that did not go under during the American railway crash of 1893.[236]

In the meantime, the associates had to contend with an enraged and frustrated Farley, who claimed that they had failed to carry out their promise to make him a partner in the Manitoba. It is not clear what, if anything, the partners had promised him in return for his services. Promising the receiver anything would have been not only wrong, but also illegal. In any event, when he was not given what he wanted, Farley went to court, charging the associates with breaking an oral contract that promised him a one-fifth share in the railway. After failing before the Minnesota Supreme Court and then the U.S. District Court, Farley appealed his case to the U.S. Supreme Court, which finally ruled in 1889 that Farley could not demonstrate that an oral contract had been made. The verdict was joyous news to the anxious associates. Notwithstanding the verdict, the fact remains that they had undoubtedly colluded with Farley and that in all probability Kennedy, Stephen, Hill, and Kittson did offer him a substantial reward, perhaps a full partnership, in return for his cooperation. Whatever happened, this unsavoury episode would long taint the reputations of those involved.[237]

The story is told that when Macdonald was looking for railway builders in 1880 to construct the long-promised transcontinental railway, John Henry Pope drew his attention to George Stephen and his associates, declaring, "Catch them before they invest their profits."[238] The remark of the next minister of railways and canals could not have been more timely, given that Stephen and his partners had just chalked up a major success in the type of enterprise that was at stake in the CPR and were now looking to the future. The associates could have contented themselves with cementing the Manitoba's hold on western Minnesota and northeastern Dakota. Instead, when confronted by the opportunity to build and operate an epic transcontinental railway in Canada, they decided to approach the Canadian government with an offer, going through Duncan McIntyre, the Canada Central Railway president. Such a move was almost inevitable since Smith and Stephen were Canadians who closely identified with Canada. For these two men, involvement in the CPR enterprise signalled not only an opportunity for further profit but also an opportunity to further the interests of their adopted country. Participation also promised them, as well as Hill and Kennedy, a western transcontinental link to the Manitoba, through Winnipeg, and access to huge new markets.

It was the prospect of obtaining a western link to the Manitoba that impelled Jim Hill to enter the Canadian Pacific syndicate despite a host of reservations about the undertaking. Hill realized that once the Northern Pacific completed its main line to the Pacific there would be a huge volume of traffic through St. Paul bound for the West Coast. If the Manitoba was to share in this business it would have to have a line to the coast too, and the Canadian Pacific would provide one. It would also furnish the Manitoba road with access to vast prairie lands that promised to produce far more wheat than the bleak Montana plains through which the Northern Pacific travelled. John Kennedy shared Hill's reservations about the project but nevertheless decided to accept Stephen's invitation to join the CPR syndicate. As it was, both men would have their confidence bolstered by the news that Sir John Rose, a partner in Morton, Rose & Company, one of London's largest banking houses, was bringing his firm into the group and that French and German capitalists would represent the Continent.[239]

Negotiations began after McIntyre approached the government and continued throughout the summer of 1880. On September 4, Macdonald finally sat down in London with Sir John Rose and his son Charles to settle the terms of a provisional contract. Just over a month later in Ottawa, on October 21, Sir Charles Tupper, minister of railways and canals, Stephen, and some of the other principals affixed their signatures to what would become the most celebrated contract in the history of Canadian transportation. Notably absent from the signing, however, was Donald Smith, whose name was prudently left out of the contract as a concession to Macdonald, who never forgave Smith for deserting the Conservatives during the Pacific Scandal and publicly denounced his sworn enemy as "the biggest liar he ever saw."[240] Later an intensely mortified and annoyed Stephen would tell Macdonald that Smith was "excited almost to a craze" by the omission.[241] Much to his chagrin, the Hudson's Bay Company official would remain a silent partner — at least initially. Nevertheless, the syndicate, with the addition of R.B. Angus, who replaced Kittson as a full associate, closely resembled the group of partners who had seized control of and reorganized the St. Paul and Pacific.

The signed contract required the Canadian government to complete and surrender to the syndicate the Pembina branch line and those stretches of the main line that had been completed or that were still under construction, that is, lines in British Columbia and between Lake Superior and the Red River valley. The government agreed to provide $25 million in direct support and a 25-million-acre checkerboard land grant subsidy, as well as generous tax and customs concessions. The CPR was also granted permission to extend its system eastward of Callander, Ontario.

As an additional concession, the railway was awarded monopoly protection. Clause fifteen, which came to be reviled by westerners, stipulated that until October 1900, the Dominion Parliament could not authorize the building of any railway line south of the CPR's main line, "except such line as shall run South West or to the Westward of South West," and even then no line could come within fifteen miles of the international border. In return, the syndicate agreed to complete the main line by constructing approximately 1,900 miles of track within a decade and to equip and operate it "efficiently" and "forever."[242]

The upholding of one section of the contract would later pit Van Horne against Hill. This was the clause that called for the CPR to run the main line from Callander to Port Arthur, north of Lake Superior. It was inserted in the contract at the behest of Macdonald, who, for political reasons, insisted that every inch of the railway be built in Canada. Although they did not really believe in this provision, the syndicate accepted the clause, thinking that perhaps the construction of this section could be postponed or later abandoned altogether. Jim Hill strenuously opposed the building of this stretch, claiming that to run a line across the wild, rock- and muskeg-strewn region north of Lake Superior would be highly impractical and wasteful. Wisdom, he said, dictated that the CPR direct its main line from either Detroit or Sault Sainte Marie to Minnesota (where ideally it would link up with a Manitoba-controlled road), and from there via the Manitoba and the Pembina extension to Winnipeg. Van Horne's future nemesis nevertheless entered the project believing that economic wisdom would eventually prevail. When Van Horne became the most trenchant advocate of an all-Canadian route and economic good sense was jettisoned, sparks flew.

In Parliament there was prolonged and fierce criticism of the contract by the Liberals, who believed that it surrendered the West's natural resources to a corporation whose influence would eclipse even that of the Hudson's Bay Company when it was at the pinnacle of its power. For weeks on end, the opposition hammered away at such features as the company's exemption from taxation, its ability to import materials duty-free, its virtually unlimited power to construct branch lines, and its monopolistic control of all traffic in the Northwest. On taxation, James Trow, the member for Perth South, huffed, "Inequality in taxation has been characteristic of despotic and barbarous nations, and in my reading of the granting of bonuses and lands to railways, I have failed to find a single instance where lands so granted have been entirely exempted, directly or indirectly, from taxation, either by State or municipal authorities."[243] Another MP, Mr. Mills, was equally scathing in his denunciation of the monopoly clause, declaring, "I venture to say that from the celebrated days of monopoly in the time of Queen Elizabeth down to our present day, so extraordinary a monopoly as that now proposed in this contract has never been submitted to any Parliament."[244]

The notorious monopoly clause even provoked opposition from within Macdonald's own caucus. Having experienced the high rates charged by Jim Hill's Red River Transportation Company, the Manitoba members claimed that the CPR, in which Hill also figured prominently, would adopt equally arbitrary policies. Their suspicions and the enforcement of the restrictions on railway construction in the Northwest would engender acrimony against the company that would last for generations to come. As a leading CPR official, Van Horne would taste some of the bitter fruits of this.

Some twenty-five amendments were proposed by the opposition and voted down by the government before the House finally passed the CPR bill on January 27, 1881. On February 16, 1881, the Canadian Pacific Railway was incorporated, and soon it began generating revenue by taking over the existing government-built lines that radiated from Winnipeg. It started construction westward on May 2.

When the new company met for the first time on February 17, 1881, George Stephen was elected president, while big-hearted but ineffectual Duncan McIntyre was made vice-president, largely because he controlled the Canada Central Railway, which the syndicate planned to amalgamate into the new transcontinental road. Angus and Hill were appointed members of the executive committee. As president, Stephen would handle finance and government relations; he would be assisted in this, and at the Bank of Montreal, by Angus. Kennedy would also assist him on the financial side, while Hill would preside as the expert in construction and operations.

No sooner was the syndicate organized than it turned energetically to its task. In addition to financing, which was Stephen's responsibility, the partners, especially Jim Hill, made route selection and the hiring of contractors their first priority. When he studied the projected western route of the CPR, Hill saw that it would cross the Prairies well to the north of Winnipeg and approach the Pacific north of Vancouver Island. This route struck him as not only expensive (because of its length) but also inimical to Canada's best interests, since it would expose the southern Prairies to invasion by predatory American roads just across the international border, roads such as the Northern Pacific, which had been itching to build into Winnipeg. In a worst-case scenario, American encroachment might lead to the American colonization of western Canada and even the secession of this part of the country from the federation.[245] For all these reasons, claimed Hill, a southern route would be far preferable to the one recommended by Sandford Fleming. The Manitoba's general manager therefore wasted no time in sending explorer and Army engineer Major A.B. Rogers to scout out practicable passes located south of Yellowhead Pass.

The impetuous and audacious Hill did not even wait for Rogers to return before setting out to convince his partners that a southern route should be adopted and that suitable passes would eventually be discovered.

In this he had to overcome two obstacles. One, a technicality, centred on the fact that the Yellowhead Pass was specified in the railway contract and could not be abandoned without Parliament's consent. The other was the widely held belief, dating from Captain Palliser's explorations, that the plains beyond the future site of Moose Jaw were desolate, arid lands unsuitable for settlement. Opposed to this view was John Macoun, Canada's best-known botanist, who argued fervently that the basin of the South Saskatchewan River was an area well suited for agriculture. In mid-May of 1881, at a meeting in St. Paul attended by Hill, Stephen, Angus, and Macoun, the botanist's assessment of the area was accepted and the momentous decision was made to adopt the southern route and to gamble on the existence of useable passes through the Rockies and the Selkirks.

In the remaining months of 1881, Hill prepared for the mammoth construction campaign that was to be mounted by the Canadian Pacific the following year. He soon realized, however, that the crushing workload imposed by building and managing the Manitoba did not allow him to devote the necessary time and effort to the CPR undertaking. He would not be able to apply to this new project his standard policy of "being where the money is being spent."[246] Although contractors were managing most of the work that was proceeding west of Winnipeg, somebody was still required to provide continual, official supervision. It was also evident that Alpheus B. Stickley had to be replaced as the CPR's general manager and Thomas L. Rosser as its chief engineer. Little work had been done west of Callander, Ontario, and in the West the two officers had succeeded in getting track built only as far as Flat Creek (now known as Oak Lake) , some 110 miles from Portage la Prairie. Moreover, it appeared that Thomas Rosser and other CPR officials in Winnipeg were furiously peddling information about the CPR's proposed route in the West to crass real estate promoters. Stickney was also suspected of land speculation, but not by Hill and Angus, who believed that the western superintendent had "kept aloof from questionable transactions."[247] Whether or not this was the case, there was general agreement that corruption and demoralization were rampant in Winnipeg and threatening to sink the whole CPR enterprise.

This certainly did not augur well for the building of the railway, so in the fall of 1881, when it became obvious that a dynamic new general manager was required, Stephen turned to Hill to find a suitable candidate. The only experienced operating railwayman in the syndicate did not have to look far. In recommending his friend Van Horne, Hill informed Stephen that he knew of "no one in the United States who had a broader imagination and a greater capacity for executive work."[248] Hill also told the CPR president that a pioneer was needed and then added, "You need a man of great mental and physical power to carry this line through. Van Horne can do it. But he will take all the authority he gets and more, so define how much you want him to have."[249] Jim Hill could not have spoken with greater prescience.

Like Hill, Van Horne could be impetuous, but not so impetuous as to accept the syndicate's job offer without first making a reconnaissance trip north of the border. He made such a trip in early October 1881, accompanied by Jim Hill and Hill's two young sons, James Norman and Louis, who went along for the excursion. From Winnipeg, which they reached on October 7, Van Horne and his party proceeded west to the booming town of Brandon. Then, after returning to Manitoba's capital, they headed along the government-built line to Rat Portage (now Kenora), located 140 miles east of Winnipeg, deep in the heart of the Canadian Shield.[250] Van Horne's appointment was confirmed on November 1,[251] and later that month, on November 17, he made a second trip to Winnipeg, this time accompanied not only by Hill but also by Angus and Samuel B. Reed, Addie's engineer cousin from Joliet.

Van Horne was evidently impressed by what he saw on his first visit north of the border, particularly by the quality of the grain on the gently rolling prairie, the abundance of the crops grown by the Red River settlers in their lush, green fields, and the promise of harvests to come. When remarking on the agricultural potential of the prairie countryside that he had seen, he could speak in only glowing terms. "He says the land is better adapted for agricultural purposes than any of the Pacific lines, and the climate is not as rigorous in the winter as is generally supposed, being about the same as St. Paul," reported the *St. Paul Pioneer Press.*[252]

No mention was made of how Van Horne reacted to the landscape that he found between Winnipeg and Rat Portage, but no doubt he was dismayed by what he saw. The huge muskegs that had been swallowing tons of gravel, miles of track, and occasionally an entire locomotive were bad enough, but even worse were the interminable ridges of rock that stretched for mile after desolate mile across the Canadian Shield. Geography, as it turned out, would present by far the greatest challenge to his railroading skills, optimism, and determination when he came to direct the progress of the CPR line in the company's so-called Eastern Section.

His first visit to Canada behind him, Van Horne wrote to Hill accepting the offer that Stephen had made to him in Chicago on behalf of the CPR.[253] When composing his letter he knew that his prospects for advancement in the United States were excellent; he probably could have had the pick of any choice railway sinecure when it became vacant. He also knew that in throwing in his lot with the CPR he was taking on an enormous risk. The company, after all, had launched itself on a giant gamble. Its main line had been diverted south of the Yellowhead Pass, but as yet nobody knew for sure how the track was to penetrate the Rockies and the Selkirks, or if it could be pushed through the Selkirks at all. On the other hand, the $25,000 salary dangled before him was certainly an incentive to accept the post. It was a princely sum for those days; in fact, it was the largest that had ever been offered to a railway man in the West.[254] Still, in accepting the offer, Van Horne was probably swayed more by the prospect of a major challenge and his love of adventure than by monetary considerations. In any event, he wasted no time in coming to his decision because on October 17 Hill wrote to his protégé saying how pleased he was that Van Horne was coming on board and pledging to assist him in every way possible.[255] As he did so, the Manitoba's general manager probably congratulated himself for not only obtaining an extremely competent general manager for the CPR but also for removing a potential rival from the Milwaukee road.

That same day Hill also dispatched a letter to Stephen in which he could barely contain his enthusiasm over the new appointment. Reported Hill, "I am fully satisfied that we could not have made a better selection than Mr. Van Horne...I have never met anyone who is better informed in the various departments, machinery, cars, operation, train services, construction and general policy — which with untiring energy and a good vigorous body should give us good results."[256]

Once news of the appointment spilled into the general press, commentators hurried to heap praise on the rising railway star. "He is recognized among railwaymen as a man of wonderful power and shrewdness," gushed the *Railway Journal.*[257] This observation was echoed by the *Manitoba Free Press*'s "Railway Ripples" column, which also noted that Van Horne was "a man so thoroughly acquainted with the details of his department, so well versed in the science of railroading, that he is never lacking in his administration of the affairs of the corporation in whose interests he is working."[258]

As for Van Horne himself, he had no time to preen over such fulsome praise, as much remained to be done before he took up his new appointment. Besides clearing up business related to his job in Milwaukee, he had to complete a great deal of preliminary work associated with his new position in Winnipeg. Heading the list was the selection of new department heads, as he was far from satisfied with the character and ability of some of the CPR departmental chiefs.[259] He also had to order equipment and material for the breathtaking construction program that was envisaged for 1882. In this connection, Angus advised Hill on December 2 that the CPR had put "Van Horne's personal matter into shape" and that he, Angus, had forwarded to Van Horne all the necessary information respecting the delivery of locomotives, cars, and other material that he had requested.[260] Not the least of the expensive hardware that had to be ordered was an official car for the railway. Before an order was placed, however, Van Horne was asked to look over the plans drawn up by the Pullman Company.[261]

When Van Horne finally did leave Milwaukee for Winnipeg and his new position he did so secure in the knowledge that he would be taking on a task with unparalleled difficulties and uncertainties. He also realized, however, that if he succeeded in his new role he would soar to even greater heights in his career and at the same time satisfy his overriding passion "to make things grow and put new places on the map."[262] Fortunately he was superbly equipped to take on this new challenge, having a practical knowledge of almost every department of railway work, from the construction of a bridge or the laying of a curve to the management of an extensive system. This encyclopedic knowledge, plus his ability to make tough decisions, would prove indispensable when it came to pushing through the construction of the CPR.

Chapter Six
Toward the Last Spike

Van Horne, accompanied by his old associate John Egan and his friend Jim Hill, left Milwaukee for Winnipeg on December 29 on a special train provided by Hill. If they had anticipated a smooth, uneventful trip they were doomed to disappointment, for as their train headed north toward the Canadian border it encountered giant snowdrifts, which so hampered its progress that two days, instead of one, were required to make the trip to Winnipeg. When the train finally did arrive it was New Year's Eve and Manitoba's raw, infant capital was awash in joyous celebrations, marked by the clamouring of church bells at midnight and the lusty horn-blowing of outrageously attired youths.

As was so often the case when assuming a new position, Van Horne eagerly awaited the new challenges and responsibilities that awaited him, but, as always, he chafed at the thought of parting from Addie and the family. With the passage of each year, it seemed, leaving behind Addie and the children became more difficult. He knew that he would also miss Thomas Shaughnessy and other colleagues at the Chicago, Milwaukee and St. Paul Railroad. On Thursday, they had presented him with a "testimonial of their friendship," much to his surprise if we are to believe the author of the "Railway Ripples" column in the *Manitoba Daily Free Press*. Whether or not Van Horne was taken aback by this gesture of respect and friendship, he managed to respond "very gracefully."[263] Two days later, on Saturday afternoon, Alpheus Stickney responded with equal aplomb when General Rosser, the CPR's discredited chief engineer, acting on behalf of Winnipeg officials, presented the departing general manager of the CPR's Western Division with a "solid silver service," purchased in Chicago at a cost of about thousand dollars, a huge sum in those days.[264]

When Van Horne and his friends descended on Winnipeg temperatures were skidding to below forty degrees Fahrenheit,[265] and the fast-growing city was teeming with newly arrived immigrants, many of whom were forced to seek accommodation in the city's immigrant sheds because they could not afford the skyrocketing rates charged by crammed hotels. In the months ahead it would not be Winnipeg's rawness and its spectacular land boom but its overcrowding that the CPR's new general manager would remark on most frequently in his hurriedly penned letters to Addie. He may have been preoccupied with railway matters, but this did not prevent him from noticing that people were pouring into the city so quickly that some hapless newcomers were forced to sleep on floors and sidewalks.[266]

The growth of Winnipeg had indeed been remarkable. From a motley collection of shacks that clustered around a general store built in 1862, it had become the queen city of the Prairies with a booming economy, some noteworthy public buildings, and an abundance of liquor stores, saloons, and prostitutes to serve its mostly male population. Gone were the days when the gateway to the West was merely a hamlet within the larger Red River Colony. It was now an incorporated city, whose population had grown from 241 in 1871, the year after Manitoba entered Confederation, to 7,985 in 1881. By 1886, it would soar to 20,238.[267] The rapidity of its growth was such that in 1881 the *Globe's* special correspondent, George M. Grant, commented, "I suppose that no city in Canada has had so rapid a growth as Winnipeg up to the point attained by it so far, and probably in the infancy of no city on the continent have town lots commanded such prices as those that are now readily paid here."[268]

The inauguration of railway service on the Pembina branch in December 1878 and the CPR's decision in 1881 to build its main line through Winnipeg virtually guaranteed a rapid increase in the city's population. Indeed, no sooner had the Pembina branch opened for business than waves of farmers and agricultural labourers from Ontario, the United States, and Europe began streaming into Winnipeg and adjoining St. Boniface. Manitoba's fledgling capital was well on its way to becoming the hub of commercial activity in Canada's Northwest.

In anticipation of Winnipeg's glowing economic future, businessmen competed for choice commercial locations in the city's developing core, and home builders vied with each other for residential sites. Van Horne had witnessed first-hand land speculation in frontier Minnesota, but what he saw there did not begin to compare with the frenzied land boom underway in Winnipeg at the time of his arrival. That January, at the height of the boom, city lots were changing hands every day at double the previous

Winnipeg, the gateway to the Canadian West, at about the time Van Horne arrived to take up his job as manager of the CPR.

day's price. Men were making fortunes, which they squandered on diamond rings, sealskin coats, and champagne in what George Ham, the well-known raconteur and colourful journalist, described as "one continuous joy ride."[269] Before it collapsed in late 1882, the boom would plunge the city into the wildest sixteen months in its history and help to ignite delirious speculation in other Manitoba towns as well as in Edmonton and Prince Albert in the North West Territories and Port Moody in British Columbia. Scenting money in the air, almost everybody, from lowly tradesmen to leading citizens, speculated madly in real estate, enticed by screaming property ads in the local press and tales of overnight fortunes to be made. That January, Winnipeggers confidently expected the boom in real estate to continue for at least another year, provided the tide of immigration into the North West continued unabated.[270] As it turned out, they were not far off in their predictions.

Of particular concern to Van Horne was the speculation centred on land that observers expected to be snapped up for townsites and CPR stations. M.F. Hurd, another experienced civil engineer relative of Addie's who had worked for the Union Pacific Railroad, was struck by the fact that all of Fort Calgary's residents, apart from the Northwest Mounted Police, were "crazy on the land question." Everyone, he informed Samuel B. Reed, was expecting to become "immensely rich," most at the expense of the CPR. "About everyone I have met yet seem to think the Co. common property and a dollar got from them no matter how is perfectly legitimate," observed Hurd in a letter penned from the tiny settlement.[271]

Seeking a fortune at the CPR's expense was a situation that clamoured for Van Horne's immediate attention, and, as had been anticipated, he wasted no time in acting. No sooner had he moved into his temporary office on the second floor of the new Bank of Montreal building than he placed a small ad in the January 2 Winnipeg papers cautioning the public against purchasing lots of prospective stations along the CPR line until he had officially announced their locations. "The permanent locations will be made with reference to the interests and convenience of the public and of the company, and without regard to any private interests whatever. W.C. VAN HORNE, General Manager," shouted the ad. His warning that real estate speculators could expect no aid and comfort from the CPR went largely unheeded, however. Oceans of type continued to trumpet unbelievable real estate bargains, and speculation continued.

Among those caught up in the orgy of speculation were senior CPR officials based in Winnipeg, some of whom indulged shamelessly in land selling and information peddling. Topping the list was engineer Thomas L. Rosser, a courtly, swarthy-looking Southern aristocrat. Described as a "fine gentleman and a capable engineer" by locating engineer Charles Aeneas Shaw,[272] Rosser had risen to the rank of major general in the Confederate Army. Following the Civil War, he became chief surveyor for the Northern Pacific and then, for a brief time, the official chiefly responsible for making land purchases for Hill's Manitoba road. A man who brought a certain élan to everything that he did, Rosser wasted little time after joining the CPR before selling his privileged information to railway land speculators and town builders along the CPR route. Since he made no attempt to do it quietly, his actions soon became known to members of the syndicate and to Van Horne.

Within a month of assuming his new position, Van Horne sacked Rosser after seeing a letter that implicated the major general in the selling of privileged information to a contractor. The blunt telegram containing the notice of dismissal immediately quashed Rosser's plans to embark on a twelve-hundred-mile survey trip in southern Saskatchewan. Instead it sent Rosser hurtling off to St. Paul, where he hoped to waylay Van Horne when he was en route from Montreal to Winnipeg. When the two men met on February 10, Rosser asked Van Horne to reconsider, but the general manager refused to back down. Van Horne told the former cavalryman that he would not go out of his way to injure his reputation; he would allow Rosser to resign after he had returned to Winnipeg.[273] The chief engineer did so on February 13, informing the press that he had had a difference of opinion with the land department and that he did not wish to conform with certain regulations relating to land speculation, etc.[274] To all appearances this was the final chapter in what R.B. Angus described as Rosser's determination to "defy authority and to set aside all sense of propriety."[275] Events, however, would prove otherwise.

Undaunted and unchastened, Rosser decided to pursue further ill-gotten rewards. Pretending still to be chief engineer, he persuaded a returning courier to hand over reports and profiles of a winter's work carried out by a CPR surveying party led by Charles Aeneas Shaw. The general, armed with the documents, then "skipped out west" for the presumed purpose of utilizing the information contained in the profiles and plans. When next Van Horne and the CPR heard of him, he was headed for Fort Calgary, intending to meet Shaw and Albert Perry, a surveyor, to secure additional information. It was not long, however, before news of Rosser's actions trickled back to Winnipeg and the company had an information laid against the general for obtaining property under false pretenses.[276] The case was eventually dropped, but not before Rosser had sued for defamation of character, claiming that when he was hired he had signed an agreement with Stickney allowing him to speculate in land. The verdict was in Rosser's favour, and he was awarded one dollar in damages.[277]

Much to his chagrin, this would not be the last encounter that Van Horne had with Rosser. On a memorable July evening, when the general manager was dining in the coffee room of the Manitoba Club, a meeting place for Winnipeg's elite, he ran into the major general and the two exchanged words, "words that would have ended in more than blows had it not been for the interference of a couple of peacemakers," reported the *Sun* of Winnipeg. According to the paper's spirited, and undoubtedly highly exaggerated, account of the incident, both Van Horne and Rosser drew pistols and an all-out battle was only averted when "the better counsels of cooler heads prevailed, and the belligerents were separated before their passions were cooled in gore."[278]

Van Horne did not stop at dismissing Rosser. In a follow-up move, he instructed Samuel B. Reed, his newly appointed superintendent of construction, to investigate the source of a continuing leak of plans and profiles, and, if necessary, to take action against Rosser's staff. Accordingly, one morning in March 1882, without giving notice or explanation, Reed fired the entire staff. Among those peremptorily dismissed were Harry Armstrong, who was then chief assistant engineer, and his chief draftsman, Stan Jukes. After leaving the office with their belongings, they sought out Van Horne and reported what had just taken place. The general manager looked surprised. Then he blurted out, "Mr. R. has been too hasty. What I told him was if he couldn't find out where the leak was <u>if necessary</u> to discharge the whole office staff."[279] Reporting on the wholesale firing and its aftermath to George Stephen, Jim Hill said, "Van Horne has made a clean sweep of the office and will only reemploy such as can show clean hands. This has already caused some feeling among those interested and some of them are in high places, against Van Horne."[280] It was evident even to Hill in St. Paul, hundreds of miles away, that his protegé was not setting out to win friends in his new post.

Armstrong's relationship with Van Horne did not end with his discharge from the CPR. In late 1883, while serving as chief engineer of the Manitoba North Western Railway, Armstrong had a chance and propitious encounter with Van Horne at the Manitoba Club. Seizing the opportunity, he asked the general manager if he had discovered who was stealing the CPR's townsites. Van Horne replied that he had, "but it wasn't you Armstrong ... I'm going to Port Arthur tomorrow and I'll write you from there." Not long afterward, Armstrong received a personal letter from Van Horne inviting him to proceed to Port Arthur and assume responsibility for a construction division on the Lake Superior section of the CPR's main line. The engineer, who became a good friend of Van Horne, promptly accepted the offer.[281]

Van Horne found his welcome in Winnipeg as frosty as the one that had greeted him when he first arrived at the Chicago, Milwaukee and St. Paul. It was not only his reputation as an iconoclast in railway operations that made tradition-loving railway men resent him — it was also because he was an American. More to the point, he was a blunt, domineering Yankee who did not refrain from telling people exactly what he thought of them, particularly if they were Britons or Canadians. The Englishman J.H. Secretan, a locating engineer who headed a CPR surveying party on the Prairies, did not mince words when describing his self-willed boss's imperious manner:

> We did not like Van Horne when he first came up to Winnipeg as General Boss of Everybody & Everything. His ways were not our ways and he did not hesitate to let us know what he thought of the bunch in a general way. At first he had no use for Englishmen or Canadians especially Engineers and told me once "if he could only teach a Section Man to run a transit he wouldn't have a single d–d Engineer about the place."[282]

There is no denying that Van Horne had a vocabulary rich in the "certainty that belongs to the Presbyterian conception of everlasting retribution, without its restraint," as D.B. Hanna, the Canadian National Railway's first president, put it.[283] This vocabulary found its fullest expression when Van Horne gave vent to his famous temper. Fortunately this was only occasionally and then it was invariably directed against carelessness and stupidity. But for all his bluntness and plain speaking, the transplanted Yankee was sensitive to the ill feeling that he invited at the office or at the Manitoba Club. Sometimes, as had been the case in Chicago, he felt the antagonism quite keenly, and on occasions such as these he would lament the fact that he was gaining more enemies than friends. Fortunately, his natural buoyancy and generosity of spirit, to say nothing of his horrendous workload, prevented his becoming unduly perturbed by the cold reception that greeted him in the opening months of his new job. In the past his charismatic presence and extraordinary ability had worked wonders and now, in Winnipeg, they would soon win the respect and admiration of those who came to know him, including that sardonic observer, Secretan.

Before winning over those in his employ, however, the "Czar of the CPR," as Secretan called Van Horne, aroused a lot of resentment by favouring the hiring of Americans. In the early days of his administration Van Horne engaged numerous seasoned American railwaymen whose work he knew and respected. Not surprisingly, many of these newcomers hailed from the Chicago, Milwaukee and St. Paul Railroad. Among them was his old colleague John Egan, the divisional superintendent and abrasive Fenian supporter, who would fire people with even more zeal than Van Horne. His appointment as superintendent of the CPR's Western Division was announced on January 3.[284] Another appointment announced the same day was that of Samuel B. Reed, Addie's cousin from Joliet, who left his job as receiver of the Chicago, Pekin and Southwestern to join the CPR.[285] He was appointed superintendent of construction, to which were added the interim duties of chief engineer after Rosser's dismissal. Still another American recruit was T.H. Kelson, the experienced storesman whom Van Horne had trained earlier in Milwaukee. Kelson was appointed general storekeeper at Winnipeg, as Van Horne had decided to import the highly effective system of centralized stores and accounts that he had implemented on the Milwaukee road.

Undoubtedly, the most important American recruit was Thomas George Shaughnessy, who was lured away from the Chicago, Milwaukee and St. Paul, where he and Van Horne had first struck up their friendship. Impressed by Shaughnessy's performance in stores on the Milwaukee Road, Van Horne had made him the railway's storekeeper on January 1, 1881. Soon the younger man became a protegé and friend of Van Horne, who lent the voracious reader books from his personal library and discussed his fossil collection with him. In early February 1882, on one of his periodic visits to Milwaukee, the CPR's general manager offered Shaughnessy the position of purchasing agent of the entire CPR system, but although the offer was tempting the young man turned it down. Later that year, however, he finally yielded to Van Horne's entreaties, and on November 2 he and his wife, Elizabeth, arrived in Montreal, where Shaughnessy lost no time in reporting to work at the CPR's head office in the financial district. The job that he took on was second only in importance to that of Van Horne, for Shaughnessy soon displayed two talents that would prove indispensable to the CPR in its construction period: a remarkable ability to get the best value for every dollar spent and an equally remarkable ability to stave off creditors in times of financial stringency.[286] Van Horne may not have been infallible in his hiring choices, but he perhaps chose better than he realized in selecting Shaughnessy, for he was destined to become the ablest of Van Horne's lieutenants and eventually his successor as CPR president.

To construct 675 miles of main line (this included clearing, grading, and track-laying) from Flat Creek, 161 miles west of Winnipeg, to Fort Calgary, the CPR syndicate hired a company headed by two Minnesota contractors, R.B. Langdon of Minneapolis and canny David C. Shepard of St. Paul, an outstanding railway builder. The company, which parcelled out the work to more than sixty subcontractors, was engaged at Hill's instigation because the American railway manager had been impressed by Shepard's exceptional capabilities and loyalty. So high was his opinion of Shepard that Hill acted decisively to ensure his friend and associate snagged the contract. When he realized that the contractor's bid was higher than a competing one, Hill conveniently left the second bid in full view on his desk in St. Paul so that Shepard, who frequently dropped into the office, could see it and resubmit an acceptable one.[287]

The fact that most experienced railway talent was American in the 1880s was not enough to forestall an avalanche of criticism of such appointments. If the CPR was not thoroughly detested in Manitoba before they arrived, Van Horne and Egan made sure that it was within months of their coming on the scene. The *Globe*, a tireless critic of the Conservative government and the syndicate, was quick to lash out at the CPR's hiring practices, claiming that the syndicate had "placed its business so entirely in the hands of the United States engineers and officials selected from their side of the line that practically no Canadians need apply."[288] Alluding to the plethora of Van Horne relatives and colleagues hired by the CPR, the paper snorted, "The Canadian Pacific is now known, conversationally, in St. Paul as the family road, it being officered by Van Horn and Egan's pinaforic relatives. Every train brings in its complement of sour-mashes, among whom a relationship exists as comprehensive and truly loyal as in a Highland clan."[289]

A letter written in white-hot fury to the editor of the *Manitoba Daily Free Press* by a dismissed CPR dispatcher perhaps best encapsulates much of the sentiment felt toward the hiring of "sour mash," as the Americans were called. The irate railway man, who ironically signed himself "J. Egan," directed much of his venom at Van Horne associates who had served with the general manager on the Southern Minnesota Railroad.

> Much comment is made here and elsewhere about the removal (by present management) of Canadians from positions on the C.P.R. and the replacing of them by Americans until there is hardly a "corporate guard" left of the Canadians. The management may say: "We do not remove except for cause; we hold the resignations of near-ly all who have left!" Yes, but only those who have gone through the mill can describe the "freezing out" process as applied to Assistant Superintendent of Traffic, Construction and Water Supply and the many others, including myself ... we (others and myself) think there is no more fitting time to protest against this outrage which is a mild name for it ... Up to the arrival of Master-mechanic Pink all positions of any standing, and nearly all inferior positions have been filled by Americans; and another coincidence is that nearly all are from the C.M. & St. P. Ry (Southern Minnesota division).[290]

Within ten days of blowing into Winnipeg, Van Horne, accompanied by Hill and the engineer in charge of the CPR's mountain division, Major Rogers, journeyed east to Montreal and Ottawa to meet the other syndi-cate members as well as leading politicians in the nation's capital. Given the general public's insatiable appetite for CPR news and its curiosity about the railway's new general manager, it is not surprising that members of the press pounced on Van Horne when his train stopped at Chicago and Toronto en route to Montreal. At Chicago, he reportedly announced that the CPR intended to construct 650 miles of road in 1882.[291] Whether the figure was 650 or 500, the number usually cited in this connection, Van Horne appeared to be promising the impossible. After all, only 161 miles of track had been laid the previous season. Much less sensational was a report out of Milwaukee. It claimed that Van Horne was dissatisfied with his new position and that the St. Paul people, knowing this, had kept his former position open in the hope that he would soon return to it.[292] If this was indeed the case, his former colleagues had not reckoned with Van Horne's more than ample ego. Nor had they taken into account his love of formidable challenges and his iron determination. Hostility and criticism, no matter how vehement, rarely succeeded in forcing him to back away from a goal or a project that he had embraced. The notable exception would be his determination to have the CPR remain above politics. When confronted by Canadian-style politics, he would bow to the inevitable and abandon some of his cherished principles.

The meeting in Montreal with CPR directors would prove to be a pivotal one, for it was during the course of this meeting that Van Horne pitted himself against Hill by arguing forcefully for the immediate construction of the Lake Superior section of the CPR's main line. When organizing the syndicate, Hill and Stephen had advocated deferring construction north of Lake Superior until there was enough settlement in the West to justify the huge costs that would be involved in building such a difficult stretch. They contended that the CPR could provide an interim, all-rail route to the West by building a branch line from Callander to Sault Ste. Marie, where ideally it would link up with a Hill-controlled line and then his own St. Paul, Minneapolis and Manitoba Railroad and its Winnipeg connection, the CPR's Pembina branch. Hill even hoped that this route would become permanent.

The former Canadian clearly had a lot to gain from such a move, for it would have invested him with a large measure of control over Canadian traffic from East to West. One can even speculate that Hill would never have joined the syndicate if he had not counted on his American road benefiting from the haulage of Canadian traffic for many years to come, perhaps even permanently if the staggering costs and the economic absurdity of building north of Lake Superior forced the eventual abandonment of an all-Canadian route.

Van Horne, however, found both of these scenarios abhorrent. They ran contrary to all his railroading instincts and his own confident estimate of his abilities. The last thing that he wanted to see was the CPR becoming dependent on Hill's line, even for a short period of time. He realized that with Hill in the strategic position that he had assigned for himself, the CPR had no chance of becoming its own master, or perhaps more to the point, he, Van Horne, had no chance of becoming its master. Moreover, from the very beginning he had not been intimidated by the yawning emptiness between Lake Nipissing and Thunder Bay. Van Horne was convinced that the difficult lake stretch could not only be built, it could be operated profitably since coast-to-coast through traffic would eventually be large enough to offset the lack of local business in this wilderness section. Besides, he was fast becoming attuned to Canadian nationalist sympathies as expressed by such leading politicians as Sir John A. Macdonald and his chief lieutenant, Sir Charles Tupper, the minister of railways and canals. From the very inception of the project they had insisted that the main line and the routing of traffic should be confined to Canada. In fact, the government had stipulated that the north of Superior route be made a condition of the CPR's contract with the government. At that Montreal meeting, then, Van Horne marshalled his well-honed powers of persuasion in support of the government position and insisted that the syndicate proceed as quickly as possible with the construction of the all-Canadian route. He then set about squelching any suggestion that the CPR planned to build a branch line to the Sault and from thence link up with an American railway.[293]

Van Horne's position vis-à-vis building north of Lake Superior did not, of course, endear him to Hill, who is reported to have sworn that he would get even with his protegé even if he had "to go to Hell for it and shovel coal."[294] The syndicate's commitment to building on the north shore as soon as possible quickly dampened Hill's enthusiasm for the CPR, but not until 1883, when it became apparent that the decision was irrevocable, did he formally withdraw from the company. Meanwhile, he would continue to play an active role in the devising and execution of important CPR policies.

If the meeting heralded a cooling in relations between Van Horne and Hill, it marked the beginning of a close friendship with Stephen, the self-confident financier and shrewd negotiator. Although their backgrounds were dissimilar, Van Horne and Stephen took to each other immediately. Perhaps it was because each recognized and admired the unbridled enthusiasm that the other brought to every undertaking that he tackled. It may also have been because each man saw his own driving ambition mirrored in the other. Whatever the reason, Van Horne and Stephen would become good friends and would remain so until Van Horne began to question Stephen's loyalty to the CPR.

This meeting also saw Van Horne convince the CPR syndicate that he could have five hundred miles of western track built during the upcoming construction season, more than any other railway company had ever laid in a single year. Speed, he felt, was essential since the CPR's land and cash subsidies were earned only as sections of its line were completed, inspect-ed, and opened for service. Money from subsidies paid for tracks on the Prairies, where costs were comparatively low, was needed to help pay for the anticipated high costs of construction in the Rockies and along the north shore of Lake Superior.

Van Horne's was certainly a laudable goal, as Stephen had already informed Macdonald that the company intended to complete the railway in half the ten-year period specified in the contract. The financier wanted, of course, to avoid tying up capital unprofitably any longer than was absolutely necessary. He also feared that the Northern Pacific might drain off a lot of western traffic if the CPR's through line was not pushed to completion swiftly. Van Horne's determination to construct the CPR's main line as quickly as possible therefore dovetailed with the thinking of Stephen and syndicate members. Nevertheless, his staggering boast that he would construct five hundred miles of western track during the upcoming construction season unleashed a volley of criticism and ridicule from anti-government papers and other critics.

At this meeting the syndicate confirmed their choice of a southern route for the railway, despite the fact that exploration expeditions had yet to turn up a practicable route through the giant Selkirks that lay between the Gold Range and the Kicking Horse Pass. The man charged with find-ing this route was Major A.B. Rogers, a small, scrawny American Army engineer, distinguished by an impressive set of white sidewhiskers, a love of picturesque profanity, and a complete disinterest in money. He was also noted for his habit of stinting on provisions when charging off into the wilds with his survey crews, a shortcoming that Van Horne would try valiantly to correct. Rogers's shortcomings notwithstanding, the general manager would develop considerable faith in the engineer. To Andrew Onderdonk, the ruthless American contractor, he observed, "While the major is somewhat eccentric and given to burning brimstone he is a very good man on construction, honest and fair dealing, and I feel sure that you will get on with him pleasantly."[295]

In February 1881, Hill had sent Rogers to seek out potential mountain crossings through the southern Rockies and the Selkirk Mountains just west of them. Despite the intimidating physical challenges that he faced, Rogers succeeded in making considerable progress in his search for practi-cable passes. But he had yet to return from the snow-choked mountains with a fuller report when the syndicate decided to adopt the southern route. This Hill-inspired recklessness and boldness could have resulted in a host of problems down the line if the Kicking Horse Pass had not proven suitable. But luck was with the associates because when Rogers returned at the end of the 1881 surveying season he was reasonably certain that the Bow River and the Kicking Horse Pass could provide a route through the Rockies and that a suitable pass could be found through the "mysterious" Selkirk Mountains. A return journey in 1882 confirmed his judgment, whereupon a jubilant Rogers hurried to Montreal, where he burst in on an elegant dinner party at George Stephens's mansion to announce the news.

Although engineering opinion favoured the Yellowhead Pass because of its easy grades, Van Horne, in the interests of both economy and speed, did not hesitate to throw his weight behind the choice of the more steeply graded Kicking Horse Pass and the southern route. Interviewed in Toronto while en route to Montreal, he declared, "We have changed the point at which the road will enter the Rockies and although the change will involve a larger expenditure it will greatly shorten the road as a through line, probably by as much as 150 miles. We expect to enter the mountains by way of the Bow River Pass."[296] This change of route provided just the ammunition that the staunchly Liberal *Globe* needed to thrust its editorial knife into Van Horne's back. Always diligent in its misspelling of the general manager's name, the paper commented, "Though Mr. Van Horn became General Manager of the Canadian Pacific Railway only a fortnight ago he has caught the tone of the Syndicate already." The waspish *Globe* then went on to chastise Van Horne for agreeing to a change of route, arguing that the only authority empowered to do this was Parliament.[297] It was a refrain that would be echoed repeatedly by critics of the CPR.

Van Horne spent two days in Montreal, then, in the company of several CPR directors, left for New York to attend to some important railway matters and to see George Stephen off to Europe, a courtesy that he would perform time and again as long as his friend headed the CPR. Unfortunately, the pressure of business prevented Van Horne from taking in much of vibrant, fast-growing New York. Still, he did manage to attend two, in his words, "state dinners." One of these was at the Knickerbocker Club, a prestigious social club located in one of New York's finest neo-federal buildings. Doting father and compulsive art lover that he was, Van Horne also found time to purchase a painting entitled "The Inspiration of Gabriel" for "our dear little Addie."[298] His business completed, he returned to Montreal, where he spent the remainder of the week before making a trip to Quebec City with Duncan McIntyre and inspecting company lines in Ontario.

On the return journey to Winnipeg, at the end of January 1882, Van Horne stopped off in Ottawa, the fledgling national capital that the highly opinionated academic and political commentator Goldwin Smith had dismissed as a "subarctic lumber village converted by royal mandate into a political cockpit."[299] In the next few years CPR business would dictate frequent trips to the city that only a few decades earlier had been dismissed as one of the most lawless communities in North America. When Van Horne was introduced to Ottawa, however, brawls between carousing Irish "Shiners" and French-Canadian shantymen were history and the city was beginning to emerge as a rather sedate capital, albeit one where there was frequent grumbling about the whining of the sawmills at the Chaudière, mud in the streets, bad smells from the drains, and stacks of lumber that sat on about every street corner.[300] But if Canada's national capital had many of the trappings of a lumber town it also had Parliament Hill, with its numerous attractions, and Rideau Hall. It also boasted some magnificent shops and a rich medley of characters. "I met there statesmen, adventurers, wild men of the woods or prairie, deputies from Manitoba, lawyers from Quebec, sharpers and honest men, all staying at one hotel; and it seemed strange to sit at dinner and see great rough fellows, with the manners of ploughmen, quaffing their costly champagne, and fancying themselves patterns of gentility and taste," reported English author Ewing Ritchie.[301]

When he visited the capital in the winter of 1882, Van Horne had to cope with "ten thousand things" that demanded his attention. Nevertheless, before resuming the long, tedious trip to Winnipeg, he squeezed in some time to admire the Gothic Revival-style Parliament buildings, which he pronounced "the finest on the continent," and to pen a letter to Addie in which he reported:

> I have just returned from a trip over the lines in this region ... I reached Ottawa (the Capital of the Dominion) on Tuesday last and was here two days before starting out on the line but so busy with the government officials and our people that I could not find a minute in which to write you. I had to decline an invitation to dine with the Minister of War [the Honourable Sir Joseph Philippe Caron, minister of militia and defence] on Wednesday because I hadn't a "swallow tail" coat but the following day I was invited to luncheon by Sir Charles and Lady Tupper and as business clothes were admissible on that occasion I went and met quite a number of prominent people ... I am quartered in the "Syndicate's cottage," a handsome and well furnished house for the use of the Syndicate when visiting the

Capitol. I get my meals at the hotel or at the Rideau Club
which is the fashionable club here ... I am very anxious to
get started westward. I have much to do there ...[302]

Van Horne's assertion "I have much to do there" barely hinted at the
enormity of the task that awaited him out west. Sealing leaks in the CPR
organization, hiring and firing employees, and providing temporary, but
comfortable, accommodation for trainmen and mechanics were but three of
the host of challenges that he faced. Before construction of the prairie section began in the late spring, he had to arrange for the freighting of huge
stores of rails and other materials to Winnipeg, the staging area. The dimen-
sions of this operation were immense. Since the St. Lawrence River would
still be frozen over when the construction season got underway, steel had to
be shipped from New York and New Orleans and then hauled to Manitoba
via St. Paul. Stone had to be ordered from every available quarry, lumber
from Minnesota, railway ties from Lake of the Woods and Rat Portage, and
rails from England and from the Krupp works in Germany.[303] The general
manager also had to monitor the whereabouts of these supplies as they made
their way from place of origin to the staging area. To do this, he arranged for
hundreds of checkers to report daily on the arrival and movement of CPR
supplies through American cities en route to Winnipeg. By this means, he
could precisely plot their time of arrival at the staging area.

Adhering to a tight timetable was no easy matter in the harsh prairie
climate. A series of fierce snowstorms and formidable snow blockades
severely hampered the delivery of materials to their destination. By March
18 only about one hundred miles or more of rails and about two hundred
thousand ties had been moved to the front.[304] This sorely tried Van Horne's
patience. So did a huge shortage of engines. As he ruefully noted to Hill
on March 18, "We are very short of motive power on account of having
been obliged to turn back all of the contract and gov't engines partly
because half of them were useless and the men that were with them were
agitating for a strike for increased wages."[305]

Van Horne's headquarters in Winnipeg was a rather dingy office, where huge
piles of paperwork always awaited him and where he usually greeted visitors
while straddling his desk chair and puffing on a giant cigar. Interspersed
with the paperwork were trips to and from St. Paul to transact business with
Hill, meet contractors, and carry on negotiations for the construction of the
line. As if this were not enough, Van Horne also had to deal with the after-

math of a major fire that broke out shortly after midnight on March 12 in a building housing a grocery store on Winnipeg's Main Street. From there the conflagration had spread to ten other buildings lying between it and the Bank of Montreal building, whose solid brick walls proved its salvation. "We thought it would certainly go with the rest and moved out all our books and papers which were soon badly mixed up and we have been busy ever since straightening them out," Van Horne informed Addie.[306]

A letter written to "my very dear little boy" on the same day made it very clear how much his father appreciated receiving a letter from Bennie and expressed the fond hope that he would write him every day. The missive, illustrated with Van Horne drawings, continued:

> Your picture is very good but I am afraid the train will run off the track as it seems to be running very fast. I dont see the engineer. He must have been shaken off. Papa would be glad to have you send him another picture when you write him another letter, which I hope you will do very soon. There are some little boys in Winnipeg but not so many as in Milwaukee. I saw one yesterday drawn along very fast by an Eskimaux dog ... The boys sleds are not like yours. They are like a board with one end curled up and are called toboggans. They run on top of the soft snow better than the kind of sleds the boys have in Milwaukee ... There are a good many Indian boys here too but they have no toboggans nor much of anything else.[307]

Fast-growing Winnipeg, no matter what the season, would certainly not have been Van Horne's choice for a place to live. One disillusioned English visitor described it as "dirty" and smelling "dreadfully."[308] Writing to Bennie in early April 1882, Van Horne reported, "The snow is nearly all gone here and mud has taken its place and it is a very sticky mud. It is hard for the little boys to wade through. I saw some of them coming from school on Friday and they almost got stuck."[309]

This raw, frontier town did have a few redeeming features, however. Heading the list was Van Horne's "warm and well ventilated" room in Syndicate House, one of a series of dwellings constructed by the CPR for its officers. For this gourmand, however, the eating left something to be desired. In Van Horne's words, it was "pretty thin," but by his own admission he was in no danger of starving. "A little meagreness in that way will not hurt me. We hope for better things soon," he confessed to Addie in a March epistle.[310]

That spring would prove to be one of the most decisive chapters in his entire career. At risk was his precious credibility, which was now constantly under attack, for it appeared that his plan to build 500 miles of track that season instead of the 161 constructed the previous year might be torpedoed right from the start by dreadful weather conditions. The March blizzards were followed by rapidly rising spring temperatures that quickly thawed the Red River system, causing disastrous flood conditions along the valleys of the Red and its principal tributaries. Traffic on the St. Paul, Minneapolis & Manitoba Railway northward to the international border, and on the CPR line north of that to Winnipeg, was brought to a standstill because large stretches of track were under water. There were also traffic stoppages on the CPR's main line between Winnipeg and Brandon following the flooding of the Assiniboine.

The result of all this was a massive blockade of traffic that interfered with the delivery of railway supplies and the transportation of incoming settlers and their goods. Particularly hard hit was the Manitoba road. Sidings on its line from St. Vincent, Manitoba, to St. Paul, Minnesota, were plugged with loaded cars for weeks. Only in May, after the blizzards had ended and the flood waters had subsided, did construction proceed apace on the CPR's main line.

The gradual let-up in the blockade nevertheless prompted an admission from R.B. Angus that staff could have been better organized at headquarters in Montreal. To Hill, he reported, "Van Horne complains with justice I fear of extraordinary delays in executing his orders for general Railway supplies. Our staff was not properly organized in the purchasing department especially. There was no lack of industry and zeal but a great want of special knowledge and system."[311] Fortunately the arrival of Thomas Shaughnessy that autumn would improve the situation immeasurably.

The delays were so numerous that few people believed that the CPR could reach its stated construction goal that season, but Van Horne, determined that it would reach its objective, went to great lengths to ensure that the contractors were accommodated in every way possible. This required, among other things, arranging for the delivery of material to construct five miles of track to the end of track daily. By June 24 there were 1,329 teams, including those engaged in transportation, and 2,232 men at work. Still, this was not nearly large enough a force to meet Van Horne's stated goal of five miles of track a day. A track organization of this size, claimed Van Horne, could not lay more than half that amount. With mounting anxiety, he wrote Jim Hill on July 2 that he did not believe that Langdon and Shepard intended to carry out their contract. Continued the irate general manager, "Unless there is a very decided change for the better within the next week or 10 days, some very decided action on our part will be necessary ... There is no good reason that I can see why the track should not be 40 miles further ahead today ... If they understand that they will be held to a strict account for the laying of the last rail in the 500 miles, and that no mercy will be shown them in case of failure, I think it will make a decided difference in their movements."[312]

When Van Horne made it abundantly clear that their contract would be cancelled if Langdon and Shepard did not live up to their obligations, the contractors responded by hiring more teams and men. The result was a whirlwind of construction described by the *Quarterly Review* as "absolutely without parallel in railway annals." By July 11, 1882, rails had been laid to a point 116 miles west of Brandon, and 4,000 men and 2,000 teams had been thrown into the job.[313] The speed with which Van Horne's army laid down the rails across the desolate Prairies was so breathtaking that both Parliament and the general public could only gape in amazement.

Bullying, cajoling, and driving the contractors into setting construction records occupied much but certainly not all of Van Horne's time during this critical period. While trying to concentrate all his energy and attention on building the railway, he also had to deal with repeated requests and advice from a pestering Hill, who, from his office in St. Paul, peppered Van Horne with suggestions and requests by letter and telegram. In Hill's eyes, Van Horne was merely an able lieutenant who owed his first step up the ladder of spectacular railway success to J.J. Hill. The American, therefore, took to dispensing advice and lectures freely to the younger man, who, not surprisingly, did not always respond with wild enthusiasm.

In the spring of 1882, the meddling Hill lectured Van Horne on the need to hire a chief engineer, impressing on him that he should not quibble about salary. Finally, in exasperation, Van Horne retorted on May 20, "I fully appreciate the importance of what you say in yours of the 16th about having a Chief Engr. quickly. I am very sorry to have missed Ross but he would not come below $12,000 and our Montreal directors thought 7,000 to 8,000 enough. These were about your figures also so I had to drop him."[314]

Van Horne finally succeeded that very month in hiring a chief engineer to replace Samuel Reed, forced by failing health to retire shortly after his appointment. By July 2, he could not contain his joy when he wrote Addie, "Our new Chief Engr has relieved me of many annoying matters and my work has lightened considerably lately — so much so that I hope to see all your dear faces before long."[315]

The return of the Manitoba road's railway cars was another source of friction between the two men. Because the CPR owed little rolling stock in 1882, it depended on the Manitoba line to send construction supplies north to Winnipeg in its cars. It took so long, however, to unload supplies in the Winnipeg yards that many of these cars jammed the road's sidings for weeks on end. Hill was fully convinced that Van Horne was badly abusing the privilege of using another railway's cars, and since these stalled flatcars represented a loss of money for the railway magnate he assailed Van Horne with a constant barrage of requests to have the cars freed up as quickly as possible.

Van Horne could, with all justice, point to mitigating circumstances. For, as Stephen explained so picturesquely to Hill, "traffic flowed into the westward extension of the CPR via Winnipeg like the sea into a hole dug into its bottom."[316] The resulting demands for cash, rolling stock, and the expansion of freight-handling facilities had caught the CPR quite unprepared, and Van Horne strove as best he could to cope with problems posed by backed-up traffic at Winnipeg, which was caused in part by delays at customs. Those delays were finally eliminated, as Van Horne had predicted to Hill they would be, when the customs officials of both countries instituted a twenty-four-hour border service.

Replying to Hill's stream of requests, Van Horne revealed that the CPR had resorted to hiring about "100 Refugee Jews" to help clear the Winnipeg yard on a June Sunday when not enough Christians were available for this purpose. "We have employed all the outside teams we could get hold of to haul freight and are applying all penalties we can think of to secure the prompt unloading of cars everywhere and the misuse of foreign cars has been made a capital offense."[317] The following week, his exasperation reaching new heights, Van Horne informed Hill, "I can only say as I have repeatedly said before, that we are doing everything possible to return them promptly. We have unloaded lumber, machinery and all freight of like character on the ground until almost every available foot in our Winnipeg yard is covered."[318]

While Van Horne struggled valiantly to cope with the problem of backed-up traffic in Winnipeg, Stephen, in his perennial role of diplomat, strove to placate Hill and to keep peace between the two men. In reply to Hill's remonstrations, the CPR president wrote on June 26:

> I am appalled by what you say as to the condition of matters in Winnipeg freight yard ... I am impressed by what

you say as to the necessity of providing at once the additional shed room you suggest. It will never do to keep
other lines' cars and use them for storage purposes, and I
will write to Mr V Horne today suggesting that he should
at once begin his preparations for building the shed. I will
not fail to be guided by your hint to avoid saying anything
to him to affect his sensibility in the matter of the retention of your cars. I fully recognize the importance &
necessity for patience & forbearance all around.[319]

It was bad enough that Van Horne had to set aside "about two-thirds
of [his] time to the exclusion of many other important matters" to attend
to Hill's barrage of requests.[320] What was perhaps even more irritating was
the older man's practice of interposing himself between the general manager and the contractors and all too often taking the contractors' side in disputes. These actions of Hill's only increased Van Horne's resentment and
made him more determined than ever to manage his own railroading show.

In his surviving letters to Addie, however, Van Horne made no mention of his mounting irritation with Hill. Letters home usually eschewed
railroading concerns and stressed the positive; his letter of June 23, 1882,
was decidedly jubilant in tone. From Winnipeg, he reported:

I returned from the West on Friday night with Mr
Stephen and party. They were delighted with all they saw.
The work is going on splendidly and we shall far exceed
the Union Pacific record: nearly double it. At the rate we
are now going we will complete 400 miles of road in the
next 115 working days and we have already made the best
30 days record. It will be a most glorious achievement ...
Am getting better "grub" now — mushrooms three times
a day. This is the greatest country on earth for them. They
grow on every vacant lot in town.[321]

The work referred to by Van Horne was carried out by a huge construction assembly line that extended for a hundred miles or more across
the open plains. At its head were the CPR engineers and surveyors who
located and then staked the route that the railway was to take. An
American engineer had once said, "Where a mule can go, I can make a
locomotive go."[322] The same could be said, of course, of his Canadian
counterparts, whose imagination and skill would be nowhere more in evi-

dence than in locating the CPR route, particularly around Lake Superior and through the Rocky and Selkirk Mountains.

To hasten progress, the engineers were followed by bridge gangs who erected trestles, Howe trusses, or, in the case of a substantial crossing, such as the one over the South Saskatchewan River near Medicine Hat, a steel structure.[323] In the wake of the bridge gangs were the contractors' grading crews, whose task was build a railway embankment four feet above the prairie, employing horse-drawn scoops and shovels, known as fresnos, to move most of the earth. The original contract had not called for such a high embankment, but Van Horne decided that the added height would shield the rails from snow blockage and thereby prevent costly delays.

After the grading crews came the track gangs, which consisted of about 182 men, most of whom were European immigrants. Working like a drill team, they followed swiftly behind the grading crews, unloading ties and rails from flatcars, cutting, laying, and spiking. Although no track-laying machines were employed in those days, the speed with which the track was laid was amazing. The previous year, small knots of men employing loaded handcars had pushed the track forward at about three-quarters of a mile a day. This leisurely pace did not suit Van Horne, who ordered the track to be advanced at five times that speed. The military precision that this necessitated astounded outside observers, who time and again that summer invoked the term "clockwork" to describe the track-laying technique that they witnessed.

To ensure that the work was completed to his satisfaction and probably to set a pace for the contractors, Van Horne organized a construction gang of his own men known as "the flying wing." It followed hard on the heels of the contractors, providing finishing touches after they had complied with the literal requirements spelled out in their contracts.

The pulse of the whole operation was the "end of track," the site where the track was actually being laid. At this location was a unique, mobile village composed of supply and office cars as well as three-storey boarding and dormitory cars, where the working crews were fed and lodged. This veritable town-on-wheels remained on the spot for the duration of only a day's work, after which it moved three or four miles west of where it had been stationed that morning.

During this period of frenzied prairie construction, Van Horne seemed to be everywhere. When not doing paperwork in his dingy Winnipeg office, he was out on the Prairies, riding on hand cars or flat cars, in a caboose or, where the rails had not been laid, in a wagon or a buckboard, which must have made for many an uncomfortable journey. Despite his portliness he moved about continually, "going like a whirlwind wherever he went, stimulating every man he met," reported Angus Sinclair, a contractor on the north shore of Lake Superior.[324] Those who saw him in action were constantly amazed by his stamina, to say nothing of his daring. They were astonished by feats of defiance that saw their boss ignore his weight and march across trestles and ties at dizzying heights. One day, while on an inspection trip, he instructed an engine driver to drive across a precarious-looking stretch of track. When the driver demurred, Van Horne, whose practised eye could well calculate degrees of danger, said, "Get down and I will take her over myself." Such was the driver's faith in Van Horne's judgment that he immediately drove the engine over to the other side himself. What the men most admired about the general manager, however, was his completely unaffected personality and his refusal to assume airs. When, for example, he could not find suitable dry clothes after an unplanned topple into a river, the general manager donned a red flannel shirt and a pair of ripped pants held together by a clothesline.

Van Horne loved to dwell on the hardships and discoveries of his early CPR days, and years after his railway construction experiences he would reminisce nostalgically about the time that he spent on the then mysterious Prairies, whose crystalline air, inhuman scale, and haunting silence made a lasting impression on him. Surrounded by an appreciative audience in his Montreal mansion, he would talk about the nights whiled away in prairie construction camps, some of them pitch black when rain pelted the tent canvas and he slept on a sopping wet mattress with the water oozing out of his blankets. The nights spent in these rude construction camps that reeked of tobacco, sweat, and drying socks certainly provided a striking contrast and counterbalance to the life that he led back East with its luxury and obeisance to convention and rigidly prescribed codes of behaviour. Still, it is easy to imagine that Van Horne did not feel out of place in these camps. It is highly probable that he preferred the company of the down-to-earth engineers and contractors with whom he associated while out on the line to that of the more stuffy and haughty members of his own circle. As one astute observer, the British art critic Roger Fry, would later remark, "[Van Horne] took his chances in society as he had taken them in the backwoods of Canada, with a genial and unpretentious simplicity of manner. He did not care to hide behind the entrenchments of etiquette and formality with which most of the newly rich protect their sensitiveness to criticism."[325]

Among the stories that he would tell in later years was one that involved his first sighting of a prairie chicken. When Van Horne spotted a giant creature strutting along the horizon line he caught himself dreaming that this was perhaps some prehistoric bird "that had been preserved for us in the unbroken solitudes and that we had made a grand discovery ..."[326] His disappointment was great when the bird's true identity was revealed. Nevertheless, to the end of his days he would continue to speak in wonder of prairie life, particularly of its silence, a silence so profound and so omnipresent that it seemed as if he could hear it.

It was rare for anyone to keep up with Van Horne during the day and virtually impossible for any colleague to keep abreast of him after the day's work was done. When the official surveys were completed, he would sketch on sun-bleached buffalo skulls or organize target shooting at them. For those interested in more strenuous activity, he would organize foot races. Nights, as was his wont, he would tell stories and play poker to dawn. Then he would wash up and go on his way.

The demands of the project required undivided attention and an abundance of focused energy, both of which Van Horne was well able to provide. In order to accomplish his goal, however, he would summarily dismiss men who were indifferent to their work or who were disinclined to carry out orders. Collingwood Schreiber, engineer-in-chief to the federal government, recalled that Van Horne would often say to him, "If you want anything done name the day when it must be finished. If I order a thing done in a specified time and the man to whom I give that order says it is impossible to carry out, then he must go. Otherwise his subordinates would make no effort to accomplish the work in the time mentioned."[327] It was a philosophy that served the general manager well because invariably those who took orders from him foresaw the end result of disputing what he said should be done.

Van Horne's somewhat autocratic manner and contempt for "the impossible" is forcefully illustrated by the well-known story retailed by J.H. Secretan, engineer and surveyor:

> One day he sent for me to his office in Winnipeg and rapidly revolving his chair squinted at me over the top of his pince-nez, at the same time unrolling a profile about one hundred miles at a time, saying, "Look here, some damned fool of an engineer has put in a tunnel up there, and I want you to go and *take it out!*" I asked if I might be permitted to see where the objectionable tunnel was. He kept rolling and unrolling the profile till he came to the fatal spike which showed a mud tunnel about 900-feet long — somewhere on the Bow River at mileage

942. I mildly suggested that the engineer, whoever he was, had not put the tunnel in for fun. He didn't care what the engineer did it for, but they were not going to build it and delay the rest of the work. "How long do you think it would take to build the cursed thing?" he asked. I guessed about twelve or fourteen months. That settled it. He was not there to build fool tunnels to please a lot of engineers. So perfectly satisfied that the matter was settled and done with, he whirled round to his desk and went on with something else, simply remarking, "Mind you go up there *yourself* and take that d–d tunnel out. Don't send anybody else."

I asked for the profile, and when I reached the door, paused for a minute and said, "While I'm up there hadn't I better move some of those mountains back, as I think they are too close to the river." The "old man" looked up for a second, said nothing, but I could see the generous proportions of his corporation shaking like a jelly. He was convulsed with laughter.[328]

Van Horne had a habit of materializing at work sites when he was least expected. One such site was Flat Creek, Manitoba, which had resumed its slumber after the construction assembly line had pushed its nose further west. In response to complaints about this point, Van Horne descended upon the unsuspecting local CPR officials like "a blizzard," reported the *Winnipeg Sun's* irreverent columnist R.K. Kerrighan, in prose that demonstrates his love of hyperbole:

> The trains run in a kind of go-as-you-please style that is anything but refreshing to the general manager. It is not for the want of officials at the end of the line, goodness knows. There are enough clerks, etc., there to build the road for that matter, if hands run short. Their chief occupation appears to be to trip over one another, and go in search of some person while the train hands go out duck shooting in the "mash", and the engineers fall asleep.
>
> ... But when Manager Van Horne strikes the town there is a shaking up of old bones. He cometh in like a blizzard and he goeth out like a lantern. He is the terror of Flat Krick. He shakes them up like an earth quake and

they are as frightened of him as if he were the old Nick himself. Yet Van Horne is calm and harmless looking. He is a she mule, and he is a buzz saw ...[329]

While George Stephen scrambled to find money to meet construction demands, Van Horne spent much of his time in the summer and autumn of 1882 prodding and inspiring his men to new heights of endurance and accomplishment. He also devoted untold hours to receiving a steady stream of directors, shareholders, and notables bent on seeing first-hand the progress of construction. In August 1882, one of these excursions took Van Horne, Donald Smith, Duncan McIntyre, John Henry McTavish, the Hudson's Bay Company accountant, and their guests to Pile o' Bones Creek, the federal government's and the CPR's choice for the future capital of the North West Territories. As it was then merely a collection of squatters' tents on a treeless, featureless plain, Pile o' Bones Creek lacked the grandeur that is usually associated with a capital city. Even its new name, Regina, selected by Princess Louise, the wife of the Governor General, in honour of her mother, did not impress the visiting party. Nevertheless, the visiting dignitaries duly christened the capital-to-be with a toast in Van Horne's private car.[330]

When the last "official grand excursion" of the season departed in late October, Van Horne heaved a large sigh of relief. To Addie, he deplored the fact that Sir Charles Tupper and the rest of the "nobs" had managed to consume every second of his time for the past ten days. Now that he was at last free to concentrate on his real job, however, he was nagged by worries concerning the home front. In what had become fairly routine for him, he took it upon himself to upbraid Addie for being a poor correspondent. "Why dont you write oftener? If I do not it is because I am out on the line and have no opportunity ... Do let me hear from you oftener. The worry of business is enough without the additional anxiety resulting from not hearing from home."[331]

Fortunately, he could seek relief from everyday cares in the opulence of official Car Number 10, which was assigned to his use in August 1882. One of seven official cars that began operating on Canadian Pacific rails that year, it boasted Turkish leather upholstery, plate glass mirrors, tapestry and silk velvet curtains, Wilton carpets, two large bedrooms, a kitchen/pantry, a dining room, and a drawing room. Even Van Horne found it "quite oppressive in its magnificence." Still, it did lack a French chef, an oversight that the general manager proposed to rectify as quickly as possible.[332] Van Horne would use Car Number 10 until he was appointed vice-president of the railway in 1884, at which time he was assigned the use of the *Saskatchewan*.

Van Horne's sojourn in Winnipeg was fast drawing to close when a cigar butt that had been tossed carelessly into his wastepaper basket ignited a major fire in the Bank of Montreal building. In the early hours of October 29, 1882, it seemed that flames would destroy the entire building, but thanks to the firemen's heroic efforts it and several adjoining edifices were saved. Damage to the bank's and the CPR's offices was so extensive, however, that both institutions had to find a temporary home for most of their operations.[333] To their rescue came nearby Knox Church, where railway officials quickly set up shop in the basement. As it turned out, though, Van Horne would see little of his makeshift office; that autumn, he had to spend increasing amounts of time in the CPR's Place d'Armes headquarters in Montreal.

Canada's most cosmopolitan metropolis, with a rapidly growing population of approximately 145,000, was essentially two cities — the English and the French. They were visibly separated, with St. Lawrence Main as the dividing line. Nearly all the population east of "the Main" were French-speaking, while nearly all those who lived west of it were English-speaking.

In 1882, Montreal was on the threshold of its three greatest decades, those that preceded the First World War. The city that would soon become the Van Horne family's new home boasted a flourishing commercial and manufacturing sector whose growth was financed in part by unprecedented quantities of capital that flowed in from Great Britain. In Montreal, much of this capital found its way to the Bank of Montreal, whose directors integrated and coordinated most of the metropolitan region's financial affairs. The Bank of Montreal, by far the largest bank in Canada, was the core of a loosely allied group that included the Canadian Pacific Railway, the Sun Life and the Royal Victoria insurance companies, the Canadian branches of British and American life, fire, and casualty companies, and the largest millers, cotton manufacturers, and shipping companies.[334] Before the century was out, Van Horne would become one of the key players in the tightly knit group of English-speaking men, many of them Scots, whose shared values and wealth enabled them to dominate Montreal's business world before the advent of the Quiet Revolution in the 1960s and the entry of French Canadians into key positions in the business and commercial sectors.

Making deals, founding companies, and amassing a fortune did not preoccupy Van Horne in the autumn of 1882, however. At that time he had very different concerns on his mind. One was the steadily escalating pressure of railway business, which weighed on him no matter where he was. It was particularly bad in Montreal, where as soon as he arrived he was inundated by requests for interviews. Whether at the office or at his hotel, there was always someone waiting to see him. The result was exceedingly long days in which he rarely got to bed before midnight.

Pressure of a different sort originated with the CPR's desire to have him transfer his headquarters to Montreal as soon as possible. In September, Van Horne had resisted the idea, not wishing to settle there until the following spring. Then, deciding that he would be too busy in the spring, he installed himself in Canada's largest city and commercial capital in late November, taking up residence in the Windsor Hotel, which had opened in 1878.[335] This venerable Dominion Square landmark would be his home until the family moved to Montreal in April 1883.[336]

Their arrival would finally spell an end to such long, extended separations as the one that had occurred earlier in the year. It had prompted his adored twelve-year-old daughter, Addie, to write plaintively from Milwaukee, "The weather is very pleasant and all the roses are in bloom. Those red roses you planted when we came here are one mass of bloom and are the admiration of everyone ... Papa, I wish you could come home, just think! it has been almost 4 months since you was [here] last, we all long to see your dear face again."[337] Before the family made the move, however, Van Horne attempted to reconcile his reluctant wife to the idea of leaving Milwaukee and the United States for Montreal and Canada. Ever conscious of costs, he decided that Montreal's cost-of-living advantages might help to sway her mind. "As Montreal is to be our future home it may please you to know that prices are very much lower for nearly everything here than in the States. For instance boots that cost me $16 in Chicago cost $8 here and are better made at that ... Will not such figures reconcile you to coming ..."[338]

When not immersed in railway business, the paterfamilias took steps to acquire a suitable family home in the city's famous Square Mile, those several blocks in central Montreal where many of the English-speaking wealthy built their stately mansions in the last half of the nineteenth century and the first years of the twentieth. To this end, he arranged for Duncan McIntyre to negotiate for the purchase of the eastern wing of the imposing semi-detached stone residence that later became known as the Shaughnessy House, after Thomas Shaughnessy, Van Horne's successor as president of the CPR. Located at the western end of Dorchester Street, in the southwestern corner of the Square Mile, it was built in 1874 by McIntyre, who lived in its west wing, and timber merchant Robert Brown, who lived in the wing that the Van Horne family would later occupy.

The Shaughnessy House, which a century later would be integrated into the Canadian Centre for Architecture, had many selling points to recommend it. Not the least of these was its location, close to Donald Smith's ostentatious residence at the corner of Fort and Dorchester Streets and not far from CPR headquarters on Place d'Armes in the heart of Montreal's financial and commercial district. Van Horne and his family would attend many a function in the Smith mansion, and on at least one of these occasions Van Horne found his "supernatural powers" put to the test. On this particular evening, he was seated at one end of the long drawing room and Sir George Stephen at the other end. Sir George was asked to make a drawing of anything he wished. Van Horne was then asked to make a drawing of the same subject. He was momentarily flummoxed, but then his formidable memory and astute powers of observation came to his aid. Suddenly he remembered Lady Stephen reporting some years before that her husband could only draw one thing, a salmon. "I cast a sly eye over to the other end of the room, and saw his hand moving quickly in small circles. The scales! So I drew a salmon as quickly as I could. And, by jinks, it was right."[339]

The Shaughnessy House was also close to the city's most attractive playground, beautiful tree-covered Mount Royal, whose commanding view of the quaint city, the St. Lawrence River, a wide swath of the Eastern Townships, and, on good days, Vermont's Green Mountains so enthralled Van Horne that he reported excitedly to Addie, "The view from the Mountain cant be equalled in the world."[340] Created a public park in 1875, 764-foot-high Mount Royal sloped gently down to Sherbrooke Street, where a mile-long section of imposing, elegant residences constituted the heart of the Square Mile, which was bounded roughly by McGill University on the east, Guy Street on the west, Dorchester Street on the south, and Pine Avenue on the north. When Van Horne was first introduced to it, the district was still relatively new, having started to take shape as recently as 1861, the year that the city began creeping up the slope of the mountain with rich, English-speaking Canadians leading the way.

South of 1149 Dorchester, only a few minutes' walk from the Square Mile, was another Montreal, where the working classes — recently arrived immigrants, the French, and the Irish — lived a strikingly different kind of existence in fetid slums with unpaved streets and tarpaper shacks. In some of these districts more than half of the residents had only outdoor privies and the accumulation of garbage was commonplace. Death rates in the slums ran as high as twenty or even forty per thousand people. By contrast, in the streets frequented by Van Horne and his friends it was twelve to the thousand.[341]

Also south of the Shaughnessy House was the financial and commercial district, which Van Horne would come to know intimately. Here,
architects had vied with each other in the economic boom of the 1860s to
design impressive facades like that of the Shaughnessy House. As a result,
many an edifice along Notre Dame and St. James Streets sported garland-
ed and carved walls, pillared porticos, and profusely decorated entrances.
Even as Van Horne descended on the scene, however, they were being
eclipsed by larger and still grander buildings, all designed to serve a growing demand for rental office space.

Perhaps even more noteworthy than the financial district was the busy
port area that abutted onto the broad St. Lawrence River. The first of the
world's ports to be electrified, Montreal now welcomed vessels from some
thirteen steamship companies, one of these being the celebrated Allan
Line, at that time pre-eminent on the Atlantic. It had been founded in
1854 by a group of friends led by Scottish-born Montrealer Hugh Allan,
later Sir Hugh Allan, of CPR fame, another resident of the Square Mile.
Presbyterian Scots, in fact, formed a majority of the denizens of the Square
Mile, the balance being made up of Irish, English, a sprinkling of
Americans, and a few Jewish and French-Canadian families. Irrespective of
origin, many would become Van Horne's friends. With his move to
Montreal he would become a prominent member of a coterie whose dom-
ination in the world of Canadian finance and business spawned power that
reached all the way to New York, London, and Paris.

In late November, the general manager's growing enthusiasm for the
house he had chosen prompted him to write Addie, "It is a very bright
and cheerful place and everything about it is nearly perfect."[342] In the
months ahead he would inspect the painting of its rooms and purchase
gas fixtures for it in New York. He would restrain himself sufficiently,
however, to await Addie's help in selecting furniture and carpeting.
Meanwhile, he would deluge her with instructions respecting the move,
insisting that she arrange to have his fossils packed in three or four
whiskey barrels and that she have a cabinet maker or other qualified person pack the furniture for shipment.

Unlike the reception that had greeted him earlier in the year at
Winnipeg, his reception at CPR headquarters in Montreal was cordial. The
warm response that greeted his return to Montreal, his move to that cosmopolitan city, plus the completion of almost five hundred miles of track
in the Northwest combined to produce a buoyant mood. In November he
told Addie:

Our people here all seem highly pleased that I have come to stay. They are not used to railway work and there is much of it to do. Their schemes are far reaching and numerous. I am going to follow a very conservative line for the present. I like the aggressive policy best but I feel that it will be unsafe for the company to attempt too much just now. The whole country is delighted with our summers work in the northwest. It is the first thing in railway building that Canada has occasion to be proud of.[343]

It was just as well that he felt undaunted and optimistic, as he would need huge quantities of optimism and determination to see him through the months ahead, when cutting costs would become an obsession because of the work in the Rockies and north of Lake Superior.

Chapter Seven
Cutting Costs

In January 1883, Van Horne could look back on a year in which, claimed the *Victoria Daily Times*, "the amount of work accomplished [had been] perfectly astonishing."[344] Although frost had stopped the grading crews on November 13, track-laying had continued until early January, a month of brutal cold on the Prairies. By that time CPR rails were in sight of what is now Maple Creek, Saskatchewan, 585 miles west of Winnipeg. Approximately 418 miles of track had been laid since work began in April. Since 110 miles of track had also been laid on the southwestern branch in Manitoba that same year, the number of main line track miles laid in 1882 totalled 528; to this total should be added a further 57 miles of sidings. Any informed observer would have to concede that the hard-driving general manager had made good on his rash boast that he would build 500 miles of track during the 1882 construction season.[345]

The previous year's accomplishments certainly gave Van Horne plenty of reason to rejoice. Nevertheless, he well knew that almost overwhelming problems still remained to be tackled. These were the difficulties and costs associated with construction in the Rocky Mountains and around the north shore of Lake Superior, that vast inland sea that seduces by its beauty and intimidates by its ferocious storms, which materialize suddenly and lash relentlessly. Of a magnitude hitherto never experienced, these construction problems would tax his determination and ingenuity to the limit during the ensuing construction seasons.

Meanwhile, in the opening months of 1883, the general manager continued to maintain a frenetic pace. In February, before the start of the new construction season, he hustled off to New York, where, he informed Addie, he was "very busy." On his return to Montreal, he plunged into a gruelling routine that called for him to toil until 1:00 or 2:00 a.m. every day, drawing up detailed reports for the government and arranging contracts for rolling stock and fuel. Then, in early March, he headed out west, stopping off in Toronto to attend to some business and then leaving the next day for Chicago. After less than a day in the Windy City he returned to Montreal for a two-day interlude before leaving for Winnipeg. It should come as no surprise, then, that when he finally stole some time to write to Addie he would confess to neglecting her shamefully.[346]

As crushing as his workload was, however, Van Horne still managed to pursue some interests not related to CPR business. In New York, he squeezed in the hours necessary to attend the sale of a celebrated porcelain collection and to select from it some pieces for shipment to Milwaukee. And in his new home city, Montreal, no matter how pressing his CPR responsibilities, he frequently inspected the Dorchester Street house and filed away in his mental notebook a list of things that had to be done before the family's move in the spring. The pace that he set for himself and his continuing absence from the family were taking their toll, however. It was enough to make him remark wistfully to Addie, "I am more anxious than I can say to get settled once more and be at home once in a while."[347]

The approach of spring not only heralded the family's move to Montreal but also signalled the beginning of a new construction season. In anticipation of this, Van Horne turned his attention increasingly to the frozen wilderness of Northwestern Ontario and to the track that had to be laid across the more than six hundred miles of remote, seemingly intractable terrain that lay between Callander and Port Arthur. This was the area dismissed by Grand Trunk supporters, who ridiculed the CPR's plans as "a perfect blank even on the maps of Canada." A pamphlet issued by these critics declared, "All that is known of the region is that it would be impossible to construct this one section for the whole cash subsidy provided by the Canadian government for the entire scheme."[348]

Van Horne entertained no illusions about the magnitude of the difficulties and costs inherent in building in this region, particularly along the rocky stretch that hugs the shoreline of Lake Superior, which he himself defined as "two hundred miles of engineering impossibilities." However, exuding his usual confidence, he added, "But we'll bridge it." Bridging it would prove a remarkable feat. Construction along this entire route would be hampered not only by steep rock cliffs that descended to the lake and by capricious ice and water conditions but also by the countryside's extremely variable topography. But these were only some of the challenges faced by grading and track-laying crews, who began their work in 1883, starting from both ends of the lake. These men found their task made even more difficult by a lack of earth with which to construct embankments and the need to repeatedly grade the roadbed. And then there were the sinkholes — ostensibly solid patches of ground that sank without apparent cause. Sometimes these suddenly gave way under the weight of a train, with costly, time-consuming results (one sinkhole collapsed seven times, swallowing miles of finished track and three locomotives).

And then there were the landslides. On one occasion a slide swept away a portion of track and thousands of dollars worth of steel rails. When the telegram conveying the bad news was handed to Van Horne at his desk in Montreal, he displayed his customary self-control by merely lifting his eyebrows and uttering a quiet exclamation.[349]

Progress would also be impeded by the lack of a dependable labour supply in 1883, as ordinary labourers deserted for higher-paying positions on the western main line. By the autumn of that year the western main line had reached the foothills of the Rockies and there was a soaring demand for day labourers to work in the mountains. In an attempt to meet it, labour agencies and ads posted by the CPR in the American Midwest offered $2.00 and $2.25 per day for ordinary labourers. Since the top daily rate paid to these workers on the Lake Superior section was $1.50 to $1.75, the CPR found itself in the awkward position of having one section competing with another for workers. Van Horne did not contemplate the situation with equanimity, but it seemed that he was powerless to do much about it, aside from urging James Ross, in charge of construction in the mountain division, to keep a lid on wages at his end.

The demon rum also hindered the progress of construction in the Lake Superior section. In the West, which was under federal jurisdiction, the sale of alcohol was banned, but it was not prohibited in Ontario, where enterprising liquor peddlers found a ready market for their wares, particularly among the toiling navvies, who frequently turned to alcohol for relief from the exhausting work that they performed and the extremely primitive conditions under which they lived. Van Horne attempted to dampen its appeal by arranging for the construction crews to be well fed, but this was not enough to stave off a chronic liquor problem that frequently spawned lawlessness and violence, such as the rioting and gunplay that erupted in October 1884. It was so serious that authorities summoned a magistrate and police from Toronto. To Van Horne's dismay, some government authorities even contributed indirectly to such lawlessness. When the general manager discovered that revenue-hungry authorities at Sault Ste. Marie had issued licences for the sale of liquor at the Michipicoten River supply base he immediately fired off a letter to the minister of railways and canals pointing out that supplies, including an enormous quantity of high explosives, were transported by train along a hundred miles of the line. Since one careless move could ignite a disaster he hoped that the licences would be revoked. He wrote in vain.[350]

Van Horne quickly realized that a great deal of heavy rock work would be required on the Lake Superior shore. Accordingly, to save time and money, he ordered that three dynamite factories, each capable of producing six thousand pounds a day, be built in the Caldwell-Jackfish area. As an economizing measure, he also pressed for the abandonment of the traditional cut and fill method. In its stead, he urged that the line be carried high and that timber trestles be built over the intervening gullies, valleys, and clefts. These would be filled later with materials brought in by rail rather than by the more costly teams. "I hope careful attention will be given to the suggestions I made as to raising the grade line and shortening the rock cuttings, using temporary trestles wherever suitable material cannot be readily borrowed for the embankments," wrote Van Horne in a letter to a construction chief. To emphasize his point, he added, "By raising the gradeline and reducing the width of the cuttings the cost of construction can be enormously decreased as also the time of completion ..."[351]

When Alan Brown, a pioneer in Ontario railway construction, saw the completed rock cuttings he pronounced them "wonderful." Brown, who travelled the line shortly after its completion, was so overcome with awe that he could barely muster the words to describe what he had seen: "It is impossible to imagine any grander construction ... Everything is synonymous with strength ... The bridges, the tunnels, the rock cuttings almost make you aghast, and after seeing the tunnel work I was not surprised to think that the Hon. Alexander McKenzie at one time spoke of them as 'impossible barriers' ..."[352]

It was during this construction phase that Van Horne imported the first "track-laying machine" to be used in Canada. It was his answer to the problems posed by track-laying, especially in inhospitable areas, such as the swampy, mosquito-infested countryside, where one day he found workers struggling to lay rails. A delivery gantry, rather than an actual machine, the American track-laying machine carried rails forward in troughs along one side of the lead car and ties on the other side.

To facilitate the delivery of supplies and men to Lake Superior's north shore, the general manager decided to locate the line as close to the lake as possible. Even locating the line was no routine undertaking since changes had to be made in the interests of saving money. This in turn delayed the letting of contracts. As a result of these delays and the horrendous construction problems, the railway line along Lake Superior's north shore was not completed until 1885.

In a move that foreshadowed the development of the Canadian Pacific's steamship service, and that incensed Hill, Van Horne ordered boats to transport supplies and workers to the north shore's work sites. An early purchase was the steam boat *Champion Number 2*, which was purchased at Quebec and delivered to Port Arthur in June 1883.[353] He also ordered the construction of three 2,300-ton steel passenger and cargo steamers, the *Alberta*, the *Algoma*, and the *Athabaska*. All were launched on Scotland's Clyde Riverin July and sailed across the Atlantic in October. After arrival in Montreal they were cut in two and reassembled on the Great Lakes in preparation for entering service when navigation opened in 1884. Eventually they were based at Owen Sound, where they became a vital link in the first-class and immigrant services that the CPR was now able to offer from Montreal to the Rocky Mountains in the summer season.

When touring the *Alberta* in June 1884, Van Horne revealed his gourmand nature and penchant for detail by taking particular notice of the food served in the 110-seat dining room. Later he informed the manager of the North-West Transportation Company, Henry Beatty, that while he found the fare excellent there were "altogether too many dishes offered." Instead of the current menu, he proposed a combination that would guide menu formats of the Canadian Pacific steamship line for the next eighty years:

> Fewer varieties, but plenty of each, I have always found to be better appreciated than a host of small, made-up dishes. Poultry of any sort when it can be had is very desirable. Two entrees will be plenty. Deep apple, peach and etc. pie should be the standard in the pastry line; and several of the minor sweets should be left out. Plenty of fresh fish ... is what people expect to find on the lakes and it is, as a rule, the scarcest article in the steamers' larders.[354]

His observations regarding the stocking of fresh fish might just as well have been made today in relation to those dining rooms that offer only frozen fish and produce when the local area abounds in the fresh version.

While Van Horne was masterminding plans for work and services around Lake Superior's north shore, Jim Hill, always a force the general manager had to reckon with, was making plans to retire from the CPR board. He finally resigned that May, along with his close associate and financial right arm, John Kennedy. Their leave-taking should have come as no surprise to Van Horne, who must have anticipated it, given the steadily worsening relationship between the CPR and Hill's St. Paul, Minneapolis and Manitoba Railway.

Relations between the two roads had undergone considerable strain in recent months, largely because Van Horne was determined to seize every possible advantage for the CPR, even if this meant straining the somewhat fragile bonds that held the old associates together. With the CPR's profit margin in mind, he had implemented a rate policy designed keep as much eastbound freight as possible from leaving Winnipeg and proceeding east via St. Paul. This infuriated Hill, who hastened to remind Stephen that as Hill's road had extended lower rates and shipping privileges to the CPR between January 1, 1882, and January 30, 1883, Hill confidently expected Van Horne to extend equally generous rebates to the Manitoba line.[355] Van Horne, however, was not prepared to do this. On the contrary, he persisted in adopting a hard-nosed approach to granting rebates to Hill's road and to sharing traffic and revenues between the two lines.

Hill responded by complaining bitterly and frequently to members of the syndicate about Van Horne's actions. After the general manager had stopped off at the Manitoba road's office in St. Paul on his way to Chicago, the American wrote to R.B. Angus, attacking Van Horne's position on the division of east-west traffic and revenues:

> The construction last year of the Canadian Pacific Road cost enormously. There should be a statement from time to time telling what the work is costing. When Van Horne passed here on Saturday I talked to him about a basis upon which both our companies would work & told him it would be necessary to have this done by the time the CP would take over the Thunder Bay Branch. I am sorry to say that Mr. Van Hornes reply was not such as would lead us to expect any reasonable or fair action on his part. His reply was substantial that he considered Winnipeg a local station on the Can. Pac. Ry and that we had no more right to look for a rate to Winnipeg than to any other point.[356]

Hill fretted about what he described as the general manager's "strange actions and decisions" while Stephen and Angus tried all the while to keep the peace between the two strong-willed, ambitious men.

But their efforts were to no avail. The squabbling continued, a reflection of the widening gulf that had developed between the two railways as they competed for traffic.

What finally precipitated Jim Hill's formal leave-taking from the CPR board was the realization that Van Horne was actually going to build around the north shore of Lake Superior. Initially there had been some doubt that track would ever be laid across the rugged, barren Canadian Shield north of the Great Lakes. Hill, in fact, was quite convinced that Stephen would postpone indefinitely the construction of this part of the main line and simply use Michigan roads and the St. Paul, Minneapolis and Manitoba route instead. This conviction was rudely shattered in early 1883 when it became apparent that Van Horne and Stephen were determined to press ahead with construction north of Lake Superior. For Hill it was unthinkable that Van Horne, the pragmatic, cost-conscious railroading man, had allowed nationalism to prevail over economics, but then Hill did not realize that his one-time protegé had bought into Macdonald's vision of Canada. Van Horne, the budding Canadian nationalist, was fast identifying with his new home and equating the CPR with Canada, the nation.

With the certitude that this stretch of road would be built came the quashing of Jim Hill's hopes that his Manitoba line would become a permanent link between the CPR's western and eastern networks. The elimination of his road from an anticipated role in the CPR's transcontinental scheme was bad enough. But the picture looked even bleaker when Hill realized that an all-Canadian route would deprive the Manitoba road of the eastbound Canadian traffic that it already carried.

Van Horne's friend found such a vision of the future decidedly abhorrent. Almost as unwelcome was the clash of interests that he foresaw between the CPR and the future transcontinental railway that he was now envisaging — the Great Northern Railroad, which would be an expansion of the Manitoba road to the Pacific coast. Competition between the two lines was not only inevitable, concluded Hill, so was a trial of strength between him and Van Horne. The prospect of further conflict between the two men and between their respective lines intensified Hill's unease and further convinced him that he should leave the CPR board. He would later sum up the situation in thirteen pithy words, "I saw that conflict was coming, and I said, 'We will part friends.'"[357] In the decade after his departure Hill would turn the Minneapolis, Manitoba and St. Paul into an American transcontinental and even take over his principal American rival, the Northern Pacific. And, in the 1890s, he would battle fiercely with Van Horne over disputed territory in British Columbia.

When Jim Hill resigned from the CPR board, track-laying on the Prairies, which had resumed on April 18, was forging swiftly ahead. By August 13, steel reached the tent and log cabin city of Calgary, Langdon and Shepard having completed their contract in fifteen months. Two weeks later, Van Horne, along with Stephen, Angus, and Donald Smith, journeyed from Winnipeg to Calgary in Stephen's private railway car on what was to be a celebratory trip to mark the arrival of steel at Calgary. Accompanying them on the seven-car train were Baron Pascoe du Pré Grenfell, one of the CPR's European backers, and His Royal Highness, Prince Hohenlohe of Germany, who was looking over the area with a view to recommending it to prospective German emigrants. Two hours after arriving, the CPR officials and their guests were joined at lunch by Father Albert Lacombe, renowned missionary to the native people in the Northwest.[358]

During the Calgary visit an incident occurred that made a profound and lasting impression on Van Horne, although later he would apologetically dismiss it as not being "exciting" or of "deep interest." It appears that after the train arrived at the log cabin settlement it was met by a large number of Natives who had been assembled for the express purpose of entertaining the visiting dignitaries. When Father Lacombe stepped off the train he asked a bystander why the Natives were there. On hearing the explanation, the Oblate priest made a signal with his hand. Almost immediately every Native vanished and was not seen again. When asked why he made the signal, the priest replied that such exhibitions were undignified and demoralizing and that he would not permit them.[359] Years later, Van Horne, who had been deeply moved by what he had seen, would recount the incident to Lacombe's biographer, Katherine Hughes.

When Van Horne met Father Lacombe, O.M.I., at Calgary, the general manager and the renowned missionary to the Blackfoot Indians were no strangers to each other. They had first met a year earlier at Rat Portage, where the rugged priest had been sent to attend to the spiritual needs of hundreds of drinking, blaspheming, and fighting railway construction workers. His first meeting with the heroic priest made a profound and lasting impression on Van Horne, who recorded his recollections of the stirring event in a painting that he presented to Lacombe in the autumn of 1894.[360] Decades later he would write about his first encounter with the priest, now a cherished friend, in a preface for Katherine Hughes's biography of Lacombe:

> Near the Lake of the Woods one morning in 1882 I saw
> a priest standing on a flat rock, his crucifix in his right

hand and his broad hat in the other, silhouetted against the rising sun which made a golden halo about him, talking to a group of Indians — men, women and pappooses — who were listening with reverent attention. It was a scene never to be forgotten, and the noble and saintly countenance of the priest brought it to me that this must be Father Lacombe of whom I had heard so much; and it was. My acquaintance with him, begun that morning, has been full of charm for me, and my only regret is that in these later years the pleasure of meeting him has come at lengthening intervals.[361]

The central figure in this memorable vignette, Father Albert Lacombe, was undoubtedly one of the most devoted, self-sacrificing, and saintly men who ever crossed paths with Van Horne. Born in Lower Canada (now Quebec) in 1827, he was ordained a priest twenty-two years later. Following his ordination he was sent to the mission of Pembina, North Dakota, where he assisted Abbé G.-A. Belcourt and studied Cree until 1850. After a year in Canada East, Lacombe returned to the West, this time to serve at Fort Edmonton and at Lac Sainte-Anne, where he joined the Oblate Order. Except for the years 1880–1882, when he served as chaplain to the CPR's construction gangs, Father Lacombe ministered to the Métis, for whom he had a special affection, and served the wandering Assiniboine, Blackfoot, and Cree, nursing them, praying for and with them, and acting as an intermediary. Because of his deep affection for the Native people and his understanding of their culture and lifestyles he became not only an invaluable interpreter and spokesman but also an effective bridge between their communities and the white population.

While serving in Calgary, Father Lacombe earned the eternal gratitude of Van Horne and the CPR for preventing a possible outbreak of violence against its workforce. The flashpoint occurred in July 1883 when railway surveyors encroached on the borders of the Blackfoot reserve east of Gleichen near Calgary. Determined to prevent an invasion of their lands, angry and indignant tribe members repulsed the workmen. Father Lacombe, informed by a younger colleague that trouble was brewing on the reserve, feared that bloodshed was imminent and wired Indian Commissioner Edgar Dewdney to come immediately. However, despite repeated appeals the commissioner failed to act. Lacombe, anticipating a massacre, rode post-haste to Crowfoot and prevailed upon the elderly and sagacious Blackfoot chief to call a council.

To this meeting, on June 19, the father brought a copious supply of sugar and tobacco as well as tea and some sacks of flour. These he distributed among the tribe members. Then, assuming the role of a government envoy, he asked his audience to let the CPR appropriate a small portion of their reserve in return for additional land, which the government would provide. Mollified by the priest's deferential courtesy and persuaded by his arguments, the tribe agreed to let the government build its railway undisturbed. A few days later, as Lacombe had announced, Dewdney finally visited the reserve and confirmed that the promise would be carried out. The flames of rebellion were quickly extinguished.[362]

The syndicate was so grateful to the priest for pacifying the Natives and allowing construction to proceed that Stephen invited him to lunch in the president's private car. Accounts vary, but it appears that during the luncheon Van Horne playfully suggested that the priest be elected president of the CPR. A directors' meeting was convened and George Stephen announced that he was resigning from his office for one hour. Angus then moved that the priest be elected to succeed him. The motion was carried unanimously and Stephen relinquished the presidency to be replaced by Lacombe. One story claims that during his brief term as CPR president, Lacombe voted himself two lifetime railway passes, free transportation of all freight and necessary baggage to the Oblate missions, and free use for himself for life of the railway's telegraph service.[363] It is difficult to assign much credibility to this tale, however, because the priest was probably too modest and self-effacing to take such action. On the other hand, we do know that Van Horne was so appreciative of Lacombe's successful intervention that he presented him with a lifetime CPR pass. If we are to believe Lady Aberdeen, that dedicated diarist, the CPR's gratitude also extended to free use of the line for all goods addressed to Lacombe.[364]

That autumn, track-laying along the western main line made such good progress that James Ross, the chief engineer, reported to Van Horne on November 23, 1883, "Our track will, at the end of this week, reach the summit of the Rocky Mountains, thus fully carrying out this year's programme of work under my superintendence nearly six weeks ahead of the time allowed for it ..."[365] This was welcome news. But overshadowing it was the knowledge that the CPR was hovering on the brink of a financial abyss as a result of construction costs and the purchase of feeder lines in eastern Canada.

The 1882 construction season alone had swallowed up a huge amount of money, a sum estimated to be at least $22 million. Stephen had initially thought that the CPR line could be built for $45 million, Sir Charles Tupper's official estimate, but the pace at which Van Horne had pushed construction across the Prairies, coupled with the topography of the land itself (broken, rolling country), ensured that construction costs would eventually overtake the estimated figure by a wide margin. This was bad enough, but in 1883, when construction began along Lake Superior's shoreline, the outlook became even grimmer. Rock excavation on only one mile of the lake's east shore would cost $700,000, while excavation along several other miles would run up to $500,000.

Financial pressure weighed so heavily on Van Horne that he frequently clashed with John Ross over the quality and expense of Ross's work along the Lake Superior shoreline. Ross, the engineer in charge of the western section of the CPR's Lake Superior construction, insisted on high-quality materials, employing masonry where Van Horne believed that timber or fill would suffice. In his letters to Ross, the general manager repeatedly stressed that not one dollar more than was absolutely necessary should be spent on construction. Structures could be built to carry trains safely for two or three years and then be replaced by permanent ones once the line was in operation and earning income.

It later transpired that Ross's threats to the budget were motivated by more than just a genuine interest in quality workmanship and materials. The engineer was systematically and ingeniously enlarging contractors' profits in elaborate railway construction frauds. When Shaughnessy realized what was going on, he informed Van Horne that in at least two cases he had admissions from contractors that they were permitted large sums of money to which they were not entitled and that "in a dozen other cases the evidence [was] so palpable that it [could not] be questioned."[366] Although he repeatedly called Ross on the carpet and grilled him, Shaughnessy never succeeded in getting an admission of guilt from the engineer. In one way the construction fraud played in Shaughnessy's favour: at a time when the CPR was hovering on the brink of financial collapse it allowed him to delay payments to both honest and dishonest contractors. In another respect, however, the frauds could not have occurred at a worse time. With Stephen striving desperately to raise funds in London and CPR shares depressed on markets everywhere, a scandal such as this would have ruined the CPR's reputation and jeopardized its future. In its wake Van Horne, Stephen, and Shaughnessy would have been ridiculed as bunglers unable to supervise their own employees properly.

The CPR therefore covered up the story, while Shaughnessy quietly fired Ross and ruthlessly pursued offending contractors.

The CPR's financial problems were further exacerbated by the syndicate's aggressive policy of gobbling up existing feeder and branch lines and constructing new ones in eastern Canada. Both Van Horne and Stephen realized that if the CPR was to survive, let alone flourish, it had to have eastern outlets and be able to tap the transportation market in Ontario and Quebec, where over 70 percent of Canada's total population lived. Settlement on the virtually uninhabited Prairies and in British Columbia, which boasted a population of little more than fifteen thousand, would eventually generate traffic. Still, this would take years to develop, and in the interval the CPR would find itself in dire financial straits if it did not attract substantial business in Canada's most populous provinces. In order to get this business, the CPR had to purchase and construct extensions in Ontario and Quebec.

Nobody believed more fervently in this system building policy than Van Horne, who was convinced that the company courted, as he put it, "absolute starvation" if it did not expand in Quebec and Ontario. No matter that such purchases and extensions were not mentioned in the original contract, they constituted part of the CPR's original plan and anybody who gave the matter any thought realized that they were as necessary as many of the local lines in the West. Without them, argued Van Horne, "the main line would have been a vast body without arms or legs — a helpless and hopeless thing and one which could not possibly live without constant Government aid."[367] In a letter defending the CPR's expansion during years of penury, Van Horne observed: "Without those acquired and constructed lines both in the East and the West the main line of the Canadian Pacific would have been of very little value to Canada and every dollar of private capital put into it would have been absolutely lost — so the company could not wait a minute. On the entire main line there was no traffic whatever save a few miles west of Winnipeg."[368]

The CPR's invasion of southern Ontario began with its acquisition of Duncan McIntyre's Canada Central Railway, which extended from Brockville, on the St. Lawrence River, north to Ottawa and from thence for a hundred miles up the Ottawa Valley. This line was targeted because its charter empowered it to build to the eastern end of Lake Nipissing, the eastern terminus specified in the CPR's charter. The Canada Central purchase was approved only weeks after the CPR came into existence, and in June 1881 it was merged with the younger road. Almost immediately work began on the extension to Callander.

A further incursion into the East occurred in the spring of 1882 when the CPR purchased the money-guzzling Montreal to Ottawa segment of the Quebec, Montreal, Ottawa and Occidental Railway. This railway, which ran west from Quebec City along the north shore of the St. Lawrence to Montreal, where it branched north to Ottawa, was owned by the financially embarrassed Quebec government, which was only too eager to sell its provincial railway system. With this acquisition, the CPR was well launched on its program to acquire or build lines affording it access to Canada's heartland between Quebec and Toronto. Imitating the example of such well-known American roads as the Pennsylvania Railroad and Van Horne's former employer, the Chicago, Milwaukee and St. Paul, Van Horne's road had embarked on system building, gobbling up feeder roads as part of a plan to create an integrated system.

That same year the CPR also began laying track on the Ontario and Quebec Railway, which had recently come into its orbit. The line under construction was to extend eastward from Toronto to Perth, where a connection would be made with the CPR. When completed, the Ontario and Quebec would provide an independent line to Toronto and connect Ontario's capital with the Credit Valley Railway and the Toronto, Grey and Bruce Railway, two roads that also belonged to the Canadian Pacific. Such a network of affiliated roads would enable the CPR to acquire a direct line to southwestern Ontario, where it could easily build a line to Detroit. Since it had already concluded a deal with William Vanderbilt's Michigan Central to carry traffic from there to Chicago, Van Horne's road was now poised to compete with the Grand Trunk in the lucrative American market.

As part of its later expansion program in Ontario and Quebec, the CPR constructed a new line linking Windsor and London. After it was opened in 1890, Van Horne, accompanied by fellow CPR directors and others, made the customary inspection trip in a special train. For this occasion, Harry Armstrong, then the CPR's chief assistant engineer, drew up a small temporary time bill that incorporated such station names as "The Puce," "Jones' Corners," and other local designations. Van Horne took a look at Armstrong's time bill and then, to all outward appearances, fell asleep in his chair, his hat pulled down over his face. Within minutes, however, he heaved himself up and said, "Call those places "Ringold, Haycroft and Elmstead." And so they were named.[369] Today these monikers still appear on official time bills.

The ultimate well-being of the CPR dictated that it expand into eastern Canada and that it complete its main line across the Prairies as quickly as possible. Nevertheless, the very speed of construction on the Prairies and the railway's incursions into Ontario and Quebec created a seemingly intractable problem that would haunt the CPR and the Macdonald government for years to come. This was the problem of finances. Periodically the railway's desperate cash position would threaten to sink the whole enterprise.

Stephen, whose financial wizardry Van Horne admired, had indirectly contributed to the situation by rejecting the all too common American practice of floating bonds and borrowing excessively on the security of bond issues to finance railway construction. Not wanting to saddle the CPR with fixed charges, its president sought to finance construction by raising funds from the stock market and by selling land grant bonds. The bonds, which represented the land subsidy, were worth a total of $25 million, the land being valued at a dollar an acre. Money accruing from their sale had to be remitted to the government, which was then supposed to dole it out to the company on the completion of each twenty-mile section of the main line. Unfortunately for the cash-starved CPR this scheme had a major weakness: the government's dilatoriness in handing over money as the land grant was earned.

To add to the CPR's misfortune, vicious attempts were made to discredit the railway lands and thereby undermine the company's reputation in American and British financial circles. The most scathing attack was launched on September 1, 1881, by an article in the influential English periodical *Truth*. A savage piece that became a benchmark for similar articles in other publications, it shredded the CPR, mocked its prospects, and stated that Canada itself was on the verge of bankruptcy. By implication, the railway's land grant, the cash subsidy, and the land grant bonds were all worthless.

Before the year 1882 was out it became apparent that it was going to be difficult to finance even a comparatively easy stretch of the prairie section. The company could not even look to the government for financial salvation because the Department of Finance, unaware that land grants had been sold, refused to authorize payments on land that had been earned. Confronted by a worsening financial situation, in December Stephen and his cousin went cap in hand to the Bank of Montreal for a short-term loan of $300,000, offering as security their New Brunswick Railway Company bonds.

This would not be the last time that the bank was approached for a financial transfusion during the money-draining construction period. In July 1883, pressing demands for money resulted in the bank lending the company $900,000 to enable it to take over the Toronto, Grey and Bruce Railway, which connected Toronto with Owen Sound on Georgian Bay.

To obtain this loan, Stephen, Smith, and some of their colleagues had to give their personal guarantees.

The fact that its board members were men of wealth who enjoyed notable reputations as railway builders and who had the backing of the federal government ought to have guaranteed the CPR an excellent credit rating. Unfortunately, it did not. In fact, the years 1882 to 1885 saw the CPR lurch from one financial crisis to another, largely because of the need to foil attempts made by rivals to deprive its line of potential traffic and to destroy the company's credit rating.

Foremost among the CPR's rivals was Van Horne's *bête noire*, the Grand Trunk Railway, a largely British-owned and -directed railway whose main line from Sarnia and Toronto to Montreal formed the backbone of the Canadian railway system in 1881. Not surprisingly, the CPR's invasion of southern Ontario and Quebec incited the wrath of the older railway. For his part, Stephen felt that CPR eastern lines that competed with the Grand Trunk constituted part of the "legitimate and necessary development" of the Canadian Pacific. Sir Henry Tyler, the Grand Trunk's president, and Joseph Hickson, its general manager, thought otherwise. As they saw it, the CPR in the East should be content with its main line and nothing more, and if it ended at Callander so much the better.

The Grand Trunk adopted this attitude as early as 1873 when it tried to frustrate Sir Hugh Allan's attempts to raise funds in London, and in the 1880s it once again entered the lists, often cultivating friends among Liberal party supporters who relished ammunition to use against the Conservatives' policies. Indeed, only days after the CPR contract had been signed, Hickson warned Macdonald that the construction of lines "apart altogether from the Pacific line proper" would invariably result in "a collision of interests and some friction" between the two companies.

In the ensuing struggle the Grand Trunk attacked on several fronts. Embarking on a policy of railway acquisition, it pitted itself against its chief rival in southwestern Ontario, the Great Western, which operated a network of lines between Toronto, Hamilton, London, and Windsor. In 1882, the Grand Trunk swallowed up the Great Western, thereby outmanoeuvring the CPR, which also wanted to acquire the railway. The Grand Trunk then followed up this coup by purchasing the eastern segment of the Quebec, Montreal, Ottawa and Occidental Railway, the "North Shore Line," in a move designed to prevent the CPR from getting into Quebec City.

Not content with outmanoeuvring the CPR in the acquisition of railways, the Grand Trunk also directed a propaganda barrage against its rival. The fruits of this could be found in such malevolent pieces as the *Truth* article, which Stephen was quick to blame on the Grand Trunk "and its paid ink slingers in London." This propaganda war would prove to be a continuing curse because of the grave threat that it posed to the CPR's reputation, and hence to the settlement of the Northwest.

Matters came to a head in early 1883, when the Grand Trunk, driven to desperation by the prospect of losing its Canadian monopoly, declared open war on the CPR. Addressing shareholders at his company's semi-annual meeting on March 29, Grand Trunk president Sir Henry Tyler accused the CPR of embarking "upon schemes of aggression" and of planning to conclude an agreement with American interests that would allow it to secure an outlet over friendly lines to Chicago, the great grain centre of the Middle West. To the charge that the Grand Trunk had fought to keep its rival out of the international money markets, Tyler replied that the company's directors "as a Board" had never done anything of the kind. He then referred to the powerful influence of the Grand Trunk's shareholders and implied that it could be brought to bear against the CPR if it tried to draw on the London market for funds to compete against the Grand Trunk in Canada.[370]

Although George Stephen regarded Sir Henry Tyler as "nothing but a bottle of stale ginger pop," he quickly rose to the Grand Trunk's challenge. In response to Sir Henry's broadside, the CPR president addressed a letter to the Grand Trunk's shareholders, pointing out the injustice of the Grand Trunk's attacks and insisting that there was room for competition between the two railways. Whether this letter had any impact is open to question. But if it did, it paled in significance to the stand that London's financial houses took toward the two railways. Stephen's plan to set up a new holding corporation to facilitate further expansion in Eastern Canada and the U.S. (the Great Central of Canada Company) and the intense competition that such a move portended alarmed those financial houses that were heavily involved with the affairs of the not too prosperous Grand Trunk. Accordingly, the market closed ranks against the CPR president and made him realize that Great Central debentures could not be sold in London.

This setback, coupled with the Grand Trunk's less than enviable financial position, was evidently enough to force George Stephen and Sir Henry to the bargaining table in London, where, against overwhelming obstacles, they managed to hammer out an agreement between their two companies. The two presidents then cabled their respective general managers to draw up an instrument that essentially reserved all Pacific-bound traffic to the

CPR, assigned Ontario to the Grand Trunk, and pledged the two companies to avoid competition and work together for their mutual benefit.

This quixotic and, as it would turn out, ineffectual attempt to end the rivalry between the two roads brought a quick response. When Stephen's colleagues in Montreal and New York saw the accord's terms they immediately repudiated them. Under no circumstances would they countenance a complete and abject surrender to the Grand Trunk's demands (Van Horne would later remark that Stephen, although an optimist in Canada, was inclined to become fearful when abroad). It is not known who led the attack, but in all likelihood it was Van Horne, whose naturally combative nature did not predispose him to be accommodating, least of all when the Grand Trunk acquired the North Shore Line from the Quebec government and thereby shut the CPR out of Quebec City. The general manager expressed his reaction to the agreement in his characteristically blunt fashion when he wrote, on April 16, 1883, with aggressive certitude, "The Grand Trunk people have been frantically attempting to force an agreement that would head off the 'Great Central' scheme but they can't do it."[371] In other words, if Van Horne had his way, the Grand Trunk would never be allowed to block CPR expansion in Canada and the United States. True to form, the CPR's general manager was not prepared to let any perceived difficulties interfere with his aims and objectives or those of his railway.

With the breakdown of negotiations with the Grand Trunk, the CPR moved quickly to firm up control of its affiliates in Eastern Canada. It abandoned the Great Central scheme (but not its objectives) and on April 20, 1883, it petitioned Parliament for authority to lease the Ontario and Quebec, the Credit Valley, and the Atlantic and North-West railways. Despite some opposition the necessary legislation became law in May. Later the company made use of convenient powers in the Ontario and Quebec charter to consolidate the various lines. In July, the Toronto, Grey and Bruce Railway was leased to the Ontario and Quebec, and in November the Credit Valley Railway was added by amalgamation. Then, the following January, the Ontario and Quebec itself plus its subsidiary lines were leased in perpetuity to the Canadian Pacific.

The equally competitive Grand Trunk did not sit passively on the sidelines while the Ontario and Quebec, along with its subsidiary lines, was being absorbed by the CPR. When Parliament was debating aid to the CPR in February 1884, Joseph Hickson, the Grand Trunk's general manager, fired off a volley of letters to Sir John A. Macdonald strongly protesting legislation "embracing assistance to lines acquired by the Syndicate outside of the objects of the Canadian Pacific charter, thus using public money for competition against private enterprise."[372] In the same letter, Hickson even urged the federal government to bring about the surrender of the CPR's acquired lines in Ontario to the Grand Trunk in exchange for the North Shore Railway between Montreal and Quebec.

When Van Horne got wind of this correspondence he immediately shot off a letter to the prime minister decrying Hickson's failure to address a business proposition directly to the CPR and pointing out that the Ontario and Quebec Railway had been leased and firmly bound to the CPR for 999 years. Carrying the war into the enemy's camp, he boldly proposed that the CPR purchase the Grand Trunk's North Shore Railway. He also reiterated a favourite theme of his, the CPR's need to operate independently of other roads:

> The necessity to the Canadian Pacific of perfect independence is manifest when the fact is considered that the Grand Trunk Company have a line of their own to Chicago, and that not one of their passengers or one pound of their freight, from any point going to the North-West, can be delivered to the Canadian Pacific at Callender, or any other point east of the Great Lakes, without direct loss to the earnings of the Grand Trunk.
>
> When the Ontario and Quebec line is completed, it will be superior to the Grand Trunk in distance, in grades, in equipment, and in every other particular, <u>and its cost will be less than one-fifth of that of the corresponding section of the Grand Trunk</u>. It will pass through a well-developed country, and will have from its opening a large local business, and will be so situated as to command its full share of traffic. I have no hesitation, therefore, in asserting that the lines by means of which the Canadian Pacific will secure independence, will not cost them one dollar, but on the contrary, will add largely to their profits.[373]

Once again Van Horne demonstrated that he would not allow the Grand Trunk to foil CPR expansion in the east and compromise its independence. Hostility between the two railways would continue, but it would not be undiluted hostility. Belying their public enmity, the two companies entered into rate-fixing agreements in eastern Canada, Van Horne suggesting that the passenger and freight agents of both companies meet regularly to discuss and adjust their differences.[374] The railways also cooperated in the transportation of immigrants from Point Lévis to Toronto and in the issuing of free passes to MPs. When Van Horne remonstrated with Hickson in the years that followed, he usually confined himself to charges that Grand Trunk personnel were breaking secret rate-fixing agreements.

Meanwhile, the CPR's financial troubles continued apace. To raise funds, the railway, in the summer of 1882, had agreed to sell a huge chunk of its land — five million acres — to the Canada Northwest Land Company for $13.5 million. The Anglo-Canadian syndicate, whose formation had been instigated by the CPR, assumed responsibility for managing townsite sales in forty-seven major communities, including Calgary, Regina, Medicine Hat, and Swift Current. When township sites were sold, the railway was to receive a percentage of the net proceeds. Initially there was a large demand in both Canada and England for the company's stock, but after the Grand Trunk's "scribblers" went to work demand for the shares plummeted, along with the syndicate's fortunes. By December 1883, the syndicate faced near collapse, and the CPR, to bail it out, agreed to take back about half of the land grant bonds that it had sold to the syndicate on time and an equivalent amount of land.

As the CPR edged closer and closer to a financial abyss in the fall of 1883, the mercurial and somewhat impulsive Stephen became almost frantic. No matter what money-raising expedient he resorted to, it failed him. Even the stock market let him down. In June of that year company shares reached a peak on the New York stock exchange, but then they slid to bargain-basement prices following the collapse of the real estate boom in the Northwest, a killing frost on September 7 that almost wiped out the 1883 wheat crop on, and the sudden bankruptcy of the CPR's latent rival, the Northern Pacific. The collapse of the Northern Pacific depressed railway shares in general and transcontinental railway shares in particular, especially those of the CPR. In fact, claimed Van Horne, the Northern Pacific's bankruptcy precipitated the financial crisis that resulted in "locking up all the cash and valuable resources of the CPR beyond recall." Faced by a desperate financial situation, Stephen decided to petition the government for relief.

Hitherto Van Horne had usually left Stephen to scramble for money, but in November of 1883, when the situation was critical, he journeyed to Ottawa with Stephen, Angus, McIntyre, and J.J.C. Abbott, the CPR's solicitor, to petition the government for funds. After arriving in the nation's capital, the mendicants went directly to Earnscliffe to outline the situation to Sir John A. Macdonald and to point out the absolute necessity of immediate government assistance. Mustering all their powers of persuasion, they asked the government to loan the company $30 million, to be paid over as construction advanced, and to be secured by a first lien on all the company's properties.

The prime minister, Van Horne later recalled, patiently heard his petitioners out, then informed them that nothing could be done. "Gentlemen, I need not detain you long. You might as well ask for the planet Jupiter. I would not give you the millions you ask, and if I did the cabinet would not agree, and if they did it would smash the party. Now, gentlemen, I did not have much sleep last night, and I should like to get to bed. I am sorry, but there is no use discussing the matter further."[375] Van Horne and his colleagues tried to argue their case, but Macdonald would not listen. Instead, he bowed them out.

Empty-handed and in despair, Van Horne and his colleagues headed for downtown Ottawa to await the departure of the 4:00 a.m. train for Montreal. As they had several hours to kill they decided on their way that they would spend the intervening time at "Bank Cottage," a Bank of Montreal residence that was then being rented to John Henry Pope. On arriving there they found Pope, the acting minister of railways and canals, lying on a couch reading, a strong habitant cigar clenched between his teeth and a glass of whiskey at his side. The minister, when he saw the gloom on the faces of his visitors, immediately asked what was up. While McIntyre danced about excitedly, Stephen conveyed the bad news. Pope then rose slowly, lit another cigar, donned his old otter cap and shaggy coat, and called for a carriage. "Wait till I get back," he said as he departed. It was then after one o'clock.

The minister returned from Earnscliffe an hour and a half later. Entering without a word, he kicked off his rubbers, removed his coat and hat, poured another glass of whiskey, and then lit a fresh cigar, all with maddening deliberation and an impassive face. Finally he broke the tension with the announcement, "He'll do it." Pope had roused Macdonald from his bed and then put the delegation's case before him, summing up his arguments with the observation, "The day the Canadian Pacific busts the Conservative party busts the day after."[376]

This was enough to trigger a complete reversal of the prime minister's position and to convince Macdonald that the government had to accede to the railway's request. Stephen, he knew, had done all that he could do to avert disaster. He had battled against his and the railway's enemies with his usual passion and energy, but then the market for railway shares had collapsed. With the failure of the investing world to come to the railway's aid, the prime minister now realized that the government had no other choice but to stand by the CPR. As Pope had reminded him, the fate of the Conservative Party was inextricably linked to that of the Canadian Pacific.

To provide the generous assistance demanded by Stephen, the government would have to push a bill through Parliament granting the railway relief, a bill that would require the support of all the CPR's friends and well-wishers. It would also require Tupper's expertise to help overcome the opposition that such a measure would evoke. Knowing this, Macdonald summoned the pugnacious minister of railways and canals home from London, where he had been serving as High Commissioner, to help pilot a relief bill through caucus and then through Parliament. In response to Macdonald's now-famous cablegram, "Pacific in trouble. You should be here," Tupper sailed promptly for Canada, where he promptly ordered a government investigation of the CPR's finances. After a searching inquiry, Collingwood Schreiber, the government engineer, and the deputy minister of inland revenue reported that they were completely satisfied with the CPR's accounts and integrity. Van Horne was thereupon summoned to a Cabinet meeting to explain his company's progress and needs.

Meanwhile, the government took steps to provide immediate assistance to the Canadian Pacific. Before Parliament met in January, Tupper came to Stephen's aid by signing a letter supporting the president's application for an extension of a current loan from the Bank of Montreal, which had refused to grant one unless it had written assurance from the government that it stood by the Canadian Pacific for repayment of the loan. As it was, the bank only granted the extension after Stephen's application had squeaked through a meeting of the bank's board of directors by the narrowest of margins.

In advance of Parliament's new sitting, Stephen and the government agreed on the terms of the aid. Essentially it consisted of a $22.5-million loan, repayable May 1, 1891, of which $7.5 million was to be made available immediately. The remaining $15 million and the balance of the cash subsidy was to be paid not on a mileage basis, as heretofore, but on the basis of work done as a proportion of the total remaining to be completed. As security for this huge loan, Stephen agreed to mortgage the entire railway, including land grant bonds and outstanding stock. The CPR president, at Van Horne's instigation, also promised to have the main line completed in half the time stipulated in the original contract. It was all too evident that the company was prepared to pay a staggering price for relief.

Later that winter Van Horne made still another trip to the nation's capital, this time to see parliamentary history in the making. Flanked by Stephen and Smith in the visitor's gallery, he watched Tupper propose the new Canadian Pacific Railway resolutions in the House of Commons on February 1, 1884. It must have been a memorable day for Van Horne, the transplanted American, to be watching proceedings in the Canadian House of Commons. But it must have been an even more memorable day for Donald Smith; on this occasion he would hear the man who had denounced him in the House in 1878 now strive to portray the CPR as a company composed of men of great wealth, unblemished honour, enterprise, and integrity.[377]

The proceedings that the men watched were the prelude to what would turn out to be one of the longest and most acrimonious debates in the history of the Canadian transcontinental railway. With the presentation of the relief bill, every agency and individual opposed to the CPR was given an ideal opportunity to unite against it. Although Blake cynically admitted that he expected the bill to pass, he and a steady parade of Liberal speakers fiercely opposed it.

The CPR, in Blake's view, could do no right. In long, turgid speeches the veteran opponent of the railway denounced its change of route, its questionable financial devices, its monopolistic construction methods, its spending on railway properties outside its contract, its invasion of other railways' territories in the east, and its own monopoly in the Northwest. As proof of what he conceived to be the railway's cavalier approach to spending, the indignant Blake quoted from an interview that a *Montreal Star* reporter had with an overly ebullient, rather reckless-sounding Van Horne the previous fall when the CPR main line reached Kamloops, British Columbia.

> "How much will it cost per mile through the Rockies?"
>
> "We don't know."
>
> "Have you not estimated the amount beforehand?"
>
> "The Canadian Pacific Railway," replied Mr. Van Horne, bracing himself and speaking as if he wanted the reporter to understand that he meant every word he said, "has never estimated the cost of any work; it hasn't time for that; it's got a big job on hand, and it's going to push it through."
>
> "Well," said the reporter, "but if you haven't estimated the cost of construction through the mountains, how do you know that you have sufficient funds to push the road, as you are currently reported to have?"

"Well, if we haven't got enough, we will get more, that's all about it."[378]

Despite threatened defections within his own Cabinet and blistering attacks from outside, a weary Macdonald managed to push the relief bill through Parliament without interruption. He only succeeded in doing so, however, by resorting to much cajoling in caucus and behind the scenes and by awarding concessions to Quebec and the Maritimes. On February 28, the measure passed the Commons and, after being passed by the Senate, it became law on March 6. A week later the Bank of Montreal debt was retired.

Van Horne claimed to have been taken aback by the frantic horse-trading and other political machinations required to keep the CPR alive. To one-time Cabinet minister Peter Mitchell he wrote, "It has always been a matter of principle with me never to enquire into a man's politics in transacting business, but I must say that our past winter's experience at Ottawa has somewhat staggered me ..."[379] He certainly had reason to be "somewhat staggered" by recent developments in Ottawa because hitherto he had not been directly involved with Canadian politics. Apart from lobbying on behalf of the Southern Minnesota, he had remained largely aloof from politics and politicians, both Canadian and American. He did not belong to any political party, and, like Stephen, he had repeatedly resisted the common Canadian practice of hiring a person on the basis of his political affiliation (to say nothing of his religion). What mattered most to Van Horne was a man's ability.

Nevertheless, Van Horne had shown that he was prepared to play the political game if this was what it took to safeguard or further the CPR's interests. One such occasion arose during the 1883 Ontario provincial election when Macdonald and the federal government solicited political assistance from the CPR. Since he was only too conscious of the railway's dependence on the government, Van Horne was quick to provide that assistance.

This election was like no other Ontario provincial election because it took place at the height of the Ontario-Manitoba boundary question, a dispute that sucked in not only the Ontario and Manitoba governments but also the federal government. At issue was the determination of Ontario's western and northern limits and the balance of federal and provincial power. The original quarrel had been between the Hudson's Bay Company and the province of Canada, but when the Dominion of Canada acquired the Company lands in 1870 the quarrel was transmuted into a new wrangle between Canada and Ontario. Manitoba was implicated in the issue in 1881 when Macdonald declared that its boundaries extended east to the disputed area claimed by Ontario.

In making this pronouncement Macdonald pitted himself and his government squarely against the Ontario government and its Liberal, provincial rights premier, Oliver Mowat. With the approach of the 1883 Ontario election, therefore, Ottawa approached friends who might help to unseat Mowat and his government. Among those allies consulted was the CPR, then feverishly pushing forward construction in the Algoma District, deep in the heart of the disputed territory. In response to Ottawa's request, Van Horne wrote Egan:

> An election in the Algoma District is near at hand and the Government at Ottawa are exceedingly anxious that we should give them some assistance.
>
> The fight is really between the Dominion and the Ontario Government and is a very important one.
>
> ... Whatever is done must be done in such a way as to avoid any grounds for a charge on their part that we have taken a hand in the matter. If you can do anything without being found out we will be glad to have you work in a few votes in the interest of our Ottawa friends.
>
> If such voters as you have east of Rat Portage are massed in the vicinity of the polling places immediately before the election it will give grounds for a charge of interference on our part but if they are worked in that vicinity for some weeks such a charge can hardly be made ...[380]

As it turned out, the Liberal candidate won. It is unlikely, however, that Van Horne was overly perturbed by the results. He took the action that he did simply for business, not ideological, reasons. Probably more than anybody else he knew on which side the CPR bread was buttered, and he was determined that the Macdonald government would continue to support the CPR.

The unpleasant experience in Ottawa certainly did not bring about Van Horne's political conversion, as has been alleged, but it did force him and his CPR colleagues to become even more politically minded. This, of course, was exactly what Macdonald wanted; the prime minister had suggested in 1883 that the CPR, in its war with the Grand Trunk, should look to its friends and, more to the point, that it had better make sure it had friends to look to. The old chieftain reinforced this point when the loan was going through: "We are going to have a regular quarrel & fight with the GTR — & they will oppose us politically all along the *line*. To meet this the CPR *must* become political & secure as much Parliamentary support as possible. The appts to the Ontario & Quebec [railway] should all be made political — There are plenty of good men to be found in our ranks."[381]

Evidently both Stephen and Van Horne agreed with these sentiments because in a letter to H.H. Smith, the Conservative organizer for Ontario, Macdonald reported, "He [Stephen] says that you had better see Mr. Van Horne who is fully aware now of the necessity of not appointing anybody along the line who has not been 'fully circumcised' — to use his own phrase."[382] In the future, lofty ideals were going to take second place to practical considerations where the railway's interests were concerned.

While Stephen strove desperately to keep the company afloat, Van Horne, contrary to the impression of frightening recklessness given by the *Montreal Star* interview, constantly struggled to reduce costs and maintain quality. His cost-cutting campaign took on a new urgency in 1883 when the sheer volume of construction sent expenditures soaring to new heights. Running rights, supplies, wages, construction approaches — everything was carefully scrutinized with cutting costs in mind.

Putting the squeeze on the St. Paul, Minnesota and Manitoba, he informed Alan Manvel, its general manager, that the CPR could not continue to dispense anything like the money it had been paying the last two years for the use of the track between Emerson and St. Vincent Transfer and for the necessary facilities at the transfer.[383] With a view to shearing construction costs, he advised the engineer in charge of the Algoma district to raise the grade line and shorten the rock cuttings, using temporary trestles whenever suitable material could not be readily borrowed from embankments. These measures, claimed Van Horne, would dramatically reduce the cost of construction and the time of completion. To drive home the point that he wanted to be kept fully abreast of developments, he concluded his letter with "I will be glad to hear from you frequently."[384]

As noted earlier, Van Horne also urged wage restraint. When he received the news that James Ross, the mountain superintendent, had advertised in Duluth for labourers to work in the Rockies for $2.00 a day, the general manager informed him that the offer had greatly demoralized the men working for John Ross on the Lake Superior section, where the best rate was then $1.50 a day. Van Horne hastened to note that with the approach of winter and the increasing scarcity of work, "you will find no difficulty in, getting on our own side of the boundary line, all the labourers you want for the rock work in the mountains and ... I believe you will find it possible to keep the rate down to $1.75."[385] He then reminded Ross that a reduction of twenty-five cents in the daily wage rate for labourers represented a potential saving of $1 to $2 million.

In any event, Ross's boss was opposed to the very idea of posting notices in the United States. "I merely wish," he said, "to call your attention to the importance of exercising very great care in dealing with employment agents in the States. They are mostly swindlers and will take advantage of you if they have the least opportunity."[386] If it was absolutely essential that Ross bring in labourers from St. Paul and Chicago, he should send one or two trustworthy men to recruit them. Under no circumstances should he advertise.

When casting about for new ways to save money in 1883, the general manager made a felicitous discovery: rerouting the main line east of Banff could result in substantial savings. Subcontractors were about to start excavation for a fourteen-hundred-food-tunnel through the aptly named Tunnel Mountain when a new survey demonstrated that a revised route would eliminate the need for a long tunnel. The elimination of the projected tunnel, it was found, could save up to a year in construction time and about $500,000.

One economy measure, however, resulted in the CPR's experiencing its first serious strike. Because of the high cost of living in the West, in April 1882 the railway granted its engine drivers and firemen bonuses of twelve dollars and six dollars a month. In December 1883, however, Van Horne decided that these would have to be chopped in half and instructed Egan to issue an order carrying out the reduction. The Brotherhood of Locomotive Engineers immediately countered with a demand that the bonuses be increased, not reduced. This ignited Egan's notorious Irish temper, and he announced that the men must accept the reductions within twenty-four hours and sign an acceptance before going back to work. The engineers thereupon went on strike, and the company closed its roundhouses and shops. Within a week the shops reopened, but the dispute with the engineers lasted a fortnight. It was eventually settled largely on the company's terms and only after a lot of bitterness had been aroused by the CPR's hiring of some outside engineers and the North-West Mounted Police's protection of CPR property and trains. Not surprisingly, this unfortunate episode only cemented Van Horne's dislike of unions and increased their hostility toward him.

In addition to cutting costs, Van Horne also sought, when financially practicable, to maintain the quality of construction. On learning in late 1883, for instance, that hewed ties were still being used in trestles west of Calgary, he wrote to James Ross saying that he could not countenance this practice except for "temporary work." All hewed ties that had been incorporated into "permanent" structures would have to be replaced by sawed ties as soon as possible. "If there is any one thing we want just right, it is the bridges and it is almost impossible to make a first class bridge with hewed ties," declared the general manager.[387]

Van Horne's insistence on quality where practicable also applied, of course, to his consuming passion — food. When Major Rogers, the redoubtable engineer, was about to set off on another expedition Van Horne hastened to write him some timely reminders. After advising Rogers to take an extra engineer in case one of his men became ill, he noted:

> It is also exceedingly important that an ample supply of good food be provided and that the quality be beyond the possibility of a doubt. Very serious reports have been made to the Government about the inadequacy of the supplies provided last year and a good many other reports have been made tending to discredit our work. The officials at Ottawa as a consequence look upon our reports with a good deal of suspicion and seem to think that we have very little to show for our two years' work in the mountains ...[388]

It was not enough that he had to allay Ottawa's suspicions about the work completed. The general manager also had to respond to a barrage of complaints and petitions from enraged westerners who bitterly resented the monopoly clause in the CPR's original contract. Since its inclusion allowed the CPR's Pembina branch and its corporate cousin, the St. Paul, Minneapolis and Manitoba Railway, to charge what the traffic would bear, the result was rates that even a CPR ally, John Henry Pope, regarded as exorbitant. This led the Winnipeg Board of Trade to fire off a letter to Van Horne in which it noted that the CPR's freight charges for all classes of goods travelling from St. Vincent on the border through Winnipeg to Regina were on average 65 percent higher than comparable rates levied by the Grand Trunk in eastern Canada. Furthermore, the Grand Trunk carried certain goods such as grain, flour, and butter at substantially lower rates. To this, the CPR replied that the cost of operating in the Northwest was much higher than that of operating in eastern Canada. Despite such arguments, however, western farmers remained convinced that the monopoly clause was responsible for the high rates.

Certainly nobody, least of all Van Horne, could deny that the infamous monopoly clause prevented the construction of rival lines. Attempts were made to build such lines, but in 1883 Macdonald, prompted by Stephen, disallowed the provincial charters of three Manitoba railways because the projected roads ran too close to the international border. The fact remained, however, that Manitoba's small communities needed more railways. So it is not surprising that various towns inundated Van Horne with letters urging the CPR to build branch lines. The general manager's response was that the railway could not afford to meet their requests; the British press, he said, had greatly exaggerated stories of the farmers' agitation, killing any chance that the CPR might have of raising additional funds in Europe. To Egan, he ruefully observed, "It is very extraordinary that people with common sense should, while demanding the construction of branch lines, with the same breath attempt to destroy the credit of the Company and render it powerless to build them."[389]

Van Horne's customary blunt replies to his correspondents did nothing to dampen the discontent. They also did nothing to pacify the *Globe,* which assailed him for addressing the people of the Northwest in a tone that resembled that "of an autocrat to serfs whose murmurings and grumblings annoyed him ... In his eagerness to apply the lash to the discontented he more than once inflicts severe blows on his associates."[390]

Concerns such as these, however, would not be uppermost in Van Horne's mind in 1884 and 1885. Nor would the loss of life as a result of the all too frequent construction accidents in the British Columbia section. Here, at the height of building activity, Andrew Onderdonk employed not only white labourers but also thousands of Chinese labourers, many of whom lost their lives to disease and injury while working, often with explosives, in the dangerous passes, canyons, and mountains that comprise this stretch of the railway. No, in those crowded months, the progress of work in the mountains, the lurking spectre of CPR insolvency, and the Riel Rebellion would jostle for Van Horne's attention as he strove frantically to push construction of the CPR through to completion.

Chapter Eight
The Final Push

In 1884 and 1885, Van Horne's mettle and managerial genius would be tested as never before. Pushing a railway through the mountains of British Columbia and along the north shore of Lake Superior, with its swamp, vast muskegs, and almost impenetrable Precambrian rock, would have tried the skills of any railway manager, even one with Van Horne's genius. But the challenges of the railway's construction did not stop there. Government policy required that he have the main line in operation by the spring of 1886. This point was driven home in Lord Lansdowne's throne speech on January 17, 1884. Speaking in "clear and distinct tones," His Excellency said, "Although the time within which the railway company is bound to finish the road will not expire until 1891, my government thought it of the greatest importance for the settlement of the North West and the development of our trade, that its completion from sea to sea should be hastened and the company enabled to open the line throughout by the spring of 1886."[391] If meeting the challenge of an accelerated schedule was not enough, the general manager would also have to grapple with problems generated by an almost chronic shortage of funds and, in 1885, with the CPR's worsening public image. In that year, CPR stock sold as low as $35.75, and in the company itself there was friction and suspicion of mismanagement.[392] Against all this Van Horne had to contend. Probably at no other time in his career would he show such superb self-control and inflexibility of purpose as he focused on the business at hand, to the exclusion of almost everything else.

Like many a modern-day manager faced by a worsening financial picture, Van Horne assigned top priority to cutting costs. The passage of a relief bill by Parliament on February 28, 1884, increased George Stephen's confidence that there would be sufficient funds to complete the railway's main line, but the general manager was less sanguine. In the ensuing months he continued his strenuous campaign to slash costs and eliminate any need for the company to return to the government for relief. Everything was on the chopping block, including that venerable railway institution, the free pass. Writing to John Egan, who had proposed cutting the number of free passes, he observed, "Nearly every pass means so much money and we need every cent. I do not think there are a dozen people in Manitoba to whom we are under sufficient obligations to justify passing them free, although I know there are some thousands who think differently."[393]

Van Horne also made it abundantly clear to his construction bosses that he wanted to economize on the immediate construction of the line and to repair any deficiencies and omissions at a later date. He would strive to get an operational line built as quickly as possible, make it pay, and then improve it when finances permitted. Under no circumstances, however, was safety to be compromised when corners were cut. "We are putting up deck spans whenever practicable ... and are using place girders up to 86 feet in length," he informed James Ross, head of construction in the mountains of British Columbia. "It will be necessary on account of our finances, as well as on account of the great uncertainty as to delivery of iron work, to use timber trestles in the mountains instead of iron, where trestles are required."[394] Funds for completing the railway were "closely limited," he told Ross, and "we do not intend to fully finish the railway as we go along. The operating department is expected to follow up the tracklayers at frequent intervals and to do just so much work toward finishing as may be necessary to make the track safe for operation and to provide only such buildings, etc, as may be absolutely necessary for the immediate future ..."[395]

These decisions were relatively easy to make. Far more problematic were certain engineering decisions relating to construction in mountainous British Columbia, where the most difficult terrain and weather along the entire CPR route was to be found. The seven-hundred-mile prairie section that lay between the Assiniboine River at Brandon and the Elbow River at Calgary had required only one major structure, the South Saskatchewan bridge at Medicine Hat. By contrast, the mountain line would require many bridges, tunnels, and snowsheds, usually on the flanks of steep granite mountains pierced by deep canyons. The descent of the Rockies' western slope, together with the climbs upward and downward to and from Rogers Pass, Eagle Pass, and Notch Hill, a distance of 169 miles, would involve a net decrease of 4,100 feet in altitude. Before construction in the mountains was completed, numerous miles would have to be cut through solid rock and countless rivers would have to be crossed, some by iron bridges over a thousand feet in length and one by a wooden bridge 286 feet above the water — the highest in North America. Moreover, no fewer than fourteen streams would have to be diverted from their natural beds by tunnelling through solid rock.[396]

This was in stark contrast to the situation on the Prairies, where the equivalent ascent had proceeded over five times the distance and had not involved any undulations. The treacherous winter weather was another factor to be reckoned with. The Prairies might experience cold arctic blasts and sudden warming chinooks, but by and large there were few extremely heavy snowfalls. In the British Columbia mountains, however, annual snowfalls averaging hundreds of inches would compel the CPR to take extensive and costly precautions.[397]

Problems posed by construction on the mountain section would prove so horrendous that two construction seasons, those of 1884 and 1885, would be required to build 169 miles of main line between the Rockies' summit at Kicking Horse Pass and the western slope of the Gold Range, located twenty miles west of Eagle Pass, where Onderdonk's crews would meet those under James Ross approaching from the east. In early 1884, when Ross's end of track entered British Columbia, Van Horne submitted to the government plans and profiles of the section of line from the summit of the Rockies down to the Columbia River. As late as May 19, however, he felt obliged to inform John Henry Pope, Tupper's successor as minister of railways and canals, that important engineering questions regarding portions of the line were yet to be settled. Highly qualified engineers had examined the projected line, and while they agreed on its feasibility they differed widely as to what should be done at certain points.[398] Van Horne thus had the unenviable task of acting as the final arbitrator with regard to these "grave engineering questions."[399]

Although cost-cutting and the continuing need to stave off creditors loomed large among Van Horne's preoccupations in the early months of 1884, they were not his only concerns. Because he was the sort of manager who poked his nose into everything, he also dealt with a wide variety of other issues, large and small. One of the more vexing problems involved a simmering feud between Egan and the western construction manager, James Ross, the extremely able, thickly bearded engineer who would go on to become a coal and steel baron, a utilities titan, a financial wizard, and one of Canada's leading philanthropists.

The trouble began after Egan's department took over the constructed mileage at the end of the season. It was Egan's practice to carry out meticulous inspections of the work done and then submit detailed reports that were rife with criticism. To add insult to injury, Van Horne's trusted lieutenant also maintained a careful watch on the issuing of passes and was on the lookout for construction materials that had not been purchased through normal channels.

The feud between the two men was really precipitated, however, by actions taken by Ross and his department. After serious delays in the delivery of some construction supplies, Ross decided to charge the cost of the delays to Egan's operating department. In retaliation, Egan charged Ross's department for work not completed to his satisfaction when the constructed mileage was turned over. By early 1884 their quarrel had escalated to the point that Ross almost resigned.[400] Hoping to mollify the injured construction boss, Van Horne informed him:

> Mr Egans relations to me are no closer than those of any other officer of the company. I have never been guilty of appointing a personal friend to office nor of favouring one man over another ... I have always thought Mr Egan a good officer and for this as well I have the same opinion of you so you need not for a minute imagine that you will not have fair play and full and cordial support in all things affecting the interests of the Company. I am exceedingly angry to learn that there is even a sign of friction. I believe that a full and frank talk between yourself and Egan will eventually settle the matter.[401]

The general manager impressed upon Ross that he had his and the directors' full support. Nevertheless, he allowed Egan to continue with his sniping.

In another personnel matter, Van Horne found himself intervening on behalf of a dismissed departmental manager. After Egan had fired the man for incompetence, the general manager suggested that the western superintendent find some "outside work" for the hapless employee, perhaps settling freight claims or something similar. "He is so well disposed to do the best he knows how that I would regret very much seeing him thrown entirely out, particularly as he has a family and probably very limited means," wrote Van Horne.[402]

Fair-minded though he no doubt was, Van Horne bore the persona of a no-nonsense, hard-boiled individual. When the situation demanded it, he could be blunt and hard-headed. In instructions to Egan, he wrote, "If Murray doesn't come up to the requirements of his office do not hesitate a minute in providing for his successor. We cannot afford to waste our strength in carrying weak men ... Any charity for weakness is out of place on a Railroad and I trust that whenever an opportunity offers to improve on any man you may have in any position you will not hesitate to do it ..."[403]

Certainly he did not suffer fools gladly. His habit of dispatching withering notes to subordinates when he thought that their conduct warranted such treatment was just one reflection of this. There was also his cherished belief in the Victorian tenet of self-help, perhaps best summed up in one of his favourite maxims, "Anyone can do anything if they begin early enough."[404] This deeply ingrained belief prevented him from feeling sympathy for those who languished on the bottom rungs of society's ladder. Still, when individual cases of hardship were brought to his attention, he invariably responded with compassion, especially if these cases involved loyal, hard-working employees or friends who had fallen on hard times. He even permitted charities other than Father Lacombe's mission to extract favours from the CPR. When a Mrs. Galbreaith of the Ladies' Aid Society of the Central Presbyterian Church wrote to Van Horne asking if the CPR would transport items of clothing free of charge, he readily agreed to her request.[405] Fittingly enough, the missive containing these good tidings was written on Christmas Day 1883, for Van Horne would not allow festivities to interfere with his heavy work program.

Van Horne could also be solicitous of the welfare of the immigrants then pouring into Winnipeg. In correspondence with John Lowe, secretary of the federal Department of Agriculture, he expressed reservations about newcomers travelling on the untested Ontario and Quebec line, which had only been completed the previous week, on May 5, 1884. Until the line was determined to be in perfect condition, he said, all passengers should be transported by the Grand Trunk, to which the CPR was turning over all its available immigrant sleeping cars without charge. Van Horne even proposed that when he was in Ottawa in a day or two's time he would discuss the matter further with Lowe.[406]

Van Horne also looked for ways to ease the lot of newcomers on the Prairies. To provide newly arrived settlers with immediate access to supplies, he had railway cars fitted up as stores that could be placed on sidings built at intervals along the line. Whenever anybody who appeared to be a good storekeeper arrived on the scene, he would be entrusted with the business and the store car would be moved to a location where it could be put to good use.[407]

Day-to-day problems such as these absorbed much of Van Horne's time during the early months of 1884 as he toiled away at his cluttered desk in Montreal, filling his letterbook daily with dozens of letters, some composed in his own hand rather than his secretary's. But even as he wrestled with cost-cutting and other immediate concerns, Van Horne spun far-reaching plans for the CPR's future, plans that encompassed more than just a well-operated, profitable road. It was his firm belief that a railway had to keep growing if it was not to die or be swallowed up by a rival road that had kept up its momentum.[408]

This view was inspired, in part, by the example set in the 1880s by senior American railway executives, who, according to business historian Alfred D. Chandler, Jr., "shifted almost simultaneously from a territorial or regional strategy to an interterritorial one in order to obtain self-sustaining systems."[409] Van Horne argued that the CPR should not restrict itself to the acquisition of railway enterprises by construction, lease, or purchase; it should also strive to become an integrated international transportation complex with ships, grain elevators, hotels, and telegraph lines. With such a network, it could compete successfully against lesser Canadian and American systems and earn top dividends for its shareholders. It can be safely said, however, that at this point he did not foresee the day in the 1990s when the CPR would flaunt its international character by displaying an American flag as part of its logo (the railway later abandoned this practice and readopted a variation of its beaver and maple leaf logo).

Van Horne was one of the first railway executives to advocate the retention of such auxiliary services as the express, telegraph, and sleeping car departments. In fact, he had no sooner arrived in Canada than he asked Stephen, "Have you given away the telegraph, the express, the sleeping cars?"[410] When the CPR president replied in the negative, Van Horne advised the company to retain these services, which he called the "side-shows." He did not want to see them relinquished to other companies or paid for on a rental basis, then a common practice among American and Canadian railways. "I expect the side-shows to pay the dividend," declared Van Horne, adding "express companies take all the cream off the parcel traffic and leave the skim milk to the railroads."[411]

When serving as general superintendent of the Chicago and Alton, Van Horne had departed from the practice of the day by arranging for that railway to operate its own dining cars. As vice-president of the CPR, he decided that this road would own not only its own dining cars but also its own sleeping and parlour cars. Many of these cars would be built by the Barney and Smith Company of Dayton, Ohio, and to his own specifications, one of which stipulated that sleeping car berths be longer and wider than those found in the Pullman cars. Comfort was not the only consideration. Since aesthetic appeal also ranked high in Van Horne's estimation, the general manager commissioned noted artists to design the interior decoration of sleeping and parlour cars.

Again with profits in mind, Van Horne arranged for the CPR to purchase control of the dormant Dominion Express Company, which had been in nominal existence since 1873, and he imported an American to manage it. He also established the Canadian Pacific telegraph service, which introduced service along each mile of railway as soon as telegraph poles were erected and wires were strung. The service accepted its first commercial telegrams in the summer of 1882, transmitting them from Winnipeg to the end of steel. An incensed Western Union, in the person of Erastus Winman, the president of the Great Western Telegraph Company, one of its subsidiaries, tried to purchase the service in 1884 at what Van Horne considered a give-away price. When the general manager objected, Winman approached Stephen, charging that Van Horne was only acting out of spite and personal motives. Winman further charged that Van Horne planned to "run out all other telegraph companies" and that his entire career revealed a desire to disregard all "vested interests or interests of those unable to defend themselves." In a spirited reply to these accusations, Van Horne wrote J.J. C. Abbot, the CPR's counsel, that when the company's directors discussed its telegraph policy, he intended to "strongly represent the great value of their telegraph privileges, and implore them to protect, develop and utilize them to the fullest extent and advantage and not in any event to part with them for less than their full value, considering all their possibilities, and not to be seduced by Mr. Winman's soft words, deceived by his false words, or frightened by his bluster into discounting one cent in price or yielding one inch in advantage ..."[412]

The CPR had already taken a step toward becoming a transportation complex when, in 1883, it acquired the passenger and cargo steamers the *Athabaska*, *Alberta*, and *Algoma*, all three designed and built to the road's specifications. Another component in the grand scheme was realized the following year. In 1884, although engaged in vigorous cost-cutting measures, Van Horne nevertheless pushed ahead with plans to build grain elevators, believing that cost-cutting should not jeopardize the future best interests of the company. The elevators, after all, would help the CPR to promote successful farming in the Northwest, and when all was said and done prosperous farmers would contribute more grist to a railway company's mill than would poor ones. His experience in the American Midwest and with the Southern Minnesota had convinced him that modern elevators were required to attract adequate volumes of grain to the railway and to facilitate the cleaning and grading of cereals. Accordingly, he encouraged private parties to erect suitably designed structures of a predetermined capacity at CPR stations and to handle and store the grain at fair and reasonable prices. He also arranged for the company to build large terminal facilities at Montreal so that grain could be loaded directly into ships' holds and the company could avoid the heavy charges on grain that had prevailed previously at this port. Further inland, he had a transfer elevator built at Owen Sound for handling grain from Great Lakes ports, while at Port Arthur and Fort William he had large grain-collection elevators erected.[413]

Increasing the CPR's traffic was, of course, one of Van Horne's constant, overriding preoccupations. Knowing full well that the railway's economic survival would depend upon the successful settlement of the Prairies, he spearheaded the establishment of an effective, large-scale promotional scheme to attract both settlers and tourists alike to the Northwest. The highlight of this program was a federally funded advertising campaign that in 1884 saw the railway's emigration department distribute publicity material in ten languages to thousands of agencies in Great Britain and to over two hundred in northern Europe.[414]

Van Horne's longstanding love of art meant that he took a special interest in the pictorial side of this project. From Sir Sandford Fleming he borrowed watercolours and photographs of northwestern scenery, which he had exhibited in any agency or hall that distributed the CPR's settlement guide. He also set out to ensure an adequate supply of photographs for the company's burgeoning publicity program, commissioning photographers like Oliver Buell and Alexander Henderson to record the progress of the CPR's construction and to illustrate the wealth of opportunity offered by the new frontier. As part of this scheme, he hammered out a deal with the well-known William Notman firm of Montreal: the firm would chronicle the advance of the CPR in exchange for free transportation for one of its photographers and an assistant; the CPR would receive a set of photographs and Notman's would retain the negatives and copyright. No sooner was this arrangement concluded than William McFarlane Notman, the eldest son of the celebrated photographer, set out in 1884 on the first of eight productive western trips that he was to make on behalf of Van Horne's company. With his characteristic attention to detail, the general manager asked that certain scenes be photographed. He was especially keen on views of the Rocky Mountains, but he also requested less dramatic images, such as those of fast-growing prairie towns, a typical CPR station, and the shops and yards at Winnipeg.[415]

Nothing, other than perhaps serving as a mentor, delighted Van Horne more than commissioning artists to serve the cause. When deciding which artists the CPR should sponsor, he showed a decided preference for prominent Canadian landscape painters, notably members of the Royal Canadian Academy (RCA). His earliest recruits included Lucius O'Brien, president of the Academy and Canada's most celebrated landscape painter, John Arthur Fraser, O'Brien's closest rival, and John Colin Forbes, O'Brien's favourite sketching companion. As far as Van Horne was concerned, their membership in the prestigious RCA sufficed to qualify them for sponsorship, but it also helped that they were familiar with the work of contemporary American colleagues whose paintings had helped to lure newcomers to the American West. One such colleague was the celebrated German-American Albert Bierstadt, whose grandiose western scenes were the sensation of their day. In a letter to Van Horne, Bierstadt alerted him to the fact that he was sending him "a box with the Van Horne range of mountains" in the hope that it would be given to Mrs. Van Horne for Christmas. If Van Horne would like some "India prints of [his] Rocky Mountains" for the Montreal office he would take great pleasure in dispatching some of those to him as well.[416]

Van Horne frequently acted as mentor to these Canadian artists/publicity agents, a role for which he was ideally suited given his knowledge of art and his love of dispensing advice and instruction. His relationship with John Fraser illustrates the close supervision under which these artists worked when employed by Van Horne. In 1883, Fraser had, on his own initiative, ventured as far west as Calgary on the CPR line, and shortly thereafter he sold two works resulting from that trip to Van Horne and R.B. Angus. Having acquired a Fraser painting for his collection, in November 1884 Van Horne asked the artist if he would illustrate a proposed CPR guidebook. The perhaps initially reluctant Fraser finally agreed the following October to take on the assignment. For this and subsequent commissions Van Horne furnished photographs and advice.

On one such occasion Van Horne was quick to show his displeasure with a sketch of Mount Stephen submitted by the artist. Fraser's patron wrote, "The black and white sketch will hardly answer our purpose, the mountain not being sufficiently imposing. I made last night a rough sketch in lamp black which will illustrate my idea: it is made mostly from memory and I have taken a great deal of license, but I do not think that anyone going to the spot without the picture in hand to compare, will ever accuse us of exaggeration."[417] It was fortunate for their relationship that the artist valued Van Horne's advice and was eager to measure up to his expectations.

When it came to justifying the sizeable investment that the CPR was making in fine arts patronage, Van Horne would claim that these works of art aided the company's campaign to promote immigration to the Northwest. This rationale seems somewhat specious, however, as it is highly improbable that landscapes by RCA members would have motivated land-poor emigrants to strike out for Western Canada. Compared to the promises of free or inexpensive land made by the CPR and Ottawa, breathtaking views of rugged mountain peaks, a favourite subject, would have had a minimal impact on would-be homesteaders. While one might question whether Van Horne really believed that these works had a role to play in immigration, there is no denying his belief that works by CPR-sponsored artists helped to promote the railway's image as a "nation-builder." This conviction alone was enough to justify his zealous promotion of fine arts patronage.

Certainly, there is no doubt how Stephen, the other CPR directors, and the CPR shareholders had come to view the general manager's performance. At the annual shareholders' meeting on May 14, 1884, Van Horne was elected to the board of directors, replacing the ineffectual Duncan McIntyre, who had declined re-election because of his grave fears about the company's financial prospects. Immediately after this meeting, a special meeting of the board of directors elected Van Horne vice-president and appointed him to the board's inner circle, the executive committee, where he joined Stephen, Angus, and Smith. With his elevation to this all-powerful committee, the general manager joined a tightly knit group determined that the CPR must not and would not fail.

After his promotion, Van Horne was assigned the use of the vice-president's private car. The *Saskatchewan*, which now sits in a car barn at the Canadian Railway Historical Society Museum in Delson, Quebec, had been manufactured by Barney and Smith. With the car's assignment to Van Horne began an association between man and car that would last until Van Horne's death in 1915. In the frantic months ahead, the *Saskatchewan* would become his home as he rushed from place to place on the line, directing operations and making important decisions affecting the CPR's future. Designed for both spectacular viewing and the ultimate in comfort, the car featured large plate glass windows at both ends and an interior elaborately finished in carved mahogany, plush upholstery, and delicately etched glass. Unlike some private cars of the period, though, the *Saskatchewan* was not outrageously flamboyant, its decor conveying the impression of solid elegance rather than oppressive magnificence. It was, in other words, ideally suited to a man of Van Horne's sensibilities.[418]

As the CPR was rushed to completion, Van Horne would find that his private car was the one place on the line where he could relax completely. Besides eating and sleeping in the *Saskatchewan*, the general manager also indulged in one of his favourite aids to relaxation, poker, and he played the game with more than one purpose in mind. Whenever his car passed through the frontier community of Medicine Hat he arranged for his winnings and those of others to be distributed to its little hospital.[419]

The series of problems that Van Horne had to deal with in the early months of 1884 resulted in his having to postpone a long-anticipated trip to British Columbia. He had wanted to look over construction in the mountains and to arrive at a decision about a location of the railway's Pacific terminus. Reaching a final decision on the terminus and engaging in hard bargaining with the provincial government to obtain the necessary lands for it would alone swallow up a lot of his time in 1884.

Although the CPR's designated terminus was Port Moody at the head of Burrard Inlet, Stephen and Van Horne had entertained serious misgivings about its suitability as a port for the railway. A first-class harbour was essential, they believed, since the CPR planned a trans-Pacific steamer service and through-traffic from Asia to America's east coast. Port Moody's tidal mud flats and lack of flat land for rail yards and industry seriously diminished its appeal. Van Horne's doubts were reinforced in the spring of 1884, when he received disquieting news from his envoy on the spot, Wellington Ross, an opportunistic real estate agent who had made a fortune in the Manitoba land boom and was now sizing up the situation in the Vancouver area. Writing to Van Horne in May, Ross reported that Port Moody's harbour was too small for the CPR's purposes but that twelve miles further west, at Coal Harbour and False Creek (an extension of English Bay) there was a superb townsite. If Coal Harbour, English Bay, and False Creek could be utilized, claimed Ross, the CPR would be well served.[420] The general manager had to wait until August, however, before he had a chance to inspect the terminus options first-hand.

In June of that year, Van Horne decided that he could finally free himself from his Montreal desk to attend to a task that he wanted to complete before journeying to British Columbia: an inspection of the line between Lakes Superior and Nipissing, which had been gobbling up appalling sums of money and would be the focus of attention in 1884. With this in mind, he found himself in July in rugged Lake Superior country. The stopover, it turned out, provided him with more opportunities than he would have appreciated to demonstrate his fabled powers of endurance, still much in evidence despite his expanding girth and his essentially sedentary lifestyle. He set off one day with Collingwood Schreiber, the government's chief engineer, on a walking tour to look over eighty-two miles of line that linked Nipigon and Jack Fish Bay. After trudging all day through fire-blackened countryside in scorching July heat, the two men finally reached an engineer's camp. Both of them were sore and limp with exhaustion. Nevertheless, irrepressible Van Horne suddenly leapt from a seat he had taken and challenged his companion to a foot race. Schreiber declined.

On their return journey by steam launch, from Jack Fish Bay to Red Rock, the vessel's boiler started to leak badly. Van Horne, always pressed for time, would not hear of putting into shore. At his insistence, he, Schreiber, and the boat's engineer spent the night paddling the launch through Lake Superior's wave-tossed waters. When the boat engineer met with an accident and had to be left on shore, Van Horne and his companion paddled the launch the remaining distance to Red Rock themselves.[421]

Van Horne's energy and vitality amazed Schreiber, and the general manager's intense interest in the work in progress also made a forceful impression on others he met in Lake Superior country. A civil engineer who worked on this section, E.G. Henderson, later recalled, "Mr. Van Horne dropped in on us here and there surveying the work, inspiring it. We never knew he was coming, but he was so completely in touch with all the work that he left the impression of being on our Section all the time."[422] This observation would be a recurring theme in the reminiscences of many who helped to build the CPR.

When Van Horne finally set off for British Columbia later that summer he travelled west via the Union Pacific and then by steamboat to Victoria. He reached the provincial capital in early August and almost immediately he headed across the Strait of Georgia to the small community of Port Moody. The village, then experiencing a mild boom, confidently expected that it would become the most dynamic city on the Pacific coast. Its inhabitants eagerly awaited Van Horne's arrival so that the laying out of the new metropolis could begin. Van Horne arrived on the evening of August 6 in the company of British Columbia's premier, William Smithe, and realtor Arthur Wellington Ross. The party stayed at The Elgin House, illuminated in their honour and bedecked with flags and welcoming banners that boldly announced the choice of Port Moody as the CPR's western terminus.[423] It was not to be. As soon as he set foot in Port Moody, Van Horne's fears about the locale as a terminus were confirmed. The next day, he travelled to the mouth of Burrard Inlet by boat, where he was assured that Coal Harbour and English Bay did provide a deep, sheltered harbour that could serve the trans-Pacific trade he hoped would generate transcontinental railway traffic. Here, he decided, just inside Burrard Inlet, would be the location of the new western terminus. After returning to Montreal, he was able to bring the directors around to his view, and soon he was negotiating with the British Columbia government for a terminus at Coal Harbour and English Bay.

Eager though Van Horne was to acquire the site in question, the CPR's desperate shortage of funds ruled out any large outlay for it. The whole amount of the government loan and subsidy was required to build the main line, and additional funds to furnish such essentials as yards, wharves, and rolling stock would be hard to come by. Van Horne spelled this out in a letter to Premier Smithe and then stated unequivocally that the CPR's directors could not see their way clear to extending the rail line beyond Port Moody and to providing the necessary docks and facilities at the new site unless the company was able to obtain sufficient property "so situated." Speaking on behalf of the directors, Van Horne wrote:

> They feel that the lands west of Port Moody recently relinquished by the Dominion Government were originally intended and set apart to aid in the construction of the Canadian Pacific Railway to English Bay and as the lands would have been so applied had the Dominion Government fixed upon English Bay instead of Port Moody as the western terminus, all of these lands should, in fairness, be granted to the Company in the event of their taking up the work where the Dominion Government has left it and continuing the line to English Bay.
>
> But our directors wish to meet your Government in a liberal spirit and to ask for no more than they believe to be necessary to cover their outlay within the near future in making their terminus all it should be in the interest of the country.[424]

The hard bargain that Van Horne drove resulted in a formal agreement that was signed on February 23, 1885. In exchange for the CPR agreeing to extend the railway from Port Moody to Granville, the provincial government undertook to give the company a long stretch of waterfront on the inlet for the railway's terminals and docks, some 480 acres on the peninsula, lots on the townsite of Granville, and a tract of land on

False Creek on which the railway could build its shops, yards, and a round-house. In short, thanks to Van Horne's bargaining skills, the provincial government agreed to give his company half the peninsula on which the present city of Vancouver now sits.

Van Horne, who took a special interest in sea captains, especially if they boasted Dutch blood, suggested that the city be called "Vancouver" for the island that had taken its name from George Vancouver, the intrepid seafaring explorer who had sailed off the B.C. coast in the eighteenth century.[425] Called upon to defend his choice of moniker, which had triggered fierce criticism in the B.C. legislature, the general manager observed, "It is very important that the terminal city should have a name dignified as well as euphonious. It should also, if possible, be made to suggest its location, and 'Vancouver' heard in any part of the world is at once approximately located. I do not see why anybody on the island should object to the use of the name. The idea seems to impress everybody in the East and England most favourably."[426]

Van Horne began his return trip by travelling along the completed stretch of the government-built line. His journey took him from the coast down through the spectacular roiling Fraser canyon, and then northeast to the railhead at Lytton, situated on the Fraser. Nearby he inspected an impressive steel cantilever bridge, the first of its kind in North America, then he clambered aboard a stagecoach for a bumpy ride along the Cariboo Road to Savona's Ferry, which marked the end of the government section. En route, he visited the new mecca of Kamloops, a one-street community of shacks, where he pronounced himself pleased to find such a "thriving and progressive look."[427] The local citizenry were so delighted to see him that they made an attempt to change the name of neighbouring Savona's Ferry to Port Van Horne. The general manager quickly quashed the idea but raised the town's spirits with the promise that Kamloops would become a CPR divisional point and the site of extensive yards and railway facilities.

The second and most arduous stage of his return journey began at Savona's Ferry, a lakeside village that Onderdonk's construction crews would later link with Eagle Pass in the Gold Range. Van Horne set off from Savona's Ferry, with his friend Samuel B. Reed and the crusty A.B. Rogers, by steamboat, heading for Sicamous Narrows. There, they exchanged their mode of transportation for a freight team that crossed the mountain lakes on a scow and carried them as far as Revelstoke. From there they travelled by pony train over the Gold and Selkirk Ranges and then up the valley of the Kicking Horse to the end of track near Wapta Lake.

It proved to be a frightful trip, marred by the summer's almost constant diet of cold rain and sleet, the rough condition of the almost unbroken mountain trail, and a series of mishaps. The trail, covered with slush from an early fall of snow, was littered with other travellers' castoffs — personal belongings, saddles, blankets, and the corpses of pack ponies. Sometimes Van Horne sank waist-deep into frigid mud, and on at least one occasion he tumbled into water that was barely above freezing. But probably even more trying was having to go without food for a couple of days, their rations exhausted after he and his companions missed one of the depots in the mountains. In a letter Van Horne wrote after his return from this gruelling expedition, there is no mention of the exploits that helped to seal his reputation for fearlessness in the face of physical adversity. For example, no matter how perilous the vantage point, when determined to see something, Van Horne ignored his bulk and went where only the most experienced workmen dared to follow. The accompanying engineer might trust only his hands and knees, but not the general manager. With complete disregard for his safety, he once strode across two loose planks thrown over the Mountain Creek Trestle, whence a few days previously several men had plummeted to their deaths. On another occasion an engineer objected to driving his train across a dangerous trestle. "Here," said Van Horne, "get down, and I'll take her over myself." Retorted the engineer, "Well, if you ain't afraid, I guess I ain't neither."[428] When describing the experience to Andrew Onderdonk, the general manager reported:

> I found the trip across the mountains a very wet one from beginning to end and grub very scarce, but both Mr. Read and myself got through in pretty good shape all but our clothes, most of which we left behind at the end of the track.
>
> The trail from Wright's camp in Eagle Pass to the East Columbia was a horrible one and we made very slow time.

After commenting on the quality of the work that he found, Van Horne then made what would prove to be an astute prediction: "I have no doubt that the meeting point between the work advancing from the east and from the west will be among the Lakes in the Eagle Pass, probably thirty miles from the Narrows."[429]

Once through the mountains and travelling across the gently rolling, interminable prairie, Van Horne could take immense satisfaction in seeing Calgary, Medicine Hat, and Regina metamorphosing from mere clusters of shacks and tents into vibrant communities pulsating with life and optimism. In Winnipeg, whose population had soared to twenty-five thousand, he met a hundred members of the British Association for the Advancement of Science, there at his invitation. Acting on the premise that seeing is believing, he had invited the scientists to visit Manitoba's capital following their annual meeting in Montreal, confident that on their return to Europe they would dispel the prevailing image of Canada as a raw, snow-blanketed country.

Van Horne had earlier rubbed shoulders with the association's luminaries and their family members in Montreal. To one of the latter — Clara, Lady Rayleigh — he had forcefully expressed his conviction that Canadians were too shy about blowing their own horn. "We are a great deal too quiet in Canada; we don't puff ourselves enough or make enough of our advantages and our doings," intoned Van Horne. He then added, "Why, we live next door to fifty millions of liars and we must brag or we shall be talked out."[430]

As the eastward-moving train ate up the miles across the Canadian wilderness, Van Horne might have reflected on this conversation. He most certainly would have reflected on what he had seen in British Columbia. Here, he had been so struck by the progress that had been made in constructing the mountain section that he had concluded that it could be completed by September 1885 and for $4 million less than the previous winter's estimates. If this calculation was on target and if, as he thought, the eastern section could be finished within the same period, a through rail service from Montreal to the Pacific coast would become a reality in a year's time.

The inspection trip had reassured the general manager in other ways as well. He could see that the syndicate had done well in choosing the more direct and southerly route, and he no longer had any lingering doubts about the mountain section, the CPR's agricultural possibilities, and western timber and mineral wealth. Moreover, as he would later report to the CPR's directors, he was now fully convinced that every part of the line from Montreal to the Pacific would "pay."[431] While Van Horne had good reason to be satisfied with the progress of construction and to be excited about British Columbia's rich coal and timber resources, he could not be optimistic about the CPR's immediate prospects. As he well knew, another financial crisis was in the making.

This crisis owed a lot to the continuing efforts of the Grand Trunk to sink the CPR. Its malicious campaign to discredit its rival had taken on a new urgency in 1884 when it realized that the CPR had constructed almost 2,500 miles of track and, funds permitting, would soon push a transcontinental line through to completion. As attacks by the Grand Trunk and other CPR enemies increased in number and ferocity, investors took alarm and the price of CPR shares, already mauled by the general depression in railway stocks, plummeted still further. The end result was that shares sold at prices that did not begin to approximate their true worth. Unable to raise adequate funds from the sale of stock, the company was forced to take on high-interest, short-term loans, but this only compounded its financial woes. In the face of these debts and an almost empty company treasury, the CPR's directors decided that thousands of the company's employees should be kept at work during the winter of 1884–85, for only if this were done, they believed, would traffic soon open across Canada and the CPR be pulled back from bankruptcy.

It was a bold course of action, one whose ultimate success depended to a significant extent on Van Horne's reputation as a sort of miracle worker. Inspired by the general manager's almost unflagging optimism, Canadian businessmen disregarded the abysmal state of the CPR's finances and continued to extend credit to the reeling company. Supplies thus continued to pour into company worksites, enabling construction to continue. In a lumbering community, a small merchant who had furnished $35,000 worth of meat on credit was asked if he was afraid he might not be paid; he replied, "I am not. Van Horne will carry this thing through. If he can't, no one can. Then I'll start all over again."[432]

In November 1884, payment of the government subsidy was delayed, further exacerbating the financial picture. By this time the margin within which the company operated had become so narrow that any hitch threatened to topple it into bankruptcy. To add to the gloom, in late December, the men on the Lake Superior section threatened to strike if they did not receive their pay. An increasingly desperate Stephen summed up the situation in a letter to Prime Minister John A. Macdonald on December 10:

> ... I have been hard at work since we parted trying to gather back into hand all the loose threads of this worrying web on which I have been working so long and I can see that we need not look for any further relief, at least to any considerable amount, from Schreiber's estimate of the value of the work to be done and I must set about at once the work of devising some plan which will at the same time provide for repayment of the loan from the Government, and also provide the capital required to carry on the business till May 1886 when the road will be

in full operation and earning enough to pay its way. I cannot tell you how sorry I am for your sake as much as my own that this could not have been postponed for another year. But the credit of the Company both at home and abroad is at the moment gone and the ability of Smith and myself to sustain it is almost exhausted: the position must be faced or failure must ensue ... and yet I feel it ought not to be so, considering the position and prospects ahead of the C.P.R.[433]

By January the condition of the CPR's finances had become so precarious that even Van Horne began to question the railway's ability to survive. In an uncharacteristic surrender to despair, but with his characteristic bluntness, he blurted out to John Henry Pope, "Why not put us out of our misery? Let us go off into some corner and bust!"[434] The minister replied that the government was so worried about what Riel and his followers might do in the Northwest that it dared not take on any further entanglements. The government, it appeared, feared a dangerous uprising in the spring. Pope then added, "I wish your CPR was through." Van Horne, recalling his experience in helping to move soldiers during the American Civil War, wanted to know when Ottawa might expect to send troops to the Northwest. When Pope replied that it might be in the first or second week of March, Van Horne informed him that he could move regiments from Kingston or Quebec, where the two permanent military units were stationed, to Qu'Appelle in ten days.[435] Later the general manager would find cause to follow up on this bold declaration.

Before that happened, however, the company acted on the correct premise that only government resources could rescue it from its plight. In the immediate future, money had to be found to pay contractors and their construction crews, not to mention the small creditors who could not wait indefinitely for the money owing them. Funds were also required to pay the company's share of the February dividend, which rumour claimed could only be met if the company's directors pledged their personal guarantee. As it was, the dividend was only paid after Stephen and Smith did just that. Meanwhile, Stephen submitted a statement of the CPR's finances to the minister of finance, while to Macdonald and the minister of public works, Sir Hector Langevin, he dispatched an outline of his proposal for relief.

In late March 1885, matters came to a head at Beaver (now known as Beavermouth), British Columbia, a wild construction camp in the Selkirk Mountains. Some fifteen hundred workers went on strike for non-payment of wages. Van Horne was not at the "head of track" when this occurred, but his friend Sam Steele was. At the time, Steele was confined to bed, gravely ill with fever. Nevertheless, the legendary North West Mounted Police officer, whose contingent had been maintaining law and order during the construction of the CPR, rose from his sickbed to read the Riot Act. Although unarmed, he succeeded by sheer force of personality in dispersing the angry mob of strikers.

When bankruptcy appeared almost imminent, Van Horne might have been tempted to unload his CPR stock, but he didn't. Replying to a query from an American investor, he wrote, "I can only say that I have a large amount of Canadian Pacific stock and that I have never sold a share of it, but that on the contrary I have increased my holding and would buy more if I had the money."[436]

It was certainly not a propitious time to petition the government for relief. Rumours of impending government assistance had already triggered a wail of protest across the country; backbenchers, always sensitive to the views of their constituents, let it be known that there was minimal support out there for another CPR loan. Macdonald fully realized that any proposal for further government aid would meet with opposition in Cabinet, but not even he anticipated how fierce and implacable that opposition would be. One of the three ministers vehemently opposed to any loan, Archibald McLelan, minister of marine and fisheries, even threatened to resign if further assistance was extended to the railway. With a rebellious Cabinet and an unenthusiastic press at his back, "Old Tomorrow" decided to postpone a decision on the CPR's appeal for aid. Shoving the contentious issue aside, the seventy-year-old chieftain bought time by pushing though a novel franchise bill that established Dominion qualifications for election to the Dominion Parliament. Meanwhile, an increasingly agitated Stephen continued to bombard the prime minister with appeals for assistance. Finally, on March 18, he officially applied to the government on behalf of the company for a loan of $5 million and asked that its unsold stock be cancelled and that the company be allowed to issue in lieu thereof 5 percent first mortgage bonds to the same amount, that is, $35 million.

A reply was not long in coming. On March 26, while in Ottawa, Stephen received what he considered to be the final rejection of his request for government assistance. Disheartened and weary, he was about to check out of the Russell House when he was waylaid by George Campbell, a CPR lobbyist, and Senator Frank Smith, one of the few Conservatives who had remained loyal to the CPR. The two men had deduced what had transpired and were now determined to prevent the railway president from leaving before another pitch had been made to the prime minister. While the CPR lobbyist stood guard to prevent Stephen's escape, Smith and Mackenzie Bowell, now a CPR convert, went to Earnscliffe. It was another midnight call, and this time Macdonald agreed to reconsider the matter.[437] Stephen, buoyed up by this development, presented a revised draft proposal to the prime minister the following day, but it would be some time before the government and the company could agree on terms.

When Stephen shuttled back and forth between Ottawa and Montreal he was often accompanied by Van Horne, who would furnish his boss with information about the progress of construction as well as figures regarding current outlays and estimates of the railway's future requirements. In the nation's capital, the general manager frequently served as the railway's spokesman and lobbyist. In this capacity Van Horne haunted the Rideau Club, then an Ottawa landmark and bastion of Victorian elitism. In this principal centre of power off Parliament Hill, he sought out leading businessmen, whom he then regaled with graphic descriptions of the rosy future that awaited the CPR once its main line had been completed and its finances restored to order. To Collingwood Schreiber and Conservative Cabinent ministers he painted an equally vivid picture of what would happen if the government turned down the company's request for assistance. He reminded them that more than $92 million had already been spent on the project, of which $55 million was government money, and he opined that nobody of sane mind could permit such an enterprise to fail for the lack of a few million dollars. At risk, should the railway collapse, was not only the Bank of Montreal but also every bank that had lent to its contractors and suppliers, as well as the large suppliers themselves. In fact, emphasized the general manager, any ensuing crash would affect the whole country and seriously jeopardize Canada's credit in the international money market.

Addie and the family saw little of Van Horne that winter and spring, so often was he away on business. In addition to his repeated pilgrimages to Ottawa there were trips to the West to inspect the mountain section and to devise methods for hastening construction. Forced to apologize for his delay in answering a letter from Joseph Hickson, he observed ruefully in early March that he had spent only one day in Montreal in nearly three weeks.[438]

And his worries about the CPR's financial predicament intruded even in the rare times that he was at home. Throughout his life Van Horne had usually succeeded in putting railway work behind him when he entered his art studio. One notable exception was the year 1885, when, as his artist friend Percy Woodcock recalled, "He was so worried about the road's condition that sometimes in the middle of a joyous bit of painting the thought of the road would come to him like a shock and hang over him, holding him totally absorbed and still."[439]

Almost as disconcerting were vicious attacks in the daily press and various pamphlets that skewered not only the company but also individual directors, singling out the CPR's general manager for special attention. Van Horne was reproached for having no Montreal antecedents, for commanding too high a salary, for hiring too many Americans, and, even more significantly, for having little or no knowledge of railway construction and engineering. One of his attackers, T.S. Higginson, launched a particularly devastating assault on Van Horne's capabilities. In May 1885, he reported:

> When coming thro' the Selkirks this last trip, I took special pains to have a good look at the location of the CPR now that the snow slides had partially disappeared and as I know a good many of the Engineers intimately, in conversation I would say how in the world can this Road be operated in Winter, not one of them expressed an opinion that it could, they would shrug their shoulders, and say don't ask me anything about winter operations — their opinion I know is that it cannot be operated in winter without much greater change in location than they have made at the summit of the Selkirks.
>
> The statement of Mr Van Horne that he would leave Montreal on 24th August in his Cr and go through to the coast is all Yankee blow, unfortunately for the Co. he knows nothing about R.R. construction or Engineering, if he did he would not talk so absurdly.[440]

Seen through the prism adopted by his attackers, Van Horne was nothing but a money-grubbing Yankee blowhard who promoted the hiring of Americans and who lacked even the basic qualifications for the important job that he had so confidently assumed. Many another man would have been quelled by such charges, but not this transplanted American. Fortunately for the work at hand, his large ego and generous supply of self-confidence would enable him to retain his self-control and continue pursuing his objectives with inflexible purpose and almost unflagging optimism. In fact, his self-confidence would contribute to an initiative that boosted the company's cause and paved the way for its salvation.

The initiative was sparked by the actions of none other than the messianic Louis Riel. The celebrated Métis leader, after spending some time in a Quebec mental hospital, had moved to the western United States to live and work among the Métis there. In 1884, however, he had returned to Canada after accepting an invitation to take up the cause of the Métis in Saskatchewan, who were then agitating for a resolution of their longstanding grievances. Riel was not long in Batoche before he appealed to the anglophone and francophone settlers, whether of mixed-blood or not, to unite in a peaceful protest to obtain such rights as free land for the settlers and provincial status for the area. A provisional government was established with the Métis leader as president, and when the federal government at last showed signs of being roused from its lethargy the rebels attacked Fort Carlton, engaging a detachment of the Northwest Mounted Police.

The Northwest Rebellion of 1885 had broken out, and for the first time in their history Canadians found themselves confronting an armed uprising on their own soil with nothing but their own resources. Macdonald could have requested the assistance of regular imperial troops but he rejected this option. Instead, the government would rely on citizen soldiers, who everywhere clamoured to enlist. And they would not have to wait until the coming of spring and the opening of navigation routes to strike out for the site of the rebellion. They could start immediately for the Northwest, courtesy of the almost completed CPR. In the weeks to come, detailed accounts of every incident, government response, and troop movement would be emblazoned across the front pages of the daily press, and urban centres across Canada would buzz with excitement.

From the nation's capital, on March 25, the *Manitoba Free Press* reported the dispatch of Batteries A and B, some four hundred men, to the Northwest. The paper noted, incorrectly, that the government had asked Washington for permission to send troops through American territory. This permission did not have to be sought, for Van Horne, recognizing a golden opportunity, had lost no time in offering the use of the CPR to transport troops from eastern Canada to the Northwest. He had insisted to Macdonald that only three conditions be met: the government would raise the troops, provide Van Horne with a week's notice of their arrival, and allow the general manager free rein in making arrangements for their transport and provisioning. For his part, Van Horne pledged to get the troops to Fort Qu'Appelle in eleven days' time.[441]

Van Horne made his offer fully aware of the good publicity that such a move would bring his railway, intuiting that the rebellion might ultimately be the CPR's saviour. In fact, he would impress upon his subordinates that not only the CPR's reputation but perhaps even its very existence would depend upon the speed and efficiency with which it could transport men and equipment to the site of the uprising. Admittedly, there was the small matter of four interruptions in the line — totalling a distance of about eighty-nine miles — north of Lake Superior, but he knew that arrangements could be made for sleighs to take the men over two of the gaps and for them to march over the remaining two twenty-mile gaps, desolate stretches of wind-whipped frozen lake.

Ottawa's abysmal lack of knowledge of the Northwest and incompetence in the militia department did not augur well, however, for the success of the troop deployment. The soldiers were to be dispatched to the Northwest from Toronto, London, Kingston, Ottawa, Montreal, Quebec, Halifax, and dozens of smaller centres, but the militia department had not considered the question of rations; nor had it provided for a telegraph cipher, let alone thought of using one. Fortunately, Van Horne could draw upon his Civil War experience in figuring out ways to move the soldiers. He also relied on the expertise of construction boss John Ross and chief engineer Harry Abbott, who routinely moved hundreds of workmen over gaps in the line during the winter months. Still, even he must have felt somewhat apprehensive when contemplating the challenge of shuttling men, horses, military supplies, and artillery pieces in brutally cold weather over primitive tote roads stretching across a frozen, forested wasteland. Horrendous as the obstacles were, however, Van Horne, Donald Smith, and Joseph Wrigley, the Hudson Bay Company's trade commissioner, successfully resolved the problems associated with provisioning over three thousand soldiers and transporting them, their horses, and their equipment over such distances.[442] Van Horne tried to do even more than that. Betraying his gourmand instincts, he arranged for the soldiers to enjoy a lavish feast at a construction camp before they began the arduous journey over the first gap, which began not far from the site of present-day White River. It was important, he told William Whyte, superintendent of the Eastern and Ontario divisions, "that the reports of the officers as to the treatment of the troops on our line should be most favourable."[443] He also saw to it that sleeping cars were made available to officers whenever possible, even though the government had not requested this.

No sooner had the first troops been deployed than the parliamentary opposition and the Toronto *Globe*, which had been sharply critical of Macdonald's handling of the trouble in the Northwest, attacked the decision to take the men around Lake Superior instead of through the United States. In the opinion of these critics, it was far preferable to have the soldiers travel in civilian clothes through the United States, their rifles and artillery pieces boxed for separate shipment in bonded cars. Huffed the *Globe*:

If the Canadian troops now struggling through the snow north of Lake Superior should be able to perform their difficult task, and if they should land at Winnipeg within six days after leaving Toronto, the utmost would be achieved that the most sanguine could hope for ... If the American roads had been used the Toronto troops would have been at Winnipeg to-day, even travelling on ordinary trains, and the two batteries would already have been at Qu'Appelle.[444]

Van Horne bridled at any suggestion that the troops be taken through his native country. In a largely illegible letter written on April 4, he spelled out with some asperity the rationale for the government's choice of route. "There is," he emphasized, "but one reason in this case and that is <u>national self respect</u>." He recalled that in the past the Americans had refused permission in a case strikingly similar to the present one, and that was why he found the very idea of again begging for such permission abhorrent. To those accusing him of serving his own self-interest, the irate general manager pointed out — somewhat disingenuously — that the CPR had nothing to gain by transporting the troops. "Quite the contrary. Our work of construction on the Lake Superior section is practically suspended while the movement is going on and we have entirely disregarded expense and trouble in carrying the troops quickly ..."[445] To all appearances, Van Horne was fast becoming a fervent Canadian nationalist. He was not prepared to see his adopted country suffer any ridicule and humiliation if it could be avoided. Nor, of course, was he prepared to ignore any opportunity to showcase the CPR's worth.

Humiliation was not an emotion that Van Horne would have felt when the Canadian soldiers were successfully transported by the CPR to Fort Qu'Appelle, near Regina, in a matter of days. By comparison, it had taken Colonel Wolsey's expeditionary force three months to journey from Montreal to Fort Garry in 1870, during the First Riel Rebellion. Without question, the CPR had demonstrated its worth by transporting troops so quickly to the site of the insurrection that it was crushed before it could set the entire West ablaze. No longer could the railway be regarded as a leech repeatedly sucking money from the federal treasury. It was finally being recognized as a real asset to the country, a steel rail binding the infant nation together. Van Horne was quick to detect the "very great change" that public opinion had undergone with respect to the need for the CPR and confidently predicted on April 4 that "in the light of the present difficulty, Parliament will deal fairly with us before adjournment."[446]

Parliament would eventually come to the CPR's aid, but not before the railway was almost pushed into bankruptcy and Van Horne had to inform Stephen of a truly desperate situation in the West. On April 16, he telegraphed the CPR president from the West that he had no means of paying wages and that the pay car could not be sent out. The results could be catastrophic for the road. Construction gangs in the mountain section, angered by the prolonged absence of the pay car, had had enough. They had left their posts and begun marching eastward, collecting as they went a force of workmen large enough to compel even those willing to work to put down their tools.

Roused to action, the prime minister asked the Bank of Montreal, at the company's request, to advance $500,000. The bank flatly refused. When Charles Drinkwater, the CPR's secretary, learned of the bank's refusal, he telegraphed Macdonald, "Sorry to inform you that Bank unwilling to act on letter. Van Horne will see you in the morning."[447] As promised, Van Horne rushed to Ottawa, where he placed the circumstances squarely before John Henry Pope. Fortunately for the CPR, the minister was sufficiently impressed by the seriousness of the situation to immediately seek out Macdonald and, with the help of Frank Smith, one of Macdonald's Cabinet colleagues and intimates, persuade the prime minister to accept the company's request for relief. As a result of this intervention, on May 1 Macdonald gave notice that he intended to introduce measures to assist the CPR. This was enough to persuade the bank to make a loan of $750,000, sufficient to allow the pay car to go out and to tide the company over this critical period. Still, not until a relief bill had been granted royal assent would the railway be yanked back from the financial precipice.

In the meantime, while Van Horne drove the line and bridge construction forward in the West, the company was fast coming to the end of its resources. On July 14, the first of several CPR debts slated to come up between then and August 1 ($400,000 to the Dominion Bridge Company) was due. This prospect, and the knowledge that the pay car had not gone out in weeks, persuaded Van Horne and Ogden, the CPR treasurer, that immediate action had to be taken. After feverishly reviewing the company's balance sheets, they concluded that the CPR was $8 million in debt. Van Horne, however, believed that if the company could acquire $5 million it could manipulate this sum in such a way as to increase its value and save the situation. With this in mind, he ordered a special train to rush him to Ottawa on July 13, the day before the first note was due and while the relief bill was still being debated in the Senate. In the nation's capital, he searched frantically for Macdonald, eventually tracking him down in his accustomed seat in the House. Van Horne sent him his card, requesting an immediate interview. Macdonald emerged from the House and somewhat testily agreed to meet with the general manager in a nearby private room. There, Van Horne informed him that the CPR would "go smash" the next day if Dominion Bridge called in its debt. The government had to do something, and fast.[448]

The prime minister could not hurry the Senate along in its deliberations, but this turned out not to be necessary in any case, because when the bridge company realized that Senate approval was imminent and that it would soon be paid it gave the company a few days' grace. On July 20 the relief bill received royal assent and the temporary loan of $5 million became available immediately. Three days later Stephen cabled from London that Baring Brothers, which had long held aloof from the CPR, had taken up the entire primary issue of $15 million of first mortgage bonds that had been placed with it. When they received this joyous news, Van Horne and Angus were ecstatic. Unable to restrain themselves, they vented their relief by capering around the CPR's boardroom and kicking its furniture.[449] For Van Horne it meant that he could at long last banish financial worries from his mind and focus on pushing the line through to completion. To Addie, who was vacationing at the Grand Hotel in Caledonia Springs, Ontario, he reported on August 2, "Am very busy at the office. We are paying our debts and 'house cleaning.'" Then, for good measure, he added, "I felt quite hurt the other day that Mary and Addie got a letter from you but none came for me."[450]

As early as August, Van Horne was convinced that the last spike in the railway would be laid by mid-October. The 212-mile government section between Port Moody and Savona's Ferry had been completed, and he thought that by September Onderdonk's forces would have finished the approximately 170-mile stretch that ran east from Savona's Ferry toward Eagle Pass. Given their present rate of progress, the chances were good that James Ross's team of tracklayers, approaching from the east, would reach the spot where Onderdonk's men ran out of rails in mid-October.

As the eagerly awaited completion date fast approached the general manager was inundated with inquiries about the date and place at which the rails would be joined. These were accompanied by a flood of requests for details of any ceremony that might be staged to mark the historic occasion. For the most part, Van Horne was courteous in replying to the inquirers that there would be no ceremony, but to a correspondent in

Charlottetown he betrayed a thinning of his impatience when he emphatically denied that there would be a special excursion for parliamentarians: "There is to be no 'golden spike' driven on the completion of the Canadian Pacific and no excursion to celebrate the event. The last spike will probably be driven by one of our track-laying gang and will be an iron one. The report about the proposed Parliamentary excursion originated in some of the newspapers without the knowledge of the Company."[451]

Van Horne had flirted briefly with the idea of staging an elaborate celebration, but he had found it impossible to limit the number of invited guests. To do so would have resulted in "a vast deal of disappointment and ill feeling," he informed a correspondent from Victoria.[452] An elaborate ceremony would also have involved considerable expense, the last thing that the company could afford at this juncture. In all likelihood, the general manager recalled the humiliating experience of the Northern Pacific's president. In 1883, this gentleman had spent $250,000 to bring "332 of the most influential men in the United States, England and Germany, riding in forty-three private cars in four trains" to Montana for a last-spike ceremony, only to have to resign short time later because the railway was in the red.[453]

Although there was to be no special parliamentary excursion or fancy completion ceremony featuring a golden spike, Van Horne did entertain high hopes that the Governor General, Lord Lansdowne, would hammer home the last spike. The able Anglo-Irish aristocrat was a likely candidate for the job. Not only was he the head of state, he had long been an interested onlooker. With this more modest ceremony in mind, Van Horne paid his respects in August to the Governor General, who later remarked, "I am very much struck with Mr. Van Horne and very glad to have met him." Indeed, the general manager's enthusiasm left him "fired with impatience to see the wonderful country thro' which we are to be carried ... "[454] It is not surprising, then, that His Excellency timed a projected trip to British Columbia and his return journey to coincide with the date that the main line was expected to be finished.

Unfortunately, Van Horne would see his carefully crafted plans for the Governor General's participation scrapped in October. Inclement weather and, despite his efforts, Lord Lansdowne's timetable were the culprits. Because rain had delayed construction on the western slope of the Selkirks, the vice-regal party, when travelling west in October, had to traverse a thirty-mile gap extending from just east of Revelstoke to the western slope of Eagle Pass. This in itself was not disastrous, but it did signal that at least another month would be required to complete construction of the transcontinental main line; consequently, since Lord Landsowne had to be back in Ottawa by October 27, he would not be able to preside at the ceremony that Van Horne was so vigorously downplaying. Somebody else would have to drive the ordinary iron spike that the general manager had in mind for the occasion.

In Montreal, on the night of October 27, Van Horne and eight-year-old Bennie boarded the *Saskatchewan* for the spot in Eagle Pass, British Columbia, where the last spike was to be driven. In another private car, behind the same locomotive, the *Matapedia*, was Donald Smith. At Ottawa, the first stop, the train picked up Sandford Fleming, who had been elected a railway director in June. A few days later, at Winnipeg, it welcomed aboard John McTavish, the land commissioner, George Harris, a Boston financier and CPR director, and J.J.C. Abbott, the company's lawyer. The train then headed west, where at Revelstoke it was held up for several days because heavy rain had again delayed the completion of construction.

As the special train of distinguished visitors headed west through the mountains, a second train, carrying another group of CPR officers, construction men, and others, headed by Major Rogers and Henry Cambie, made its way from Port Moody to the selected meeting place, which Van Horne, with an appropriate sense of drama, had named Craigellachie. He had decided on the name years ago, when he had first joined the company, after having heard Donald Smith employ the moniker when the syndicate was being formed. In response to the suggestion that the new venture spelled trouble for their old age and that they ought to think twice before committing themselves irrevocably, Smith had retorted, "Craigellachie!" This reference to the rock in Banffshire, Scotland, where the Clan Grant had rallied when in battle against its enemies, stirred Van Horne's imagination, and he decided that if he was still with the company when the last spike was driven, the spot would be marked by a station named Craigellachie.[455]

The development that Van Horne had set his sights on for so long unfolded on a dull November day, when the cedars and dark firs at Craigellachie dripped with wet snow. At six o'clock on Saturday morning, November 7, track-laying began on the last half-mile of the line, and by nine o'clock weary navvies had brought forward and measured for cutting the last rails required to make the connection. They cut and placed one rail and left the other to await the arrival of Van Horne and his party.[456] In anticipation of this, the ceremonial train headed west from Eagle Pass at seven-thirty. When Van Horne, Bennie, and the train's other passengers descended to a spot close to the ends of track they were greeted by the legendary Major Rogers, James Ross, and others who had surveyed the route and overseen construction. Behind them crowded some of the men whose toil had built the line and a bevy of other curious onlookers. Conspicuous by his absence was Andrew Onderdonk, who was represented by his Irish superintendent, Michael Haney.

Van Horne had insisted that there be no extravagant ceremony, and his wishes were respected. Since the Governor General could not be present, and George Stephen, the next logical choice, was in England on CPR business, the task of hammering in the last spike devolved on Donald Smith. Smith accepted a maul, and, with the men flanking him, he swung at the tie held in place by Major Rogers. His first blow bent the spike badly. Frank Brothers, the roadmaster, who would later help build the Cuba Railway, quickly replaced it with another, and on his second attempt Smith succeeded. His audience, seemingly overawed by what was taking place, remained absolutely silent for a moment or two, then shattered the solemnity with an explosion of cheering. This was followed by still more cheers and by the shrill whistles of locomotives. Chips from the last tie were scooped up as mementoes by many of the onlookers. Earlier they had indulged in a great deal of speculation on what the length of the last rail would be, waging considerable sums of money in the process. The length proved to be twenty-five feet, five inches.[457]

Courtesy of the Norman Photographic Archives, McCord Museum of Canadian History, Montreal, MP-000.25.971

Perhaps the most famous Canadian photo. It shows Lord Strathcona driving the last spike at Craigellachie. The bearded, corpulent figure on his right is Van Horne.

Van Horne, called on to make a speech, made a characteristically terse pronouncement: "All I can say is that the work has been well done in every way." While the occasion required that he say something along these lines, his words begged the truth. He knew very well that in the interests of saving money, large sections of track had been left unballasted and huge wooden trestles had been substituted for steel ones. Nevertheless, Van Horne had succeeded in pushing 2,400 miles of railway through the Canadian wilderness in far less time than had generally been predicted. Alexander Mackenzie, for example, had announced when speaking at Sarnia in

Van Horne in 1886, when he was vice-president of the CPR.

October 1875 that the road "could not likely be completed in ten years with all the power of men and all the money of the Empire."[458] The government had allowed ten years for the construction of the line, but the general manager had built it in less than five. Moreover, the job had been done with little help from the Empire. Instead, it owed its completion to an amazing blend of iron determination, financial acumen, political lobbying, government assistance, reckless gambles, and the toil of legions of anonymous labourers.

In later years, Van Horne would minimize his own role in the CPR's construction, insisting that George Stephen's had been the more difficult. "My part was easy," he observed. "I only had to spend the money, but Stephen had to find it when nobody in the world believed in it but ourselves."[459] As for Stephen himself, he was quick to assign the larger share of the credit to the vice-president. Replying to a congratulatory message sent by Van Horne, the president wrote:

> As for myself I am grateful for what you say in your message but I must honestly disclaim any merit in connection with our work except perhaps that I have never lost

confidence in the intrinsic merit of the enterprise from first to last always feeling, if we could only carry the project to conclusion, success was certain & acting on that belief I had no hesitation in risking everything to attain the end in view. Whatever Mr Smith & I may have been able to do in the way of sustaining the credit of the coy in its days of adversity would all have been of little avail had you not been at hand to practically carry on the work we were struggling to complete. Though never to you personally, I have to others time & again during the last three years said that but for your aid the contract could never have been carried out by us. It is you, in a far more direct sense than can be said of us, that is the author & builder of the CPR.[460]

This was certainly lavish praise. Indeed, in the eyes of at least one observer, it was probably too lavish. Thomas Shaughnessy, that gifted and astute administrator who could accurately gauge the worth of both men and goods, would later remark that although Van Horne was a "tower of strength" in the CPR's construction days, he failed to "give due credit to the Managers of Construction and the men engaged in the operation of completed mileage, who contributed so much to his success, and without whose active cooperation he would have been helpless."[461]

It is hard to know what Van Horne was pondering as he stood behind Donald Smith and watched his associate hammer the last spike into place. The celebrated photo of the event shows a portly figure attired in his customary garb (a homburg and a dark suit), his hands thrust deep in his pockets, his face a solemn, inscrutable mask. Was he thinking of his beloved mother, who would have rejoiced in the event but who had died that month? Was he perhaps drafting in his mind the contents of the telegrams that he would send to the prime minister and to Addie? Or was he impatiently awaiting the departure of the special train for the Pacific? One can only hazard a guess. In any event, when he did telegraph Addie, he reported, "Last rail laid this Saturday morning at 9:22 a.m. Quite well and very happy."[462] To the prime minister, he telegraphed this somewhat disingenuous message: "Thanks to your farseeing policy and unwavering support the Canadian Pacific Railway is completed. The last rail was laid this (Saturday) morning at 9:22."[463] The policy might have been farseeing, but Van Horne could not in justice describe the support as unwavering.

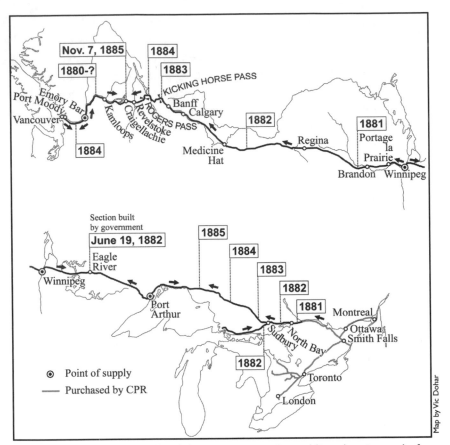

Construction of Canadian Pacific's main transcontinental line showing end of track at year's end."

As soon as news of the epochal event was received at 149 Dorchester Street young Addie hastened to write her beloved father, saying how delighted the family was to hear about the last spike ceremony. However, so well observed had been her father's wishes about having no fanfare for the event that she and the family had yet to learn who had actually hammered in the last spike. They hoped, she said, that he had performed the task, for unquestionably he deserved the honour "better than anybody else." Then she reported, "Mr. Stephen has received congratulations from the Queen, the first time, it is said, that she has congratulated the colonies on any work accomplished by them ..." Brimming with pride, young Addie concluded her letter with the injunction, "If you see any more nice articles about your dear self, please send them to us, and remember that no one congratulates you more heartily than little Addie."[464]

The ceremony completed, Van Horne, Bennie, and other members of the official party and their guests scrambled aboard the special train that would wind its way along the Thompson River Valley and down through the scenic Fraser Canyon to Port Moody. There they boarded the steamer *Princess Louise*, which took them on a tour of Burrard Inlet and English Bay and then across to Vancouver Island for a round of congratulatory speeches in the provincial capital before their return to the mainland. On the morning of November 12, after returning to the mainland, the party boarded the special train to be carried east toward Winnipeg.

On the return journey, Van Horne no doubt amused himself thinking about a scheme he had concocted for celebrating the road's completion in style, involving an elaborate practical joke on Donald Smith. Among the several Canadian residences owned by Smith was Silver Heights, located a few miles outside Winnipeg. The house had remained closed and without servants in recent months because business cares had forced its owner to divide his time between London and Montreal. Van Horne had conceived the idea of staging a celebratory party at the residence and keeping the preparations a secret from Smith. He had had a spur built from Winnipeg to the house, cooks and domestics hired, and food and drink sent up. Within a week the preparations were complete. All that was required was the presence of the official party.

Close to noon on November 15, when the special train entered the spur, the party was deep in conversation and Smith did not notice that the engineer had reversed the engine. When the director at last looked out the window he observed that the train was backing up. Then he saw "a very neat place" and some Aberdeen cattle. Thinking that he was the only person who owned cattle like that, he remarked, "This is really very strange." Suddenly the house came into view. This was enough to jolt him into thinking that he must be going crazy. In all the many years that he had lived in the area he had never noticed another place "so exactly like *Silver Heights*." Smith only realized what was happening when the conductor called "Silver Heights" and the car stopped. Members of the entourage burst out laughing, and Smith, glancing outside again, began to laugh too.[465] Van Horne's imaginative practical joke had struck just the right note for the occasion. He could be justifiably proud.

Van Horne would experience even greater pride when he watched the first transcontinental passenger train from Montreal to the Pacific depart from Montreal on the evening of June 28 the following year. Anticipating the soon-to-arrive day when bales of silk would be arriving from China and Japan, the city fathers had hung silken banners on the engine and ordered a fifteen-gun salute. As the smoke-belching train drew slowly out of the Dalhousie Square station, bound for Port Moody, Van Horne heard the guns of the Montreal battery boom and the assembled crowd cheer madly. But before this happened he would find himself rebuilding the line that had been "completed" on November 7 and attempting to solve the multitude of problems that arose with the opening of a transcontinental line in a country with a harsh climate and a rugged landscape.

Chapter Nine
All That Grant Was to the U.S.A.

On his return from Silver Heights to Montreal, Van Horne found a letter from his old friend and admirer Jason Easton, the Wisconsin banker, who was also a director of the Chicago, Milwaukee and St. Paul Railroad. "I am counting the time when your five years' engagement with the Canadian Pacific will be up," wrote Easton, who then informed Van Horne that he was going to be offered a railroad presidency, "and your acceptance would make me the happiest man in America."[466] Easton did not become the happiest man in America with this, his first attempt to lure Van Horne back to the United States. Nor did he with his second try in early 1887. This time the bait was the presidency of the Milwaukee road. "The question of salary will cut no figure and will of course be very large, and you will have all freedom of action ... If you give me any encouragement and things work out as I now expect, I will go to New York at once ... I can't sleep nights until this is off my mind," wrote Easton, by now desperate to have Van Horne back on his old stomping ground.[467]

Almost any other ambitious railroading man would have found such an offer irresistible, but not Van Horne. His refusal prompted an immediate reply from a chagrined Easton: "Your telegram of this evening is about what I might expect ... If the St. Paul Company could have secured you as its head it would have had the ablest railroad general in the world, all that Grant was to the U.S.A."[468]

Easton was not the only party alerted to Van Horne's intentions. When rumours circulated in New York that he would be appointed president of the C.M. & St. P., Van Horne hastened to inform Sir George Stephen that the rumours were completely false. "I have no thought or intention of going there. I was asked some time ago if I would favourably consider an offer from the St. Paul Co. and I promptly replied that I could not. I made the same reply to a second inquiry a few weeks later and since Mr Eastons visit I am sure those who wanted me clearly understand that it is impossible," he wrote.[469] Having assured the CPR president that he could always count on his remaining with the CPR, Van Horne then thanked the ardent salmon fisherman for a "fine salmon."

Even if he had been at liberty to leave the CPR in either 1885 or 1887 — his contract expired in 1886 — Van Horne would not have been tempted to return south of the border. He had come to love Canada, concluding that there was no better place in which to put his seemingly inexhaustible supply of ener-

George Stephen (later Lord Mount Stephen). The Scottish-born financier was the first president of the Canadian Pacific Railway, in which capacity he became a good friend of Van Horne.

gy and talent to work than this raw and expansive country with its myriad of possibilities and challenges. Leaving aside all the reconstruction that still remained to be done on the line, there was the tantalizing prospect of the CPR presidency. Van Horne realized that Stephen did not intend to remain CPR president indefinitely, and being an ambitious man it is highly likely that he had his sights firmly trained on this position.

Van Horne's ambition was probably not the only factor that figured in his decision, however. No doubt he attached almost equal importance to the more congenial railroading climate that he found in Canada. As a man of integrity and sensitivity, he could not help but find the bare-knuckle competition south of the border distasteful. In the American railway system, as Van Horne's long-time friend John Wesley Powell pointed out, there was not much room for men of fine feelings, that is, men who were true gentlemen. As viewed by the well-known ethnologist and geologist, railroading in the United States at its best had little to commend it except the money that it brought to a man's wallet and the enormous power and prestige that it delivered to those who occupied the higher rungs. From top to bottom, this world resembled a huge ladder, up which climbed an army of men, each one of whom stomped on the fingers of the individual on the rung immediately below him. Van Horne, observed Powell, was capable of clambering up that ladder to the very top, but although he excelled in all the arts that make for success, Powell ventured that his friend would sooner not bring some of them into play.[470] Powell also observed that Addie, a woman of refinement, would feel at home in a cosmopolitan Canadian city like Montreal. So, it was for a host of reasons, not just one, that Van Horne resolved to cast in his lot with Canada's.

When addressing the CPR's shareholders in June 1885, Stephen, in a burst of enthusiasm, had confidently predicted that by early spring 1886, the main line would "be finished and in perfect condition, thoroughly equipped, possessing every requisite facility for doing its work economically and efficiently, and at least equal to the best of its competitors in all respects; particularly as to curves and gradients, permanent way and rolling stock; the quality and character of the railway being far above the standard fixed in the contract with the Government."[471] As it turned out, the quality and character of the line built by the CPR did exceed the standards fixed in the contract with the government. Nevertheless, construction had proceeded so rapidly that the railway had made use of many temporary structures and other shortcuts.

Van Horne, the practical railroading man, would never have delivered Stephen's rosy forecast. Whenever he went out on the line it was driven home to him that it had been merely slapped down and that for hundreds of miles it comprised little more than the ties and the two rails that lay across them, with a row of telegraph poles along one side. On the Prairies, it had little or no ballast, and in more rugged country, particularly in the western mountains, it skirted many minor obstructions instead of barrelling through them. North America's first true transcontinental railway was therefore amazingly crooked in places and full of curves. To further complicate matters, the railway trestles that had been built of timber instead of masonry or iron were often so rickety that trains had to crawl across them. Divisional points boasted only a minimum of essential equipment, and many a station house, loading dock, or warehouse had to be rebuilt or enlarged. By every qualification, the CPR was a typical pioneer railway.[472] Although the heavy construction work of the previous five years was over, Van Horne would have his work cut out for him supervising its rebuilding and lobbying for government funds with which to do it. He would also have to wrestle with

211

the fallout from disputes and litigation with contractors on the Lake Superior section and with the government regarding the rugged stretch from Yale to Kamloops Lake, built by Andrew Onderdonk.

As always, countless little details that related peripherally to the running of the railway competed for his attention. There was, of course, the usual barrage of requests for free passes and the steady stream of inquiries about employment opportunities. Notable among them were endearing queries from Father Lacombe, the priest whom Van Horne treated as his "own brother" and "special friend." In response to one such missive, Van Horne promised that he would do his best to reduce ticket fares and provide a "convenient" car for a priests' excursion. An "Emigrant Sleeper" would be furnished free of charge, but if the gentlemen in question aspired to a first-class sleeper, the charges would be considerable. In any event, the CPR would transport free of charge certain trunks of clothes from Montreal to Calgary.[473]

The CPR's adoption of standard time was another issue that demanded attention. In the hectic spring of 1886, when he was frantically readying the line for the inaugural passenger run, a letter arrived on Van Horne's crowded desk from the surveyor and engineering genius, Sir Sandford Fleming. Since resigning as the government's chief engineer in 1880, Fleming had been energetically campaigning for worldwide adoption of uniformity in timekeeping and an end to the confusion caused by hundreds of local times. His letter queried Van Horne about the steps the CPR was taking to introduce standard time in its passenger service. In his reply, Van Horne reported that although "a tremendous accumulation of business" had prevented him from doing "anything about the standard time matter," CPR circulars were nevertheless almost ready for distribution and he was using his "spare minutes at home" to figure out a new timetable.[474]

Most North American railways had adopted standard time in November 1883 as a result of an agreement reached at the General Time Convention, initiated and sponsored by American railroads. By the time the first scheduled transcontinental train departed from Montreal on June 28, 1886, however, the CPR had taken the additional step of introducing twenty-four-hour-system timetables in the Western and Pacific divisions. This meant the use of a.m. and p.m. had been abandoned and the hours after noon had been designated as 13:00, 14:00, etc. up to 24:00. Later this new system of notation would be extended to the Eastern and Ontario divisions.[475]

The master of operational detail also found himself caught up in the planning of transcontinental train journeys undertaken by leading figures of the day, including the spirited Agnes Macdonald. Sir John's devoted wife had long nursed a dream to see Western Canada, and in December 1885, when her husband was vacationing in London, England, she set off by private railway car for the summit of the Rockies, accompanied by her friends Judge and Mrs. Brooks, a maid, a butler, and a porter.[476]

Following her return to "dull grey Ottawa," a rejuvenated and ecstatic Agnes informed Van Horne, "Nearly five thousand miles have we travelled — so safely easily & comfortably that it all seems a dream and I can hardly yet realize how much space we really traversed because it was done without any trouble or fuss or anxiety whatever." Agnes continued:

> As for the C.P.R. it is of course marvellous. A strong adjective but simply true. To find oneself travelling over half a continent hardly yet known in such a style & at such a rate certainly does impress me deeply ... You must allow me to say that the perfect <u>control</u> of the whole thing astonished me much. The working was all so orderly. Even at those remote points so systematic so quiet so punctual. No <u>nonsense</u> (to use a woman's word) anywhere.

This resounding testimony to the smoothness of CPR operations would have delighted Van Horne, who was, no doubt, equally impressed by Agnes's own admission that she had been seized by Western fever and wanted "to go & live in Calgary & have nothing to do with Eastern life any more!"[477]

Later that year, on July 10, both Macdonalds embarked on a trip to the West. The pressure of business had prevented the prime minister from travelling on the first scheduled transcontinental train trip. When Sir John was finally able to leave Ottawa for his first and only visit to the Great West he and his party travelled in the private car *Jamaica*, which Van Horne had outfitted with fine-meshed window screens to keep out mosquitoes and dust. As further evidence of his thoughtfulness, he had also arranged for little travelling to be done at night because he wanted Sir John to have ample rest and to see the entire line by daylight.[478] As it turned out, the prime minister would have no trouble seeing the passing countryside as the train averaged a stately 20.86 miles an hour while making its way from Ottawa to the West Coast.

It was on this historic trip that the indefatigable and adventurous Agnes made her celebrated ride on a locomotive cowcatcher. Sir Joseph Pope, Macdonald's private secretary, later recalled, "Lady Macdonald, with characteristic imprudence, occupied the cowcatcher most of the way between Canmore and Port Moody, a distance of nearly six hundred miles."[479] After her escapade, which could have proven fatal if rocks had thundered down a mountain slope onto her, Agnes informed Van Horne:

> I travelled on the Buffer beam from Laggan [Lake Louise] to Pt. Moody. Every step of the way. Mr. Egan made me a lovely seat with a box and cushions, right in front of the Engine, and down the Kicking Horse Pass, he and I and Mr. F. White [of the Mounted Police] flew on the big Engine in delightful style. I was not at all afraid. I don't know how I am going to ride in a car, like a Christian, any more, after the delights of a cushioned cowcatcher!
>
> Even among those wonderful loops near Rogers Pass, or on the steep grade of the Kicking Horse, or on the sharp curves of the magnificent Fraser Canyon, so steady was the Engine that I felt perfectly secure and the only damage we did from Ottawa to the sea, was to kill a lovely little fat Pig, whom an error of judgment led under the engine near Nicomen, yesterday morning.
>
> I shut my eyes while he flew up and past, striking Mr. Pope who was sitting at my feet.[480]

The last week of that memorable July saw Van Horne embark on what would be the first in a series of annual inspection tours from Montreal to the West Coast. In the years to come he would invariably be accompanied by some co-directors and personal friends, and occasionally by family members, such as Bennie. These trips quickly earned a reputation for good company and good cheer, much of it provided, of course, by Van Horne himself. During the day, he would take up his post at the back of the well-appointed *Saskatchewan*, where he would review the railway's operations with the divisional superintendent and engineer of each division over which the train passed. At night, when the *Saskatchewan* sat quietly on a siding, he would throw himself into games of poker while regaling his audience with stories and anecdotes, usually colourful narratives of incidents in which he himself had participated or that he had witnessed; and he told them with a quiet drollery all his own, enlivening his performance with an abundance of mimicry and gesture.

On these trips Van Horne's guests would often be treated to boyish practical jokes, a legacy of his youth. In these harmless pranks he had an apt conspirator in Jimmy French, his incomparable black porter. A short, thickset man with a highly mobile face and a quick wit, French was devoted to the CPR, Van Horne, and his family. When Addie was ill in 1891, he made repeated trips to Van Horne's Montreal home to inquire about her health and pitch the case for a reviving trip in the *Saskatchewan* under his care.[481] But Jimmy was more than just a servant. He was also a confidant, whose behaviour transcended the usual strictures of a master-servant relationship. Strangers were amazed by the apparent liberty with which French gave full vent to a rich vocabulary of profanity. But between porter and master there was complete understanding. Following a hail of vituperation from Van Horne for some neglect of duty, Jimmy would seat himself a few minutes later on the arm of his master's chair and start punctuating the game of poker with droll remarks.[482]

On the inaugural trip Van Horne was accompanied by George Olds, the CPR's general traffic manager, two New Yorkers, and Sir George and Lady Stephen, whose private car, the *Matapedia*, was attached to the regular express along with Van Horne's, which was placed at the rear of the train.[483] For Van Horne and Stephen this would be their first opportunity to inspect the whole road since it had become fully operational.

The train steamed out of Montreal on Saturday evening, July 24, headed for open countryside, where it chugged along the north shore of the Ottawa River to Ottawa. From there it headed southwest, then northwest toward North Bay and the rugged, lake-strewn countryside around Lake Nipissing. Surveying the northeastern Ontario landscape from the wide, curtained windows of the *Saskatchewan*, Van Horne was struck by the numerous clearings that he saw in what had recently been heavy bush. What was most remarkable, however, was the dramatic change that had occurred in areas adjacent to some of the CPR stations. Where previously there had been only station buildings, there were now substantial villages, notably at Sturgeon Falls. North Bay, which two years ago had comprised only a dozen or so houses, was now a sizeable town surrounded by large areas that had been cleared in anticipation of spectacular growth.

The train threaded its way through the dense forests of the Laurentian Shield, then hugged the rocky and indented north shore of Lake Superior, where in places cliffs rose hundreds of feet above sections of the track. Across the entire Lake Superior section, Van Horne watched men and equipment engaged in widening cuttings, raising and widening embankments, ballasting, and filling trestles. Once again, he was reminded of the tremendous challenges posed by the construction of the line across the Archean Age Canadian Shield, where seemingly endless rock knobs alternate with rock basins filled with swamps or lakes.

On Tuesday morning, July 27, two and a half days after leaving Montreal, the train rolled into prosperous Winnipeg, destined, predicted one optimistic observer, to become the Chicago of the Canadian Northwest. At the train station, Western Canada's first major railway terminal, Van Horne spent the day receiving business men and deputations and, according to the *Manitoba Daily Free Press*, "inspecting things generally." This involved touring every arriving train and carefully scrutinizing the sleeping cars of the Atlantic Express, the CPR's eastbound transcontinental.[484]

On the morning of July 30, Van Horne and his colleagues boarded the train for the trip across gently rolling, seemingly interminable Prairies, where stops would be made at Austin, to inspect a farm, and then at Virden, where one of George Stephen's Scottish cousins and his sons worked a large, prosperous farm. The first important town that the train reached was Portage la Prairie, a well-established and thriving centre surrounded by the finest agricultural land in Manitoba. Next in importance was Brandon, founded in the early days of the line's construction and now the location of several mills and elevators owned by Montreal merchants. Between it and Gleichen, situated a few miles east of Calgary, the verdant, treeless prairie stretched like an ocean toward a limitless horizon, its vastness punctuated here and there by prize wheat crops, grazing cattle, and infant settlements. Just west of Gleichen and the Blackfoot Indian reserve, however, the country took on the appearance of a barren waste, although settlers would claim that twenty or thirty miles north or south of the railway line was the finest grazing land to be found anywhere in the world. As the landscape glided past, Van Horne pondered plans for settling this agriculturally rich swath of Canada, then receiving immigrants not only from the older provinces and the British Isles but also from Germany, Scandinavia, and Hungary.

No doubt the transformation undergone by Calgary, the town of the North West Mounted Police and his friend Father Lacombe, yielded the greatest surprise for Van Horne. Two and a half years earlier it had consisted of only a few log huts on one side of the Bow River. Now, in July 1886, it was a thriving town with a population of some fifteen hundred people, most of whom were in the ranching business.

West of Calgary, the land rose up into foothills and then into craggy, snow-capped mountains. After entering the mountains the train followed the broad and gently ascending valley of the Bow River for most of the way to Silver City, once a booming mining town, but in 1886 completely deserted. Leaving this eerie ghost town behind, the train climbed steadily until it reached the summit of the Rockies and majestic Mount Stephen, named after George Stephen, upon whom Queen Victoria had conferred a baronetcy in January of that year. The descent from this lofty peak was rapid, the train running alongside the Kicking Horse River, which tumbles and roars through canyons until it reaches what is now the village of Field but was then just a stump-littered townsite. From Field the train followed the valleys of the Otter Tail and Columbia rivers, then began climbing again until it reached Rogers Pass, located at the summit of the Selkirks. As the Selkirks were then being ravaged by forest fires Van Horne may or may not have been able to see the grandest of all its peaks, Mount Sir Donald, which looks down on the pass and commemorates Donald Smith, who was knighted not long after George Stephen.

Having passed two peaks named after his CPR colleagues, did Van Horne begin to rue the fact that there was no peak to serve as an enduring monument to his own memory? Although he had seen fit to name many points along the line after individuals who had rendered services to the CPR — Secretan, Crowfoot, Schreiber, Tilley, Langevin, and Bowell, to name but a few — he had not allowed a landmark to be named after himself. In 1884, when the enthusiastic citizens of Kamloops had attempted to change the name of nearby Savona's Ferry to Port Van Horne, he had quashed the idea. Matters would only be rectified in 1887 when Dr. Vaux, an alpine climber from Philadelphia, named a range of mountains on the outskirts of Field the Van Horne range.

In the mountains, Van Horne observed burning forests and huge hundred-foot-high trees that had been transformed into pillars of fire. Elsewhere, he saw workers erecting wooden snowsheds to protect the line against avalanches, always a danger in the winter months, particularly in the Selkirks, where snow in Rogers Pass averaged fifty feet during the winter. Up to nine feet could fall in a single storm. The threat of avalanches thundering down the mountains' high peaks was recognized even before the line was completed, and Van Horne had stationed observation teams in the Selkirks over the winter of 1885–86. Although the winter turned out to be comparatively mild, one team recorded that, in one area alone, nine winter avalanches had buried the track. In another spot, thirty-nine feet of snow had blanketed the line.[485]

The solution was one that Van Horne was undoubtedly familiar with, since it had been adopted in 1868–69 by the Central Pacific Railway: snowsheds. Following a series of engineers' reports, designs were drawn up for more than thirty snowsheds, some of which Van Horne saw being constructed in the summer of 1886. The estimate of the cost of the complex and time-consuming work, $1,126,034, must have staggered him. If it did, it still did not dissuade him from authorizing the expenditure of addi-

A view of the Van Horne range, located on the outskirts of Field, British Columbia.

tional funds to lay non-essential tracks alongside the long sheds on the descent from Rogers Pass to the foot of the Illecillewaet Glacier. When passenger trains used these tracks in summer, passengers would not have their views of the west slope's Illecillewaet and Asulkan glaciers blocked by miles of sheds on the summit of Rogers Pass, a prospect that was sheer anathema to Van Horne, the irrepressible showman.[486] Eventually he would suggest a system of triangular glance-works to guide the avalanches and direct their course right and left of the openings that served as fire-breaks between the sheds.[487] Still, avalanches would continue to pose a threat and create problems on the Revelstoke stretch. In 1910, therefore, the CPR invested in a five-mile tunnel under the pass to reduce the danger of avalanches and the recurring problem of extremely heavy snows.[488]

The train journey came to an end at Port Moody, since the railway extension to Vancouver would not be completed until May 1887. Vancouver itself was now making a second attempt to get established. Once the decision to build an extension had been made developers and investment funds had poured onto the townsite, where some five hundred structures were erected by mid-June 1886. Clearing was underway for the construction of many more when, on the afternoon of Sunday, June 14, a wind sprang up and fanned the flames of some brush fires that had been set to aid the clearing operations. In no time shanties and tents in the west end of the city, now Stanley Park, were engulfed in flames. Within an hour and a half, the city of Vancouver was burnt to the ground. Reconstruction began immediately, however, and by the time that Van Horne arrived at the town-site docks were being built according to plans that he had sketched out the previous year for Henry Cambie, Onderdonk's engineer and surveyor.

When describing the inspection trip to Addie, Van Horne did not squander words. "Our trip," he informed her in a letter dispatched to the Maine coast, "was a hot dusty and uneventful one and the forest fires hurt the mountain scenery." Having summarily dismissed the inspection tour, he then mentioned that he had arranged for the family to accompany him out west in late September. "We cant start much before the end of the month of September as Miss Smith is to be married to Mr. Northcote late in the month. The engagement is known only to a few here as yet. It was a surprise all around." Of even greater import as far as Van Horne was concerned, however, was John Egan's imminent departure, which rated more than a bare mention in the letter. Referring to the CPR's western superintendent and trusted colleague who had served him well for so many years, Van Horne reported dejectedly, "Mr Egan leaves us at the end of this month and Mr. McKinnon will take his place. Egan goes to the St. PM & M road [St. Paul, Minneapolis & Manitoba Railway]. I don't like it at all but it cant be helped."[489]

With the conclusion of his inspection tour in the second week of August, Van Horne plunged once again into the management of the CPR's day-to-day operations, focusing his attention on developing traffic. This would become his all-important goal, for only if there were enough traffic would there be sufficient earnings to meet the line's huge financing charges.

Since Van Horne now had full operational control of the company — Stephen concerning himself only with financing and larger policy questions — many of the initiatives taken to create a market and build up traffic would bear his imprint. Over the years these would see him diversify the company's operations by moving it into non-rail sectors such as grain elevators, flour mills, express and telegraph operations, port facilities, maritime fleets, agricultural and timber lands, and tourist services, including hotels. When it came to actual rail operations, Van Horne continued the company's policy of acquiring a network of rail lines in the settled industrial regions of eastern Canada. At the same time he also strove to develop rail links to established markets in New England and the American Midwest.

In the grand vision that Van Horne and George Stephen entertained the CPR was more than just the first pan-Canadian corporation — it was part of an integrated transportation network that would girdle the globe. "Canada is doing business on a back street," the general manager once observed. "We must put her on a thoroughfare."[490] Doing that would require the company to operate steamships on both the Atlantic and Pacific oceans, but to realize even part of what would be a highly ambitious and costly undertaking, an imperial subsidy was essential.

Shortly before the last spike was driven, the British government had invited tenders for a mail service between Hong Kong and Vancouver. In response, Van Horne had drawn up an official memorandum that furnished detailed information on trade possibilities and mail subsidies. The memorandum was followed a few months later, in May 1886, by a formal tender to provide a first-class fortnightly service for an annual subsidy of £100,000, using chartered steamships in 1887 and the CPR's own steamships in 1888. "We could make a beginning in the business immediately by means of sailing vessels and tramp steamers as the Northern Pacific has been doing for sometime back, but the freight taken by slow vessels does not pay much and we have not thought it worthwhile to compete for the business until we are in a position to establish a regular line as it would only have a tendency to demoralize rates without any immediate profit," Van Horne informed Jim Hill in April 1886.[491]

Notwithstanding the CPR's best efforts, all the deliberations came to naught because of a change of government in Britain and opposition on the part of the venerable P. & O., which was determined to retain its subsidy for carrying mails to the Far East via the Suez Canal. A trans-Pacific mail service would be delayed for another five years and would only be instituted after the CPR had concluded long and complicated negotiations with the British and Canadian governments. This did not occur until December 1887, and the contracting parties did not sign the agreement until some time later. No sooner was the contract awarded, however, on July 15, 1889, than the CPR ordered the three liners needed to maintain the monthly service, the *Empress of India, Empress of Japan,* and *Empress of China.* Van Horne named all three ships, choosing the designation "Empress" to reflect the vessels' superiority over all anticipated competition. Aesthetically pleasing, mechanically sound, and efficient to operate, these ships proved ideal for their intended service. Moreover, since they boasted solid hardwood and silk-panelled walls, richly carpeted floors, and finely upholstered furnishings, they earned a reputation that other lines found difficult to equal.[492]

Before the first *Empress* came into service, Van Horne pursued other prospects for a trans-Pacific steamship service. An examination of the manifests of sailing vessels and steamers transporting cargo between San

Francisco and Australia convinced him that 90 percent of these shipments could be furnished by either farmers or manufacturers in Canada, and he immediately spearheaded the establishment of a temporary service between Port Moody and Japan, using chartered sailing ships. As the first scheduled transcontinental passenger train pulled out of Montreal on June 28, 1886, a small, wooden-hulled, three-masted barque, the *W.B. Flint*, worked her way eastward across the north Pacific with the first cargo from the Far East for shipment on the CPR. Thirty-five days out of Yokohama, she sailed into the Royal Roads anchorage off Victoria, carrying chests of tea consigned principally to Toronto, Hamilton, Chicago, and New York. Among those who greeted her was Van Horne.

With the docking of this first cargo vessel from the Far East, Van Horne set out to arrange advantageous shipping rates for large importers in New York and other large eastern centres. It would not be long before CPR employees came to realize that the speeding trains carrying tea and silk eastward were only slightly less important to the general manager than the CPR's passenger trains.

The following year, a new service employing three small, retired Cunard steamships was inaugurated between Vancouver and the Far East. George Stephen labelled the service "poor and transient."[493] Nevertheless, the CPR could not discount its contribution to rail revenues. In a three-year period between 1888 and 1890, the three aging liners, supplemented occasionally by other steamers, managed to unload a sizeable amount of cargo at Vancouver. From there, most of it travelled by train to other locations, thereby making a significant contribution to the railway's coffers during what were depression years.[494]

Van Horne was very proud of what he had managed to accomplish on the West Coast. Indeed, he could not resist congratulating himself on the results of his farsighted policies when, in July 1888, he visited Vancouver, the fast-growing and increasingly sophisticated town that he had founded. As he gazed out the windows of his Hotel Vancouver room across Burrard Inlet to the snow-tipped Cascade Mountains and eastward toward towering Mount Baker, he let his emotions spill over into a letter to Addie: "The surroundings are very beautiful and the town is already a handsome and important one. We have had four China steamships in port within ten days besides many others. I take special pride in all this because it is the result mainly of my work."[495]

He would experience an even greater sense of pride on April 28, 1891 when the graceful, clipper-bowed *Empress of India* docked in Vancouver. The first to be completed of the famous majestic Empress liners that would

sail the seas for eighty years, she had sailed from Liverpool for the Pacific
by way of the Suez Canal on February 8, 1891. More than a hundred first-
class passengers had booked passage for what would be the closest thing to
a world cruise that had yet been offered. When she docked at Vancouver,
Van Horne (who was by now president of the CPR) and some of the directors were on hand to welcome her. As part of the welcoming festivities, a
grand banquet and ball were staged at the Hotel Vancouver, but Van
Horne, who disliked such functions, departed for Montreal in the afternoon. Ironically, it was Edward Blake, one of the harshest critics of the CPR
during its construction days, who assumed the role of guest of honour.[496]

Years later Van Horne was queried about the red and white checker-
board house flag that the *Empress of India* flew — and that would be flown
by all Canadian Pacific ships for eighty years. He replied, "Yes, I designed
the house flag — partly to differ from any in use and partly that it might
be easily recognized when hanging loose. It has no historical or heraldic
significance. Somebody has suggested that it meant 'three of a kind' but
that would not be a big enough hand for the C.P.R. for which a 'straight
flush' would only be appropriate."[497]

Under the heading "CPR gossip," the *Manitoba Daily Free Press*
announced on May 31, 1886 that the CPR was "going into the business
of building hotels at prominent places along the line." The *Free Press* continued, "A magnificent building is now going up at Vancouver ... and two
others will be shortly erected ... one at Banff ... and the other in the Selkirk
range in the centre of the most picturesque scenery through which the line
runs." The picturesque mountain hotels were all part of Van Horne's grand
scheme to create traffic for the railway and make the line's costly mountain section pay for itself. "Since we can't export the scenery, we'll have to
import the tourists," he is reported to have said when contemplating the
stunning mountain landscape, which only a few years earlier had been
uninhabited, trackless bush. Luring tourists to this part of the world
would be accomplished by furnishing first-class train travellers with excellent dining, parlour, and sleeping cars, by erecting hotels that commanded the choicest views in the Selkirks and the Rockies, and by advertising
the mountains as "the Switzerland of America."

The tourists that Van Horne hoped to entice to western Canada were
well-off North Americans with the leisure time to travel and an interest in
health, new knowledge, relaxation, thrills, and adventure; in other words,
the North American equivalent of the affluent tourists who were starting to
vacation in the European Alps. Fortunately for him, the period between the
American Civil War and the end of the nineteenth century — a period that

came to be labelled, in Mark Twain's sardonic phrase, the "Gilded Age" — produced increasing numbers of Americans and Canadians fitting this description. Instead of heading to Europe, however, they sought out attractive, railway-accessible destination sites in the United States and Canada that featured mineral springs, natural wonders, and mountain scenery. This was Van Horne's target audience, and he wooed it assiduously.

The CPR's entry into the hotel business began, however, not with the building of full-fledged hotels but with the erection of three "hotel dining stations," intended to substitute for the railway's early dining cars, which were too heavy to be hauled economically up and down the steep grades of Kicking Horse and Rogers passes. In 1886, work began on Mount Stephen House at Field in the Kicking Horse Valley, the Fraser Canyon Hotel at North Bend, and Glacier House, near Rogers Pass and the summit of the Selkirks. Mount Stephen House was ready for business in the fall of 1886, and the other two in early 1887. Although designed primarily to serve meals to first-class passengers, each of the three buildings had six or seven bedrooms for the few travellers likely to stay over. For first-class tourists who did not stop over, the trains arrived at mealtimes and stopped long enough for passengers to enjoy a good meal, the mountain scenery, and bracing fresh air.[498]

By contrast, Banff Springs Hotel, the most celebrated of all the CPR's mountain hostelries, was built as a hotel, owing its construction indirectly to the discovery of several natural hot springs on the flanks of Sulphur Mountain by three CPR workers prospecting for minerals in 1883. The co-discovers staked a claim and sought ownership of the springs but were informed that their claim would not be allowed because the mountains had not been surveyed. Word of the springs meanwhile reached other parties who wanted a share in any bonanza that might be generated by development of the site. The uproar ignited by a series of conflicting claims and counterclaims attracted the attention of the federal government, which dispatched an agent to inspect the situation. Early in 1885, Van Horne visited the hot springs, now known as the Cave & Basin, and immediately sized up the tourist potential of the springs, reportedly remarking, "These springs are worth a million dollars."[499]

Van Horne strongly endorsed the federal government's attempts to reserve the springs for public use and to make them the core of what would become Canada's first national park. He also decided to build a top-notch hotel near the springs, at the confluence of the Bow and Spray Rivers. To design the hostelry, he hired New York society architect Bruce Price. Construction of the 250-bed hotel began in the autumn of 1886 and ended in the spring of 1888, when it opened its doors. The work did not proceed without at least one conspicuous mishap. When Van Horne visited the construction site in the summer of 1887, he was horrified to see that the contractor had oriented the hotel backwards, thereby providing the kitchens with the best view. His wrath aptly illustrated a colleague's observation: "Van Horne was one of the most considerate and even-tempered of men, but when an explosion came it was magnificent."[500]

Fortunately, his solution was simple: Van Horne sketched a rotunda pavilion on the spot and directed that it be situated to provide hotel guests with a coveted view. After the hostelry was completed, Van Horne, satisfied that the building did justice to the magnificent view, boasted that it was the "Finest Hotel on the North American Continent."[501] With its steep hipped roofs, turrets, bay windows, and balconies (one observer described it as being in the "Schloss style of the Rhenish provinces"), the hotel attracted more than five thousand visitors in the year after it opened and became the jewel in the CPR crown. Whatever its defects, it initiated the chateau style that came to characterize many of the hotels erected by the CPR and other railways, as well as railway stations, apartment complexes, and several large government buildings in Ottawa.

Van Horne also commissioned Price to design the CPR's principal terminal and administrative headquarters, Windsor Station. Built in 1888–89, this Montreal landmark is a fine example of "Richardsonian Romanesque," a style that acknowledges American architect Henry Hobson Richardson's adaptation of forms inspired by Spanish and northern Italian architecture. To decorate the cavernous two-storey waiting room (alterations would later cut it in half), the CPR commissioned art nouveau practitioner Edward Colonna. Colonna, however, would have to share credit with Van Horne. Reported a Montreal journal of the day:

> The idea of the decorated ceiling and the mosaic pavement for the large waiting room at the Windsor Station belongs to Mr. Van Horne, and Mr. Colonna, the designer for the CPR, is carrying it out. The whole design is aesthetic in a high degree. Mr. Van Horne has a soul for the beautiful. There are brown, and terracotta, and gold combinations which are very sweet. The pavement is to be a joy ... When the ceiling and floor are finished, this waiting room will be the finest in America.[502]

Van Horne was so proud of the station that on its completion he placed a sign on the building that proclaimed in six-foot-high letters, "Beats all Creation — the New CPR Station!"

It is impossible to know just how much Van Horne contributed to the Banff Springs Hotel and Windsor Station designs. But we do know that he considerably influenced the planning of another Bruce Price commission — Quebec City's Chateau Frontenac. Van Horne, who became president of the railway in 1888, watched over every stage of the hotel's design. One day, he reportedly took Price out on the St. Lawrence River in a small boat to make sure that the elevation of the building's central feature, an imposing round tower, was "sufficiently majestic."[503] Five years after the hotel had opened its doors in December 1893, the CPR was able to inform its shareholders, "Your Company's Hotel at Quebec — the Chateau Frontenac — has been most successful, and a large addition was made to it last year to meet the requirements of the travel it had so largely stimulated. It has not only become profitable in itself, but has from its beginnings added materially to your passenger earnings."[504]

Van Horne's architectural flair was also put to good use designing the prototype for a CPR log station. When CPR officials could not decide what should replace the boxcar that had been serving as a primitive station at Banff, Van Horne, after discussing the problems with his officials on the spot, grabbed a sheet of paper, sketched a log chalet, and, gesturing in the direction of the mountain slopes, announced, "Lots of good logs there. Cut them, peel them, and build your station."[505] Thus was born the design for the CPR's quaint log stations in the mountains of British Columbia.

In later years, Van Horne came to regret some of the changes that had overtaken what he referred to as the "Mountain Hotels." His misgivings were shared by one of the most fascinating members of society in both Montreal and St. Andrew's, New Brunswick — Kate Reed. Reed was a woman of tremendous energy and executive ability who parlayed an extensive knowledge of antiques and paintings into a flourishing business that advised wealthy clients, one of whom was Van Horne. Their friendship and her marriage in 1894 to Hayter Reed, who became manager of the newly created CPR's hotel division the following year, eased the way for her to obtain choice CPR decorating contracts. Her first CPR commission involved the purchase of paintings, antiques, and furniture in Europe for Quebec City's Chateau Frontenac. Later she was commissioned to redecorate CPR hostelries in Banff, Lake Louise, Field, Emerald Lake, and Sicamous Junction.

Reed wrote to Van Horne in September 1905 bemoaning the transformation that the mountain hotels' interiors and architecture had undergone over the years: "How I wish I could talk to you! I can't half write what I would like to, of my feelings when I got to Emerald Lake for instance. I haven't seen Glacier yet, but my sister says my hair, just turning grey, will go snow white there! In a so-called chalet far up in the mountains, the first thing my eyes rested on, was a chimney piece of? on coat after coat of varnish, until you can see your face in it!"[506]

Van Horne, who readily concurred with her opinion, replied:

> I quite agree with all you say and I hope your visit out there [the British Columbia mountains] will result in better things. The mountain hotels are becoming of enormous importance to the C.P.R. — and of sufficient importance to justify making them all they should be and they should be appropriate to their purpose and free from all vulgarity — clean, simple and picturesque, which they are far from being now. Field and Glacier House — the former especially — have been getting worse and worse.[507]

In short, Van Horne was repelled by what he considered to be an excess of frills and ornamentation in the early twentieth-century mountain hotels.

Close to Van Horne's heart was the commissioning of artists to produce art for installation in company hotels or the private collections of CPR directors. In the summer of 1889, Van Horne dispatched Albert Bierstadt, the celebrated American painter, and several other artists westward with instructions to paint large oil canvases of designated landmarks along the railway line. From 1890 to 1891, Bierstadt worked on a large painting of Mount Baker that Van Horne had commissioned on behalf of his colleague and friend, George Stephen. Not content with commissioning the painting, Van Horne instructed Bierstadt as to the precise subject and the vantage point from which to paint it, scheduled the artist's trip, and arranged for his transportation and accommodation. He also judged the final product despite the fact that Bierstadt was one of the most respected of all Rocky Mountain landscape painters and Stephen himself was a connoisseur and patron of fine art.[508]

When it came to advertising the Rockies and the Selkirks as the "Switzerland of America," Van Horne quickly recognized the need for catchy slogans. As an active participant in the design of the company's promotional material, he succeeded in coming up with slogans that captured people's attention. The witty, gregarious George Ham, whom Van Horne enticed away from the *Manitoba Free Press* in 1891 to become the CPR's general passenger agent and subsequently its "Ambassador-At-Large," recalled that when the CPR's passenger service was inaugurated, people in Montreal, Toronto, and other large centres were puzzled and astonished one morning to see billboards featuring such slogans as: "Parisien Politeness on the CPR," "Wise Men of the East Go West on the CPR," and "By Thunder-Bay passes the CPR." According to Ham, these slogans of Van Horne's created quite a stir at the time. Twenty-five years later, however, when he recalled the ads, an advertising man ventured the opinion that they were quite idiotic. "And yet you remember them for a quarter of a century?" Ham asked. The mere fact that the advertising man remembered the derided slogans testified to their effectiveness.[509]

Van Horne also threw himself into the CPR's large-scale promotional campaign to attract settlers to the Northwest, inaugurating special efforts to persuade Maritimers and Quebeckers, who were still pouring into the New England states, to settle instead in the Northwest. To encourage the recruitment of French Canadians toiling in New England factories, priests were appointed colonizing agents.

One feature of this campaign was the establishment of the Canada Northwest Land Company, which Van Horne served for years as president. Prior to 1882, the CPR was primarily interested in the settlement of its lands, not in the sale of sizable tracts to speculators who would let them remain unoccupied for years, appreciating in value but not generating traffic-producing revenue. In 1882, however, the company's pressing need for working capital forced it to abandon its opposition to large land sales and to instigate the establishment of the Canada Northwest Land Company, the Anglo-Canadian consortium that was organized in Great Britain and that brought together British capitalists and close associates of the CPR in Canada. A key figure was shrewd Toronto financier Edmund Boyd Osler, a friend of Van Horne's who had been instrumental in forming the Ontario and Quebec Railway in 1881 and who would be elected to the CPR board of directors in 1885. Initially land sales were brisk, but then they dropped substantially, resulting in the liquidation of the original company and the incorporation of a new one in Canada with the same name. In September 1893, the shareholders elected Van Horne president and Osler vice-president.[510]

Van Horne had pronounced views on land settlement, and central to his thinking was the belief that homesteaders should be grouped in settlements and not separated from each other by large unoccupied spaces. "You have no doubt observed," he wrote in 1906 to his friend Rudyard Kipling, "that the largest buildings in the new western states and in western Canada are usually insane asylums." Isolation, Van Horne told his friend, had contributed more than any other factor to filling these buildings. For the man who was "out all day busy with his work" isolation didn't present a major problem, but it did to "the woman who eats out her soul in loneliness," claimed Van Horne. In his opinion, the problem of isolation might have been overcome had he succeeded in persuading the Canadian government to change its system of surveys in the Northwest to provide for triangular farms and roads that radiated from small centres of settlement that in turn clustered around a larger village. Insisting that "such a thing had not been done before," the Canadian government rejected his farsighted plan. As a result, many settlers lacked close neighbours. In many cases this led to extreme loneliness, which all too frequently gave rise to mental illness.[511]

Notwithstanding the CPR's energetic attempts to recruit settlers for the Northwest, the returns were discouraging. Several factors contributed to the West's slow growth in these years, chief of which was worldwide adverse economic conditions between 1873 and 1896. Grain prices were relatively low from 1874 to the mid-1890s, and in the West, with its low rainfall and short growing season, farming became more risky and experimental, especially outside Manitoba's Red River district. High freight rates to ship grain to the Lakehead were another drawback. Van Horne and the CPR watched in dismay as many settlers headed for the American West, which besides offering better farming conditions also boasted a more complete transportation system. Canada's immigration prospects and western land sales only began to improve in the late 1890s, when there was a general economic recovery in both North America and Europe, an increased demand for Canadian foodstuffs, and a population explosion in Europe.

Hotel construction, land sales, and recruitment of settlers were just some of the Northwest-related issues that competed for Van Horne's attention in these years. Another was the condition of the government-built section, which extended from Port Moody through the Fraser River canyon to Savona's Ferry at the western end of Lake Kamloops. From time to time during its construction, reports of inferior work had trickled eastward to Ottawa and Montreal, alarming George Stephen and providing political fodder for the ever-vigilant leader of the Opposition, Edward Blake. In February 1885, Blake noted that there had been landslides near Maple Ridge on the Fraser River and questioned the condition of the government section. It was extremely important, he told the House of Commons, "that there should be such an efficient oversight of the work in these final stages" that the railway company would have no difficulty accepting the work when it was completed. John Henry Pope, who had succeeded Sir Charles Tupper as minister of railways and canals, replied that the government engineers had "always expressed themselves very well satisfied with the work done." He then added that his chief engineer, Collingwood Schreiber, had been over the line personally every year and would do so again.[512]

Van Horne did not share Pope's view that the government section was soundly built. Neither did George Stephen. After inspecting the section in 1886, he, like Van Horne, concluded that only extensive and hugely expensive reworking would bring it up to line standards. The question then became, who would be liable for an outlay estimated to be as high as $12 million?

When Pope stood his ground the stage was set for a protracted feud between him and Van Horne. Relations between the minister and Van Horne, whom he came to positively dislike, became especially bitter in 1887 when the Canadian Pacific launched a multimillion-dollar claim against the government, contending that the disputed section handed over to the company did not measure up to the required standards outlined in the Act of 1881. An injured Pope took strong exception to this move, for although he had not been minister at the time of construction, he believed that the charge reflected poorly on him and on his work. Even more importantly, he felt that the claim was completely unjustified. All the evidence submitted by the government's engineers, he predicted to Macdonald in August 1888, "will go to show that it is a very good road — better, in fact, than the part that the other fellows built and that it is a safe road with careful running ..."[513] So convinced was the hard-working, conscientious minister of the validity of his position that he dismissed the Canadian Pacific's claim as merely a scheme on the part of Van Horne and his associates to extort more money from the government.[514]

The government could not countenance the huge sum demanded by the CPR since the Liberals would have assailed it as still another subsidy to the company. Nevertheless, Macdonald realized that some compensation would have to be paid. In an effort to prod the government in this direction, Van Horne arranged for a minimum of work to be done on the disputed section and repeatedly called attention to its shortcomings. In March 1887, for example, he informed Macdonald that he had received reports of "three extensive breaks in the embankments, three bridges gone and four heavy rock slides" on the Onderdonk section. He then added that it would be exceedingly dangerous to delay work on it.[515]

The whole vexing question weighed heavily on the shoulders of John Henry Pope who, while defending the government's position, was also struggling with an illness that would kill him two years later. On August 22, 1887, the troubled minister wrote Macdonald, "Every day that passes is making the matter more difficult for us, as they will charge us with all they do, much of which is just ordinary running repairs ... I wish you would write or wire me what you would do. Van Horne will stop at nothing to gain his point."[516]

Pope could not have been more correct in his assessment of his adversary. To drive his point home about the unsafe condition of the Onderdonk section, Van Horne took some lawyers and other parties interested in the case on an inspection tour of the line. For good measure, he also invited some newspapermen to accompany them. At Canmore, Alberta, Van Horne took it upon himself to interview the engine driver, Charles Carey. "We will show these fellows that our line is fit to run on, though the Onderdonk is not," announced Van Horne. "I'll go just as fast as you want," replied Carey, who enjoyed a reputation for skill and daring. "Then give these fellows a merry ride, just to let them know that they are on a railroad; run her as fast as you like, provided you don't ditch them," instructed his boss.[517] Before long the cars were rocking along and chairs and loose furniture in the private car were hurtling across the floor into a pile. Van Horne was jubilant.

Eventually both parties agreed to arbitration, but although the arbitrators began their sittings in February 1888, it was not until 1891 that an arbitration agreement was drawn up. It had been estimated that between $6 million and $12 million would be required to improve the section, but rather than drag out the controversy any longer the CPR decided to accept the verdict (the amount of the award was only $579,225) without appeal. During the course of the seemingly interminable investigation arbitration counsel and witnesses spent weeks at a time along the disputed portion of the line, often holding court at sidings or way stations. Van Horne, of course, was the chief witness and, as such, was subject to searching cross-examination by leading legal figures of the day. During some of the most interesting inquiries he filled the dual role of both witness and recorder, drawing illustrations of the chief participants. On one occasion he sketched the whole court, producing an excellent portrait of Chancellor Boyd.[518]

In late June 1888, Van Horne journeyed west to Vancouver, where the court's sessions would continue day after day in the Hotel Vancouver. When delivering his opinion of the contested work, Van Horne was characteristically blunt, if not reckless. His assessment, in fact, led one of the arbitrators to remark out of court that if one half of what the vice-president said were true the government ought to stop operating the line immediately. Collingwood Schreiber, who was also in attendance, went so far as to tell

Pope that by decrying the government construction and claiming that the section was dangerous, Van Horne had placed himself in an untenable position, "as he could not show that he had taken a single precaution of a general nature to guard against accidents so that should an accident occur he would find it difficult to keep outside the walls of the Penitentiary."[519]

When it came to making demands upon Van Horne's attention, however, the arbitration proceedings could not compete with the agitation in Manitoba for "free-for-all" railway construction and the criticism levelled at Van Horne and George Stephen by the agitators. The very real threat of American competition had led the CPR to insist that its charter include a monopoly clause forbidding other federally chartered companies from building south of the CPR's main line, except in the direction of southwest or to the westward of southwest, and even then no competing line was to come within fifteen miles of the international border. No other provision in the charter was better calculated to rouse the ire of a province where there was a patent lack of railway facilities, especially for farmers wishing to get their products to market. Manitobans therefore protested vigorously against the monopoly clause, goaded by their endemic fear of monopolies and high freight rates and their growing sense of alienation from eastern Canada.

Before John Norquay became Conservative premier in 1878 he asked the electors to endorse a policy that called for the provincial government to encourage "local efforts in the direction of railway construction by granting power to municipalities to bonus such enterprises and by every other means in their power."[520] Before the session of 1881 closed, the Manitoba legislature passed the Emerson and North-Western Railway Act, the Manitoba Tramway Act, and the General Railway Act of Manitoba. On November 4, 1882, however, the federal government disallowed all three acts on the grounds that they contravened its contract with the CPR. A storm of indignation immediately swept across Manitoba as meetings were convened everywhere to protest against the perceived outrage and to draw up plans to prevent a repetition of it. Unfortunately, the completion of the CPR made Manitobans and the people of the Northwest feel more estranged than ever from industrialized eastern Canada, for it made possible the development of a new metropolitan-hinterland relationship that, in many cases, did not favour Manitoba and the Northwest.

By the spring of 1887, Manitoba had become a hotbed of disallowance agitation and railway plotting. A scheme that envisaged the building of a rival road from Winnipeg to the border had barely seen the light of day when it died. Meanwhile, Manitoba's Conservative premier, John

Norquay, promised to put through a charter for any company that demonstrated it could execute the terms. For his part, George Stephen continued to impress upon Macdonald the need to uphold the policy of disallowance. When it appeared that the provincial government might construct a line to the boundary to connect with a projected Northern Pacific extension, the CPR president attacked the Norquay administration directly. In a telegram of protest that he fired off to the premier that May Stephen made sure that Norquay and Manitobans fully appreciated the implications of their actions:

> If the mischievous agitation in favour of diverting the business of the Northwest into American channels is continued and the Canadian Pacific Company is to be treated as a public enemy by the people of Winnipeg, the company will at once take steps to establish their principal workshops at Fort William, which, from an operating point of view has many advantages, leaving nothing at Winnipeg but the ordinary division shops. Pray do not be mistaken. This is not an idle threat, it is a fixed purpose, taken after full consideration.[521]

By the end of that month the CPR's arrogance and stupidity had resulted in Stephen's becoming, in Winnipeg's eyes, the most unpopular man in Canada. A close second was Van Horne, who is reported to have said that when the Winnipeggers burnt Sir George in effigy one mattress sufficed, while two would be required to do justice to him.[522] To make matters worse for the two associates, Stephen's wire to Norquay had no effect whatsoever on the provincial premier's plans. In June, the legislature chartered the Red River Valley Railway, to be built as a government project, and voted $1 million to be raised by the sale of provincial bonds for its construction. In a further move to lessen Manitoba's dependence on the CPR, the legislature passed an act that guaranteed interest on $4.5 million, to be employed in the construction of a railway to a port on Hudson Bay (the Hudson's Bay Railway).

The introduction of the Red River Valley Railway bill in the Manitoba legislature triggered an immediate downturn in the price of CPR shares on the London market. In view of the continual attacks on the company and the serious threat to its credit, Stephen began to wonder if perhaps the monopoly clause was not harming the CPR more than it was aiding it. Accordingly, he suggested to the prime minister that when the bill was disallowed the government should intimate that it planned to negotiate with the CPR to have the monopoly clause cancelled. This, however, Macdonald was reluctant to do. As far as he was concerned, it was too soon for the CPR to surrender its monopoly rights in Manitoba.[523]

Disallowance of the Red River Valley Railway bill only roused the province to new heights of indignation and made it more determined than ever to proceed with its railway. After CPR influence blocked the province's attempts to secure funding in London, Manitoba went looking for money in New York and even in Winnipeg itself. With the arrival of winter everything came to a halt, including Norquay's Conservative government, which was forced out of office in December over the Hudson's Bay Railway transaction. In January 1888, the Conservative government was succeeded by a Liberal administration headed by Thomas Greenway, whose choice for commissioner of railways was Joseph Martin, his belligerent and hotheaded attorney general. Although both men were pledged to complete the construction of the Red River Valley Railway, they decided that the government should not build and operate the road itself but should lease it to a private company. Much to the indignation of the CPR, they chose the Northern Pacific. It was to build the line, which, upon completion, would be leased to a provincially incorporated subsidiary, the Northern Pacific and Manitoba. News of this arrangement produced a furor, critics of the government alleging that a corrupt bargain had been stuck between the Northern Pacific and the Greenway administration. The government's actions became even more suspect when it was learned that Joseph Martin had been named a director of the Northern Pacific and Manitoba Company. Nevertheless, the Manitoba legislature quickly passed an amended Red River Valley Act, which provided for the line to be built not only to the border, but also from Winnipeg to Portage la Prairie.

Fortunately for the Greenway government there would be no disallowance of the railway act. For by now Macdonald had concluded that the use of disallowance to advance his government's policy did not always pay off politically. His government had therefore negotiated with the CPR to surrender the monopoly clause in its charter in return for a federal guarantee of $15 million in CPR bonds, the money to be used for perfecting the main line, building branch lines, and purchasing rolling stock. After much haggling over the terms, legislation was presented to Parliament in April 1888.

Although the CPR had surrendered its monopoly, the company and Van Horne had not lost their capacity or desire for retaliation, which centred on the Northern Pacific's Portage la Prairie line. Ordinarily such a line would not have made news headlines, but because it entered the heart of

CPR territory it ignited Van Horne's fury and led to the conflagration known as the "Battle of Fort Whyte." About fifteen miles from Winnipeg, the line had to cross the tracks of the Manitoba and South Western, a CPR branch line. Before this happened, however, the Northern Pacific was required to obtain permission from the Railway Committee of the Privy Council at Ottawa. Knowing that it would take some time to complete the necessary legal formalities, Joseph Martin wrote to Van Horne on September 20, 1888, asking if he would allow crossings to be laid before the legal authority for doing so had been obtained. Van Horne vetoed Martin's request. "While I should be glad personally to oblige you," wrote the CPR president, "I am constrained by the interest of this Company to withhold my assent and am therefore unable to comply with your wishes."[524]

Notwithstanding Van Horne's response and the lack of official permission to cross the CPR line, the Northern Pacific and Manitoba continued to lay track and installed a diamond crossing in the dead of night. CPR men ripped it out the next day. Then Van Horne instructed his general superintendent at Winnipeg, William Whyte, to take appropriate action. An old CPR engine was ditched at the point of crossing and a force of some 250 men from the company's Winnipeg shops was summoned to the spot to prevent its removal. By October 20, 1888, developments had escalated to crisis proportions. Track-laying had proceeded steadily in the direction of the "killed" engine (dubbed Fort Whyte), and CPR officials, fearful that the tracklayers might respect neither the engine nor its guardians, sought an injunction from the courts forbidding the contractor from laying his rails across CPR tracks.

Winnipeg was aflame with excitement, and Van Horne, waging a game of bluff from his Montreal office, was subjected to some of the harshest criticism he had ever received. The *Manitoba Daily Free Press* reported, "Everyone condemns unreservedly the conduct of the Canadian Pacific in taking advantage of a miserable technicality in order to block for this year the development of a competing railway line; and the vigor and point of the expressions about him would probably make even the imperturbable Van Horne wince."[525] A St. Paul paper, speaking from experience, urged its Canadian neighbours to calm down, noting that the situation was one of "ineffable absurdity."[526] Manitoba's railway commissioner, however, did not share this opinion. On the fifth day of the standoff, Joseph Martin called out the militia and had three hundred special constables sworn in to put in the crossing by force should circumstances dictate this. In faraway, subdued Ottawa, the Railway Committee of the Privy Council referred the issue to the Supreme Court of Canada.

Attempts were made to construct a crossing elsewhere on the line, but all were foiled by Whyte's diligence. Finally, after two weeks of tension, the battle ended abruptly when the Supreme Court ruled in favour of the Northern Pacific. The potential combatants, who had traded nothing more than insults, dispersed, track was laid, and the crossing was made. Faced by a legal decision from on high, the CPR had surrendered, but Van Horne's reckless actions constituted a public relations disaster for the CPR. Whatever meagre support it had left in Manitoba vanished because of his blundering arrogance.

The Battle of Fort Whyte was the first major challenge faced by Van Horne after his elevation to the CPR presidency on August 7, 1888, when he had been unanimously elected to the position at a board of directors' meeting in Montreal. George Stephen, who resigned from the position after seven years of almost constant anxiety and struggle, deemed it right that somebody more experienced in railway administration should take his place.

In September 1889, Stephen left for England. Before departing from Canada, however, he took pains to smooth the way for Van Horne in his dealings with the prime minister. In a letter to Macdonald, Stephen beseeched the prime minister to be perfectly open and frank with Van Horne on matters of mutual concern. Stephen wrote:

> You may be sure of one thing, Van Horne wants nothing from the Government that he is not on every ground justified in asking. You are quite "safe" in giving him your whole confidence. I know him better, perhaps, than anyone here and I am satisfied that I make no mistake when I ask you to trust him and to dismiss from your mind all suspicion that would lead you to look upon him as a sharper bound to take advantage of the Government every time he gets the chance.[527]

Four years later, Stephen made his permanent home just outside of London, in Hertfordshire, where he could savour to the full the English countryside's well-ordered beauty and enjoy a social life that frequently brought him into contact with members of the royal family. In Hertfordshire, near Hatfield, he leased Brocket Hall from Earl Cowper, son of Lord Palmerston. A large, red brick country house situated on an eminence in a spacious park, it had once been the home of Lord Melbourne, Queen Victoria's prime minister, and Lady Palmerston, to whom it passed after Melbourne's death in 1848. Stephen would make this mansion, with its exceptionally restrained exterior and opulent interior, his permanent country abode until his death in 1921.[528]

Most observers believed that the railway magnate had retired because of ill health and exhaustion, and it is true that he was sunk in depression when he left for a holiday in England in the fall of 1888. Not only was he deeply hurt and depressed by the apparent apathy and at times even hostility of Canadians toward the CPR, he was also extremely worried by the prospect of some great calamity befalling the CPR's shareholders. The financier, however, was far from broken and incurably exhausted. For the next twenty years he would be intimately involved with James Jerome Hill's business empire, and from his Hertfordshire mansion he would dispatch a steady stream of letters to Van Horne, who used him as a sounding board and the CPR's direct link to the British financial markets, going to great pains to keep his predecessor abreast of CPR developments, employing cablegrams and letters couched in a formal style that belied the two men's long and close association. Thanks to Van Horne's powers of persuasion, Stephen would continue serving as a CPR director and member of the company's executive committee until his resignation in May 1893.

In proposing Van Horne as his successor, George Stephen had informed the meeting that the CPR had in Van Horne a "man of proved fitness for the office in the prime of life, possessed of great energy and rare ability, having a long and thoroughly practical railway experience, and above all entirely devoted to the interests of the company."[529] *The Gazette* in Montreal certainly concurred with this assessment of the new president, informing its readers, "His abilities have long been recognized. He has great foresight, executive talents of high order, and is filled with confidence in the value and the future of the property over which he will hereafter preside ..."[530] *The Globe* of Toronto, a Liberal paper, not surprisingly took a somewhat jaundiced view of Van Horne's new appointment. With the customary asperity with which it dealt with Van Horne and CPR-related issues, it reported, "In the course of conversation on the street to-day on the event which, in view of the official prevarications, took the public somewhat by surprise, every one was considerably exercised over the idea of Canada having paid about a hundred millions for a road that was to be run by Americans to satisfy whom Sir George Stephen goes out and Mr. Van Horne goes in as president."[531] Anti-Americanism also figured prominently in the avalanche of criticism from London that greeted his promotion. Labelling Van Horne "a foreigner and an alien," and alleging that "the road, though built with Canadian money, is intended for foreigners," the Grand Trunk's president, Sir Henry

Tyler, and his supporters urged the Canadian government to take over the CPR and divide the profits with the company.[532]

Van Horne's elevation to the CPR presidency did not, of course, result in an increase in his responsibilities. He was already in full control of company operations and had been for years. Still, the announcement of his new appointment must have filled him with pride. At the comparatively young age of forty-five he had become titular head of a railway system that comprised over 5,000 miles of line, owned 14,000,000 acres of land, and boasted assets of $180,000,000. Already it had forged strong connections with Minneapolis and Duluth in the American Northwest, New England, China and Japan, the Maritimes (through the Short Line nearing completion, which would connect Montreal with the Maritime provinces), and the Wabash system (by means of a recently concluded alliance). Compared, however, to the great systems that entered New York, Philadelphia, and Chicago, the Canadian Pacific was relatively insignificant. Nevertheless, because it was a world-girdling system in the making, it had the incomparable advantage of affording unlimited challenges for the ever ambitious and creative Van Horne. As its new president, he occupied not only its top position but also the leading post in the Canadian railroading world. From this lofty summit, he would preside over the continued expansion of the CPR, pursuing, along with members of the directors' executive committee, a strategy that represented a judicious blend of expansion and economy and aimed for the lowest possible costs.[533]

Although Van Horne's elevation to the railway's presidency did not lead to an increase in responsibilities, it did result in substantial boost in salary. In August 1889, a special committee, struck to adjust his salary, informed Van Horne that his annual salary would be raised from $30,000 to $50,000, retroactive from the beginning of that year. "As it would undoubtedly be injurious to the interests of the company if the terms of this agreement were to become known," advised the special committee, "they suggest that you continue to draw your salary monthly at the former rate of thirty thousand dollars per annum; adjusting the difference by quarterly or half quarterly vouchers."[534] Clearly, the directors approved of Van Horne's management of the company. For them to announce an increase in his salary would have been impolitic, however, since the country was then in the throes of a prolonged recession and the CPR's future was far from assured. The last thing that these canny directors wanted to do was to furnish the CPR's critics with additional ammunition with which to attack the company.

With his elevation to the presidency of the CPR, Van Horne had the continuing support of able and hard-working colleagues, chief of whom was assistant general manager Thomas G. Shaughnessy, whose love of minutiae, talent for administration, and business acumen had been abundantly demonstrated over the years. Van Horne's trust in the dependable, predictable Shaughnessy was such that he would substantially increase his responsibilities during the period between 1885 and 1891. Van Horne and Shaughnessy, who became assistant to the president in 1889, were assisted by a team that included George Olds and David McNicoll, in charge of traffic, and I.G. Olden, an outstanding accountant who filled the office of comptroller. George Mackenzie Clark, an able and shrewd lawyer and a man of great integrity, was the company's chief solicitor.

Stephen was correct in thinking that the CPR was in need of sound, practical management. In the years ahead, the company would experience financial problems because of the depression, but it would never hover on the brink of bankruptcy. Moreover, even during the worst years of the depression, 1894 and 1895, Van Horne and the company knew that it was bound to prosper once economic conditions picked up. Meanwhile, it required prudent management, and this it would receive from its new president, Van Horne's protegé, Thomas Shaughnessy.

Chapter Ten
Van Horne at the Helm

During the years that he presided at the helm of the Canadian Pacific Railway, Van Horne faced a prolonged depression that gripped Canada for most of this period. The seemingly interminable economic downturn forced him to tone down expansion, and when the depression reached its lowest point in 1894, he had to introduce stringent economy measures. Nevertheless, until the depression bottomed out, expansion in one form or another remained the order of the day, the CPR spending huge sums of money not only to improve the main line but also to construct or acquire lines linking it to parts of western Manitoba and the northern Prairies.

Van Horne was dedicated to expansion. It was a maxim of his that a new railway had to grow in order to avoid being swallowed up by a competing road or, worse, going bankrupt. This belief was only reinforced by his managerial experience, acquired during a period of great consolidation among North American railways. Desirable as expansion was, however, making the CPR grow by means of acquisitions and new construction was not always straightforward and painless.

Typical of the costs and problems of expansion were those associated with the piece-by-piece assembly of the "Short Line," destined to run from Montreal through central Maine to Saint John, New Brunswick. Far-sighted industrialists and politicians had contemplated such a railway for years, and as a first step in the realization of that dream they had constructed a line that ran from Sherbrooke, Quebec, to Megantic, about seventy-five miles to the east. Chartered in 1870, the St. Francis and Megantic International Railway was completed in 1879, but it would be another decade before it became an operating component of the Short Line.[535] Meanwhile, the completion, in 1871, of the European and North American Railway, from New Brunswick to Portland, Maine, made it possible for passengers to travel from

Montreal via the Grand Trunk to Portland and from there via the European and North American to Saint John, Moncton, and Halifax. When the government-owned Intercolonial Railway was completed in 1876, passengers and freight could travel to Halifax by an all-Canadian route that followed the St. Lawrence River Valley northeastward for many miles before turning south to New Brunswick.

Such a circuitous route made for an excessively long journey and highlighted the need for a more direct alternative, but it was not until the CPR was nearing completion that the idea of a short line to New Brunswick was revived. Stephen, determined that the railway would have direct access to an all-weather Atlantic port, met civic officials in Portland in 1883 to discuss the idea of making Portland the CPR's Atlantic terminus. No deal was concluded, but by that time the CPR president had opted for another route, one that would make use of the Atlantic and Northwest Railway Company, a CPR subsidiary.[536]

Not surprisingly, Stephen's dalliance with Portland triggered a storm of opposition in the Maritime provinces, which deplored the idea of the CPR acquiring an American terminus. Although both Halifax and Saint John were much further from Montreal than Portland, Maritimers pointed out that the distance could be reduced significantly if a line were built across the central part of Maine, hence the origin of the designation "Short Line." Among the most impassioned supporters of such a scheme were Sir Charles Tupper, a Nova Scotian, and his successor as minister of railways, John Henry Pope, an unflinching supporter of the CPR during the most difficult and turbulent of its construction years.

The CPR faced mounting pressure to take over the Short Line project after Parliament, in 1884, approved the awarding of a cash subsidy to assist in the line's construction. No sooner was the last spike driven at Craigellachie than the government awarded a contract for the Short Line to the International Railway (formerly the St. Francis and Megantic Railway). A year later, when the road was purchased by the Atlantic and Northwest Railway, the contract was transferred to the CPR. With this move, and government assurances that the Intercolonial would extend its facilities to the CPR, the way was made clear for the various pieces of the new line to fall into place. Van Horne and Stephen would nevertheless always insist that it was only with the greatest reluctance that the CPR embarked on the Short Line project. The deciding factors appear to have been a threat by Maritime members of Parliament to oppose additional financial assistance to the CPR and Stephen's high regard for John Henry Pope.[537]

Even before the Short Line opened in June 1889, Van Horne and Stephen had cause to regret that the CPR had ever become involved in the enterprise. The line's construction placed the company under a heavy financial obligation, and to make matters worse, once the new line opened for traffic the Intercolonial, instead of cooperating with the CPR, treated it as a competitor, refusing to grant it free and unrestricted access to Halifax, an essential condition of the company's obtaining a contract from the imperial government to provide mail service to the Far East.

The problems unleashed by the building and early operation of the Short Line caused Van Horne great distress. Frustrated almost beyond words, he deluged the prime minister with letters about the troublesome railway. "This is far from the treatment that this Company had reason to expect when it undertook the building of the 'Short Line.' Nearly nine millions are now invested in that line which such an attitude on the part of the officers of the Intercolonial Railway will make absolutely valueless, or worse than valueless," exploded Van Horne in a missive to Sir John A. Macdonald in July 1889, only one month after the line began operating.[538] And in October of that same year the irate president declared, "The CPR has been grievously wronged." Continuing his fulminations, he noted that the Intercolonial's train conductors had been instructed to refuse CPR tickets sold from points east of Saint John and that its agents had been forbidden to check CPR baggage on them.[539] With the CPR losing more than $400 a day operating the Short Line, and with its efforts to do business in Halifax frustrated, Van Horne had ample reason to apply steady pressure on the prime minister to give the CPR access to the Intercolonial Railway on terms that the CPR thought had been agreed upon. For whatever reason, however, Macdonald was either unwilling or unable to accede to his request. Not until the summer of 1890 was an agreement finally worked out, at which time Stephen informed Macdonald that Van Horne had wired him, before leaving for the "Coast," that "a satisfactory settlement had at last been reached on the short line matter ..."[540]

CPR expansion in Ontario continued to rouse the ire of its long-time antagonist, the Grand Trunk Railway. In their attempts to make mutual concessions in the interests of greater harmony and the smooth execution of their respective expansion plans, Van Horne and Joseph Hickson, the GTR's forceful general manager, met face to face in sometimes gruelling negotiating sessions.

Hickson was a Northumberland man who had begun his railroading career at a young age as an office clerk with the York, Newcastle and Berwick Railway. By dint of sheer hard work and enterprise he had clawed his way up the railway hierarchy, becoming chief accountant of the Grand Trunk Railway in 1862 and its general manager in 1874.[541] Inspired by the great consolidation movement then underway among North American railways, Hickson embarked on an ambitious expansion program that led to the GTR obtaining independent access to Chicago in 1880. After the CPR started invading the GTR's backyard, Ontario, the GTR's enterprising general manager devoted most of his attention to business in that province, where between 1881 and 1890 he took control of fifteen companies, including the GTR's greatest rival up to that point, the Great Western. Hickson was not only a man of vision, he was also a shrewd, patient, and tenacious negotiator.[542] As such, he would prove a formidable adversary in any negotiations, even when pitted against the redoubtable Van Horne.

In one of their negotiating sessions, on June 11, 1888, two months before Van Horne assumed the CPR presidency, the two men begged, cajoled, bluffed, and argued for four hours. Among the issues discussed was the CPR's determination to take immediate steps to secure its hold on Ontario traffic to and from points west of Lake Superior. The Grand Trunk's acquisition of the Northern Railway and the abrogation of the CPR monopoly in the Northwest made such action absolutely necessary, insisted Van Horne when opening the negotiations. Hickson replied that if the CPR wanted the Grand Trunk's full cooperation it should sell its existing Ontario and Quebec lines to its rival and enter into a stringent agreement binding the GTR to give the CPR at North Bay its entire Ontario traffic for the country west of Lake Superior. Van Horne did not welcome this suggestion, knowing full well that the CPR's directors would not stomach the idea of surrendering to the Grand Trunk in eastern Canada. Hickson inquired about trackage to Sault Ste. Marie and proposed an exchange of trackage rights. Van Horne opined that this would not be satisfactory to the CPR, for if his road had to build its own line from Sudbury to Toronto and fight Hickson and the Northern Pacific for the Northwest business, its board would probably refuse to handle Hickson's traffic or to grant him trackage rights.

The marathon negotiating session was not a complete waste of these busy executives' time. When Van Horne registered strong objections to the GTR having shut the CPR out of Hamilton, viewed by the company as Canada's third most important city, Hickson claimed that he too had been "very angry" that his officials had taken this action and said that the situation would be corrected. In another coup for Van Horne, the two men arranged for the CPR to begin sending its Ontario freight via North Bay on substantially the same terms that Van Horne had proposed earlier to Samuel

Barker of the North and North Western Railways, two new acquisitions of the GTR. Inevitably, there was prolonged argument over many minor points, but Van Horne hastened to assure George Stephen, now Lord Mount Stephen, that it was conducted in "a most friendly spirit,"[543] a surprising comment given the public displays of deep enmity between the two rival roads. Still, negotiating with Hickson could be an extremely frustrating business. During one round of negotiations, an exasperated Van Horne forwarded a copy of a Hickson letter to Stephen, fuming, "It has been a repetition of the old story — carrying on the negotiations up to the very last minute and then raising a new point relating to an outside matter."[544]

Van Horne's reference to the Grand Trunk's acquisition of the Northern Railway was a painful admission that his rival had outsmarted him in a strategic area. When handling its growing traffic from Ontario to the Northwest and the Pacific coast the Canadian Pacific laboured under the serious disadvantage of having to use its line through Smiths Falls, a very roundabout route. In an effort to overcome this disadvantage, Van Horne had proposed utilizing the Northern and Northwestern, two relatively small roads that provided a connection between Toronto and North Bay, the latter situated close to Sudbury Junction on the CPR's main line. Use of these lines would allow the CPR to shave off considerable mileage when hauling its freight from Toronto to Sudbury. The Grand Trunk, however, had absorbed the lines in 1884 and had thus checkmated him. Van Horne had thereupon arranged for surveys to be made for a direct line between Sudbury Junction and Toronto, one that would serve not only main-line traffic but also the traffic of the lines through Sault Ste. Marie. A favourable route had been found, but Van Horne had then decided not to build such a line, preferring to avoid additional capital outlays. When he negotiated with Hickson in June 1888 to have the Grand Trunk handle CPR traffic from Toronto to North Bay over its two new lines he hoped that the benefits to both parties would be such that construction of the line could be put off for years. The armistice notwithstanding, Van Horne at the CPR's annual meeting in 1889 lashed out at the "senseless hostility" of the Grand Trunk and the "mendacious and absurd statements" and "unscrupulous attacks" of its president, Sir Henry Tyler. He then promised to cooperate fully with the Grand Trunk "in any effort to induce the Government to put a stop to the subsidizing of competing lines."[545] In view of all the aid that the Canadian government had doled out to the CPR, especially when it came to subsidizing numerous duplications in Ontario, this last remark was certainly indefensible.

CPR expansion in the United States led, not surprisingly, to a renewal of clashes with Van Horne's friend and railroading rival James Jerome

Hill. Their rivalry took on a new dimension after the CPR acquired the Duluth, South Shore and Atlantic and the Minneapolis, St. Paul & Sault Ste. Marie, commonly referred to as the Soo line.

The Soo traced its beginnings to 1883 when the citizens of Minneapolis, determined to mill all the wheat that the Northwest could produce, incorporated the Minneapolis, Sault Ste. Marie & Atlantic Railway to construct a line that would carry their flour eastward from Minneapolis to Sault Ste. Marie ("the Soo"). The following year, many of these same men, led by W.D. Washburn, a Minneapolis luminary and powerful figure in the milling industry, incorporated the Minneapolis & Pacific Railway to build a line northwestward into the wheat-growing areas of Minnesota and North Dakota. These two roads, along with two others, would be consolidated into the Minneapolis, St. Paul & Sault Ste. Marie Railway in 1888.[546]

Hill, always alert to any possible moves against the St. Paul, Minneapolis & Manitoba Railroad, watched these developments with an increasingly apprehensive eye. When he learned of the millers' plans to build the westbound Soo line he did not become overly perturbed; after all, the group's repeated trips to the money markets of Boston and New York had failed to produce any financing. He became truly alarmed, however, when he heard that Washburn and his cronies had obtained sufficient funds to build a Soo line east of St. Paul and that the necessary capital had come from the Bank of Montreal, in which Stephen and Smith continued to play an influential role. Hill fired off a stern letter to Stephen, demanding an explanation:

> I have to request that yourself and Mr. Smith as directors of the Manitoba Company, will ascertain if possible, and advise me if it is true that they are getting their money from Montreal. It would hardly seem possible that the Bank of Montreal would loan money for this enterprise on its own merits. We have no controversy with the Sault road, but when they undertake to build into territory served by our lines, it becomes this company to take whatever steps are necessary to prevent the success of their enterprise.[547]

It was, indeed, true that the Bank of Montreal had provided capital for the project, but Stephen told Hill most emphatically that he had not realized that the line east of St. Paul was to be involved in any way with the line being built west of that city and that it would be in direct competition with the St. Paul, Minneapolis & Manitoba Railway. In fact, claimed

Stephen, he had been unaware that any company was building into that area. Although the Bank of Montreal had advanced funds to the Soo undertaking east of the Twin Cities, he swore that no Canadian funds were being invested in the scheme to the west.[548]

If these developments — the construction of the eastbound Soo line (it would open in 1887) and the source of its funding — raised Hill's hackles, they positively alarmed George Stephen. While it was true that this road and the Duluth, South Shore and Atlantic Railway, which connected Duluth with Sault Ste. Marie, might deliver traffic to the CPR if the two roads fell into the hands of a rival, they might just as easily divert traffic into other channels. When anticipating potential rivals one did not have to look further than the Grand Trunk Railway, a road that had consolidated its hold on various Canadian lines leading to Sault Ste. Marie and that was all too ready to join forces with the interests that were constructing the eastern Soo line. If it succeeded in obtaining control of this road and the impoverished Duluth, South Shore and Atlantic or in establishing a link with them, the GTR would pose a grave threat to the main Canadian Pacific line north of Lake Superior. To add to Stephen's fears, there was the possibility that Vanderbilt interests might obtain control of the financially strapped Soo line. In Vanderbilt hands, Stephen wrote Sir John A. Macdonald, the Soo line would be "a most potential instrument for diverting traffic from the Canadian channels and drawing it forever into U.S. channels. The supreme importance of the 'Soo' line to Canada ... though felt in a languid sort of way by most Canadians is to me so clear that the bare idea of its being turned against us oppresses me almost beyond endurance."[549]

With a view to scotching such a possibility, George Stephen and Donald Smith came to the rescue of the Soo line at "their own cost and individual risk," as Stephen phrased it. By negotiating a pact with the entire Soo enterprise and the South Shore line the two men were able to provide the Canadian Pacific with perpetual traffic agreements with the two roads and control over an essential sphere of railway influence. When he and Smith came to the rescue of the Soo, Stephen confidently expected that Hill would take over the line and associate it with the St. Paul, Minneapolis and Manitoba (the future Great Northern). The Minnesota railway magnate, however, had lost interest in anything east of St. Paul. Thus the Soo remained Stephen's and Smith's responsibility until 1890. By then the Canadian Pacific was in safer financial waters and able to step in and relieve the two men of their burden. Along with the Soo, the CPR also snapped up the Duluth, South Shore and Atlantic, securing control of it and the Soo by means of agreements that guaranteed the principal and interest of the companies' funded debt. With control of the two lines now firmly in its hands, and Van Horne's acquisition, in 1892, of a small, inconspicuous road, the Duluth and Winnipeg, the CPR was poised to compete aggressively with Hill's Great Northern.

The ensuing rivalry that developed between the Canadian Pacific and the Great Northern soon became a personal struggle, at first between Hill and Van Horne, and then between Hill and Van Horne's successor, Thomas Shaughnessy. Hill enjoyed the decided advantage of having, for the most part, complete control of his road, whereas Van Horne was beholden to his friend George Stephen and the other members of the CPR's four-man executive committee. As long as Van Horne confined the subjects of his frequent consultations with Stephen to the company's internal operations, there were few problems. Stephen, of course, was principally interested in finance and overarching policy, while Van Horne, the practical railroading man, was engrossed above all in day-to-day operations. When, however, the interests of the CPR and those of the St. Paul, Minneapolis and Manitoba (later the Great Northern) clashed, problems arose because of the divided loyalties of three members of the executive committee. Until 1892, this elite CPR committee comprised Van Horne and three substantial shareholders in Hill's railway, Stephen, Smith, and Angus. Although Stephen and Smith had resigned from the St. Paul board in 1883, both had rejoined it in 1889 and both staunchly supported Hill in his plan to extend the Manitoba road to the Pacific Ocean. Smith even served as vice-president of Hill's road for a time and continued as a director until 1895. Stephen withdrew from the executive committee in 1892 and left the board in 1893, but he continued to maintain a close friendship with Hill for many years. Given these circumstances, Van Horne could not always anticipate full cooperation from the CPR's executive committee.

Hill's celebrated transcontinental road, the Great Northern Railway, would become one of the most profitable of the world's major railways. It got its start in 1889, when the St. Paul, Minneapolis and Manitoba was reorganized. In its new guise, the road immediately began planning and preparing to fling itself across the Rockies and the Pacific Northwest to the Pacific Ocean, where the terminus would be the ambitious small city of Seattle. Hill hoped and expected that when the line was completed in 1893 it would significantly improve his bargaining position with the Canadian Pacific.

Meanwhile, Van Horne's road was conducting an efficient transcontinental business in Canada, even snatching westbound freight in the

American East and Midwest from under the noses of American carriers and delivering it to San Francisco. The CPR's acquisition of the Soo line played a large role in making this possible, especially after the line completed a long extension in 1893 that crossed North Dakota in a northwesterly direction and stretched as far north as the Canadian border, where it met a branch that linked it with the CPR's main line near Moose Jaw. From there, Van Horne planned to build a new line that would run through Macleod and the Crow's Nest Pass to a network of lines that would cross British Columbia just above the international boundary. With the completion of these far-ranging plans, the Canadian Pacific would acquire one of the shortest routes from St. Paul, Minneapolis, and Chicago to the Pacific coast and an alternative line through the Rockies. This would enable it not only to protect itself from invasion by Great Northern spurs but also to thrust down into the Spokane, Washington area, part of Hill's territory. If necessary, the extension could be employed as a club against both the Great Northern and the Northern Pacific should either of these roads deal unfairly with the Soo lines.

With the completion of the extension as far as St. Paul, the CPR acquired a through route to St. Paul independent of the Great Northern. No sooner had its incursion into the GN heartland been accomplished than the Canadian Pacific trumpeted the line as the "shortest line from Minneapolis and St. Paul to the Pacific coast."[550] This, of course, only served to further infuriate Hill and to furnish him with still another reason for railing against Van Horne, the Soo lines, and the government-subsidized Canadian Pacific.

The problem of international railway relations in the Northwest could have been resolved by the cementing of a contract that would see the traffic divided equitably between Hill's road and the CPR. There was no difficulty in making one, Hill explained to Sir Donald Smith in the spring of 1890. "It is like a pledge to temperance, entirely depending on the intention of the parties from time to time."[551] Unfortunately, in any joint undertaking involving Hill and Van Horne the intention of each party would be continually suspect. There was also the complicating factor of Van Horne's views of any joint arrangement, no matter with whom it was concluded. As he readily confessed to his American railroading friend F.D. Underwood, he did not think much of joint arrangements because "the higgling of accounts and all sorts of little questions growing out of them takes time from more important matters."[552]

Van Horne and Hill, by their own admissions, admired one another. In their personal dealings, they would exchange railway passes, visit each other's roads, call on each other when visiting each other's home city, and swap news about their latest art purchases (Van Horne's collection contained at least one work acquired from Hill, a painting by Eugene Delacroix).[553] But when it came to operating rival railway systems the two dynamos engaged in fierce, bare-knuckled competition. Contemplating the looming struggle with the Great Northern, Van Horne remarked in 1892 to Thomas Skinner, the London financier and CPR director, "I think just as much of Mr. Hill personally as it is possible for me to think of anybody who is opposed to the Canadian Pacific, but I would see him hung, drawn and quartered rather than have the Canadian Pacific lose ten cents through his Great Northern Railway."[554]

Strange as it may seem, their mutual regard for each other somehow survived the tensions of bitter competition. Van Horne intimated as much in a letter to Allen Manvel, Hill's general manager. "I have some very decided opinions about matters that have occurred between the two companies," he wrote, "... but I would like it to be understood that whatever personal feelings I have is against the actions of your company and not against Mr. Hill or anybody else.... When I damn you or him for your numerous sins as, unhappily, you give me frequent occasion to do so, I beg to assure you that you are damned in a strictly official sense."[555]

When the Great Northern was beginning its thrust toward the Pacific in 1890, and storm signals were being hoisted, Van Horne visited Hill in New York to discuss a permanent and peaceful traffic arrangement between the CPR and Hill's road. He left the meeting, however, fully persuaded that Hill entertained no friendly intentions for the future.

Writing to Stephen in early 1891, Van Horne provided a frank assessment of his foe:

> I have, as you know, ever since Mr. Hill's apparently
> favourable change of heart, looked with friendly eyes on
> his doings, believing him in the main to be sincere. But
> for a year back I have been rapidly loosing faith. I have
> passed the stage of distrust and feel sure now that he has
> neither the good will nor good intentions towards the
> Canadian Pacific, whatever his inside feelings towards
> yourself and Sir Donald may be. I was confidently
> warned some months ago by a friend who is on rather
> intimate terms with Mr. Hill to look out for him — that
> his apparently friendly disposition towards the C.P.R.
> came from his need of the assistance of yourself and Sir
> Donald in carrying out his Montana and Pacific Coast

plans and from nothing else, and that this game was to get you both in so far that you couldn't draw back or stop when the effect of his plans should become apparent.[556]

Hill's seething frustration with both the CPR and Van Horne sometimes led him to act in ways that were detrimental to his own best interests. This happened with increasing frequency after the CPR, by dint of its ownership of the Soo, became firmly entrenched in the heartland of the Great Northern's territory and Van Horne brought the Duluth and Winnipeg into the CPR fold. Van Horne had earlier entertained strong reservations about the small and impoverished D & W, but in late 1892, in what appeared to be a brilliant tactical move, he scooped it up. A 108-mile road that ran northwestward of Duluth, the D & W owned 18,420 acres outright and leased even more of the iron-rich land in the Mesabi and Vermilion ranges of Minnesota. Extended by means of spur lines, the road would have access to valuable iron ore, which could be delivered to the financially troubled South Shore line. Viewed in terms of grand strategy, the D & W had even more potential. With its ideal location, it was perfectly situated to drive all the way to the Pacific coast and thereby provide the Canadian Pacific with another transcontinental line that could threaten the Great Northern.

Unfortunately, Van Horne did not know at the time that a loan that the D & W was striving valiantly to pay off had been advanced by Hill, who had also set his sights on the line. Hill, through intermediaries, had been buying up the railway's debt, believing that the property would be worth fully $3 or $4 million more than the estimated $2 million it would cost him. The American tycoon's wrath can only be imagined when he learned that the CPR had outsmarted him by advancing just over a million dollars to the CPR's Duluth, South Shore and Atlantic to enable it to obtain control of the D & W.

The purchase of the Duluth and Winnipeg heralded four years of trying frustration for Van Horne. Hill wanted the road, and wanted it desperately. No sooner had Van Horne acquired the D & W than a furious Hill fired off an indignant telegram to Stephen attacking Van Horne for securing control of the line. Not content with this, he also threatened his old adversary with a boycott of the South Shore road. This prompted Stephen to observe, "It is extraordinary that he should have so little control over his temper as to permit himself to indulge in such childish language. As I have already wired you, it will be a very good thing for him and for his railway that he should realize that the

C.P.R. is much too strong an antagonist for him to tackle without great injury to himself."[557]

Stephen then attempted to check Van Horne's competitive instincts. Playing the role that he so often played when intervening in struggles between the two antagonists, the veteran conciliator urged his friend to adopt a policy of caution and diplomacy when dealing with Hill. "I am glad," he wrote, "that you recognize the necessity of avoiding everything calculated to increase his apprehension and his jealousy, and I have no doubt when he gets time to cool down, he will become amenable to reason, and I am sure you will see the necessity and wisdom of doing everything you can to pay the way for my suggested treaty of peace."[558] Stephen proposed that Donald Smith, who was closer to Hill than Stephen was, Van Horne, and Hill should meet in Hill territory, St. Paul, to try to arrive at some solution to the steadily escalating dispute. Smith would be the peacemaker. Then, if Hill boycotted the Duluth, South Shore and Atlantic at Duluth he could not legitimately complain if that line expanded through the Duluth and Winnipeg in quest of traffic that he had refused to bring it.

Van Horne did journey to St. Paul to negotiate with Hill, but the interview proved fruitless. In response to Van Horne's overtures, Hill produced a sketch of a road that he was planning to build east into Duluth. Whether this was a bluff or a threat, Van Horne responded coolly that when Hill's line was completed the CPR's South Shore road would have to go in search of business for the D & W.

As the 1890s wore on, Van Horne lost patience with Hill's tactics, which consisted largely of talking around an issue, hoping that his adversary, owing to impatience or sheer exhaustion, would cave in and agree to give him what he wanted. Describing the conclusion of still another futile meeting between the two contestants, this time in Montreal in 1894, Van Horne wrote Stephen:

> I reminded him that we had only an hour left for the discussion of the Duluth and Winnipeg matter, and we started out fairly well on that question for a few minutes ... then he soon wandered away from the subject ... we did not get back to the D. & W. until he had to start for his train. Then he said he would think it over, and if I would try to think out some scheme, we could discuss it at St. Paul on my way back from the Pacific coast. I promised to do so; and then taking me affectionately by the arm, he said, "Van, it is a very nice thing that

although we may disagree about business matters, our personal relations are so pleasant. We would do anything for each other." (the Skunk.)[559]

Van Horne, determined to make the Duluth and Winnipeg a paying proposition, worked out comprehensive plans for its extension, but when he submitted these to Stephen his reaction was not encouraging. When he was first apprised of Van Horne's purchase, Stephen had described it as a wise move, but with the passage of time and the sharp economic downturn in 1894 he began to express doubts and to inch away from his earlier assessment. This inspired Van Horne to write some veiled criticism of his friend's contrary opinion, one of the few occasions in their extensive correspondence in which he felt compelled to do so. As diplomatically as he could, Van Horne informed Stephen on July 27, 1894, that he believed that the man on the spot should be the best judge of the situation: "Difficulties and dangers always look greater to everybody at a distance and I think I have noticed or thought I noticed a good many times in the history of the company that where you were full of belief here you were more or less of a pessimist in London.... I believe it impossible for anybody in London to make a correct diagnosis of conditions in Canada, however familiar he may have been with the country two years ago ..."[560]

As it turned out, economic developments in Canada probably did more to shape Stephen's views vis-à-vis the retention of the Duluth and Winnipeg than did Van Horne's missive. By 1894, the United States was experiencing the ravages of the severe economic downturn that had begun in the middle of 1893. A feeble monetary system, an obsolete banking system, and several years of agricultural distress had transformed the financial panic of that year, 1893, into the cruellest economic crisis that Canada's neighbour had seen up to that time. During the calamitous summer of 1893, Wall Street had been gripped by terror as stock prices collapsed and depositors rushed to banks to demand their money; it had looked as though fortunes, old and new, would be wiped out. Every part of the country experienced hard times, but none more so than the West since President Grover's decision to take his country off the silver monetary standard spelled disaster for the region's mining industry. Industries failed, profits dried up, commodity prices plunged, and America's railways, highly indebted and extended after the 1880s building boom, faced the threat of receivership. More railways, in fact, would default during the 1890s than at any other time in American history. Indeed, by 1898, a third of the nation's track mileage would be in foreclosure.[561]

From his vantage point in Minneapolis, Ty Hurd, Addie's brother, heaped blame for the economic catastrophe on the recent change in government. Exploded Ty in a letter to his sister in August 1893:

> The people of the U.S. asked for a change of administration. They sought with all their ability, clamor and demagogism to accomplish such a change. They knocked! Hell has opened for them, banks breaking, manufactories closed, all employers of men reducing forces, wages everywhere being cut and the end not yet. Silver robbers, fanatical thieves and demagogues are still a thick as mosquitoes in a Jersey swamp or flies on a Democratic cadaver.[562]

Canada was soon caught in the fallout from the American panic. According to Van Horne, the sharp economic downturn experienced in 1894 was "not due to any constitutional weakness, but [had] been caught, like the itch from our neighbours," where "the business storm" had driven one third of the railway mileage into the hands of receivers.[563] He further noted that American manufacturers, "in the absence of a home market, dumped everything they could into Canada, making our own manufacturers sick and disturbing our business generally; and at the same time their securities of all kinds were so greatly cheapened that foreign capital was soon attracted to them and away from us."[564] He neglected to mention that the financial cyclone had also smashed the western grain market, leading to a steep plunge in Canadian wheat prices and a flattening of the wallets of hard-hit western grain farmers. In fact, the torpid American economy contributed to reduced sales of all Canadian agricultural products and lumber in the United States.

The inevitable outcome of the downturn was a reduction in CPR train travel and a decrease in its freight traffic; the latter, when measured in ton-miles, declined nearly 10 percent in 1894, the worst year of the depression. The result was a slide in the CPR's revenues and an alarming and precipitous fall in the price of its stock. The company was dealt still another blow when it was forced to suspend transcontinental traffic for forty-one days in 1894 because its tracks in the lower Fraser River Valley had been washed out by severe flooding. To add insult to injury, when Van Horne rushed to the scene of the disaster he had to complete his journey over the Great Northern. After finally making it to the flooded area, he surveyed the devastation and exclaimed, "Hell! This means all the money in the treasury is gone." The loyal engineer who had brought him there responded, "Well, Sir, we'll run the road whatever comes."[565] When the CPR was finally able to resume through freight traffic in early July, Van Horne remarked to Thomas Skinner, "I did not think such an interruption of traffic was possible. It has been a sad blow to our pride."[566]

Faced with "hard times," the CPR let go a large number of employees and chopped 10 percent off salaries between $1,000 and $2,000 and 20 percent off those above $2,000.[567] Only loyalty to the railway, still regarded as a national institution, enabled it to keep operating. One aspect of this loyalty is well illustrated by the recollections of the engineer who accompanied Van Horne to the flooded area of the Fraser Valley in 1894. Twenty years afterward he recalled that salary or no salary, the men would have stood by Van Horne, so strong was his hold on them.

As he surveyed the Canadian Pacific scene from afar, Stephen became gloomier and gloomier about the company's prospects. Some of his dismay may be attributed to a loss of confidence in Van Horne's judgment and managerial abilities. Van Horne, on the other hand, never appears to have second-guessed his own management decisions, and he certainly never for one moment doubted the long-term prospects of his beloved company: he revered the CPR only slightly less than he revered Addie and his children. Despite his misgivings about Stephen's position on the Duluth and Winnipeg, and even though Stephen had left the CPR board in 1893, he continued to correspond faithfully with his old friend. Van Horne, however, could no longer approach the task as enthusiastically as he had previously, relations between the two men having become markedly strained thanks to Stephen's loss of faith in the CPR. Van Horne was "greatly irritated by Mountstephen's default in loyalty, not so much to him [Sir William] himself as to the Railway," Van Horne's close friend, Robert Horne-Payne, the English financial assistant of railway promoters, would recall decades later. "I well remember Lord Strathcona coming to Montreal ostensibly to open up his house for the reception of some guests ... but in reality as Sir William told me with a quizzical smile, to try and restore the former relations between Sir William and Mountstephen."[568]

Van Horne went to some lengths to try to bolster confidence in the beleaguered CPR and his management of it. In the depths of the depression, when criticism was flying from every quarter, even from members of the CPR board, he wrote to Stephen, "Our expenses were less in our most extravagant year than have been those of any of the other lines." Then, later in the same afternoon, he declared in a second letter, "I do not believe that any important railway in the United States can possibly get down to our figures."[569] To his confidant, Thomas Skinner, he pointed out that the

CPR had "withstood without any embarrassment whatever, a storm which has put into bankruptcy one-third of the railway mileage of the United States ... Beyond our current accounts we owe nothing to any bank or anybody, and I think we have more money on deposit than any railway on this side of the Atlantic."[570]

Van Horne's financial restraint during the depression and his desperate and persistent efforts to maintain dividend payments earned him plaudits from the world of international finance, but not from western farmers, who were among the CPR's biggest customers. As far as the irate farmers were concerned, he and his company were ogres. Reeling from the lowest international grain prices in years, they accused the CPR of expecting them to carry its investors and creditors on their backs. Van Horne retorted that rates for carrying wheat had been steadily reduced and that, in fact, they compared favourably with rates anywhere in North America. The western farmers, however, refused to be placated by such claims and continued their attacks on the CPR.[571]

Van Horne also had to contend with Hill's efforts to play up the desperate condition of the Duluth and Winnipeg and to increase financial pressure on it. In March 1894, after meeting with Stephen in London, Hill announced that he had obtained financing to build a new line that would run from Fosston, Saskatchewan, to Duluth, in direct competition with the D & W. "The right of way into Duluth has been secured and work will begin early in the spring. The move will compel the Canadian Pacific to extend the Duluth and Winnipeg to the West," reported the Associated Press.[572]

Hill could not have timed the announcement of his threat more brilliantly. Although Van Horne had already drawn up plans for the Duluth and Winnipeg's extension, Hill was goading him into undertaking the extension at the worst possible time, in the depths of the depression. Railroad financing, already depressed by the financial panic, seemed to have dried up completely after the Northern Pacific had once again become insolvent. Even that financial genius Stephen was finding it impossible to raise money for the CPR. Nevertheless, Van Horne drew up a bold plan to sell construction bonds in the North Dakota and Minnesota towns that would be served by the extension. Whenever he visited a town to promote the sale of the bonds, however, Hill's minions doomed his efforts by "spending a large sum in cash," as a gleeful Hill later reported to J.P. Morgan, America's leading capitalist and proponent of railway consolidation.[573]

Still incensed at his failure to obtain control of the Duluth and Winnipeg, J.J. Hill went out of his way to attack his rival. He not only boycotted the Soo lines, he embarked on an orgy of rate cutting, using his recently completed transcontinental line, the Great Northern. Surveying the damage done to CPR revenues, Van Horne commented, "Hill seems to be like a boy with a new pair of boots & bound to splash into the first mud-puddle so that he may have an excuse for showing their red tops."[574] In a still more provocative move, Van Horne's old foe stalled trains at the international boundary so that they arrived in Winnipeg too late for passengers to connect with the westbound CPR train. Hill even went so far as to bribe members of the Interstate Commerce Commission to make tariff rulings that were damaging to the CPR.

What probably upset Van Horne the most, however, were Hill's devious and underhanded attempts to slander his reputation and that of other CPR officials. The celebrated Canadian civil and military engineer Sir Casimir Gzowski saw first-hand a sample of Hill's tactics while attending a dinner at Government House in Toronto in the late spring of 1894. On this occasion, American financier Dudley Ryder, fresh from a visit to Hill in St. Paul, seized the opportunity to spread "the most scandalous and false statements" about the CPR and its officials. Gzowski was so disturbed by this outrage that he immediately informed Van Horne about it in a letter. When Stephen got wind of what Hill was up to he fired off a telegram to Gaspard Farrer, the young British establishment figure at Baring Brothers who was a good friend of Hill's. In the telegram, Stephen pleaded with Farrer to warn Ryder and his firm not to accept as true anything that Hill said about the CPR or its officials, explaining that the St. Paul tycoon had been bitterly opposed to the CPR for years and would stop at nothing to injure it.[575] Stephen then sent a copy of the telegram to Van Horne.

The discovery that his old antagonist had been circulating malicious lies about him and other CPR officials deeply wounded Van Horne and sent him hurrying to his desk to unburden himself in a letter to Thomas Skinner:

> While I am naturally more than indignant at his personal slanders upon myself I am only anxious at the moment to prevent any injury to the CPR from his talk. It hurts particularly because he is supposed to be on such friendly terms with Lord Mount Stephen and others prominently connected with the company and because his poison is always administered with an appearance of friendship for them ... Hill knows as well as anybody my scruples concerning the use of one's position in such a company for his personal profit and he lied maliciously.[576]

In light of Stephen's reaction to Hill's manoeuvres, Van Horne was bewildered when, two months later, he received a letter from his predecessor lavishing praise on Hill for his economical management of the Great Northern. Once again, he unburdened himself to Skinner: "I am quite unable to understand on what Lord Mount Stephen's fear that the Canadian railways will suffer in traffics is based. We are doing business on both sides of the international boundary and are in constant touch with the business of the Northern and Western States, and I am sure that we are much better off than they are; and I can't see that their prospects for the immediate future are any better than ours."[577]

James Jerome Hill was not Van Horne's only American foe in the ruthless railway expansion game. In pressing his competitive edge so fiercely, Van Horne also attracted the hostility of other American roads, specifically those that felt threatened by the CPR's success in forging strategic American connections. Van Horne's acquisition of the Soo lines and the Duluth, South Shore and Atlantic crystallized much of this opposition. Indeed, it stirred up the waters of agitation so effectively that in 1889 the Senate's Interstate Commerce Committee (ICC) embarked on a study of Canadian railway operations in the United States. As Senator Cullom explained, the acquisition of the Soo lines provided the Canadian Pacific with a monopoly over the St. Mary's Bridge, enabling it to ignore and defeat the operation of the Interstate Commerce Act in letter and in spirit.[578]

A variety of broadly based interests lay behind the disparate agitation that culminated in the Senate inquiry. One group suggested retaliatory legislation against Canada because of its treatment of American fishing vessels, another demanded that Canadian railways should be kept out of the United States as a means of ensuring increased Canadian interest in annexation with that country, and a third — most important — group, comprised of railway interests, used Canadian competition as an excuse to agitate for the legalization of pooling and the repeal of the unpopular long- and short-haul clause of the Interstate Commerce Act.

In their determination to hit back, lines that had been injured by Canadian competition lobbied Congress to pass legislation rescinding the bonding privileges that allowed Canadian railways to carry American freight in bond across Canada. This was necessary, claimed the American roads, because Canadian lines were not subject to the jurisdiction of the newly created Interstate Commerce Commission and could therefore make secret rebates and compete unfairly with American roads. When pursuing their cause, irate railroading men lashed out at the CPR by circulating exaggerated and erroneous statements about its land grants, government loans, subsidies, and political inclinations.

In an effort to set the record straight and quell opposition, Van Horne engaged an American lawyer, Alonzo C. Raymond, to look after CPR interests in Washington, and he himself journeyed to the American capital to present his company's case. In his appearance before the Senate committee, Van Horne quickly tossed aside the argument that the CPR strategy was politically motivated, observing that the principal interest of the company's shareholders and directors was "to make the most money they can out of the Canadian Pacific Railway for their shareholders. They are not moved by sentiment or political considerations very much."[579] He observed that relations between the CPR and Canada's federal government were no closer, if not less close, than those between the Pennsylvania Railroad and the government at Washington, and he hastened to disabuse congressmen of the ridiculous idea that the CPR was a pampered pet of the Canadian government. The only assistance that the CPR received from the federal government was compensation for carrying the mails, and as for the subsidies that the CPR gave to Pacific steamships, they bore no relationship whatsoever to competition with American lines.

Since the Senate committee made only one recommendation relating to railways and the U.S. Congress failed to take decisive steps regarding Canadian competition, American agitation continued for years. In the face of one particular storm, Van Horne arranged for the Canadian Pacific's case to be presented directly to President Benjamin Harrison, who had been threatening to issue a proclamation against Canadian roads. After the president finally withdrew his threat, Stephen was quick to commiserate with Van Horne. In all likelihood, the American president had been misled by the "hired agents" of Van Horne's rivals, he observed, speculating that the attacks in the New York papers upon the CPR had undoubtedly been inspired by the railways on "whose toes" Van Horne had been treading. Uppermost in Stephen's mind, no doubt, was Hill, who had earlier warned a Senate committee that the British government was subsidizing the Canadian Pacific in order to guarantee Britain an alternate route to Asia besides that of the Suez Canal. Stephen also drew Van Horne's attention to another *bête noire* of the CPR and Canadian railways. "What you say about the Annual Report of the Interstate Commerce Commission is disgusting, and I am afraid the Commissioners have been got at in some way," he wrote. "It is very satisfactory to find that your record in so clear and clean. In the meantime [January 1893] it is very annoying and trying to be obliged to suffer from grumbles and unfair interpretations."[580]

Not all American papers and interests took a dim view of Van Horne's tussles with the CPR's American competitors in these years. Commenting on the rivalry, a New York paper, *The Commercial Advertiser*, ventured the opinion that "although he [Van Horne] had many a lively tilt with his United States rivals, few lances were broken and no personal bitterness was engendered."[581]

Railway competitors were not the only antagonists that Van Horne had to deal with in these years. He also had to confront the organizers of a railway strike that erupted in 1892. On this occasion, as in previous strikes, Van Horne trotted out his anti-union prejudices. The clash began in late 1891, when a joint committee of unionized conductors and trainmen of the CPR's Western Division submitted a request for improved wages to the divisional superintendent, William Whyte. Whyte responded by instructing the committeemen to return to their jobs until he had had an opportunity to study their appeal. When the men refused to do so, he presented them with an ultimatum: report for duty immediately or be fired. The committee thereupon telegraphed their international headquarters for assistance, and two union officials travelled from the United States to Winnipeg to negotiate a settlement. Confronted by the Grand Chief of the Order of Railway Conductors, Whyte backpedalled frantically, explaining that only Van Horne, in Montreal, could grant all of the requests of the committee. Although they questioned Whyte's assurances that the committeemen had not been threatened with dismissal, the union officials persuaded the men to return to work and to await the outcome of further negotiations before taking any action.

The talks resumed at the beginning of March 1892, but then broke down completely when the company presented proposals that included reductions in wages for some job categories. Once again the committee wired the American headquarters for assistance, and once again Whyte opened negotiations with another offer. This one was accepted by the committee, but head office, in the person of Van Horne, refused to ratify it. The CPR president was convinced that some American union officials were devising a plot against Canadian railways and that the negotiations were merely part of their grand scheme. He also believed that most Western Division conductors and trainmen, given a choice, would support the company. Resolved to strike the "first blow," Van Horne instructed Whyte to require all these men "to pledge themselves to stand by the company in any emergency."[582] Although he must have resented Van Horne's long-distance appraisal of the situation, Whyte met with the committee and, as instructed, demanded immediate acceptance of the CPR's offer.

With the survival of the two unions at the CPR now at stake, the dispute took a new turn. The end result was a final ultimatum and the decision of the two brotherhoods to strike the CPR's Western Division on March 16 at midnight. Since Van Horne had always attached the utmost importance to company — and family — loyalty, what happened next was almost inconceivable: all but a handful of the two brotherhoods' members on the Western Division went out when ordered to do so. Furthermore, as a gesture of sympathy, a number of non-unionized CPR switchmen also struck.

The strike might well have dragged on for an unseemly length of time had it not been for the intervention of the local engineers' grievance committee. Although sympathetic to the strikers, it was eager to see an end to their walkout and therefore offered its services as a mediator. Both brotherhoods accepted the offer, but the company, confident that it could bring in new men to replace the strikers, did not. By now the strike had spread to the Pacific Division and the first contingent of strikebreakers had arrived in the West from Eastern Canada. Not content with recruiting strikebreakers, the CPR also employed special police to guard its property during the strike and had auxiliary police sworn in by cooperative police magistrates in almost every major centre that the company served. On March 21, Van Horne and Shaughnessy raised the ante still further by ordering company officials to administer a loyalty oath to workers in the CPR's Eastern Division. This decided the issue for the men of Northern Ontario, who, despite having no prior grievances against the company, voted to go out on strike. As a result, Van Horne and other company officials awoke on March 22 to the news that another 752 miles of track had been tied up.[583] Faced with this setback, Van Horne and the company capitulated. Thanks to the assistance of the engineers' committee, which acted as a mediator, Whyte and the brotherhoods' two Grand Officers negotiated an agreement that represented an outstanding victory for the unionists. The agreement was ratified on March 23 by Van Horne, who had reluctantly, but pragmatically, concluded that further resistance would only be drawn-out and costly. He had wanted to destroy the trainmen's and conductors' organizations on his road; instead, he found himself granting them formal recognition and the first signed contract with the CPR.

Van Horne was in the prime of life in 1894. Fifty-one years of age, he typified the experience of most people in that he had put on weight over the years. The stocky body of his youth had yielded to spreading girth, the result of too many hours at his desk, lack of exercise, and a gargantuan appetite (although, as he confided to Addie, not even he could live up to the image of him held by their two housekeepers, who expected him to dispose of a whole melon, a boiled chicken, a porterhouse steak, ham and eggs, and two pounds of hash at a sitting).[584] The receding hairline of his young manhood had long since been replaced by a bald pate, and his clipped beard was now flecked with grey. In fact, his resemblance in these years to the third Marquis of Salsbury, then Britain's prime minister, was so pronounced that Van Horne's prominent Liberal friend J.D. Edgar once drew his attention to a "very flattering portrait" of the marquis, thinking that it resembled Van Horne.[585]

Notwithstanding the signs of middle age, Van Horne continued to be a high-voltage dynamo, driven by ambition and determination. He still toiled incredibly long hours, whether at his desk or rushing hither and yon across the continent. But his body, which he had used and abused so often, was now registering the occasional protest. The year 1894 saw the first of these, a prolonged attack of bronchitis that threatened to take up "permanent quarters" with him if he did not escape to a warmer climate. His once seemingly invincible body and superhuman vitality had let him down. No longer could they remain unaffected by extended periods of stress. And the last two years had been riddled with stress owing to the financial pressures generated by the panic of 1893.

In the hope of regaining his health, Van Horne left Montreal for New York on December 3, 1894, intending to sail for London on December 5 and then make his way to the Mediterranean. He planned to be away five or six weeks. Normally he would have relished the prospect of a lengthy visit to London, but on this trip he proposed to spend a minimum of time in England's capital. His health was one reason for the abbreviated visit. But what he described as "unfavourable inferences that might be drawn from any long stay there"[586] was another factor that came into play. He did not explain what he meant by these inferences, so one is left to speculate wildly.

A letter from Stephen had warned Van Horne that he might be called upon to answer inconvenient questions from disgruntled shareholders. But the prospect of fielding anxious questions did not faze him; after all, as he explained to Thomas Skinner, the mail brought an unending stream of questions in any case. Van Horne's stock reply was that the Canadian Pacific, in common with nearly all the western American railways, and especially the transcontinental lines, had staggered under the weight of hard times, but not nearly as badly as the American lines had. Besides, beyond its current accounts, his road was not in debt to any institution or individual.[587]

During his brief sojourn in England, Van Horne made an obligatory visit to his friend Robert Horne-Payne. A financial genius who was frequently called upon to handle the financial needs of Canadian railways, Horne-Payne shunned London whenever possible for his country estate, Merry Mead, in Essex, and it was there that Van Horne probably visited him. At Merry Mead, the two men undoubtedly discussed the Canadian economy and Horne-Payne undoubtedly boasted of the accuracy with which he could predict how many stocks or bonds a particular English town or hamlet would take in a Canadian venture.[588] What is known for sure is that Van Horne, either at this meeting or at an earlier one, introduced his friend and protegé to the exciting commercial possibilities afforded by the exploitation of electrical power and traction. At any rate, this is what a grateful Horne-Payne recalled years later, remarking that since that pivotal visit he had "pushed himself well to the front in this branch of finance."[589]

While in England, Van Horne may have retraced his steps to Brocket Hall, that historic mansion once owned by Lords Melbourne and Palmerston, but now the home of his friend George Stephen. Whether or not he did, he certainly planned to meet with his old friend in London in mid-December, before he left for the Continent.[590] If the primary aim of such a get-together was to banish any reservations his friend may have had about Van Horne's management of CPR affairs, it failed conspicuously. No less an authority than Stephen himself made this unequivocally clear to Van Horne's able lieutenant, Thomas Shaughnessy:

> It is quite evident that Sir William, either from failing health or from allowing other things to occupy his mind, is no longer able to give the affairs of the company his undivided attention. His want of grasp and knowledge of the true position of the Company was, painfully, twice shown at our conference on Tuesday last, and can only be explained on the assumption that he had never given his mind to the matter ... His actions gave me the impression that he felt like a man who knew he was in a mess and had not the usual courage to look his position in the face. His apparent indifference and inability to realize the gravity of the position I can account for in no other way.
>
> From what I have thus said you will see that all my confidence in the ability of Sir William to save the

Company has gone, and it is to you alone that I look, if disaster is to be avoided.[591]

In London, it poured rain. To make matters worse, a mistake on the part of the Canadian High Commission led to Van Horne missing the requiem mass for Prime Minister Sir John Thompson. He had slumped over dead on December 12 at the luncheon table in Windsor Castle, where earlier he had been sworn in as a member of the Imperial Privy Council by Queen Victoria. About the only cheerful news that the railway president could report from London concerned the price of CPR shares. It had gone up 3 percent since his arrival.[592]

Paris proved more inviting. The weather may have been raw and wet, but at least in the "City of Light" Van Horne could visit the Louvre, hobnob with art dealers, and dine with friends at the celebrated Paris restaurant Joseph's. There, Joseph himself, "the most famous cook in the world," attended to him and his party in person.[593] The result, claimed Van Horne, was a "revelation."[594] Unfortunately, the weather did not improve in Italy. Still, this did not preclude frenetic rounds of sightseeing, Van Horne and his travelling companions hurtling from church to church, from palace to palace, and from one set of ruins to another. The frantic pace prompted the observation, "It has been pretty hard work bumping along as we have been doing. I wouldnt like to try it again without twice as much time."[595]

The weather continued to disappoint. In a desperate search for warmth, Van Horne and his party persevered through a snowstorm to Naples and then travelled on to Sorrento, the famous seaside resort across the bay from Naples. Notwithstanding the raw cold, Van Horne was captivated by the picturesque town, so much so that he would have liked to rent a villa so that he might spend a year or so there. Seduced by the resort's charm and a "capital" Italian dinner, he even let himself admit that he liked Italy and its people. "Both are better than I expected," he wrote Addie.[596]

While her husband vacationed in the Mediterranean, Addie endured the travails of a distinguished man's wife in frigid Montreal, albeit not without protest. Accustomed as she was to organizing countless dinners and weekends for all manner of guests, there were times when she was tempted to rebel overtly against the role of dutiful wife. The arrival of an Aberdeen entourage on her doorstep in December 1894, shortly after her husband's departure for Europe, was especially irksome. Although the party did not include Lady Aberdeen, the wife of Canada's then Governor General, it was bound to cause a stir because it was there at the instigation of Lady Ishbel, the zealous social crusader who had won over legions of Canadians.

Addie, quiet and unassuming, was not one of Lady Ishbel's great admirers, at least not at this juncture. In reaction to this visit, she let all her pent-up frustration boil over in a letter to Van Horne, written two days after Christmas.

> Your dear letters to Addie & myself came by this mornings post. I am sorry you did not see more of London. How I wish you could go once & not be obliged to meet "high Commissioners" & others on business. Let us plan to enjoy life a little before we get too old or infirm. We are always waiting on other people & I am tired of it. I was quite willing Mr Eaton shd paint one picture of Lady Marjory [Lady Marjorie Pentland, the daughter of Lady and Lord Aberdeen, Canada's Governor General from 1893 to 1898], but two is asking quite a good deal. Yesterday Lady Marjory, the lady secretary & the three boys & two dogs came in & up in the billiard room meanwhile one of the dogs left his <u>cards</u> in the hall & poor Mrs Dunn had to clean it up. I told [?] when they came in again to tell the children to please not let the dogs in as they were apt to make trouble.[597]

Courtesy of the Norman Photographic Archives, McCord Museum of Canadian History, Montreal 11-89974

Mrs. William Van Horne in 1889. The Canadian novelist William A. Fraser described her as "the most gracious woman I ever met in my life."

In May of 1894, it was Lord Aberdeen who informed Van Horne that an honorary knighthood could be his for the taking. This was the third time that Van Horne had been offered a knighthood. On the first two occasions, in 1891 and 1892, he had turned down Queen Victoria's proposed honour. Explaining his refusal in 1892, Van Horne told Prime Minister Sir John Abbott that he felt it would be a great mistake for him to accept a knighthood in the near future. He had reached this conclusion after considering several factors, "the chief one being the probability of renewed attacks on the CPR in the United States" and his refusal to countenance any honour that might cost the CPR "an ounce of advantage."⁵⁹⁸ It has been suggested that Van Horne was far from honest in ascribing his refusal to such motives, and that in actual fact he rejected the offer because he felt very uncomfortable with the idea of "Sir William." If we take him at his word, he really did believe — at least initially — that he could better defend the interests of the CPR in anti-British Washington without such a special mark of royal favour as a knighthood.

When the offer was made for the third time, almost six years after he had become a naturalized British subject, Van Horne accepted it. As a result, the Queen's birthday list of honours that spring announced his appointment as an Honorary Knight Commander of the order of St. Michael and St. George. The actual announcement was made on Saturday, May 26.⁵⁹⁹ Lord Aberdeen expressed the hope that it would be generally recognized in Washington and elsewhere that "this mark of distinction has reference to your career as a whole, & is in no sense an impulsive act or one prompted by any event or contemporaneous circumstances."⁶⁰⁰

Van Horne was at first decidedly uncomfortable with his new title. Walking to his Windsor Station office on the morning that his knighthood was announced, he was repeatedly accosted by acquaintances and friends offering hearty congratulations. This could be tolerated, but it was the last straw when his elderly office attendant, who for years had greeted him with a friendly salute, now made a servile bow and intoned, "Good morning, Sir William!" Completely flummoxed, Van Horne muttered "Oh, Hell," and beat a hasty retreat.⁶⁰¹

Still, there was nothing Van Horne could do to prevent an avalanche of congratulations from the exalted and the humble. His friend John W. Mackay, the successful American business tycoon and railway director, telegraphed from New York, "Congratulations both to the order of St. Michael and St. George and yourself."⁶⁰² Far less trenchant was a congratulatory letter from Sir John A. Macdonald's son, lawyer Hugh John Macdonald, who would be made a Knight Bachelor in 1913. From Winnipeg, he wrote:

> It is gratifying to know that the people of England are beginning to realize the great advantage that the construction of the CPR has been not only to Canada but to the Empire at large and I must say that it would have been hard for the Government to have discovered a more graceful way of showing their appreciation of what has been done in this respect than the one they have chosen, by honouring the

man who was mainly instrumental in carrying through this
great work to a successful completion ...[603]

Van Horne was probably more moved by another letter that came
from Winnipeg, that hotbed of anti-CPR agitation. It was penned by a
Miss Esther Nichol, who recalled that eight years earlier, when she had
written to Van Horne requesting a pass to travel east, he had very kindly
issued her a very inexpensive ticket. This had enabled her to take a trip
that gave her a new lease on life, and for this she would be eternally grateful to the CPR president. "No one," she wrote, "wishes you more happiness, and prosperity than I."[604]

Not surprisingly, Van Horne's acceptance of a knighthood buttressed a
widely held belief that he had lost all love for his native country, the United
States, and had become one of its most intractable opponents. This riled the
railway magnate, and he went to some lengths to squelch this misconception
and make it clear that when he acted against American interests it was simply because of his love of the Canadian Pacific. When the rabidly anti-CPR
New York Sun described him as "originally an American but now a fierce
Tory hater of all things American," he dispatched a bristling letter of protest
to the editor, declaring that no act or thought or word of his had ever justified such a statement. He continued: "I am as proud of the United States as
you are, Mr. Dana, and I know that this is saying very much. For many years
I have been entrusted with important interests by the Canadian Pacific
Railway Company and I have done my best to protect and develop these
interests ... Pray put me down not as an enemy of things American but as
one who loves the Canadian Pacific Railway.[605]

When it came to furthering the welfare of the Canadian Pacific, Van
Horne was quite prepared to accommodate certain American interests. On
at least one occasion this involved the routing of the direct line of the Soo
extension. Eager to perform favours for his friend General Thomas and
Senator Casey, the CPR president urged the Soo's general manager, his
friend Frederick D. Underwood, to arrange for this line to pass via
Carrington. To General Thomas, Van Horne reported, "I am very glad of
an opportunity to oblige Senator Casey and yourself."[606]

Canada was still in the grip of hard times when Van Horne returned
to Montreal in January 1895. Although relieved to be cured of his bronchitis, he felt only dismay when contemplating the "world of care," to use
Addie's phrase, that he now faced. Commenting on the trials confronting
Van Horne, Addie informed her sister-in-law, Ethel Hurd: "The financial
depression has at last reached Canada & the CPR has been one of the chief

sufferers. Will's individual enterprises are at a standstill & of course he has occasion for anxiety all around."[607]

Van Horne had been confident the previous September that the Soo's earnings would increase substantially by the end of the year and that the Canadian Pacific would show a substantial improvement in its balance sheet as well, but in early 1895 he was forced to concede that times ahead continued to look dark. The economic climate was so grim, in fact, that on February 16, Stephen dispatched a coded cablegram to Van Horne suggesting that the CPR suspend payment of its proposed dividend. "Nothing can now restore lost confidence but proof that Company can earn enough money to pay all its obligations," he gloomily predicted.[608] One week later, at a Saturday meeting, the CPR directors decided to reduce 1894's half-yearly dividend on the preference shares from 4 percent to 2 1/2 percent and to stop paying a dividend on the common shares altogether. "This decision," commented the *Montreal Gazette*, "has not been unexpected. The decline in the earnings of the company has been almost continuous for more than a year past, and although all economy consistent with efficient service has been practised, it has been found impossible to realize profits that would justify the payment of a dividend on the common stock for the last half year."[609] According to Toronto's *Globe,* it was a "source of gratification to the general public that the energetic management [had] not descended to the too common practice of paying dividends to the impoverishment of capital account." The devout Liberal paper went on to opine that "it would have been a great mistake to have allowed the road to fall from its high state of efficiency and excellent condition that the shareholders might draw dividends on their stock."[610] Certainly there was no pillorying of Van Horne and the CPR management in these quarters or along Montreal's St. James Street and Toronto's Bay Street.

Whether it was because he had lost all faith in Van Horne's management or because he was setting out to help paralyze the CPR and advance the interests of the Great Northern, Stephen began advising CPR shareholders to sell. In this he was joined by Van Horne's confidant Thomas Skinner. Reliable evidence of the treachery of these men has been provided by no less an authority than Van Horne's British friend R.M. Horne-Payne:

> One morning, on arrival at my office, I found two ladies who had invested in a few C.P.R. shares at my advice waiting in different rooms to ask me whether they had not better sell at once in consequence of advice they had received

from Mount Stephen. After reassuring them, I went across to Skinner's office to enquire what it all meant.

On my approaching the subject Skinner became very excited, and in effect said the C.P.R. was in a critical condition, and could not avoid bankruptcy, and that the accounts rendered by Sir William were misleading and dishonest, especially in the matter of a certain Reserve Fund. He applied the epithet of "old blackguard" to Sir William.

A heated altercation ensued, and although I have been forced to meet him on business from time to time, I have never spoken in a friendly way to Skinner from that day to this.[611]

Thanks to the machinations of individuals like Stephen and Skinner and rumours suggesting that CPR directors were selling short and organizing bear raids on the stock, share prices slid from $76 to $63 in less than two months and then plummeted to $35, an all-time low. They would have skidded even lower but for the purchases made by German capitalists, who were advised by Van Horne's friend Adolph Boissevain, the Dutch financier whose Amsterdam firm floated CPR shares in European financial markets.

Fortunately, by the autumn of 1895 business had recovered. Westbound traffic was starting to pick up, livestock shipments had increased, the harvest was good, and the Soo line was performing splendidly. "Indeed," Van Horne wrote Boissevain in October, "all the clouds in our sky seem to have disappeared. We are in very good shape for business although we are likely to be very short of freight cars and locomotives."[612] By 1896, gross and net earnings had almost returned to their 1892 levels. The CPR had reeled under the weight of hard times, but it had not collapsed. It had weathered the storm and, just as Van Horne had foreseen, would soon return to profitability.

The improvement of the CPR's financial position in 1896 was not the only development in that year calculated to improve Van Horne's outlook on life. Another was the federal Liberal Party's accession to power after an eighteen-year Conservative reign during which immigration, a field in which Van Horne naturally took a keen interest, received short shrift. Given his past performance, Van Horne might have been expected to intervene directly in the campaign of 1896, but he did not. This was in striking contrast to his deportment in the 1891 campaign, when reciprocity with the United States had been the central plank of the Liberal Party and trade policy the burning question. That campaign had seen Van Horne fling caution to the winds and dispatch a long letter vehemently denouncing reciprocity to the chairman of the Conservative Party in Montreal, Senator G.A. Dandurand. "I am well enough acquainted with the trade and industries of Canada," Van Horne had declared, "to know that unrestricted reciprocity would bring prostration and ruin." Realizing that he might be "accused of meddling in politics," he had added, "but with me this is a business question and not a political one, and it so vitally affects the interests that have been entrusted to me that I feel justified in expressing my opinion plainly; indeed, since the opposite views have been attributed to me, I feel bound to do so."[613]

This impulsive gesture returned to haunt Van Horne. In fact, the magnitude of his blunder had been driven home to him one morning in February 1891, when he had discovered, to his horror, that his letter had been reproduced in the *Gazette*. In the interests of damage control, he had asked Shaughnessy, a former politician, if it would be prudent to write another letter. His second-in-command immediately shot down this suggestion, contending that "nothing could now be done to modify the intense animosity of the Liberal Party who, if they came to power, would leave nothing undone to hamper and harass the Company."[614]

Since the CPR had already been tarred with a political brush, Shaughnessy contended that the company should come out into the open and render all possible assistance to the Conservatives. Van Horne had agreed, and having decided to throw the massive weight of their company and its purse behind the Conservatives, the two men had then set about organizing a highly effective piece of election machinery, "to which," Shaughnessy had later boasted, "Sir John Macdonald owed his success in that campaign."[615]

The CPR's fragrant partisanship had stirred the Liberal *Globe* to new heights of animosity against the CPR and Van Horne. "Mr. Van Horne," the paper had huffed, "is a very able man, but his fulminations carry little weight. Everyone knows that he is not an unbiased authority. The corporation, of which he is the head, has drawn $100,000,000 in cash from the public treasury, to say nothing of land grants, loans and other easements. It is the Tory government on wheels."[616]

At least one observer had been impressed by Van Horne's bold, frontal assault on the Liberals and his vigorous defence of the National Policy. Writing to the prime minister during the height of the 1891 campaign, Stephen had remarked, "I believe Van Horne really believes the best thing for Canada is a high wall between it and the United States. Van Horne's courage is greater than mine."[617] Van Horne, of course, had placed his faith in the National Policy; he truly believed that if the policy were replaced by one of unrestricted reciprocity Canada's infant manufacturing sector would be doomed and its economy ruined. Viewed in the eyes of critics, however, Van Horne's stance had been disingenuous and untenable. As the *Globe* had pointed out, while Van Horne had been trying to discourage trade with the United States, claiming that Yankees were poor and growing poorer and that trade with them would not be profitable, he had at the same time been investing "large sums" of his own money in "properties and business in Chicago."[618]

In the 1896 contest, by contrast, Van Horne and the CPR remained on the sidelines. Nevertheless, observers found it difficult to swallow his repeated denials of CPR intervention. Reflecting on this, Van Horne told Robert Jaffray of the *Globe* a few weeks later, "We were somewhat in the position of a girl who had once been whoring, but who had reformed and was trying to lead a correct life — it was difficult to make everybody believe it."[619] During the election campaign Van Horne also felt it necessary to assure Wilfrid Laurier, "I am doing my best to keep on the fence although it turns out to be a barbed wire one."[620]

As it turned out, the railway's reform was not quite complete, for in Winnipeg CPR personnel actively supported the Conservative candidate, Hugh John Macdonald, a CPR counsel and a personal friend of the company's officers in that city. In the fallout from the blatant soliciting, Van Horne was taken to task by at least one western Liberal politician, Joseph Martin, and probably by others. This prompted the CPR president to retort, "When we undertook to maintain a position on the fence it was not to be implied that we would not get down and kick any individual who might throw stones or rather eggs at us. We hold ourselves free to do that and neither the Liberal nor the Conservative party have a right to object."[621] Van Horne's ire, it would appear, had been raised by the demagoguery of Winnipeg's Liberal candidate, who, according to the CPR president, was blatantly hostile "to the Canadian Pacific Railway and everybody associated with it."[622]

But if Van Horne remained on the sidelines during the 1896 election it was not because he was not vitally interested in the outcome. Quite the contrary: he had a deep and abiding interest in the handling of several important issues, and he frequently approached politicians with his views and concerns about their treatment of questions that concerned him. Immigration, of course, was one of them.

Although nominally a Conservative, Van Horne deplored the Conservatives' tepid performance in recruiting immigrants. A strong proponent of immigration, he described the government's work in this area as "hardly visible" and devised a settlement scheme of his own. This called for the federal government to allocate $15 million to settling 12,000 British families in the Northwest. In spelling out his plan to Archer Baker, the CPR's general European traffic agent, Van Horne explained that the sum that he had in mind would provide each family with $1,250. This would pay for their transportation and furnish them with a "small but comfortable house of 3 or 4 rooms, a small stable, a team, a cow and enough implements and furniture etc to make a start with; as well, seed, a season's provisions and the cost of breaking, say 20 acres in advance of their coming." What remained would be left in the hands of the government, to be used to help the settlers over a bad season in case of misfortune. Betraying his contempt for politicians, Van Horne insisted that the administration of the undertaking be entrusted not to them but instead to three trustees, who would be "men of the highest standing."[623] Regrettably, the Conservative government never adopted his ambitious plan, and as a consequence Van Horne never saw this particular dream realized.

Since he fully expected the new Laurier government to give immigration the same short shrift, the immigration enthusiast used elements of his original plan in lobbying the Liberals, mounting a campaign to have immigration "administered by a special commission of three men in whom the entire country would have confidence, removing this work from the jurisdiction of any individual minister and from the soporific influence of the civil service."[624] Fortunately, Van Horne's fears were somewhat misplaced. Clifford Sifton, appointed minister of the interior in 1896 at the age of thirty-six, proved to be a dynamic member of Laurier's Cabinet, fully prepared to dedicate his relentless drive and celebrated energy to his powerful portfolio. A born organizer, he quickly set about revamping the lacklustre immigration service that he had inherited and filling the empty Prairies with suitable agriculturists, many of whom came not from Canada's traditional sources, the United States and northwestern Europe, but from central and eastern Europe. Sifton had the added distinction of being a western politician who was willing to shed the typical westerner's reflexive suspicion or hatred of the CPR and cooperate with the company in such mutually advantageous areas as grain handling and the movement of immigrants. Van Horne thus had good grounds for admiring and respecting this most important member of Cabinet, second only to Laurier himself. Indeed, after the Liberals swept into office, Van Horne wrote to his newly acquired Liberal friend, James Edgar, "I hope Mr. Laurier will realize that Sifton is the only man who can settle the school question and that he will make sure of having him in his cabinet."[625]

As much as he respected Sifton, however, Van Horne took strong exception to Canada's choice of immigrants during this period. In his typically blunt fashion, he outlined his concerns to a parade of newspaper editors. One of these was a personal friend, Sir John Willison, editor of the *Globe* from 1890 to 1902 and of the *Toronto News* from 1903 to 1917 as well as advisor to Laurier before converting to the Conservative side and becoming advisor to Prime Minister Robert Borden. Van Horne's friendship with Willison dated from 1895, when Sir John had published a long and glowing article on western Canada's potential and a grateful Van Horne had promptly ordered 250,000 copies of the issue in which it appeared.[626]

When corresponding with Willison, Van Horne loved to pontificate on controversial issues of the day, which, of course, included immigration, a perennial hot topic. Of particular concern to him was the growing anti-Chinese agitation then sweeping the Pacific Coast. It had originated, claimed Van Horne, "a good many years ago with the saloon-keepers of San Francisco, whose places were not visited by the Chinese and who conceived the idea that if the Chinese labourers were replaced by white men they would sell more liquor."[627] Diligently fanned by the worst class of local politicians, the movement had spread north along the coast until it had reached British Columbia, where it was growing steadily.

Van Horne feared that the anti-Chinese agitation would culminate in increasingly restrictive legislation against Chinese immigration, a prospect that he could not stomach. Like other Canadian industrialists, Van Horne wanted access to a plentiful supply of cheap, hardworking labour, and the Chinese fitted the bill admirably. "We must have in British Columbia a good supply of digging machines which, unlike steam shovels, can climb hills and go down into mines. These can be most cheaply and readily had from China," he informed Willison when trying to persuade him not to adopt an anti-Chinese stand in the *Globe*. To reinforce his argument for admitting Chinese immigrants, Van Horne pointed out that the Chinese:

> ... have an infinite contempt for all people but their own, and show not the least disposition to adopt our ways, even when they are here among us. As I see it, it is an argument in favour of their coming, rather than against it, that they do not become citizens or permanent residents of the country. That, it seems to me, is decidedly in their favour as against the Sicilians, Danubian Jews, and other worthless European people, who are let in without a word of objection ....[628]

There was nothing underhanded about Van Horne's relationship with Willison and the *Globe*. Without question, his dealings with this well-known publisher and his paper were above board. The same cannot be said, however, of the railway president's involvement with the *Call* and the *Manitoba Free Press*. Van Horne had become involved with the *Manitoba Free Press* in 1888, when he and Donald Smith became its proprietors. Desperately short of funds, the *Free Press* had earlier accepted a five-year loan from Donald Smith, for which the CPR director received 796 shares as collateral.[629] A few months later, Van Horne, who had by now succeeded Stephen as CPR president, was persuaded to purchase the organ. Lest word of the directors' association with the paper leak out and trigger an avalanche of criticism, the deal was kept a secret, albeit an open secret to any well-informed observer. Nevertheless, a letter to Sir John A. Macdonald makes it clear that subterfuge made Van Horne distinctly uncomfortable. When advising the prime minister of the pending sale of the *Call* to the *Free Press*, Van Horne reported that he had poured all he could into the money-losing *Call*, but to no avail. The paper had failed to do good "either to the Government or the Company." He continued, "I feel sure that we will be able to keep the Free Press in hand but that of course should be a profound secret as should our past dealings with the 'Call.' I would not have that known for the world — it is something I am very much ashamed of."[630]

As it turned out, Van Horne would have little success in getting W.F. Luxton, the *Free Press*'s editor, to comply with his wishes. In fact, Luxton inspired one of the most brutal letters ever written by the CPR president. As a man of the people and a sincere radical, Luxton was not amenable to taking direction from capitalists. Even Van Horne admitted as much when he informed Edgar Dewdney, lieutenant-governor of the Northwest Territories, "I have once in a while been able to reason with Luxton, but I gave him up long ago. In my later attempts I have not even been able to save my dignity."[631] Although he was repeatedly accused of editing a CPR organ, Luxton nevertheless persisted in attacking Manitoba's Liberal government under Thomas Greenway — with which, meanwhile, Van Horne was attempting to establish friendly relations. The editor eventually sealed his fate, when, without consulting the paper's shareholders, he entered into secret negotiations with representatives of the Greenway government regarding the paper's reorganization.

After news of this betrayal reached Van Horne, Luxton was unceremoniously ejected from the *Free Press*. The journalist was as deeply devoted to the newspaper as Van Horne was to the CPR, and he was not too proud to make several attempts to regain the paper's editorship, all of which Van Horne spurned. Finally, the CPR president relented and arranged for the *Free Press's* business manager to approach Luxton with an offer for his return. The terms of the offer were such, however, that Luxton had to shed his last ounce of pride to accept them. He sent Van Horne a copy of his letter of refusal to the business manager, and the CPR president shot back this response to him:

> I trust that you will read to the end what I have to say, for it is perhaps the last letter I will ever write to you and I would not take the trouble did I not have some regard for you and a sincere desire to help you.
>
> I think you are the damnedest — I was going to say the damnedest fool I have ever known, but I can't say that because I have known two or three others who completed their record by dying in their foolishness, while your record is still incomplete and there is a faint chance that you may yet make a turn and end under suspicion of having had some sense ...[632]

Such bluntness would not have served Van Horne well in the semi-diplomatic role that he was called upon to play from time to time. When acting as a quasi-ambassador to Washington Van Horne had to curb his more aggressive instincts and hone his diplomatic skills, not one of his strong points. His friendship with leading American senators and members of the McKinley administration frequently led the new Laurier government to ask him to probe the Yankee frame of mind during a period of increasing tension between Canada and the United States. The drastic McKinley tariff of 1891 and the still more uncompromising Dingley tariff of 1897 ranked high on the list of irritants poisoning the relationship between the two countries. So did the Bering Sea dispute, a disagreement that originated in the mid-1880s from the rival claims of the American and Canadian fur seal industries. It was the tariff question, however, that directly involved Van Horne in his role as unofficial Canadian government emissary to Washington. After introducing the two-tiered Fielding tariff in 1897, the Laurier government appealed to Van Horne to ascertain if the American government would institute reprisals or admit Canadian goods at a rate equivalent to the minimum Canadian tariff. His mission completed, Van Horne informed Ottawa that there was no possibility of the United States entertaining any reciprocity proposals.[633]

Always didactic, Van Horne could not resist the urge to advise Laurier of his views on the export of certain agricultural products. When the federal government was seeking a reduction of American duties on hay and potatoes, he informed the prime minister:

> Exporting hay is a good deal like living off one's own blood. I hold that no community can do it and prosper and that the conditions with such a community must constantly grow worse ... If the export of hay from the Province of Quebec could be absolutely stopped and the farmers of that province taught (as might easily be done) how to utilize their land to the best advantage, a few years would make them as prosperous as those of the Province of Ontario Peninsula.[634]

Van Horne's services were also enlisted in the potentially dangerous Alaska Boundary dispute. Various attempts had been made to determine the boundary between Canada and Alaska after the United States acquired the territory in 1867. By 1898, the boundary was basically agreed upon except for a stretch of the line that ran south of Mount St. Elias in the panhandle, and this was where the problem arose. With the discovery of gold in the Klondike in 1896, this portion of the boundary became subject to dispute between the two countries. Canadian and American interests were in conflict in two places in the panhandle: Observatory Inlet and Lynn Canal (especially the latter). The Canadians believed that if the confusing provisions of the Anglo-Russian Treaty of 1825 were implemented Canada would acquire control of the headwaters of the Lynn Canal, an important route to the gold fields. On the other hand, no matter what the treaty said, the United States was in de facto control of the Lynn Canal headwaters and hence of all the trade to and from the Yukon. In other words, more than just the determination of a boundary line was at stake. Of utmost importance was which of the two countries controlled the huge trade in goods and gold into and out of the Yukon.[635]

Prior to heading off to Washington in late 1897, Van Horne got in touch with his friend and business associate Russell Alger. To the honest but hopelessly incompetent American secretary of war, Van Horne wrote, "I would be glad of a confidential hint from you as to the filing of plans covering the United States end of the line from the Lynn Canal in Alaska to the Five Fingers Rapids..."[636] On his return from Washington that December, Van Horne informed Laurier, "The authorities at Washington wish to consult with the Dominion authorities concerning Yukon matters, and, among other things, I understand that they wish to get permission to send United States troops to the Fort Cudahy district through Canadian territory. This will afford a good opportunity to open up the other two questions Mr. Sifton is so anxious to have settled ..."[637]

Following his return to Canada, the Laurier government's emissary also saw fit to advise Sir Charles Tupper about conditions in the Klondike mining community. In his letter to the leader of the Opposition, Van Horne warned that even a seemingly trivial ill-advised move by Ottawa could trigger another Boston Tea Party, only this time in the Yukon. Every male entering the territory, Van Horne pointed out, was armed with a rifle and a revolver, and 95 percent of them had no interest in or sympathy for Canada. Moreover, none of them liked the federal government's levy on gold. As soon as their numbers were large enough, these hardy, self-reliant miners would refuse to "pay the royalty to the Dominion gov't or anybody else." Lacking a "big enough army," Canada, Van Horne predicted, would be powerless to enforce the law.[638]

No sooner was Van Horne's mission completed than James Edgar let his friend know that he believed him largely responsible for the Americans' renewed interest in cooperation. "I rather suspect your handiwork in the most cordial way [as the reason] they are all working with Sifton about the Klondike matter," wrote the prominent Liberal, whose warm friendship with Van Horne had helped keep the CPR out of the Conservative camp in the 1896 campaign.[639]

Van Horne's intervention in the Klondike question occurred in the same year, 1897, that he was persuaded to relinquish the Duluth and Winnipeg to his old adversary, Jim Hill. Van Horne was bent on retaining the road despite the copious amounts of CPR money it was gobbling up. "The D. & W. is the best property we have and this year will demonstrate that," he wrote to Thomas Skinner as late as April 1896. "It is moreover our only weapon of defence against the Great Northern and Northern Pacific and we must keep it." Still, despite the force of Van Horne's arguments, Stephen's contrary view prevailed in the executive committee, and some months later the road became a Hill possession.[640] Hoping to salvage some advantage from the deal, Van Horne secured an undertaking from Hill that he would give the Duluth, South Shore and Atlantic (the Soo) his eastbound traffic. Hill, however, chose not to observe the agreement.

"A blunder of the worst possible description," Thomas Shaughnessy would later describe the Duluth and Winnipeg transaction. When recalling the money-losing undertaking, he placed the blame for it squarely on Van Horne:

Van Horne was induced to invest a very large sum of the Company's money in this enterprise without having any of the information to warrant him doing so. The condition of D & W affairs were misrepresented to him from the beginning, with the result that in 1894 we were compelled to pass our dividend for the last half of 1894, although one year previously the Shareholders had been assured that a fund of Four Million dollars had been deposited in the Bank to meet dividend requirements. A large part of this sum had been invested in the unfortunate D & W and the Company had little to show for it, excepting lawsuits.[641]

The CPR's relinquishment of the Duluth and Winnipeg to Hill intensified competition between the Canadian Pacific and Hill's lines. In the United States, the CPR's Soo line hounded the Great Northern mercilessly, prompting Hill to harass the CPR in ore-rich British Columbia, more in mischief and in the hope of forcing an overall compromise than in the interests of constructive competition.[642] Eventually Jim Hill would build eleven spurs into the province and lock horns with the CPR in the Kootenays, where the two companies engaged in a game of charters, buyouts, mergers, and bluffs.

Hill's challenge and various other pressures convinced the CPR of the wisdom of opening up the southern reaches of British Columbia and the Okanagan Lakes and purchasing mines and refineries in the Kootenays. In response to the company's moves, the humorous weekly tabloid *Grip*, published in Toronto, declared:

> There is a great deal of uneasiness manifested in British Columbia over the grabbing policy now being carried out by the C.P.R. with the consent of the Provincial Government. The Napoleonic Van Horne (W.C. Van Horne, principal builder of the C.P.R.) seems to have set his heart on taking possession of the entire mining region in the "Sea of Mountains," and several great slices of territory have already been reserved in connection with the railway to the Kootenay district, which is, of course, controlled by the Canadian Pacific.[643]

The CPR was also persuaded that the Crow's Nest Pass should be built. Van Horne had anticipated that mining developments in the Kootenay region of southeastern British Columbia in the late 1880s and 1890s would encourage American rival carriers to divert mining traffic to the United States. Indeed, he feared a "permanent diversion southwards of the greater part of the ores of the Kootenay and adjacent districts" if a Crow's Nest Pass railway were not built without delay.[644] He therefore began as early as 1893 to press the government for the building of a railway from Lethbridge, Alberta, through the Crow's Nest Pass to Nelson, British Columbia. For several years Van Horne had zealously pursued this goal, knowing that the project could only be viable if the federal government provided a substantial subsidy. Initially, he made little headway, but following the Liberals' resounding victory in 1896, the stage was set for serious negotiations with Ottawa. The following year, in September 1897, these culminated in a deal with the Laurier administration. In the Crow's Nest Pass Agreement, solidified by federal statute, the Canadian Pacific received a hefty subsidy to help in the construction of a railway through the Crow's Nest Pass. In return, the company undertook to reduce its rates on grain shipped to Thunder Bay and its charges on many westbound items. The company was bound by statute never to raise these rates. This, of course, would have enormous long-term implications, but for the present Van Horne could exclaim enthusiastically over the mining traffic that the Crow's Nest Pass Railway would bring the CPR.

Unfortunately, success did not crown Van Horne's efforts to realize another cherished goal, the establishment of a fast Atlantic steamship service. Year after frustrating year, the "Atlantic Steamship question," as Van Horne phrased it, weighed on his mind, involving him in long hours of study and fruitless negotiation. To Prime Minister Sir John Abbott, the former CPR counsel, he wrote, in November 1891:

> Mr. Shaughnessy's necessary departure for China this week which will leave me alone during the coming winter has compelled me to hurry around and clear up outside matters and I have been unable until now to give any time to the Atlantic Steamship question ... I have studied this Atlantic question with a great deal of care for the past eight years; have discussed it hundreds of times with steamship people of large experience; have considered it in every way from our railway standpoint, and I am satisfied that you will never be able to induce anybody to put money into a trans-Atlantic line which must make its absolute terminus at Halifax during half of the year even if you increase the subsidy vastly beyond anything that has yet been suggested or discussed ...[645]

By general consensus, the CPR, rather than the Grand Trunk, was the logical railway to operate a fast Atlantic service, but much to Van Horne's chagrin, efforts to secure such a service for Canada would not bear fruit during his regime. Not until 1902, when Shaughnessy was president, would a modified version of Van Horne's dream begin to unfold. In that year, the CPR submitted an offer to the Canadian government to provide what the company believed to be "the best and most practical service under existing conditions."[646] Following the conclusion of successful negotiations, the CPR, in 1903, purchased eight passenger and seven cargo liners from the Elder Dempster Company. With a speed of between twelve and thirteen knots, none of these vessels approached Van Horne's vision of "twenty knots to Canada," but the CPR did, at long last, have the nucleus of a fleet with which to begin operating its own Atlantic service.

To discerning friends and colleagues alike, it was readily apparent in the 1890s that Van Horne's enthusiasm for his job was waning. A highly critical Shaughnessy would later inform Walter Vaughan: "During the last seven or eight years of his Presidency, Van Horne's loss of interest in his work was most pronounced. He had ceramics, pictures, and other things artistic on his mind almost continuously, and a wandering artist, of whom there was a drove always following his trail, could take his time and attention from Canadian Pacific matters of great importance."[647]

This loss of interest in the job can undoubtedly be ascribed to several setbacks, notable among them Van Horne's failure to establish a fast Atlantic steamship service, the fallout from the financial panic of 1893, and the mortifying surrender of the Duluth and Winnipeg Railway to Hill. There was also his deteriorating health, brought on by years of overwork and self-indulgence in food and smoking. More than anything else, though, it was probably the lack of scope for his creativity that robbed Van Horne of his enthusiasm for the presidency and let competing interests interfere with the day-to-day demands of the job. Van Horne was essentially a "constructor" who loved building for its own sake. Once the CPR was nearing completion he began to lose interest in it and to find management details more and more distasteful. The music and drama critic, newspaper editor, and author Augustus Bridle revealed just how perceptive he was when he observed:

> Whatever the philosophy of Van Horne it was probably
> not equal to the task of administering the system which he
> had done the major share to create. He had shot his bolt

in projecting the system. To carry it further, with all its bewildering complications of freights and tariffs, steamship lines, palace hotels, irrigation advantures, land policies, immigration agencies, and concurrent wrestling with both governments and Railway commission, needed the hand of a man with greater concentration of purpose and more patient with conflicting details. To manage the CPR in competition with other transcontinental systems was no work for a man of Gargantuan hobbies ...[648]

In the final years of his presidency Van Horne talked increasingly of retiring, only to be thwarted by Shaughnessy, who was "anxious to see our affairs in fairly good shape during his Presidency."[649] In 1897, Van Horne told the president of the Soo line that he did not intend to leave the Canadian Pacific until "it was quite out of the woods."[650] By 1899, he believed that that condition had been fulfilled. The CPR was paying substantial dividends and its earnings were largely exceeding its dividend requirements; moreover, its stock was selling at par.

Before resigning from the CPR presidency, however, Van Horne decided to treat himself to an extended vacation trip. As a possible destination, Japan had a lot of appeal and had, in fact, been beckoning him persistently for years. Van Horne knew that he was guaranteed a royal reception there, thanks to the inauguration of the Pacific steamship service, which had earned him the gratitude of the Japanese emperor and government officials. As one of Japan's best friends, he was highly respected by such well-known figures as the Marquis Ito, a Choshu native who had drafted Japan's first constitution and then become the country's first prime minister in 1885. "The Marquis Ito has often spoken of you, and with great estime," reported an Imperial Government Railways official to Van Horne in 1898.[651] Van Horne, for his part, regarded the marquis as the greatest statesman of his time. Despite his many Japanese friendships, however, Van Horne had qualms about being on the receiving end of lavish attention and hospitality. He disliked ostentation of any kind and cringed at the thought of the ceremonial observances that would mark a visit to that country. As a result, he decided to postpone a visit to that far-distant land and travel instead to southern California, hoping that its heat would "burn out" his bronchitis.

With a party of friends, he set off in the *Saskatchewan* in April 1899 for San Francisco, planning to be away three or four weeks. En route, they stopped off at Salt Lake City, where Van Horne was warmly received by Brigham Young the Second and other Mormon Church officials.

"Some of their people are settled in Alberta and more are going and it had been reported at Salt Lake City that I had been kind in some way to those who had gone there and therefore everybody wished to show their appreciation of it," he wrote Addie.[652] In San Francisco, John Mackay, the Dublin-born head of the Commercial Cable Company, booked the finest rooms in the luxurious Palace Hotel for them, stocked them with fine cigars, and adamantly refused to allow anyone to pay for anything, be it a week's hotel accommodation or newspapers. Not content with this outpouring of generosity, Mackay also set aside the whole of each day to escorting members of the party around San Francisco and introducing them to "everybody" that they did not already know. Among the leading citizens that Van Horne met was a Miss Flood, who invited him and Mackay to dinner one Friday evening. Van Horne did not fail to note that this was "quite a rare event in San Francisco" and "that the enormous home was in pretty good taste throughout which [he could not] say of the other great houses [he] saw."[653]

After a week of festivities in San Francisco, Van Horne's friends returned to the East, and Van Horne, along with John Mackay and the manager of the Southern Pacific Railroad, took the train to Monterey, stopping first at Palo Alto, thirty-five miles south of San Francisco. In this infant city, one day to be known as the birthplace of Silicon Valley, he marvelled at Mrs. Stanford's great stock farm "with its hundreds of famous horses" and Stanford University's magnificent buildings and grounds. If McGill University were to be compared to Stanford, it would look "like a lot of barns in a barnyard," Van Horne grumbled to Addie, noting that when Stanford's edifices were completed they would be unequalled.[654] At Alma, another stop on the trip south, Van Horne lunched with his close friend Otto Meysenburg, now a retired businessman. It was an occasion to savour as the two men's friendship probably dated from the early 1870s, when Van Horne had lived in St. Louis, Meysenburg's hometown until he moved to Chicago.

While in Monterey, Van Horne experienced a revelation of sorts. As he expressed it:

> I went out on the verandah [of his hotel] and sat down, and smoked a big cigar. Then I got up, walked around the verandah, and looked at the scenery. It was very fine. Then I sat down again and smoked another cigar. Then up again; another walk around the verandah, and more scenery. It was still very fine. I sat down again, and smoked another cigar. Then I jumped up, and telephoned for my car to be

coupled to the next train; and, by jinks, I was never so happy in my life as I was when I struck the C.P.R. again.[655]

Shortly after his return to Montreal, Van Horne took the bold step he had been contemplating for ages: on June 12, 1899, he resigned from the CPR presidency. The move was not a complete surprise to outside observers as they had been anticipating his resignation for some time. Their suspicions had earlier been confirmed when a newspaper reporter, acting in response to rumours, had inveigled an admission from Van Horne that he intended to resign. No date had been supplied. Nevertheless, the published account of the interview precipitated a sell-off of Canadian Pacific stock. In both London and New York, the price of the company's shares dropped several points. Confidence in the CPR was only restored when its officers issued a denial of the newspaper story.[656]

The denial would not stand for long. The occasion chosen for Van Horne's formal resignation was the regular monthly board meeting of the CPR directors held in Windsor Station. When they assembled in June, the directors accepted Sir William's resignation as president and then proceeded to elect Thomas Shaughnessy to succeed him. In a press release, Van Horne paid his successor a handsome tribute, noting that "one of my chief reasons for asking our directors to permit me to relinquish the duties of the office of president was to secure the well earned promotion of Mr. Shaughnessy, whose services to the company have been beyond estimation, and whom I look upon as all that could be wished for as the chief executive officer of a great corporation — honourable, capable, energetic and fair-dealing."[657] Van Horne would retain his directorship and be appointed to the newly created office of chairman of the board. Since the chairman was an *ex officio* member of the CPR executive committee, he could continue to play a significant role in formulating company policy.

When Van Horne had come to the conclusion that it was time for him to go, he had sat down and written a lengthy letter to Lord Strathcona, expressing his concern about the horrendously heavy workload that Shaughnessy would inherit. To prevent his successor from "breaking down," and plunging the company into disarray, Van Horne suggested that the CPR adopt the practice of major American railways and appoint several vice-presidents. "In our own case we [the board of directors] all think that three vice-presidents should be provided for — one for general executive duties, one in charge of traffic and one in charge of operation ... The plan which finds approval with the Board is to make me Chairman of the Board, with duties chiefly of an advisory nature and to make Mr. Shaughnessy President."[658]

With Shaughnessy's elevation to the presidency, and as other qualified individuals became available, Van Horne's proposal was gradually put into effect.

Van Horne could regard with justifiable pride and satisfaction the legacy that he turned over to Shaughnessy. His high opinion of the road was revealed in his report to CPR shareholders at the annual meeting in the spring of 1898:

> An analysis of the traffic of the various sections of the main line, the branch lines, and the auxiliary services on the sea, lakes and rivers, shows that practically no mistakes have been made in the development of the system so far as we have gone. Some things have had to be done ahead of time in order to protect our future, and we have had to wait for a good many vacant spaces on our lines to become productive, but nearly all these spaces are now yielding revenue and practically all our branch lines are self-supporting.[659]

In spite of the prolonged depression that gripped Canada during most of his term as president of the CPR, Van Horne managed to improve and expand the system significantly. In fact, by the end of 1899, the railway's mileage had increased to seven thousand miles. If the controlled American lines were included, the increase from 1888 exceeded 3,500 miles, or 65 percent.[660] In summing up his achievements as CPR president, the *Globe*, in an unsigned editorial, written, no doubt by Van Horne's friend John Willison, said, "Under the management of the retiring President this great Canadian enterprise has prospered beyond the expectations of its most sanguine supporters a few years ago. Much can be said of the public bequests in both money and land, but great as they were they would not have carried the road through its period of adversity without a courageous, energetic, and, above all things, enterprising direction."[661] A no less enthusiastic assessment of Van Horne's presidency was provided by the editors of the 1935 edition of the *National Encyclopedia of Canadian Biography*. They concluded that during these years "the road sprang into first and permanent prominence among the struggling roads of Canada ..."[662] Despite competing interests and his deteriorating health, Van Horne had indeed succeeded admirably in making the Canadian Pacific Railway a powerful force in the Canadian economy.

Chapter Eleven
Art for Art's Sake

V an Horne had a deep love of beauty and art, a love that dated from the days of his childhood, when he had drawn pictures on the whitewashed walls of the family home in Chelsea. Now, whenever time permitted, he took up one of his favourite pursuits: painting. At Covenhoven he retired to a large, well-lit studio to paint realistic, somewhat ethereal landscapes rich in browns and yellows, frequently inspired by the primeval woods, fields, and shores of Minister's Island. A rapid worker, he would frequently complete his canvases — usually large oils — in a single evening from notes made earlier in the day. He did not labour over his work or spend much time preparing for it since it was his firmly held conviction that great art was the product of feeling, not intellect. As he himself expressed it, with his customary bluntness, "There is no place for intellect in art. Art is wholly a matter of feeling. As intellect enters art goes out ... All of the great artists who acquired temporary fame but subsequently lost the esteem of the world were intellectual. Many of the great artists have been weak-minded or lunatics, or sodden with drink or debauchery."[663]

Whether Van Horne truly believed that rapidity of execution made for spontaneous and inspired art is open to question. There is no doubt, however, that he revelled in the speed with which he completed his canvases. Nothing gave him greater pleasure than to astonish his friends with the revelation that he had completed a picture in one, two, or three hours, or even in half an hour. "Sir William," reported his friend Robert Wickenden, who frequently joined him in painting sessions, "wanted to paint by telegraph."[664]

On one occasion some admiring friends were dumbfounded to learn that a large canvas depicting birch trees in their autumn glory had been completed in only eight hours and, as was his customary practice, entirely indoors under artificial light. "Yes, but I know what a birch tree looks like," Van Horne replied in response to their exclamations. "Why should I sit outside in the cold to do it. I know the dip of its branches; I know the curl of its leaves; I know the colour of it where the sun touches it in autumn."[665] Sir Martin Conway, the English art expert and alpinist, echoed these sentiments when summing up his friend's appreciation of trees. "His trees are not inventions but old friends," wrote Sir Martin in an article for *The Connoisseur*. "He knows a whole army of them between Montreal and Vancouver, and can draw the likeness of any one you ask for. It is in their autumn livery that he loves them best, or rising naked out of the snowy mantle of winter."[666]

Van Horne signed most of his work with his initials, WCVH. Occasionally he substituted "Enroh Nav." This enabled him to indulge in one of his favourite jokes, passing off a work of his as either a masterpiece executed by a prominent artist or a work painted by an insignificant one. Robert Paterson, a young Scot and an amateur artist, was probably one of a handful of viewers who was not completely taken in by this ruse. According to Paterson's account, when he visited Van Horne's Montreal home he had stopped transfixed in front of a canvas signed Enroh Nav.

"Who's this by?" he had asked.

"Oh that's by an artist of very little account," his host had replied.

"Yes, but it's very clever — it reminds me of the work of L'Hermitte, the French landscape painter, but it's signed Enroh Nav. Oh, it's your own. By jove, that's good, I didn't realize you were a painter — this has ability." Van Horne had chuckled, had looked pleased, and with a "humph" had passed on.[667]

Sometimes Van Horne's Montreal studio — located in an immense attic lit by arc lights — was shared by Canadian artist Percy Woodcock, who has provided us with a vivid snapshot of Van Horne the self-taught artist at work:

> Van Horne painted as birds sing, as naturally and enjoyably. It was a form of relief to his creative faculties that were continually seeking an outlet. In the studio his railway work was put entirely behind him — except in 1885, when he was so worried about the road's condition that sometimes in the middle of a joyous bit of painting the thought of the road would come to him like a shock and

hang over him, holding him totally absorbed and still. But when he presently threw it off, you would think that he had no other interest in life than painting. To live close to a personality so winning and so strong was as surely to become submerged in it as the women of his household were ... I became so attached to him that in our repeated talks on art I found myself leaning too strongly towards his views. His makeup was so positive that he exerted a tremendous influence on anyone less positive. I wanted to keep my art, whatever it should be, as my own, and I often had to deliberately stay away from his studio until I left for Europe.[668]

Because of the demands of his job, Van Horne, when in Montreal, usually painted at night under artificial light. According to artist Robert J. Wickenden, his friend compensated for the resulting false chromatic effects by paying more attention to his colour combinations. While doing so, he comforted himself with the belief that while the "surrounding majority of finer minds [were] asleep his benefitted by the stimulus of their liberated magnetism."[669] Whether or not such "liberated magnetism" played a role in his work, the fact remains that he was not static.

When sketching outdoors at St. Andrews, Van Horne was sometimes accompanied by George Innes, Sr., the American Romantic artist noted for the poetic, mystical landscapes of his later years. Innes, not surprisingly, found one of his choice subjects in a Passamaquoddy Bay bathed in moonlight. Van Horne, it seems, was likewise inspired, producing a canvas entitled "Moonlight on Passamaquoddy Bay."[670]

Scottish-born G. Horne Russell, an artist who churned out publicity material for the CPR but who was noted chiefly for his portraits of prominent Canadians, was another painting companion. So, too, was Canadian artist William Hope, R.C.A. Hope lived on the Bar Road in an Edward Maxwell – designed house that boasted an attractive painting studio where "gentlemen artists," but no women, sometimes met. One wonders if this select circle included large, burly, cigar-smoking Van Horne, eagerly delivering his firmly held convictions on art and doling out generous gobs of advice to other artists and collectors.

Although he loved to paint landscapes and found inspiration from one end of Canada to the other, Van Horne did not restrict himself to this genre. Occasionally he ventured into the realm of portraiture, sometimes without having his subject sit for him. Van Horne did a portrait of Cleo de Merode, the celebrated Parisian opera dancer, although he had never met her. The incredibly beautiful dancer so fascinated him that he painted her portrait with the aid of photographs.[671]

In the 1970s, when fifteen of Van Horne's oil canvases were offered for sale at the Robert Manuge Gallery in Halifax, restorer and artist Dusan Kadlec commented that the best of the tycoon's work was superb. Kadlec was obviously moved by the scope of Van Horne's vision. "He had an inner quality ... looked at big things in a special way and interpreted what he saw in a powerful manner ... and he was a genius in composition."[672] This, of course, was not surprising since even as a young man Van Horne had been a skilled draftsman and had daily used pencil and pen to convey ideas.

Although his work was decidedly uneven in quality, there is no question that much of it was, in the words of that seminal British art critic and friend of Van Horne, Roger Fry, "marvellously effective and on the spot ..."[673] Some canvases, perhaps only a few, were even outstanding in their portrayal of nature. Nevertheless, friends could not persuade him to exhibit publicly. He only painted, he claimed, for his own enjoyment and for that of his family and a few favoured friends. Today, five of his oils and one of his watercolours are in the National Gallery of Canada's collection.[674] Another twenty-seven of his works, some donated by his estate and ten by Imperial Oil Ltd., form part of the province of New Brunswick's art collection.[675]

Given his love of art and his instinct for collecting, Van Horne quite naturally took up the pastime of collecting art, a hobby that he shared with James Jerome Hill. In this respect Van Horne was typical of many late-nineteenth-century North American gentlemen of wealth, some of whom sought to veneer their *arrivisme* with the cultural trappings of the Old World. Many of these were American "smokestack" titans who had amassed huge fortunes in railroads, industry, and finance during the period of aggressive expansion that followed the Civil War. In fact, the flow of European art into the United States between 1870 and the First World War paralleled the flood of human immigrants that reached a peak in the United States, as it did in Canada, in 1913. Many aristocratic families in Great Britain and Europe had an excess of ancestry but a dearth of cash and they were eager to sell their Old Masters to new American magnates who had an abundance of cash but lacked ancestry. The purchasers of these canvases and sculptures — multimillionaires like J. Pierpont Morgan (who qualified for inclusion in both the old and the new elites), Henry

Clay Frick, Clarence Mackay, and P.A.B. Widener — filled their homes with countless real and occasionally dubious masterpieces that they had obtained with the help of international art dealers. The most celebrated of these was Joseph Duveen. Less well-known, though one of the most prominent members of this select group, was international art dealer R.F. Knoedler, the first European dealer to open a showroom in New York and one of several dealers whom Van Horne dealt with.[676]

Montreal, then Canada's leading centre of commerce, also spawned its share of notable art collectors. In addition to Van Horne, they included such distinguished Canadians as his CPR colleagues Lord Strathcona and R.B. Angus, CPR construction boss James Ross, and Charles Hosmer. Also heading the pack of dedicated collectors were Sir George Drummond, a politician and financier who became one of Canada's most influential men as president of the Bank of Montreal, and Edward Black Greenshields, financier, Bank of Montreal director, co-founder of the Royal Trust, and head of the largest dry goods firm at the turn of the century. It has always been acknowledged, though, that Van Horne amassed the most outstanding Canadian collection of his day. And he did so with his customary self-confidence, audacity, and independent judgment.

Goaded by his insatiable curiosity and love of acquisition, Van Horne seized every opportunity to study and acquire art (he wrote in reference to a monumental book on Corot that R.F. Knoedler had sent him from Paris, "It is a perfect mine of information and I am exceedingly glad to have it").[677] He built up a comprehensive library on art history, greedily absorbed details of the lives of favourite artists, and scooped up coveted paintings on his many business trips to the world's art centres. He would purchase only works that he had fallen in love with, for as he once informed a Montreal friend, "A picture that you do not feel you really want is always an incubus and a source of dissatisfaction."[678]

It is difficult to establish exactly when Van Horne started assembling a collection. The diaries of pioneer American art dealer Samuel P. Avery record that he purchased a Theodule Ribot for six hundred francs in Paris from a Van Horne in 1871.[679] It is possible that William Cornelius Van Horne sold a Ribot to Avery in 1871, but since he was then only twenty-eight and there is no evidence that he visited Paris before settling in Montreal, it is highly unlikely that he was the party referred to in the Avery diary. It is much more probable that Van Horne began collecting — at least seriously — in the mid-1880s when he was living in Canada's largest metropolis and pulling in a large CPR salary. Certainly by 1892 he had acquired enough confidence as a collector to begin cataloguing his most prized paintings in a notebook, which is now in the archives of the Montreal Museum of Fine Arts. Its auspicious title reads: "Catalogue of My Oil Paintings at 6 December 1892. (This book contains only those which I regard as of superior class)."

On the frequent trips that he made to London, the Continent, and New York between 1891 and 1914, Van Horne had plenty of opportunity to indulge his passion for buying art. Fortunately the considerable fortune that he had amassed since his arrival in Canada allowed him to do this, albeit not on the scale of a Vanderbilt or a Widener. His sortie to Britain and the Continent in 1911 was one such excursion. That March, he crossed the Atlantic on the CPR's *Empress of Ireland*, a magnificent ship that would meet a tragic end three years later when it collided with a Norwegian freighter in the St. Lawrence and sank to the depths of the river along with 1,012 people. In 1911, however, nothing detracted from the sublime comfort of Van Horne's voyage, not even bad smells, which, though he tried, he was unable to detect anywhere on the five-year-old ship. Equally impressive was the ship's food, which Van Horne pronounced "decidedly better" than that offered on the *Empress of Britain*.[680]

In England, Van Horne spent most of his time in London. There, if he followed his usual practice, he undertook a frenetic round of engagements and swept through one exhibition, gallery, museum, and private collection after another. After several supercharged weeks in Britain's capital and its environs, he made his way across the Channel to France and then to Paris, where he visited many friends and, in his words, saw "oceans of pictures."[681] Well-known among both the artists and art critics of Paris, he probably descended on artists' studios to view some of these works. Undoubtedly, he stopped off at the gallery of Roland Knoedler, Daniel Cottier's showroom, and the gallery owned by the German-born Paris dealer Stephan Bourgeois.

On one of his jaunts to New York City, in 1905, Van Horne went on a buying spree, purchasing eight paintings at auction on March 31 and April 6 and 7. Among the works snapped up was a portrait by the well-known British portraitist George Romney, for which he paid $3,650.[682] On another pilgrimage to New York Van Horne dropped into an art dealer's showroom (this could have been William McGuire's or the Blakeslee Galleries, two New York dealers Van Horne patronized) that was displaying a fifteenth-century bust attributed to Donatello and said to represent Niccola Pisano. He immediately fell in love with the work, but on finding that the price was "hideous," he gave a melancholy shake of his head and departed, angry and frustrated. He returned a few hours later, only to find that the piece had been sold. When the dealer refused to divulge the identity of the purchaser, Van Horne responded with, "I am fortunate in having friends." He thereupon traced the whereabouts of the piece, which had been acquired by a collector in Boston. Van Horne considered offering the collector the original "hideous" price, plus 10 percent, but he was advised against making such a move. Such an offer would be resented, and his opportunity might be lost.

The art lover thereupon gave his agent blanket instructions to await the advent of a financial recession. When this happened, he should offer the original price. Years passed and the inevitable crisis arrived. Van Horne's offer was made and accepted. "But," recalled Van Horne in recounting the saga to Ellery Sedgwick, the editor of the *Atlantic Monthly*, "Niccola did not come a moment too soon. I was ill, very ill, so low in spirit that I thought of turning my face quietly to the wall." When the news arrived that the bust was available, he responded immediately. "Hurry," said his telegram. When the bust arrived at the Sherbrooke Street mansion, it was quickly unpacked and then trundled into the sickroom, where it was placed beside Van Horne's pillow. "And," said Van Horne ending his story, "I threw my arm around his neck, laid my cheek against his, and slept like a child."[683]

The Donatello became part of a collection that featured works from the early Dutch, Flemish, and Spanish schools (Velázquez, Frans Hals, Albert Cuyp, Rembrandt) and boasted canvases by such eminent British painters as Hogarth, Turner, Reynolds, Constable, and Gainsborough. And, contrary to what has often been remarked about it, the collection also included many modern works; in fact, all but two of the forty-nine works listed in Van Horne's 1892 catalogue are from the nineteenth century.[684] In making his nineteenth-century purchases, Van Horne concentrated almost exclusively on French artists with a Realist bent — Theodule Ribot, Honoré Daumier, Georges Michel, and members of the Barbizon school (the initiators of landscape painting in nineteenth-century France), including Charles François Daubigny, who anticipated Impressionism and actually associated with members of the younger group, Camille Corot, the most gifted and most independent member of the school, Théodore Rousseau, the school's nominal head, and Constant Troyon.

Interestingly enough, Van Horne's collection in 1892 contained works by several nineteenth-century American artists, namely John Brown, Robert Newman, Frederic Remington, and that most original and individualistic of the nineteenth-century Romantics, Albert

Pinkham Ryder. Introduced to Ryder in New York by Daniel Cottier, Van Horne became one of his stalwart supporters, buying his work, promoting it to friends, and even entertaining the artist in his Montreal home. Such unexpected manna must have been intoxicating to Ryder, an eccentric recluse who lived in a debris-littered room in a New York City tenement and who, in the 1880s, could count on his fingers the number of artists and dealers who did not scorn his "poor drawing" and his "slovenly execution."[685]

Van Horne's patronage of Ryder was not without its drawbacks. When it came to his dealings with the Montreal collector, the painter had to be prepared to accept criticism and advice, an inevitable by-product of any relationship with Van Horne. Like another well-known art collector, William H. Vanderbilt, Van Horne loved to instruct. "Aim at the big broad, simple & strong effects & dont add one touch without a definite reason & you will surprise everyone in a year or two," he advised one unidentified amateur painter.[686] To Ryder, he dispensed advice about the treatment of a boat. The painter acknowledged the criticism when he wrote his patron in 1895:

> I give you credit, that the criticism you made was good, as I am bound to admit that the picture is better for the change ... I trust you will find the boat all right now; I lowered the rail as you suggested and as much as I dared, as the lifting and rolling of the boat by the sea is made somewhat by the line of the gunwale, and the weight is more in the other end of the boat. I hope Lady Van Horne and your charming daughter will be pleased with the picture, and Benny I feel quite sure will for old acquaintance sake.[687]

Not surprisingly, Van Horne also loved to dispense advice to fellow art collectors. Among those who benefited from his advice was the well-known Canadian financier and industrialist Sir James Dunn. In December 1911, when Dunn was a mere novice in the art-collecting game, Van Horne wrote him:

> I am glad to hear of your purchase of the magnificent Jacob Morris.
>
> I am sure that you will never regret it, for I feel sure that it will some day rank as one of the half dozen world's

masterpieces in landscape, and will be spoken of with Rembrandt's Mill and Vermeer's View of Delft.

It is better to buy one such picture than a hundred average things. A half dozen of their class will in themselves make a famous collection. I hope you will stick to the "top notchers'" and keep your eyes shut to the second class. Two such great things quite fill a room. They need space and it is a sin to force inferior company on them.[688]

In the world of art, Van Horne distinguished himself by being not only the foremost Canadian collector of his day but also by being the only one in Montreal to purchase works by post-Impressionists. Timid Montreal collectors shied away from paintings by these artists, but Van Horne was audacious enough to acquire works by French painter, graphic artist, and poster designer Henri de Toulouse-Lautrec, Mary Cassatt (usually regarded as America's most famous female painter), and outstanding pioneer French painter Paul Cézanne. The dealer credited with introducing Van Horne to the work of Toulouse-Lautrec and Cézanne, Stephan Bourgeois, later played a vital role in arranging for Van Horne's two Toulouse-Lautrecs and his Cézanne portrait of Madame Cézanne to be hung in the first major modern exhibition of art to be held in the United States, the mammoth, ground-breaking Armoury Show of 1913.[689]

At a time when contemporary Canadian artists were being shunned by other collectors, Van Horne was bold enough to invest in their work. In 1906, for example, he paid the munificent sum of $100 for a study of an ox by Canadian master Maurice Cullen, R.C.A.[690] James Wilson Morrice was another Canadian artist in whom Van Horne took an interest. Born to a wealthy Montreal family, Morrice was able to overthrow the conventions of a staunchly Presbyterian upbringing and become one of the world's leading early-twentieth-century artists. But his journey to artistic acclaim was not easy. His family grudgingly tolerated his youthful sketching and only accepted his choice of career when the French government and Parisian connoisseurs started to buy his paintings, but that was after he had left for Europe in about 1890 and after Van Horne had spoken glowingly to his father about his son's artistic talent.[691]

As a private collector, Van Horne played a significant role in encouraging Canadian artists, but it was in his capacity as a CPR official that he made his greatest contribution. Before the beginning of the twentieth century he issued free passes or reduced-fare tickets to thirty-three prominent artists on more than one hundred occasions. During this same period he also commissioned and/or purchased at least fifty-six landscape canvases on behalf of the CPR.[692]

Van Horne maintained extremely close ties with the Canadian art world during the closing years of his CPR career. As an honorary member of the Royal Canadian Academy, he frequented that organization's annual meetings and openings.[693] He became actively involved in the Art Association of Montreal (later the Montreal Museum of Fine Arts), and on December 13, 1901, he was elected president of the association.[694] Although he was decidedly niggardly when it came to making charitable contributions, he nevertheless managed to donate $5,000 in 1910 toward the purchase of land and a building for the Montreal Museum of Fine Arts. This enabled him to meet the minimum qualifications for a bene-factor, an honour he shared with his CPR colleague R.B. Angus, who gave $20,000, and CPR construction boss (now multimillionaire financier) James Ross, who gave $150,000.[695]

When building his collection — "You stagger me with the list of your new acquisitions," wrote one correspondent in 1912[696] — Van Horne was in touch with a number of internationally known art connoisseurs and critics. One of these was Bernard Berenson, a Lithuanian-born Jew who specialized in Italian Renaissance art.

Roger Fry was another international art figure who had dealings with Van Horne. On November 30, 1905, when he was curator of paintings at New York City's Metropolitan Museum, Fry boarded the train for Montreal and a "very tough day's picture seeing." Commenting on works painted by Van Horne himself, Fry later wrote his wife, Helen: "One has to admire them for the short time that he took to do them, but he's such a wonderful person and so astounding in his capacity that one willingly stretches a point in favour of his paintings."[697]

After Van Horne's death, Fry summed up his impressions of the collection that he had viewed. "It was," he wrote in *Burlington Magazine*, "full of out of the way and curious things which other collectors would have overlooked, but as far as I recollect it was not a choice collection, and contained few indisputable masterpieces ..."[698] Fry was ready to admit, however, that he may have underestimated the collection since he had only seen it once and that had been nine years earlier, at which time he had found Van Horne himself more interesting and arresting than any of the objects that he had acquired. On the other hand, after viewing the collection in 1936, Toronto art critic Graham C. McIness rated it as the finest private collection in Canada. McIness, who championed the work of the Group of Seven as well as that of the newer figurative artists, informed his *Winnipeg Free Press* readers that the Van Horne collection's "richness and variety almost take away one's breath ..."[699]

As a financier, with a financier's keen interest in investments that appreciate in value, Van Horne was quick to recognize the valuable role that publicity could play in enhancing his collection's reputation. And so he welcomed an international army of fellow collectors and scholars to his Sherbrooke Street mansion. Here he would personally escort them around his collection, often winding up the tour with a long and knowledgeable discussion about art in his sanctum sanctorum. On one occasion (and there were no doubt others) he gave up the whole day to introduce his collection to a complete stranger, C.T. Currelly, later the first curator of the Royal Ontario Museum.[700] Sometimes Van Horne would even seek out a stranger if he had learned that the man was interested in art. This was how he came to meet the artistically talented Scotsman Robert T.G. Paterson, who had been dispatched to Montreal in 1892 to open up a business for an Edinburgh manufacturing firm. Somehow Van Horne came into possession of some of Paterson's quick sketches and on that basis decided that he would like to meet the young man who had created them. He arranged for Paterson to be driven to the Sherbrooke Street mansion, where he gave him a personal tour of his art collection.

Conducting tours of his collection was one way that Van Horne could expose it to a wider audience. Another was to lend pieces to public exhibitions, many of whose curators would have heard about the collection from Bernard Berenson and other art scholars with whom Sir William was in contact, notably Sir Martin Conway, Wilhelm Bode, and August L. Mayer. Over the years, starting in about 1887, Van Horne pictures were lent to such prominent dealers and museums as the Metropolitan Museum of Art in New York, M. Knoedler & Co. in New York, and the Art Association of Montreal.

In an era when collectors were gulled by dishonest dealers, art experts questioned the authenticity of some of Van Horne's purchases. Van Horne's immediate reaction was to vigorously defend the works whose authenticity was disputed as he had little faith in the infallibility of judgments delivered by most of the so-called experts. He would go so far as to admit that he regretted having paid a Rembrandt price for a Ferdinand

Bols, but he reminded the experts that they often did not agree among themselves and that some of their members had even questioned the authenticity of several works attributed to Velázquez in the world's leading art museums. As far as he was concerned, "pictures are inherently good or bad, and it doesn't matter a damn whether a great man painted the poor one or an unknown man painted the fine one."[701]

When, however, he became convinced that a painting was of doubtful attribution or a poor example of a good painter's work, he was quite prepared, unlike some of his fellow collectors, to ruthlessly cut his losses. Notwithstanding his massive ego, he did take advice, but he preferred that it be given indirectly, in conversation. When an opinion contrary to his own was pronounced too plainly he could become quite fierce in his displeasure. Stephan Bourgeois was one authority who never failed to deliver his views directly, and surprisingly enough, they invariably met with a mild reception. On one visit to the Sherbrooke Street mansion, he advised Van Horne to dispose of some twenty canvases. And his client did just that.[702]

It was painful for Van Horne to admit that he had been duped by a dealer. But his spirits would immediately soar if he later learned that the dealer had met with some misfortune. Editor Dick Wilbur recalled the sad end of one such individual who had gotten the better of Sir William:

> Sir William, like all great men of parts, was a little inclined to be dogmatic, in his likes and dislikes, and ranking high amongst these was his deep seated love for motor cars. He loved them. Oh yes! He loved them!! He loved them with the serene undying affection that the late Mr Terence McSweeney had for the Union Jack. He was broad enough to admit, though, that occasionally they proved useful — he said this on reading of the death of a certain art dealer who had done him badly in a picture trade a year or so before. The dealer had been run over and killed by one.[703]

After Van Horne's death, his art collection, which had been valued at $1,235,050 in 1914, remained intact, in the care of young Addie and Bennie. After Addie's death in 1941 (ten years after her brother's), her one-quarter share of the collection (about sixty paintings) was bequeathed to the Montreal Museum of Fine Arts. The rest remained in the hands of her nephew, William. Five years later, in 1946, after his death, the heirs of that portion of the estate consigned twenty of the most noteworthy nineteenth-century paintings to auction.[704] As a result, works from the Van Horne art collection became widely dispersed.

The possibilities of connoisseurship also led Sir William to collect Japanese pottery and porcelain. Although he had never been to Japan, he abandoned fossil-collecting in the 1880s and began instead to collect fine and rare pieces of Japanese pottery and porcelain. Pieces of pottery featuring accidental effects resembling natural forms are especially admired by the Japanese. The Japanese connoisseur likewise admires objects that appear misshapen and glazes that reveal what would be regarded as serious imperfections in China and the West.[705] As a Western student, therefore, Van Horne had to learn and adopt new criteria of judgment in pursuit of this hobby, one that he cultivated assiduously in the 1890s and the opening years of the twentieth century. With his usual attention to detail, he catalogued each acquisition by painstakingly producing a miniature watercolour of its design, painting the image with such firmness and accuracy that it seemed, under a magnifying glass, to grow in distinctness and beauty.[706]

Van Horne began collecting Japanese pottery and porcelain at a time when these pieces were being studied and admired by coteries of artists and collectors in Paris, notably Samuel Bing, the art dealer and orientalist. In the two and a half centuries of the Tokugawa shogunate, Japan had been so insular that leaving the country was considered a crime punishable by death. Only two countries had trading rights with it, China and the Netherlands, and then their merchants were confined to a single port in a single island. But in 1854, Commodore Perry and his ships steamed into Yokohama, and Japan was forced open at gunpoint.[707] With the opening of the country to Western influences came a reciprocal awakening of the Western mind to Japanese culture, and objects from Japan began flowing into the West, attracting attention because of their very different aesthetic. Among members of the American arts community influenced by Japanese culture was American painter John La Farge, who played a major role in introducing Japanese aesthetic ideas and methods to American art and who counted himself among Van Horne's correspondents.

The fad for all things Japanese may have inspired Van Horne, like fellow collector Edward Black Greenshields, to take up the hobby. In all likelihood, though, it was the CPR's inauguration of a temporary service to the Far East in the late 1880s that whetted his interest in Japanese culture, especially its pottery and porcelain. Certainly his collection benefited from the CPR's establishment of a regular passenger service to the Far East in 1891; thanks to this development Van Horne became acquainted with Japanese statesmen and prominent businessmen who, learning of his deep interest in Japanese art and ceramics, would inform him of choice pieces for sale and sometimes present him with valuable gifts of pottery and porcelain.

Van Horne's love of showing off his knowledge and his boyish desire to humbug his friends and acquaintances found a perfect outlet in his Japanese porcelain and pottery collection. A frequently employed stunt was to palm off a small, common grease cup as a rare Japanese piece. He would wrap this lowly item in silk coverings and store it in the corner of one of his cabinets, then produce it with great pomp and ceremony at a propitious moment. Probably the first authority to spot the fraud was a Professor Morse of Boston, the only Japanese porcelain and pottery expert and collector deferred to by Van Horne. Morse, in fact, was the source of many of the bottles, tea sets, bowls, cups, and sake dishes in Van Horne's Japanese pottery and porcelain collection.[708]

Van Horne would handle his Japanese pieces with great "loving kindness" and carefully polish them with a piece of soft silk before displaying them to a visitor. He himself loved to contemplate the form and the glaze of each specimen and would often stand enraptured for minutes at a stretch before a favourite piece. His knowledge of the subject was so extensive that even when blindfolded he could usually identify by his sensitive touch the specimens brought to him. On one occasion, Japanese art dealer Bunkio Matsuki arrived at the Sherbrooke Street home with a number of pieces to show him. He arranged them on Van Horne's massive billiard table, placing a beautiful tea bowl in the centre, and issued this challenge: "Sir William, there is a mark on the foot of that bowl, and if without looking at the mark or feeling it, you will tell me who made the bowl, I will give it to you." Van Horne studied the piece from all angles, pondered his own collection, and then began discussing a completely unrelated topic. Suddenly, without warning, he announced, "Matsuki, I don't see who could have made that bowl except the second Rokubei." The dealer, conceding that Van Horne had met the challenge, gave him the bowl.[709]

When seeking new finds, Van Horne sought precise information from every available source, including helpful friend and lawyer Howard Mansfield (who visited dealers in Paris), an agent in Japan, and the friends he was fast cultivating among Japanese businessmen and statesmen. As soon as he became aware of a choice specimen he would instruct his agent or a friend to negotiate its purchase. If a satisfactory agreement could be reached, the piece would be incorporated into a collection that grew steadily in size and value throughout the 1890s and the opening years of the twentieth century.

There inevitably came a time when the collection's representation of Japanese master potters was almost complete. When this happened, Van Horne turned his attention to still rarer Chinese and Korean pottery and porcelain. Among the Chinese pieces that he acquired was a stunningly beautiful, tall, graceful vase made of mottled glass. One of his most prized acquisitions, it had once belonged to Samuel Bing, Sr. Stephan Bourgeois, from whom Van Horne purchased it, claimed that during Bing's lifetime Whistler had journeyed several times from London to Paris just to see it, believing that the vase had no equal. It was, he said, "the Venus de Milo of vases."[710] The purchase of such a magnificent piece further enhanced the value of the overall collection, whose Japanese component was then believed by Roger Fry to constitute the finest Japanese pottery and porcelain collection outside Japan.[711]

In August 1914, in response to a request from Van Horne, the H.E. Boucher Manufacturing Company, specialists in the manufacture of marine models for yacht owners, steamship companies, and the American government, dispatched to Van Horne a list of ship models and other items purchased from a Mr. Oatway.[712] Van Horne apparently needed more than an internationally renowned private art collection and a world-class Japanese pottery and porcelain collection to satisfy his collector and connoisseur instincts. In the decade or so before his death, Sir William also assembled a collection of ship models, one that came to boast some very important old votive models of European origin — seventeenth- and eighteenth-century Dutch and Hanseatic cogs, Mediterranean types, and a fine nineteenth-century French model.[713] But, as a later Canadian expert, John Stevens, revealed, the collection included models whose "obvious anachronisms would taint them in the eyes of anyone at all familiar with old time ships."[714] Whether or not they fooled Van Horne is open to question. In any event, their presence in various rooms and halls throughout the Sherbrooke Street mansion helped to make it truly a domestic museum.

Today, "Renaissance" is an overworked label when used in relation to individuals. When applied to Van Horne, the architect, painter, and collector, however, it is entirely fitting. It is also fitting that a man so gifted should find outlets for his prodigious energy and talent in so many different pursuits. While these diversions satisfied his collector's instinct and artistic bent, they also served another important function: they provided him with an escape from the many worries and burdens of his job as CPR president and later as head of the Cuba Company, the Laurentide Paper Company, the Canadian Salt Company, and the Canadian Sardine Company.

Chapter Twelve
Family Matters

On April 30, 1890, a pleasant but chilly Saturday, the Van Horne family moved from their Dorchester Street West home to a much larger stone residence at the foot of Mount Royal, deep in the heart of Montreal's Square Mile. In their new home, Van Horne's sister Mary went to work unpacking boxes, directing servants, and instructing workmen. Still, despite her exhaustion at the end of that frantic, chaotic day, the conscientious schoolteacher managed to summon up enough energy to pen a terse entry in her small, leather-bound Collins Handy Diary, the journal in which she sporadically recorded favourite sayings and the day's highlights. In her fine, elegant hand, Addie's invaluable helpmate wrote, "First dinner in new home, no lights and furnace not working properly."[715] It had been nine years since she, William, Addie, the children, and Addie's mother, Mrs. Hurd, had moved to Montreal, and this would be the second and last home that they would occupy in Canada's largest, most vibrant city.

This move, like all the others, was instigated by Van Horne. Unlike previous moves, however, this one was not made for career-related reasons. Van Horne simply wanted a larger house in which to display his burgeoning art and pottery collections. With this in mind, he began a search for larger premises, finally settling on a neo-classical stone mansion located on the northeast corner of Sherbrooke and Stanley Streets. The house, which was probably built in the late 1860s, originally belonged to Merchants Bank president and senator John Hamilton, who occupied it from 1869 to 1890. Van Horne purchased the property in 1890 and immediately embarked on alterations, with a view to providing the additional space required. Indications are that he refitted the whole of the ground floor and possibly the first floor, creating generous walls for pictures, well-proportioned rooms, and a spacious orderliness throughout.[716] After the family settled in, the mansion acquired a comfortable, lived-in look, which was in stark contrast to the museum-like interiors of so many other Square Mile residences in this period.

To carry out the remodelling, Van Horne hired someone whose work he knew and liked. This was Edward Colonna, best known as a pioneer of art nouveau, the decorative movement that featured long, sinuous curves of vegetal-inspired forms and that was regarded in 1890s Europe as "Modern Style." Ultimately the German-born designer would fade into obscurity and suffer a long, debilitating illness before dying in France and being buried in an unmarked pauper's grave in 1948. In the 1880s and 1890s, however, his career was flourishing and he was making a name for himself among the patrician citizens of first Dayton, Ohio, and then Montreal.

Colonna had studied architecture in Belgium before immigrating to the United States, where he settled in New York City. There, he found employment first with Louis C. Tiffany, a leading decorating consultant, and then with celebrated architect Bruce Price, who drew up the plans for several CPR hotels. Through Price, Colonna found a position as chief designer for the well-known railway car builder Barney & Smith Manufacturing Company of Dayton, Ohio. It was while working for Barney & Smith between 1885 and 1888 that he probably had his first dealings with Van Horne, who would have had a hand in the CPR's purchase of passenger cars from that company.

The Van Horne mansion on Sherbrooke Street West in Montreal. Derided by critics for resembling an armoury, it was razed in 1973 despite a furious campaign to save it.

Following his stint with the railway car builder, Colonna stopped off briefly in New York City, then headed north in 1889 to Montreal to open his own office and renew his contact with Van Horne, who would frequently invite the designer and his wife, Louise, to meals at the family home.[717] After moving to Montreal, Colonna continued to design Canadian Pacific's parlour and sleeping cars, some of which were still being produced by Barney & Smith. His main focus, however, was on architectural design, and it was this expertise that he put to work in designing a large portion of what would become one of the most sumptuous residential interiors in the country. In so doing, he provided Canada with an almost unique example of art nouveau decoration and Van Horne with a ground floor interior that reflected his essentially "modern" taste. It is not surprising that Colonna and his wife were among the first guests entertained in the Van Hornes' new home. In fact, they joined the family for Sunday lunch only days after the move.[718]

When the paterfamilias moved his family into the renovated residence at 917 (later 1139) Sherbrooke Street in 1892, the Square Mile was at the peak of its influence, a powerful anglophone community nestled smugly in a predominantly francophone province. Probably few other neighbourhoods in the British Empire were more British than the Square Mile. Lady Drummond, wife of Sir George Drummond, one of Canada's most influential men, summed it up well when, speaking for herself and her Montreal-born friends, she remarked, "The Empire is my country. Canada is my home."[719]

In slavish imitation of London society, the Square Mile's denizens rode to hounds, imported servants from the old country, staged elaborate dinner parties, hired governesses for their children, copied British social mores, and occupied mansions that were surrounded by acres of lawn, orchard, and garden on the hillside a mile or so from St. James Street's cathedrals of commerce. The well-known Canadian writer Stephen Leacock, himself a resident, labelled the place "Plutoria-under-the-elms,"[720] alluding to the tall elms and maples that lined its unpaved streets.

In 1892, Montreal, with a population of approximately 260,000,[721] was by far Canada's largest city and, in terms of financial clout and entrepreneurial spirit, the capital of Victorian Canada as well. A century earlier the North West Company had brought wealth and power to the city from the west. Now the Canadian Pacific Railway would do likewise. But this would happen only after the interminable stagnation of the Great Depression ended and prosperity returned to both the United States and Canada. When this occurred, in 1897, the city and the province embarked on a period of renewed prosperity and rapid industrialization. By 1914, *Lovell's Directory* could boast that Montreal was still the largest city in Canada, and the ninth largest in North America. It was also the largest port on the continent. In fact, Montreal was well on the way to becoming a second New York.[722]

Montreal's commercial aristocracy, most of whom lived in the Square Mile, controlled not only the province of Quebec but also two-thirds of Canada's wealth and most of the country's major corporations, including the CPR. Collectively, these tycoons bore scant resemblance to Europe's fading aristocrats or the sophisticated socialites of the New York 400 set. Although Sir John A. Macdonald's National Policy and the building of the Grand Trunk, the Intercolonial, and Canadian Pacific Railways had helped to create a moneyed class based largely in Montreal, most, if not all, of its members had been raised in far from privileged circumstances. Fairly typical of this class were the CPR duo Donald Smith and George Stephen, both of whom rose from humble origins. Donald Smith was the fourth child of a hard-drinking saddler. George Stephen, his cousin, was born the first child of a carpenter who had a large family to support. Another CPR director, Square Mile resident, and Van Horne friend, Robert Mackay, was the son of a crofter. All three men had been born in Scotland, but even those members of the Square Mile aristocracy who could not claim Scotland as their homeland were Scottish "to the marrow of their souls, and whatever their backgrounds or religions, they knew how to parlay endurance of the spirit into earthly salvation," claims Canadian journalist and author Peter C. Newman.[723]

Certainly Van Horne knew how to parlay endurance of the spirit into earthly salvation. Nevertheless, the fearless optimism that governed most of his life and his extravagant displays of affection for his family, to say nothing of his gambling instincts and his delight in sybaritic living and big practical jokes, rule out any claim to his being Scottish to the marrow of his soul.

Like most Victorian men, Van Horne was the authority figure in his family. As the individual who controlled the family purse he made all the important decisions, although admittedly he did consult Addie from time to time. Unlike so many other men in his circles, however, Van Horne doted on his wife and children. Indeed, his devotion to his family "was so pronounced as to be quite unique," observed Thomas Shaughnessy in a letter to Walter Vaughan.[724] Not for Van Horne the role of remote husband and father. Perhaps because his father died when he was only eleven years of age, leaving his family in straitened circumstances, Van Horne craved a sense of security. And what could better nurture this than the enveloping love and respect of a devoted wife and closely knit family. Family, as a result, became all-important to him. Addie, who was distinguished by "a serenity of spirit rare in modern times,"[725] and his family became indispensable restoratives for Van Horne's soul, and when he was away from them he fretted constantly about their well-being, distributing concern and instructions in equal measure in letters to his wife.

In these missives to Addie, Van Horne would frequently chastise her for being a poor correspondent and would fret about her health. "I am much distressed by your letter of yesterday as I know you have been and are still seriously ill. I trust that you have not failed to call the doctor," he wrote Addie in October 1872, just after he had moved from Chicago to St. Louis to become manager of the St. Louis, Kansas City and Northern Railway. "If you have not done so do it at once. You must take no risks nor trifle with your health," he continued. Then, to drive the home the point that his instructions must be obeyed, he added, "I am very busy but am so nervous on your account that I can hardly do anything. Do not fail to let me hear from you every day. Now my Treasure, do not forget that I am anxious about you and that I will be in agony if I do not hear from you and if I do not hear that you have called the doctor."[726] Unfortunately, there is no indication in this or subsequent letters of the nature of Addie's illness. Nor are there any hints in later correspondence as to why Addie's health should be a source of recurring concern to family members. For whatever reason, Addie Van Horne was generally thought to be "far from strong," the phrase employed by young Addie in a missive to her father, in which she reports that she rejoices at the prospect of Aunt Mary returning home, "where she is such a help to dear Mamma whose cares are many..."[727]

Addie was indeed fortunate in having Mary as an indispensable helpmate in running the Van Horne household, no light task in a day when the standard of housekeeping was high. However polished the butler and however efficient the housekeeper and the large staff, Addie was expected to take a personal and informed interest in her kitchen, linen room, and garden. To her aid came able Mary. Van Horne's sweet-tempered sister not only played a leading role in numerous local organizations, such as the Natural History Society, she also rendered invaluable assistance to Van Horne's wife, helping out with grocery shopping, raising the children, and entertaining the countless guests who passed through the doors of the Sherbrooke Street mansion and Covenhoven. Her death on July 17, 1904, at age forty-eight after a serious illness, left a yawning void in the family.

Van Horne was certainly conscious of the magnitude of his wife's responsibilities, but although very solicitous of her welfare, Van Horne was not inclined to lavish favours on her. His parsimony, in fact, upset young

Addie, who, when just shy of twenty, pointed out to her adored father that his wife was "the only lady in Montreal of high position who has not her own horses and you know it does not look well for the wife of the President of the C.P.R. to go calling in cabs or what is worse for her on foot."[728]

For her part, Addie Van Horne was devoted to her demanding, restless husband. A quiet, kind, and intelligent woman, whom the Canadian novelist William A. Fraser described as "the most gracious woman I ever met in my life,"[729] she was ideally suited to providing the solace and support that Van Horne so desperately needed in his harried, frantic life. It is a reflection of how highly he regarded her intelligence and judgment that he consulted her about major career-related decisions. Despite her college education and musical talent, however, Addie was content to play the role of the model late Victorian wife and remain in her husband's shadow. For her, home was where she belonged, and, if given a choice, she would have shunned the glamour and glitter of stuffy Montreal society altogether in favour of a family-centred home life. In what was undoubtedly a rare fit of pique, she confided that she did not care for people or theatres.[730] To her absent husband Addie once reported, "It will be four or five long weeks before we see your dear face. Time was never so long before. If I cared for people or theatres I could while the time. As it is I prefer home & it is dreadfully lonely ..."[731]

Because she disliked society, Addie Van Horne avoided creating a stir in the wider world. In this respect, she differed from other socially prominent women of the day. Neither trained nor expected to do anything useful, except perhaps to organize household servants and play the role of charming hostess, these women made the social whirl the centre of their lives or employed their spare time and surplus energy in organizing church, charitable, and social organizations.

Addie Van Horne was in many ways the antithesis of a not infrequent and certainly most renowned visitor to 917 Sherbrooke Street, Lady Ishbel Aberdeen. An earnest late Victorian reforming liberal of unlimited energy and commanding presence, she was as outgoing and dominating as Addie Van Horne was quiet and retiring. From the moment that Lady and Lord Aberdeen, the newly appointed Governor General, set foot in Rideau Hall in the autumn of 1893, it was evident that Government House would be set on its ear. "It is not so much what is done or what is said," Lady Aberdeen wrote on her first evening in Canada. "It will be the tone which will make itself felt, and in this every member of the Household, even down to the smallest child, will have a share."[732] Since she was a fervent Presbyterian and an ardent liberal who believed strongly that liberalism was the Christianity of politics, Lady Aberdeen immediately set out to use the office of Governor General as an instrument for social reform. While in Canada she would found the Victorian Order of Nurses, to commemorate the Diamond Jubilee of Queen Victoria, and, against tremendous odds, the National Council of Women, of which she became president. She would also lend her ardent support to the leader of the Opposition, Wilfrid Laurier, a great admirer of the tenets of British liberalism.

Tall, buxom Lady Aberdeen was clearly the dominant partner in her marriage. Fortunately, Aberdeen, a slight, rather delicate-looking man, was quite prepared to follow where she led. Indeed, it has been suggested that this formidable woman was really the Governor General and he was her consort. In an age when a woman was expected to be a mere appendage of her husband, Lady Aberdeen brazenly flaunted convention and dared to express her influence openly. To some women like Addie, who were comfortable in the traditional role, this could be vexing. Her lack of appreciation for this role reversal and the Aberdeens' verve and energy in performing good works is hinted at in the letter that she dispatched to Van Horne in December 1894 following the visit of an Aberdeen entourage to 917 Sherbrooke Street West. Utterly fed up with the demands made on Van Horne and herself, Addie wrote, "The Aberdeens only care for themselves anyway & the work they have in hand. They are to be respected for their charity certainly but I have quite enough of distinguished guests."[733] Outside the home, Addie Van Horne would content herself with serving as vice-president of the women's branch of the Antiquarian Society, attending the music recitals of notable artists, and exhibiting regularly at flower shows.[734]

Although satisfied to linger in her husband's shadow, Addie Van Horne was not always prepared, as we have seen, to perform the role of dutiful wife uncomplainingly. Nor did she always meekly accept her husband's views. Like so many successful men, Van Horne could be very opinionated and dogmatic: he always knew what was best. This, of course, could annoy people, including his wife, who was not loath to prove her beloved Will wrong. One such opportunity arose after Addie had viewed a display of wedding presents received by a Miss Lonsdale, who married her cousin John Lonsdale Gilmins on December 31, 1885. Writing to her sister-in-law, Mary, a gleeful Addie reported:

> The presents were many, pretty and useful — I selected a beautiful card receiver — best plate. I showed it to Will who said "No one ever sent plate. I might throw that away." So I changed it for a pie knife solid only a trifle

more & not half as pretty. There were ever so many plated silver articles — There was a coffee & tea service from Mr Gilman's mother & a pretty silver five o'clock tea set from Mr and Mrs Finlay. I asked Mrs F if the large service was solid. She replied "She thought not hers was not." So I looked closely at the rest & concluded mine was among the few solid pieces. So I quite enjoyed telling Will he was sometimes mistaken.[735]

Addie Sr. was often forced, by circumstances, to play the role of gracious hostess, a role expected of the wife of a Square Mile resident, especially someone as prominent as her husband. Nevertheless, because Van Horne, like Lord Strathcona, gloried in it, entertaining was elevated to a high art in the Van Horne home. With strangers and mere acquaintances, and in formal social situations, Van Horne could be cold and austere, if not downright shy, but personally, with friends, he was genial and gracious. As some one who revelled in the role of courtly host and paterfamilias, the railway magnate orchestrated countless dinners, Sunday lunches, and overnight visits. When away from home, he would pepper Addie with instructions regarding plans he had for entertaining friends and business associates upon his return. "Mr — will remain in Montreal until Sunday afternoon and I would like very much to have him to lunch at 2. I have written him. It may be well to invite Mr and Mrs James Ross also. I think they are at the Windsor and I would like them for special reasons. If not then Mr and Mrs Colonna might come in addition to the others ..."[736] People from all walks of life and occupations figured in his entertainment plans. CPR contractors, judges, railway magnates, artists, politicians, financiers, diplomats, industrialists, writers, all were the recipients of lavish and warm hospitality at 917 Sherbrooke Street and Covenhoven, his beloved New Brunswick estate.

When he was in New Brunswick in the late 1880s to negotiate the lease of the New Brunswick Railway Company to the Canadian Pacific Railway, Van Horne stopped off in the small resort town of St. Andrews in the southwestern part of the province. It was to prove a pivotal visit, as the railway magnate was so struck by the beauty of Passamaquoddy Bay and its islands that he soon set about acquiring property on Minister's Island, a five-hundred-acre strip of verdant land located just a half-mile offshore and around a point from St. Andrews. Nestled in the protective crook of land that forms Passamaquoddy Bay, the island

A partial view of the family home at Covenhoven, the impressive Van Horne estate on Minister's Island, New Brunswick. Dignitaries from across North America and around the world visited here during the summer months.

exists in a salubrious microclimate that allows lilacs to bloom three weeks longer than they bloom in Montreal and lilies to blossom three weeks earlier, a selling point that no doubt did not escape Van Horne the avid gardener. Over the next couple of decades he would put his diverse talents and still formidable energy to work transforming four hundred acres of the island into a self-sustaining estate that included not only a large summer home and sprawling gardens but also an impressive working farm and assorted outbuildings. Until the end of his life, Covenhoven would be Sir William's refuge, the haven to which he would retreat during the summer months and early autumn in search of rest and creative renewal.

Founded in 1783 by Loyalist refugees, St. Andrews had once been a thriving port dependent on international trade in lumber. Its fortunes began to wane in the mid-nineteenth-century following the decline of the Maritimes' traditional timber trade with Great Britain and the failure of a scheme to link the town to Quebec City by means of a railway. By 1870, the town was merely a quaint, insignificant port with a population of approximately three thousand.[737]

Notwithstanding its shabbiness, St. Andrews did have its boosters. Among the most visionary were the newspaper editors who touted summer resort development as the key to the town's economic survival. For inspiration they had to look no further than fashionable Newport, Rhode Island, which had been a summer resort for hundreds of years, attracting first the colonial gentry and then, from the 1870s on, America's wealthy families. Having "discovered" Newport, the Astors, Vanderbilts, Geolets, Berwinds, and Oelrichs purchased property in the tiny Atlantic coast town and proceeded to erect palatial estates, modelled on those of European aristocracy.

In Canada, however, it was not until 1883 that summer visitors began to arrive in appreciable numbers at St. Andrews, drawn by the natural beauty of the area, the healthy air, and, in the case of hay fever sufferers, the absence of ragweed. Van Horne found the place to be the "sleeping beauty of the seaside,"[738] well on its way to becoming a booming summer resort patronized by the newly rich, long-time rich, and once rich of the Canadian and American eastern seaboard. Leading the parade was Sir Samuel Leonard Tilley, a minister in the first Macdonald government. In 1871, he purchased and renovated a striking brick mansion. He was joined by wealthy Robert S. Gardiner, president of the Rand Avery Supply Company of Boston, who arrived in 1887, then returned the following year with a select group of friends in tow. Known as the American Syndicate, this group became a driving force behind the town's evolution into a luxury seasonal resort and a summer enclave for the wealthy.[739] Gardiner, in fact, has been credited with being the person who sparked Van Horne's interest in St. Andrews as a summer retreat. The two men had struck up a friendship through the dealings between their respective businesses, the CPR having purchased printed railway tickets and menus from the Rand Avery Supply Company.[740]

Van Horne acquired his Minister's Island property piecemeal, starting in 1891. That year, he bought 150 acres at the most southerly end of the island for $3,500 from Adelina and Edwin Andrews, the latter a descendent of the "Minister," the Reverend Samuel Andrews, who had purchased the island in 1791. Five years after his first purchase, Van Horne bought 250 acres for $5,000 from Henry Pultz Timmerman and his wife, Alice Maud. Lady Van Horne would acquire the island's remaining hundred acres in 1926.[741]

Shortly after acquiring his first parcel of land, Van Horne spoke enthusiastically about Minister's Island to Lord Strathcona, announcing that he intended to construct a summer house on it. When his friend spoke wistfully of a desire to acquire his own seaside home, Van Horne offered to divide the property with him at cost if he would build on it. "I was particular about this because I did not wish to take any chance of having an undesirable neighbor later on," Van Horne would later recall.[742] Strathcona immediately sent Van Horne a $1,500 cheque, but Van Horne just as promptly returned it. The cheque then bounced back and forth between the two men until Van Horne finally retained it on the understanding that should Strathcona fail to build on the island within a reasonable time the $1,500 would be returned to him and the arrangement would be considered concluded. In the late 1890s, Lord Strathcona asked Van Horne to treat the whole property as his own and to proceed with any improvements upon it that he thought necessary. He, Strathcona, would make good any costs should he himself build, and in the event of his not building within a reasonable time he would renounce any claim to the property. With this assurance, Van Horne embarked on a decade-long series of improvements to the property. Lord Strathcona never got around to selecting a site for a seaside home, and Van Horne, despite Herculean efforts, never succeeded in persuading his CPR colleague to make a move toward building one. The matter was only settled after Lord Strathcona's death in 1915, when his daughter agreed to Van Horne's acquiring his friend's interest in the property on the terms Van Horne had suggested some years earlier. Van Horne thereupon remitted a cheque representing the principal sum and interest compounded at 5 percent annually for twenty-four years.

Once he had purchased his parcels of land, Sir William set out to design a summer home, which he named Covenhoven in salute to his father and his Dutch ancestry. The actual construction began in 1898, but unidentified problems soon arose. Forced to seek assistance, he turned to a young Montreal architect, Edward Maxwell. After an apprenticeship with the well-established Montreal architect Alexander Dunlop, Maxwell had worked in Boston with the prominent architectural firm Shepley, Rutan & Coolidge, "heirs to the prestigious practice of H.H. Richardson (1838–1886)."[743] Although it is unlikely that Edward ever met the celebrated American architect, Richardson's influence was readily apparent in the planning, massing, materials, and decoration of Maxwell's early country and city houses.

In 1891, the gregarious and self-confident Edward returned to Montreal to supervise one of the Boston firm's commissions, the construction of the imposing new Board of Trade building. This provided him with an entrée into Montreal's business community, and when private commissions began to flow in, Edward opened his own office in the city. Ten years later, in 1902, he would be joined by his younger brother William, and the two brothers would go on to create one of the most significant architectural practices in Canadian history.

When Van Horne issued his call for help, Edward Maxwell hurried to St. Andrews to rectify the construction problems.[744] His intervention succeeded, and he no doubt pleased Van Horne, for when Van Horne accompanied the architect to the St. Andrews railway station at the work's conclusion he drew Maxwell's attention to a field en route and suggested that Maxwell purchase the property for a summer retreat of his own. Maxwell took Van Horne's advice and in 1899 acquired five acres of land opposite Minister's Island. There, he would build his country house, Tillietudlem.[745]

The house that Van Horne designed was a modest one, a long, one-and-a-half-storey building with a shingled roof that extended over a veranda whose piers, like the house's exterior walls, were made of red sandstone quarried from the southern tip of the island. Centred in the roof was a four-windowed dormer that repeated the symmetry of the French windows flanking the ground-floor entrance. From the front door one walked into a central hall onto which opened four bedrooms. To the rear were service rooms and a kitchen.

When Van Horne decided the following year to enlarge the house he again called upon Edward Maxwell, this time to design a wing that would harmonize with the main part of the building. The architect obligingly produced a plan that artfully managed to promise a house that was large and bulky like his client, triple the current dwelling's size. Van Horne, though, was not satisfied and asked for a revised scheme. After he approved the second set of architectural drawings the original building was extended in length by both a service wing and a wing similar to that suggested in the first set of plans. Also added to the structure was an L-shaped wing that included a studio and a magnificent dining room on the ground floor and bedrooms on the upper floor.[746] In due course, the impressive dining room was furnished with Persian rugs, English furniture, paintings by Old Masters, and numerous landscapes executed by Van Horne himself. One of the most striking of these was a work depicting a full moon emerging from a bank of light clouds in a star-studded sky above water. Its composition and style suggest that the work was at least partly influenced by Van Horne's study of Japanese and Chinese masterpieces.

Further additions and modifications to the house were undertaken in subsequent years. All were closely supervised by Van Horne, who sometimes found it necessary to drop everything in Montreal and hurry to Minister's Island to inspect new construction. He made one such turnaround trip in late March 1902, travelling to the island with his wife and his sister Mary to check on recently completed additions to the main house and to measure windows for curtains. News of the house's radical transformation reached young Addie in New York City, where she was visiting friends and soaking up art (she ranked an exhibition of the Society of American Artists below its Canadian counterpart).[747] In short order, she dispatched a letter to "Mamma," inquiring plaintively, "Will you not ask Papa, if we cannot have inside blinds on the dining room windows? If we had, they could be closed between meals and the windows opened and the flies would crawl out & the dining room and the table would not be in the usual disgraceful condition during the fly season."[748]

Of all the wings that were added to the main house, the addition that had a tower at the junction of the roofs and that also contained young William's nursery was probably the one that most involved Van Horne's attention. It was in the nursery, after all, that he so lovingly painted the joyous mural for small William. This room also featured at least one mantel constructed of Dutch picture tiles specially ordered from Montreal. The first order of tiles had been incorrectly filled — something Van Horne had recognized at once — and to prevent further errors he prepared a careful diagram of the projected installation and mailed it to the supplier.[749] Minor setbacks such as this, however, did not diminish Sir William's enthusiasm for the new addition. When it was finally completed he wrote on July 8, 1910, to his friend Governor Smith: "We have just got well settled here for the summer and are very much pleased at the way our recent improvements have turned out. I should very much like to get you down for a little while to see what the place is like."[750]

Besides helping to design the original house, Van Horne also turned his hand to designing the farm manager's house, one of several buildings that would constitute part of the large working farm that he envisaged for Minister's Island.[751] He may also have helped Edward Maxwell draw up plans for the other farm buildings, but the evidence is not clear on this point. There can be no disputing the fact, however, that the most impressive farm building on the property was the massive barn that was the centrepiece of the Minister's Island operation. Three storeys in height and built on a stone foundation, it had twenty-five windows on the ground floor alone. Among its other features were a high, shingled roof with vents and flared gable ends (a Maxwell trademark) and two huge grain silos topped by dovecotes with conical roofs. This remarkable building even included a kitchen equipped with an elevator that provided access to the floors above. Two immaculately kept floors in this barn would house Van Horne's prized herd of Dutch belted cattle, so called because this breed has a large band of white over the shoulders. Over the years they won many show ribbons, some from the Royal Winter Fair in Toronto.

Determined to make Minister's Island as self-sufficient as possible, Van Horne provided for a supply of fresh water, the growing of vegetables and fruit, the raising of sheep, cattle, pigs, turkeys, and guinea fowl, and the manufacture of gas for lighting fixtures. A windmill, assisted by kerosene-fired engines, pumped water from an artesian well to the main house through a system of hydrants. Carbide gas for lighting and cooking was supplied by an adjoining plant; carbide pellets were dropped into water and the resulting gas collected and piped from the plant into the family home. Back-to-the-land pioneers could have learned much from a tour of Covenhoven, especially if the tour had been conducted by the inveterately didactic Van Horne. Still a tour was not necessary to drive home some of the lessons that Sir William wanted to impart while he was in charge. Wishing to impress upon the New Brunswick government the importance of promoting the export of processed agricultural products, he dispatched some Covenhoven ham and bacon to its secretary of agriculture in March 1909. "It does not cost much more to produce what would bring very fancy prices than the ordinary Chicago products cost, and the right kind of hams and bacon put up in good style would find a ready market at twice the Chicago prices," he informed the minister.[752]

Even when not at Covenhoven, Van Horne immersed himself in a myriad of details relating to the estate's operation. Letters from the manager invariably requested decisions on a welter of issues. Should a certain bull be castrated or registered? Should certain mares be bred to Sir Robert (a prize stallion) again? What about the grading of turnips for sale or for feed? Since the estate employed one head gardener, four assistant gardeners, one head stockman, one assistant stockman, three teamsters, a weir manager, a farm hand, a head field hand, poultry hands, carpenters, plumbers, and painters as part of its outdoor staff alone, Covenhoven was essentially a medium-sized business. As such, it required the services of not only a paid manager but also the frequent attention of Van Horne, the ultimate decision-maker. In his capacity of micromanager, Van Horne not infrequently took on tasks that could have been performed by the paid manager. A case in point involved Van Horne's attempt to interest a member of the Boissevain family in purchasing a three-year-old Covenhoven bull named Hugo Van Covenhoven. The bull, Van Horne told Louis Boissevain, had an "uncommonly good belt" and was "quite free from any white hairs about the feet and from any defects. He is the son of 'Nicholas of Covenhoven,' the head of my herd — the finest belted bull I know."[753]

Van Horne always claimed that one of Minister's Island's main attractions for him was its relative inaccessibility from the New Brunswick mainland. Still, he could not be long without the company of stimulating friends. Besides, he loved to show people around his beloved estate. And

One of Van Horne's prize bulls. The railway magnate raised pedigreed stock at Covenhoven and at his East Selkirk, Manitoba, estate.

so they came, by train or yacht — leading Canadian and American businessmen, railway barons, Japanese royalty, retired generals, and spinster friends like Maud Edgar, principal of a Montreal private girls' school.

Invitations to Covenhoven were not restricted, however, to well-known members of Canadian, American, or international society. Sometimes they were extended to lesser mortals such as a Mrs. S. Baines, who, despite her lower station in life, was made to feel quite special by Van Horne, the consummate host and teacher. Following a visit to Covenhoven in 1895, Mrs. Baines informed her hostess, "On my trip down & back I was favored with Sir William's valued consideration as only a perfect host could benefit a guest. He must have found me dull enough knowing as little as I do of the great world he lives in & understands so well. But he enriched me with many a new idea & fact ... He amazes me with his knowledge & power & it was good of him to spare to me so much time."[754]

Visitors to Sir William's beloved summer retreat usually crossed to Minister's Island at low tide on the natural gravel bar that links the New Brunswick mainland with the island. Once on the island, they would journey for half a mile through woodland before emerging onto the estate's expansive grounds. There, waiting for them under the mansion's porte cochère, would be Van Horne, who would inevitably intone his customary welcome, "Gentlemen, you may have champagne or milk — the price is the same."[755] Guests were royally entertained at Covenhoven. Dutch wagons, beach wagons, buckboards, and surreys would bounce them across the island on sightseeing tours and transport visitors to the shore for bathing parties. At mealtime, in the spacious dining room with its exposed beams and green marble and tile fire place, there would be sumptuous repasts featuring fresh produce, meat, and fowl from the estate. For those interested in more than meals and conversation there would also be games of poker or ping pong with Sir William and other guests, strolls along the island's twelve miles of paths and roads, and perhaps a sketching trip.

At home in Montreal, as at Covenhoven, guests often saw Van Horne perform in the role of storyteller. From his position at the head of a long dining room table, adorned with flowers and silver, an animated Van Horne would recount tales to an appreciative audience of friends and family, all the while toying with a heavy silver fork balanced on his forefinger. By all accounts he was an entertaining storyteller, although in his later years he had a tendency to exaggerate. When reflecting on his friend's all too human qualities, Sir John Willison, the urbane *Globe* editor, described Van Horne as a "gracious host who talked much but was never dull or commonplace. Decisive in judgment and confident in opinion, his sentences were so picturesque and so penetrating that even his rasher statements were seldom challenged."[756]

Although Sunday was a favourite time to entertain, it was not uncommon for William and Addie to entertain on weekdays. Nor was it uncommon for the couple to lunch with friends at 917 Sherbrooke Street and then meet the same people elsewhere that day for dinner. Often they accepted written invitations — some delivered the day of the function — to a meal at Lord Strathcona's. The bearded CPR financier had come a long way since toiling for three decades as a Hudson's Bay trader in the Labrador wilderness and acquiring what Lord Minto, the Governor General, contemptuously referred to as a "squaw wife."[757] As befitted a man of wealth and social position, he now owned a huge sandstone and smooth-dressed stone mansion that occupied two lots at Dorchester and Fort Streets and featured a magnificent three-storey mahogany staircase, a second-floor ballroom, an orchid-filled greenhouse, and a dining room that opened into a garden that could hold more than two thousand people. Over its lifetime, the house would be rebuilt and enlarged three times. One of these ambitious transformations inspired Lady Aberdeen to write in her diary that Strathcona was "princely in all he does." She then recounted how he had ordered a large expansion to his mansion after discovering the night before that it was not spacious enough to accommodate all the guests that he had entertained that evening.[758]

Whether a Sunday luncheon or a weekday meal at Lord Strathcona's or the Van Hornes', the menu was extensive. Thanks to one of Mary Van Horne's intermittent diary entries, we know that eighteen people assembled around the Van Hornes' Montreal dining room table on January 3, 1893, a Tuesday, to consume a dinner consisting of consommé, boiled cod with anchovy sauce, partridge pates, ox palates with mushrooms, saddle of mutton, turkey with celery sauce, potatoes, peas, celery-root, English pheasants with port wine sauce, frozen chestnut pudding, celery and cheese, Neapolitan ice cream, pineapple water ice fruit, coffee, and tea.[759] Only slightly less daunting was the menu served at a May 1896 luncheon, which included Sir Wilfrid Laurier and the premier of New Brunswick, Andrew George Blair, who would become the federal minister of railways and canals after the Liberals' June election victory. The fare at that May luncheon consisted of consommé, haddock with mayonnaise sauce, mushrooms on toast, spring chicken, potato and spinach salad, salad of stuffed tomatoes, frozen pudding, and strawberries and sweets, including dried persimmons.[760] To meals of this nature, if not to Van Horne's customary unrestrained diet, must go much of the credit for his growing portliness and the onset of diabetes.

Such excess was not found only in the dining room; conspicuous consumption also took to the waves. James Jerome Hill, when visiting Montreal in June 1906, shortly before Bennie's marriage, arrived on his substantial yacht, *Wacouta*, which was rarely used except for trips to his Canadian fishing haunt, the Saint John tributary of the St. Lawrence River. A *Gazette* reporter who spotted the vessel lying just off the Bonsecours Market referred to it as "a perfect floating palace of luxury." Since the yacht was 243 feet in length and boasted 10 staterooms, a steam laundry, and a 43-member crew, this was an apt description.[761]

Rudyard Kipling was another notable entertained at 917 Sherbrooke Street. In late September 1907, this complex, enigmatic figure and his wife, Carrie, sailed on the *Empress of Britain* for Canada, where plans called for them to take a transcontinental train trip and for Kipling, the devoted Imperialist, to give rousing speeches on imperial unity to Canadian Clubs. Repeating a gesture that he had made fifteen years earlier, Van Horne arranged for the couple to have the use of a special green velvet and mahogany "private car," which could be hitched to the rear of any train, thereby enabling the Kiplings to stop en route at major towns. In 1915, Van Horne recalled, "Rudyard Kipling was at my house in Montreal for several days but I only had a chance to see him for a few hours. He has improved very much since we met before & has become more human & sociable. He is really interesting & knows a lot about everything."[762]

As for Kipling, he had mixed feelings about his Canadian visit. Despite his encounter with Van Horne and his visit to Rideau Hall, then occupied by Lord Grey and his family, Kipling found Canada a "constipating land," where he had to speak in what we would now label "soundbites" since Canadians could not "carry anything more than three and a half lines in their busy heads." Canadians' one redeeming feature, it seems, was "a certain crude material faith in the Empire, of which they naturally conceive themselves to be the belly-button."[763] Although Kipling was probably at his most introverted when he expressed these sentiments, his international reputation was at its peak. For in November 1907, when he was working on his Canadian articles for the *Morning Post*, he received word that he had been awarded the Nobel Prize for Literature. Ten years later, in November 1927, when addressing a Canadian Club dinner in London, "The Bard of Empire" would pay a marked tribute to Van Horne's memory with the observation that his one-time Canadian host "was as big and full of vision as Cecil Rhodes" and that "he and Rhodes were the two biggest men" that Kipling had ever met in his life.[764]

Samuel S. McClure, who published *McClure's* magazine, was another Van Horne admirer and visitor to 917 Sherbrooke Street West. The two men struck up a friendship before the publisher inaugurated the literature of exposure that did much to discredit the reputation of American big business, which Van Horne, the staunch capitalist, venerated. McClure became a trailblazer in January 1903 when, in an editorial in his magazine, he announced that three of its articles constituted such an "arraignment of the American character as should make every one of us stop and think."[765] McClure's stable of skilled and meticulous investigative journalists, such as Lincoln Steffens and Ida M. Tarbell, helped to make McClure the leading publisher of muckraking articles. In 1906, however, he suffered a serious setback when several of his top writers, disillusioned with the literature of exposure, left the magazine to found a new publication, the progressive *American Magazine*. When he became financially strapped, McClure sought advice from Van Horne, who, of course, was only too happy to provide it. Subsequently, McClure declared that he would not borrow money under any circumstances and would not do anything without the approval of his Canadian friend.[766]

Another popular literary figure entertained by the Van Hornes was Gilbert Parker (later Sir Gilbert), who, with his wife, spent a couple of days at the Sherbrooke Street mansion in April 1896.[767] Van Horne knew little, if anything, about classical literature and rarely read novels, contemporary or otherwise, but he enjoyed the company of writers. He probably became a friend of the Canadian-born author because Parker had endeavoured to interpret the Northwest in short stories, albeit romantic and melodramatic ones that betrayed his lack of first-hand knowledge of the area. A prolific author of short stories, novels, poetry, and sonnets, Parker eventually settled in England, where he became a member of Parliament in 1900. He was knighted six years after he partook of Van Horne hospitality in Montreal and became a baronet in 1915, by which time he had become the most popular novelist in the British Empire.[768]

A less exalted figure entertained by the Van Hornes was the Canadian artist Wyatt Eaton. Eaton had been overwhelmed when he saw Jean-François Millet's *Woman with a Lamp* at a large Paris exhibition in the summer of 1873, and when he returned to Canada he continued to be impressed by the Barbison school and the Millet tradition. The Phillipsburg, Quebec, mayor's son had gone on to become an accomplished portrait painter, painting numerous portraits in Montreal between 1892 and 1893. Among his subjects were Van Horne and Addie, whose home he shared for months on end. From New York, in 1896, the year of his untimely death, Eaton wrote Addie, "Let me say by letter again what I have already said by word. I owe this avoidance of another complete 'break down' and the completion of my work entirely to your kindness dear Lady Van Horne and Mrs Eaton also feels this to be a fact."[769]

Another prominent visitor was well-known Métis poet and entertainer Emily Pauline Johnson. Between 1892 and 1910, this beautiful daughter of a Mohawk chief and an English gentlewoman undertook a series of speaking tours in Canada, and it was undoubtedly during one of these tours that Van Horne first met her. Like so many other spectators at Pauline's performances, he would have been mesmerized by both her beauty and her combination of aristocratic hauteur and daintiness. At any rate, he (or Addie?) invited her to lunch one day at the Montreal mansion. This provided Pauline with an opportunity to admire Van Horne's art collection ("His pictures are glorious. Rosseau, Corot, Doré, Reynolds — all the great names," she wrote to a friend) and to be impressed by her host's refined taste and homespun charm.[770]

Even individuals subjected to volleys of withering criticism by Van Horne were prepared to accept his hospitality. General William D. Washburn, a leading citizen of Minneapolis, a member of Congress, and an initiator of the CPR-owned Soo line, was one such victim. On June 30, 1896, his blunt, no-nonsense friend Van Horne advised him:

Nobody has said or thought, so far as I know, that you are unfit for the Presidency of the Soo Company, & to make clear what is in my mind & what is in the minds of a good many among your friends, I may illustrate it by pointing out that nobody thought Mr. Sherman or Mr. Allison unfit for the Presidency of the United States, but all things considered, it was thought best to nominate Mr. McKinley. His nomination did not mean that he was thought to have more ability or that he was held in higher esteem by those who knew him ... it was only a question of expediency... Only the weak excite no antagonisms. It is a common characteristic of the strong to quarrel with their best friends. That is one of your characteristics & you do not know it ...[771]

Yet a month after firing off this missive to Washburn, Van Horne entertained the Minneapolis businessman and his family at Sherbrooke Street. Three years later Van Horne had occasion to employ even more blunt and colourful language when addressing his friend. Incensed and wounded by misstatements Washburn had attributed to him, Van Horne wrote accusingly, "You knew when you wrote that letter that the words attributed to me were falsely quoted. You are vain enough to think that you may throw mud at your friends when it suits your purposes of the moment and that they will meekly take it as from Divine hands; but they do not and I will not, and you may go to Hell."[772]

Among the art critics who made their way to the Sherbrooke Street mansion was a Lithuanian-born Jew who wore perfectly cut, pale grey suits with a dark red carnation in the buttonhole. Bernard Berenson was a sensitive aesthete who had chalked up a brilliant academic career at Harvard University before going on to become a world-renowned art critic and connoisseur of Italian Renaissance art. In December 1904, when he was thirty-nine, he and Van Horne had a "lively night out" in New York. A decade later, in the winter of 1914, the critic and author, this time accompanied by his wife, Mary, his collaborator and a connoisseur in her own right, visited the Van Horne mansion in Montreal, where they saw Van Horne's collection, but not the man himself. Van Horne was laid up with "inflammatory rheumatism," a condition that would incapacitate him for months during the winter of 1914–15.

Following their ill-starred visit to the Van Horne home and to the homes of other Montreal collectors, Mary Berenson unburdened herself in a letter to the Berensons' friend and patroness Isabella Stewart Gardner, the well-known Boston art collector. It was, indeed fortunate, wrote Mary, that Isabella had decided not to accompany the Berensons to Montreal because all she would have found there was provincialism. Provincialism was everywhere, but especially in the homes of Square Mile millionaires, who built "hideous brownstone houses" and "hung in their multifarious and overheated rooms a vast collection of gilt-framed mediocre pictures, often spurious and almost always, even if authentic, poor ..." Only time spent with Van Horne could have helped to redeem the visit. "I am sure it would be far more interesting — not the collection but the human situation — if Sir Wm. van Horne were not laid up with inflammatory rheumatism. We haven't seen him. His son is a powerful and intelligent man, but of course doubly busy," she wrote[773]

The Berensons' dismissive attitude toward the art collections that they viewed in Montreal is not too surprising given that the couple was most knowledgeable and interested in Italian Renaissance art. What is really striking is Mary Berenson's description of thirty-six-year-old Bennie Van Horne. "Powerful" and "intelligent" are not the usual adjectives applied to Van Horne's only son, who had a good mind but who was destined by his upbringing and his father's lofty stature to become spoiled and cynical.

Perhaps because he was the only son to survive early childhood, Bennie ("Benj" to intimate friends) fell victim to an overpowering, and ultimately destructive, love. From his earliest years, he was the centre of attention, doted on by Addie, who fretted about him constantly (she referred to him as "my dear precious boy" when he was in his twenties), and continuously instructed by Van Horne, who, of course, expected great things of him. "My Dear Little Boy ... I hope you will be very careful and not cause Mama any anxiety. She worries a great deal about you. Dont go into the deep water and when you are on the train coming home dont go out on the platform," enjoined Van Horne in a letter written to ten-year-old Bennie, then vacationing in St. Andrews.[774] The following summer, although caught up in the weighty CPR arbitration proceedings, Van Horne nevertheless snatched time to bombard his wife with instructions relating to their son's welfare. From the Hotel Vancouver, on June 24, he instructed, "Don't let Bennie break his little neck or get sun stroke this summer."[775] This was followed six days later by "Don't let Bennie get ill again by over exerting himself in the hot sun. He should make some trips of ten miles or so in the country with his pony. If there is a swimming school in Montreal he ought to take lessons."[776] Counselled an agitated Van Horne just over a week later, "I hope Bennie has not suffered from the hot weather. You must run down to the sea shore with him and your mother during August. I hope you will plan to do that soon after my return. You must not waste your strength unnecessarily by remaining at Montreal during the very hot weather."[777]

Bennie's illnesses, no matter how insignificant, were a source of great anxiety for both parents. They became especially alarmed when he contracted typhoid fever in Cuba in the summer of 1902. The fact that he was hospitalized for eleven weeks suggests that he may have developed severe complications from the disease or, alternately, that Van Horne insisted on prolonged hospitalization in order to avoid any possibility of a relapse. In any event, while Bennie languished in a New York City hospital, day-to-day life for the Van Horne family took on a new sense of urgency, with telegrams flying back and forth between New York and Montreal and all three immediate family members rushing to Bennie's bedside. During this anxiety-wracked period, Van Horne hurtled back and forth between Montreal and St. Andrews, Montreal and New York, and even made a trip to the Northwest, only interrupting the press of business to consult doctors about Bennie and to instruct Addie about his well-being. "I assume that you had the doctors permission to give Bennie grapes. Dr Wylie told me he was more afraid of them than any-

thing else for they were the cause of many relapses — the seeds and pieces of skin. Don't take any chances," he wrote Addie when she was ministering to Bennie in New York.[778] Fortunately, the invalid recovered and was able to return to Cuba and his job with the Cuba Railroad.

Bennie, who appears to have been as weak as his father was strong, reacted as one might expect to the smothering parental love and the Van Horne wealth. He became unmotivated, lazy, and spoiled. With a view to toughening up his son and improving his academic performance, Van Horne arranged in the

Bennie Van Horne, Van Horne's only surviving son. Although very gifted, he failed to realize his potential and to live up to his father's demanding expectations.

Courtesy of the National Archives of Canada, E000945218.

early 1890s for him to attend Dr. Holbrook's Military School in Sing Sing, New York. But even here there was no escaping the steady torrent of parental advice and lectures. Thoroughly fed up, Bennie dispatched a letter to his grandmother Hurd, expressing displeasure with his mother's moral lectures and insisting that they be buried. For good measure, he included a sketch of the lectures' grave.[779] Sketching, in fact, came naturally to Bennie, who, like his father, was an accomplished artist. When the mood struck, this artistically talented son could produce devastatingly witty and biting caricatures of his grotesquely large sister, Addie, or well-executed, sombre self-portraits in oils.

What Bennie required, of course, was distance from his family, particularly from his father, who, no doubt, was at pains to hide his bitter frustration with him. If "Mamma's own forlorn, deserted but happy lamblet," as he once labelled himself, had struck out on his own after graduating from McGill University in applied science (today referred to as engineering) he might have enjoyed a rosier future. However, when not gainfully employed in Cuba, he remained at home, assiduously cultivating the air of a ne'er do-well who enjoyed liquor, running up bank overdrafts, and gambling.

There is no question but that Bennie wanted to acquit himself better in the eyes of his parents. He as much as admitted this when, at age twenty-four, he wrote from the Chicago Club, "I can somewhat appreciate how you feel about it, but really, Mamma, I have been doing a lot of thinking during the past year, and I fully realize that I have been far from what I should have been, and I really am trying to be a credit to you all, especially since I have found what it is to be really in love with a sweet nice girl."[780]

Although she is only identified as Jeannette, the object of his affections was undoubtedly an American who did not meet with his parents' approval. Bennie did not marry her. Instead, in on June 12, 1906, in Montreal's St. George Church, he married Edith Molson, the only daughter and first child of Dr. William Alexander Molson, scion of a large Montreal brewing fortune, and Esther Shepherd, daughter of R.W. Shepherd, who owned a steamship line, the Ottawa Navigation Company.

Van Horne was delighted with this match, which would link the Van Hornes with one of Montreal's most respected and powerful families. Moreover, he was fond of his new daughter-in-law. As a token of his affection, he presented her with two Chinese porcelains on the occasion of her marriage and signed his letters to her, "with much love." His joy can well be imagined when, on July 10, 1907, he learned that she had been safely delivered of a son. The boy, the couple's only child, would be christened William Cornelius Covenhoven Van Horne.

In June 1906, Van Horne took time out from a visit to New York to pen a letter to Addie. "It has occurred to me," he wrote, "that Bennie and his wife should make their home with us for a while until their plans and arrangements are all made and that Edith might feel some delicacy about this unless cordially asked to do so by you. Will you not write them."[781] With this missive, the stage was set for the young couple to move into the Van Horne mansion after their return from their honeymoon. It would become their permanent home, for it seems that Van Horne was incapable of weaning Bennie — or anyone for that matter — from his close control. And, for his part, Bennie was incapable of steering a course of his own.

This arrangement, of course, was not in either their best interests or those of their only child. "Little William" or "Small William," as he was frequently called, became Van Horne's adored grandson. Van Horne loved children, but the love that he lavished on this child was so intense that it was beyond reason and ultimately destructive. The boy was only four months old when his grandfather began to mould his tastes. As he later wrote, "I wished him to have artistic tastes, so I carried him around to see the pictures. He noticed some things in them from the start. Already [at a year and a half] he can tell ships and birds and the sea, calls them by name, pats them."[782]

When away from home, Van Horne wrote regularly to William. If he failed to do so it was only because the most urgent and pressing business scuttled his good intentions. This happened at least once, in December 1909, when he was visiting Cuba. Swamped by work and engagements, he advised Addie: "... I have even had to neglect my letters to Small William." He then added, with a touch of pride, "Everybody here asks about the dear little man. The President was especially interested concerning him for he expects him to be the future great man of Cuba."[783] It appears that no matter where Van Horne travelled, people always inquired about his grandson.

Interestingly, it was in the spring of that year that Van Horne dispatched illustrated letters to his grandson that would become immortalized in a book assembled by Canadian author Barbara Nichol and published in 2001. Entitled *Trunks All Aboard: An Elephant ABC*, it reproduces twenty-six postcards that Van Horne painted on hotel stationery while he, Addie, and young Addie were visiting England and the Continent. Since he had an extraordinary fondness for elephants (was this because there was a certain elephantine quality to him and he wanted to draw attention to it?), Van Horne made an elephant the subject of each postcard. He signed his charming watercolours "Grandpa" and depicted his elephants in a whimsical way — carrying a framed painting, smoking a cigar on the deck of the *Empress of Britain*, taking dancing lessons, etc.

In the book, the cards are accompanied by droll captions written by Nichol, who has used each painting as an excuse to alphabetize an elephant from Ahmed to Zinnia.

When at home, Van Horne spoiled his grandson shamelessly, indulging him even more than he had his own son. When young William expressed an interest in his grandfather's Model T Ford, Van Horne immediately arranged for an exact, child-size replica to be made for him. At St. Andrews, the doting grandfather would order six or more model ships at a time for his grandson from Captain Maloney, an expert craftsman and maker of model vessels. Young William would float the ships on the Covenhoven lily pond. Then, taking aim with his toy gun, he would shoot at them. After all the vessels had been sunk or sufficiently battered, Van Horne would order more.[784]

Predictably this foolish indulgence played no small part in helping to create a very self-centred, pompous youngster. It is possible that his parents tried to provide a mitigating influence, but it is unlikely as Bennie was struggling with his own demons — drink and gambling — and Edith had her hands full trying to cope with her husband's upsetting behaviour.

Fortunately young Addie had no demons to fight. A shy woman who had inherited her father's big frame and beautiful blue eyes, she appears not to have protested openly at playing second fiddle to Bennie, although there were times when she undoubtedly resented the inordinate attention lavished on her younger brother. There are certainly hints of this in a letter written when she and her aunt Mary were on an extended visit to the Continent and Addie was trying to reconcile herself to the idea that her father might not be able to be able to join her there and accompany her home. To her grandmother Hurd, Addie confessed, "I am very much disappointed of course that there is a possibility that Papa may not come, for it would be delightful for him and for me, think how lovely for me to travel a little with Papa, a pleasure which I have never had."[785]

This, Addie's first trip to Europe, had been instigated by her aunt, who believed that her niece's needs had been too long overlooked and that to prepare for her entry into society Addie should exchange her hitherto quiet, retiring life for a year of travel abroad.[786] Van Horne had finally accepted the idea, but then found that the demands of the CPR arbitration proceedings in Vancouver would prevent him from returning east in time to wish his beloved daughter goodbye. Nevertheless, in between daily sessions of the arbitration panel and consultations with CPR counsel, he found time to write young Addie: "I am unable to get away from here and the sorrowful conclusion that I cannot see you again before you go has settled down upon me and I can only console myself with the reflection that

I will be almost certainly obliged to cross the Atlantic before the end of the year and that I will then be sure to see you and Mary in Dresden. Will you not make it a rule to write me once a week? Such a weekly letter will be a source of great happiness to me."[787]

Only three months earlier, Addie had written somewhat wistfully and poignantly to her adored father, "It has been a long time since I received any of your lovely illustrated letters but I know well you are too busy to write very much and when you do have a leisure moment I always like to have you look at and enjoy your pictures ..."[788] Looking at pictures was certainly a pastime that Addie could identify with because she loved art. It was a passion that she shared with her father, along with a love of collecting and identifying fungi.

The doting daughter was a conscientious letter writer, often seizing the opportunity in her missives to stoke her father's ego. Writing in November 1888 she declared, "I tell you Papa our house is more palatial and our drawing rooms are furnished with more magnificence and taste than any palace or castle in Europe that I have yet seen." Young Addie followed this with a plea to Van Horne to take a month off to visit "the wonderful art treasures of the Old World." To reinforce her plea, she asserted, "I am sure you are working too hard. It is too much for one man altho' he is the strongest and cleverest and dearest man in the world to bear such a load of responsibility."[789]

Partly because of his deprived youth, Van Horne focused nearly all of what little private life he had on his family. The tragedy is that although it usually provided badly needed solace for his sensitive but restless soul it also provided him with the deepest disappointment of his life: Bennie's failure to realize his potential and to measure up to his father's demanding expectations. Regrettably, Van Horne would never learn that he couldn't micromanage people's lives the way he could a railway. At some subconscious level, he may have grasped this basic truth, but if he did he was never be able to submerge his intensely controlling instincts. The resulting fallout would reverberate down through the decades.

Chapter Thirteen
Cuba Beckons

The trip to the West Coast in the spring of 1899 reinforced Van Horne's view that he would rather not devote his remaining years to the plethora of hobbies that had hitherto enthralled and delighted him. When heading the Canadian Pacific Railway he had only been able to spare the occasional hour for them, and therein had lain much of their attraction. Once he had resigned from the CPR presidency, however, they failed to kindle any interest whatsoever. The situation might have been different, he confessed to his old friend Otto Meysenburg, if he "had knocked off ten years ago." In semi-retirement, however, he discovered that great gobs of leisure time only made all those pastimes "flavourless."[790] Although he had predicted otherwise, he now recognized that hobbies could not fill his life.[791] Even less could communion with nature, the route chosen by Meysenburg, who, in his retirement in Alma, California, found himself hungering for the "might of silence and the brotherhood of stars in cool, calm spaces on the mountain height."[792]

Van Horne conceded that his health had been "in an uncertain state for several years."[793] Nevertheless, there was still too much restless energy churning in his massive fifty-six-year-old frame to allow him to settle into a life of comparative ease that centred on his hobbies and various business ventures. What he seemed to need more than anything else at this juncture was a major challenge, one capable of taxing his problem-solving abilities to the utmost and giving a new edge to life. Or, by his own admission, a project that involved "working out schemes."[794] Fortunately, such a challenge came to Van Horne's rescue, and, not surprisingly, it took the form of another railway enterprise: the building of the Cuba Railroad.

Van Horne, the poker player, had certainly taken on a tremendous gamble when he agreed to mastermind the construction of the CPR, but this was nothing compared to the audacity he would demonstrate in organizing and completing the construction of a railway in Cuba, a developing nation that had just emerged from four centuries of colonial dependence on Spain to a state of quasi-colonial dependence on the United States.

Like nineteenth-century Canada, Cuba had a commodity-based economy, with sugar and tobacco as the tropical island's agricultural mainstays. Of the two, sugar was by far the most important. In the interests of getting their sugar speedily to market, Cuban planters had built Latin America's first railway in 1837. Soon a hodgepodge network of railways transported sugar from all major sugar refineries to Cuba's ports for shipment abroad — chiefly to the United States, Cuba's principal market. In 1900, when Van Horne first visited the island, Cuba supplied 2.7 percent of the world demand for this commodity, a figure that would soar to a dominant 21.1 percent in 1925.[795]

Despite its stranglehold on the nineteenth-century Cuban economy, sugar production never realized its full potential because of a lack of capital, the ineptitude of the Spanish administration, and an archaic royal land grant system. These factors also contributed significantly to the Cuban economy's lacklustre performance, which in turn fuelled the numerous frustrations that nurtured Cubans' growing desire for independence. Eventually these frustrations boiled over in a series of minor rebellions and skirmishes that culminated in the War of Independence from 1895 to 1898.

The last stages of the overall struggle for independence (the Ten Years' War, 1868 to 1878, and the War of Independence) were so costly that when Spain relinquished control of the island to the United States in December 1898, starvation, anarchy, and devastation had become widespread. Visible signs of the war's impact were everywhere, from closed schools and abandoned farms and plantations to wretched shabbiness and stench in the national capital, Havana. And there were noticeably fewer people on Havana's streets.

Largely because of the war and Spain's practice of herding the rebels' allies into disease-ridden "reconstruction camps," the island's population had plummeted from approximately 1.8 million in 1895 to 1.5 million in 1899.[796] The end result was an alarming shortage of labour. This was accompanied by a huge shortage of horses and oxen, their numbers having been decimated by the hostilities.

The bureaucratic nightmare in which the country operated after Spain's departure also worked against a flourishing economy. Corrupt courts and tangled land-holding laws were everyday facts of life, as was a chaotic monetary system. Combined with the devastation and disease caused by the war, they presented a daunting challenge to the military government when it took office in January 1899.

Notwithstanding such drawbacks, Cuba was a country brimming with investment opportunities. In the aftermath of war, its economic and urban infrastructures were in dire need of rebuilding. Streetcars, bridges, warehouses, telephones, sugar storage facilities, and sugar plantations all needed extensive renovation. In fact, no sooner had the smell of gun smoke vanished from the air and shipping been restored than hordes of entrepreneurs began descending on the island eager to pluck whatever development plums they could.

Among these promoters were Canadians who had carved out a niche for themselves in what had become Canadian specialties: the insurance, utility, and transportation fields. Seeking new investment opportunities, the intrepid Canadians came armed with capital from the British and American capital markets and from Canadian financial institutions suddenly overflowing with cash as a result of Canada's extended economic boom.

Competing with the Canadians were American entrepreneurs, among whom was a young man who would link up with Van Horne and play a pivotal role in the construction of the Cuba Railroad. He was thirty-four-year-old Percival Farquhar, a Quaker and a trained engineer and lawyer who had become a good friend of several Cubans during his years at Yale College. Good-looking and suave, he could have become a favourite guest of the leading New York dowagers at whose dinners and balls he circulated so gracefully. Instead Farquhar left New York and a career as a Wall Street speculator to pursue capitalist dreams in Cuba and ultimately to become a representative of some of the worst excesses of finance capitalism.

After arriving on the island in the summer of 1898, Percival Farquhar focused his sights on a scheme to electrify Havana's streetcars, then drawn by emaciated mules and horses. The deplorable state of the city's transportation system also attracted the notice of a coterie of Van Horne's business friends, notably two American cronies who were already involved in business ventures with him: General Alger, who resigned from his position as secretary of war in 1899, and Garret Hobart, who died in 1899 after serving two years as vice-president of the United States. Gonzalo de Quesada, the well-known Cuban diplomat, writer, and orator, was probably another friend who sniffed out investment opportunities in Havana and sought to alert Van Horne to the possibilities for making money in that city's transportation system. Van Horne, in fact, would later claim that it was Quesada who first drew his attention to investment opportunities in Cuba.[797]

In any event, Quesada or one of the Americans, probably General Alger, suggested that Van Horne employ his genius developing an electrical transportation system for Cuba's capital. This idea had little appeal for the former CPR president, but what did interest him was the investment return such an undertaking offered.[798]

As they had in the past, the twin themes of transportation and money-making opportunities had an irresistible appeal for Van Horne. Indeed, he was so excited by the prospect of reaping huge returns from a scheme to electrify Havana's tramway system that he immediately invited a restless corporate empire builder who was always alert to the main chance, William Mackenzie, and other associates from similar enterprises to form a syndicate to pursue one of the two transit concessions up for grabs. Writing to General Alger, Van Horne noted pungently, "... Mackenzie thinks there are 'millions in it' if we get it into reasonably secure shape. It has been a long hunt and we musn't miss it now. Only Mackenzie and I know of your connection with it."[799]

The hunt for a suitable Caribbean investment scheme may have ended, but it did not bring the anticipated rewards. As luck would have it, Mackenzie's and Van Horne's group went down to defeat in the dramatic, bitterly contested fight waged by several syndicates for the two prizes. The victorious group was headed by Farquhar and Tiburcio P. Castaneda, a Cuban lawyer. Still, not all was clear sailing for the winners since their concessions were opposed in the Havana courts by rival business buccaneers.[800] Eventually Leonard Wood, the American military governor, forced a compromise that led to the establishment of the Havana Electric Railway, in which Farquhar held stock but no position. In early January 1900, Van Horne accepted an invitation to sit on its board of directors.[801] If he had not succeeded in his first attempt to establish a business beachhead in Cuba, he had at least emerged with a consolation prize.

No sooner was he on the board, however, than Van Horne learned from a Cuban source that there was a "good deal of unfavourable gossip about the Company's work." The source, a prominent Havana businessman whom Van Horne met in New York, reported that construction payrolls contained the names of many fictitious workers. This alarmed Van Horne, who suggested that the matter be investigated, informing the company's president, Edwin Hanson, "The method of robbery referred to is not peculiar to Cuba. We have to carefully guard against it even here in honest Canada."[802] Unfortunately, the company would attract so much hostility that Van Horne would try to hide his involvement with it, even going to such lengths as to refuse the presidency when it was offered to him.[803]

Once he had nailed down the electrification franchise, Farquhar went in search of a more ambitious project. This turned out to be a trunk railway that would run down the spine of Cuba, linking the sea port of Santiago at the island's east end with Havana at the west end and reducing the travel time between the two ports from ten days to one. As the only trunk railway serving eastern Cuba, it would help to open up the country's rich interior and in doing so generate wealth. In this largely undeveloped interior were areas that contained not only extensive deposits of copper, iron, and other minerals but also vast territories of land superbly suited to the cultivation of sugar cane and tobacco, the raising of cattle, and the growing of invaluable groves of cedar, mahogany, and ebony. Spain, the colonizing power, could have exploited these potential riches, but it had opposed the construction of a trans-island railway, fearing that such a vital transportation link would help to promote Cuban national integration. Spain also dreaded the fierce opposition of Spanish coastal shipping interests to any railway.[804]

With the installation of an American military government in January 1899, Farquhar felt free to pursue his plans for the railway of his imagination. In an attempt to convert dream to reality, he formed a syndicate that, in the summer of 1899, offered $5 million for the small Matanzas Railroad, located east of Havana. Just when it appeared that negotiations were reaching a successful conclusion, however, the Boer War broke out and British investors, the syndicate's chief backers, "drew back."[805] When he realized that the war would last longer than anticipated, the ambitious entrepreneur began searching for an investor to replace the English dropouts. It was then that he approached Van Horne and asked if he would assume the leadership of the syndicate.[806]

Van Horne was no stranger to Farquhar. The two had already been introduced to each other by General Samuel Thomas, who was a mutual friend, a syndicate member, and an ex-president of several American railways. Farquhar may have attempted to bring Van Horne on board at that first meeting, but this is unclear. What is clear is that the ex-Wall Street speculator began lobbying Van Horne in earnest as early as the spring of 1899, pitching his idea to him in person when the two of them met in New York, and by letter when Van Horne was in Montreal.

Initially Van Horne had a lot of qualms about Farquhar's proposal and resisted the idea of becoming involved, informing the American, "The information I gathered about your scheme was not encouraging and I came away disinclined to go into it for the reason that the possible profit did not seem to justify the risk; but I have great confidence in Gen Thomas's judgment in such matters and if he sees a favorable conclusion I am quite prepared to revise my views."[807] The following day, March 30, 1899, he spelled out why he had turned down the proposal in a letter to Andrew Onderdonk, the American railway contractor. His chief concern was the prohibitive cost ($30,000 per mile for the major line and its branches and $5,000 per mile for improvements and equipment). Other deterrents included the conspicuous shortage of Cuban labourers, the possibility of disaffection, and the years of "bushwhacking" that would be involved in such an undertaking. Van Horne climaxed his arguments with the observation that "Cuba has a liberal supply of artistic liars and several of them are interested in selling their railways."[808]

Because he too had come to entertain reservations about it, General Thomas withheld his blessing from the railway project. Van Horne therefore decided not to have anything to do with it — at least for the time being. Nevertheless, he kept a sufficiently open mind on the subject to ask Farquhar to go to Cuba and explore the situation further. For nine months the scheme languished, only to be revived when the young man returned to New York with a more favourable report on Cuba's outlook. Convinced that the time was ripe, he urged Van Horne to go to the island and take stock of the situation himself.[809] This encouragement and his recent election to the board of the Havana Street Railway were all the persuasion that Van Horne needed to embark on his first visit to Cuba, a decisive fact-finding tour that heralded the opening of a new and exciting chapter in his life.

Once in Cuba, Van Horne was forcefully struck by how poorly served the island was by its railway system. To serve a country equal in size to Pennsylvania, there was only 1,135 miles of track, 90 percent of which radiated out from Havana. Additional track encircled the populous seaport of Santiago, but only one hundred miles or so of railway served the largest and richest provinces in the country, Santa Clara, Camaguey, and Oriente. For the most part, these sugar-rich eastern provinces, comprising three-quarters of the island's area, could be reached only by water.

Weighed against this infrastructural weakness were the immense natural advantages Cuba enjoyed. If he had been less of a visionary, Van Horne might have failed to grasp the significance of these unlimited resources and the prospects for Cuba's development. But with his business acumen and characteristic optimism he saw a thinly populated, undeveloped island transformed out of all recognition by the construction of a railway that linked Havana with Santiago and the city of Camaguey (then known as Puerto Principe), the largest city in the interior. In pushing the CPR through to completion he had helped to transform western Canada. Perhaps he could now make things happen in Cuba. But he only hinted at this irresistible prospect when he reported to Joseph Todd, president of the small Cuba Central Railway: "During a visit to Cuba some six months ago I was struck by the great need of a railway connection between Havana and the eastern end of the island, and I was at the same time much impressed by the possibilities of the future in the country that would be opened by such a railway ..."[810] What he neglected to mention was that he had fallen in love with Cuba and its people. Cuba, it would appear, had so beguiled Van Horne that he was prepared to ignore many of the drawbacks that had earlier discouraged him from embracing Farquhar's railway scheme.

Still, he knew that there were many shoals to be navigated before he could realize his goal. One of these, and unquestionably the leading obstacle as far as he was concerned, was the Foraker Act. Enacted by the U.S. Congress in 1899, it was designed to protect Cubans and the military government from exploitation by carpetbaggers and irresponsible land speculators, such as those who had descended on Winnipeg in 1881. The act thus prohibited the granting of franchises or "concessions of any kind whatever" to foreigners during the American occupation. As long as this act was in place, any company that attempted to build a railway in Cuba could only be described as reckless, for in embarking on such an undertaking it would have to proceed without the power to expropriate lands for right-of-way or to construct track across navigable waters, public property, or public roads. To further complicate matters, any railway project that Van Horne launched in Cuba would have to proceed without a government subsidy or land grant. These roadblocks, coupled with those cited in his letter to Onderdonk, should have been enough to make him consider a Cuban railway venture doomed from the start, but since timidity was foreign to his nature, Van Horne would not let something like the Foraker Act and the other obstacles stand between him and the Cuban railway that he envisaged.

Van Horne now regarded the projected road as a challenge, a challenge made to order for his inventive mind and his appetite for adventure and one-upmanship. In fact, no sooner had he determined to build a railway than he began to ponder ways of overriding or evading the Foraker Act, albeit with a view to ultimately serving the best interests of the Cubans themselves. He studied the Foraker Act at length and reached the conclusion that perhaps the act's franchise provisions could be circumvented if an individual or a corporation bought individual parcels of private land and then built a railway on these strips. The solution seemed at hand when he checked with a lawyer friend, Howard Mansfield, and learned that there was nothing in Spanish law, which still operated in Cuba, even under the U.S. military government, to prevent such acquisitions. With this assurance, one of the few implicit in the projected scheme, Van Horne charged full steam ahead.

Van Horne was fortunate in having the support of the second military governor, General Leonard Wood, who believed that without such a railway, eastern Cuba would be inaccessible to what he regarded as the immeasurable "civilizing" and "modernizing" benefits of economic development and close ties to the United States.[811] He therefore aided and abetted the undertaking after receiving assurances that it would benefit Cuba and not merely enrich a few already wealthy individuals.[812] Wood and Van Horne, in fact, developed a close friendship.

A military surgeon who had graduated from Harvard's medical school, Wood had taken up his new appointment in December 1899, just a month before Van Horne arrived on the scene. The governor's appointment had been recommended to President McKinley by Secretary of War Elihu Root, who was convinced that the surgeon was the best man available for the difficult task of establishing good relations with the Cubans and getting them on their feet. The energetic Wood certainly justified this faith in him. In 1902, he would depart from Cuba with laurels, having made a significant contribution to its reconstruction.

Accompanied by his friend General Dodge and bolstered by Wood's endorsement of his railway, Van Horne journeyed to Washington in March 1900 to seek the support of the American government. He did not anticipate any problems in marshalling this support, although in a letter to General Wood he questioned how long it might take to arrange matters.[813] His faith in the American government was not misplaced, for President McKinley quickly approved the plans once the scheme had been outlined for him. It would have been difficult for him to do otherwise, since the construction of such a railway promised immediate employment for large numbers of Cubans. And once completed, the road would serve as an indispensable catalyst for the development of Cuban resources.

Less than two months after his departure for Cuba, Van Horne was back in Montreal, working feverishly to set up a company to build the railway. For guidance in this new venture, he looked to certain painful lessons culled from his CPR experience. One involved the thorny issue of financing. As he remembered all too painfully, the cautious conservatism of the CPR's directors had complicated the already daunting challenge of obtaining funds for expansion. This time around, he decided, he would labour under no such constraints.

In forming the new company, Van Horne decided to approach only very wealthy personal friends and acquaintances, men who could afford to wait indefinitely for a return on their money and who could put up capital during those difficult periods when funds and enthusiasm ran low, an all too common experience in railway construction.[814] To ensure that control remained in such hands, he fixed the capital stock at $8 million, divided into 160 shares of $50,000 each, and stipulated that no shareholder could subscribe to more than eight shares. As a further indication of his shrewdness, he inserted a penalty clause stipulating that shareholders who did not contribute an additional 40 percent when called upon to do so would have to sell their shares.[815] Unfortunately, recurring shortages of funds would later cause him to regret that he had not asked for more start-up capital. As men of enormous wealth, the Cuba Company's shareholders could easily have provided it for the asking in 1900.

To line up the necessary capital, Van Horne made a pilgrimage to New York, where, as he informed his friend Adolphe Boissevain, he found himself "in the position of a small boy with his pockets full of bonbons, and all the shares [he] would not let go willingly were taken away from [him]."[816] Although he did not expect much more than half of those he approached "to go in," everyone invited to take out stock did so. Van Horne even found himself asking some of the larger subscribers to drop a few of their shares in order to accommodate the wishes of parties who had not taken out a subscription. His appeal was largely rejected.[817]

The enthusiastic capitalist was so successful in attracting interest in the venture that he returned to Montreal stripped of all shares but a small holding for himself. He had accomplished his task in only a few hours.[818] Although he had made it clear that he was looking for ultimate results rather than quick profits,[819] Van Horne succeeded in lining up probably the most impressive list of subscribers ever associated with any commercial enterprise in the Americas. Such a remarkable achievement testifies to the huge respect he commanded in North American railroading and business circles. It also testifies to the tycoons' belief that, in the illuminating words of Henry Frick, the coal baron, "Railroads are the Rembrandts of Investment."[820]

Thanks in no small part to Van Horne's reputation and acumen, the list of shareholders that he recruited reads like a who's who of American capitalism, including such names as John W. Mackay, president of the Commercial Cable Company of London, England, and his old railroading rival James J. Hill. It must have taken Van Horne's formidable powers of persuasion to induce Mackay to become a subscriber because the cable company president had earlier declined to be associated with the enterprise, claiming that he was too busy with other commitments.[821] Skilful lobbying plus the extremely high regard in which Mackay held Van Horne likely decided the issue.

It is less clear why Van Horne decided to bring in Hill. Even Farquhar, who was to become Van Horne's right-hand man in the Cuba Company, was surprised at the railway tycoon's inclusion. If he had disregarded their railway rivalry, however, Farquhar would have quickly realized that the two men were good friends. Indeed, if pressed to admit it, Van Horne would probably have said that he secretly admired and respected his old antagonist, if for no other reason than that Hill was a master of humbug, an art that Van Horne venerated, especially when, as in Hill's case, it was put to good use. But even more important, Van Horne respected Hill's genius in all things pertaining to railroading. On learning that his railroading rival would subscribe to only four shares instead of eight, Van Horne informed him, "Most of those whose names I sent you subscribed for 8 shares each and I kept out 8 for you in case you should want that many; but 4 will be just as satisfactory as 8. I want you in the thing: that is my only wish ... I am planning for a board of 7 all of whom can be got together on short notice if required. I don't imagine that you would care to go on the Board?"[822]

Besides Mackay and Hill, the list of subscribers included: Samuel Thomas, the one member from Farquhar's original syndicate to join; Levi P. Morton, the banker and Congressman who had been a United States vice-president; E.H. Harriman, chairman of the Union Pacific, the Illinois Central, and the Chicago and Alton Railway boards; General Grenville Dodge, the legendary railroading man much admired by Van Horne; William L. Elkins, an oil promoter who organized gas and street railways in Philadelphia and other cities; Henry Flagler, a pioneer in Florida hotel development and a partner in Standard Oil; William C. Whitney, an American lawyer who had known remarkable triumphs as a politician (President Cleveland's secretary of the navy) and as a speculator in electric railways; Peter A.B. Widener, the former butcher and Philadelphia entrepreneur who had giant holdings in public utilities; and Thomas F. Ryan, the financier and promoter who had amassed a huge fortune in street railways and tobacco and was at the centre of New York City finance capitalism. Included for good measure were Van Horne's CPR colleagues R.B. Angus, Thomas Shaughnessy, and Charles Rudolph Hosmer.

Thomas Ryan, a master of stock market legerdemain, was another American Medici who did not jump at the opportunity to join the roster of subscribers. Ryan, whom Kate Reed labelled a "money machine,"[823] initially ridiculed Van Horne's bold gambit, contending that "it was a great waste of time for Van Horne to turn his back on an Empire and go chasing a Rabbit...."[824] He thought that Van Horne's legendary energies should be deployed in a much more promising and productive undertaking, a scheme that would produce a real empire for him to rule over. As outlined at a dinner given by Henry M. Whitney, the Boston financier and utilities magnate, it called for Ryan and some of his associates to obtain control of the CPR and then to invite Van Horne to return to it as president. Reinstalled in the presidency, Van Horne would work with Ryan's group to extend the CPR further into the United States and thereby secure for the railway a virtual monopoly of railway activity in North America.

When this scenario was laid before him, Van Horne was both startled and appalled. Then, regaining his composure, he told Ryan that his proposal made a mockery of everything that the CPR's builders stood for and that for him to participate in such a scheme would reek of the most vile treachery. Canadians, he curtly informed the financier, regarded the CPR as the backbone of their country and they would go to any lengths to prevent it from falling under American control. Under no circumstances would he, Van Horne, have anything to do with Ryan's proposal.[825]

Van Horne's strong rebuff must have irritated the American promoter, but if it did it was not enough to prevent him from doing an about-face. Succumbing to Van Horne's magnetism, the vice-president of the Morton Trust Company purchased shares in the newly formed company and supplied it with the backing of the Morton Trust. Unfortunately for Van Horne and the Cuba Company, this move did not portend a long-lasting, happy relationship. Only a few years down the line the actions of the noted robber baron would jeopardize the very future of the Cuba Railroad.

Perhaps because he wanted to run a one-man show, Van Horne adopted a somewhat cavalier approach to making board appointments to the Cuba Company. A case in point is that of Grenville Dodge. Van Horne only informed his friend some months after the fact that he had been made a company director and a member of its executive committee.[826] Dodge, in fact, would enjoy a brief reign as company vice-president.

Van Horne located the Cuba Company's head office in New York, but incorporated the company itself in permissive New Jersey, whose lenient corporate tax policies and antitrust laws were well suited to the company's purposes. In doing so, Van Horne arranged for articles of incorporation that allowed the company to "do pretty much anything." However, it did not follow, he told Joseph Todd, chairman of the Cuba Central Railroad, "that we have everything in view that is provided for."[827] The new company president had chosen New Jersey because its laws were well adapted to the multiplicity of purposes he had in mind for his new undertaking. They had to be, because Van Horne saw the building and operation of a railway as the first step in his plans for Cuba's overall development. Just as the CPR had spawned a host of subsidiary enterprises, so would the Cuba Company. Should his dream be realized, the holding company would develop not only a pioneering railway but also resource-based industries, telegraphs, ports, hotels, and townsites. All would be grist for the island's economic transformation and, not incidentally, profit for the company's shareholders.

Van Horne made it perfectly clear that his new company intended to adopt the CPR's modus operandi. To Joseph Todd, he announced that the Cuba Company planned to adopt and to perfect the methods that had enabled the Canadian company to build up a not just supporting but also-profitable traffic in only a few years. In emulating the CPR's methods, the Cuba Company would enjoy a decided advantage over the Canadian company, whose traffic had been developed in a sparsely populated country and under conditions "infinitely less favourable than those presented in Cuba."[828]

Not surprisingly, the Cuba Company adopted virtually the same system used by Canadian and American railways to procure supplies. Essentially this called for a purchasing agent to obtain the best available materials and equipment at the best possible prices. In the Cuba Company's case, the agent was based in New York and the managing officers, who placed the requisition orders, were based in Cuba. Aided by a staff of inspectors and clerks, the agent made the purchases and then oversaw their shipment to the company's storekeeper in Cuba.[829]

In assembling the management team for the new company, Van Horne assigned top spot to Percival Farquhar, who had conceived the idea of a railway to serve Cuba's interior and who had then worked so diligently to interest Van Horne in building one. Farquhar's unflagging optimism, drive, creative spark, and presence made him the ideal candidate to be Van Horne's second-in-command and field commander. Moreover, his generous and mild temperament, the product of his Quaker upbringing, equipped him well for dealing with proud and sensitive Latin Americans. Van Horne was probably influenced, though, by more than the young man's qualifications. It is quite possible that he saw something of his younger self in the intrepid entrepreneur, who had just demonstrated his prowess in besting wily American robber barons.

As for Farquhar, he would develop a great admiration both for his boss's personal life and for his operating methods. Van Horne's lightning calculations of the outlay required for bridges, fill, and cuts made an especially deep impression on the young man. It appears that Van Horne was even speedier at making these calculations than the railway line's contractors, May, Jekyll, and Randolph, members of that tough American breed known as "tropical tramps."

Although the two men admired and respected each other, their relationship was not always unruffled. For his part, Van Horne strongly disapproved of Farquhar's fondness for making highly speculative ventures, and on at least one occasion he made his views known in no uncertain terms. In defending himself, the younger man accused his boss of being "a little unjust." His speculations, claimed Farquhar, took neither time nor thought away from Cuba Company business. Still, rather than jeopardize their good relationship, which he valued more than Sir William realized, Farquhar would not invest in any other Cuban venture while he was a Cuba Company official. If he strayed from this intention, said Farquhar, it would be only because Van Horne was involved in the venture in question or had requested Farquhar's assistance with it.[830]

Farquhar would prove indispensable to Van Horne in the building of the Cuba Railroad. One observer who took stock of this was Minor Keith, the magnetic head of the United Fruit Company. Impressed by his role in opening up the eastern half of Cuba, Keith prevailed upon him to leave the Cuba Company at the end of 1903 for Guatemala to help him complete the long-neglected Guatemala Railroad.

No sooner was the Cuba Company up and running than Van Horne set off on still another trip to Cuba. In the years to come he would shuttle back and forth to the island two to three times a year to see how his various Cuban enterprises were faring and to deliver what his son, Bennie, described as "the regal opinion" on matters demanding his attention.[831] Sometimes he made the journey in the company of family members, notably Bennie, using the United Fruit Company boat the SS *Admiral Sampson*, out of Philadelphia, or, in later years, a vessel that sailed from New York. But usually Van Horne travelled with business or railway cronies whom he had persuaded to make the trip. As a rule he travelled straight through from Cuba to Montreal, but occasionally he would interrupt his trip at Miami or Palm Beach to rendezvous with the likes of Henry Flagler, who relished visits from Van Horne and General Dodge.

Travel associated with his Cuban interests alone should have sufficed to rescue Van Horne from his incurable restlessness. In this connection he made countless trips each year to New York, where much of the Cuba Company business and its annual meetings were conducted. Here, he would put up at one of the large hotels, often the Manhattan, where he would make himself accessible to anyone in the saloon prepared to down innumerable tankards of German beer throughout the night and listen to him expound on such disparate topics as Japanese pottery, Dutch art, cattle breeding, bacon curing, Chinese script, and the ideal planning of cities.[832]

Van Horne also mounted missions to Washington to consult with Americans prominent in Cuban affairs and to lobby on behalf of his railway. Stopping off in New York on his return to Montreal in late March 1900, he informed the ever-vigilant *New York Times* that reports claiming that he had acquired all of Cuba's railways were "very much exaggerated." Then he added, "I am very much impressed with the excellent condition of affairs down there, principally due to the efforts of General Wood and I believe that when the United States gets ready to grant self-government to that people, they will very well be able to take care of themselves."[833]

No matter how sanguine he was in public about conditions in Cuba, however, Van Horne was enough of a realist to know that political uncertainty did pose a threat to his enterprise. While the military government, headed by General Wood and his predecessor, General Brooks, had done an admirable job of relieving the starving population, disarming the combatants, and controlling yellow fever, much remained to be done before power could be assumed by the Cuban people. A legislative authority had not yet been convened; nor had an assembly to design a constitution. Nevertheless, Van Horne and the Cuba Company were determined to forge ahead with their plans, fully prepared to risk having the future government revoke or confiscate the project.

Chapter Fourteen
Building the Cuba Railroad

First on the agenda was the purchase of an existing railway, the launching of surveys, and the acquisition of land. This was to be followed by construction, Van Horne contending that when the necessary authority could be obtained both to cross roads, rivers, and other public property that lay between the company's parcels of land and to operate a railway, very little would remain to be done.[834] In other words, he hoped — and probably expected — that once an elected legislative body had been established the railway would be so far advanced that no authority could or would want to kill it. Van Horne conceded, however, that his company was taking a great risk in plunging ahead, fully realizing that developments could interrupt its work "temporarily, and possibly for a long time."[835] But there was no time to be lost. More to the (unspoken) point, if the company did not move quickly — before the end of the American occupation — it risked the possibility of having to submit a competing bid for the construction of a central railway.

Before proceeding with construction the company purchased a majority of the stock of the Sabanilla & Moroto Railroad, which ran from Santiago to San Luis, a distance of twenty-nine miles (together with a branch line of twelve miles).[836] Van Horne regarded this railway as the key to the whole enterprise, not only because of its location but also because of its charter, which gave it practically a monopoly in the vicinity of Santiago.[837] The acquisition of this road would enable the Cuba Company to build its trunk line as quickly as possible from Santa Clara to a connection with the Santiago Railway at San Luis, a distance of 337 miles. When the need arose, branches would be constructed from this trunk line to areas of the country being opened to development.[838]

West of Santa Clara, however, the company would rely on established railways for all necessary traffic connections. This ran contrary to Van

Horne's earlier plans for the railway, which had called for the Cuba Company to buy up their lines and then use them to extend its railway westward from Santa Clara to Cuba's capital. The prospect of a costly purchasing program, however, soon led him to jettison this idea and instead to opt for obtaining running rights on already operating track west of Santa Clara.[839]

Among the Cuba Company's first emissaries to Cuba were engineers and land examiners who arrived in the spring of 1900. The results of their preliminary survey inspired an enthusiastic report from the chief engineer, Miller Smith, who remarked that the country, although very undeveloped and thinly inhabited, was "the finest and most admirably adapted to agriculture of any equal amount of territory that it has ever been my fortune to examine." Smith was also impressed by the topography of the projected line. Its light grade, he noted, would allow heavy freights to be transported long distances at minimum cost and permit the establishment of an immense central sugar factory at some convenient location. Smith hastened to point out, though, that labour would have to be imported, as would most of the railway ties and bridge timber. Moreover, because of the prevalence of tropical diseases, notably malaria, hospitals would have to be maintained for the men. It was also likely that most of the water would have to be hauled or else wells would have to be dug to supply the construction camps.[840]

By the late spring of 1900, developments were unfolding so rapidly that Van Horne found himself busier than he had been in years, his new project inspiring the same sort of zest and enthusiasm that he had brought to the construction of the CPR. From both Montreal and Covenhoven he dispatched a steady stream of letters, including one addressed to Meysenburg, in which he confessed, "The Cuban matter is the most interesting one that I have ever encountered and I am looking forward to a great deal of pleasure in carrying it through, and perhaps profit as well — a few dozen Rembrandts and such things, which I think will quite fill my capacity for enjoyment."[841]

As the undertaking gathered momentum Van Horne found himself indulging his usual passion for detail. Just about everything, it seemed, came under his scrutiny, from the unexpected to the mundane. When one of the project's engineers was taken fatally ill, Van Horne monitored the situation closely, instructing the attending physician to spare no expense and keeping the engineer's wife, Mrs. Brothers, up to date on all developments. But just as he could engross himself in non-routine developments, so could he lose himself in questions of a routine nature. Nothing escaped his attention. The treatment of railway ties, plans for wooden culverts, the disposition and care of three hundred mules, raw sugar refining processes

— these were just a few of the day-to-day questions that utterly absorbed the Cuba Company president.

Even paint schemes had to pass scrutiny. Realizing that Cuba's vegetation is green year-round, he countermanded a requisition for dark olive green paint. To his way of thinking, such a colour was highly unsuitable for use on Cuba's buildings and water stations. Only mineral red would serve the purpose.[842]

On the other hand, when dealing with the Cubans themselves, he was not the legendary Van Horne. In Cuba, whose culture and mores differed markedly from Canada's, he went to great lengths to assert the gentler, more sensitive side of his nature, the side that had been rarely revealed when he swooped down on construction sites on the Canadian Prairies. Instead of resorting to his usual bluntness, he demonstrated a remarkable finesse and subtlety. To have done otherwise, of course, might have imperilled the whole undertaking, since, as Van Horne knew all too well, he could not construct a railway without land expropriation powers unless the Cubans gave their blessing to the enterprise and were prepared to provide the land for it.

Van Horne also knew that this goodwill had to be assiduously cultivated because the Cubans were an intensely proud, sensitive people who deeply resented the brash, condescending behaviour displayed toward them by some foreigners, particularly Americans. As a foreigner frequently mistaken for an American, Van Horne also had to take into account the Cubans' suspicions of American motives, especially their deeply ingrained fear that Americans wanted to see Cuba annexed to the U.S. Much to his annoyance, a few ardent, somewhat hysterical Cuban patriots even voiced the fear that his projected railway would constitute a military machine that would be used against them.

The "Terror of Flat Krick," therefore, became a model of courtesy and diplomacy in his dealings with the Cubans, persuaded that they would respond favourably to such treatment. When doing his rounds on the island he always took off his hat when he met a Cuban, and when one of them bowed to him he returned the bow twice. He also curbed his swearing, rarely bellowing imprecations when in their midst.[843]

Van Horne also urged Cuba Company employees to show the same courtesy and consideration. Writing to his chief engineer, Van Horne declared that he wanted all company officers operating in Cuba to deal politely with the Cubans no matter what the provocation, for "we cannot afford to antagonize even the humblest individual if it can be avoided."[844] Since it was important that the company's objectives be clearly understood, Van Horne also appointed two influential Cubans to act as local agents. In their role as advance men, Gonzalo de Quesada and Horatio Rubens, who would later head the Cuba Railroad, journeyed by horseback and buggy across the country, explaining the company's objectives, dispelling any mistrust that might have arisen, and attempting to deflect any opposition from already established roads. They were aided in this mission by two local lawyers, Teodoro de Zaldo and Manuel Manduley, who also obtained rights of way by gift or purchase.[845]

As for the company's objectives, Van Horne made it abundantly clear to company officials that they must eschew any involvement with politics. "The Cuba Company," he reminded them, "is a strictly commercial enterprise; it has nothing to do with politics and will not so long as I am connected with it ... Under no circumstances will we have anything to do with politics or political parties, and if we cannot build our railway now without mixing in such things we will wait until we can."[846]

In short, Van Horne was determined that the Cuba Company and its offspring, the Cuba Railroad, would adopt the CPR's official policy of non-involvement in politics, a policy that had been thrown overboard only occasionally, most noticeably during the Canadian general election of 1891 when Van Horne had thrown caution to the winds and fiercely attacked the idea of reciprocity with the United States.[847] Still, non-involvement with politics did not rule out cultivating good relations with General Wood and his administration. But in this, as in so many other domains, circumspection was the watchword. When the military governor invited Farquhar to accompany him on a trip, for example, Van Horne counselled his right-hand man to turn down the invitation, explaining, "The fact of your having travelled about with him might be made use of by his enemies or ours later on ... I am sure it will be best for us and for him to give the public no sign of any intimacy at present."[848] Van Horne's refusal to buy any men or influence had certainly not been the traditional way of doing business in Cuba. If anything, it was a rarity. But, as the cost-conscious railway builder readily pointed out, it certainly had "the merit of cheapness."[849]

Although he steered clear of overt politicking, Van Horne nevertheless conducted his own public relations campaign. Often this took the form of soothing letters to the governors of the various provinces through which the railway would run. To assuage any fears that might be entertained about the scheme, the letters outlined the Cuba Company's objectives and observed that its shareholders were both American and Canadian capitalists who had the greatest faith in Cuba's future. Company plans, it was pointed out, included not only the building of a railway but also the development of timber resources, the promotion of sugar planting and other industries, and the encouragement of immigration of "the most desirable type," notably from Galicia and the Canary Islands.[850]

In the summer of 1900, Van Horne drew up railway specifications that called for a standard gauge of 4 feet, 8 1/2 inches and 34-foot cars of a 40,000-pound capacity "with the simplest and best automatic couplers." The cars, to be provided by American Car and Foundry Company in Chicago, were to be equipped with air brakes, another safety device that had become mandatory during his CPR regime.[851] A couple of months later, in the early fall, grading and construction of the railroad began at both the Santa Clara and Santiago ends and proceeded as rapidly as possible, using a labour force of up to six thousand men.

For the most part, these men were paid well and assigned fair working hours. Ten hours constituted a day's work, except on Saturday, when they worked nine hours. In 1902, pay ranged from $110.00 a month (engineers on construction trains) to $40.00 a month (nurses). Carpenters were paid $1.50 to $2.00 a day and labourers were paid $1.00 a day. Employees engaged by the month could, if they so chose, board in the company's camps.[852] By comparison, the average daily wage rate for carpenters in the Toronto area in 1902 was $1.85, while that for labourers was $1.38.[853]

No sooner had work begun, however, than Cuban newspapers launched an attack on the Cuba Company for not employing Cubans. To his chagrin, Van Horne had to acknowledge that the charge was far from groundless. In his company's defence, he pointed out that it had to hire American engineers with experience working in the tropics. Whenever possible, though, he wanted preference given to hiring locally. "If we do not make a good deal of effort in this direction," he informed one correspondent, "we are likely to create a sentiment which may in important ways be damaging to the Company."[854] And to Miller Smith he wrote:

> ...it would be very desirable to work in some competent Cuban engineers if any are to be found. There must be some competent transit men or levellers among them, and there may be one or two who would be useful in the preliminary studies of the country and as chiefs of parties. I hope you will be able now to work in quite a number of Cubans because it has already become a matter of reproach that we are employing none of them.[855]

The Cuba Company had additional good grounds for hiring locally. When it imported non-Spanish-speaking "operating men" to serve as railway engineers and firemen it had to hire interpreters "to wait on them." Even then the men got into trouble, prompting Van Horne to consider the advisability of instituting a cadet system to educate young Cubans for operating service.[856] In any event, there were never enough Cubans available to do the jobs that had to be done. As a result, the Cuba Company found itself importing significant numbers of both Spaniards from the Galicia region of Spain and Canary Islanders who had gone to Venezuela in search of work. Despite this recourse to off-island labour, however, the company always experienced a shortage of workers.[857]

This problem might have been overcome if the Cuba Company had been prepared to import Jamaicans, but Van Horne strenuously opposed the importation of black labour into racially sensitive Cuba. As cosmopolitan in outlook as he was, he could not countenance the idea of the Cuba Company, or any other company for that matter, bringing in blacks, be they Jamaican blacks, whom he described as "undesirable people," or American blacks. Consequently, when rumours were rife in the racist Cuban press that the Cuba Company intended to hire Jamaican labour, he resorted to vigorous denials.

To Gonzalo de Quesada, he stated emphatically that the company had never entertained any intention of engaging Jamaican workers. Moreover, it would fight attempts by others to do so since the introduction of large numbers of Jamaicans would do irreparable harm to Cuba's prosperity and undermine the success of the Cuba Railroad.[858] Dealing with the emotionally charged issue of black labour was no easy matter, as Van Horne and other company officials were to discover. It would become particularly trying when the company went back on its promises and, for convenience, began importing black workers from Jamaica and Florida. Not surprisingly, this gave rise to widespread annoyance with the company, especially in the Santiago de Cuba area.[859]

Raiding the CPR's ranks for a desired employee was also vetoed unless it could be proven beyond a doubt that he was not required in the CPR's service.[860] When it came to hiring family members, however, Van Horne found himself reluctantly giving in to Bennie's wishes to join the Cuba Company. It was not, of course, what he had in mind for his son, but nevertheless he found himself capitulating to the young man's wishes because Bennie seemed "quite set" on becoming assistant to the manager of construction.[861]

In this new position Bennie strove valiantly to prove himself in his father's eyes, all the while tipping off Van Horne as to what was happening in the field. Evidently the new-found independence that the job brought was enough to galvanize the errant son into meaningful activity. Away from the anxious scrutiny, the overdose of advice, and the intimidating presence of his father, Bennie demonstrated that he could meet a challenge and work hard, so diligently that in July 1902 G.R. Ward, the superintendent of construction, recommended Bennie's appointment rather than that of another candidate for the position of superintendent engineer in charge of the engineering and roadway departments. When making his recommendation, Ward advised Van Horne, "Ben has many manly and admirable qualities, and has worked loyally faithfully intelligently and well; and I believe will fill the position offered him with credit to himself, and in a manner acceptable to the Company."[862]

Bennie's testing would have to be postponed because in mid-summer of 1902 he was stricken with typhoid fever. This required that he be hospitalized, and on Farquhar's recommendation, he was sent to a New York hospital. There he languished for eleven weeks, during which time he was visited by both his mother and his sister. These were months of undiluted anxiety for Van Horne. Required to be in Montreal for most of this period, he looked to a steady stream of telegrams dispatched by his wife and daughter to keep him abreast of his son's progress. It was mid-September before Bennie was released, at which time a fretting Van Horne arrived to supervise the details of his return to Montreal.

In November 1900, Van Horne returned to Cuba for a memorable five-week inspection tour that cemented his love for the island and its people. The visit had many highlights, but two in particular would linger in his memory. One was the lavish dinner given in his honour by the Cosmopolitan Club of Santiago, which, according to the *New York Times*, staged the "most brilliant" function in that city since the beginning of the American occupation of Cuba.[863] The visit's other highlight was the trip that Van Horne made into the rugged interior of the province of Santiago (now called Santiago de Cuba), where the Cuba Company had acquired nearly one hundred square miles of land that it planned to subdivide into small farms or units for sale to settlers.

Accompanied by Bennie, Farquhar, and others, including, at the start, an escort of prominent Santiago men, Van Horne rode horseback from San Luis across the island to Nipe Bay and Banes Bay. Even a young person would have found this trip through the tropical forests of sparsely settled eastern Cuba a real trial of strength. So it is not surprising that corpulent, middle-aged Van Horne found the journey along a rough trail, in blistering heat, and with the flies swirling around him and the sweat pouring down his face, "pretty rough."[864] An even rougher trip was in store for him when he returned by steamer to Santiago, leaving Bennie to make the return trip by horseback.

When he stopped off in New York City in mid-December, on his return to Montreal, a *New York Times* reporter waylaid him in his old stomping ground, the Manhattan Hotel. Attacking recent rumours swirling around the Cuba Company, Van Horne told the reporter, "The rights of way have been cheerfully accorded to us for nothing by the owners of the property through which our line passes, and the reports that there is local hostility against the road are untrue."[865] Then, warming to his subject even further, he added, "I travelled a good deal in Cuba, and I think it is the richest country I have ever seen. The time will surely come — that is, when yellow fever has been stamped out on the seaboard, as it has been already in the interior — when Cuba will be the Riviera of the U.S. Wealthy Americans will build villas there by the hundreds and enjoy an ideal winter residence."[866]

One of the wealthy Americans who came to mind was his railroading friend Henry Flagler, entering his seventh decade in 1900. Born the son of a poor Presbyterian minister, Flagler was only fourteen when he left his home in northwestern New York State to make his way in the world. Ambitious, hardworking, and determined, he succeeded in building up a very profitable grain brokerage business in Cleveland in the halcyon years before the Civil War. While doing so, he struck up an acquaintanceship with John D. Rockefeller, then a fellow grain broker but soon to be a pioneer in the oil refining business. Rockefeller admired Flagler's drive, unflagging optimism, and marketing ability so much that when he came to establish his oil refining venture after the Civil War he asked the older man to join him. Over the next fifteen years the two partners worked side by side to found Standard Oil, the largest, most profitable, and perhaps most notorious corporation ever established.[867]

Having amassed a huge fortune, Flagler then decided to combine business with pleasure, pleasure being associated with the development of a frontier region, in this case the state of Florida. In the early 1880s, he embarked upon the building of an opulent Mediterranean-themed hotel, the Ponce de Leon, as a refuge for his wealthy friends. If divine intervention could have been invoked, Van Horne would have arranged for Flagler to move his hostelry "bodily" from St. Augustine to Havana. "It would be so appropriate there, and ... would pay most handsomely the year round," Van Horne told Flagler.[868]

In summoning up shimmering images of a Cuban Riviera, Van Horne was voicing his genuine optimism about the island's future. But he was no doubt also hinting at a growing desire to escape the brutal cold and snow of

Montreal's winters and pamper his aging body. In time he would set out to realize this dream by constructing a magnificent villa, San Zenon de Buenos Aires, on the outskirts of Camaguey, an old town with a population of thirty thousand and a rich store of beautiful colonial architecture. Nearby he would also establish a large experimental farm, emulating the example of the large stockbreeding farm that he had set up in East Selkirk, Manitoba.

By January 1901, the Cuba Company and its railway undertaking had come to be regarded as benign, if not positive, additions to the island scene. Bennie informed his father, "All the really influential, conservative and stable people seem to be in favor of the road here ..."[869] The same could not have been said of the situation when construction began. In those early months many Cubans — perhaps most — were suspicious of the company's intentions, regarding it and Van Horne as merely agents of the U.S. government. Since the early days, however, his method of conducting business in Cuba and the perceived benefits of his projected railway had won increasing numbers of Cubans over to his enterprise. As a result, the Cuba Company was placed in the enviable position of being able to obtain most rights-of-way and land for stations and yards by gift or at minimal cost.

This good fortune was frequently offset, however, by problems in obtaining clear legal title to the acquired properties. It was a situation that spurred Van Horne to remedial action. Convinced that a loose system of land titles would hamper future settlement in Cuba, he recommended to General Wood as early as August 1900 that Cuba implement the Torrens land registration system, which was then in use in Australia and two western Canadian provinces. "The existing maps of Cuba are pretentious but very inaccurate, and the lines I suggest will enable them to be very quickly corrected in their main features,"[870] he pointed out to his new friend after suggesting changes to some Cuban maps.

Notwithstanding the Cuba Company's relative ease in obtaining rights-of-way and land for stations, there was growing offshore opposition to Van Horne's road. This occurred principally in Washington, where the Cuba Relations Committee received many complaints about Van Horne's undertaking, some parties charging the Cuba Company with being a monopoly.[871] When he was secretary of state under Theodore Roosevelt, Elihu Root had to endure the harassment of senators who had been pitted against Van Horne by aggressive American promoters seeking railway franchises in Cuba. Some of these legislators went to such lengths as to table anti–Van Horne resolutions in the Senate.

Even more disquieting was a complaint against Van Horne that New York lawyer Luis R. Perozo forwarded to Root and Senator Foraker. The complaint, delivered by Cuban promoter General Jose Lacret, accused Van Horne of "flagrantly violating with audacious subterfuges" the Foraker Act and Cuban rights.[872]

There is certainly no validity to the charge that Van Horne was violating Cuban rights. From the very start, he sought to build a railway that would aid Cuba's development without depriving Cubans of their territorial rights and independence. And this he succeeded in doing. But there is also no question that in constructing a railway on private and federal land, Van Horne resorted to ingenious and audacious means to subvert the intent of the Foraker Act.

The need for this was highlighted in March 1901 when the Cuba Company encountered its first real "hold-up," a setback that Van Horne suspected had been inspired by Central Cuban Railway officials. It occurred at a private narrow-gauge railway whose nominal owner doggedly refused to permit the Cuba Company to cross either the railway or the plantation on which it was located. Initially the question defied solution. But then company lawyers earned their pay package by finding a way out of the difficulty.[873] Nevertheless, this temporary setback dramatized Cuba's lack of a railway law, which would have militated against such developments.

Fortunately for Cuban railway interests, Van Horne had already set to work drafting such a law. He had been driven to act by the news that General Wood intended to apply the Texas Railroad Law in Cuba, a law Van Horne detested because in his view its application was a licence to confiscate existing railway properties. Implemented in Cuba, it would ruin every railway interest except his own as yet-to-be-completed road. And since he was determined to rescue Cuba from such a fate, Van Horne embarked on a self-appointed mission to convince the General to substitute a clear and simple railway law (embodying the best features of Canadian and American railway laws) for the Texas model.[874] He succeeded. Accordingly, in the summer of 1900, he set to work on a railway law designed to govern the organization of Cuban railway companies and the building and operation of their lines. On his frequent visits to New York in these years, he and Farquhar would often work on the law at opposite ends of the large desk that they shared at 80 Broadway.[875]

Most of the groundwork for the law was done by Van Horne. The company's legal counsel, Mandulay, translated the English draft into Spanish, omitting everything that was already covered by Cuba's general corporation laws and adapting the rest to Cuban needs. This Spanish draft was then retranslated into English and the English version forwarded to Root for his suggestions.[876]

To lobby for its adoption, Van Horne set off in February 1901 for Washington, where he presented his case to senators Platt and Aldrich and other legislators prominent in Cuban affairs. In the American capital, he also had a long talk with an overworked and frail Root, who, although interested in Van Horne's project, showed little inclination to move on it.[877] Still, Van Horne was convinced that his friend Governor Wood would enact the law if Root and Foraker provided even a modicum of encouragement. He therefore telegraphed General Dodge with the request that he raise the matter with the two men.[878]

Unfortunately all this strenuous lobbying was to little avail. Despite repeated trips to Washington to plead his cause, Van Horne could make little progress. The politicians who were deeply involved in Cuban affairs were too preoccupied with the friction that had developed between the American government and delegates to the constitutional convention that met at Havana between November 5, 1900, and February 21, 1901.

Underlying the strained relations was a series of demands known collectively as the Platt Amendment, which had been proposed by the outspoken expansionist Orville Platt. A rider to the Army Appropriations Act of 1900, the amendment required the Cuban constitutional convention to incorporate certain provisions in its constitution as a condition of American acceptance. Among the distasteful provisions was one that allowed the United States to intervene in Cuba to protect liberty and property. Another allowed Washington to purchase or lease naval stations on the island.

While these matters were being hotly debated in the convention, Van Horne wrote to Root predicting the probable fate of the Platt Amendment. His sources, he reported, led him to believe that Cuba would grant the United States practically everything that it wanted. But always mindful of Cuban sensibilities, he suggested to the Secretary of War that both the Cuban and American flags be hoisted over Cuban forts occupied by American troops. "It would help enormously towards the settlement of this very delicate question — and I do not believe that anything else would go so far towards soothing the pride of the Cubans," he wrote.[879]

When the Platt Amendment was first submitted to the constitutional convention it was defeated. However, since its adoption was indispensable to American evacuation of the island, convention delegates eventually swallowed their nationalist objections and incorporated the amendment in the new constitution. Nine days later the constitution was adopted and the following May American troops withdrew from the island, leaving Cuba an independent nation in name, but in fact an American protectorate.

Largely as a result of the storm created by the Platt Amendment, Van Horne's railway law did not come into force until February 1902 and then only after it had undergone several revisions. While the tedious and laborious task of revision was underway Van Horne made repeated trips to Washington, where on at least one occasion he met with the president. In January 1902, thanks to the advance work of Senator Proctor, Van Horne was able to see President Theodore Roosevelt, who, like his visitor, was a man of many interests and facets. The moral idealist and militant imperialist greeted Van Horne warmly as his "fellow Dutchman" (Roosevelt's father was descended from an old New York Dutch family) and spent a considerable amount of time with him despite the large number of legislators queuing outside his office for an audience.[880]

In the draft's final stages Van Horne rarely saw the light of the Caribbean day as he and a phalanx of lawyers toiled away in Havana, putting their final touches to the legislation. The time was well spent, for the fruit of their labours was a model law based largely on Canadian railway law rather than on Texan railroad law, which General Wood had favoured. "General Dodge and I dined one evening with the military governor and that is all that has happened," Van Horne grumped in a letter to Addie late in January 1902 as he chafed at the bit to get away on a trip over the railway line.[881] Finally, however, the legislation was finalized. A short time later, on February 7, it was promulgated by General Wood.

The occasion was one of rejoicing for Van Horne, who confidently predicted that the new law was "going to make the finishing up of our enterprise quite easy — giving us a solid foundation to work upon."[882] It certainly achieved this goal in as much as it allowed the Cuba Company to save about $25,000 by providing for expropriation against some unreasonable parties. But that is about the only purpose that the legislation served at this late stage of the railway's construction.[883]

Before the law was implemented Van Horne had had recourse to extraordinary measures to overcome the obstacles presented by the absence of such a piece of legislation. One of these was the revocable permit or licence that allowed a railway to cross federally owned lands and roads. This fortuitous device came to mind when Van Horne pondered the question that had vexed him and Cuba Company officials for months: How, in the absence of a general railway law, could his railway obtain the right to cross public highways and rivers? Van Horne decided that the revocable permit was the answer. He also concluded that since the Foraker Act said nothing about an revocable permit, the military governor could award one to any builder who was prepared to assume the risk of having that permit modified or cancelled by the yet-to-be elected Cuban government. With visions of the revocable permit saving the day, the Cuba Company president set about marshalling support for his idea. Initially this support came from Washington officials, whom Van Horne met during his February visit. They conceded that such a permit could, indeed, be granted.

With a view to invoking the revocable permit for his purposes, Van Horne visited Havana, where he saw the governor and asked for what he knew he would not get, namely unconditional permission for the railway to cross public highways and rivers. As anticipated, General Wood replied that he could not grant such a concession. Despite his pro-railway stand and a barrage of petitions from Cubans, his hands were effectively tied by the Foraker Act. Van Horne then withdrew and hastily sought out the Cuban official who was Governor Wood's confidant and trusted advisor on such issues. Before this illustrious official Van Horne mentioned the revocable permit and intimated that if the advisor and General Wood could not devise a better solution, he, Van Horne, was prepared to continue construction if the governor would issue a revocable permit for the crossing of public roads, lands, and waters. Van Horne's strategy succeeded admirably. The official communicated the suggestion to Wood, who, unaware that it originated with Van Horne, granted the licence. The way was thus paved for construction to proceed without further interruptions.[884]

An obliging General Wood later furnished Van Horne with some additional ammunition. Before boarding his yacht at Covenhoven, where he had stopped briefly, the General gave his host "the strongest possible assurances concerning the road crossing permits, saying that we might rely with absolute necessity on having them in the form proposed, if it could not be done in an even stronger form."[885] Wood would later expand the revocable permit. Years down the line, a grateful Van Horne would resort to hyperbole when telling his friend that the Cuba Railroad owed its existence largely to him.[886] As for Wood, he would later claim that his role, since it was not American policy to alienate any state property or "rights of Cuba," was only to issue a revocable permit to cross public areas. Because of the fair and just procedures adopted to build the railway, the Cuban government later confirmed Wood's acts as governor and enacted the necessary legislation to give the road a continuous right of way.[887]

The revocable permit offered a possible solution to one problem. But there remained the question of how to obtain permission for the railway to cross municipal and provincial roads. Van Horne decided that he would meet this challenge by appealing directly to the Cuban people. The force of public opinion was brought into play, and by ingenious means. Whenever he could not obtain the necessary permissions or concessions, Van Horne simply brought all railway construction to a halt and threatened to bypass the municipal business districts. With local labourers thrown out of work and merchants and farmers reeling from the loss of American dollars, the Cubans hastily signed petitions calling for the necessary permission. Invariably it was forthcoming.

Van Horne's inventive turn of mind, celebrated powers of persuasion, and cordial demeanour solved two problems. But where inter-railway rivalry and misunderstanding were involved, he had to rely on his finely honed powers of conciliation. These he invoked in his dealings with London-based officials of the Cuban Central Railways, who insisted that he had no right to build his railway further west than Sancti Spiritus and who opposed even more strongly his decision to build into Santa Clara, where the Cuban Central had its terminus. Van Horne met these protests in his most conciliatory manner, deploring any misunderstanding that might have developed on the part of its railway officials and insisting that he had taken great care never to conceal anything from Cuban authorities, from the public, or anybody else concerning the Cuba Company's operations.[888] To General Dodge, he confided that his replies to the London officials were "as sweet and friendly as possible" and that he fully intended to keep the correspondence going all summer across the Atlantic until such time as the road had advanced beyond their interference.[889].

The Cuba Company had informed Cuban Central officials that it intended to restrict its operations to developing the countryside east of Santa Clara. But this did not preclude the company from safeguarding its best interests west of this point. With its railway line terminating at Santa Clara, the company would be in a better position to negotiate satisfactory running rights over track running to Havana and other points west. Failing satisfactory terms, it could "easily secure freedom," but at Placetas or at Sancti Spiritus it would be "bottled up." As Van Horne wryly noted, Santa Clara was chosen as the company's western terminus for the very reason that Cuban Central Railway officials objected to its presence there.[890]

Van Horne deplored the failure of London railway directors to grant their Cuban officials adequate decision-making powers. Just as this management weakness had roused his ire when he had had to deal with distant London directors in his early days with the CPR, now it would do so once again. Only this time it would involve questions about the new railway law and the board of railway commissioners, which had been established to regulate and control railway rates.

In the interests of badly needed railway reform, the military government had asked Cuba's railways to draw up and submit a uniform schedule of classifications and tariffs. The request was largely ignored. Canadian and American railways had long ago voluntarily harmonized their classifications and tariffs, but Cuban roads, it appears, were not prepared to emulate the North American example. Nearly all of them fought the proposal, citing what they deemed to be their rights under their Spanish concessions.[891] Confronted by the railways' refusal to act, the government set about framing a schedule that Van Horne acidly described as "approximating the old Missouri classification of plunder and lumber."[892] Once again, he felt obliged to trot out his special expertise, this time to help the railway commissioners draw up an improved schedule.

The new version, which prescribed maximum rates below those of the prevailing tariffs, was welcomed by the Cuban people but vehemently opposed by the railway companies, which instructed their Cuban officials to ignore it. This prompted Van Horne to again take a hand in matters. Recalling his earlier attempts to establish harmonious relations with railway directors in London, he wrote to some of his London business friends asking them to prevail upon these boards to abandon their "supreme belief in the efficacy and fitness of the rules and instructions laid down from London."[893] London boards, he declared, should give their Cuban managers sufficient authority to act promptly and decisively in railway matters raised with the government. If they were not prepared to do this, they should at least "very quickly send out the best & broadest-minded men they have among them to do it. They should by all means avoid sending out one of the narrow-minded, self-sufficient, damned fools so often sent out from London to various countries in such cases."[894] The celebrated bluntness had evidently lost none of its razor edge.

It appears that the railways eventually scuttled attempts to reform the tariff schedule because in June 1902, the railroad commission revoked all tariff rates and restored the former ones. But in an about-face, those same companies that had strenuously opposed the railway law later fought for its retention and opposed any modification of its provisions.[895]

In 1902, Van Horne and the Cuba Company faced a host of daunting challenges. Not the least of these was a glaring shortage of funds, triggered by delays in the delivery of rolling stock and soaring construction costs.

A cutting being excavated on the Cuba Railroad, which began operating in 1902.

Both were largely attributable to Van Horne's insistence on perfectionist Canadian Pacific standards. Although such standards were a rarity in frontier regions, especially those in Latin America, the Cuba Company president insisted that they be enforced in Cuba. These standards decreed that railway equipment be the equal of that employed by the best railways in the United States. Cars the equivalent of those in general use in Cuba would not suffice. However, to satisfy such requirements, orders had to be placed with the few American manufacturers that could do the work, and because they were operating at overcapacity they would not accept a contract with penalties for delay.[896] The inevitable happened: delays occurred, throwing many a kink into Van Horne's timetable and producing cash shortages. Indeed, soaring costs swallowed up all remaining funds for railway construction.

When the CPR was being built, it was George Stephen who scrambled for funds. Now Van Horne had to shoulder the burden of fundraising, and it proved to be an onerous responsibility. Faced by the financial crisis, he asked the twenty-two shareholders to put up an additional 40 percent or sell their shares as stipulated in the company's incorporation agreement. Much to his distress, not all the shareholders were prepared to produce additional funding. In fact, a small group of dissidents, led by Thomas Ryan, bailed out.[897] Later, when recalling the failure of these shareholders to pony up additional funding, Van Horne observed ruefully that they "got scared and could not be found when they were wanted."[898]

The defection of Ryan, Elkins, and Widener made it difficult for Van Horne to raise new capital, but the problem was temporarily resolved when Farquhar took him to lunch one day at the Lawyers' Club in New York. On spotting Robert Fleming, the British financier, in these hallowed precincts, Van Horne announced, "He's our man. Fleming will take the $3,000,000 of stock despite Ryan and his crowd."[899] Van Horne worked his charm on Fleming and succeeded in getting him not only to take over the dissidents' shares but also to put up an additional $3 million. The shrewd Scot, who was then the principal of London-based Robert Fleming and Company, eventually succeeded in enlarging his share of the Cuba Company and thereby gaining control, obliging Van Horne to appoint a young Fleming protegé, George Whigham, as a director.

Once the financial squeeze had passed, construction proceeded rapidly. But later that spring unusually severe rains intervened, badly eroding clay embankments and cuttings. Finding it too expensive to maintain track just to move materials, Van Horne ordered a halt to all track-laying east of Puerto Principe and instructed that time and money be deployed in rock ballasting.[900] This development, along with a delay in the delivery of bridge structures from the American manufacturers, completely disrupted the construction timetable.

With this setback, it became patently obvious that the main line between Santiago and Santa Clara would not be completed before the end of May, as Van Horne had predicted in January while on one of his inspection tours with General Dodge.[901] Instead, he could now anticipate a much delayed completion date, soaring costs during the last phase of track-laying, and more rigorous retrenchments.[902]

These delays and retrenchments troubled Van Horne no end. From Covenhoven, in July 1902, he fired off a series of cables to managers in Cuba that reflect his agitation. To Ward, he instructed, "Read my two cables twelfth carefully reply fully clearly definitely immediately. Cant wait letter." And in a cable to the contractor, Jekyll, he ordered, "Cable at least every third day situation. Am quite in dark concerning what doing and force employed."[903]

Van Horne confronted a very different challenge at Puerto Principe, the ancient town that was to become the site of the railway's headquarters and its new car-building workshops. Here, in early 1902, he ran up against a wall of resistance when he convened a well-advertised sod-laying ceremony to inaugurate construction of the workshops. Because the owners of the small Neuvitas Railroad had mounted a successful attack against the Cuba Company, the residents of Puerto Principe boycotted the ceremony. Only a few people showed up, one being a reluctant mayor, who arrived with his brother-in-law and the latter's small daughter. Fortunately this frosty reception did not faze Van Horne. Despite the pitifully small attendance, he carried on as if nothing had disrupted his carefully laid plans. Adopting his most courtly and charming manner, he asked the young girl if she would turn the first sod.[904] To his great delight, she obliged.

Van Horne decided that this young stand-in should receive some tangible recognition of his gratitude. Accordingly, on his return to New York in March, he laid a portrait of *la nina* Adelina Esther Barreras before a meeting of the Cuba Company's board and asked it to tender a vote of thanks to her for "so graciously inaugurating [the company's] work of construction at Puerto Principe." He then followed this up with a request to the directors to approve the forwarding of a suitably inscribed gold watch to the young girl.[905] Van Horne did not go so far as to select the watch himself, but he did supervise its purchase, instructing Sandford Beaty, the Cuba Company's secretary, to look for one "downtown" rather than at Tiffany's and to make sure that the timepiece had a cover on its face.

On his return to Puerto Principe, Van Horne brought the watch and an engraved vote of thanks on parchment with him.[906] This time he met with quite a different reception, for by now sentiment in Puerto Principe had swung strongly in favour of his railway. Nowhere was this change more evident than at the outdoor ceremony convened in young Adelina Esther's honour. On this occasion, instead of just a few sullen observers, a crowd of people craned their necks to watch Van Horne present his company's tributes to the mayor's niece.

Van Horne had even greater reason to rejoice that autumn. On November 11, the last spike in the railway's main line was driven,[907] and to mark this landmark event, the Cuba Company president made a return trip to Cuba. He disembarked at Havana on November 12 after a routine voyage, marred only by the presence of "some loud Americans who were far from pleasant."[908] No sooner had he set foot on Cuban soil than he embarked on a frenetic social schedule that included a call on President Estrada Palma, who received him warmly, and a visit with the Archbishop of Santiago, the Primate of Cuba. A ball at the Presidential Palace topped off the day.

The next major undertaking was a trip over the line, which took him from Santa Clara to Santiago and then back to Ciego de Avila, where the company's principal construction headquarters were then located. It proved to be an inaugural inspection tour rife with good omens, for all along the line he was enthusiastically received. Indeed, the outpouring of goodwill was such that he even dared to feel "quite cheerful" about the road's prospects.[909] Van Horne had good reason to feel buoyant when travelling along the line to Santiago, but he had even greater grounds for feeling cheerful when making the return trip to Ciego de Avila, located 108 kilometres west of Puerto Principe. En route, when he stopped at Puerto Principe he was feted at a banquet given in his honour. When he finally reached Ciego de Avila, he was greeted by practically the whole town, including some seven hundred enthusiastic schoolchildren. Never able to resist an opportunity to be with children, he took time out the next day to visit the youngsters' large school.

The spate of public appearances and tributes did not stop there. Further recognition came from a local Spanish club, which entertained Van Horne and subsequently made him its first honorary member.[910] The municipality of Puerto Principe (it adopted the Native name Camaguey in 1903) also rose to the occasion. Before the year was out, it conferred the title "Adoptive Son of Camaguey" on Van Horne for all that he had done to encourage the city's advancement and prosperity.[911]

This collective tribute sent Van Horne's spirits soaring and convinced him that perhaps all the worry and setbacks had been worth it. It certainly made young Addie glow with pride. She wrote at the first opportunity to congratulate her father on completing his newest railway and to let him know how much she would have enjoyed seeing "the ovation, and the enthusiasm, the confetti and everything!"[912]

The railroad that was generating so much attention was now operated by a separate company, the Cuba Railroad Company, which had been established in 1902 to take over and operate the Cuba Company's railway properties. The Cuba Railroad Company had purchased the railway as it existed on September 19 of that year from the Cuba Company for $4 million worth of first mortgage bonds, $6 million of Cuba Railroad preferred stock, and $6 million of its common stock.[913]

In the first three weeks of January 1903, the railway carried more than 2,700 paying passengers, despite running only local trains by daylight and on alternate days. This encouraging start led Van Horne to predict a huge increase in traffic when daily service was introduced between Havana and Santiago de Cuba at the end of February.[914] By this time, approximately $10.5 million had been spent in building and equipping the railway.[915] The size of this outlay and Van Horne's adoption of perfectionist standards did not, however, blind the American War Department's agent in Cuba, Frank Steinhart, to what he perceived to be certain realities. After viewing

Courtesy of the National Archives of Canada, E002107474.

A locomotive employed by the Cuba Railroad.

the line in mid-1903, he concluded that the railway would have to implement many more expensive improvements to complete its ambitious program and meet North American standards.[916]

Van Horne meanwhile was shuttling back and forth to Cuba, where, as Bennie wryly observed, his august presence seemed "to create more of a panic than a yellow fever epidemic."[917] Frequently Van Horne was accompanied by American business cronies. Henry Whitney, the Boston utilities magnate, and a Mr. Dewey from Boston joined him in January 1903. So did Bennie, who planned to inspect some property that his father had purchased for him in Yaragua.[918] On a return voyage to the island in March, Van Horne was accompanied from New York by the Cuba Company's lawyer, Howard Mansfield, and his brother, Franklin B. Lord, a prominent New York lawyer and the proprietor of the *Hartford Courant*. Mansfield would later recount the story of the memorable tour that they took on the new railway line. In his opinion, the highlight was the food served up to the visiting dignitaries. One Sunday the men devoured three breakfasts between morning and mid-afternoon. But that did not end the feasting because at Zaza Junction, a fourth breakfast and a brass band awaited them![919]

Food might have been readily proffered, but not so funds for the expansion of the railway and the construction of sugar mills. From the very beginning Van Horne had envisaged the erection of sugar mills as part of his grand scheme for the development of that part of the island through which the railway ran. With this in mind, he fixed upon Jatibonico as the site of the Cuba Company's principal mill and embarked upon an exhaustive study of the sugar industry. But all his elaborately laid plans started to unravel when the financial recession of 1903 intervened, drying up funds for both mill construction and the building of feeder lines for his railway. Only when the end of the recession freed up funding was he able to forge ahead with his ambitious program.

One of the first items on the agenda was the construction of the large mill at Jatibonico, located almost in the centre of the island. As it neared completion in January 1906, Van Horne waxed ecstatic, pronouncing it to be "the finest in the world — a work to be proud of."[920] By 1910, when it had been joined by other mills, the Jatibonico mill's profits would be more than sufficient to pay interest on the entire funded debt of the Cuba Company and to justify a doubling of mill capacity.[921]

He was equally enthusiastic about a resort hotel in Camaguey, which he had reconstructed from old barracks that had been occupied by Spanish troops. Described by a piece of puffery as one of the "most charming hotels to stay at,"[922] it became a showplace for plants and flowers personally selected by Van Horne for its patio and gardens. The results impressed even cynical Bennie, who was forced to admit that the Hotel Camaguey was "certainly beautiful" and that everybody who visited it left "perfectly delighted."[923]

Not too long after it opened, Van Horne was photographed standing in front of the hostelry's main entrance. The photograph shows a portly figure with a capacious belly, a moustache, and a well-trimmed white beard. Attired in a jacket and straw hat, he holds a cane and gazes into the distance, possibly pondering the hotel's menu, a source of some concern to him. It annoyed Van Horne that the Hotel Camaguey served a much greater variety of dishes than the Chateau Frontenac, "the most popular hotel in Canada." Writing to a Cuba Company official, Van Horne suggested that in the interests of quality and economy the Hotel Camaguey emulate the example of the Chateau Frontenac's dining room, which earned plaudits by serving a few well-prepared dishes in style. After all, noted Van Horne, "the cost between well prepared dishes and badly prepared is exceedingly small."[924]

Santiago's Casa Grande Hotel, which the Cuba Railroad Company had reconstructed and refurbished, and the Hotel Antilla also claimed his attention.[925] And as plans proceeded for the Casa Grande's rejuvenation, the Cuba Railroad Company began negotiating for the establishment of a steamship service between Santiago de Cuba and Jamaica.[926]

As he had during his CPR days, Van Horne spearheaded the establishment of an effective promotional campaign to increase his railway's passenger traffic. His target audience was the leisure class of Americans, which he hoped to attract to the island by placing illustrated articles on Cuba in selected magazines like *Harper's* and by distributing advertising material in winter resorts in Florida and the Gulf states.[927]

Van Horne did not always resort to skilfully placed advertising to promote his various Cuban ventures. Not infrequently he employed his keen sense of good public relations and his genuine love of the Cuban people in small acts of charity that helped to burnish his image and that of his companies. Such was the case when he instructed the Cuba Railroad Company to arrange school excursions to various sugar mills and plantations during the grinding season. "I am sure that these excursions will be of great advantage to the school children and bring much happiness to them, besides resulting to the good of the Company," he remarked in March 1908.[928]

A somewhat similar gesture involved the purchase of a bell for a picturesque old church in Camaguey. This particular philanthropic act, however, originated with an affront to Van Horne's aesthetic sensibilities. When he learned that the parish priest wanted to have thick coats of paint and varnish applied to the church's walls Van Horne was so horrified that he offered to give the parish a new bell if the priest's plans were shelved. The offer was taken up and the railway magnate arranged for the purchase and shipping of a bell to Father Martinez's church. In characteristic fashion, he oversaw all the details, even instructing the Cuba Railroad Company manager to have the freight and duties charged to his own account.[929]

While overseeing the refurbishing of the parish church, Van Horne was also supervising the creation of extensive gardens on the grounds of each of the Cuba Railroad's stations. Such attractive displays, he hoped, would not only advertise the railway but also help to educate nearby residents in fruit culture.[930] Education was also the goal of the Cuba Company's agriculture department, which carried out experiments on Cuban fibres and other products, issued bulletins, and corresponded with manufacturers who were potential buyers of these products.[931]

As townsites sprouted alongside the railway's main line, branch lines began to snake out into the undeveloped countryside. First off the drawing board was one that linked the main line with Antilla on Nipe Bay, headquarters of the recently incorporated United Fruit Company, which had snapped up ninety thousand acres of virgin territory in 1900. After the line was opened to traffic in 1904, terminal wharves were built and a beginning was made on laying out a town according to a plan that Van Horne had drawn up.

Repeated shortfalls of capital, however, played havoc with Van Horne's plans to forge steadily ahead with branch line construction. The cash shortage can be attributed partly to Van Horne's lack of foresight, but this is not the entire explanation. In the post-1902 years other factors were also at work — one, of course; being the recession of 1903. Another was the insurrection that erupted against President Estrada Palma's administration in the summer of 1906.

Fomented by the Liberals, who accused the Moderates of stealing the December 1905 and March 1906 elections, it spread rapidly through the countryside. This prompted the president to request intervention by the United States, which dispatched commissioners to mediate. When mediation failed and the president and his entire government resigned, the Americans returned to Cuba. The resulting provisional government, headed by a civilian judge, Charles Magoon, lasted from September 1906 until April 1909 and inaugurated a period of great humiliation for the Cubans.

The insurrection of 1906 scared away investors and precipitated a drought of investment capital. For Van Horne, this meant putting all his plans for branch line construction on hold. As late as July 1908, he was bemoaning the stagnation of business in Cuba and the deleterious effect that this was having on the railway's earnings.[932]

Still, the picture was not all bleak. While the insurrection was in progress, it produced striking evidence of the high esteem in which Van Horne and his companies were now held. To his delight, Van Horne saw his determined efforts to establish good relations with the Cuban people amply rewarded by the refusal of the insurrectionists to interfere with his railway's operations. These same insurrectionists, however, also warned the railway's manager that "they would be obliged to resort to the blowing up of bridges" if the company provided any aid and succour to the government.[933]

After civilian rule returned under President Jose Miquel Gomez, Van Horne found himself waging a dogged campaign to improve the image of his beloved Cuba and dispel rumours of new insurrections. It infuriated him that most reports about the island were "if not defamatory at least patronizing or Pharisaical."[934] In a 1909 letter, he lamented the fact that most Americans anticipated the worst in Cuba once the American army was withdrawn. Then he added, "While I have not the least doubt that Cuba must in time become part of the US, I do not see any possible reason for intervention at this time, nor do I see any good reason at present for the annexation of the Island."[935]

Intervention rumours the following summer gave him further cause for alarm and once again ignited his indignation. "The so-called disturbances in Cuba," he huffed in a letter to Gonzalo de Quesada, "are quite imaginary, existing only in the small brains of the Northern Press."[936] Then he shot off a missive to a representative of the press, berating his paper for publishing press dispatches describing an insurrection in Cuba. Noting that there was no sign of trouble anywhere on the island, Van Horne continued in vintage Van Horne prose:

> There are in Cuba a good many left-over representatives of the northern press who might well be classified with the unemployed; indeed, I think they are the only unemployed people in Cuba at this time. They must have news items occasionally to justify their existence and to them a "General" leaving town without apparent reason is "taking to the woods" to start an insurrection; a bar-room brawl is an actual insurrection, and a movement of a detachment of the rural Guard is a movement of the Cuban army.[937]

Fighting rumours of insurrections paled in significance, however, to the continuing struggle to raise money for the Cuba Railroad. On several occasions the Royal Bank of Canada provided loans. Its best customer in Cuba, in fact, was the Cuba Company and the Cuba Railroad.[938] Robert Fleming also came to the rescue with loans. But still, other financing avenues had to be pursued.

Chief among these was the Cuban government itself. In recognition of the valuable role played by the railway, President Estrada Palma's administration loaned money for branch line construction in 1905. Using this as a precedent, Van Horne lobbied for the introduction of a Congressional measure that would provide for a program of subsidies to finance the construction of branch lines in the eastern provinces. His efforts paid off when, in May 1906, the Cuban Congress passed a subsidy bill that authorized the president to grant $6,000 per kilometre, payable in six annual instalments, after the completion of the railway.

In 1910, Van Horne looked to the Subsidy Act for financial relief, only to receive a rude shock. Although he had settled for a reduced subsidy (Van Horne had wanted the money earlier and agreed with the president to accept a contract that reduced the subsidy to $5,000 a kilometre on condition of its being paid in two instalments) and had strong assurances from

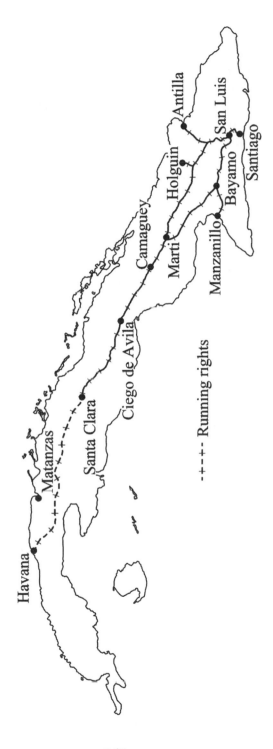

THE CUBA RAILROAD IN 1910

Havana

Matanzas

Santa Clara

Ciego de Avila

Camaguey

Marti

Holguin

Antilla

San Luis

Santiago

Bayamo

Manzanillo

-+-+- Running rights

Map by Vic Dohar

the president that Congress would approve a modified contract, he was not able to obtain one.[939]

The Cuban Congress's failure to grant even a reduced subsidy plunged Van Horne into a bout of gloom and despondency. He was so upset by this perceived breach of faith that he put off acknowledging two letters relating to the issue, thereby violating his usual practice of quickly responding to correspondence. To the author of these letters, he reported, "I am very much discouraged and feel that I am very much to blame for having, in attempting to meet the President's wishes and in the faith of his strong assurances, put our Company in a position which is not only embarrassing but dangerous."[940] Van Horne's disgust and disappointment were so great that he asked for a list of names of those members of Congress who had voted for and against the subsidy bill, and he became even more dismayed on noting that a good many of the Camaguey members were against it.[941]

Notwithstanding all the setbacks, by June 30, 1910, the railway boasted eight branches in addition to its main line, which ran from Santiago de Cuba to Santa Clara via Camaguey and Alto Cedro. The total mileage — one quarter of Cuba's total railway mileage — was 568.559 miles (915.10 kilometres). The company's rolling stock included 65 passenger cars, 1,473 freight cars, 42 maintenance-of-way cars, and 58 locomotives.[942] Noticeably absent from an inventory listing was any mention of dining cars, which had yet to put in an appearance on the line. Meanwhile, passengers could take meals at picturesque little restaurants, which had been designed under the supervision of Van Horne, who looked to Cuban rural architecture for his inspiration. True to form, he insisted that the food served by these wayside stations be excellent in both quality and quantity.[943]

The railway's net earnings for 1910 were $1,107,299.37, an increase of $157,210.56 over the year before. The proportion of working expenses to gross earnings was 56.73 percent, as compared with 55.95 percent the previous year.[944] By way of comparison, the CPR's ratio of operating costs to revenue averaged about 60 percent before 1900.[945]

With one notable exception, Van Horne found Cuba to be generally prosperous in 1910. The exception was Cuba's poor, who had been impoverished by the national lottery, designed to supplement the incomes of top government officials. Given his way, Van Horne would have abolished this sinkhole of disposable income on the grounds that "no country ever continued in prosperity with a legalized lottery."[946]

If Van Horne had not been an optimist he would probably have been defeated by the seemingly insurmountable challenges that he faced in Cuba. It is just possible, however, that if he had not been so doggedly optimistic he might have established a firmer financial foundation for his Cuban enterprises and thereby avoided some of the financing headaches that were to plague him. He conceded as much when he remarked to Gonzalo de Quesada, "I have perhaps been too optimistic and gone too fast for I have no sooner got out of one financial hop than I have got into another."[947]

Toward the end of his life, Van Horne admitted that Cuba had involved him in far more work and worry than he could ever have imagined when he first succumbed to its siren call. And although the admission was painful, he had to confess that he had yet to reap any return from the large amount of money that he had invested there between 1900 and 1909. Nevertheless, he conceded that he could take much comfort in the realization that he had been of some use in "helping the people of that lovable island."[948]

When he donned his mantle of optimism once again, Van Horne could point to the noticeable transformation that the districts east of Santa Clara had undergone as a result of the railway's presence. He could also console himself with the knowledge that the Cuba Railroad's earnings were improving. Three years later, his perusal of the railway company's latest report would prompt Percival Farquhar's father, A.B. Farquhar, to write Van Horne, "Your prophecies in regard to that road are coming true, and I presume in the very near future you will be paying dividends on the original Cuba Company shares. And I recollect what you told me some years ago in regard to the value of the stock of the Canadian Pacific Railroad. That prophecy has also come true."[949]

To the Cuba Company and the Cuba Railway must go a great deal of credit for opening up a hitherto undeveloped part of the country and serving as a catalyst for the development of many new enterprises. As a result of the two companies' direct outlays, sugar mills had been built, timber properties developed, townsites created, and new hotels opened. In 1910 Van Horne could boast that he "had drawn to Cuba in one way or another, about $30,000,000 besides what has come indirectly as a result of our work."[950] Some of this money was, of course, straight out of Van Horne's own pocket. Among his own investments was a part interest in a 56,380-acre timber property known as Demajagual Barbacoas, located in the province of Santiago de Cuba. In this venture he was joined by R.B. Angus and Edward Clouston, the general manager of the Bank of Montreal.[951] He also invested in and served as president of the Havana Docks Company, which had its head office on Wall Street.[952]

When all is said and done, though, the Cuba Company's investments had not ripened sufficiently before Van Horne's death in 1915 to reap much in the way of returns for its shareholders. That would only occur after the First World War destroyed European beet sugar production and the price of Cuban sugar skyrocketed from two cents a pound to twenty-three cents.

Chapter Fifteen
Chasing the Money

"Mackenzie thinks there are 'millions in it' if we can get it into reasonably secure shape. It has been a long hunt and we musn't miss it," wrote a jubilant Van Horne to his friend General Alger in 1898.[953] Van Horne was writing about a scheme to electrify Havana's tramway system, but the railway magnate could just as easily have been referring to one of numerous other overseas and Canadian projects in which he became involved at the close of the nineteenth century and the opening years of the twentieth. These were the years in which Van Horne dedicated himself to making money and savouring the excitement that so often accompanies the discovery of new money-making opportunities; however, unlike his adroit and suave financier friend Thomas Ryan, he did not find joy in stuffing securities away in a safe. For Van Horne, money was a means to an end, a way to renovate a house, perhaps, or to purchase a coveted work of art.[954] This in itself, of course, is not remarkable. What is striking is the staggering number of companies in which he became involved before he decided to relinquish many of his directorships. By some estimates he was a director of at least forty companies and invested in countless more.[955] After he retired from the presidency of the CPR, he not only collected directorships he also played an active role in the management of several enterprises — the Cuba Company, of course, being the most conspicuous of these.

Van Horne, a capitalist par excellence, would have subscribed to the view of capitalism expounded by that great Napoleon of the West, Clifford Sifton, who contended, "The capitalistic system has grown up and it is in use because, and only because, the experience of mankind has proven it to be the best way of doing what has to be done."[956] Van Horne not only venerated the business corporation, he regarded it as the very foundation of modern civilization. He once told his newspaper friend Sir John Willison that corporations "have souls — composite souls — larger and purer than any individual soul that ever was or ever will be." He added, "I have sat at the Directors' table in corporations for many years and have yet to hear the first deliberately mean suggestion on the part of a Director on any matter of policy, and have yet to see the first case in which, as between two lines of policy, the fair and liberal one was not adopted."[957] Van Horne allowed that corporations should pay "their fair proportion of taxes," but he contended that they "should be taxed precisely the same as individuals are taxed." He saw no valid reason "for making them pay for the privilege of being a corporation for that privilege is a public necessity and a public good."[958]

Much to Van Horne's indignation, his benevolent view of corporations was not shared by everybody else, especially groups in the United States that traditionally resented state authority: labour, farmers, small businessmen, and the growing middle class. So strong was their objection to the dominion of big business they began turning to the government for protection in the opening years of the twentieth century. No president was better suited to take advantage of this political climate than the activist and moral crusader Teddy Roosevelt. As governor of New York he had advocated the regulation of big business, and after he ascended to the presidency in 1901 he moved fast. Taking direct aim at the United State's financial oligarchy — John D. Rockefeller, Edward H. Harriman, and James Jerome Hill, to name just some of the leading lights — the president prosecuted Morgan's Northern Securities Company under the Sherman Act as an illegal restraint of trade. Later, large railway systems bent on extending their territorial dominion became targets. They took a direct hit in 1906, when Congress passed the Heburn Act. Designed to plug loopholes in the legislation that established the Interstate Commerce Commission in 1887, it gave the commission power to set maximum railway rates. Four years later, in 1910, the Mann-Elkins Act, which extended the jurisdiction of the Interstate Commerce Commission over means of communication as well as transportation, restored the long-haul/short-haul clause of the original act.

When the railways requested a rate increase of about 15 percent in 1910, they had to justify their case before the commission. Faced by inflation that was driving up their costs and the need to attract capital to continue to make physical improvements, they nevertheless stumbled badly when presenting their case, as they had no idea of their costs or their return on investment. The ICC's response to the request, therefore, was a resounding no.[959] It was heard all the way to Covenhoven, prompting Van Horne to fire off a letter to A.B. Farquhar decrying the attacks on the railways. "At present I feel that I would rather be interested in railways anywhere than in the United States," wrote a dismayed Van Horne, who predicted that the "attitude of the Gov & the people towards such properties must, if persisted in, bring widespread disaster ..."[960]

As for Van Horne the capitalist, he was always on the lookout for legitimate ways to make money, eagerly seizing on investment tips provided by colleagues and friends and supplementing these with timely commercial intelligence supplied by the telegraph line. The returns from real estate properties and eventually from his extensive holding of CPR shares (in August 1883 he had 3,905 shares, a holding that he would add to over the years[961]) coupled with his large CPR salary, enabled him to amass a fortune. As a dedicated capitalist, he would devote himself unreservedly to nurturing this fortune and making it grow.

Fortunately for Van Horne his move to Canada opened up an abundance of investment opportunities, particularly at the turn of the century, for these years coincided with a striking improvement in the Canadian economy. Hitherto stagnant, it was now entering a period of unprecedented growth that would last, with only two minor interruptions, until 1913. During these buoyant years Canada grew faster than any other nation, the United States included. Practically every Canadian indicator soared upward — population, railway mileage, exports, construction, homestead entries. With its economy growing so rapidly, this country became a more attractive country of destination for both immigrants and investment capital. Thanks to Clifford Sifton's aggressive immigration policies, technological developments, and the lifting of the long depression, newcomers from Europe and the United States poured into Canada, settling on the virtually empty Prairies and taking up employment in the rapidly multiplying rail yards and factories of the fast-growing cities.

As a staunch proponent of immigration, Van Horne would have been expected to welcome the arrival of so many new settlers. Nevertheless, just as skeptical observers in the 1960s and the early years of the twenty-first century would question Canada's ability to absorb large numbers of new immigrants, so did Van Horne. When living in the "Western States and Territories" he had witnessed firsthand the "ill effects of rushing the settlement of new districts," and he did not want to see anything like this occur in the Northwest, he informed a correspondent in 1901.[962]. In 1901, when immigration was just beginning to pick up steam, he probably did not foresee the day in 1913 when immigration would rocket to over four hundred thousand.

Once arrived in their new country, homesteaders could turn the prairie sod with chilled steel ploughs and successfully till semi-arid prairie lands by means of dry farming techniques. With the rebound in the economy, they and other farmers across the country could anticipate better returns from their grain, butter, cheese, and bacon as these were finally fetching higher prices in North American and European markets. From the lofty heights of a captain of industry, Van Horne delivered his pronounced views on how Canadian farmers should conduct their operations. Always didactic, he wrote at length to Laurier protesting the failure of Canadian farmers to fully exploit their opportunities. He was especially critical of their practice of shipping agricultural produce, especially turnips, to New England. New Brunswick and Nova Scotia farmers should utilize turnips to make "beef and butter which would give them three times as much profit," Van Horne declared. It was sickening, he continued, "to go through New Brunswick and see how magnificent opportunities in this way are wasted, just as it is to see how Manitoba and Eastern Assineboia have been denuded of young cattle by American buyers who have taken them south...for the purpose of feeding them and shipping many of them abroad in competition with Canadian cattle growers ..."[963] While other parties lobbied strenuously for a reduction of American duties on Canadian agricultural products, Van Horne took the view that Canada's interests would be best served if the country abandoned its efforts to secure reciprocal trading arrangements or a reduction of duties on certain agricultural products. Canada, he informed Laurier, would be better off if Washington doubled or tripled the Dingley tariff on Canadian cattle, hay, root crops, and lumber. He declared:

> Exporting hay is a good deal like living off one's own blood. I hold that no community can do it and prosper and that the conditions with such a community must constantly grow worse...If the export of hay from the Province of Quebec could be absolutely stopped and the farmers of that province taught (as might easily be done) how to utilize their land to best advantage, a few years would make them as prosperous as those of the Province of Ontario Peninsula ...[964]

When it came to investing his money, this capitalist looked to railways, real estate, and companies with tangible assets or intrinsic value, not stock market speculation, to bring the desired returns. His real estate investments included a building (the so-called New York Block), located on one of Vancouver's main arteries, Granville Street, and shares in the Montreal Land and Improvement Company and Winnipeg-based Norwood Improvement Company (he was the largest shareholder). Outside of the CPR, however, Van Horne's railway investing was confined to offshore roads, largely in Central and South America. Besides real estate and railways, he invested in a huge number of Canadian companies with a tangible product to sell.[965] In the final years of his CPR presidency and the opening years of the twentieth century, he began to focus more and more time and energy on his business affairs. His success was such that before his death he would be acknowledged as a multimillionaire and one of the most influential businessmen of his generation.

Van Horne began purchasing stock and dabbling in real estate when he was still a young man making his way up the railway hierarchy in the United States. He was a partner for several years in a Chicago car works, had a one-tenth interest in the Canada Foundry Company, and before he retirement from the CPR presidency sold his interest in the American Car and Foundry at a handsome profit.[966] His participation in the business world took on a new dimension, however, in 1894 and 1895. With the enthusiastic approval of the CPR's board, he became actively involved in organizing the Canadian Salt Company, whose product line would eventually include not only salt but also caustic soda and bleaching powder. Destined to carry out business in Windsor, Detroit, and Sandwich, it was intended to secure for the CPR its share of the Ontario salt traffic.[967] He would remain president of the company until his death. The salt company, however, was but one of several business ventures that justified his being labelled an "activist entrepreneur." With typical Van Horne enthusiasm, he threw himself into the organization and management of several companies in the closing years of the nineteenth century.

Conspicuous among these was the Laurentide Pulp (later the Laurentide Pulp and Paper) Company, located in northern Quebec. The company traced its beginnings to 1877, when a farsighted Montrealer of Scottish origin, John Foreman, sought to capitalize on Quebec's huge supplies of fast water and spruce forest by establishing a pulp mill at Grand Mère, twenty-five miles north of Trois-Rivières on the St. Maurice River. Unfortunately, Foreman's company was plagued by capital shortages, transportation problems, and inadequate technology. As a result, the mill, although able to make pulp, could not operate at a profit.[968]

The company's potential, however, attracted the attention of Van Horne's friend and fellow business tycoon General Russell Alger. The former Michigan governor, who had made a fortune in lumber before becoming secretary of war in William McKinley's Cabinet, began investing in Canada's forestry industry when he realized that the American mass media's insatiable appetite for paper would soon lead to a shortage of pulp wood in the United States. After his son, Russell Alger, Jr., was appointed manager of the Laurentide mill, Alger began regularly offering advice on building and operating procedures.[969] His frequent visits to the mill site and company headquarters in Montreal convinced him that the Laurentide could be made profitable. Accordingly, he enlisted the aid of various business colleagues, including Van Horne, and set about organizing the Laurentide Pulp Company, capitalized at over $1.5 million and boasting some 1,500 square miles of white spruce timber at Grand Mère.

Van Horne became a company director at the urging of Alger, who thought it desirable to have some Canadians associated with him in the enterprise.[970] No doubt Van Horne was one of the first Canadians that came to mind, for the Van Horne name certainly added lustre to any company masthead. For his part, Van Horne acceded to his friend's request because he wanted to see more traffic generated for the CPR, whose Piles branch ran from Trois Rivières northward. He was also, of course, not averse to making some money for himself, and the Laurentide operation, properly capitalized and managed, promised to do just that. After all, the outlook for wood pulp and paper sales could not have been more promising. No less a figure than J.R. Booth, Ottawa's towering lumber and railway magnate, testified to this when he observed, "there is not likely to be found any substitute for spruce for paper making, and with our unlimited spruce forests, our greatest water power in the world and our various means for making acids, we should become the paper makers for the world."[971] Van Horne probably would not have thrown in his lot with the company, however, had he not thought highly of Alger as a businessman and as a man of wealth and stature. Alger's stature in the business community alone sufficed to persuade Van Horne that the undertaking had excellent long-term investment prospects. Indeed, when lobbying the Laurier government for a lowering of the duty on imported American paper-making machines, he described the undertaking to the prime minister as "the most important one of any description in Canada."[972]

Van Horne was not content to be a mere company director. He also became Laurentide's president, taking an active interest in the erection of pulp mills and power plant and in the production and sale of the company's product. Furthermore, as a demonstration of his faith in the enterprise, he sank a lot of money into it — over $350,000 by July 1900.[973] Perhaps even more important, he persuaded a large number of his friends, such as R.B. Angus and other CPR cronies, to become fellow investors. Their involvement would return to haunt him, however, when the company misjudged its profits and suffered one setback after another. "So far as I personally concerned [sic], my summer two years ago was spoiled by the first fire at the Mills, my last summer was spoiled by the second fire, and I have not enough summers left to spare another," wrote a dispirited Van Horne in an anguished letter to Alger in June 1902.[974] In 1902, Van Horne would have severed his connection with the calamity-prone company altogether had he not felt obligated to the investors whom he had induced to buy its stock.

That same year, however, steps were taken to reverse Laurentide's fortunes. Following a visit by American experts, the company was reorganized and the decision made to focus on the manufacture of paper, utilizing a newly discovered process that made paper from a pulp of ground wood rather than from reconverted waste materials such as rags and straw. Since state-of-the-art paper mills required a huge outlay of funds, Van Horne took on the laborious and time-consuming task of trying to raise additional capital. He would later report that he found it "the most difficult job of the kind" he had ever undertaken.[975] Nevertheless, despite the recessions of 1903 and 1907, all the money was subscribed by 1908. By 1910, the fortunes of the company had improved so dramatically that it was paying an annual dividend of between 6 and 8 percent and Van Horne was able to boast to his young American protegé, Percival Farquhar, "The Laurentide Paper Company, of which I have been president for a good many years, is the most successful one in the country and its preferred and common stocks stand at something like 200."[976] Van Horne was still president of this worldwide exporter when he died in 1915, at which time it was the largest paper-making concern in Canada and its president, according to *Canadian Railway and Marine World*, had earned the reputation of being the "Dominion's greatest business authority on the pulpwood question."[977]

If reorganizing one such operation was not challenging enough, Van Horne, Alger, and other investors involved from the beginning in the Laurentide operation also established related undertakings in the Maritimes. In 1898, with the backing of the town of Grand Falls, New Brunswick, and the New Brunswick government, they began setting up a company known as the Grand Falls Water Power and Boom Company. When describing its potential to Alger, an ecstatic Van Horne wrote, "The water power company at Sault Ste. Marie are expending $3,000,000 to get forty thousand of horse power, while we will have at Grand Falls nearly twice the power at a good deal less than one tenth the cost."[978] The power company's site was certainly ideally suited to a paper-making operation, located as it was on the St. John River, which drains into the forests of northern Maine and is close to year-round shipping facilities on the Atlantic. In fact, Van Horne, several Canadian associates, such as R.B. Angus and Sir Herbert Holt (a colossus of Canadian business who had been a successful CPR contractor), and a few American friends, such as Redfield Proctor and G.W. Underwood of the International Paper Company (which was to control half the new operation), established the Grand Falls Company with a view to erecting a paper-making mill whose eventual capacity would make it "by far the largest paper mill in the world."[979]

Implementation of their ambitious plans was frustrated, however, by a series of roadblocks. In 1912, newspaper reports of plans to erect a large paper manufacturing plant at Grand Falls fuelled hopes that a plant would be in operation in the not-too-distant future, but in June 1914 a plant engineer had still to be appointed and as late as the spring of 1915 a weary Van Horne was still "chasing a lot of unwilling people" for money.[980] Just two months before his death, he was protesting the New Brunswick government's insistence that he, Sir Herbert Holt, and G.W. Underwood as licence holders proceed with timber cutting while they were attempting to conserve valuable timber. He grumbled to company lawyer H.A. Powell in July 1915:

> If the Deputy Minister of Public Lands will consider the value to the Province of unmanufactured timber exported as compared with the export of paper made from it and consider the large population that every first call paper-mill brings with it I feel sure that he will see where the true interests of the Province lie. Perhaps the Government thinks that the Grand Falls Company has been idle and it may be well for you to inform them of the extensive purchases of lands in the immediate vicinity of Grand Falls for the purpose of carrying out its extensive works — purchases aggregating considerably more than $100,000 within the past eighteen months.[981]

Neither of these ventures could be described as highly speculative and unethical. On the other hand, some of the others in which Van

Horne became involved were "extra hazardous." As such, they reeked of the shady business practices and imperfect competition so characteristic of the finance capitalism that dominated North American industry before the crisis of 1929. In this era of unregulated business, capitalist barons frequently watered and/or manipulated stock, or diverted shareholders' and policyholders' money into extremely speculative undertakings. Van Horne certainly did not instigate such practices and schemes. Next to losing a family member, he dreaded nothing more than having his good name sullied by any hint of scandal. Nevertheless, he did allow his name to be associated with some questionable ventures and companies.

Heading the parade were schemes initiated by that peripatetic American and young Van Horne protegé, Percival Farquhar. Like other bravura entrepreneurs of his ilk, Farquhar constantly sought new ways to make money, be it organizing a new railway, installing an electrified trolley line, or establishing an electric power distribution system. An avid risk-taker (known in the parlance of the day as a "plunger"), he shuttled restlessly around the Atlantic in his quest for new money-making prospects, all too often found in undeveloped Latin America, where gullible politicians were often hungry for modern development. Whenever his search turned up a promising-looking project, he would assemble a syndicate that would provide the necessary funds for implementing the scheme. Members of the syndicate — bankers, investment dealers, and well-heeled capitalists — and the institutions with which they were affiliated would then acquire large blocks of bonds to which was attached bonus stock. As soon the undertaking was well established and reporting earnings, the stock would be listed on the stock exchange and the bonus stock released gradually onto a managed market. By proceeding in this fashion, the promoter realized his gains and freed up capital for another round.[982]

Percival Farquhar was a driven man. In fact, his father, a Pennsylvania businessman with extensive interests in Cuba, frequently fretted about his son's health in letters to his friend Van Horne. The frenetic pace, constant worry, and continuous travel demanded by company promotion were, he felt, taking an undue toll on young Farquhar's health. No doubt Van Horne shared the elder Farquhar's worries, but of even greater concern to him was the recklessness of some of the young man's schemes. When Farquhar was based in Cuba, serving as Van Horne's chief lieutenant in the Cuba Company, Van Horne gently reproached him for indulging in some pretty speculative ventures. These reproaches, however, were nothing compared to the charges that Van Horne levelled against him, albeit reluctantly, in later years when Farquhar was pursuing money-making opportunities in Brazil, Guatemala, and Mexico.

Invariably, Van Horne was sucked one way or another into Farquhar's schemes, sometimes to his great regret. Such was the case with a railway project in Guatemala. This undertaking was first drawn to his attention by Farquhar, who had become a friend of Minor Cooper Keith, the magnetic, if unscrupulous and rapacious, vice-president of the United Fruit Company. Brooklyn-born Keith regarded railways as indispensable to the expansion of his rapidly growing fruit empire, and, having helped to build a railway under horrendously difficult conditions in Costa Rica, he set his sights on a railway project in Guatemala. In response to Keith's and Farquhar's invitation to participate in a Guatemala railway project, a harassed Van Horne wrote in August 1903:

> My only fear is that I shall be unable to give this enterprise very much attention if I go into it, for I am simply overwhelmed with work in connection with various other things, the care of which has mostly fallen upon me with the result that I am so pressed that I do not know which way to turn. In better times I might get out of a lot of them, but just now it is impossible, and, in addition to all of my time, they require all of the money I can rake up. I feel at this moment that I should be very foolish to embark in any new enterprise requiring either time or money. However, I shall be very glad if I can possibly do it to join Mr. Keith in this matter.[983]

In another letter to Farquhar that September, Van Horne made it quite clear that his only object in joining this loose syndicate was to enable Farquhar "to make something worthwhile."[984] No doubt his friendship with Farquhar and his debt of gratitude to him for his services to the Cuba Railroad decided the issue because at this juncture Van Horne was truly feeling weighed down by his many onerous responsibilities and the steady stream of demands being made on his pocketbook. In any event, he unwisely decided to throw in his lot with Keith and another railway promoter, General Thomas Hubbard, president of the Guatemala Central Railroad. On July 12, 1904, all three parties signed a syndicate agreement that incorporated the Guatemala Railway in New Jersey for the purpose of constructing, leasing, maintaining, and operating tramways and terminals in Guatemala.[985] Van Horne would become chairman, Keith president, and Farquhar vice-president.

Keith had been impressed by Farquhar's role in opening up the eastern half of Cuba. Indeed, he was so impressed that he invited the young entrepreneur to go to Guatemala and obtain a railway contract to acquire banana lands in Guatemala's unused lowlands and complete a long-interrupted stretch of rusting railroad from Puerto Barrios, the country's principal seaport on the Caribbean coast, to Guatemala City, its capital and the centre of its trade. Farquhar accepted the challenge, and in late 1903, acting on behalf of Keith and Van Horne, he travelled to Guatemala to secure the sought-after contract from Guatemala's ruthless dictator president, Manuel Estrada Cabrera. To Farquhar's and the syndicate's chagrin, the tyrant temporized for two months. At this point, Van Horne's lieutenant warned that unless a contract was signed the next day giving his group perpetual ownership of the 135-mile "streak of rust" to Puerto Barrios built by the government and of 50,000 acres of banana land, he would leave. This produced the desired results: a remarkably generous contract and concession, which were signed on January 12, 1904. Having overcome this hurdle, Van Horne and his associates advanced sufficient funds to rehabilitate the existing line and begin construction of the new one. Forging the new sixty-mile link between Guatemala City and El Rancho to the northeast would be a daunting undertaking, however, as the line had to be laid through steep, rain-drenched mountains plagued by landslides. The syndicate would not have taken comfort in the knowledge that every previous contractor who had attempted this feat had gone bankrupt.

If the terrain across which the new link was to be laid posed one set of problems, political strife and open warfare posed another. Manuel Estrada Cabrera's re-election to the presidency in 1906 unleashed widespread discontent, which in turn led to war with Honduras, Salvador, and Costa Rica, accused by the president of aiding his political enemies. The strife came to an end only after President Roosevelt of the United States and President Diaz of Mexico intervened. Meanwhile, all outside funding for railway construction was cut off. As a result, members of the syndicate had to dig into their own pockets to find the necessary funds for the road's completion. When viewed in terms of railway outlays, the amount was not large, but because he had invested more than he had intended to in Cuba, Van Horne probably found it more difficult to shoulder his share of the new financial obligation than Keith and Hubbard. In fact, he was so pressed for funds that he had to unload some of his investments in Mexico and elsewhere. He even resorted to selling one-half of his interest in the Guatemala Railroad to Keith and Farquhar in January 1910 and another share of his interest to his Scottish financier friend Robert Fleming.[986]

When corresponding with Van Horne on the subject of the railway, Fleming could not refrain from commenting, "I sometimes think you Americans are very careless & reckless but you seem cat like & will I think land on your feet this time."[987] Two years later, Van Horne would reiterate his belief to the fruit company magnate that the financially strapped syndicate should not attempt to buy the Guatemala Central. Still, if Keith was determined to do so, Van Horne would prefer to sell his remaining interest in the Guatemala Railroad at half its actual cost to him rather than prevent his friend from making the purchase.[988]

Van Horne allowed that he had "suffered severely" from his involvement in the Guatemala undertaking and the sacrifices that he had been required to make in assuming his share of the burden. These included not only money but also time. "I am unable to understand the slow progress of track ... and I shall be glad if you will tell me how many ties you are putting in the old line per kilometer," Van Horne wrote in 1906 to the railway's general manager, with whom he corresponded routinely about progress profiles and cost-cutting measures.[989] Before confessing, however, to the heavy toll that the project had taken on his pocketbook and his time, he had the satisfaction of making a triumphal tour of the line in April 1907. Accompanied by Keith and Charles Hopkins Clark, editor of the *Hartford Courant*, he travelled by mule from end of track to Guatemala City, riding along the most precipitous cliffs with a fearlessness that astonished his companions. The arduous trip was physically demanding, but his all-consuming interest in the road under construction enabled him to tolerate the journey's hardships better than his younger and more slender companions. The enthusiastic and deferential welcome that he received at every depot and engineers' camp the party visited also bolstered his powers of endurance.

On his return to Canada Van Horne reported that Guatemala City was the "handsomest" of the Spanish American cities he had yet seen, "beautifully situated, with fine streets and buildings and with many signs of prosperity and growth." Even more important, he was "very much impressed by the high character and ability" of Guatemala's president. While in Guatemala City, Van Horne and his associates submitted "ten matters of importance" to the dictator, "all of which he agreed to, and in less than two hours the necessary decrees had been issued. Some of our northern governments might learn something there."[990] Further homage awaited the celebrated railroader the following January in Guatemala City.

There, during a two-week fiesta held to mark the completion of the northern line, he and Keith drove the ceremonial golden spike.

Van Horne's association with the Guatemala Railway and initially with another project of Farquhar's, the Brazil Railway, served only to increase his apprehension about his protegé's modus operandi. The lack of attention that the promoter paid to the Guatemala railway project was of utmost concern to Van Horne. Farquhar was expected to spend most of his time on the scene supervising the railway's progress. Instead, he was off chasing opportunities in Brazil, Colorado, and Alaska. With rising indignation, Van Horne wrote to his intrepid friend, "Success is only possible in taking up one thing and sticking to it exclusively, until it is worked to a conclusion. I regard failure as certain in every one of those enterprises which depend largely on you."[991]

Equally upsetting to Van Horne was Farquhar's failure to keep him and W.L. Bull, the New York investment banker, fully informed about the exact conditions and limitations of franchises associated with the Brazil Railway Company undertaking. Farquhar's evasions and attitude so disturbed Van Horne that he was spurred to write, "I doubt if you fully realize the gravity of what you are asking us to do. I do not wish to be captious, and I am sure that Mr. Bull does not, but speaking for myself I do not wish to take any chance at being smirched by this or any other transaction, nor of incurring any serious responsibility."[992] This letter was followed the next day by one in which Van Horne stated unequivocally that he wanted to resign from the "Brazil Railway Committee as soon as possible."[993] Thereafter he denounced attempts to have his name associated with the Port of Para (port works at Belém in Amazônia) and the Brazil Railway Company, both headed by Farquhar and both incorporated in Maine. Indeed, in 1907 Van Horne saw fit to warn his young friend that "the air in New York" was full of "adverse talk" about his various South American schemes and that Paris and London likewise buzzed with unfavourable gossip about his wildly speculative ventures.[994]

In response to concerns voiced by Robert Fleming, Van Horne replied to the financier in December 1907:

> I quite appreciate what you say about the use of my name in connection with the Brazil Railway Company. To oblige Mr. Farquhar I consented about two years ago to act as one of his underwriting committee in connection with Mr. Keith and Mr. Bull, but the functions of that committee ended a long time ago and I declined

positively to have anything further to do with the matter. Finding that my name was being used in connection with that enterprise I wrote Mr. Farquhar months ago telling him plainly that I would not submit to anything of that kind. He assured me that my name had been used without his knowledge and that he had taken the necessary steps to prevent any further use of it and sent me copies of a lot of letters that he had written to various parties interested which were as explicit as I could wish.[995]

Despite Van Horne's insistence that his name be expunged from all Brazil Railway Company publicity material, the name Van Horne still appeared on the Brazil Railway Company's list of directors four years later, by which time the road had built over three thousand miles and had almost two thousand either under construction or to be constructed.[996] In 1911, the enterprise appeared to be flourishing, but in 1913 and 1914 disaster would strike in the form of an economic slump, delays in Brazil's large payments for the construction of traffic-generating subsidiaries, and the outbreak of the First World War. Having sought to gain control of his companies by speculating in his own securities, Farquhar had only a paper fortune, estimated at approximately $25 million, with which to counter these threats. The inevitable happened: the railway collapsed.[997] Events did indeed prove that Van Horne had had good reason to protest the association of his name with the enterprise.

Problems of a different sort confronted Van Horne in his association with two enterprises in the Maritimes. As a director of both the Dominion Coal Company and the Dominion Iron and Steel Company, he became closely associated with the fortunes of the two jointly owned companies during a turbulent time in their history. The coal operation was founded in 1893 after Van Horne's Boston friend Henry Whitney and a coterie of Nova Scotia businessmen consolidated numerous small collieries into the Dominion Coal Company, located in Sydney, Nova Scotia. To provide an outlet for so-called slack coal (the finest screenings of coal produced at the mine but unusable for fuel unless cleaned), Whitney spearheaded the establishment of the Dominion Iron and Steel Company in 1899. Two years later, in 1901, he sold control of both producers to prominent financier and railway builder James Ross. In 1903, Ross, in turn, ceded control of the steel company to another financier, J.H. Plummer, a Torontonian and assistant general manager of the Bank of Commerce.

Central to the companies' turmoil were the actions of James Ross. Scottish-born and trained as an engineer, Ross had been manager of construction of the mountain division of the CPR before settling in Montreal and turning his attention to the reorganization, electrification, and expansion of street railways in Canada, the United States, Mexico, South America, the Caribbean, and the United Kingdom. In addition to seeking riches as a street railway promoter, the rising tycoon served on the board of directors of the Bank of Montreal, its sister institution, the Royal Trust Company, and numerous other businesses affiliated with the CPR. In his role as a major developer of Cape Breton's coal and iron industry, he also headed the consortium that purchased the Dominion Coal Company and the Dominion Iron and Steel Company from Henry Whitney.

To Van Horne's great consternation, both companies became embroiled in a long and bitter dispute that sent shudders through the business community, rattled the nerves of investors, and grabbed newspaper headlines. At issue was a formal contract that the coal company signed in 1899 with the iron and steel company to furnish large quantities of high-quality coal at prices well below those prevailing on the market. In 1902, the coal company was leased by the steel company with the provision that the original contract, signed in 1899, be revived in modified form should the lease be cancelled. The lease was cancelled in 1903, at which time Ross resigned from the steel company presidency, confident that the coal company had sufficient legal grounds to get out of its onerous contract.[998] Control of the company passed to the Plummer syndicate and a new ninety-nine-year contract was signed. Disputes then arose as to the quantity and quality of the coal delivered. Three years later, on November 1, 1906, after years of mounting tension, the steel company withdrew from a provisional agreement, claiming that the quantity of coal delivered in August, September, and October of that year had been reduced without reason and that after that date it was unfit for the purposes for which it was required. Tensions escalated still further on November 9 when the coal company declared the contract null and void. This resulted in the steel company having to shut down its works for a short time, and although a working compromise was arrived at in December, the company entered a suit in Nova Scotia's Supreme Court for huge damages.[999]

Van Horne went to battle after Ross, as head of the coal company, rescinded the formal contract without consulting his board of directors. Ross's move enraged Van Horne, who regarded it as "unwarranted, dishonest and highly dangerous."[1000] As he saw it, the mogul had acted with a view to "wrecking the Steel Company and then buying up its major securities, foreclosing against the rest and securing the property for a very small fraction of its actual value — an often repeated proceeding in olden times in the United States but happily, until now, unknown in Canada."[1001] After trying in vain to persuade Ross to agree to settle the dispute by arbitration, Van Horne withdrew from the coal company altogether in November 1906. Attempts were made to have him return to its board, but he stoutly refused to retract his resignation. Instead, he began vigorously championing the interests of the steel company, in which he had invested about $100,000. In the months ahead he would fight its battles with all the fervour he could muster, goaded on, no doubt, by a falling out that he and Ross had had in a business transaction some seven or eight years previously. Van Horne could never forgive a betrayal, and his belief that Ross had cheated him was enough to sharpen his combative instincts and make him a formidable foe in the ensuing struggle.

The legal dispute degenerated into a protracted and bitter battle. Round one was played out in Nova Scotia's Supreme Court, where the suit came to trial on July 31, 1907. Responding to J.H. Plummer's invitation, Van Horne journeyed to Sydney to serve as a witness and to do "all he could to help the Steel Company."[1002] While a settlement was still pending in the courts, he also fired off a letter to Lord Grey arguing the steel company's case and attacking Ross and his "piratical" move. "The questions now are, on the part of the Steel Company, simply whether a deliberate contract entered into between two companies ... will be enforced by the Courts of this country, and whether a party finding himself with a losing or undesirable contract can get out of it or force the other party to a cancellation or modification of it through such a high handed course as that taken by Mr. Ross," declared Van Horne.[1003]

Whether or not Van Horne's evidence played a pivotal role in determining the outcome of the case, the court found unanimously in the steel company's favour and awarded the company damages. The case was immediately appealed, and when no compromise was reached it went all the way to the Judicial Committee of the Privy Council in London (then Canada's highest court of appeal) in October 1908. Although recognizing that the contract was unbalanced, the committee found the contract to be legally binding. It upheld the Dominion Iron and Steel Company's case and ordered the two companies to carry out further negotiations to settle damages and other financial details. Following his defeat, Ross resigned from the Dominion Coal Company, thereby paving the way for the two firms to merge in 1910 as the Dominion Iron and Steel Company, from which Van Horne would receive $1,250 twice a year for his services as vice-president.[1004] He had lamented the litigation and had tried desperately to avert it. Once involved, however, he had revelled, as he had in his old railway battles, in detecting and defeating his adversary's moves.

Over the years Van Horne would wage more battles on behalf of the iron and steel company. Most of these were inspired by the crippled financial condition in which the company found itself as a result of years of litigation, providing for a permanent coal supply, increasing transportation costs, and expanding its plant to meet the challenges posed by global competition. In 1913, the company's vice-president struck a decidedly desperate note when he beseeched Prime Minister Robert Borden's government to assist the company. "Whether the results of mistakes or not the Dominion Steel Corporation is as I said in my former letter 'under the shadow of the Synagogue and only your Government can help out,'" Van Horne wrote.[1005] To present-day observers the appeal has a decidedly familiar ring.

Van Horne demonstrated his national vision by also investing in British Columbia, where he became a late subscriber in the British Columbia Lumber Company. His interest in the firm was sparked by the knowledge that legendary John Rudolphus Booth, Senator Robert Mackay, and other parties had invested substantial sums of money in it. Van Horne made a point of conferring with the senator, a fellow CPR director, about the firm's prospects for, as he readily admitted, he had "very much confidence" in the Senator's judgment. This is not surprising, as his friend was ranked as one of twenty-three titans pre-eminent in the Canadian financial community in the opening years of the twentieth century.[1006]

Another British Columbia venture in which Van Horne took an interest traced its roots to the annual inspection trip he made out west. When his train was delayed for some hours at Yale, British Columbia, Van Horne and his party decided to try their hand at panning the river soil for gold. Under the guidance of a veteran California miner, they washed and discovered gold in their pans. This led immediately to the suggestion that each member of the party invest $8,000 in a hydraulic mining plant. Thus was born the Horsefly and Hydraulic mining companies. They struggled along for several years conducting placer mining operations in British Columbia before being wound up after much more than the original investment had been lost.[1007]

The conduct of the British Columbia companies may not have generated newspaper headlines, but not so that of the New York-based Equitable Life Assurance Society, another company in which Van Horne had an interest. The shenanigans of its principals were just made to sell newspaper copy.

The unwelcome publicity did not occur, however, until several years after Van Horne joined the Equitable's board at the invitation of the company's founder, Henry Hyde, who died in 1899. Van Horne had no hesitation in lending his name to the board because it boasted several leading American financiers whom he knew well. Confident that the company was in good shape and meeting its obligations, he attended board meetings only occasionally and only in a perfunctory way.

Great was his shock, then, when the society, along with the Mutual and New York Life, the other two big life insurance companies, became the subject of screaming newspaper headlines and eventually a New York State legislature investigation. The problem arose when a wealthy Boston speculator and stockbroker, Thomas W. Lawson, published a series of articles in *Everybody's Magazine* in which he charged the "racers," as the three leading insurance companies were called, with systematically bribing regulators and politicians, using "captive" trust companies to conduct illegal financial operations, and investing policyholders' money in risky ventures instead of "safe" government bonds.

The Equitable gained notoriety after young James Hyde, who had inherited 51 percent of its stock in trust from his father, invested much of the society's surplus capital in corporate securities. Although the company profited from this new investment policy, its conservative president, James Alexander, declared that insurance was a "sacred trust," not a "monster money-making scheme," and began to entertain fears that Hyde would sell out in 1906, when he reached thirty and inherited his shares. Like vultures spotting potential carrion, prospective buyers began circling overhead.

On January 31, 1905, Hyde staged an extravagant costume ball at Sherry's restaurant in New York. With complete disregard for the public's mounting distaste for vulgar displays of wealth, he had the restaurant's grand ballroom transformed into the palace of Versaille's Hall of Mirrors, hired the Metropolitan Opera orchestra and the French actress Gabrielle Réjane to provide entertainment, and invited friends from around the world to attend. No sooner had the press reported — incorrectly — that the "orgy" had cost the Equitable $200,000 and that Hyde was having an affair with the actress than the battle for control of the company was catapulted onto the front pages of the nation's newspapers.

As a result of the uproar, both Hyde and Alexander lost the confidence of the Equitable's board, and the following month its directors appointed a panel of lawyers headed by Elihu Root to mutualize the company, and thereby vest control in its policyholders. Root deep-sixed the plan. And, if this were not bad enough, a committee of Equitable board members proceeded to find the company guilty of financial misconduct and "moral oblique-ness." Root then arranged for one of his own clients, Thomas Fortune Ryan, to acquire young Hyde's majority holding in the company. Ryan paid Hyde $2.5 million in 1905, which was far more than the par value of the stock but considerably less than the company's apparent market value.[1008]

Later that same year, a New York State investigative committee began to take evidence about the insurance scandals. Its revelations of mismanage-ment and irregularities helped to inspire the establishment of a similar body in Canada, the Royal Commission on Insurance, appointed in February 1906. In Canada, the call for action was led by the *Toronto World*, which cru-saded vigorously against Canada's leading insurance companies, particularly Canada Life, in the opening months of 1906. The paper's strident appeals on behalf of the "injured and the outraged" and its insistence that Canada conduct an investigation similar to that being conducted in New York would prove remarkably effective in stirring up local agitation for a Canadian investigative body.[1009] The result was the establishment of a royal commission that turned up some headline-grabbing findings. None was more explosive than the revelation that Senator George Cox (president of both the Bank of Commerce, Canada's second largest bank, and the Canada Life Assurance Company, the second largest business of its type) and other officials made liberal use of the life insurance premiums at their disposal to underwrite and accommodate stock market operations in numerous com-panies, including Dominion Coal and São Paulo Tramway.[1010]

Van Horne was not only shocked by the revelations of misconduct on the part of the North American insurance industry he was also mor-tified, so much so that he began to question the propriety of retaining directorships in companies where he exercised no control.[1011] In 1907, therefore, he decided that he would begin retiring as gracefully as he could from many of them. This still left many firms, however, in which he retained an interest.

Several of these, not surprisingly, involved transportation in one form or another, notably street railways and railways. Like other railway tycoons of this era, Van Horne invested in electric street railways, which began replacing horse-drawn trams as a mode of public transit in the late 1880s. In this, he was motivated not just by investment considerations but also by an interest in seeing Canadian urban electrification schemes integrated with CPR freight and passenger services. When accepting invitations to participate in these projects he often joined forces with the wily, crafty, and blunt-speaking William Mackenzie, one of Canada's best-known entrepre-neurs in the first two decades of the twentieth century.

Van Horne's friendship with Mackenzie dated from the years that the Kirkfield, Ontario, native worked as contractor for the CPR. Mackenzie, who had been born in a North Eldon Township shanty in 1849, had started making his mark as a contractor in the mid and late 1870s when he worked with some of his brothers in a contracting business that served the hamlet of Kirkfield and the surrounding community. His association with the CPR began in 1884 when, thanks to his friendship with James Ross, he and his partner, John McDonald, acquired a contract to construct bridges for the CPR in the Rockies. In due course they would also build telegraph offices, water tanks, a gunpowder factory, and coal sheds. When Donald Smith drove the last spike at Craigellachie in 1885, Mackenzie, then recognized as a competent contractor, was among the crowd of spectators who craned forward to watch the proceedings. The following January he and his partner strode into Van Horne's office in Montreal to collect their profits, about $200,000 for each of them for two years' work.[1012] Mackenzie would later team up with a fellow CPR contractor, Donald Mann, to build a segment of the CPR's "short line" through Maine and to assemble prairie charters and railway lines that would comprise the nucleus of the transcontinental Canadian Northern Railway.

Although remembered primarily as a railway magnate, Mackenzie also devoted his formidable energy to assembling an urban utilities empire comprising electrical power generating stations and transportation companies. His first foray into this sector occurred in 1891, when he and three partners purchased the horse-drawn Toronto Street Railway. As its president, he participated in the inaugural run of its first electric trolley, a dark chocolate-coloured vehicle with spring-cushioned seats and handcrafted maple interior. Throngs of excited Torontonians caught their first glimpse of the car when it glided past them on August 10, 1892.[1013] Soon Mackenzie and his associates controlled public transit in Montreal and Winnipeg as well, operating the street railways as ruthlessly as they could in order to generate the cash flow required to finance their hydroelectric projects. Among Mackenzie's associates in the Winnipeg enterprise was Van Horne. He became a director of the Winnipeg Electric Railway Company, formed by the amalgamation of the Winnipeg Electric Street Railway Company, incorporated in 1892 in Manitoba, and the Winnipeg General Power Company, incorporated in 1902. The Electric Street Railway Company showed that it meant business when, shortly after its opening on September 5, 1892, it launched a price war with Winnipeg's decade-old horse car line. Following two years of invective and court battles, the outclassed horse car company was forced to sell out to Van Horne and William Mackenzie's aggressive syndicate.[1014] In 1912, Van Horne owned 2,201 shares of the amalgamated company while young Addie and Bennie each owned 85.[1015]

When their friendship was still intact, Van Horne and James Ross had bid on the property of the Consolidated Electric Company of Saint John, New Brunswick, when it had come on the market in the spring of 1894. The two erstwhile partners went to some lengths to hide the fact that they were the actual bidders. At Van Horne's behest, E.S. Clouston, the Bank of Montreal's general manager, instructed the Bank of Montreal's manager in Saint John to bid on the property, ostensibly on behalf of the bank but in fact on behalf of Ross and Van Horne. If necessary, the bank could bid as high as $100,000. Events proved that this would not be necessary, for Van Horne later thanked Clouston for advising him of the purchase of the property for $92,000.[1016] As a director of the Saint John enterprise, Van Horne became actively involved in the modernization of street railway transportation in that Maritime city.

Aggressive utility entrepreneurs and financiers that they were, Mackenzie and Ross did not confine their operations to Canada, where there were comparatively few opportunities to exploit and the cities to be served were relatively small. In the belief that their technical and managerial skills could generate much higher returns elsewhere, where local politicians were perhaps more gullible and hungrier for modern development, the intrepid duo began in 1895 to look outside Canada for investment opportunities. Initially they focused on the United States, but they soon discovered that their American competitors were not only numerous but also very aggressive and frequently litigious. It also did not help their cause that Canadian investors could only receive minority shareholders' returns from the enterprises in which they invested. Mackenzie and Ross, therefore, led the way in turning investors' attention to investment opportunities abroad.[1017]

Among those investors who followed their lead was, of course, Van Horne, whose many Latin American investments also included the Demerara Electric Company. It was established by a syndicate that Van Horne joined in 1899 to install an electric lighting and trolley system in Georgetown, British Guiana. The company, which was capitalized at $850,000 and financed by a $600,000 loan from his friends at the Bank of Montreal, built a power plant to provide power and laid down tramlines. Van Horne and his fellow investors, however, had not anticipated that the company's rather primitive wiring would seriously disrupt the provincially owned telephone system. As a result of this and other unforeseen obstacles, the small undertaking limped along until it was reorganized toward the end of the decade.[1018]

The Mexican Light and Power Company was another offshore enterprise in which Van Horne invested. Although incorporated by a group of Halifax lawyers in 1902, it became a predominantly Montreal property when the Mexican government signed a revised concession and the company's head office was moved from Halifax to Montreal. On January 20, 1903, the Halifax directors resigned, to be replaced by Van Horne, E.S. Clouston, George Drummond (former president of the Bank of Montreal), James Ross, F.L. Wanklyn (general manager of James Ross's and William Mackenzie's Montreal Street Railway), and four Torontonians: William Mackenzie, J.H. Plummer, George Cox (of Canada Life), and E.W. Wood (a stockbroker and president of the Central Canada Loan and Savings Company).[1019] With James Ross as president, the company metamorphosed into a major venture that soon turned its attention to acquiring other companies with a view to creating an integrated distribution monopoly that would transmit power into Mexico City.

Given his outstanding railway expertise and the lure of his name, it was inevitable that Van Horne would be deluged with invitations to participate in various railway ventures. One such invitation originated with a no less exalted party than the American government, now a colonizing power thanks to its decision to retain possessions awarded to it by the December 1898 Treaty of Paris with Spain. One of these possessions was the Philippines, where guerrilla war continued to devastate the colony's countryside and play havoc with its economy long after the treaty had been ratified. In the belief that improved transportation might help to allay this unrest, the American government began to consider various railway schemes for the islands. Immediately the Cuba Company's success in building a railway in Spanish-speaking Cuba came to mind. In January 1903, therefore, Elihu Root invited Van Horne to come to Washington to discuss a similar undertaking in the Philippines.

Van Horne accepted the invitation and journeyed to the American capital, where he was asked if the Cuba Company would be interested in building a railway in the colony. Van Horne told Root that he felt sure his associates would agree to such an undertaking, provided the American government furnished the necessary assistance.[1020] Thus began Van Horne's involvement with an undertaking that was doomed to failure. That it never got off the ground was not due to any lack of interest and effort on his part. The challenge of building a railway in the war and cholera-ravaged Philippines was no less appealing than the one that drew him to Cuba. Fired up by the prospect of duplicating his success in Cuba, he approached various financiers, including Thomas Ryan, and in 1903 dispatched a party of engineers to the island of Luzon to investigate railway conditions and draw up a preliminary report.

Further progress, however, was derailed by an English railway company, the Manila Railway Company, which had been awarded two concessions by Governor William Howard Taft to build lines along the routes that Elihu Root had in mind for Van Horne. Van Horne attempted to negotiate with the Manila Railway Company's chairman, C.J. Cater Scott, for the two concessions awarded by Governor Taft (later Root's successor as secretary of war) but met with resounding failure. The company's chairman adamantly refused to discuss his road's future until claims it had against the United States and Philippines governments were settled. This led Van Horne to believe that the company had secured the two concessions for the sole purpose of blocking the American government's plans and forcing a settlement of its claims.[1021] Despite these setbacks, Van Horne continued to express an interest in building a road in the Philippines, even drawing up a memorandum suggesting how the work should be accomplished. Finally, six months later, in September 1904, he was forced to concede that the time and money he had spent on the project had been wasted. Writing to a London friend, he reported:

> I do not know what the outcome of the general railway project of the Philippines is likely to be, and I am beginning to doubt that anything of consequence will be done, notwithstanding all of Secretary Taft's expressions in that direction. He is an extremely good-natured gentleman who makes promises without much consideration and is too honourable to go back on them, and therefore he has got himself and his railway projects into such a muddle that I doubt if he will ever find his way out.[1022]

Fortunately the Latin American railway undertakings in which Van Horne became involved were carried through to completion. One of these, the Argentine Railway Company, was spearheaded by a ten-member syndicate formed in 1901 and managed by George B. Hopkins, the New York stockbroker, who supplied Van Horne with Virginia hams as well as stock tips.[1023] Van Horne served as a director, for which he received a quarterly director's fee of $725.00 from the company in 1913.[1024]

In Brazil, a vast, undeveloped country brimming with promise, Van Horne became associated with various enterprises blazed by another well-known promoter of the day, Fred Pearson. A brilliant and innovative engineer, Pearson was consumed by a desire to live the life of a business tycoon. As the first step in realizing this ambition, he completed scientific studies at Tufts College in Medford, Massachusetts, and then immediately joined the college faculty, where he capitalized on a pioneering program in electrical engineering to master the rudiments of that discipline.[1025] While designing and managing electric lighting systems in the Boston area, he was hired by Henry M. Whitney to direct the electrification of six Boston-area horse railways that Whitney had consolidated into the West End Railway in 1887. Two years later, the engineer took on his first Canadian assignment when his Boston firm was hired to construct a gas plant in Halifax for lawyer and promoter Benjamin Franklin Pearson. Since the plant was designed to convert goal into gas, and since both Fred Pearson and H.M. Whitney sought inexpensive fuel for their electrical operations in the Boston area, they linked up with Benjamin Pearson and J.A. Grant in an effort to obtain coal fields in Cape Breton. This resulted in the founding of the Dominion Coal Company with Whitney as president and Fred Pearson as engineer-in-chief.[1026] Once established in Canada, the energetic Pearson soon became the Canadians' most sought-after consulting engineer, furnishing staff and expertise for assorted enterprises and gradually assuming a leading role in the promotion of new undertakings not only in Canada but also in the Americas.

The engineer's attention was first drawn to Brazil by a promising hydropower concession owned by an Italian-born contractor friend of James Ross, Antônio Gualco. Located in the heart of rich coffee-growing country, just outside the prosperous and expanding city of São Paulo, Gualco's concession required the provision of an integrated system of generation, transmission, and distribution. Unfortunately, Gualco and his Brazilian partner, Antônio de Souza, met with little success in their quest for capital to exploit the concession, so, desperate to obtain financial backing, Gualco went to Montreal, where he persuaded James Ross to look at his concession. Ross was sufficiently impressed that he took the concession to William Mackenzie. The frontier entrepreneur in turn brought in Fred Pearson, who arranged for a technical expert to investigate the concession on the spot. The enthusiastic report produced by R.C. Brown persuaded Mackenzie to enter wholeheartedly into sponsoring the project. Always on the lookout for more profits in the utilities field, he enlisted the aid of other members of Toronto's financial community, who in due course were joined by some of their cronies in Montreal, among them Van Horne.

Ownership of the assorted concessions assembled by Gualco and his partner over the years was eventually transferred to Mackenzie and his associates. For their part, Pearson and a young Toronto lawyer, Alexander Mackenzie (no relation to William Mackenzie), worked feverishly to tailor the principal Gualco concession to meet the needs of North American promoters. Once their petitions to legislative authorities had achieved the desired results, the two men took just over two months to transform the original Gualco concession into an all-embracing concession that provided for the right to generate and distribute electrical power to industrial and domestic users, as well as to a tramway.[1027] To reassure investors and take advantage of lax Canadian laws relating to corporations and securities, William Mackenzie arranged for Alexander Mackenzie's legal firm of Blake, Lash and Cassels to obtain an Ontario charter for the São Paulo Tramway, Light and Power Company Limited.

The public utilities company was established with a view to making profits for its shareholders, which it did. But at the same time it also furnished inexpensive, efficient power and thereby became one of the most constructive forces in the life of São Paulo. Encouraged by the outcome of this venture, Pearson and Alexander Mackenzie turned their attention to Rio de Janeiro, where they planned to repeat their success. After obtaining the necessary concessions and franchises, they established a second firm, the Rio de Janeiro Light and Power Company Limited, and in June 1904 obtained a federal charter for it in Ottawa. Since they wanted to avoid attracting attention to the company's ultimate aim of seizing control of Rio's scattered tramway companies, they deliberately avoided including "tramways" or "traction" in the company's name.[1028] In November of 1904, Van Horne took his place on the new company's board, along with William Mackenzie, F.S. Pearson, Z.A. Lash, New York financier W.L. Bull, E.R. Wood (a financial associate of prominent central Canadian businessman and senator George Cox), and Frederic Nicholls, a Toronto electrical promoter. William Mackenzie was elected president.

Eight years later, in 1912, the Rio and São Paulo companies were amalgamated under a holding company known as Brazilian Traction, Light and Power Company Limited, headed by William Mackenzie as chairman and Fred Stark Pearson as president. One of the directors appointed to its first board was Van Horne, who undoubtedly took satisfaction in the knowledge that Brazil's largest utility company was making a substantial contribution to the economic development of southeastern Brazil's industrial heartland. At the time of his death Van Horne was still a director, receiving $500 a quarter for his services.

Closer to home, Van Horne became actively involved in the fortunes of the Robin Hood Powder Company, located in Swanton, Vermont. The company was founded in 1900, after F.W. Heubach, a one-time CPR employee, and E. Dickson journeyed to Montreal to consult with Van Horne about the manufacture of shot-shells. Van Horne told his visitors that he knew nothing about the business, but suggested that they scout out a suitable location for manufacturing shells and establish a company for this purpose. He agreed to invest in the proposed company and at a subsequent meeting he also agreed to prevail upon his Montreal friends to invest in the enterprise.[1029] True to form, he resorted to a practice that served finance capitalism so well: he placed the money among a posse of his friends, in this case Thomas Shaughnessy, R.B. Angus, Lord Mount Stephen, and Charles Hosmer. In addition to becoming shareholders, Lord Mount Stephen and Hosmer also became directors, while Van Horne agreed to take on the presidency. Unfortunately, neither its star-studded board nor Van Horne's direction resulted in the company becoming profitable during his lifetime.

Launching new companies in an era of an unregulated and unscrupulous financial system and scraping together funds to keep some of them going would have been enough to tax the energies of most men Van Horne's age. It wasn't enough for Van Horne, however. In the late 1890s he decided to expand his role as a hobby farmer. Preoccupied with the fortunes of his beloved CPR, he started a stock farm at East Selkirk, Manitoba, gateway to the Prairies. He began assembling land for the operation in 1898 while he was still president of the company. The farm, suitably sited and designed, was intended to draw attention to the district's potential and thereby attract settlers, who were, of course, grist for the CPR mill. Van Horne alluded to this when he wrote to a municipal official to protest the building of a proposed road. "I am obliged to say," reported Van Horne, "that the road you propose would very largely defeat the object I had in view in starting the farm in East Selkirk, which was to draw attention to that district by making the land for as long a distance as practicable on both sides of the railway as attractive to people reaching the Red River Valley by the C.P.R., and I have laid out everything for a distance of over four miles with this object in view."[1030]

Since the farm was to be a showplace, Van Horne arranged for the "cultivation and ornamentation" of the CPR's right-of-way that stretched the over four-mile length of the property. He also hired Edward Maxwell to draw up plans and specifications for the farmhouse, horse barn, cattle sheds, and root house, for it was important that the buildings have a certain cachet. As the farm's first manager Van Horne chose Fred W. Barber, who was advised on the selection of staff by the owner of a Winnipeg farm equipment firm, Joseph Maw. Urged Maw in June 1899:

> Referring to the help, I would strongly recommend that you secure the greater portion of your help in the East, particularly the women, as it is very hard to get girls in this country to work. If you can get good men that you know I would advise you to secure them also. It might be advisable to pick up one good western man who is acquainted with the country, and the way to start in, but secure the greater portion of you help in the East.[1031]

An inventory compiled in 1912 records $41,967.50 worth of purebred shorthorns, Clydesdales, Yorkshires, Dutch-Belted cattle, and sheep. Nevertheless, despite Van Horne's efforts and those of various managers the enterprise never measured up to expectations. James Yule, who managed the farm from 1903 to 1912, hinted at this in a letter to his boss in which he reported, "As to me being tempted with money, it is not the case, for it is nearly two years since Mr. Emmert made me the offer of $2,500, but I have always thought it best to stay with you for less money, thinking that things would advance here. But I have never made this farm go as I would like to, and feel that I never can."[1032]

It appears that prospects never did improve for the Selkirk farm. Still, its steady drain on his purse did not diminish the enjoyment that Van Horne derived from a new pastime that the farm opened up for him. He was introduced to stockbreeding by his Scottish manager, Yule, who had developed a penchant for snapping up prizes at agricultural fairs. Determined that he would also become a champion exhibitor, Van Horne set out with his usual determination to obtain the best stock and beat rival contenders in the game. With this in mind, he sent Yule on frequent trips to England and Scotland to purchase top animals from the choicest herds. The end result was a prize herd of shorthorns that took blue ribbons at shows in Winnipeg, Chicago, and elsewhere.

The stock farm's drain on the purse was imitated by another venture of Van Horne's, a giant undertaking to harvest and can the sardines of Passamaquoddy Bay. Van Horne had been much impressed by the bay's rich store of fish, and in 1911, less than two months after the reciprocity election, he announced the formation of the Canadian Sardine Company, with plans to build a huge cannery and a model residential village at Ross's Point at Chamcook, just outside of St. Andrews.[1033] Van Horne and the company's backers, the usual consortium of current and retired CPR magnates, were convinced that such a cannery would fill a real need because the American ports of Lubec and Eastport were then handling most of the Canadian herring catch, and Connors Brothers of Black's Harbour was only a tiny operation.

To obtain skilled workers who were knowledgeable about the fishery, the consortium advertised in Norway, touting the wonderful opportunities to be found in the coastal Canadian fishery. The campaign bore fruit in August 1912. Eager for adventure and lured by the promise of liberal pay and fine housing, twenty-eight young men and one hundred young women sailed on the *Empress of Ireland* for Quebec, where, equipped with complimentary CPR passes, they boarded a train for St. Andrews.

Unfortunately, the news that greeted them at St. Andrews heralded the first of many setbacks associated with the enterprise. Upon their arrival the young adventurers learned that their promised accommodation was still under construction and that the new cannery had still to begin operations. As a result, the girls had to be billeted in an old clam factory located on the steamer wharf in St. Andrews.

Plans called for the Norwegians and their French-Canadian counterparts (the company drew upon both Norway and French Canada for the desired class of employees) to pack sardines during the fishing season and, in the winter months, kippered herring, fish balls, clams, baked beans, and brown bread. This would be accomplished, boasted the newly appointed managing director, Francis McColl, with "the latest labor-saving devices for manufacturing the highest quality of goods at a low cost."[1034]

Unfortunately for Van Horne and his fellow investors, their rosy hopes for the enterprise were never realized. A host of factors combined to doom it from the start, one being McColl's lack of management experience. Hitherto he had only managed a sardine-packing plant, not a large cannery and residential village under construction. The cost of the buildings and machinery was grossly underestimated, prompting Van Horne, in late 1912, to order a sharp reduction in expenses. "The necessity is upon us of stopping every possible item of expense instantly," he wrote the managing director that November.[1035] In response to his memorandum, McColl slashed furiously, but it was not enough to save the day. In late July 1913, Van Horne's private secretary, who was also the company's secretary treasurer, W.F. Lynch, issued a circular letter in which he reported, "We have got beyond the limit of our bank advances, and against these advances the bank holds our entire issue of bonds — $300,000 — together with our oils & other manufacturing materials as collateral."[1036] After conferring that summer with the company's bankers, management shut down operations, which, due to a scarcity of fish, did not resume.

Matters came to a head when creditors rejected a proposal to reorganize and refinance the company in February 1914. Two months later, in April, a notice of foreclosure was served by trustees representing the bondholders and a receiver was appointed by the Court of New Brunswick. Van Horne still hoped that new capital could be found to restart the business, but the outbreak of the First World War in the summer of 1914 destroyed any remaining chance for the company's resurrection. Aside from the amount that he had originally subscribed in stock, he lost about $100,000 in the venture.

Van Horne admittedly lost money in some of the projects in which he was involved, notably the Guatemala Railway, his East Selkirk ranch, and the Canadian Sardine Company. In launching the last two ventures, he demonstrated that although he was an enterprising entrepreneur, he all too often lacked the time or skills to carry out these schemes effectively. Still, he was among those fortunate individuals who reaped large dividends from the Laurier boom. Max Aitken, the financial wunderkind from rural New Brunswick, was another. Like Van Horne, who lent him a helping hand, Aitken had a passion for making money. Born in 1879 in Maple, Ontario, Aitken was raised in a Presbyterian manse in Newcastle, New Brunswick. He started on his road to millions by working as a bond salesman in the Maritimes, specializing in the bonds of Canadian-based utilities and growing industries. Within five years of joining the Royal Securities Corporation as a manager in 1902, he was a millionaire. He then moved to Montreal, where he concentrated on promoting new companies and merging established ones.[1037] While adjusting to life in the big city, "the little man with the big head" was helped by some of Montreal's most powerful citizens, people like Sir Edward Clouston, Herbert Holt (president of the Bank of Montreal), and, of course, Van Horne. All of them respected the young man's financial acumen and used their influence to open doors for him.[1038] Van Horne would certainly have been only too happy to use his influence in this way, as he admired anybody imbued with a strong will to succeed, particularly a colleague who had had to overcome adversity from an early age.·

Van Horne was certainly a businessman with vision. His association with the Laurentide Pulp and Paper Company and his establishment of the ill-fated sardine cannery and the East Selkirk ranch testify to that. On the other hand, it is obvious that this multimillionaire lacked the business instincts necessary to accumulate a huge fortune. Even if he had possessed the acumen and the necessary skills, however, his restlessness and wide diversity of interests would have prevented him from focusing his attention on a handful of promising undertakings and fully exploiting the opportunities that they presented. When all is said and done, though, the railway magnate was highly respected by his peers and much sought-after as a company director. Perhaps this is why, in early 2000, a blue-ribbon panel of judges assembled by the Canadian Business Hall of Fame voted him the most outstanding business leader of the twentieth century. One could question this choice, but there is no denying that the railway genius erected a far-ranging financial edifice. The Montreal *Star* was right on the mark when, in 1911, it described him as one of Canada's most influential financiers and promoters.

Chapter Sixteen
Dodging the Grim Reaper

In the spring of 1906, Van Horne took Scottish peer and CPR share-holder Lord Elphinstone and Bennie to dinner at Henri's, a celebrated Parisian restaurant frequented by King Edward VII, who would dine there incognito, with Lord Elphinstone in attendance. When the Van Horne party arrived, the head waiter rushed forward to receive them, and the orchestra, to Van Horne's great embarrassment, struck up "God Save the King." Such was the price that the railway magnate occasionally paid for resembling, at this period in his life, the portly British monarch.

Although neither a crowned monarch nor a member of the British or European landed aristocracies, Van Horne, in 1906, was nevertheless a leading member of Canada's financial aristocracy and one of this country's most influential men. Such a lofty position resulted in his frequently being invited to accept honours. Because of his strange shyness in formal social situations and his dislike of public speaking, he just as frequently turned down these invitations. However, when it came to a less conspicuous form of recognition, such as serving on a committee charged with arrangements for a royal tour, Van Horne, despite his visceral dislike of pomp and cere-mony, was not loath to become involved.

One such tour took place in the early autumn of 1901, when the Duke and Duchess of Cornwall (the future King George V and Queen Mary) arrived in Canada. As a member of the general reception commit-tee that helped to make arrangements for the royal couple's visit to Montreal, Van Horne had a role to play in the two days of ceremonies and festivities that unfolded in that city. Since the "new imperialism," with its stress on the superiority of the Anglo-Saxon race and Great Britain's civi-lizing mission in the world, was then in full swing, no effort was spared to cement still further Montrealers' ties to Great Britain and the Empire.

The formalities got underway as soon as the royal train backed into Place Viger station at precisely 3:00 p.m. on Wednesday, September 18. After alighting from their private car, Their Royal Highnesses were greeted by Lord Minto, the Governor General, who then presented Mayor Préfontaine, Madame Préfontaine, Senator George A. Drummond, head of the reception committee, Mrs. Drummond, and the Roman Catholic archbishop of Montreal, Archbishop Bruchesi. Van Horne, accompanied by Addie, joined other dignitaries awaiting the royal couple's arrival in the station.

After the initial presentations, the royal party proceeded through the station to banner- and flag-bedecked Viger Square, where approximately twenty thousand Montrealers had assembled. Many had been waiting under sombre skies since early morning to catch a glimpse of Their Royal Highnesses, and when the royal party crossed the street from the station to a raised platform the crowd broke into loud cheers, or, in the words of a *Gazette* reporter, "unmistakable outbursts of loyalty and enthusiasm." Following several addresses, the duke's acknowledgment, and the presentation of South African medals to nine officers and 131 non-commissioned officers and men, the royal procession formed. Accompanied by the Royal Scots regiment, complete with pipe band, it made its way along an elaborately decorated route to Lord Strathcona's Dorchester Street residence, which would be Their Royal Highnesses' home during their Montreal stay. That evening, Van Horne, Addie, and Mary attended a dinner for the royal couple hosted by Lord Strathcona. It was held in the garden, where a temporary structure had been erected to accommodate up to two thousand people. On this occasion it accommodated ninety or so dignitaries, including His Excellency the Governor General and Lady Minto, Sir Wilfrid and Lady Laurier, and the Anglican and Roman Catholic archbishops of Montreal.[1039]

The following morning, Van Horne affixed assorted medals to his chest, put on his coat, and then strode over to McGill University's Victoria College, where the McGill convocation was to take place. En route, he met Captain Arthur Cecil Bell, aide-de-camp to Major-General Hutton, general commanding officer of the militia. Van Horne asked Bell whether he should wear his ribbons and star, and on learning that the duke would be wearing none, he removed his. The aide-de-camp "offered to help him undo the hook behind his neck, but Van Horne was too impatient, and simply tore the whole thing off."[1040]

That evening, Van Horne and Addie attended another dinner for the royal couple hosted by Lord and Lady Strathcona, but this one was a much less ambitious affair as its guest list included, in addition to the Van Hornes,

only Sir William Macdonald, the wealthy tobacco manufacturer and phi-
lanthropist, and Lord Mount Stephen's sisters, Mrs. Meighen and Mrs.
Cantlie. Lord Strathcona had planned a large function, but this was abruptly cancelled because of the obsequies following the assassination of American
President William McKinley, who had been shot on September 6 while visiting the Pan-American Fair in Buffalo and had died eight days later.[1041]

When the Montreal segment of the royal tour ended on Friday morning, Van Horne rose early and went to Windsor Station to see the duke
and duchess board a special train to Ottawa. Although he must have
chafed at the large dose of formality that he had been subjected to in
recent days, he must have taken pleasure — and pride — in the royal train
that stood in the station. It featured seven special cars that the CPR had
built for the transcontinental royal journey. Two, the royal coaches, boasted not only crests on the exterior but also elaborate interiors complete with
telephones and electric lights.

Four years later, Van Horne again had a hand in arrangements for a
royal visit. Prince Louis of Battenberg, grandfather of Prince Philip, Duke
of Edinburgh and an officer in the Royal Navy, visited Montreal in the
autumn of 1905. From there, he left on October 27 for a visit to
Fredericton and then St. Andrews. A flurry of telegrams and letters regarding the use of Van Horne's private car for part of the Maritimes visit preceded the event. "It is intended to drive Prince Louis of Battenberg and
suit through town on Saturday. If so, the citizens would like to show their
respects for him and you by a display of bunting," telegraphed J.S. Magee,
correspondent of the *Saint John Daily Sun* on October 26, 1905.[1042] Three
days later, Prince Louis himself wrote Van Horne, "Thanks to your kindness, the railway journey which has just come to an end has been one of
the pleasantest in my experience, and I hasten to tell you how glad I am at
having met you and seen your charming island."[1043]

Although he was now in his sixties, Van Horne found himself even busier
than he had been as CPR president. At the Olympian heights of his career,
he was committed to a daunting number of undertakings. These involved
his participation, whether active or peripheral, in a staggering number of
business enterprises; his supervision of the Cuba Company and the construction of the Cuba Railroad, which entailed two or more visits to Cuba
each year and hurried trips to New York; the administration of his estates
in New Brunswick, Manitoba, and Cuba; and his participation in various
schemes of municipal and national advancement. There were times, even

for Van Horne, when the demands made by these various commitments seemed overwhelming, especially when his health left a lot to be desired. In a letter to Beckles Willson, he hinted at his mounting frustration when faced by so many responsibilities: "I wonder if you know what it is like to have, from one years end to another, not one minute of time without something pressing to be done — not a minute of free time from the demands of business."[1044]

One of the highly touted federal schemes in which Van Horne became involved was a project promoted by Canadian farmers and politicians. Van Horne dismissed as impractical the idea of building a railway to Hudson's Bay, but, to the surprise of many who thought it might compete with the Canadian Pacific, he took up the long-simmering cause of the Georgian Bay Canal. This scheme traced its distant beginnings to 1819, when Royal Engineers, prompted by military considerations, drew up a plan that would see boats move up the Ottawa River and cut across what is now Algonquin Park, using lakes, rivers, and new canals to reach the Great Lakes and further west. Their plan came to naught, but it was revisited in the 1860s when senior military officers took an exploratory trip along the Mattawa River, Lake Nipissing, and French River route. The well-known Canadian engineer Walter Shanly completed a survey of the route in 1863, but for various reasons it was not acted upon. Not until 1884 did the scheme show real promise. In that year, Member of Parliament Joseph Kavanagh Steward succeeded in having Parliament incorporate the Montreal, Ottawa, and Georgian Bay Canal Company. By the terms of incorporation, the company was empowered to construct a shipping canal from Montreal to Georgian Bay via the Ottawa and Mattawa rivers, Lake Nipissing, and the French River, using a system of dams, locks, and dredging. As envisaged, the canal would permit most ocean-going vessels to use a route 282 miles shorter and nearly three days faster than the Welland Canal route between Montreal and Port Arthur. In 1898, the Senate investigated and commended the scheme, and in 1904, Laurier publicly committed the government to providing funding for it. Four years later the prime minister repeated the government's intention to proceed when resources permitted.[1045]

Van Horne initially embraced the scheme warmly and did whatever he could to make it a reality. When Robert Perks, an English shipbuilder, arrived in this country to explore the feasibility of constructing the canal, Van Horne eagerly assisted him in whatever way he could. In July 1907, he even arranged for an interview with Laurier on the subject, astutely selecting Senator George Cox, a Laurier-appointed senator, to accompany him as a fellow lobbyist.[1046]

When he studied the scheme more closely, however, Van Horne began to doubt the feasibility of constructing a canal twenty-eight feet or more in depth and of adapting facilities at lake ports. Still, he did not believe that the project should be scrapped altogether. In a lengthy memorandum to Laurier, Van Horne suggested that a barge canal twelve to fourteen feet in depth be built but in such a way that it could be easily converted to a deeper canal when traffic warranted.[1047] Notwithstanding its endorsement by such high-profile Canadians as Laurier, Robert Borden, and initially Van Horne, the canal scheme never saw the light of day. In fact, in 1917, it was voted down by the special Commons Committee on Railways, Canals and Telegraph Lines.

Notwithstanding the enthusiasm with which he embraced and investigated new schemes, there is no denying the fact that age was catching up with Van Horne and that he was keenly aware of its relentless progress. His awareness manifested itself in various ways, not the least of which was his relinquishment of numerous company directorships in the wake of the Equitable Life Assurance Society fiasco. He began to sever his ties from one company after another until by the spring of 1910 he had withdrawn from about thirty boards. Only in one severance did he experience any pang of regret and that was when at age sixty-seven he resigned from the chairmanship of his beloved Canadian Pacific Railway. "I am getting old and it is irksome to watch the clock and it may become depressing and therefore I do not wish to keep up even the appearance of attending to business. Consequently I am getting out of everything that may make the least demand upon my time or freedom," he informed the press when announcing his resignation from the CPR chairmanship on April 25, 1910.[1048]

When Van Horne had retired from the presidency, the company's stock sold for $110.00 a share. Ten years later, on his resignation from the chairmanship, it fetched $181.50 a share. An optimist by nature, he had always believed in the CPR's prosperity, even in the depths of the financial panic of 1893 to 1894, when the outlook for company's future had been far from rosy. Now, in 1910, it seemed that his unwavering faith in its prospects was more than justified. Two years later, he could rejoice in the glowing account of a transcontinental trip taken by a friend from his Chicago, Milwaukee and St. Paul days who waxed enthusiastically about the CPR's development since he had last travelled on the railway six years earlier. The progress made by the road in the intervening years "was simply marvellous," as was the transformation undergone by near and more distant farms. "It was such a comfort to me to find that while you were not in active service any longer that the spirit that I had witnessed years ago in

Courtesy of the National Archives of Canada.

Van Horne at Lardo City, Kootenay Lake, June 1903. He's the portly figure striding purposefully forward.

the Chicago, Milwaukee and St. Paul Railway, later on the C.P.R. was still in evidence on that Great Railway."[1049]

After his retirement from the CPR chairmanship, friends expected that Van Horne would devote more time to public service. The Laurier government had pointed the way in 1903, when it offered him the chairmanship of the National Transportation Commission. The temptation to accept was great. "The only public position I could think of accepting is the chairmanship of the Transportation Commission in the work of which I feel a very deep interest," Van Horne wrote the prime minister.[1050] Nevertheless, he declined this invitation, as he would do others, claiming that prior commitments would absorb his attention "for the next eight months at least." Still, he did take on some additional responsibilities. At the request of Sir Lomer Gouin, Quebec's premier, he agreed to become a member of Montreal's Metropolitan Parks' Commission, established when a wave of enthusiasm for city planning, garden suburbs, and parks was sweeping across Canada. The impetus for this movement, which came to be called the City Beautiful Movement, came from the United States, where it originated with the park movement associated with Frederick Law Olmsted's work. When the celebrated landscape architect and Calvert Vaux had created New York's Central Park they established a precedent that other cities were eager to follow. One of these cities was Montreal, which, in the 1870s, commissioned Olmstead to design a large park to cover a magnificent site atop Mount Royal.

It was not until after the World's Columbian Exposition (more commonly known as the Chicago World's Fair) in 1893, however, that the City Beautiful Movement really gained momentum. The pragmatic and aesthetic lessons that the fair touted had an enormous impact on both American and Canadian urban planning.[1051] In Quebec, the Province of Quebec Association of Architects' preoccupation with Montreal's appearance led in 1906 to the creation of a group, the Municipal Improvement Committee, which not only discussed city beautification but also oversaw the production of some ambitious urban plans for the fast-growing metropolis. With the support of a revitalized reform movement led by citizens' committees, in 1909 the PQAA presented its urban schemes to the first meeting of the City Improvement League of Montreal. The following year, the provincial government, acting partly on the demands of well-to-do citizens' groups battling an inept city administration, established the Metropolitan Parks' Commission. Composed of political leaders and businessmen, it was charged with recommending plans and measures for creating new recreational areas, thoroughfares, residential neighbourhoods for the working class, and public facilities such as baths.[1052]

Van Horne was an ideal choice for the commission given his long-standing interest in the beautification of towns and cities and his passion for designing structures, be they railway stations, hotels, or buildings on his private estates. Because he harboured a deep distrust of political bodies and believed that municipal development should be treated like a business, he welcomed the new commission and the opportunity to serve on it. He saw it as a means whereby he could participate actively in the beautification of his adopted city and at the same time indulge in one of his favourite pursuits, working on plans for structures and gardens.

Van Horne spelled out his views in July 1910 to W.D. Lighthall, the well-known lawyer, author, and Westmount mayor who had spearheaded the erection of a monument to the memory of Montreal's founder, Paul de Chomedy Maissoneuve. To Lighthall, Van Horne confessed his "almost entire ignorance" about the commission's status.[1053] He was certainly not unmindful, however, of the city's appalling slum conditions, conditions that provoked visiting British Member of Parliament Henry Vivian to predict, "Unless preparations are constantly made for caring for your population, Montreal will become one of the greatest cesspools of human depravity in the world."[1054] With the city's working-class neighbourhoods uppermost in mind, Van Horne told Lighthall that he agreed that the first priority of the commission should be to work toward "the improvement of conditions in the districts occupied by the poorer classes, which are as a rule the breeding places of diseases which often threaten the whole community ..."[1055] As he saw it, the commission's first plans should be "quite modest in their scope although forming part of a comprehensive plan to be carried out year by year." He also believed strongly that the commission's influence would depend largely on its making effective use of a comparatively small amount of money. If they approached their mandate in this fashion, declared Van Horne, the public would have confidence in its "good sense, its conservatism and its character."[1056]

Regrettably, the commission's work was hobbled by a perpetual lack of municipal funding and by the failure of the Quebec government to make any appropriation for its expenses. To add to the commission's difficulties, the recession of 1913 intervened. As a result, the body in which Van Horne had invested so much hope was unable to discharge its ambitious mandate. For four years it tried desperately to obtain funds, but it failed to obtain any financial assistance whatsoever, "not even," as Van Horne expressed, it, "a postage stamp." Disheartened, his goodwill utterly exhausted, he eventually suggested, in April 1914, that the commission should use personal contributions from its members to defray any expenses it had incurred and then dissolve.[1057] The whole experience was certainly a disillusioning one, made even more so by the recent collapse of his sardine fishery enterprise. Fortunately, the other public causes with which he was associated did not entail frustration of this order. These included the Royal Victoria Hospital, which he served as a governor, the Protestant House of Industry, McGill University, on whose board of governors he sat, and the St. John Ambulance Association, which he served as vice-president.[1058]

Outside the public sphere, Van Horne was able to put his philanthropic impulses, such as they were, to effective use in assisting Maud Edgar to realize her dream of establishing a private girls' school in Montreal. Maud had taught at Havergal Ladies' College, a leading private girls' school in Toronto, where private schools were the preferred choice of Anglo-Protestant elite families who sought an upper-class education in the British tradition for their daughters. At Havergal, she had found a soulmate in English-born Mary Cramp, who shared her ideals and advanced views about teaching, namely that the literature, history, and art of a period and a country should be taught together, that each pupil should progress at her own rate in each subject, and that students should be encouraged to matriculate at McGill.

The two friends began to dream of establishing a private girls' school grounded in their teaching philosophy, and in pursuit of this dream they started searching for a suitable building, which they finally found at 507

Guy Street on the western edge of Montreal's Square Mile. Located in a spacious garden, the building was a huge family residence that belonged to the Carsley family, a name long associated with a leading Montreal dry goods establishment.

The edifice was available and soon negotiations were underway with Samuel Carsley, son of its builder, Cecil Carsley. Was it for sale or for rent? Maud Edgar and Mary Cramp did not lack enterprise, but they did lack financial resources. Furthermore, they were not too knowledgeable about the complexities of leases, titles, risk capital, and the uncertainties of tenure. Van Horne was, however, and he soon came to their rescue.[1059] He did so with his customary zeal because both he and young Addie had become personal friends of Maud, the Edgar and Van Horne families having lavished hospitality on each other at their respective homes in Toronto and St. Andrews. Besides, Maud Edgar's plight offered Van Horne, the father-like figure, the ideal opportunity to play a role in which he revelled, that of mentor or advisor.

Van Horne was determined to do all that he could to provide his young friend with some peace of mind and security when she embarked on her new venture. Accordingly, he purchased the Carsley property for $67,000 in the summer of 1909 and assumed a lease that Maud had taken out with Samuel Carsley. Writing to Cecil Carsley in August of that year, Maud Edgar's new landlord reported, "As to the homologation. I have felt all along that the price of the entire property was an extreme one and that it discounted the future a considerable number of years, and I should not have thought of paying such a price but for my desire to remove Miss Edgar's fear of being turned out in the course of a year or so."[1060]

Disaster struck in late January 1913, when a fire raced through the school, allowing boarders and its two founders only time to escape with "little on but their night clothes." In the early hours of the morning, Maud Edgar and Mary Cramp made their way to the Van Horne mansion, where Addie, young Addie, and a servant hastened to provide them with warm milk, overnight accommodation, and clothes.[1061] Van Horne was in Cuba, but when notified of the conflagration he immediately contacted insurance adjustors and his favourite architect, Edward Maxwell, whom he wanted to direct the necessary repairs. Next he instructed Bennie to look after the Carsley house in his absence, keeping in mind that Van Horne was "anxious to help Miss Edgar in any possible way without throwing away money."[1062] As the notation for a $500 cheque to "Miss Edgar" in a daily journal indicates, however, Van Horne continued to assist the schoolteacher as late as January 1914.[1063]

Maud Edgar was undoubtedly very grateful to Van Horne for all his assistance, as were other friends to whom he extended timely financial and other help. The Quebec author and enthusiastic sportsman George Moore Fairchild was one of these appreciative friends. Fairchild, who was no slouch himself when it came to being a generous host, entertaining droves of visiting writers and artists in his Cap Rouge home, wrote Van Horne in April 1900, "I have received so many kindnesses at your hands and have made so little return that I am somewhat bewildered at the extent of my obligation."[1064] When it came to assisting personal friends experiencing financial and other hardship Van Horne could, indeed, be generous.

Van Horne could be less generous in his treatment of personal employees. A young secretary of his, Richard Harlan, after working for Van Horne for three months, was reduced to writing a "begging letter" to his employer. In requesting a "substantial increase" in wages, he noted that he and his wife had used up their slender stock of savings and now found it impossible "to come anywhere near to making both ends meet" on his small salary.[1065]

Van Horne was downright stingy when it came to making charitable contributions to schools, colleges, hospitals, welfare organizations, and other institutions that served the community. Nothing illustrates this better than his will, presumably a sound indicator of his pattern of charitable donations. Drawn up in January 1915, it makes no provision for bequests to friends, family retainers, non-profit organizations, or charities. By contrast, the will of his wealthy CPR colleague Lord Strathcona lists an eye-popping number of generous bequests to colleges, college chairs and professorships, and hospitals in Canada, the United States, and the United Kingdom. During his lifetime Van Horne did make one or two noteworthy donations to public institutions, but this does not detract from the fact that he hated to part with money that could be used to purchase another painting or Japanese vase.

It is hard to reconcile this meanness with his lavish hospitality and his warm nature, but, as his biographer Walter Vaughan has recalled, Van Horne's finer instincts did occasionally rebel. From time to time he would confide to a friend that he intended to do this or that when "my ships come home," but invariably when the ships did dock he had pledged their profits to some new venture or used the money to reduce a bank overdraft or buy a work of art that he coveted. Sometimes he actually succeeded in raising expectations with his good intentions, but just as quickly he sought to dispel them. One night, when travelling in his private car, he talked animatedly about helping to finance the cost of an addition to a public institution. The next morning, however, when parting from his companion, he exclaimed, "I say, Doctor, I must have been very drunk last night."[1066]

In the final decade or so of his life Van Horne continued to shuttle constantly back and forth between Montreal and New York and Montreal and Havana. Interspersed with these sorties were transatlantic voyages in luxuriously appointed ships, undertaken more frequently now that he was retired from the CPR presidency. When Van Horne made the crossing to England he had primarily business, the renewal of old friendships, and art viewing in mind. Often he would also purchase made-to-measure clothes from the London haberdasher Pooles, but perhaps not with the same degree of enthusiasm as he had in the summer of 1891 when he ran up an order for several suits and shirts as well as forty-eight neckties.[1067]

Sometimes trips to England had other objectives. A visit in March 1906 was dictated partly by a desire to acquire a new Shorthorn bull and sows for the East Selkirk operation. There's no escaping the smug self-satisfaction in Van Horne's letter to Addie, in which he reported that Yule, his East Selkirk farm manager, "had found nothing better in Scotland than I have." In the hope of adding to his finds, Van Horne planned to travel to Windsor to see the King's Shorthorn herd and, if possible, to Wiltshire to look over another herd. Meanwhile, he was kept well occupied in Scotland with a visit to the Fairfield shipyard to inspect two eighteen-knot liners, the *Empress of Britain* and *Empress of Ireland* (the first liners to be ordered by the CPR for its Atlantic service), and a trip by train to Kirkcudbright to inspect Clydesdales and purchase a first-rate horse for East Selkirk.[1068]

Van Horne sometimes took Bennie with him on these overseas junkets, and on one occasion, the spring of 1909, he arranged for Addie and young Addie to accompany him on the *Empress of Britain* to England. From London they made their way to Paris and Amsterdam, Van Horne scooping up several new works of art for his collection. On their return from the Continent to England, the party spent Whitsuntide with Mary Humphry Ward at her rural home near Tring in Hertfordshire, just outside of London. Van Horne would have been enthralled by the incomparable beauty of the springtime countryside, but one wonders if he was equally impressed by Mrs. Ward's views on women's suffrage. Only the year before the popular novelist had agreed to head the Anti-Suffrage League, and at the time of the Van Hornes' visit she was campaigning furiously to prevent women from being granted the vote. Thomas Arnold's eldest daughter believed in the need to help the less fortunate in society, but at the same time she was adamantly opposed to women's suffrage. In her view the "vast growth of the Empire, the immense increase of

England's imperial responsibilities... and the increased complexity" of the issues faced by her statesmen created problems that could only by resolved by "the labour and special knowledge of men whose burden should be left unhampered by the political inexperience of women."[1069]

Not surprisingly, death took its toll among his siblings and friends as Van Horne strode toward his senior years. His old friend Otto Meysenburg, the Chicago businessman, died in early 1901 at his retirement home in Alma, California. On learning of the death, Bennie hastened to offer condolences from Cuba, where he was then working on the Cuba Railroad. "I was awfully sorry to hear of Mr. Meysenburg's death which must be a great loss to you," wrote the young engineer in an effort to console his grieving father.[1070] Over a decade later, Van Horne would bemoan the "unnecessary & inexcusable loss" of six friends.[1071] They perished when the seemingly unsinkable *Titanic* struck an iceberg on April 14, 1912, and sank in the North Atlantic, 590 kilometres southeast of Newfoundland. Among those who lost his life on the ship's maiden voyage was railway magnate Charles Hays, president of the Grand Trunk Railway.

After the Titanic's plunge to the ocean floor, Van Horne mused that the occasional disaster might be the price man paid when he employed speed and technology in travel. The saving of time more than compensated for "the shortened lives resulting now & then from speed," and he, for one, would continue to employ the fasted mode of transportation available.[1072]

Memorable for quite different reasons was the holiday that Van Horne took in the summer of 1912. In the first week of July, he, Addie, and young Addie returned to Joliet to participate in a homecoming festival timed to coincide with July 4 festivities. It had been forty-eight years since he had left the town where he had spent a good part of his youth and where his last job had been that of ticket agent and telegraph operator for the Chicago and Alton Railroad. Now, as "the man who had done more for Canada than any other man in the world," he was the centre of attraction at a public meeting held in the town's library, where he regaled his audience with boyhood recollections of his first visit to Joliet and lauded a book about Joliet written by a Universalist minister.[1073]

What most impressed those who had known him half a century earlier was Van Horne's lack of pretension. He was still the same Will Van Horne that they recalled from earlier days, a man of rough-and-ready comradeship. Before he returned to Joliet, however, speculation had been rife about how to address him. Should he be addressed as "Sir Van Horne" or plain "Mr. Van Horne"? For a Solomon Williams, the problem was quickly resolved when he met his old friend in front of the First National

Bank. "Why, hello, Bill," he cried, and Van Horne replied, "Well, well, if it isn't Sol" and hustled him into a car where they proceeded to reminisce about old times.[1074]

During his Joliet visit, Van Horne consorted with surviving members of the Agassiz Club and swapped stories with elderly engineers and trainmen who had known him when he worked in the "Cut Off" office. In the evenings, he presided on the veranda of a relative's home, enthralling admiring friends with lessons learned from his remarkable life and describing some of his unfulfilled and far-fetched dreams. Conspicuous among these was his vision of a fleet of triple-hulled steamers that would carry people back and forth across the Atlantic. Built in the Bay of Fundy by the CPR and operated by that company, they would boast cafés and theatres and be capable of carrying up to thirty thousand people each on a single voyage.[1075]

The Joliet reunion was so exhilarating that Van Horne returned to Montreal feeling decidedly rejuvenated. It was with renewed vigour that he turned his attention to the construction of his Cuban home, San Zenon de Buenos Aires. When completed, it would be the lair to which he could retreat during Montreal's long, harsh winters, a lair made all the more desirable because of its location on the outskirts of Camaguey. The previous summer he had drawn up plans for the property, all the while nursing fond memories of Camaguey with its warm sunshine, old colonial charm, and membership in the prestigious Cosmopolitan Club. Now, in the summer of 1912, he occupied himself with the myriad details relating to the actual building of the house itself.

From Covenhoven, as he had so many previous summers, Van Horne dealt with a wealth of details regarding his assorted far-flung enterprises. In Montreal, meanwhile, Harlan struggled manfully with a small Spanish dictionary to decipher letters and cablegrams arriving from Cuba. Those requiring Van Horne's attention were then forwarded to his boss at St. Andrews. That summer, communications, some in code, poured in from the Cuba Company. But there were also communications from a wide variety of other sources, including a letter from freewheeling Jimmy Dunn, relating to a shale enterprise in New Brunswick, and a photograph of an old painting that had just been received by Stephan Bourgeois.

Van Horne also continued to take a lively interest in the fate of the CPR, to which he was still fiercely attached. Any perceived threat to it immediately roused him to action, as did any implied threat to Canadian manufacturers or Canada's ties with Great Britain. So it is not surprising that when reciprocity resurfaced as an issue in 1911, Van Horne marshalled all his forces to fight it.

At the beginning of 1911, the Laurier government appeared to be as strong as any government could hope to be after being in power for four-teen consecutive years. The Liberals had won four general elections in a row, and Laurier himself was regarded as a national institution. Yet before 1911 was over the silver-tongued orator would lose a bitterly contested election because of fears generated by two major decisions that he made. One involved his naval policy, the other reciprocity in trade between the United States and Canada.

Of the two issues, it was reciprocity that grabbed Van Horne's atten-tion and spurred him to shove aside his distaste for public speaking and re-enter the political arena. The issue traced its immediate origins to 1907, when Ottawa had granted a newly established intermediate tariff to France in return for reciprocal concessions. No sooner was the French treaty con-cluded than Americans began hurling charges of commercial discrimina-tion against Canada. With the threat of American tariff reprisals looming large, representatives of the American and Canadian governments met in 1910 to arrange a face-saving compromise and to pave the way for more ambitious negotiations. William Howard Taft, the newly elected American president, suggested a general trade treaty. Laurier and his minister of finance, William Fielding, eagerly embraced the idea, believing that reci-procity would gain support from agrarian interests, whose resentment of Canada's protected manufacturers knew no bounds. The result was a for-mal agreement, the so-called "Reciprocity Treaty" of January 1911, which eliminated duties on a wide range of natural products and lowered them on a selected list of fully manufactured and semi-finished articles. Plans called for the treaty to be implemented by concurrent legislation in the two countries, but ultimately only the United States, in a special session of Congress, provided the necessary approval.

In Canada, the treaty's first public exposure came on January 26, 1911, when an enthusiastic Fielding presented it to Parliament. Most Liberals were surprised and elated. Ottawa, after all, had been begging for reciprocity of decades, only to see each plea insolently rejected by Washington. Now, Washington had not only come to Ottawa on bended knee but had successfully pushed for a broad agreement on freer trade between the two countries. As for the Conservatives, led by lawyer Robert Borden, they were dumbfounded. Even more important, they feared that the treaty's proposals would prove so attractive that the Laurier govern-ment would be returned to office at the next election.[1076] Presented with a golden opportunity, the Conservatives began to stir up opposition to the treaty's thinly veiled implications for the imperial connection, predicting that increasing orientation toward the United States would mean a move away from Great Britain, if not the actual severance of Canada's ties with the mother country. Nobody employed these arguments more effectively than Canadian businessmen, who became the shrewdest lobbyists against the accord. Hitherto supporters of the Laurier government, they suddenly broke with it when they felt that their interests in national transportation, industrial, and commercial policy were being threatened. On February 20, eighteen Liberal Toronto businessmen and financiers issued an anti-reciprocity manifesto that claimed the agreement would weaken Canada's ties with the Great Britain and make it more difficult to avoid political union with the United States. In making this move, the Torontonians voiced sentiments identical to those expressed weeks earlier by the Montreal Board of Trade when it declared that it considered it the bounden duty of every Canadian "to resist to the last anything" that endangered Canada's ties with Great Britain.[1077]

The prospect of reciprocity both alarmed and depressed Van Horne. One of the National Policy's most ardent supporters, he considered high tariffs essential for the nurturing of Canada's infant industries. As he viewed it, the agreement would destroy Canada's fiscal independence with regard to tariffs. Not only that, it "would loosen the bonds which bind Canada to the Empire and ultimately destroy them" as well.[1078] He therefore jumped into the fray early, telling a reporter, "I am out to do all I can to bust the damn thing."[1079] In his determined effort, he went to work attempting to convert friends and acquaintances to an anti-reciprocity position. To Sir John Willison, former editor-in-chief of the *Globe*, he sent a photo of the Canadian Pacific fleet in 1910, believing that it provided a most telling argument against reciprocity. The fleet, Van Horne reported, had been practically completed between 1891 and 1910, during which period the Allan Line ships had increased in number and the tramp fleet plying to Canada had expanded enormously. "I have shown this picture to a good many people within the past few days who were inclined to favor reciprocity or who viewed the question with indifference, and it has worked an instant cure in every case," claimed Van Horne. To friends and acquaintances in London, he discoursed at length on the accursed accord. "I have been in very much of a whirl all the week," he reported to Addie while on a visit to Britain's capital in March 1911. "Wednesday I was at luncheon at lady Northcotes, meeting the Duke and Duchess of Connaught and Princess Patricia, Lord Salisbury, the Earl Stanhope, Lord and Lady Salton and Lord Hamilton. I was the only commoner. I had to explain the reciprocity question at length to his R.A. and afterwards the Duchess had lots of questions to ask about it and kept me nearly twenty minutes."[1080]

As a capitalist and the head of several Canadian enterprises, it was to be expected that Van Horne's interpretation of the treaty would fill him with consternation. Protecting his assorted commercial ventures was the least of his concerns, however. He perceived in the agreement Canada's trading away of its industrial achievements for a "few wormy plums." He denounced the treaty as a one-sided proposal. "Our trade," he declared, is "$97 per capita; that of the United States, $33. In other words, the water in our millpond stands at 97, theirs at 33; and they want us to take down the dam."[1081]

To prevent an opportunistic J.J. Hill from making further raids into the Northwest and to keep the dam standing, Van Horne resorted to what was an extreme measure for him: he took to the public platform. He did so reluctantly, because he loathed public speaking. Given his public persona, one would have expected him to be a competent public speaker, but Van Horne never succeeded in overcoming the agonies of stage fright he endured on the public platform. Although an excellent raconteur in the company of friends, he always spoke awkwardly in public, lacking what one admirer termed "fluidity of speech."[1082] Only his deep conviction that the treaty signalled disaster for his adopted country persuaded him to summon up the necessary courage to address meetings in Montreal, St. Andrews, and Saint John. When planted before audiences in these centres he would trot out the familiar anti-reciprocity arguments and then observe:

> Canada is now the most prosperous country on the face of the earth and is increasing in prosperity from day to day, and I say let well enough alone and don't monkey with the machine that has worked so well ...She has found herself and scorns the crumbs of her neighbours...Do you imagine for a minute or have you seen anything in the commercial policy of the United States towards Canada to indicate that they would press upon us such a bargain for our advantage? Not a bit of it. We shall lose money in trade, in manufactures, in independence, in self-respect and in the respect of others.[1083]

With politics polarizing around the old issues of free trade versus protectionism, north-south orientation versus the pull of the British Empire, and nationalism versus continentalism, splits in party ranks were inevitable.

Van Horne predicted as much when, in an interview he gave to a *Montreal Star* journalist, he declared that there was going to be a "flare-up" within the Liberal party. Prominent Liberals, he said, were going to secede openly, and if reported, Van Horne's predictions would take away some of the ammunition that the disaffected Liberals were going to use in their speeches.[1084] Van Horne was proven right when Clifford Sifton denounced reciprocity in the House of Commons and Lloyd Harris, a Liberal MP and Ontario manufacturer, crossed the floor.

In the face of defections from the Liberals' ranks and the willingness of recalcitrant Liberals to join him in fighting reciprocity, Robert Borden's stance changed. From being somewhat hesitant and confusing in his opposition to the reciprocity bill, Borden determined to filibuster it in the House of Commons. Debate in the House was only adjourned to allow Laurier to attend the Imperial Conference in London. It resumed in July after his return to Canada and ended on July 29, when the prime minister, who by now had had enough, asked for the dissolution of Parliament. In the general election of September 21, the Laurier government was defeated, winning only 87 seats to the Conservatives' 134.

From Nova Scotia, where he received the joyous news of his party's victory, Borden wrote Van Horne, acknowledging "the splendid aid" which he had given him "in this great battle."[1085] Certainly Van Horne's friend Joseph Gilder, a New York journalist who was then editing the *New York Times Review of Books*, considered Van Horne's contribution to Borden's victory invaluable. Van Horne's influence was so great, Gilder claimed, "that in some quarters it was credited with being the chief factor, at least one of the chief factors, in the defeat of reciprocity between the United States and the Dominion."[1086] Be that as it may, Van Horne was ecstatic when he learned of the election results, declaring that "Canada's first great trial is ended and she now stands out in brilliant sunshine without a cloud in the skies."[1087]

Van Horne was quick to offer the new prime minister advice on how he should run his government and which men he should appoint to certain powerful cabinet positions. Despite his warm regard for Laurier, Van Horne, like many other observers, deplored the corruption ("audacious plundering," in his words) reported to be widespread in the Laurier government. Van Horne fervently hoped that the new prime minister would have nothing to do with anyone who was the least bit tainted or under suspicion and that he would be the unmistakable leader. "A benevolent dictator is what we need — one who will not hesitate to kick friend or foe," wrote Van Horne.

> The Conservatives of Canada have been long enough out
> of power to have lost the office holding habit and there are
> very few "leftovers" to claim anything. You can therefore
> commence with new and sound materials and build an
> enduring structure and one that will stand as a model for
> future governments and you can establish a new standard
> of political [sic] which will make such rotteness as that of
> the first ten years impossible for decades to come.[1088]

To help create this enduring structure, Van Horne plugged for E.B. Osler, one of Toronto's shrewdest capitalists, for the position of finance minister. Osler, whom he had known for nearly thirty years, would make the best finance minister that Canada had ever had, predicted Van Horne. J.A.M. Aikens, who "knows the Northwest well" and "is in every way capable, absolutely honest and a man of the highest character" would make a good minister of the interior, while Collingwood Schreiber, a man of "pure gold," would be a good choice to head the government commission in charge of the Grand Trunk Pacific settlement.[1089] Not content with advising on cabinet appointments, Van Horne even urged Borden to look at a proposal made by "a very clever architect" for a Canadian government building in London. "I am convinced that what Mr. Swales proposes would make the Australian effort on the Strand look like thirty cents," wrote the tireless promoter.[1090]

Neither of Van Horne's suggestions for cabinet positions, it should be pointed out, was acted on. He also met with a deaf ear when he suggested to Borden that the money-losing Intercolonial Railway be administered by three competent commissioners along strictly business lines and that it be made to contribute to the national treasury.

Notwithstanding his position as a pre-eminent businessman and railway manager, Van Horne could be politically naive when it came to cabinet formation and the fulfillment of election promises. He entertained no doubt whatsoever that the prime minister would carry out his promise to improve transportation so that the Maritime provinces could tap into Cuban, Caribbean, and central American markets. And he was convinced the new government would encourage ship building in Canada and the growth of a merchant navy.

While Van Horne zealously promoted his choices for the new Borden cabinet, newspapers promoted Sir Wilfrid Laurier and Van Horne for the position of High Commissioner to the United Kingdom. In response to this press campaign, a Van Horne admirer, J.F. Tufts, impressed upon

Borden the need for constructive statesmanship and hence the desirability of having Van Horne appointed High Commissioner. By way of explanation, Tufts noted that Van Horne, with his involvement in railway construction and the establishment of "industrial enterprises," had done more than any other man in Canada to weld the provinces together. He then added, "Sir Wm Van Horne may not have the fluidity of speech that will grace the platform but he can think in chapters and by his forcefulness of character bring his ideas to fruition."[1091]

Van Horne, of course, was never given this opportunity to become High Commissioner to Great Britain. He remained in Canada, where, undeterred by Borden's continuing disregard of his advice, he continued trying to influence the prime minister's thinking on various issues of the day.

The subject of family deserters was one of these. The thought of men deserting their wives so upset Van Horne that he urged Borden to see that legislation was changed to allow the extradition of American deserters to the United States. "It seems to me that the despicable characters who abandon their families to want and suffering, are even less desired in Canada than common thieves, and that they should be just as easily reached by extradition," he wrote Borden in early 1914.[1092]

Van Horne was no social democrat, believing that just about anything could be accomplished through effort, determination, and goodwill. To one interviewer, he observed that able men have always "appropriated a large amount" of the world's goods and that to deny them these just rewards "would be to send us back to chaos."[1093] As a devout family man, however, he was prepared to lobby for legislation that would, he thought, help to preserve the family, the basic unit of Canadian society.

Countless individuals wrote to Van Horne soliciting donations for a charitable enterprise or his help in starting a new business. Although he was no longer at the helm of the CPR, many individuals still sought his help or guidance in company-related matters. Canadian and American editors asked him to write articles on such subjects as the CPR and the Northwest Rebellion. He invariably turned them down, as he did invitations to address various organizations and public bodies.

He also spurned any suggestion that he write an autobiography. "I don't believe in autobiographies. I think Mark Twain is a good judge of the fitness of things, of the time that should elapse, as it were, between funeral and flowers. He has just finished writing 'Leaves from the Life of Adam.'"[1094] Van Horne was equally dismissive of biographies. He informed Beckles Willson, "Authorized lives of men are always and justly regarded with suspicion for the words suggest that they have been cooked, pruned glossed and furbished up to suit somebody and therefore they lose their value and fall flat. For my part, I would not waste time in reading the authorized life of anybody."[1095] To the editor of the *Daily Mail & Empire*, he declared that he strongly objected to an "ante mortem biography. "I do not think it wise to hold up living people as examples for youth; such examples are never safe until they have been dead and buried for a reasonable time." He then noted that too many biographical subjects, paraded as examples for youth, had ended in failure or disgrace, thereby sowing doubts in "the youthful mind" and creating much harm.[1096]

On the other hand, Van Horne believed strongly in the value of a good liberal arts education. Years of helping many young men get launched on a successful business career had convinced him that the ability to express one's self clearly, concisely, and "with some degree of elegance" was essential for achieving success in any career. It was clear to him, however, that many college and university graduates lacked good communications skills. And the explanation was simple: they had been exposed to the flawed "modern system of education," which was deficient in writing instruction.[1097]

This aging mogul also attached a great deal of importance to ambition, a powerful force in his own career. Van Horne believed that there "should be no bounds to ambition." Nevertheless, he anticipated the day arriving when labour leaders and legislators would make "conditions desperate for men of ambition." This, he predicted, would happen only in the distant future. Still, the mere prospect of its becoming a reality horrified him.[1098]

Although he set great store by ambition, Van Horne was nevertheless not prepared to treat men as pawns to be sacrificed ruthlessly in order to accomplish his own goals. Admittedly, he loved to best friends, colleagues, and acquaintances, but this passion usually took the harmless form of humbugging. He loved to give the impression that he possessed supernatural powers, which is why he so relished his stunts as a mind reader, someone capable of knowing the unknowable. In performing these feats, however, he relied only on his amazing memory and the astuteness of his observations.

As someone who loved children, Van Horne was quick to respond to requests for a message for young people. One such request came in 1913 from the flamboyant and controversial Sam Hughes, who two years previously had asked Van Horne to write or wire Borden endorsing him as minister of the militia. "You remember several times you and I talked over military matters and our views always harmonized, even to plans for defense of the Empire," recalled Hughes when lobbying for Van Horne's support.[1099] Politics and the militia had been Hughes's primary and inseparable interests since his early manhood, and so it is not surprising that when Borden's minister of militia and defence again wrote to Van Horne, this time in April 1913, it was on a military matter. "It is my desire in issuing drill instructions, etc., to the Cadet Corps to publish some maxim, or brief expression from you to inspire the young lads of Canada," wrote this tireless proponent of the citizen-soldier.[1100] Van Horne obliged by furnishing Hughes with the motto, "Discipline is the foundation of character and the safeguard of liberty."

In fact, discipline, along with industry, undivided attention to duty, and unswerving loyalty to family, friends, and the CPR were the tenets that governed Van Horne's life. But of these he attached primary importance to discipline, for to him, it was the foundation of character. It had made possible his climb to such lofty heights. He also believed, however, that to reach great heights men had to be masters of humbug. "The greatest men of the past were all Masters of Humbug, and so are the greatest men of to-day, including our friend J.J. Hill, and I don't say this in any derogatory sense, for I feel a real respect and admiration for him, because in the main he has applied his mastery of Humbug to very useful purposes ...," wrote Van Horne in 1909.[1101] Other prominent men of the day would have dismissed humbug as a factor in their ascendancy and instead ascribed a leading role to religion. Not so the self-made Van Horne. A non-religious man, the railway baron nevertheless entertained strong views on man's mastery of his fate. Using for inspiration the style of the moralist and prophet Zoroaster, whom he called by the corrupt Greek form of the old Iranian name Zarathustra, Van Horne encapsulated some of these views in a passage he entitled "Ormath (Ormazd) to Zarathustra," Ormath being "a sort of Persian Buddha." With a nod to Nietzsche's 1893 work, *Also sprach Zarathustra*, Van Horne wrote, "Thou talkest much, Zarathustra, of what I taughtest thee, but obscureth and distorteth all with words and false reasoning. My teachings are plain and simple that a child may know them." Van Horne then spelled out his convictions that man creates his own gods and his own hell here on earth, that there are as many gods as men, and that strength makes for good and weakness makes for evil.[1102]

While engaged in a stunning array of activities, Van Horne had to cope with recurring health setbacks and the nagging and painful realization that his overall health was far from good. Indeed, he was prepared to admit as early as 1899 that his health had been "in an uncertain state for several years."[1103] There had been the serious attack of bronchitis in the late autumn of 1894. It had revisited him three years later, plaguing him throughout the entire winter of 1897–98 and prompting the remark to his friend Meysenburg in March 1898, "... when our annual meeting is over I hope to be able to run out to Pasadena to bring my wife and daughter home. Perhaps I will be able to leave my bronchitis there; I fear however that I will not get rid of it so easily."[1104]

Potentially much more serious was the onset of diabetes and glomerulonephritis, labelled "Bright's Disease" by Van Horne. Since this latter condition involves inflammation of the glomeruli (filtering units) of both kidneys, thereby hampering the removal of waste products, salt, and water from the bloodstream, it can have serious complications. On the other hand, mild forms of the disease may produce no symptoms and may be discovered only when a urine sample is tested for some other reason. In all likelihood, Van Horne experienced only a mild form, because in a letter to Borden, composed in 1915, he wrote, "I should tell you what nobody suspects, save a few physicians — not even my own family — that for years back I have been contending with Diabetes and more recently with Brights Disease."[1105] What is most revealing about this disclosure is not that Van Horne suffered from diabetes or glomerulonephritis (the latter may have been caused by a common tropical disease that he contracted in Cuba) but that he kept these conditions hidden from his beloved family.

Certainly he could not hide the illness that struck him on November 17, 1913, following an address that he had been persuaded to give to a Canadian Club luncheon in Toronto. That evening he became ill at the King Edward Hotel with what has been described as a "chill followed by a sharp attack of inflammatory rheumatism."[1106] Although he had intended to spend the remainder of the week in Toronto, he abruptly changed his plans and boarded a train for Montreal before midnight. His hurried departure aroused the curiosity of the press, with the result that an alarming piece appeared in the next edition of Montreal's *Gazette*. "Becoming ill while at the King Edward Hotel tonight, Sir William Van Horne had to be rushed to Montreal shortly before midnight," reported the paper. Then the inevitable happened: when he alighted from his train the following morning, Van Horne was besieged by a crowd of reporters. This so annoyed him that he walked the length of St. James Street to demonstrate how well he was. His inflamed leg rebelled against such treatment, however, and when he arrived home he was forced to bed.

Thus began a lengthy period of confinement to bed and home. For a man of seemingly unflagging energy, who had to be in control, his illness meant weeks of not only pain and discomfort but also humiliation. The fact that one day his spirits would be buoyed by a slight improvement in his condition and then dashed the following day by a setback only added to his torment. Writing in December to his Vermont friend Governor Smith, Van Horne said, somewhat disingenuously, "This is my first experience of any kind of illness and perhaps that is the reason I find it so very hard."[1107] To George Whigham later in the month, the invalid reported, "I have not yet dared to ask you to come up because of the vagaries of my rheumatism, which one day give me encouragement and the next day set me back ..."[1108]

Van Horne had recourse to a variety of touted remedies. A Japanese friend journeyed to Montreal to administer poultices made from the nuts of Cape Jessamine, while friends in Cuba sent him some green coconut water, a beverage that he had become very fond of while in that country. An old friend from his Missouri railroading days, Isaac Cate, travelled from Baltimore with his own osteopathic physician. Whether any of these interventions did any good is open to question, but if nothing else they reveal the degree of concern his loyal friends felt for him and the lengths to which some of them would go in an effort to provide him with relief and comfort.

By the end of January, after being laid up for ten weeks, Van Horne was able to sit up for a few hours each day, but although "very much better" his "working machinery" was not yet in very good order.[1109] Unfortunately, after the rheumatism abated a carbuncle developed on his knee, confining him to his bedroom. Not a submissive patient, he openly defied his physician's order not to smoke more than three cigars a day. "See how I circumvent the doctor," he said to a visitor as he showed a cigar about a foot in length and an inch and a half in diameter. "I have had these specially made for me and smoke three of them a day; and each of them gives me a good smoke for two hours."[1110]

Finally, by mid-February he was able to hobble about the house on crutches. At that time, he told Borden, with whom he was corresponding on family desertion and non-support law, that he was beginning to feel quite himself again. Nevertheless, it was a couple of months before he could substitute a cane for his crutches and resume his normal life. He then ignored his physician's advice to seek out some curative springs and instead headed directly for his beloved Cuba. This proved to be a wise move, for the island's salubrious climate and his preoccupation with beautifying San Zenon hastened his recovery. As a result, he returned to Montreal with "one leg not yet in dancing form," but declaring that he had never felt better or more cheerful.

Only days later, on June 4, he left for Europe. Accompanied by Bennie, he set sail for London on the SS *Alsatian*, which he described as a "very fine ship in every way and considerably larger than the Empresses." As was now his wont, he revelled in the comfort of a well-appointed stateroom with its own "fine private bath room."[1111] Luxuriating in such comfort would help prepare him for the rigors of an action-packed visit to the throbbing centre of the British Empire and travels on the Continent.

On this, his last visit to London, Van Horne realized that the metropolis had changed a great deal since he had first descended on it in the early nineties. No longer did a solemn, righteous air prevail. Elderly Queen Victoria had long since died, and her grandson, George V, now occupied the throne. The pace of progress had accelerated greatly, changing London's aspect every day. "Electric picture palaces" and tube railway stations now dotted its landscape. Nowhere was the pace of progress more evident, however, than in the city's busy streets, where old landmarks were being ruthlessly replaced by "improvements" and where the hansom and the "growler" had surrendered to the taxi. "There are very few horses to be seen in London now — taxi cabs have almost entirely taken their place and the streets are full of them dodging about," Van Horne wrote his grandson, whom he addressed as "my dear little man." These same streets were also noisy. The previous Wednesday, a Salvation Army parade had taken the entire afternoon to file by the Piccadilly Hotel, where Van Horne and Bennie were putting up. That same day some ten thousand boy scouts had also strutted their stuff, looking, according to William's doting grandfather, "very proud."[1112]

Business matters absorbed much of Van Horne's attention in London, where he spent the better part of a day in discussion with financier Robert Fleming. Time was also set aside, however, for a meeting with Lord Mount Stephen, an interview with Stephan Bourgeois, the art dealer, and a visit to the theatre to see a play selected by Bennie. The next day father and son were to journey by car to Oxford to see, among other notables, Canadian-born William Osler, the most revered, beloved, and influential physician of his era. Created a baronet in 1911, Osler now lived with his wife and son in Oxford, serving as Regius professor at the university and working as a busy consultant. It is not known why Van Horne wanted to see Osler, but one can speculate that he planned to consult with the transplanted Canadian about health matters.

No sooner had Van Horne and Bennie returned to Montreal, after visiting the Continent, than the First World War broke out. Van Horne had earlier predicted that there would be no war with Germany. "The great wars of the future will be in trade and commerce," he had boldly declared.[1113] This view was no doubt based partly on his high regard for

Van Horne with small William, the grandson whom he spoilt shamelessly.

Kaiser William II, the ambitious and melodramatic German head of state. In an interview, Van Horne had expounded for an hour on the Kaiser's perceived business acumen and skills, recalling that the German emperor had once stolen a march on him by obtaining information about the Laurentide Pulp and Paper Company before even Van Horne himself had been sent a copy of the report.[1114] Having placed so much faith in the man he regarded as the greatest emperor of all time, Van Horne must have watched in disbelief as the assassination of Franz Ferdinand of Austria on June 28 gave way to ultimatums, mobilizations, and declarations of war by Austria, Russia, and Germany, and then the German march across Belgium that culminated in the British government's declaration of war against Germany on August 4.

421

War had been uppermost in Van Horne's mind when his friend Samuel McClure raised the topic with him in 1910. At the time, the publisher had been greatly perturbed by the mounting tension in Europe, so much so that he had written to Senator Elihu Root about Germany's intentions and proposed that the senator and America's unofficial central banker, J. Pierpont Morgan, form a hundred-member, blue ribbon committee to seek out a peaceful solution to the evolving crisis. McClure sent copy of the missive to Van Horne, who, it seems, did not share the publisher's view of peace. As he made clear in his response, Van Horne had no use for universal peace and nothing but praise for war as a promoter of man's highest qualities. If worldwide peace reigned, he wrote Samuel McClure:

> I feel sure that it would result in universal rottenness ... All the manliness of the civilized world is due to wars ... All of the enterprise of the world has grown out of the aggressive, adventurous and warlike spirit engendered by centuries of wars. Divest the enterprise of the past three or four centuries of its military features and you would have common robbery and murder, which would long ago have brought chaos.[1115]

Not many people shared Van Horne's view of war as a beneficent agency. On the other hand, probably many, including a French diplomat, shared his belief that the Kaiser sincerely desired peace. "I know your views as to Emperor William's desire for peace, and I agree with them," wrote J. Klechzkowski, the French consul in Montreal. The diplomat tried to persuade Van Horne, however, that "overpopulation" in the German empire would inevitably lead to expansion, which posed a real threat to Germany's less-favoured neighbours.[1116]

The First World War had been underway only a month when Van Horne informed his journalist friend Beckles Willson, "The devlish wars have added much to my work for they caught me with much washing hung out to dry and I have had to hustle to avoid serious loss and damage ... Business is demoralized here and as much so in the tropics and money has ceased to be."[1117] Still, in the opening weeks of the war, Van Horne, like most other Canadians, clung to a basic belief in the sanity of man and assumed that the conflict would be over by Christmas. He watched with interest and pride as volunteers for the Canadian Expeditionary Force formed into numbered battalions, which then assembled at Valcartier, Quebec, where his friend Sam Hughes had constructed a mobilization camp boasting four miles of streets, rifle ranges, buildings, lighting, telephones, and sanitary conveniences. As a former railwayman, he speculated on how the allies would respond to the great efficiency shown by the Germans in moving their troops by rail to all fronts. But his serenity soon evaporated, as did his once firmly held belief that battle was an essential catalyst for the development of mankind's highest qualities. Both were shattered by the horrendous realities of modern warfare. When he came to realize how ghastly were its engines of destruction and how tragic was its annihilation of promising young men, some of whom had served in the CPR and whose record he knew, Van Horne did an about-face on his attitude toward war.[1118]

To escape from the shadow of war and the harsh cold of a Montreal winter, where he was fighting rheumatism, he hurried off to Cuba. He made his first wartime visit in December, accompanied by luggage containing bottles of sour milk culture ordered from Clay, Paget & Co Ltd. in London and bottles of Langdale Concentrated Medicinal Essence of Cinnamon imported from E.F. Langdale Wholesale Chemist, another London supplier. ("I am pleased to inform you that my Cinnamon preparations are now largely used by the troops at the front with most beneficial results," reported E.F. Langdale to Van Horne.)[1119] The following year, he made two more visits, one in February and the last one in May.

Before embarking on his last visit to Cuba, however, Van Horne and "small William," now seven years old, explored New York together. When Van Horne could snatch time away from business, he swept his grandson off to leading attractions deemed to have child appeal. Heading the list was the Bronx Park zoo, which so captivated small William that Van Horne told Addie the youngster was "delirious with joy."[1120] Another landmark was the recently opened Woolworth Building. Commissioned by Frederick W. Woolworth, owner of the five-and-dime retail chain, and designed by architect Cass Gilbert, it was then the tallest building in the world. In one of the central tower's high-speed elevators, grandfather and grandson zipped from the three-storey stone base past fifty-two storeys clad in cream-coloured terra cotta to the top of the three-storey roof. A far less exhilarating exercise was planned for the following morning, when young William was scheduled to tour the Hippodrome. On Saturday, he was expected to attend a performance recommended by Mrs. Charles Meredith. This was the same day that Van Horne was scheduled to set sail on the SS *Havana* for Cuba.

Van Horne in a characteristic pose.

In between visits to Cuba and a tour of New York with his beloved grandson, Van Horne busied himself in Montreal, all the while regretting that his advanced years and deteriorating health prevented his playing an active role in the war effort. However, this did not preclude putting his fertile mind to work in aid of the Allied cause. To this end, he wrote Donald Macmaster, a British MP with whom he had been corresponding over the years, about a method of detecting submarines. Van Horne reported that he had been interested in the Submarine Signal Company of Boston and had even tested some of their equipment while he had been sitting on a Boston wharf. This had involved dropping a "telephone cap" and "receiver" into the water and observing that they detected the presence of a tugboat making for south Boston. When he made this discovery, Van Horne hypothesized that the approach of a submarine might easily be detected by employing the same method.[1121] Accordingly, he created a detection device that would enhance the Allies' ability to hunt German submarines. He forwarded his suggestion to the British Admiralty, then experimenting with the training of sea lions to perform this function. After considering his proposal, however, the Admiralty referred it to the "Lusitania" inquiry, which concluded that it wouldn't work.

Fortunately, another avenue of service opened up to Van Horne. This was the chairmanship of a commission whose establishment Borden was spearheading in late June 1915. The prime minister had recognized the need to stimulate greater production in Canada, particularly in the field of agriculture, then being severely tested by wartime conditions. His government had therefore advanced the idea of a commission that would examine not only agriculture but also immigration, transportation, the borrowing of capital, and the marketing of food products. Borden looked to Van Horne to head the inquiry, for probably no other nationally known figure had more qualifications for the job or a deeper interest in the topics to be covered.

Van Horne accepted Borden's invitation, telegraphing, on June 28 from St. Andrews, that he was unreservedly at the prime minister's disposal in any matter in which he could be of use. This was before he had fully grasped the nature and scope of the Production Commission, however. When he studied its mandate more closely, Van Horne realized that his health would not allow him to devote all the time and energy he considered necessary to fill the chairmanship properly. A thorough study of all the questions, or even of two or three of the most important ones, he concluded, would entail at least two years of almost continuous work and an inordinate amount of travelling.

Although he did not shrink from this, Van Horne feared that his required absences in Cuba during the winter months might jeopardize the commission's work. The spending of his winters in Cuba "has been a matter of 'dodging the reaper' rather than the carrying out of business enterprises, these enterprises having been taken up only to make my stays there more tolerable," he confided to Borden.[1122] This admission and his revelation that he suffered from diabetes and Bright's Disease might have persuaded Borden to withdraw his offer, but they didn't. Knowing that Van Horne's name would lend influence to the commission's work and report, he repeated his invitation, saying that arrangements could be made to accommodate Van Horne's visits to Cuba. With this assurance, Van Horne cabled the prime minister on July 9 that he was willing "to take chances" if Borden thought that best.[1123]

Events would conspire, however, to rob Van Horne of this coveted challenge. Shortly after his return from Europe he came down with a fever that baffled his physicians and forced periods of rest on him. When his activities were not sharply curtailed by the fever, he made several visits to Covenhoven and continued to manage his widely scattered business interests. The affectionate father-in-law also arranged for a portrait to be painted of his daughter-in-law, Edith. This was only accomplished with increasing difficulty, however, as he was becoming progressively weaker.

In early August, Van Horne made plans to begin a history of the CPR and even contemplated a visit to Cuba in the immediate future. But none of this was to be. Following a week of observation and tests in Montreal, he was rushed to the Royal Victoria Hospital on the night of August 22. There, at 2:30 the next morning, he was operated on for a huge abdominal abscess. To the great relief of family and anxious friends, the operation was judged a success. Bennie, who had rushed up to Montreal from St. Andrews, reported to Edith, who had remained there, "We found Papa looking splendidly considering what he had gone through. The doctors are very pleased at the way he came through the operation, and although his condition is still serious of course, think he had better than a fair chance of pulling through."[1124] Legions of friends inundated the family with telegrams and letters, with the Duke of Connaught inquiring on behalf of King George V.

More encouraging news followed on August 26, when Percival Farquhar, then in New York, was informed by Van Horne's private secretary, "I am glad to be able to tell you that Sir William is progressing wonderfully and is practically out of immediate danger. We are now able to hope for an ultimate recovery."[1125] Having rallied from the shock of the operation, Van Horne began receiving visitors, some of whom he entertained with plans of the new type of hospital he would build when he regained his health. On September 7, however, he took a turn for the worse, and four days later he died. He was seventy-two.

"William Van Horne Dies At Montreal. Pushed CPR Through with Masterful Force," screamed bold type on the front page of the September 13 edition of the *Globe*. The paper then observed that Van Horne had risen "from base to top of the railway ladder by sheer grit, organizing resource and brain power. There was no royal road to success with him.

The circumstances were none too rosy in his favour, but he rose above them and stamped his impress on what he did in a remarkable way."

From around the world poured messages of sympathy, while across the far-flung CPR system, from Montreal to London and Hong Kong, flags on company buildings drooped at half-mast. Across Cuba, the country that he had fallen in love with, church bells tolled for the passing of one who "in little more than one year had done a greater work for Cuba than the Spanish government had accomplished in four hundred and fifty years."[1126]

The funeral took place on the morning of Tuesday, September 14, from his Sherbrooke Street home, where the service was conducted in the great drawing room by the minister of the Church of the Messiah, Addie's and his sister Mary's church. Van Horne had never embraced formal religion — he had once said, "All my religion is summed up in the Golden Rule, and I practise it"[1127] — so the choice of a Unitarian Church service was eminently fitting. There was no eulogy. Instead, the minister read passages from the Bible and an extract from the poem "Threnody" by the celebrated American poet, essayist, and philosopher Ralph Waldo Emerson. Among those who packed the drawing room were representatives of the Governor General, the federal and Quebec governments, and the Japanese and Cuban governments; Sir Thomas Shaughnessy; a large number of CPR officials and directors; and leading members of the judiciary, transportation, banking, manufacturing, and other commercial sectors. Many who could not cram into the drawing room stood in the front hall.

After the service concluded, the funeral procession began its journey to Windsor Station, passing down Stanley Street, which was thronged with onlookers, many of whom had been standing for hours. In the somewhat flowery words of a *Gazette* reporter, "The classes were abundantly represented, but the masses were there in the thousands. Sir William was not, perhaps, known to the generality of the public, but so large, commanding and picturesque a personality had won upon the imagination and his passing was of concern to all."[1128]

Four flower-laden carriages headed the procession. Next came the hearse, followed on foot by Bennie, small William, and Van Horne's brother Augustus Charles, who had come from Joliet for the funeral. They were followed by Shaughnessy, R.B. Angus, Sir Edmund Osler, Charley Hosmer, George Bury, and other vice-presidents and heads of CPR departments, as well as hundreds of other dignitaries. It was remarked that never had so many flowers been seen at a public funeral in Montreal, testimony to Van Horne's great love of flowers, particularly lilies and roses.

At Windsor Station, the deceased's remains were transferred to a special train headed by locomotive 2213, suitably draped in black crepe. The train departed at 11:00 a.m. for Joliet, where Van Horne was to be buried. The last car on the train was the official car, the *Saskatchewan*, which Van Horne had used since 1884. On board the train were Bennie and his wife, Edith, Van Horne's brother, and W.F. Lynch, who had been Van Horne's private secretary for many years and was now purchasing agent for the Cuba Company in New York. Addie and young Addie remained in Montreal.

As the funeral train made its way across Canada, groups of men who revered Van Horne's memory greeted it at station after station. In homage to him, all traffic on the system was suspended at an appointed hour.

Van Horne's last journey ended at 10:00 a.m. the next day at Joliet, where every flag was at half-mast. At the station the train was met by Colonel Fred Bennet, one of Van Horne's oldest friends, and a delegation of members of some of the oldest families of Will County, many of whom had known Van Horne since he was a boy. Thousands of local residents lined Cass Street when the coffin was escorted to Oakwood Cemetery. As the casket was lowered into the ground in the family plot, the presiding minister intoned, "From a humble beginning, he rose by his energy and prophetic foresight to a high place in the esteem of his fellow men."[1129]

A year after Van Horne's death, George Tate Blackstock, K.C., of Toronto, who was his friend and counsel during the frenetic years of 1885 to 1892, wrote, "Canadians even to-day, have no realization of the work he did or of what they owe him. He was a Napoleonic master of men, and the fertility of his genius and resource were boundless, as were the skill and force with which he brought his conceptions to realities."[1130] It has been written that "every life is not only a string of events: it is also a myth."[1131] In Van Horne's case it was a huge myth.

Afterword

In his will, Van Horne stipulated that his wife, Addie, within six months of his death, "relinquish, renounce and abandon in favour of his estate all rights of dower, community rights and other rights whatsoever, if any, arising out of marriage." In lieu of such rights and in addition to certain bequests, she was to have the use and the enjoyment of the Sherbrooke Street mansion and its contents for three years after his death should she survive him. He also bequeathed to Addie the sum of $30,000 per annum to maintain the residence. Addie subsequently renounced all matrimonial rights and accepted the legacies made in her favour.

Van Horne also provided under his will for the maintenance of his Sherbrooke Street mansion. "I should like said house and premises to continue to be used as a family residence (unless the neighbourhood should for any reason become undesirable for such purpose) for my wife and children and the survivors of them but this is only a suggestion and not obligatory."

To his beloved daughter Addie, Van Horne conveyed Covenhoven, its furniture and art collections, the animals, and all his real estate on Minister's Island. He bequeathed all the residue of his estate to his wife "for one third or four twelfths (4/12)," to "Bennie (or his issue representing him par souche) for five twelfths (5/12)" and to his daughter "(or her issue representing her par souche) for three twelfths (3/12)," thereby making his wife, daughter, and son his "Universal Residuary Legatees & Devisees in full ownership" from time of death with the exception of one third of each of his son's and daughter's shares, which were to be held in trust by the Royal Trust Company.

Van Horne also made provision for his cherished grandson, stipulating that the sum of $20,000 be placed in the hands of the Royal Trust and held in trust for William. The sum was to be invested by the company and the interest used for the education and support of his grandson until he reached the age of twenty-one. At that time any surplus revenue was to be added to the principal and invested in interest bearing securities and the capital amount plus all accumulations of revenue were to paid over to William when he reached twenty-one

In accordance with the wish expressed in his will, family members continued to occupy the mansion on Sherbrooke Street West after Van Horne's death. It was in this home, which some observers had likened in appearance to an armoury, that Addie Sr. died on January 24, 1929. A private funeral, conducted by the minister of the Church of the Messiah, was held at the family residence. Only immediate family members and a few friends attended. Following the service, Addie's remains were taken in the private CPR car *Van Horne* to Joliet for burial beside her husband.[1132]

Bennie devoted himself after his father's death to looking after Van Horne family railway and plantation interests in Cuba. This required that he spend a great deal of time on the island as well as in New York, where his chauffeur, Sammy Taylor, became his friend and companion. In the late 1920s, Bennie distinguished himself by laying out $1.5 million for a huge yacht, the *Intrepid*, which had a crew of twenty-seven and was brought to St. Andrews for one summer.[1133]

A fondness for drink and partying probably contributed to Bennie's early death. He was only fifty-four when he died on August 20, 1931, after a two-week illness while staying at St. Andrews. Following the funeral, which was conducted at Covenhoven, his remains were taken to the St. Andrews Rural Cemetery for burial. The following year, his widow, Edith, married the Honourable Randolph Bruce, former lieutenant governor of British Columbia and later Canadian minister to Japan.

Bennie and Edith's only child, William (Billy), was married on November 29, 1928, to Audrey Fraser. They had one child, a daughter, Beverley Ann. When she was still an infant, in August 1934, her mother, Audrey, was killed in a car accident at St. Andrews. Billy married again, this time Margaret Hannon (also nicknamed Billy) from Montreal. When in that city, the Billy Van Hornes lived in the Sherbrooke Street mansion, although during the Second World War they spent much of their time at St. Andrews, occupying a house on Augustus Street that they had purchased. Regrettably, William Cornelius Covenhoven Van Horne took to alcohol like his father, but unlike Bennie, he never did succeed in holding down any kind of a job. He attempted to work for the Navy at Cornwallis, Nova Scotia, but when that ended in failure he spent much of his time stationed at the end of the St. Andrews wharf, looking for submarines. Billy was only thirty-nine when he died in 1946 in Montreal. He was buried beside his father at St. Andrews.[1134]

Unlike her brother or her nephew, Addie Van Horne was not dragged down by alcohol. An intelligent, well-educated woman with a deep knowledge of and interest in art, she led an exemplary life, maintaining her father's art and pottery collections, supporting various charities, and managing the house, farm, and staff at Covenhoven. Because of her great bulk, young Addie was regarded as rather shy, but nevertheless she could be very much at ease with people, especially younger people and individuals she knew well. Certainly nothing gave her greater pleasure than receiving appreciative visitors and showing them works of art and pieces of pottery from her father's renowned collections. So encyclopedic was her knowledge that even when she was almost blind she could locate every exhibit and, if questioned, describe the features of every piece. She died on February 24, 1941, at age seventy-three and was buried, like both her parents, in the Van Horne plot in Joliet's Oakwood Cemetery.

The sad saga of the Van Horne family played itself out in the 1960s, by which time it evolved into the saga of the Van Horne family home at 1139 Sherbrooke Street West. Margaret Van Horne, Billy's widow, was the sole family member to occupy the house after her mother-in-law, Edith Bruce, died, an incapacitated octogenarian, in 1962 (the Honorable Randolph Bruce had died in 1942). A woman who shunned publicity, Margaret Van Horne was, like her sister-in-law, Addie, dedicated to preserving Van Horne's memory, and accordingly she devoted much of her time and energy to maintaining his various collections. Indeed, she so admired her father-in-law that she seriously contemplated writing a biography of him.

Unfortunately, her deep attachment to the Van Horne legacy was not shared by her step-daughter, Van Horne's great-granddaughter, Beverley Ann, who had inherited Covenhoven from her Aunt Addie and who was a revenue beneficiary of Addie's estate.[1135] But even if she had identified with the family legacy, Beverley Ann was probably not in a position to maintain either the huge Sherbrooke Street residence or sprawling Covenhoven. She therefore sold the Minister's Island property in 1961. It would pass through several hands before being acquired at auction in 1977 by the Province of New Brunswick. It was subsequently designated a protected historic site. Since being sold by Beverley Ann, however, the house had been stripped of most of its original furnishings. Nevertheless it did survive intact, albeit almost empty and looking very forlorn. The same could not be said for 1139 Sherbrooke Street West.

Its fate was sealed in 1967, when the Royal Trust Company, executors of the Van Horne estate, put the Montreal residence up for sale. As it had been designated a historic site by Montreal's Jacques-Viger Commission, heritage aficionados hoped that it would be retained as such and preserved for future generations. To ensure this, Montreal architect Michael Fish and other like-minded individuals embarked on a struggle to see that the house was not demolished. Their fight took on a new sense of urgency in 1973, when a multimillionaire developer, David Azrieli, made a $750,000 offer for the mansion. When the Polish-born self-designated architect and designer applied for a permit to demolish the house the fight became critical.

In the wake of these developments, the last phase of the struggle to save the house got underway. Those fighting for the building's retention advanced a powerful case for its survival, noting that the house possessed the only known Colonna-designed interior in the world and that it was a prime example of a nineteenth-century house embodying the fundamental ideas and ideals of its age. Moreover, the Jacques-Viger Commission had repeatedly recommended that the building be conserved. Its sentiments had also been echoed by the provincial Biens Culturels Commission, which had recommended, unanimously, that the Van Horne house be classified — that is, designated a property that could not be altered, restored, repaired or changed, either inside or out, without the Commission's authorization.

An extraordinary effort was made to save the house, but it would prove futile. In September 1973, the City of Montreal issued a demolition permit, and within a few hours wreckers were on the site. Michael Fish would later describe the levelling of the mansion as "one of the great cultural tragedies of my time."[1136]

It was more than that, however. With the razing of the house one of the most visible reminders of Van Horne's personal legacy was consigned to history's trash bin.

Not even the Cuba Company and the Cuba Railroad Company have survived to the present day. In 1923, the Cuban senate passed legislation providing for the consolidation of railway transportation on the island. The device finally chosen to carry this out, Ferrocarriles Consolidados de Cuba, acquired the stock of the three amalgamating companies, one of which was the Cuba Railroad, which retained its identity and administrative autonomy. The controlling shareholder of Ferrocarriles Consolidados was the Cuba Company, which received 60 percent of Ferrocarriles Consolidados's common stock and 66 percent of the preferred stock. One of the two junior members of its board was Bennie Van Horne.[1137] However, in 1959, in the wake of the Fidel Castro revolution, the Cuba Company was dissolved and its stock transferred to Ferrocarriles Consolidados and the Compañía Cuba, which thereby became independent entities.[1138] The following year, 1960, Ferrocarriles Consolidados and its subsidiaries were nationalized.

Bibliography

Manuscript Sources

National Archives of Canada
Sir William Van Horne Papers (identified in endnotes as MG29 A60).
Sir John A. Macdonald Papers.
Sir Wilfrid Laurier Papers.
Sir Robert Borden Papers.
Sir John Willison Papers.
Katherine Hughes Papers (these include a draft biography of Van Horne).
Gonzola de Quesada Papers.
Lord Shaughnessy Papers.
Canadian Pacific Presidents' Letterbooks (identified in endnotes as CPPL).

James Jerome Hill Reference Library
James J. Hill papers.

Library of Congress
General Wood Papers

McCord Museum
Kate Reed Papers

Theses and Typescripts
Allen, Gale. *Building the Railroad of the Minnesota Valley.* Typescript produced by the Minnesota Historical Society, 1947.
Baldwin, Fayette. *The Economic Development of Joliet, Illinois,* 1830–1870. Ph.D. dissertation, Harvard University, 1933.

Bell, Rodney E. *A Life of Russell Alger, 1836–1907*. Ph.D. thesis, University of Michigan, 1975.

Vince, Margaret. *Sir William Van Horne and Canadian Economic Relations in the Caribbean, 1900–1915*. M.A. thesis, Smith College, 1949.

Unpublished Works

Armstrong, Harry. *One Canadian, 1853–1933*. Unpublished memoir, MG30 B26.

Government Publications

Canada. House of Commons Debates.
Canada. Sessional Paper #31, Sessional Papers, 1884, #9, vol. 17.

Books

A Retrospect. Montreal: Old Girls' Association of Miss Edgar's and Miss Cramp's School, 1984.

Armstrong, Christopher and H.V. Nelles. *Southern Exposure: Canadian Promoters in Latin America and the Caribbean, 1896–1930*. Toronto: University of Toronto Press, 1988.

Artibise, Alan. *Winnipeg: An Illustrated History*. Toronto: James Lorimer & Company, 1977.

Ashdown, Dana. *Railway Steamships of Ontario*. Erin, Ontario: The Boston Mills Press, 1988.

Beaufort, Madeleine Fidell, Herbert L. Kleinfield and Jeanne K. Welcher, editors. *The Diaries of Samuel P. Avery, Art Dealer*. New York: Arno Press, 1979.

Beaverbrook, Lord. *Courage: The Story of Sir James Dunn*. Fredericton: Brunswick Press, 1961.

Berton, Pierre. *The Great Railway, vol. 1: The National Dream, 1871–1881*. Toronto: McClelland and Stewart, 1970.

Berton, Pierre. *The Great Railway, vol. 2: The Last Spike, 1881–1885*. Toronto: McClelland and Stewart, 1971.

Black, Martha. *My Seventy Years*. London: Nelson, 1938.

Bliss, Michael. *Northern Enterprise: Five Centuries of Canadian Business*. Toronto: McClelland and Stewart, 1987.

Brooke, Janet. *Discerning Tastes: Montreal Collectors, 1880–1920*.

Montreal Museum of Fine Arts, 1989.

Brown, Robert Craig and Ramsay Cook. *Canada, 1896–1921: A Nation Transformed.* Toronto: McClelland and Stewart, 1974.

Canada 1939: The Official Handbook of Present Conditions and Recent Progress. Ottawa: Dominion Bureau of Statistics, 1939.

The Canadian Encyclopedia, 2nd. edition, vol. 11. Edmonton: Hurtig Publishers, 1988.

Chandler, Jr., Alfred D. *The Visible Hand: The Managerial Revolution in American Business.* Cambridge and London: The Belknap Press of Harvard University Press, 1977.

Collard, Edgar Andrew. *Montreal Yesterdays.* Toronto: Longmans Canada, 1962.

Corliss, Carlton. *Main Line to Mid-America: The Story of the Illinois Central.* New York: Creative Age Press, 1950.

Creighton, Donald. *John A. Macdonald: The Old Chieftain.* Toronto: The Macmillan Company of Canada Limited, 1955.

Cruise, David and Alison Griffiths. *Lords of the Line.* Markham: Viking, 1988.

Currie, A.W. *The Grand Trunk Railway of Canada.* Toronto: University of Toronto Press, 1957.

Dempsey, Hugh A., ed. *The CPR West.* Vancouver: Douglas & McIntyre, 1984.

Donald, David Herbert. *Lincoln.* New York: Simon & Schuster, 1995.

Eagle, John. *The Canadian Pacific Railway and the Development of Western Canada.* Montreal: McGill-Queen's University Press, 1989.

Engelbourg, Saul and Leonard Bushkoff. *The Man Who Found The Money: John Stewart Kennedy and the Financing of the Western Railroads.* East Lansing: Michigan State University Press, 1996.

Fleming, R.B. *The Railway King of Canada: Sir William Mackenzie, 1849–1923.* Vancouver: University of British Columbia Press, 1991.

Gauld, Charles. *The Last Titan: Percival Farquhar American Entrepreneur in Latin America.* Stanford: California Institute of International Studies, 1972.

Genealogical and Biographical Record of Will County. Chicago: Biographical Publishing Company, 1900.

Gibbon, John Murray. *Canadian Mosaic.* Toronto: McClelland and Stewart, 1938.

Gibbon, John Murray. *Steel of Empire: The Romantic History of the Canadian Pacific Railway, The Northwest Passage of Today.* New York: The Bobbs-Merrill Company, 1935.

Gilbert, Heather. *The End of the Road: The Life of Lord Mount Stephen.* Volume 2. Aberdeen: Aberdeen University Press, 1977.

Goodfield, Joyce D. *Before the Melting Pot: Society and Culture in Colonial New York City, 1664–1730.* Princeton: Princeton University Press, 1992.

Gray, Charlotte. *Flint & Feather: The Life and Times of E. Pauline Johnson Tekahionwake.* Toronto: HarperCollins Canada, 2002.

Grodinsky, Julius. *Transcontinental Railway Strategy, 1869–1893: A Study of Businessmen.* Philadelphia: University of Pennsylvania Press, 1962.

Gwynn, Sandra. *The Private Capital: Ambition and Love in the Age of Macdonald and Laurier.* Toronto: McClelland and Stewart, 1984.

Hadley, Rollin Van N., ed. *The Letters of Bernard Berenson and Isabella Stewart Gardner 1887–1924. With Correspondence by Mary Berenson.* Boston: Northeastern University Press, 1989.

Hall, D.J. *Clifford Sifton, vol. 1, The Young Napoleon, 1861–1900.* Vancouver: University of British Columbia Press, 1985

Hall, Roger, Gordon Dodds, and Stanley Triggs. *The World of William Notman: The Nineteenth Century Through a Master Lens.* Boston: David R. Godine, 1993.

Ham, George. *Reminiscences of a Raconteur.* Toronto: The Musson Book Company Ltd., 1921.

Hamilton, Robert M. and Dorothy Shields, *Canadian Quotations and Phrases.* Revised and enlarged edition. Toronto: McClelland and Stewart, 1979.

Harper, J. Russell. *Painting in Canada A History.* Toronto: University of Toronto Press, 1966.

Hart, E.J. *The Selling of Canada: The CPR and the Beginnings of Canadian Tourism.* Banff: Altitude Publishing, 1983.

The Historical Guide to North American Railroads. 2nd edition. Waukesha: Kalmbach Publishing Company, 2000.

The History of Will County, Illinois. Chicago: William Le Baron, Jr. and Company, 1878.

Hitchman, James. *Leonard Wood and Cuban Independence, 1898–1902.* The Hague: Martinus Nijhoff, 1971.

Holbrook, Stewart. *The Story of American Railroads.* New York: Crown Publishers, 1947.

Hopkins, J. Castell. *The Canadian Annual Review of Public Affairs. 1907.* Toronto: The Annual Review Publishing Company Limited, 1908.

Jenkins, Kathleen. *Montreal: Island City of the St. Lawrence.* Garden City: Doubleday & Company, Inc., 1966.

Jensen, Richard J. *Illinois: A Bicentennial History*. New York: W.W. Norton & Company, Inc. and Nashville: American Association for State and Local History, 1978.

Jessup, Philip. *Elihu Root*. New York: Dodd, Mead and Company, 1938.

Jones, David Laurence. *Tales of the CPR*. Calgary: Fifth House, 2002.

Josephson, M. *The Robber Barons: The Great American Capitalists, 1861–1903*. New York: Harcourt, Brace and Company, 1934.

Kalman, Harold. *A History of Canadian Architecture*. Toronto: Oxford University Press, 1994.

Kaplan, Justin. *Walt Whitman: A Life*. Toronto: Bantam Books, 1982.

Knowles, Valerie. *First Person: A Biography of Senator Cairine Wilson*. Toronto: Dundurn Press, 1988.

Lamb, W. Kaye. *History of the Canadian Pacific Railway*. New York: Macmillan Publishing Company, 1977.

Larkin, Oliver. *Life and Art in America*. New York: Rinehart & Company, 1950.

Lavallée, Omer. *Van Horne's Road: An illustrated account of the construction and first years of operation of the Canadian Pacific transcontinental railway*. Montreal: Railfare Enterprises Ltd., 1974.

Lemly, James. *The Gulf, Mobile and Ohio: A Railroad That Had to Expand or Expire*. Homewood: Richard D. Irwin, 1953.

Licht, Walter. *Working for the Railroad: The Organization of Work in the Nineteenth Century*. Princeton: Princeton Universityi Press, 1983.

Lycett, Andrew. *Rudyard Kipling*. London: Weidenfeld & Nicholson, 1999.

MacBeth, R.G. *The Romance of the Canadian Pacific Railway*. Toronto: Ryerson Press, 1924.

MacGregor, James A. *Father Lacombe*. Edmonton: Hurtig Publishers, 1975.

MacKay, Donald. *The Square Mile: Merchant Princes of Montreal*. Toronto/Vancouver: Douglas & McIntyre, 1987.

Malone, Michael P. *James J. Hill: Empire Builder of the Northwest*. Norman: University of Oklahoma Press, 1996.

Martin, Albro. *James J. Hill and the Opening of the Northwest*. New York: Oxford University Press, 1986.

Martin, J. Edward. *On a Streak of Lightning. Electric Railways in Canada*. British Columbia: Studio E, 1994.

McDonald, Donna. *Lord Strathcona: A Biography of Donald Alexander Smith*. Toronto: Dundurn Press, 1996.

McDowall, Duncan. *Quick to the Frontier*. Toronto: McClelland and Stewart, 1993.

McDowall, Duncan. *The Light: Brazilian Traction, Light and Power*

Company Ltd. Toronto: University of Toronto Press, 1988.

McKee, Bill and Georgeen Klassen. *Trail of Iron: The CPR and the Birth of the West.* Vancouver: The Glenbow-Alberta Institute in association with Douglas & McIntyre, 1983.

McPherson, James. *Battle Cry for Freedom: The Civil War Era.* New York: Oxford University Press, 1988.

National Encyclopedia of Canadian Biography. Toronto: Dominion Publishing Company, 1935.

Newman, Peter C. *Canada 1892: Portrait of a Promised Land.* Toronto: Madison Press Books for Penguin Books Canada Limited and McClelland and Stewart, 1992.

Origo, Iris. *Images and Shadows: Part of a Life.* Boston: David R. Godine, 1999.

Pole, Graeme. *The Canadian Rockies: A History in Photographs.* Banff: Altitude Publishing, 1991.

Pope, Maurice, ed. *The Memoirs of Sir Joseph Pope.* Toronto: Oxford University Press, 1960.

Pope, Sir Joseph. *The Tour of Their Royal Highnesses The Duke and Duchess of Cornwall Through the Dominion of Canada in the Year 1901.* Ottawa: S.E. Dawson, the King's Printer, 1903.

Pratte, France Gagnon. *Country Houses for Montrealers 1892–1924: The Architecture of E. and W.S. Maxwell.* Montreal: Meridian Press, 1987.

Reed, Robert C. *Train Wrecks: A Pictorial History of Accidents on the Main Line.* New York: Bonanza Book, 1968.

Reynolds, Agnes. *Agnes: The Biography of Lady Macdonald.* Ottawa: Carleton University Press, 1990.

The Routledge Historical Atlas of American Railroads. New York: Routledge, 1999.

Samuels, Ernest. *Bernard Berenson: The Making of a Legend.* Cambridge: The Belnap Press of Harvard University, 1987.

Saywell, John, ed. *The Canadian Journal of Lady Aberdeen, 1893–1898.* Toronto: Champlain Society, 1960.

Schofield, F.H. *The Story of Manitoba.* Montreal, Vancouver, Winnipeg: The S. J. Clarke Publishing Co., 1913.

Secretan, J.H., *Canada's Great Highway. From the First Stake to the Last Spike.* London: John Lane, The Bodley Head Limited, 1924.

Skelton, O.D. *Life and Letters of Sir Wilfrid Laurier.* Toronto: Oxford University Press, 1921.

Stover, John F. *American Railroads.* Chicago: The University of Chicago Press, 1965.

Strouse, Jean. *Morgan: American Financier.* New York: Random House, 1999.

Sutton, Denys, ed. *Letters of Roger Fry.* Volume 1. London: Chatto & Windus, 1972.

Taché, Louis J.C.H., ed. *Men of the Day: A Canadian Portrait Gallery.* Montreal, 1890.

Thompson, Norman and Major J.H. Edgar. *Canadian Railway Development From the Earliest Times.* Toronto: The Macmillan Company of Canada Limited, 1933.

Trubek, Amy B. *How the French Invented the Culinary Profession.* Philadelphia: University of Pennsylvania Press, 2000.

Turner, Robert D. *The Pacific Expresses: An Illustrated History of Canadian Pacific Railway's Express Liners on the Pacific Ocean.* Victoria: Sono Nis Press, 1981.

Urquhart, M.C. and K. A. Buckley, Eds. *Historical Statistics of Canada.* Toronto: The Macmillan Company of Canada Ltd., 1965.

Vance, Jr., James E. *The North American Railroad: Its Origin, Evolution and Geography.* Baltimore and London: The Johns Hopkins University Press, 1995.

Vaughan, Walter. *The Life and Work of Sir William Van Horne.* New York: The Century Company, 1920.

Waite, Peter B. *Canada 1874–1896: Arduous Destiny.* Toronto: McClelland and Stewart, 1971.

Walker, Willa. *No Hay Fever & A Railway.* Fredericton: Goose Lane Editions, 1989.

Wilbur, Dick, ed. *A Collection of Old St. Andrews Sketches.* St. Andrews: E. Williamson, 1983.

Willison, Sir John. *Reminiscences Political and Personal.* Toronto: McClelland and Stewart, 1919.

Willson, Beckles. *From Quebec to Piccadilly and Other Places, Some Anglo-Canadian Memories.* London: Cape, 1929.

Wood, Charles R. and Dorothy M. Wood. *Milwaukee Road West.* Seattle: Superior Publishing Company, 1972.

Zanetti, Oscar and Alejandro García. *Sugar and Railroads: A Cuban History, 1837–1959.* Translated by Franklin W. Knight and Mary Todd. Chapel Hill: The University of North Carolina Press, 1987.

Zaslov, Morris. *The Opening of the Canadian North 1870–1914.* Toronto: McClelland and Stewart, 1971.

Articles

"Chicago." *Encyclopedia Britannica*, volume 5. Chicago: William Benton, 1970.

"The Death of Sir William Van Horne." *Canadian Railway and Marine World.* October 1915.

"The Diary of Arthur Rowe Miller." *Saskatchewan History*, vol. X, #2, Spring 1957.

The Magazine of History With Notes and Queries, Extra No., #102, vol. 26, #1 and vol. 26, #2.

Angus, Fred. "The Saskatchewan." Canadian Rail, #375, July–August 1983.

Armstrong, Elizabeth Metzger. "Where We Live: Alton." Published by the Missouri Historical Society and reproduced on the Internet.

Chandler, Jr., Alfred D. "The Railroads: Pioneers in Modern Corporate Management." *Business History Review*, No. 1, 1965.

Lindsey, J. "Sir Joseph Woelsey Flavelle." *The Canadian Encyclopedia*, 2nd edition, volume 2. Edmonton: Hurtig Publishers, 1988.

Macnaughtan, S. "Sir William Van Horne." *The Cornhill Magazine*, vol. XV, January–June 1916.

Mosgrove, J.H. "Famous Railway Head Has Brush With Notorious Bandit Gang." *Edmonton Bulletin*, October 6, 1934.

Newman, Peter C. "Sir William Van Horne the Nation Builder." *The Montrealer*, June 1959.

Schermerhorn, Jr., Richard. "Representative Pioneer Settlers of New England and their Original Home Places." *Immigrants to the Middle Colonies: A Consolidation of Ship Passenger Lists and Associated Data from the New York Genealogical and Biographical Record*, Michael Tepper, ed. Baltimore: Genealogical Publishing Co., 1978.

Smith, Gene. "The Last Rebel Ground." *American Heritage*, April 1999.

Stanton, Jeffrey. "Coney Island — Early Years (1609–1880)." Reproduced on the Internet.

Sterling, Robert E. Excerpts from a history of Joliet on the City of Joliet website.

Vaughan, Walter. "Sir William Van Horne." *The Maker of Canada Series*. London and Toronto: Oxford University Press, 1926.

Newspapers

Alton Telegraph
The *Gazette* (Montreal)
The *Globe* (Toronto)
The *Joliet News*
Manitoba Free Press
The *Montreal Star*
The *New York Times*
The *Ottawa Journal*
St. Paul Dispatch
The *Sun* (Winnipeg)

Notes

1. *Northern Enterprise: Five Centuries of Canadian Business*, 599.

2. This is a reference to the American railway barons James J. Hill and Edward H. Harriman.

3. J.H.F. Secretan, *Canada's Great Highway: From Stake to the Last Spike* (London: John Lane, The Bodley Head Ltd., 1924), 96.

4. Van Horne to F. Tennyson Nealy, July 28, 1910 (Van Horne personal letterbook, No. 11, MG29 A60, vol. 56), 1201.

5. Van Horne to Dr. P. Desvernine, August 24, 1910 (MG29 A60, vol. 6, file 1).

6. Van Horne to Manuel Diaz, August 27, 1910 (MG29 A60, vol. 6, file 1).

7. Van Horne to Lady Nicholson, July 13, 1913 (MG29 A60, vol. 96, genealogical notes, pt. 3, n.d., 1913–26).

8. Richard Schermerhorn, Jr., "Representative Pioneer Settlers of New Netherland and their Original Home Places," in *Immigrants to the Middle Colonies: A Consolidation of Ship Passenger Lists and Associated Data from the New York Genealogical and Biographical Record*, edited by Michael Tepper (Baltimore: Genealogical Publishing Co. Inc.), 11.

9. Joyce D. Goodfriend, *Before the Melting Pot: Society and Culture in Colonial New York City*, 1664–1730 (Princeton, New Jersey: Princeton University Press, 1992), 3.

10. Walter Vaughan, *The Life and Work of Sir William Van Horne* (New York: The Century Company, 1920), 5.

11. *The Christian Intelligence* (genealogical notes, pt.1, 1840–1916 MG29 A60, vol. 96).

12. Richard J. Jensen, *Illinois: A Bicentennial History* (New York:

W.W. Norton & Company, Inc. and Nashville: American Association for State and Local History, 1978), 32.

13. *The History of Will County, Illinois* (Chicago: William Le Baron, Jr. and Company, 1878), 498.

14. *The History of Will County*, 498–99.

15. Cornelius Van Horne to Abraham Van Horne, February 12, 1840 (genealogical notes, pt.1, 1840–1916, MG29 A60, vol. 96).

16. Vera Martin (genealogical notes, pt. 1, 1840–1916, MG29 A60, vol. 96).

17. Alfred D. Chandler, Jr., *The Visible Hand: The Managerial Revolution in American Business* (Cambridge and London: The Belknap Press of Harvard University Press, 1977), 81.

18. Gene Smith, "The Last Rebel Ground," (*American Heritage*, April 1999), 90.

19. Chandler, *The Visible Hand*, 91.

20. Chandler, *The Visible Hand*, 82–83.

21. Chandler, *The Visible Hand*, 87.

22. Van Horne, draft letter to his grandson, n.d. (MG29 A60, vol. 102).

23. Ibid.

24. Vaughan, *The Life and Work of Sir William Van Horne*, 11.

25. Robert E. Sterling, "History of Joliet, Illinois," reproduced on the City of Joliet website.

26. Vera Martin (genealogical notes, pt.1, 1840–1916, MG29 A60, vol. 96).

27. Sterling, "History of Joliet, Illinois."

28. S. Macnaughtan, "Sir William Van Horne," (*The Cornhill Magazine*, vol. XL, January–June 1916), 240–41.

29. Vaughan, *The Life and Work of Sir William Van Horne*, 12.

30. J. Lindsey, "Sir Joseph Wesley Flavelle," *The Canadian Encyclopedia*, 2nd edition, vol. 11 (Edmonton: Hurtig Publishers, 1988), 789.

31. David Herbert Donald, *Lincoln* (New York: Simon & Schuster, 1995), 27.

32. Van Horne, draft letter to his grandson (MG29 A60, vol. 102).

33. Macnaughtan, "Sir William Van Horne," 243.

34. Vaughan, *The Life and Work of Sir William Van Horne*, 38.

35. Vaughan, *The Life and Work of Sir William Van Horne*, 15–16.

36. Vaughan, *The Life and Work of Sir William Van Horne*, 16.

37. Macnaughtan, "Sir William Van Horne," 241–42.

38. Macnaughtan, "Sir William Van Horne," 241–2.

39. Vaughan, *The Life and Work of Sir William Van Horne*, 18.

40. John Parsons to Van Horne, October 20, 1856, MG29 A60, vol. 87, file miscellaneous.

41. John F. Stover, *American Railroads* (Chicago: The University of Chicago Press, 1965), 45.

42. Carlton Corliss, *Main Line to Mid–America: The Story of the Illinois Central* (New York: Creative Age Press, 1950), 79–80.

43. Fayette Baldwin, *The Economic Development of Joliet, Illinois, 1830–1870*, (Ph.D. dissertation, Harvard University, 1933), 121.

44. Katherine Hughes mss., (MG30 D71, vol. 2. file 11.2).

45. Vaughan, *The Life and Work of Sir William Van Horne*, 20.

46. Macnaughtan, "Sir William Van Horne," 243.

47. Vaughan, *The Life and Work of Sir William Van Horne*, 21.

48. Van Horne, undated letter to his grandson (MG29 A60, vol. 102).

49. James McPherson, *Battle Cry for Freedom: The Civil War Era* (New York: Oxford University Press, 1988), 12.

50. Ibid.

51. Tyrus Hurd to Addie Hurd, September 15, 1857 (MG29 A60, vol. 95, Hurd family 1846–1904).

52. John F. Stover, *The Routledge Historical Atlas of the American Railroads* (New York: Routledge, 1999), 20.

53. Alfred D. Chandler, Jr., "The Railroads: Pioneers in Modern Corporate Management," (*Business History Review*, #1, 1965), 16.

54. Vaughan, *The Life and Work of Sir William Van Horne*, 22–23.

55. Vaughan, *The Life and Work of Sir William Van Horne*, 23.

56. Justin Kaplan, *Walt Whitman: A Life* (Toronto: Bantam Books, 1982), 261.

57. Van Horne to S.S. McClure, January 31, 1910, MG29 A60, vol. 74, S.S. McClure, 1909–14.

58. McPherson, 274.

59. Sterling, "History of Joliet, Illinois."

60. Sterling, "History of Joliet, Illinois."

61. McPherson, 308.

62. Jensen, *Illinois*, 67.

63. John F. Stover, *The Routledge Historical Atlas of the American Railroads* (New York: Routledge, 1999), 28.

64. Macnaughtan, "Sir William Van Horne," 244.

65. James Lemly, *The Gulf, Mobile and Ohio: A Railroad that Had to Expand or Expire* (Homewood: Richard D. Irwin, 1953), 316.

66. Stewart Holbrook, *The Story of American Railroads* (New York: Crown Publishers, 1947), 320–21.

67. Vaughan, *The Life and Work of Sir William Van Horne*, 27.

68. Van Horne to Addie Hurd, January 14, 1865 (MG29 A60, vol. 87, file n.d., 1865–66).

69. Information supplied by Gene Glendinning, author of *The Chicago & Alton Railroad: The Only Way* (DeKalb: Northern Illinois University Press, 2002).

70. G. Mercer Adam, ed., *Prominent Men of Canada* (Toronto: Canadian Biographical Publishing Company, 1892), 473.

71. Van Horne to Addie Hurd, January 14, 1865 (MG29 A60, vol. 87, file n.d., 1865–66).

72. Vaughan, *The Life and Work of Sir William Van Horne*, 28–29.

73. Van Horne to Addie Hurd, January 14, 1865 (MG29 A60, vol. 87, file part 1, n.d., 1865–66).

74. Vaughan, *The Life and Work of Sir William Van Horne*, 29.

75. Van Horne to Addie Hurd, December 5, 1865 (MG29 A60, vol. 87, file (part 1), n.d., 1865–66).

76. MG29 A60, vol. 96, file comet sighting 1868.

77. *Genealogical and Biographical Record of Will County* (Chicago: Biographical Publishing Company, 1900), 554.

78. Tyrus Hurd to Addie Hurd, April 10, 1860 (MG29 A60, vol. 95, Hurd Family 1846–1904).

79. Vaughan, *The Life and Work of Sir William Van Horne*, 30.

80. Katherine Hughes mss. (MG30 D71, vol. 2, file 11.2).

81. Henry Beckles Willson, *From Quebec to Piccadilly and Other Places, Some Anglo–Canadian Memories* (London: Jonathan Cape Ltd, 1929), 55.

82. Oakwood Cemetery records.

83. Ethel Hurd to Anna Hurd, May 18, 1868 (MG29 A60, vol. 95, Anna Hurd: Family corr., 1868–1892).

84. Lombard University 1889–90 catalogue.

85. *The Magazine of History With Notes and Queries*, Extra Number, #102, vol. 26, Number 1, 135, and vol. 26, Number 2, 8.

86. Mrs. Henry Sanderson to Addie Van Horne, Sr. August 26, 1908 (MG29 A60, vol. 89, miscell. corr. (part 4), 1896–99).

87. Addie Van Horne Sr. to Mrs. Henry Sanderson, n.d. (MG29 A60, vol. 89, miscell. (part 4), 1896–99).

88. Vaughan, *The Life and Work of Sir William Van Horne*, 30.

89. Addie Hurd to Van Horne, October 12, 1864 (MG29 A60, vol. 86, file Lucy Adeline Hurd 1864–65).

90. Van Horne to Addie Hurd, March 4, 1865 (MG29 A60, vol. 87,

n.d., 1865–66).

91.   Van Horne to Addie Hurd, April 24, 1866 (MG29 A60, vol. 87, file (part 1), n.d., 1865–66).

92.   Robert C. Reed, *Train Wrecks A Pictorial History of Accidents on the Main Line* (New York: Bonanza Book, 1968), 17, 27.

93.   Van Horne to Addie Hurd, April 24, 1866 (MG29 A60, vol. 87, file (part 1), n.d., 1865–66).

94.   Van Horne to Addie Hurd, October 2, 1866 (MG29 A60, vol. 87, file (part 1), 1865–66).

95.   Van Horne to Addie Hurd, April 18, 1866 (MG29 A60, vol. 87, file (part 1), n.d., 1865–66).

96.   Van Horne to Addie Hurd, June 30, 1866 (MG29 A60, vol. 87, file (part 1), n.d., 1865–66).

97.   Addie Hurd to Van Horne July 9, 1866 (MG29 A60, vol. 86, Lucy Adeline Hurd, 1866 (part 2).

98.   Anna Hurd to her daughter, March 10, 1867, and May 26, 1867 (MG29 A60, vol. 88, file Anna Hurd, n.d., 1859–69).

99.   Addie Hurd to Van Horne, December 27, 1866 (MG29 A60, vol. 86, Lucy Adeline Hurd, 1866, part 1).

100.   Van Horne to Addie Hurd.

101.   Addic Hurd to Van Horne, March 6, 1867 (MG29 A60, vol. 86, Lucy Adeline Hurd, 1867).

102.   Copy of marriage certificate issued by the county court of Will County, Illinois, and *Joliet Signal,* March 26, 1867.

103.   Van Horne to his wife, April 2, 1867 (MG29 A60, file 1867–72 (part 2)).

104.   Addie Van Horne to her husband, April 2, 1867 (MG29 A60, vol. 86, file Adeline Van Horne, 1867).

105.   Van Horne to his wife, July 6, 1867 (MG29 A60, vol. 87, file 1867–72 (part 2)).

106.   W.H. Stennett to Van Horne, April 4, 1912 (Microfilm M7494, 82.5.653).

107.   Walter Licht, *Working for the Railroad: The Organization of Work in the Nineteenth Century* (Princeton, N.J.: Princeton University Press, 1983), 157.

108.   Appointment notice (MG29 A60, vol. 87, file 1867–72).

109.   Printed announcement under the signature of JC McMullin (MG29 A60, vol. 79, chronological corr., 1866–69).

110.   Van Horne to a cousin, June 8, 1868 (MG29 A60, vol. 95, Van Horne family miscellaneous).

111.   Elizabeth Metzger Armstrong, *Where We Live: Alton*. Published by the Missouri Historical Society and reproduced on the Internet, http://www.ezl.com/~jtsgeneralstore/where.html

112.   Van Horne obituary, the *Alton Telegraph*, September 13, 1915.

113.   Van Horne to his wife, February 16, 1869 (MG29 A60, vol. 87, file 1867–72 (part 2)).

114.   Lemly, 316; and Gene V. Glendinning, *The Chicago & Alton Railroad: The Only Way* (DeKalb: Northern Illinois University Press, 2002), 68.

115.   Vaughan, *The Life and Work of Sir William Van Horne*, 33.

116.   Article on Chicago in the Encyclopedia Britannica, vol.5 (Chicago: William Benton, Publisher, 1970), 481–482, 489; The Chicago Historical Society and the Trustees of Northwestern University, "The Great Chicago Fire and the Web of Memory," on the Internet; and Martha Black, *My Seventy Years* (London: Nelson, 1938), 26–27, 29.

117.   *Chicago City Directory*, 1871 census edition, 1128; and Vaughan, *The Life and Work of Sir William Van Horne*, 33, 34.

118.   Black, 29.

119.   Vaughan, *The Life and Work of Sir William Van Horne*, 34.

120.   Van Horne to Addie Van Horne, September 19, 1870 (MG29 A60, vol. 87, file W.C. Van Horne (part 2) 1867–1872).

121.   T.B. Blackstone to Van Horne, July 8, 1872 (MG29 A60, vol. 79, chronological corr., 1872–79).

122.   Van Horne to his wife, August 28, 1872 (MG29 A60, vol. 87, file 1867–72 (part 2)).

123.   Van Horne to Addie Van Horne, July 10, 1872 (MG29 A60, vol. 87, file 1867–72 (part 2)).

124.   J.H. Mosgrove, "Famous Railway Head Has Brush With Notorious Bandit Gang" (*Edmonton Bulletin*, October 6, 1934).

125.   Jean Strouse, *Morgan: American Financier* (New York: Random House, 1999), 152.

126.   Vaughan, *The Life and Work of Sir William Van Horne*, 36.

127.   Vaughan, *The Life and Work of Sir William Van Horne*, 37.

128.   Peter Newman, "Sir William Van Horne the nation builder" (*The Montrealer*, June 1959), 43.

129.   Charlotte Eaton, "Sir William Van Horne" (n.d., 17, MG29 A60, vol. 102); and Vaughan, *The Life and Work of Sir William Van Horne*, 39.

130.   Van Horne to his wife, June 28, 1874 (MG29 A60, vol. 87, file

1876–1882 (part 3)).

131. D.W. Thomas to Van Horne, June 30, 1874 (MG29 A60, vol, 79, chron. corr., 1872–79).

132. Copy of resolution in board minutes (MG29 A60, vol. 79, chron. corr., 1872–79).

133. J.P. Hall to Van Horne, July 11, 1874 (MG29 A60, vol. 79, chron. corr., 1872–79).

134. Father O'Reilly to Van Horne, July 1, 1874 (MG29 A60, vol. 79, chron. corr. 1872–79).

135. Van Horne to his wife, July 14, 1874 (MG29 A60, vol. 87, W.C. Van Horne (part 3), 1876–82.

136. Van Horne to his wife, July 14, 1874 (MG29 A60, vol. 87, file 1876–82 (part 2)).

137. Van Horne to his wife, August 10, 1874 (MG29 A60, vol. 87, file 1876–82 (part 2)).

138. John F. Stover, *The Routledge Historical Atlas of the American Railroads* (New York and London: Routledge, 1999), 32.

139. Gale Allen, *Building the Railroad of the Minnesota Valley* (typescript produced by the Minnesota Historical Society, 1947).

140. Chandler, *The Visible Hand*, 151.

141. Van Horne to T.B. Blackstone, March 25, 1876 (Southern Minnesota letterbook, 1876–78, MG29 A60, vol. 58), 55.

142. Vaughan, *The Life and Work of Sir William Van Horne*, 41–42.

143. Van Horne to A.P. Mann, August 26, 1876 (MG29 A60, vol. 59, Southern Minnesota letterbook, 1876–78), 247.

144. Van Horne to Cornelius Gold, February 14, 1875 (MG29 A60, vol. 58, letterbook 1875–76), 38–39.

145. Van Horne to Cornelius Gold, November 5, 1877 (MG29 A60, vol. 59, Southern Minnesota letterbook, 1876–78), 762.

146. Vaughan, *The Life and Work of Sir William Van Horne*, 42.

147. Van Horne to his wife, January 22, 1876 (MG29 A60, vol. 87, file 1876–82 (part 3)).

148. Van Horne to Cornelius Gold, March 11, 1876 (MG29 A60, Southern Minnesota letterbook, 1876–78, vol. 59).

149. Van Horne to Cornelius Gold, June 11, 1876 (MG29 A60, vol. 58, Southern Minnesota letterbook, 1875–76), 116.

150. Vaughan, *The Life and Work of Sir William Van Horne*, 44–45.

151. Van Horne to Cornelius Gold, June 2, 1876 (MG29 A60, vol. 58, Southern Minnesota letterbook, 1876–78), 90.

152. Van Horne to Peter Myers, June 1, 1878 (MG29 A60, vol. 59,

Southern Minnesota letterbook, 1878–79), 13–14.

153. Annette Akins, *Harvest of Grief: Grasshopper Plagues and Public Assistance in Minnesota, 1873–78* (St. Paul: Minnesota Historical Society, 1984), 15.

154. Vaughan, *The Life and Work of Sir William Van Horne*, 45.

155. Van Horne to Cornelius Gold, August 26, 1876 (Southern Minnesota letterbook, 1876–78, MG29 A60, vol. 59).

156. Van Horne to Cornelius Gold, January 15, 1878 (MG29 A60, vol. 59, Southern Minnesota letterbook 1876–78), 859.

157. Van Horne to Cornelius Gold, January 15, 1878 (MG29 A60, vol. 59, Southern Minnesota letterbook, 1876–78), 862.

158. Katherine Hughes draft mss. (MG30 D71, vol. 2, 11.31), 63.

159. Van Horne to Peter Myers, July 22, 1877 (MG29 A60, vol. 59, Southern Minnesota letterbook, 1876–78), 592.

160. Van Horne to Peter Myers, July 22, 1877 (MG29 A60, vol. 59, Southern Minnesota letterbook, 1876–78), 593.

161. Katherine Hughes draft mss. (MG29 A60, vol. 2, 11.31), 63.

162. Van Horne to J.B. Dumont, February 8, 1876 (MG29 A60, vol. 58, Southern Minnesota letterbook, 1875–76), 395.

163. Van Horne to J.B. Dumont, February 9, 1876 (MG29 A60, vol. 58, Southern Minnesota letterbook, 1875–76), 403.

164. Van Horne to J.J. Mitchell, May 22, 1876 (MG29 A60, vol. 59, Southern Minnesota letterbook, 1876–78), 86.

165. Van Horne to P.M. Myers, November 9, 1877 (MG29 A60, vol. 59, Southern Minnesota letterbook, 1876–78), 772.

166. Van Horne to P.M. Myers, March 24, 1876 (MG29 A60, vol. 59, Southern Minnesota letterbook, 1876–78), 31.

167. *St. Paul Dispatch* (vol. X, #276, January 21, 1878), 2.

168. Van Horne to the Hon. F.A. Day, February 10, 1878 (MG29 A60, vol. 59, Southern Minnesota letterbook, 1876–78), 887.

169. Katherine Hughes manuscript (MG30 D71, vol. 2, 11.3), 70–71.

170. Van Horne to J.C. Easton, November 18, 1877 (MG29 A60, vol. 59, Southern Minnesota letterbook, 1878–79), 783.

171. Van Horne to P.M. Myers, March 6, 1876 (MG29 A60, vol. 59, Southern Minnesota letterbook, 1876–78), 10.

172. Van Horne to Cornelius Gold, March 5, 1876 (MG29 A60, vol. 59, Southern Minnesota letterbook, 1876–78), 8.

173. Van Horne to Cornelius Gold, January 16, 1878 (MG29 A60, vol. 59, Southern Minnesota letterbook, 1876–78), 857.

174. Van Horne to Cornelius Gold, February 10, 1878 (MG29 A60,

vol. 59, Southern Minnesota letterbook, 1876–78), 889.

175. Van Horne to Cornelius Gold, March 8, 1878 (MG29 A60, vol. 59), 905.

176. Ibid.

177. Van Horne to Cornelius Gold, March 8, 1878 (MG29 A60, vol. 59, Southern Minnesota letterbook, 1876–68), 906–07.

178. Katherine Hughes draft mss, MG30 D71, vol. 2, 11.3, 67–68.

179. James J. Hill to O.N. Mackintosh, October 22, 1915 (J.J. Hill letterbook, 5/27/11 – 6/10/16), 895.

180. Albro Martin, *James J. Hill and the Opening of the Northwest* (New York: Oxford University Press, 1986), 293.

181. Van Horne to Cornelius Gold, April 21, 1878 (MG29 A60, vol. 59, Southern Minnesota letterbook, 1876–78), 920.

182. James P. Shannon, *Catholic Colonization on the Western Frontier* (New York: Arno Press, 1976), 54 and ix.

183. Van Horne to Cornelius Gold, May 4, 1878 (MG29 A60, vol. 59, Southern Minnesota letterbook, 1876–78), 939.

184. Anonymous, "Illinois Central Telegraph Boy Won Fame as Rail Builder" (*Illinois Central Magazine,* vol. 43, May 1955), 18.

185. Van Horne to his wife, March 31, 1878 (vol. 87, W.C. Van Horne, 1876–82, part 3).

186. Adaline Van Horne to her husband, April 1, 1878 (MG29 A60, vol. 86, Lucy Adaline Van Horne, 1876–82).

187. Van Horne to Cornelius Gold, July 22, 1878 (MG29 A60, vol. 59, Southern Minnesota letterbook, 1878–79), 32–33.

188. Van Horne to J.J. Mitchell, May 22, 1876 (MG29 A60, vol. 58, Southern Minnesota letterbook), 86.

189. Jeffrey Stanton, "Coney Island — Early Years (1609–1880)" (http://naid.sppsr.ucla.edu/coneyisland/articles/earlyhistory.htm)

190. Van Horne to his wife, September 12, 1878, (MG29 A60, vol. 87, W.C. Van Horne, 1876–82, part 3).

191. Stanton, "Coney Island — Early Years (1609–1880)."

192. William R. Marshall to Van Horne, September 22, 1878 (MG29 A60, vol. 79, chron. corr., 1872–79).

193. Lemly, 316.

194. Vaughan, *The Life and Work of Sir William Van Horne*, 30.

195. Lemly, 316.

196. Information provided by Gene V. Glendinning of the Baltimore and Ohio Historical Society.

197. Katherine Hughes draft mss. (vol. 2, 11.3), 75.

198. Katherine Hughes, draft mss., 75–76.

199. Vaughan, *The Life and Work of Sir William Van Horne*, 51–53.

200. Vaughan, *The Life and Work of Sir William Van Horne*, 62.

201. Vaughan, *The Life and Work of Sir William Van Horne*, 63.

202. Mrs. Van Horne to Mary Van Horne, October 27, 1878 (MG29 A60, vol. 95, Hurd family 1846–1904).

203. Mrs. Van Horne to Annah McKee, June 8, 1879 (MG29 A60, vol. 95, file Annah McKee, 1846–1881).

204. MG29 A60, vol. 84, Freeborn County, Minn., 1877–81 and Faribault County, Minn., 1876–80.

205. Promissory note signed by Van Horne (MG29 A60, vol. 84, Freeborn County, Minn., 1877–81).

206. Charles R. Wood and Dorothy M. Wood, *Milwaukee Road West* (Seattle: Superior Publishing Company, 1972), 15.

207. Julius Grodinsky, *Transcontinental Railway Strategy, 1869–1893: A Study of Businessmen* (Philadelphia: University of Pennsylvania Press, 1962), 127.

208. S.A. Miller to Van Horne, January 6, 1880 (MG29 A60, vol. 87, file fossils (part 1), 1874–80).

209. Van Horne to William Arnold, December 3, 1879 (MG29 A60, vol. 59, Southern Minnesota letterbook, 1878–79).

210. Van Horne to Cornelius Gold, October 28, 1879 (MG29 A60, vol. 59, Southern Minnesota letterbook 1878–79), 429.

211. Appointment notice from S.S. Merrill (MG29 A60, vol. 70, file Chicago, M.)

212. Van Horne to S. Stein (?), October 31, 1879 (MG29 A60, vol. 59, Southern Minnesota letterbook, 1878–79), 423; and Van Horne to St. Stein, November 24, 1879 (MG29 A60, vol. 59, Southern Minnesota letterbook, 1878–79), 447.

213. Frank H. Taylor, "Through to St. Paul and Minneapolis 1881" (scrapbook, n.d., 1885–89, MG29 A60, vol. 104).

214. Ibid.

215. Van Horne to his wife, January 2, 1880 (MG29 A60, vol. 87, W.C. Van Horne, 1876–82, part 3).

216. Van Horne to his wife, January 2, 1880 (MG29 A60, vol. 87, file 1876–82, part 3).

217. Vaughan, *The Life and Work of Sir William Van Horne*, 55; and *The Historical Guide to North American Railroads*, 2nd edition (Waukesha, Wisc.: Kalmbach Publishing Company, 2000), 164.

218. Charles R. Wood and Dorothy M. Wood, 21.

219. Vaughan, *The Life and Work of Sir William Van Horne,* 56.

220. Vaughan, *The Life and Work of Sir William Van Horne,* 57.

221. Frank Underwood to Katherine Hughes (MG30 D71, vol. 1, corr. Pierce–Worley).

222. John A, Eagle, *The Canadian Pacific Railway and the Development of Western Canada* (Montreal, Kingston, London: McGill–Queen's University Press, 1989), 11.

223. Vaughan, *The Life and Work of Sir William Van Horne,* 58.

224. Van Horne to Cornelius Gold, January 27, 1875 (MG29 A60, vol. 58), 17.

225. Vaughan, *The Life and Work of Sir William Van Horne,* 59–60.

226. W. Kaye Lamb, *History of the Canadian Pacific Railway* (New York: Macmillan Publishing Co. Inc., 1977), 14.

227. Donald Creighton, *John A. Macdonald: The Old Chieftain* (Toronto: The Macmillan Company of Canada Limited, 1955), 238–39.

228. Albro Martin, 248.

229. Michael P. Malone, *James J. Hill: Empire Builder of the Northwest* (Norman: University of Oklahoma Press, 1996), 7.

230. James Shannon, *Catholic Colonization on the Western Frontier* (New York: Arno Press, 1976), 1.

231. Albro Martin, 125.

232. Albro Martin, 115.

233. Donna McDonald, *Lord Strathcona: A Biography of Donald Alexander Smith* (Toronto: Dundurn Press, 1996), 263.

234. Maury Klein, review of *The Man Who Found the Money: John Stewart Kennedy and the Financing of Western Railroads* (*Business History Review,* vol. 71. no. 2. summer 1997), 326.

235. Van Horne to Beckles Willson, September 10, 1914 (MG30 D5, file Beckles Willson, corr. gen., Strathcona, 1 1897–1915).

236. Peter B. Waite, *Canada 1874–1896: Arduous Destiny* (Toronto: McClelland and Stewart, 1971), 107.

237. Malone, 62.

238. Lamb, 63.

239. Albro Martin, 239.

240. Creighton, 301.

241. Lamb, 71.

242. Bill McKee and Georgeen Klassen, *Trail of Iron: The CPR and the Birth of the West* (Vancouver/Toronto: The Glenbow–Alberta Institute in association with Douglas & McIntyre, 1983), 18.

243. *House of Commons Debates* (Session 1880–81, January 27, 1881), 732.
244. *House of Commons Debates* (Session 1880–81, January 26, 1881), 725.
245. Malone, 68.
246. Albro Martin, 241.
247. R.B. Angus to Hill, February 10, 1882 (MG29 A28, Book 2), 53.
248. James J. Hill to O.N. Mackintosh, October 22, 1915 (JJ Hill letterbook, 5/27/11 – 6/10/16), 895.
249. Vaughan, *The Life and Work of Sir William Van Horne*, 74.
250. *Manitoba Free Press,* October 8, 1881.
251. *Manitoba Free Press,* November 2, 1881.
252. *The St. Paul Pioneer Press* (reported in the *Manitoba Free Press,* November 12, 1881).
253. J.J. Hill to George Stephen, October 17, 1881 (J.J. Hill letterpress books, 1866–1916, series R, 1877–98), 107.
254. Katherine Hughes (MG30 D71, vol. 2, file 11.4), 99.
255. J.J. Hill to Van Horne, October 17, 1881 (J.J. Hill letterpress books, 1866–1916, Series R 1877–98), 110.
256. J.J. Hill to Stephen (J.J. Hill letterpress books, 1866–1916, Series R, 1887–98), 107.
257. *The Railway Journal* (Carroll Ryan, *Men of the Day: A Canadian Portrait Gallery,* edited by Louis J.C.H. Taché, Montreal, c.1890), 345.
258. *Manitoba Free Press,* November 18, 1881.
259. R.B. Angus to Duncan McIntyre, November 14, 1881 (J.J. Hill letterpress books, 1866–1916, series R, 1877– 98), 117–18.
260. R.B. Angus to Hill, December 2, 1881 (J.J. Hill general corr., November 1 – December 10).
261. Angus to Van Horne, December 6, 1881 (MG29 A28, letterbook 2), 10.
262. Vaughan, *The Life and Work of Sir William Van Horne*, 75.
263. *Manitoba Daily Free Press,* January 3, 1882.
264. *Manitoba Daily Free Press,* January 2, 1882.
265. R.G. MacBeth, *The Romance of the Canadian Pacific Railway* (Toronto: Ryerson Press, 1924), 79.
266. Van Horne to his wife, February 13, 1882 (MG29 A60, vol. 87, 1876–82, part 3).
267. Censuses of Canada 1871–1971. Reproduced in Alan Artibise, *Winnipeg: An Illustrated History* (Toronto: James Lorimer &

Company, 1977), 202.

268. "Our Prairie Empire," *The Globe* (Toronto, August 26, 1881).

269. George Ham, *Reminiscences of a Raconteur* (Toronto: The Musson Book Company Ltd., 1921), 51.

270. *Manitoba Daily Free Press* (January 4, 1882).

271. M.F. Hurd to Samuel B. Reed, January 23, 1882 (MG29 A60, vol. 95, Hurd Family, 1846–1904).

272. Raymond Hull, ed., *Charles Aeneas Shaw: Tales of a Pioneer Surveyor* (Don Mills, Ontario: Longman Canada Ltd., 1970), 91.

273. Pierre Berton, *The Great Railway, vol. 2: The Last Spike, 1881–1885* (Toronto: McClelland and Stewart, 1971), 90.

274. *The Manitoba Free Press* (February 14, 1882), 6.

275. R.B. Angus to J.J. Hill, February 10, 1882 (MG29 A28, letter-book 2), 52.

276. Van Horne to J.J. Hill, March 18, 1882 (copy of Minnesota Historical Society original letter in the J.J. Hill papers, general corr., March 13–25, 1882).

277. Harry Armstrong, *One Canadian, 1853–1933* (Unpublished memoir, MG30 B26), 128–29.

278. *The Sun* (Winnipeg, July 13, 1882).

279. Harry Armstrong, 127.

280. J.J. Hill to George Stephen, April 6, 1882 (J.J. Hill letterbook, 9/24/79 – 7/20/82), 423.

281. Harry Armstrong, 133.

282. J.H. Secretan, to Katherine Hughes, March 14, 1916 (MG30, D71, vol. 1, corr., Pearce–Worley).

283. D.B. Hanna, *Trains of Recollection Drawn from Fifty Years of Railway Service in Scotland and Canada, as told to Arthur Hawkes* (Toronto: The Macmillan Company of Canada Ltd., at St. Martin's House, 1924), 40.

284. *Manitoba Free Press* (January 3, 1882).

285. Ibid.

286. Lamb, 84.

287. Malone, 70.

288. *The Globe* (Toronto, February 4, 1882), 16.

289. *The Globe* (June 23, 1882), 5.

290. *Manitoba Free Press* (May 4, 1882).

291. *Manitoba Free Press* (January 1,6 1882).

292. "Railway Ripples" (*Manitoba Free Press*, January 16, 1882).

293. *Manitoba Free Press* (February 16, 1882).

294. Malone, 72.

295. Van Horne to Andrew Onderdonk, September 10, 1884 (CPPL, Letterbook 7, M2252), 482.

296. *The Globe* (Toronto, January 12, 1882, quoted in "Railway Ripples," the *Manitoba Free Press*, January 18, 1882).

297. *The Globe* (Toronto, January 14, 1882).

298. Van Horne to his wife, January 19, 1882 (MG29 A60, vol. 87, file WC Van Horne, part 3, 1876–82).

299. Robert M. Hamilton and Dorothy Shields, eds., *Canadian Quotations and Phrases*, revised and enlarged edition (Toronto: McClelland and Stewart, 1979), 650.

300. Sandra Gwynn, *Tapestry of War* (Toronto: Harper Collins Publishers Ltd., 1992), 73.

301. Charlotte Gray, *Sisters in the Wilderness: The Lives of Susanna Moodie and Catherine Parr Trail* (Toronto: Penquin Books, 1999), 324.

302. Van Horne to his wife, January 29, 1882 (Van Horne papers, MG29 A60, vol. 87, 1876–82, part 3).

303. Pierre Berton, *The Last Spike*, abridged version (Toronto: McClelland and Stewart, 1974), 296.

304. Van Horne to J.J. Hill, March 18, 1882 (J.J. Hill Papers, general corr., 13–25 March 1882).

305. Ibid.

306. Van Horne to his wife, March 15, 1882 (MG29 A60, vol. 87, file 1876–82, part 3); and *Manitoba Daily Free Press* (March 13, 1882).

307. Van Horne to Bennie Van Horne, March 15, 1882 (MG29 A60, vol. 94, W.C. Van Horne 1882).

308. "The Diary of Arthur Rowe Miller" (*Saskatchewan History*, vol. X, no. 2, spring 1957), 65.

309. Van Horne to his son, April 9, 1882 (MG29 A60, vol. 97, W. C. Van Horne 1882).

310. Van Horne to his wife, March 15 (1882, vol. 87, file 1876–82, part 3).

311. R.B. Angus to J.J. Hill, June 18, 1882 (J.J. Hill papers, general corr., 19–29 June 1882).

312. Van Horne to James Hill, July 2, 1882 (Manitoba Historical Society original in the J.J. Hill papers, general corr., June 30 – July 10, 1882).

313. *Manitoba Daily Free Press* (July 11, 1882).

314. Van Horne to J.J. Hill, May 20, 1882 (Minnesota Historical Society original reproduced in the J.J. Hill papers, general corr., May 15 – June 16, 1882).

315. Van Horne to his wife, July 2, 1882 (MG29 A60, vol. 87, 1876–82, part 3).

316. George Stephen to J.J. Hill, June 26, 1882 (J.J. Hill papers, general corr., June 19–29, 1882).

317. Van Horne to J.J. Hill, June 19, 1882 (Minnesota Historical Society original in the J.J. Hill papers, general corr., June 19–29, 1882).

318. Van Horne to J.J. Hill, June 26, 1882 (Minnesota Historical Society original in the J.J. Hill papers, general corr., June 19–29, 1882).

319. George Stephen to J.J. Hill, June 26, 1882 (J.J. Hill papers, general corr., June 19–29, 1882).

320. Van Horne to J.J. Hill, June 26, 1882 (Minnesota Historical Society original letter in J.J. Hill papers, general corr., June 19–29, 1882).

321. Van Horne to his wife, June 23, 1882 (MG29 A60, vol. 87, 1876–82, part 3).

322. Stephen E. Ambrose, *Nothing Like it in the World: The Men Who Built the Transcontinental Railroad 1863–1869* (New York: Simon and Schuster, 2000), 25.

323. George H. Buck, *From Summit to Sea: An Illustrated History of Railroads in British Columbia and Alberta* (Calgary: Fifth House Ltd., 1997), 20.

324. Katherine Hughes manuscript (MG30 D71, vol. 2. file 11.4), 110.

325. Roger Fry, *Burlington Magazine* (No. CLI, vol. XXVII), 39.

326. Charlotte Eaton, interview with Van Horne (MG29 A60, vol. 102), 14.

327. Katherine Hughes manuscript (MG30 D71, vol. 2, file 11.4), 115.

328. J.H. Secretan, *Canada's Great Highway: From the First Stake to the Last Spike* (London: John Lane The Bodley Head Limited, 1924), 104–105.

329. *Winnipeg Sun,* 10 June 1882.

330. McDonald, 309.

331. Van Horne to his wife, October 28, 1882 (MG29 A60, vol. 87, 1876–82, part 3).

332. Fred Angus, "The Saskatchewan" (*Canadian Rail,* No. 375, July August 1983), 117; and Van Horne to his wife, August 19, 1882 (MG29 A60, vol. 87, 1876–82, part 3).

333. *Manitoba Free Press* (October 30, 1882), 8.

334. Christopher Armstrong and H.V. Nelles, *Southern Exposure: Canadian Promoters in Lain America and the Caribbean 1896–1930* (Toronto: University of Toronto Press, 1988), 8.

335. *The Gazette* (Montreal, November 23 and 25, 1882).

336. Mary Van Horne, daily journals, 1893–96 (MG29 A60, vol. 95, April 30, 1896).

337. Young Addie Van Horne to her father, July 23, 1882 (MG29 A60, vol. 87, Adaline Van Horne, n.d., 1880–1914).

338. Van Horne to his wife, 14 September 1882, MG29 A60, vol. 87, file 1876–82, part 3.

339. Edgar Andrew Collard, "Montreal Yesterdays: More Stories from All Our Yesterdays" (Montreal: *The Gazette*, 1989), 6.

340. Van Horne to his wife, 14 September 1882, MG29 A60, vol. 87, file 1876–82, part 3.

341. "Van Horne's other legacy" (*The Montreal Star*, August 4, 1973).

342. Van Horne to his wife, November 27, 1882 (MG29 A60, vol. 87, file 1876–82, part 3).

343. Ibid.

344. *The Victoria Daily Times* (November 7, 1885), 4.

345. Omer Lavallée, *Van Horne's Road: An illustrated account of the construction and first years of operation of the Canadian Pacific transcontinental railway* (Montreal: Railfare Enterprises Ltd., 1974), 83.

346. Van Horne to Addie Van Horne, February 20, 1883 (MG29 A60, vol. 87).

347. Ibid.

348. Vaughan, *The Life and Work of Sir William Van Horne*, 91.

349. *The Globe* (Toronto, June 13, 1899), 5.

350. Lamb, 113–14.

351. Van Horne to Middleton, September 10, 1883 (CPPL, Letterbook #2, Microfilm M2248), 827, 829.

352. Berton, *The Last Spike*, 272.

353. Van Horne to the chairman of the Board of Steamboat Inspection, June 25, 1883 (CPPL, Letterbook #2, Microfilm 2248), 184.

354. Dana Ashdown, *Railway Steamships of Ontario* (Erin, Ontario: The Boston Mills Press, 1988), 241.

355. Hill to George Stephen, August 10, 1883 (J.J. Hill letterbook, 8/1/83 – 1/11/84), 174–78.

356. J.J. Hill to R.B. Angus, April 3, 1883 (J.J. Hill letterbook, 3/15/83 – 7/31/83), 21.

357. U.S. Senate Commission on Interstate Commerce Commission

(51st Congress, 1st Session, Report #847, 1890), 168.

358. James A. MacGregor, *Father Lacombe* (Edmonton: Hurtig Publishers, 1975), 261.

359. Van Horne to Katherine Hughes, January 27, 1911 (MG29 A60, vol. 73, file Katherine Hughes).

360. John Saywell, ed., *The Canadian Journal of Lady Aberdeen, 1893–1898* (Toronto: Champlain Society, 1960), 138.

361. Preface that Van Horne wrote for a biography of Father Lacombe by Katherine Hughes (MG29 A60, vol. 73, file Katherine Hughes, 1911–15).

362. Vaughan, *The Life and Work of Sir William Van Horne*, 94; and MacGregor, 259–60.

363. Berton, *The Last Spike*, 245.

364. Saywell, 138.

365. James Ross to Van Horne, November 23, 1883, reproduced in Sessional Paper Number 31, p. 41 (Sessional Papers, 1884, No. 9, vol. 17).

366. David Cruise and Alison Griffiths, *Lords of the Line* (Markham: Viking, 1988), 188.

367. Van Horne to Robert Glasgow, March 27, 1915 (VH personal letterbook, MG29 A60, vol. 58, file 16), 533–34.

368. Ibid.

369. Harry Armstrong, 177–78.

370. Lamb, 99.

371. Van Horne to ?, April 16, 1883 (CPPL, Letterbook #2, Microfilm M2247), 577.

372. Joseph Hickson to Sir John A. Macdonald, February 7, 1884 (Macdonald papers, vol. 129, 53670).

373. Van Horne to Sir John A. Macdonald, February 14, 1884 (Macdonald papers, vol. 129, 53688).

374. Van Horne to Joseph Hickson, March 21, 1885 (CPPL, Letterbook # 10, Microfilm M2254), 730.

375. O.D. Skelton, *Life and Letters of Sir Wilfrid Laurier.* (Toronto: Oxford University Press, 1921), vol. 1, 272.

376. Berton, *The Last Spike*, 251–52.

377. McDonald, 316.

378. House of Commons Debates (Session 1884, vol. 1, February 5, 1884,) 127.

379. Van Horne to the Hon. Peter Mitchell, April 21, 1884 (CPPL, Letterbook #5, Microfilm M 2250), 675–676.

380. Van Horne to Egan, September 10, 1883 (CPPL, Letterbook #2, Microfilm M2248), 838–40.

381. Macdonald to Stephen, February 18, 1884, in Waite, 136.

382. Waite, 137.

383. Van Horne to Alan Manvel, October 26, 1883 (CPPL, Letterbook #3, Microfilm 2249), 367.

384. Van Horne to Middleton, September 10, 1883 (CPPL, Letterbook #2, Microfilm M2248), 827–29.

385. Van Horne to James Ross, September 10, 1883 (CPPL, Letterbook #2, Microfilm M 2249), 845–47.

386. Ibid.

387. Van Horne to Ross, November 8, 1883 (CPPL, Letterbook #3, Microfilm M2249), 435–436.

388. Van Horne to Rogers, February 6, 1883 (CPPL, Letterbook #2, Microfilm M2247), 279.

389. Van Horne to Egan, May 13, 1884 (CPPL, Letterbook #6, Microfilm M2251), 58–59.

390. Berton, *The Last Spike*, 256.

391. *The Gazette* (Montreal, January 18, 1884).

392. Sir John Willison, *Reminiscences Political and Personal* (Toronto: McClelland and Stewart, 1919), 339–40.

393. Van Horne to Egan, April 28, 1884 (CPPL, Letterbook #5, Microfilm M2250), 757.

394. Van Horne to Ross, May 17, 1884 (CPPL, Letterbook #6, Microfilm M2251), 131–32.

395. Van Horne to Ross, May 17, 1884 (CPPL, Letterbook #6, Microfilm M2251), 135–36.

396. *Manitoba Daily Free Press* (November 9, 1885), 1.

397. Lavallée, 173.

398. Van Horne to John Henry Pope, May 19, 1884 (Macdonald papers, vol. 129, 53640–44).

399. Ibid.

400. T.D. Regehr, "Letters From End of Track" (*The CPR West*, edited by Hugh A. Dempsey, Vancouver: Douglas & McIntyre, 1984), 39.

401. Van Horne to James Ross, May 17, 1884 (CPPL, Letterbook #6, Microfilm M2251), 122–23.

402. Van Horne to Egan, April 28, 1884 (CPPL, Letterbook #5, Microfilm M2250), 755–56.

403. Berton, *The Last Spike*, 297.

404. Macnaughtan, "Sir William Van Horne," 246.

405. Van Horne to Mrs. M. Galbreaith, December 25, 1883 (Letterbook #4, Microfilm M M2249), 31.

406. Van Horne to John Lowe, May 11, 1884 (CPPL, Letterbook #6, Microfilm M2251), 69–74.

407. Berton, *The Last Spike*, 298.

408. Katherine Hughes mss. (MG30 D71, vol. 2), 120.

409. Chandler, *The Visible Hand*, 167.

410. Walter Vaughan, "Sir William Van Horne," *The Maker of Canada Series* (London and Toronto: Oxford University Press, 1926), 142.

411. Vaughan, "Sir William Van Horne," 143.

412. Berton, *The Last Spike*, 300.

413. Van Horne to A.S. McClellan, February 6, 1885 (CPPL, Letterbook #10, Microfilm M2254), 53–58.

414. Allan Pringle, "William Cornelius Van Horne: Art Director, Canadian Pacific Railway" (*The Journal of Canadian Art History*, vol. X111/1 1884), 50.

415. Roger Hall, Gordon Dodds and Stanley Triggs, *The World of William Notman: The Nineteenth Century Through a Master Lens* (Boston: David R. Godine, 1993), 21.

416. Albert Bierstadt to Van Horne, December 16, 1889 (MG29 A60, vol. 87, miscell., 1867–1915).

417. David Laurence Jones, *Tales of the CPR* (Calgary: Fifth House Ltd., 2002), 181.

418. Angus, "The Saskatchewan", 121–22.

419. Katherine Hughes mss. (MG30 D71, vol. 1, file 11 (b)), 1.

420. Summary of correspondence between A.W. Ross and Van Horne, May–December 1884, (Microfilm M7493, 82.5.13–14).

421. Vaughan, *The Life and Work of Sir William Van Horne*, 108.

422. Hughes mss. (MG30 D71, vol. 2, file 11.5), 133.

423. Berton, *The Last Spike*, 303–04.

424. Lamb, 125.

425. John Murray Gibbon, *Canadian Mosaic* (Toronto: McClelland & Stewart, 1938), 200; and Walter Vaughan, *The Life and Work of Sir William Van Horne*, 109.

426. Van Horne to John Nicholson, March 7, 1885 (CPPL, Letterbook #10, Microfilm M2254), 515.

427. Berton, *The Last Spike*, 311.

428. Vaughan, *The Life and Work of Sir William Van Horne*, 110–11.

429. Van Horne to Andrew Onderdonk, September 10, 1884 (CPPL, Letterbook #7, Microfilm M2252), 481.

430. Clara, Lady Rayleigh, Journal and Letters (London: British Association for the Advancement of Science, 1885, microfiche), 51.

431. Van Horne's report to the CPR directors, September 16, 1884 (CPR Reports, 1881–89), 76.

432. Vaughan, *The Life and Work of Sir William Van Horne*, 114.

433. Heather Gilbert, *Awakening Continent: The Life of Lord Mount Stephen, vol. 1* (Aberdeen: Aberdeen University Press, 1965), 167.

434. Skelton, vol. 1, 276.

435. Skelton, vol. 1, 276..

436. Van Horne to an American investor, February 18, 1885 (CPPL, Letterbook #10, Microfilm M2254), 247.

437. McDonald, 320.

438. Van Horne to Joseph Hickson, March 9, 1885 (CPPL, Letterbook #10, Microfilm M2254), 558.

439. Vaughan, *The Life and Work of Sir William Van Horne*, 179.

440. T.S. Higginson to A.W. Burgess, May (?) 20, 1885 (Macdonald papers, vol. 256, 116024–25).

441. McDonald, 322.

442. McDonald, 322.

443. Van Horne to William Whyte, April 23, 1885 (CPPL, Letterbook #11, Microfilm M2254), 239.

444. The *Globe* (Toronto, April 2, 1885).

445. Van Horne to White (?), April 4, 1885 (CPPL, Letterbook #10, Microfilm M2254), 901.

446. Van Horne to S.J. Ritchie, April 4, 1885 (CPPL, Letterbook #10, Microfilm M2254), 906.

447. C. Drinkwater telegram to Sir John A. Macdonald, April 1885 (Macdonald papers, vol. 129, 53591).

448. Van Horne memorandum (MG30 D5, file Beckles Willson, general corr., Strathcona, 1897–1915).

449. Vaughan, *The Life and Work of Sir William Van Horne*, 130.

450. Van Horne to his wife, August 2, 1885 (MG29 A60, vol. 87, file W.C. Van Horne (part 4) 1883–93).

451. Van Horne to a Charlottetown correspondent, August 29, 1885 (CPPL, Letterbook #13, Microfilm M2256), 31.

452. Van Horne to C. McLagan, September 10, 1885 (CPPL, Letterbook #13, Microfilm M2256), 268.

453. Lamb.

454. Landsdowne to Mr. Kippen, August 26, 1885 (MG29 A60, vol. 87, miscell., 1867–1915).

455. Van Horne memorandum (MG30 D5, file Beckles Willson, general corr., Strathcona, 1897–1915).

456. *Manitoba Daily Free Press* (November 9, 1885), 1.

457. *Manitoba Daily Free Press* (November 9), 1.

458. Katherine Hughes papers (MG30 D71, vol. 2, 11 (b)),1

459. Vaughan, *The Life and Work of Sir William Van Horne*, 134.

460. George Stephen to Van Horne, November 21, 1885 (MG29 A60, vol. 79, chronological corr., 1882–89).

461. Thomas Shaughnessy to Walter Vaughan, May 8, 1920 (MG30, A130).

462. Van Horne to his wife, November 8, 1885 (Van Horne personal corr., Microfilm M7494: 82.5.42).

463. Van Horne to Macdonald, November 7, 1885 (Macdonald papers, Microfilm C1558, 53567).

464. Young Addie Van Horne to her father, November 8, 1885 (MG29 A60, vol. 87, file Adeline Van Horne).

465. Vaughan, *The Life and Work of Sir William Van Horne*, 135; and McDonald, 327–28.

466. Vaughan, *The Life and Work of Sir William Van Horne*, 137.

467. Vaughan, *The Life and Work of Sir William Van Horne*, 148.

468. Vaughan, *The Life and Work of Sir William Van Horne*, 148.

469. Van Horne to George Stephen, June 21, 1887 (MG29 A60, vol. 89, file Lord Mount Stephen 1915).

470. Arthur Burgess to Van Horne, May 28, 1894 (Van Horne personal corr., Microfilm M7493, 82.5.197).

471. *Report of the Directors of the Canadian Pacific Railway Company, submitted at the Adjourned Annual General Meeting of the Shareholders, held at Montreal on the 13th June, 1885*, 18.

472. Lamb, 138.

473. Van Horne to Father Lacombe, February 23, 1886 (CPPL, Letterbook #15, Microfilm M2258), 483.

474. Van Horne to Sir Sandford Fleming, May 22, 1886 (CPPL, Letterbook #16, Micrfilm M2259), 723.

475. Lavallée, 250.

476. Louise Reynolds, *Agnes: The Biography of Lady Macdonald* (Ottawa: Carleton University Press, 1990), 105.

477. Agnes Macdonald to Van Horne, January 16, 1886 (MG29 A60, vol. 87, file Lady Macdonald 1885–1890).

478. Maurice Pope, ed., *Public Servant: The Memoirs of Sir Joseph Pope* (Toronto: Oxford University Press, 1960), 52; and Creighton, 459.

479. Pope, *Public Servant*, 56.
480. Lavallée, 289.
481. Mary Van Horne to Bennie, July 25, 1891 (MG29 A60, vol. 94, Sir William Van Horne, 1898–1913).
482. Vaughan, *The Life and Work of Sir William Van Horne*, 184.
483. "Railway Magnates," *Manitoba Daily Free Press* (July 28, 1886).
484. "Railway Magnates."
485. E.J. Hart, *The Selling of Canada: The CPR and the Beginnings of Canadian Tourism* (Banff: Altitude Publishing, 1983), 11.
486. Lavallée, 241.
487. Vaughan, *The Life and Work of Sir William Van Horne*, 145.
488. James E. Vance, Jr., *The North American Railroad: Its Origin, Evolution, and Geography* (Baltimore and London: The Johns Hopkins University Press, 1995), 277.
489. Van Horne to his wife, August 19, 1886 (MG29 A60, vol. 87, file W.C. Van Horne (part 4), 1883–93).
490. Vaughan, *The Life and Work of Sir William Van Horne*, 146.
491. Van Horne to James J. Hill, April 21, 1886 (J.J. Hill papers, general correspondence, 21–23 April 1886).
492. Robert D. Turner, *The Pacific Empresses: An Illustrated History of Canadian Pacific Railway's Empress Liners on the Pacific Ocean* (Victoria: Sono Nis Press, 1981), 21–23.
493. Lamb, 152.
494. Lamb, 152–53.
495. Van Horne to his wife, July 8, 1888 (MG29 A60, vol. 87, file 1883–93, part 4).
496. Lamb, 154.
497. Lamb, 154.
498. Harold Kalman, *A History of Canadian Architecture*, vol. 2, (Toronto: Oxford University Press, 1994), 492.
499. Graeme Pole, *The Canadian Rockies: A History in Photographs* (Banff: Altitude Publishing, 1991), 16.
500. Vaughan, *The Life and Work of Sir William Van Horne*, 151.
501. Kalman, 495.
502. Jones, *Tales of the CPR*, 29–30.
503. Lamb, 183.
504. Kalman, 497.
505. Vaughan, *The Life and Work of Sir William Van Horne*, 152–53.
506. Kate Reed to Van Horne, September 5, 1905 (Van Horne personal corr., Microfilm M7494, 82.5.492.1).

507.	Van Horne to Kate Reed, September 3, 1905 (Box 4, folder 2, Reed papers, McCord Museum, Montreal).

508.	Pringle, 68.

509.	E.J. Hart, "See this World Before the Next," *The CPR West: The Iron Road and the Making of a Nation*, edited by Hugh A. Dempsey (Toronto: Douglas & McIntyre, 1984), 155.

510.	Eagle, *The Canadian Pacific Railway and the Development of Western Canada*, 178.

511.	Van Horne to Rudyard Kipling, April 12, 1906 (Van Horne personal corr., Microfilm M7494, 82.5.896); and Vaughan, *The Life and Work of Sir William Van Horne*, 173.

512.	*Canada: House of Commons Debates* (1885, vol. 1, February 23), 204.

513.	John Henry Pope to Sir John A. Macdonald, August 10, 1888 (MG26 A, vol. 256, 11652–53, Microfilm C1675).

514.	Waymer S. Laberee, "John Henry Pope: Eastern Townships Politician" (M.A. thesis, Bishop's University, 1966), 132.

515.	Lamb, 140.

516.	John Henry Pope to Sir John A. Macdonald, August 22, 1877 (MG26A, vol. 256, 116115, Microfilm C1675).

517.	Norman Thompson and Major J.H. Edgar, *Canadian Railway Development From the Earliest Times* (Toronto: The Macmillan Company of Canada Limited, 1933), 179–80.

518.	*The Globe* (Toronto, June 13, 1899), 5.

519.	Collingwood Schreiber to John Henry Pope, July 22, 1888 (Macdonald papers, MG26A, vol. 256, 116139, Microfilm C11675).

520.	F.H. Schofield, *The Story of Manitoba* (Montreal, Vancouver, Winnipeg: The S.J. Clarke Publishing Co., 1913), 355.

521.	*Winnipeg Morning Call*, May 21, 1887, in Gilbert, *Awakening Continent*, 211.

522.	Gilbert, *Awakening Continent*, 213.

523.	Gilbert, *Awakening Continent*, 214–15.

524.	Van Horne to Hon. Joseph Martin, September 26, 1888 (CPPL, Letterbook #27, Microfilm M2267), 801.

525.	*Manitoba Daily Free Press* (October 20, 1888).

526.	Walter Vaughan, *The Life and Work of Sir William Van Horne*, 158.

527.	Heather Gilbert, *The End of the Road: The Life of Lord Mount Stephen, vol. 2* (Aberdeen: Aberdeen University Press, 1977), 28.

528.	John Julius Norwich, *The Architecture of Southern England*

(London: Macmillan, 1985), 284–85.

529.   *New York Times* (August 8, 1888), 2.

530.   *The Gazette* (Montreal, August 8, 1888), 2.

531.   *The Globe* (Toronto, August 8, 1888), 1.

532.   Vaughan, *The Life and Work of Sir William Van Horne*, 165.

533.   Michael Bliss, *Northern Enterprise: Five Centuries of Canadian Business* (Toronto: McClelland and Stewart, 1987), 294.

534.   George Stephen, R.B. Angus, and other members of the special committee, letter to Van Horne, August 15, 1889 (MG29 A60, vol. 79, chronological correspondence, 1882–89).

535.   Fred Angus, "The Eightieth Anniversary of 'The Short Line" (*Canadian Rail*, # 211, June 1969), 161.

536.   Lamb, 168.

537.   Lamb, 169-170.

538.   Van Horne to Sir John A. Macdonald, July 10, 1889 (Macdonald papers, vol. 288, Microfilm C1689, 131868).

539.   Van Horne to Sir John A. Macdonald, October 31, 1889 (Macdonald papers, vol. 288, Microfilm C1689, 132102).

540.   George Stephen to Sir John A. Macdonald, July 6, 1890 (Macdonald papers, vol. 272, Microfilm C1682, 124429).

541.   Peter Baskerville, "Joseph Hickson" (*Dictionary of Canadian Biography, vol. XII 1891–1900*, Toronto: University of Toronto Press, 1990), 432–43.

542.   Berton, *The Last Spike*, 132–33.

543.   Van Horne to George Stephen, June 12, 1888 (CPPL, Letterbook # 26, Microfilm M2266), 255–57.

544.   Van Horne to George Stephen, October 4, 1888 (CPPL, Letterbook # 27, Microfilm M2267), 475.

545.   A.W. Currie, *The Grand Trunk Railway of Canada* (Toronto: University of Toronto Press, 1957), 318–19.

546.   *The Historical Guide to North American Railroads*, 2nd. ed. (Waukesha: Kalmbach Publishing Co., 2000), 393.

547.   James J. Hill to George Stephen, May 11, 1886, in Cruise and Griffiths, 195.

548.   Albro Martin, 288.

549.   George Stephen to Sir John A. Macdonald, January 26, 1888, in Lamb, 167.

550.   Malone, 174.

551.   James Jerome Hill to Donald Smith, March 11, 1890, in Albro Martin, 474.

552. Van Horne to F.D. Underwood, October 21, 1894 (CPPL, Letterbook # 47, Microfilm M2284), 749.

553. Van Horne's catalogue of his oil paintings, compiled December 6, 1892, in the Montreal Museum of Fine Arts.

554. Van Horne to Thomas Skinner, March 2, 1892 (CPPL, Letterbook # 40, Microfilm M2277), 30.

555. Van Horne to Allen Manvel, November 12, 1894, in Lamb, 203.

556. Van Horne to George Stephen, 1891, in John Murray Gibbon, *Steel of Empire: The Romantic History of the Canadian Pacific, the Northwest Passage of Today* (New York: The Bobbs–Merrill Company, 1935), 338.

557. Mount Stephen to Van Horne, January 28, 1893 (Van Horne personal corr., Microfilm M7493, 82.5.147).

558. Ibid.

559. Lamb, 203.

560. Van Horne to Mount Stephen, July 27, 1894, in Lamb, 204.

561. Strouse, 320.

562. Ty Hurd to his sister, August 13, 1893 (MG29 A60, vol. 89, miscell. corr. (part 3), 1892–96).

563. Van Horne to Sir Charles Hibbert Tupper, November 6, 1894 (CPPL, Lettterbook #47, Microfilm M2284), 867.

564. Van Horne to Colonel John Maclean, January 16, 1912 (MG29 A60, vol. 74, Mc & Mac Miscell., 1908–13).

565. Vaughan, *The Life and Work of Sir William Van Horne*, 237.

566. Van Horne to Thomas Skinner, July 5, 1894 (CPPL, Letterbook #46, Microfilm M2283), 932.

567. Van Horne to Mr. Fritch, March 28, 1895 (MG29 A60, vol. 52, personal letterbook, 1893–96), 178.

568. Robert Horne–Payne to Katherine Hughes, July 24, 1917 (MG30 D71, vol. 1, corr. A–Pam).

569. Van Horne to Mount Stephen, February 16, 1894, in Cruise and Griffiths, 214.

570. Van Horne to Thomas Skinner, November 27, 1894 (CPPL, Letterbook # 47, Microfilm M2284), 996.

571. D.J. Hall, *Clifford Sifton, vol. 1 The Young Napoleon, 1861–1900* (Vancouver: University of British Columbia Press, 1985), 102.

572. Cruise and Griffiths, 216.

573. Cruise and Griffiths, 216.

574. Cruise and Griffiths, 212.

575. Copy of a telegram sent by Mount Stephen to Gaspar Farrer, June 18,

1894 (Van Horne personal corr., Microfilm M7493, 82.5.203).

576. Van Horne to Thomas Skinner, June 20, 1894 (MG29 A60, vol. 52, personal letterbook, 1893–96), 41–43.

577. Van Horne to Thomas Skinner, August 27, 1894 (CPPL, Letterbook #47, Microfilm M2284), 339.

578. Rosemary Lorna Savage, "American Concern Over Railway Competition in the Northwest, 1885–1890" (*Canadian Historical Association Annual Report and Historical Papers* 1942), 82.

579. Savage, 82.

580. Mount Stephen to Van Horne, January 24, 1893 (Van Horne personal corr., Microfilm M7493, 82.5.144).

581. *The Commercial Advertiser* (New York, July 26, 1902, MG29 A60, vol. 41, file 41).

582. J.H. Tuck, "Canadian Railways and Unions in the Running Trades, 1865–1914" (*Relations Industrielles/Industrial Relations,* 1981, vol. 36, No. 1), 117.

583. Tuck.

584. Van Horne to his wife, September 2, 1888 (MG29 A60, vol. 87, file 1883–93).

585. J.D. Edgar to Van Horne, January 2, 1898 (Van Horne personal corr., Microfilm M7493, 82.5.254).

586. Van Horne to Thomas Skinner, November 27, 1894 (CPPL, #47, Microfilm M2284), 995.

587. Van Horne to Thomas Skinner, November 27, 1894 (CPPL, letterbook # 47, Microfilm M2284), 995.

588. Duncan McDowall, *The Light: Brazilian Traction, Light and Power Company Limited, 1899–1845* (Toronto: University of Toronto Press, 1988), 59.

589. Robert Horne–Payne to Van Horne, January 1901 (MG29 A60, vol. 95, Van Horne family: misc. 1868–1932).

590. Van Horne to his wife, December 14, 1894 (MG29 A60, vol. 87, Sir William Van Horne (part 1), 1894–1901).

591. Cruise and Griffiths, 218.

592. Van Horne to his wife, December 14, 1894 (MG29 A60, vol. 87, Sir William Van Horne (part 1), 1894–1901).

593. The Joseph referred to may have been French–born Joseph Favre (1849–1903), who, by the end of his career, was known not only as a great chef but also as an indefatigable organizer on behalf of his profession. See Amy B. Trubek, *Haute Cuisine: How the French Invented the Culinary Profession* (Philadelphia: University of

Pennsylvania Press, 2000), 69.

594. Van Horne to his wife, December 22, 1894 (MG29 A60, vol. 87, Sir William Van Horne (part 1), 1894–1901).

595. Ibid.

596. Van Horne to his wife, January 6, 1895 (MG29 A60, vol. 87, Sir William Van Horne (part 1), 1894–1901).

597. Addie Van Horne to her husband, December 27, 1894 (MG29 A60, vol. 86, Lady Van Horne, 1894–1901).

598. Van Horne to Sir John Abbot, July 3, 1892 (MG26C, vol. 6).

599. Mary Van Horne (MG29 A60, vol. 95, Miss Mary Van Horne: Daily journals, 1893–96).

600. Lord Aberdeen to Van Horne, May 22, 1894 (MG29 A60, vol. 96, Sir William Van Horne: Knighthood 1894).

601. Vaughan, *The Life and Work of Sir William Van Horne*, 239.

602. John W. Mackay to Van Horne, May 26, 1894 (MG29 A60, vol. 96, Knighthood: Congratulations, 1894).

603. Ibid.

604. Ibid.

605. Vaughan, *The Life and Work of Sir William Van Horne*, 240.

606. Van Horne to General Thomas, March 4, 1892 (CPPL, Letterbook # 40, Microfilm M2277).

607. Addie Van Horne to Ethel Hurd, April 23, 1895 (MG29 A60, Hurd Family, 1864–1904).

608. Mount Stephen to Van Horne, February 16, 1895 (Van Horne personal corr., Microfilm M7493, 82.5.230).

609. Editorial, *The Gazette* (Montreal, February 25, 1895).

610. Editorial, *The Globe* (Toronto, February 26, 1895).

611. Cruise and Griffiths, 222.

612. Lamb, 189.

613. Lamb, 192.

614. Eagle, 16.

615. Cruise and Griffiths, xv.

616. Editorial, *The Globe* (Toronto, March 2, 1891).

617. Gilbert, *The End of the Road*, 32.

618. Editorial, *The Globe* (Toronto, March 2, 1891).

619. D.J. Hall, *Clifford Sifton, vol. 1*, 115.

620. Van Horne to Wilfrid Laurier, June 10, 1896 (MG26G, vol. 11, Microfilm C740), 4330.

621. Van Horne to Joseph Martin, June 17, 1896 (MG29 A60, vol. 52, personal letterbook, 1896–97).

622. Van Horne to Laurier, June 10, 1896 (MG26G, vol. 11, 4330, Microfilm C740).

623. Van Horne to Archie Baker (CPPL, letterbook # 47, Microfilm M2284), 454–56.

624. D.J. Hall, *Clifford Sifton, vol. 1*, 131–32.

625. Van Horne to James Edgar, June 29, 1896 (CPPL, letterbook # 51, Microfilm M2287), 548.

626. Willison, 221.

627. Van Horne to Sir Richard Cartwright, July 6, 1899 (MG29 A60, letterbook 56), 583.

628. Van Horne to Sir John Willison, September 24, 1896 (the Willison papers, vol. 46, 33824).

629. D.J. Hall, *Clifford Sifton, vol. 1*, 212.

630. Van Horne to Sir John A. Macdonald, January 28, 1889 (Macdonald papers, vol. 288, Microfilm C 1689, 131915–918).

631. Van Horne to Hon. Edgar Dewdney, March 1, 1892 (CPPL, Letterbook # 39, Microfilm M2277).

632. Vaughan, *The Life and Work of Sir William Van Horne*, 245.

633. Vaughan, *The Life and Work of Sir William Van Horne*, 256.

634. Van Horne to Wilfrid Laurier, January 6, 1899 (MG26 G, vol. 97, Microfilm C762), 2940.

635. Robert Craig Brown and Ramsay Cook, *Canada 1896–1921: A Nation Transformed* (Toronto: McClelland and Stewart, 1974), 35–36.

636. Van Horne to Russell Alger (MG29 A60, vol. 52, personal letterbook, 1897–98), 203.

637. Vaughan, *The Life and Work of Sir William Van Horne*, 257.

638. Van Horne to Sir Charles Tupper, February 17, 1898 (CPPL, Letterbook # 54, Microfilm M2290), 746.

639. Robert M. Stamp, "J.D. Edgar and the Liberal Party: 1876–96" (*Canadian Historical Review,* vol. XLV, No. 2, June 1964), 115; and James Edgar to Van Horne, January 17, 1898 (Van Horne personal corr., Microfilm M7493, 82.5), 254.

640. Lamb, 204.

641. Thomas Shaughnessy to Walter Vaughan, May 8, 1920 (MG30 A130), 3.

642. Malone, 173.

643. "Van's Reserve Pudding" (*Grip,* February 13, 1892).

644. Van Horne to John Willison, April 11, 1896 (MG30 D29, vol. 46), 33811.

645. Van Horne to Sir John Abbott, November 10, 1891 (M26, vol. 2), 484.

646. George Musk, *Canadian Pacific: The Story of the Famous Shipping Line* (London: David & Charles, 1981), 22.

647. Thomas Shaughnessy to Walter Vaughan, May 8, 1920 (MG30 A130).

648. Augustus Bridle, "Baron Shaughnessy" (*Sons of Canada*, Toronto: JM Dent & Sons Ltd., 1916), 55.

649. Bridle, "Baron Shaughnessy," 55.

650. Vaughan, *The Life and Work of Sir William Van Horne*, 259.

651. Tadamada Hayshi to Van Horne, July 29, 1898 (MG29 A60, vol 87, miscellaneous).

652. Van Horne to his wife, May 1, 1899 (MG29 A60, vol. 87, Sir William Van Horne (part 1), 1894–1901).

653. Ibid.

654. Ibid.

655. Vaughan, *The Life and Work of Sir William Van Horne*, 262.

656. Vaughan, *The Life and Work of Sir William Van Horne*, 260.

657. Eagle, 73.

658. Van Horne to Lord Strathcona, February 7, 1899 (MG29 A60, vol. 52, letterbook 1898–99), 150–52.

659. Lamb, 226.

660. Lamb, 176.

661. *The Globe* (Toronto, June 13, 1899).

662. Jesse Edgar Middleton and W. Scott Downs, eds., *National Encyclopedia of Canada* (Toronto: The Dominion Publishing Company, 1935), 82–83.

663. "Concerning the Philosophy of Style," handwritten, undated notes (MG29 A60, vol. 102).

664. Vaughan, *The Life and Work of Sir William Van Horne*, 270.

665. Macnaughtan, "Sir William Van Horne," 239–40.

666. Robert J. Wickenden, "Sir William Van Horne as an Artist and Collector" (typescript, 6, MG29 A60, vol. 101, file Adaline Van Horne estate, 1940–84), 9.

667. Roger Paterson, biographical sketch, (MG29 A60, vol. 102, biographical sketches, n.d., 1915), 5.

668. Vaughan, *The Life and Work of Sir William Van Horne*, 179.

669. Wickenden, "Sir William Van Horne as an Artist and a Collector."

670. Willa Walker, *No Hay Fever & A Railway: Summers in St. Andrews,*

       Canada's First Seaside Resort (Fredericton: Goose Lane Editions, 1989), 96.

671.   Beckles Willson, 55.

672.   Elizabeth Hiscott, "Art and Van Horne" (*The Atlantic Advocate,* January 1977).

673.   Denys Sutton, ed., *Letters of Roger Fry* (London: Chatto & Windus, 1972), vol. 1, 275.

674.   Reported to the author by National Gallery spokeswoman Helen Murphy, February 5, 1996.

675.   Information supplied by Janet Toole, New Brunswick provincial archivist.

676.   Ernest Samuels, *Bernard Berenson: The Making of a Legend* (Cambridge, Mass.: The Belnap Press of Harvard University, 1987), 152.

677.   Van Horne to R.F. Knoedler, 1909 (MG29 A60, vol. 56, personal letterbook, No. 11), 10.

678.   Van Horne to H.V. Meredith, February 1, 1910 (MG29 A60, vol. 56), 457.

679.   Madeleine Fidell Beaufort, Herbert L. Kleinfield, and Jeanne K. Welcher, eds., *The Diaries of Samuel P. Avery, Art Dealer* (New York: Arno Press, 1979), 29.

680.   Van Horne to his wife, March 11, 1911 (MG29 A60, vol. 88, file Sir William Van Horne (part 4), 1910–11)

681.   Van Horne to his wife, April 11, 1911 (MG29 A60, vol. 88, Sir William Van Horne (part 4), 1910–13).

682.   Information supplied by Michael Pantazzi, curator of European art, National Gallery of Canada.

683.   Edgar Andrew Collard, "Sir William Van Horne as an Art Collector" (*Montreal Yesterdays,* Toronto: Longmans Canada, 1962), 258–260.

684.   Janet Brooke, *Discerning Tastes: Montreal Collectors,* 1880–1920 (Montreal: Montreal Museum of Fine Arts, 1989), 20.

685.   Robert J. Wickenden, "Sir William Van Horne as an Artist & Collector", 11; and Oliver Larkin, *Life and Art in America* (New York: Rinehart & Company, 1950), 269.

686.   Biographical sketches (n.d., MG29 A60, vol. 102), 6.

687.   Albert P. Ryder to Van Horne, August 1895 (MG29 A60, vol. 87, miscellaneous file).

688.   Lord Beaverbrook, *Courage: The Story of Sir James Dunn* (Fredericton: Brunswick Press, 1961), 232–33.

689. Brooke, 22.

690. Receipt dated January 5, 1906 (MG29 A60, vol. 87, miscellaneous file).

691. J. Russell Harper, *Painting in Canada A History* (Toronto: University of Toronto Press, 1966), 248.

692. Pringle, 73–74.

693. Pringle, 73.

694. Secretary, Art Association of Montreal, to Van Horne, December 13, 1901 (MG29 A60, vol. 79, chron. corr., 1900–05).

695. Montreal Museum of Fine Arts Annual Report, 1910.

696. M. Ward (?) to Van Horne, December 27, 1912 (MG29 A60, vol. 87, file miscellaneous).

697. Roger Fry to Helen Fry, December 2, 1906, in Sutton, ed., vol. 1, 275.

698. Fry, 40.

699. G. Campbell McInnes (*Winnipeg Free Press*, December 15, 1936), 13.

700. Collard, "Sir William Van Horne as an Art Collector", 257.

701. Vaughan, *The Life and Work of Sir William Van Horne*, 268–69.

702. Collard, "Sir William Van Horne as an Art Collector", 254.

703. Dick Wilbur, ed., *A Collection of Old St. Andrews Sketches* (St. Andrews: E. Williamson, 1983).

704. Brooke, 23.

705. *Encyclopedia Britannica* (Chicago: William Benton, 1970), vol. 18, 358.

706. Unidentified author, Biographical sketches (n.d., 1915, MG29 A60, vol. 102), 6.

707. William Deresiewicz, reviewing *The Great Wave* (*The New York Times Book Review*, July 20, 2003), 7.

708. Van Horne Japanese pottery catalogue (Montreal Museum of Fine Arts archives).

709. Howard Mansfield Reminiscences of Van Horne (NAC, Microfilm M7394: 82.5.896).

710. Wickenden, "Sir William Van Horne as an Artist and Collector," 11.

711. Robert Wickenden, "The Collector" (typescript, MG29 A60, vol. 101, Adaline Van Horne: Estate 1940–1984); and Roger Fry to Helen Fry, in Sutton, ed., vol. 1, 275.

712. H.E. Boucher to Van Horne, August 7, 1914 (MG29 A60, vol. 104, file ship models, 1907–59).

713.	Margaret Van Horne to Mr. Dery, May 14, 1955 (MG29 A60, vol. 104, file ship models, 1907–59).

714.	John Stevens to Margaret Van Horne, February 6, 1948 (MG29 A60, vol. 104, file ship models, 1907–59).

715.	Mary Van Horne's daily journal for 1892 (MG29 A60, vol. 95, Miss Mary Van Horne: Daily Journals 1892).

716.	Paper furnished the author by architect Michael Fish.

717.	"Edward Colonna, 1862–1948," www.mcrwy.com/collectn/wood-pas/mlsw63/colonna.html, summarized from Martin Eidelberg, "E. Colonna" (Dayton, Ohio: The Dayton Art Institute, 1983).

718.	Mary Van Horne's diary (MF29 A60, vol. 95, Mary Van Horne: Daily Journals 1892).

719.	Donald MacKay, *The Square Mile: Merchant Princes of Montreal* (Toronto/Vancouver: Douglas & McIntyre, 1987), 157.

720.	MacKay, 8.

721.	The 1891 population was 256,723, as reported in *Canada 1939: The Official Handbook of Present Conditions and Recent Progress* (Ottawa: Dominion Bureau of Statistics, 1939), 13.

722.	Kathleen Jenkins, *Montreal: Island City of the St. Lawrence* (Garden City: Doubleday & Company, Inc., 1966), 447.

723.	Peter C. Newman, *Canada–1892: Portrait of a Promised Land* (Toronto: Madison Press Books for Penquin Books Canada Limited and McClelland & Stewart Inc., 1992), 17.

724.	Thomas Shaughnessy to Walter Vaughan, May 8, 1920 (MG30, A 130).

725.	Observation of the Rev. Lawrence Clare, quoted in the *Montreal Gazette*, January 26, 1929.

726.	Van Horne to his wife, October 8, 1872 (MG29 A60, vol. 87, file 1867–72 (part 2)).

727.	Young Addie to her father, November 20, 1888 (MG29 A60, vol. 87, file Adeline Van Horne).

728.	Young Addie to her father, April 1, 1888 (MG29 A60, vol. 87, file Adeline Van Horne).

729.	W.A. Fraser to Van Horne, January 16, 1898 (MG29 A60, vol. 87, miscellaneous).

730.	Addie Van Horne to her husband, December 27, 1894 (MG29 A60, vol. 86, Lady Van Horne, 1894–1901).

731.	Ibid.

732.	Sandra Gwynn, *The Private Capital: Ambition and Love in the Age of Macdonald and Laurier* (Toronto: McClelland and Stewart

Limited, 1984), 276.

733. Addie Van Horne to her husband, December 27, 1894 (MG29 A60, vol 86, Lady Van Horne, 1894–1901).

734. Obituary, *Montreal Gazette* (January 25, 1929).

735. Addie Van Horne to Mary Van Horne, January 4, 1886 (MG29 A60, vol. 95, Hurd Family, 1846–1904).

736. Van Horne to his wife (n.d. MG29 A60, vol. 87, W.C. Van Horne, pt. 1).

737. Andrew Sackett, "Inhaling the Salubrious Air: Health and Development in St. Andrews, N.B., 1880–1910" (*Acadiensis*, XXV, 1, Autumn 1995), 55.

738. Sackett, 54.

739. Sackett, 57.

740. Walker, 123.

741. Janet Toole, oral history archivist, New Brunswick, and New Brunswick archival documents, including deed of conveyance and Crown Grant Sheet no. 161.

742. Van Horne to Edinburgh solicitors, March 28, 1915 (MG29 A60, vol. 86, file St. Andrews: Lord Strathcona).

743. Ellen James, "The Education and Training of Edward Maxwell" (*The Architecture of Edward & W.S. Maxwell*, catalogue produced by the Montreal Museum of Fine Arts, 1991), 29.

744. France Gagnon Pratte, *Country Houses For Montrealers 1892–1924: The Architecture of E. and W.S. Maxwell* (Montreal: Meridian Press, 1987), 132.

745. Pratte, 132, 149.

746. Pratte, 134–35; and *The Architecture of Edward & W.S. Maxwell*, 145.

747. Addie Van Horne Jr. to her mother, Easter Sunday 1902 (MG29 A60, vol. 88, Adeline Van Horne (part 2), 1893–1902).

748. Mary Van Horne's daily journal, 1900–02, March 27 and 28, 1902 (MG29 A60, vol. 96); and Addie Van Horne to her mother, Easter Sunday, 1902 (MG29 A60, vol. 88, Adeline Van Horne (part 2), 1893–1902).

749. Van Horne to Castle & Son, July 21, 1910 (MG29 A60, vol. 56, Van Horne personal letterbook, 1909–10, no. 11), 1175–76.

750. Van Horne to Governor Smith, July 8, 1910 (MG29 A60, vol. 56, Van Horne personal letterbook, 1909–10, No, 11), 1155.

751. Van Horne to Edward Maxwell, June 22, 1899 (MG29 A60, vol. 52, Van Horne personal letterbook, 1898–99), 328.

752. Van Horne to W.W. Hubbard, April 4, 1909 (MG29 A60, vol. 73, W.W. Hubbard, 1909–1912).

753. Van Horne to Louis Boissevain, May 10, 1898 (MG29 A60, vol. 69, Boissevain Brothers).

754. Mrs. S. Baines to Lady Van Horne, July 15, 1895 (MG29 A60, vol. 89, (part 3), 1892–96).

755. Unidentified newspaper clipping (MG29 A60, vol. 101, Margaret Van Horne, 1966–82),.

756. Willison, 341.

757. McDonald, 448.

758. MacKay, 170.

759. Mary Van Horne, daily journals, 1893–96 (MG29 A60, vol. 95).

760. Ibid.

761. *The Gazette* (Montreal, June 9, 1906), 5; and Malone, 191.

762. Biographical sketches (n.d., MG29 A60, vol. 102, 1915), 7.

763. Andrew Lycett, *Rudyard Kipling* (London: Weidenfeld & Nicholson, 1999), 378.

764. Wickenden, "Sir William Van Horne as an Artist and Collector," 5.

765. Strouse, 454.

766. Samuel S. McClure to Van Horne, October 13, 1913 (MG29 A60, vol. 74, S.S. McClure, 1909–14).

767. Mary Van Horne, daily journals (MG29 A60, vol. 95).

768. Norah Story, ed., *The Oxford Companion to Canadian History and Literature* (Toronto: Oxford University Press, 1967), 626.

769. Wyatt Eaton to Lady Van Horne, April 27, 1896 (MG29 A60, vol. 89).

770. Charlotte Gray, *Flint & Feather: The Life and Times of E. Pauline Johnson, Tekahionwake* (Toronto: HarperCollins Canada, 2002), 220.

771. Van Horne to General William Washburn, June 30, 1896 (CPPL, letterbook #51, Microfilm M2287),555.

772. Van Horne to General Washburn, December 13, 1899 (MG29 A60, vol 59, outgoing business corr. 1899–1900).

773. Rollin Van N. Hadley, ed., *The Letters of Bernard Berenson and Isabella Stewart Gardner 1887–1924 With Correspondence by Mary Berenson* (Boston: Northeastern University Press, 1989), 504–505.

774. Van Horne to his son, September 3, 1887 (MG29 A60, vol. 87, file 1883–93).

775. Van Horne to his wife, June 24, 1888 (MG29 A60, vol. 87, file 1883–93, part 4).

776. Van Horne to his wife, June 30, 1888 (MG29 A60, vol. 87, file 1883–93, part 4).

777. Van Horne to his wife, July 8, 1888 (MG29 A60, vol. 87, file 1883–93, part 4).

778. Van Horne to his wife, 11 September 1902 (MG29 A60, vol. 87, Sir William Van Horne (part 2), 1902–04).

779. Bennie Van Horne to Anna Hurd, October 28, 1892 (MG29 A60, vol. 95, Anna Hurd: Family corr., 1868–92).

780. Bennie Van Horne to his mother, December 17, 1904 (MG29 A60, vol. 88, file Richard Benedict Van Horne (part 7), 1903–07).

781. Van Horne to his wife, June 1906 (MG29 A60, vol. 87, file 1905–09, part 2).

782. Unidentified biographical sketch (MG29 A60, vol. 102, biographical sketches, n.d. 1915).

783. Van Horne to his wife, December 11, 1909 (MG29 A60, vol. 87, file 1905–09, part 3).

784. Walker, 163.

785. Young Addie to Anna Hurd, May 20, 1889 (MG29 A60, vol. 95, Anna Hurd: Family corr., 1868–1892).

786. Mary Van Horne to her brother, September 3, 1888 (MG29 A60, vol. 87, file Mary Van Hornc).

787. Van Horne to young Addie, July 4, 1888 (MG29 A60,vol. 87, file 1883–93, part 4).

788. Young Addie to her father, April 1, 1888 (MG29 A60, vol. 87, file Adeline Van Horne).

789. Young Addie to her father, November 20, 1888 (MG29 A60, vol. 87, file Adeline Van Horne).

790. Van Horne to O.W. Meysenburg (MG29 A60, vol. 59, outgoing business corr., 1899–1900).

791. C. Lintern Sibbley, "Van Horne and His Cuban Railway" (*Canadian Magazine*, 41, no. 5, September 1913), 444.

792. Meysenburg to Van Horne (n.d., MG29 A60, vol. 60, business corr., 1895–1900 M).

793. Van Horne to Lord Strathcona, February 7, 1899 (MG29 A60, vol. 52, Letterbook, 1898–99), 150.

794. Sibbley, 444.

795. Duncan McDowall, *Quick to the Frontier: Canada's Royal Bank* (Toronto: McClelland and Stewart, 1993), 167.

796. Hugh Thomas, *Cuba: The Pursuit of Freedom* (New York: Harper & Row, 1971), 423.

797. Van Horne to Gonzalo de Quesada, April 21, 1901 (MG29 A60, vol. 76).

798. Katherine Hughes mss. (MG30 D71, vol. 2, file 11(b)).

799. Van Horne to General Alger, November 12, 1898 (MG29 A60, vol. 52, VH personal letterbook, 1898–99), 39.

800. Charles Gauld, *The Last Titan: Percival Farquhar, American Entrepreneur in Latin America* (Stanford: California Institute of International Studies, 1972), 16.

801. Van Horne to Edwin Hanson, January 6, 1900 (Van Horne personal letterbook, 1900–01, MG29 A60, vol. 52).

802. Van Horne to Edwin Hanson, July 24, 1900 (Van Horne personal letterbook, 1900–01, MG29 A60, vol. 52).

803. Theodore D. Regehr, "Sir William Cornelius Van Horne," *The Dictionary of Canadian Biography*, Vol. X1V, 1911–1920 (Toronto: University of Toronto Press, 1998), 1035.

804. Gauld, footnote, 49.

805. Percival Farquhar to C.A. Johnson, October 25, 1902 (MG29 A60, vol. 61, business corr., F (part 2), 1902).

806. Ibid.

807. Van Horne to Farquhar, March 29, 1899 (Van Horne personal letterbook, 1898–99, MG29 A60, vol. 52), 228.

808. Van Horne to Andrew Onderdonk, March 30, 1899 (Van Horne personal letterbook, 1898–99, MG29 A60, vol. 52), 231–33.

809. Katherine Hughes papers (MG30 D71, vol. 2, file 11(b)), 4.

810. Van Horne to Joseph Todd, August 28, 1900 (MG29 A60, vol. 41, file 1, A).

811. Juan C. Santamarina, "The Cuba Company and the Expansion of American Business in Cuba, 1898–1915" (*Business History Review*, vol. 74, no. 1, spring 2000), 44–45.

812. James Hitchman, *Leonard Wood and Cuban Independence, 1898–1902.* (The Hague: Martinus Nijhoff, 1971), 69.

813. Van Horne to General Wood, March 6, 1900 (MG29 A60, vol. 52, letterbook, 1899–1900).

814. Vaughan, *The Life and Work of Sir William Van Horne*, 281; Gauld, 29; and Van Horne to Joseph Todd, August 28, 1900 (MG29 A60, vol. 41, file 1, A).

815. Gauld, 29.

816. Van Horne to A.A. Boissevain, April 28, 1900 (MG29 A60, vol. 52), 348.

817. Van Horne to H.M. Whitney (MG29 A60, vol. 59, file outgoing

corr., 1899–1900).

818. Van Horne to Senor da Galda, March 6, 1900 (MG29 A60, vol. 52, personal letterbook, 1899–1900), 207.

819. Van Horne to Edwin Post, June 23, 1900 (MG29 A60, vol. 52), 463.

820. M. Josephson, *The Robber Barons: The Great American Capitalists, 1861–1903* (New York: Harcourt, Brace and Company, 1934), 343.

821. Mackay to Van Horne (n.d., MG29 A60, vol. 60, business corr., 1895–1900 M).

822. Van Horne to J.J. Hill, April 15, 1900 (J.J. Hill papers, general correspondence, April 14–16, 1900).

823. Kate Reed to Van Horne, December 5, 1905 (M7494: 82.5.492).

824. Vaughan, *The Life and Work of Sir William Van Horne*, 282.

825. Vaughan, *The Life and Work of Sir William Van Horne*, 282–83.

826. Van Horne to Grenville Dodge, June 8, 1900 (MG29 A60, vol. 52, personal letterbook), 422.

827. Van Horne to Joseph Todd, January 2, 1901 (MG29 A60, vol. 1, file 1).

828. Van Horne to Joseph Todd, August 28, 1900 (MG29 A60, vol. 41, file 1).

829. Van Horne to Joseph Todd, April 8, 1902 (MG29 A60, vol. 1, file 3).

830. Farquhar to Van Horne, July 10, 1902 (MG29 A60, vol. 61, business corr. (F pt. 1), 1902).

831. Bennie Van Horne to his father, March 6, 1901 (MG29 A60, vol. 60, business corr., 1898–1901).

832. Fry, 39.

833. *New York Times* (March 30, 1900), 8.

834. Van Horne to the governor of the province of Santa Clara, October 3, 1900 (MG29 A60, vol. 1, file 1).

835. Van Horne to Senor Diaz, October 2, 1900 (MG29 A60, vol. 1, file 1).

836. Van Horne to Joseph Todd, August 28, 1900 (MG29 A60, vol. 41, file 1); and memorandum prepared for Robert Fleming (MG29 A60, vol. 101, Van Horne Estate: Cuba 1902–1957).

837. Van Horne to Senator Proctor, June 24, 1900 (MG29 A60, vol 52, VH letterbook, 1899–1900), 459.

838. Van Horne to Joseph Todd, August 28, 1900 (MG29 A60, vol. 41, file 1, letterbook), 2.

839. Van Horne to M.L. Diaz, October 2, 1900 (MG29 A60, vol. 1, file 1).

840. Miller Smith's survey report (MG29 A60, vol. 70, The Cuba Company, 1900–13).

841. Van Horne to Meysenburg (MG19 A60, vol. 59, outgoing business corr., 1899–1900).

842. Van Horne to R.G. Ward, May 26, 1902 (MG29 A60, vol. 1, file 3), 685.

843. Memorandum for Doctor Justiz (MG29 A60, vol. 102, biographical sketches).

844. Van Horne to Miller Smith, September 1, 1900 (MG29 A60, vol. 41 file 1).

845. Van Horne to Farquhar, October 5, 1900 (MG29 A60, vol. 1, file 1); and Gauld, 30

846. Van Horne to Horatio Rubens, October 23, 1900 (MG29 A60, vol. 1, file 1), 107.

847. Van Horne to Grenville Dodge, June 17, 1902 (MG29 A60, vol. 2, file 1), 1.

848. Van Horne to Farquhar, July 24, 1900 (Cuba Company letterbook, No. 1, MG29 A60, vol. 1).

849. Ibid.

850. Van Horne to the governor of the province of Santa Clara, October 3, 1900 (MG29 A60, vol. 1, file 1).

851. Van Horne to E.F. Curry, July 25, 1900 (MG29 A60, vol. 1, file 1).

852. Booklet relating to construction in the Western Division (MG29 A60, vol. 9, 9–16 general corr., W, January–September 1902).

853. M.C. Urquhart and K.A.H. Buckley, eds., *Historical Statistics of Canada* (Toronto: The Macmillan Company of Canada Ltd., 1965), 111, table Series D471–484.

854. Van Horne to C.A. Johnson, September 29, 1900 (MG29 A60, vol. 41, file 1), 73.

855. Van Horne to Miller Smith, September 29, 1900 (MG29 A60, vol. 41. file 1), 68.

856. Van Horne to F.D. Underwood, December 24, 1900 (MG29 A60, personal letterbook, 1900–01), 282.

857. Van Horne to Gonzalo de Quesada, July 16, 1901 (MG30 A12); and Van Horne to Grenville Dodge, April 7, 1902 (MG29 A60, vol. 1, file 3), 631.

858. Van Horne to Quesada, July 16, 1901 (MG30 A12).

859. *The Ottawa Journal* (August 2, 1901).

860. Letter to E. Alexander, July 18, 1901 (MG29 A60, vol. 56), 709.

861. Van Horne to his wife, December 1, 1900 (MG29 A60, vol. 87, file 1894–1900).

862. G.R. Ward to Van Horne, July 23, 1901 (MG29 A60, vol. 70, the Cuba Company, 1900–1913).

863. *New York Times* (November 29, 1900), 2.

864. Van Horne to his wife, December 1, 1900 (MG29 A60, vol. 87, file 1894–1901).

865. *New York Times* (December 16, 1900), 5.

866. Ibid.

867. Les Standiford, *Last Train to Paradise: Henry Flagler and the Spectacular Rise and Fall of the Railroad That Crossed an Ocean* (New York: Crown Publishers, 2002), 38–39.

868. Van Horne personal letterbook, 1899–1900 (MG29 A60, vol. 52), 285.

869. Bennie to his father, January 14, 1901 (MG29 A60, vol. 87, file R.B. Van Horne).

870. Van Horne to General Wood, August 21, 1900 (MG29 A60, vol. 1), 22.

871. Hitchman, 72–73.

872. Gauld, footnote 13, 43.

873. Van Horne to General Wood, March 11, 1901 (MG29 A60, vol. 1, file 2).

874. Van Horne to Joseph Todd, May 24, 1902 (MG29 A60, vol. 1, Cuba Company letterbook, No. 3), 662–63.

875. Gauld, 33.

876. Van Horne to Senator Proctor, February 20, 1901 (MG29 A60, vol. 1, file 1); and Van Horne to Farquhar, February 8, 1901 (MG29 A60, vol. 1, file 1).

877. Van Horne to Farquhar, February 8, 1901 (MG29 A60, vol. 1, file 1).

878. Van Horne to Dodge, February 14, 1901 (MG29 A60, vol. 1, file 1).

879. Van Horne to Elihu Root, February 22, 1901 (Cuba Company letterbook, No. 1, MG29 A60, vol. 60).

880. Van Horne to his wife, January 28, 1902 (MG29 A60, vol. 87, file 1902–04).

881. Van Horne to his wife, January 28, 1902 (MG29 A60, vol. 87, file 1902–04, part 2).

882. Van Horne to his wife, February 13, 1902 (MG29 A60, vol. 87, file 1902–04, part 2).

883. Van Horne to Joseph Todd, May 24, 1901 (MG29 A60, vol. 1, Cuba Company letterbook, no. 3), 662.

884. Sibbley; and Vaughan, *The Life and Work of Sir William Van Horne*, 291.

885. Van Horne to Farquhar, August 26, 1901 (MG29 A60, vol. 1, file 2).

886. Van Horne to General Wood, July 21, 1910 (MG29 A60, vol. 5, Cuba Company letterbook No. 13).

887. Leonard Wood to Katherine Hughes, June 7, 1918 (MG30 D71, vol. 1, corr. Pearce–Worley.)

888. Van Horne to Joseph Todd, May 20, 1901 (MG29 A60, vol. 1, file 2).

889. Hughes mss. (MG29 A60, vol. 102), 286.

890. Van Horne to General Dodge, April 6, 1901 (MG29 A60, vol. 1, file 2).

891. Van Horne to F.L. Govett, February 1, 1902 (MG29 A60, vol. 1, file 3).

892. Vaughan, *The Life and Work of Sir William Van Horne*, 293.

893. Van Horne to F.L. Govett, February 1, 1902 (MG29 A60, vol. 1, file 3).

894. Ibid.

895. Frank Steinhart to General Wood, June 19, 1902, and June 25, 1902 (General Leonard Wood papers, vol. 206, 1902, Library of Congress).

896. Van Horne to Senator Bravo, August 22, 1902 (MG29 A60, vol. 2, file 1).

897. Armstrong and Nelles, 153.

898. Gauld, 35 and 36.

899. Gauld, 35 and 36.

900. Van Horne to Morgan Jones, July 24, 1902 (MG29 A60, vol. 2, file 1).

901. Van Horne to General Alger, January 15, 1902 (MG29 A60, vol. 53, personal letterbook), 76.

902. Van Horne to General Dodge, June 17, 1902 (MG29 A60, vol. 2, file 1); and Van Horne to de Quesada, June 21, 1902 (MG30, A12).

903. (MG29 A60, vol. 2, file 1, July 17, 1902), 109.

904. Macnaughtan, 248–49; and Sibbley, 446.

905. Extract from board minutes of the Cuba Company, March 26, 1902 (MG29 A60, vol. 1, file 3), 605.

906. Ibid.
907. Van Horne to his wife, November 12, 1902 (MG29 A60, vol. 87, file 1902–04, part 2).
908. Ibid.
909. Van Horne to his wife, November 21, 1902 (MG29 A60, vol. 87, file 1902–04, part 2).
910. Van Horne to his wife, November 27, 1902 (MG29 A60, vol. 87, file 1902–04, part 2).
911. MG29 A60, vol. 41, file 25.
912. Addie Van Horne to her father, November 26, 1902 (MG29 A60, vol. 87).
913. Memo for Robert Fleming, December 21, 1903 (MG29 A60, vol. 101, Van Horne estate: Cuba 1902–03).
914. Van Horne to General Alger, February 9, 1903 (MG29 A60, vol. 53, personal letterbook, 1901–03), 38.
915. Gauld, 37.
916. Gauld, 37.
917. Bennie to his mother (n.d., MG29 A60, vol. 88, file R.B. Van Horne (part 7), 1903–07).
918. Van Horne to his wife, January 27, 1903 (MG29 A60, vol. 87, file 1902–04, part 2).
919. Mansfield's reminiscences of Van Horne (NAC, Microfilm M 7394: 82.5.896).
920. Van Horne to his wife, January 20, 1906 (MG29 A60, vol. 87, file 1905–09, part 3).
921. MG29 A30, vol. 5, file 3, 629–30.
922. Florence Stoddard, "The Canadian Invasion of Cuba" (*Busyman's Magazine*, vol. XIX, no. 4), 38–39.
923. Bennie Van Horne to his mother (n.d., MG29 A60, vol. 88, file R.B. Van Horne (part 7), 1903–07).
924. Van Horne to D.A. Galdos, May 3, 1910 (MG29 A60, vol. 5, Cuba Company letterbook, No. 13, 762–763).
925. Van Horne to Dr. Desvernine, July 28, 1910 (MG29 A60, vol. 5, file 2).
926. Van Horne to Ambrosio de Grillo, September 16, 1909 (MG29 A60, vol. 5, Cuba Co. letterbook, no. 13), 274.
927. Van Horne to D.A. Galdos, August 28, 1914 (MG29 A60, vol. 28, file 4).
928. Van Horne to D.A. Galdos, March 30, 1908 (MG29 A60, vol. 41, file 26).

929. Stoddard, 33–39; and Van Horne to D.A. Galdos, April 7, 1908 (MG29 A60, vol. 5, file 1).

930. Van Horne to Professor John Gifford, February 8, 1901 (MG29 A60, vol. 1, file 1), 422.

931. Van Horne to the editor of *Tropical Life*, February 26, 1911 (MG29 A60, vol. 28).

932. Van Horne to Robert Fleming, July 9, 1908 (MG29 A60, vol. 5, file 1).

933. Katherine Hughes mss. (MG30 D71, vol. 2, file 11(c).1), 308.

934. Van Horne to James Creelman, September 14, 1909 (MG29 A60, vol. 5, file 3), 262.

935. Van Horne to James Creelman, September 14, 1909 (MG29 A60, vol. 5, file 3), 263.

936. Van Horne to Gonzalo de Quesada, July 16, 1910 (MG30 A12).

937. Van Horne to *Star* editor, July 28, 1910 (MG29 A60, vol. 56, personal letterbook, no. 11), 1195–96.

938. McDowall, *Quick to the Frontier*, 179.

939. Van Horne to Robert Fleming, January 24, 1910 (MG29 A60, vol. 5, file 3), 607–08.

940. Van Horne to Dr. Pablo Desvernine, July 13, 1910 (MG29 A60, vol. 5, file 2), 901.

941. Van Horne to Dr. Desvernine, July 13, 1910 (MG29 A60, vol. 5, file 2), 896.

942. MG29 A60, vol. 27. file 21.

943. Margaret Vince, *Sir William Van Horne and Canadian Economic Relations in the Caribbean, 1900–1915* (M.A. thesis, Smith College, 1949), 74.

944. Cuba Railroad Company earnings 1910 (MG29 A60, vol. 27, file 21).

945. Bliss, 294.

946. Van Horne to de Quesada, July 16, 1910 (MG30 A12).

947. Van Horne to de Quesada, November 28, 1910 (MG 30 A12).

948. Van Horne to de Quesada, April 21, 1909 (MG30 A12).

949. A.B. Farquhar to Van Horne, October 15, 1912 (MG29 A60, vol. 71, file A. B Farquahr, 1910–1912).

950. Van Horne to de Quesada, July 16, 1910 (MG30 A12).

951. Van Horne to Edward Clouston, October 26, 1903 (MG29 A60, vol. 53, personal letterbook, 1901–03), 565.

952. MG29 A60, vol. 41, files 9 and 13.

953. Van Horne to General Alger, November 12, 1898 (MG29 A60,

vol. 52, personal letterbook, 1898–99), 39.

954. Kate Reed to Van Horne, September 5, 1905 (Van Horne personal papers, Microfilm M7494, 82.5.492).

955. Regehr, "Sir William Cornelius Van Horne," 1035.

956. Hamilton and Shields, eds., 169.

957. Van Horne to Sir John Willison, May 14, 1897 (MG30 D29, vol. 46, folder 315, 33833–34).

958. Van Horne to Horatio Rubens, September 8, 1900 (Cuba Company letterbook No. 1, MG29 A60), 46–47.

959. Richard Saunders, Jr., *Merging Lines: American Railroads 1900–1970* (DeKalb, Illinois: Northern Illinois University Press, 2001), 32–33.

960. Van Horne to A.B. Farquhar, August 6, 1910 (MG29 A60, vol. 71, A.B Farquhar 1910–12).

961. Sessional paper, no. 31, vol. 17, 1884, no. 9.

962. Van Horne to Col. Richard Morgan, August 30, 1901 (MG29 A60, letterbook 56), 725–26.

963. Van Horne to Wilfrid Laurier, January 6, 1899 (MG26 G, vol. 97, Microfilm C762), 29441.

964. Van Horne to Wilfrid Laurier, January 6, 1899 (MG26 G, vol. 97, Microfilm C762), 29440.

965. Van Horne to Messrs. Richards & Akroyd, May 30, 1905 (MG29 A60, vol. 75, New York Block: Vancouver Property 1905–1909); and CPR solicitor, Winnipeg to Van Horne, November 20, 1906 (MG29 A60, vol. 75, Norwood Improvement Company).

966. Van Horne to E.B. Osler, January 24, 1900 (MG29 A60, vol. 52, 1899–1900); and Vaughan, *The Life and Work of Sir William Van Horne*, 262.

967. Van Horne to Thomas Skinner, June 20, 1894 (MG29 A60, vol. 52, personal letterbook, 1893–96), 72; and Van Horne to Mr. McGraw, July 16, 1895 (MG29 A60, vol. 52, personal letterbook, 1893–96).

968. Bliss, 323; and Guy Gaudreau, "Progress on Paper" (*Horizon Canada*, vol. 9, no. 107), 2561.

969. Rodney E. Bell, *A Life of Russell Alger, 1836–1907* (University of Michigan PH.D thesis, 1975), 324.

970. Van Horne to H.R. Sperling, July 11, 1896 (CPPL, Letterbook #51, Microfilm M2287), 628.

971. Morris Zaslow, *The Opening of the Canadian North, 1870–1914* (Toronto: McClelland and Stewart, 1971), 174.

972. Van Horne to Sir Wilfrid Laurier, March 7, 1898 (MG26G, vol. 68, Microfilm C754), 21317.

973. Van Horne to Senator Proctor, July 26, 1900 (MG29 A60, vol. 52, personal letterbook, 1900–01), 29.

974. Van Horne to Russell Alger, June 25, 1902 (MG29 A60, vol. 53, personal letterbook, 1901–03), 324–25.

975. Vaughan, *The Life and Work of Sir William Van Horne*, 311.

976. Van Horne to Percival Farquhar, January 4, 1910 (MG29 A60, vol. 56, personal letterbook 1910–12), 171.

977. "The Death of Sir William Van Horne" (*Canadian Railway and Marine World*, October 1917), 380.

978. Van Horne to Alger, September 3, 1898 (Van Horne letterbook 1897–98, MG29 A60, vol. 52), 456.

979. Van Horne to H.H. McLean, January 13, 1899 (MG29 A60, vol. 52, personal letterbook, 1898–99), 124–25.

980. Van Horne to G.F. Underwood, May 4, 1915 (MG29 A60, vol. 72, Grand Falls Co.: G.F. Underwood, 1912–1915).

981. Van Horne to H.A. Powell, July 24, 1915 (MG29 A60, vol. 72, Grand Falls Co.: H. A. Powell).

982. Armstrong and Nelles, 21.

983. Van Horne to Percival Farquhar, August 22, 1903 (MG29 A60, vol. 53, personal letterbook, No. 4), 507–08.

984. Van Horne to Percival Farquhar, September 10, 1903 (MG29 A60, vol. 53, personal letterbook, no. 4), 545.

985. MG29 A60, vol. 50, file 43.

986. Van Horne to Farquhar, May 23, 1911 (MG29 A60, vol. 56, personal letterbook 1910–12), 748; and Robert Fleming to Sir E. Stacey (?) (n.d., MG29 A60, vol. 72, Robert Fleming, 1907–1912).

987. Robert Fleming to Van Horne, August 19, 1910 (MG29 A60, vol. 72, Robert Fleming, 1907–1912).

988. Van Horne to Minor Keith, January 6, 1912 (MG29 A60, vol. 50, file 39).

989. Van Horne to F.G. Williamson, November 4, 1906 (MG29 A60, vol. 54, letterbook 8), 107.

990. Van Horne to Robert Fleming, April 20, 1907 (MG29 A60, vol. 72, Robert Fleming, 1907–1912).

991. Van Horne to Percival Farquhar, October 31, 1906 (MG29 A30, vol. 54, letterbook No. 8), 96.

992. Van Horne to Percival Farquhar, October 30, 1906 (MG29 A60,

vol. 54, letterbook No. 8), 89–90.

993. Van Horne to Percival Farquhar, October 31, 1906 (MG29 A60, vol. 54, letterbook No. 8), 96.

994. Van Horne to Percival Farquhar, March 26, 1907 (MG29 A60, vol. 54, letterbook No. 8), 530.

995. Van Horne to Robert Fleming, December 26, 1907 (MG29 A60, vol. 72, Robert Fleming, 1907–1912).

996. MG29 A60, vol. 69, Brazilian Railway Co.: Annual Reports, 1911–1912.

997. Gauld, 161.

998. Theodore D. Regehr, "James Ross," *Dictionary of Canadian Biography*, vol. XIV, 1911–1920 (Toronto: University of Toronto Press, 1998), 898.

999. J. Castell Hopkins, *The Canadian Annual Review of Public Affairs 1907* (Toronto: The Annual Review Publishing Company Limited, 1908), 56.

1000. Van Horne to Lord Grey, September 2, 1907 (MG26G, vol. 476, Microfilm C851, 128549).

1001. Ibid.

1002. *The Gazette* (Montreal, July 31, 1907), 1.

1003. Van Horne to Lord Grey, September 2, 1907 (MG26G, vol. 476, Microfilm C851, 128552–53).

1004. Van Horne's secretary (?) to E. Alexander, December 14, 1914 (MGA60, vol. 68, E. Alexander).

1005. Van Horne to Robert Borden, May 12, 1913 (Borden papers, Microfilm C4202), 2750.

1006. Van Horne to Walter Whigham, September 3, 1913 (MG29 A60, vol. 34, file 348); and Valerie Knowles, *First Person: A Biography of Senator Cairine Wilson* (Toronto: Dundurn Press, 1988), 30.

1007. Vaughan, *The Life and Work of Sir William Van Horne*, 263.

1008. Strouse, 543–45.

1009. Hopkins, 215.

1010. Armstrong and Nelles, 21.

1011. Vaughan, *The Life and Work of Sir William Van Horne*, 233.

1012. R.B. Fleming, *The Railway King of Canada: Sir William Mackenzie, 1849–1923* (Vancouver: UBC Press, 1991), 22.

1013. Fleming, 30.

1014. J. Edward Martin, *On a Streak of Lightning: Electric Railways in Canada* (British Columbia: Studio E, 1994), 133.

1015. List of shareholders, Winnipeg Electric Railway 1912 (MG29 A60, vol. 78).

1016. Van Horne to E.S. Clouston, April 9, 1894 (MG29 A60, vol. 53, personal letterbook, 1893–96), 43.

1017. Armstrong and Nelles, 88.

1018. Armstrong and Nelles, 38.

1019. Armstrong and Nelles, 87–88.

1020. Van Horne to Hon. William Taft, March 17, 1904 (MG29 A60, vol. 75).

1021. Van Horne to Charles H. Allen, March 6, 1904 (MG29 A60, vol. 75, Philippine Railways 1900–1904).

1022. Vaughan, *The Life and Work of Sir William Van Horne*, 308.

1023. Official document (MG29 A60, vol. 69, Argentine Railways, 1901–13).

1024. MG29 A60, vol. 68, E. Alexander 1910–15.

1025. Armstrong and Nelles, 43.

1026. Duncan McDowall, "Pearson Frederick Stark" (*Dictionary of Canadian Biography*, vol. XIV, Toronto: University of Toronto Press, 1998), 830–31.

1027. McDowall, *The Light*, 43.

1028. McDowall, *The Light*, 137.

1029. Van Horne to A.S. Richardson August 10, 1902 (MG29 A60, vol. 59), 259.

1030. Van Horne to the secretary–treasurer, St. Clements, October 20, 1899 (MG29 A60, vol. 52), 1.

1031. Joseph Maw to Fred W. Barber, June 20, 1899 (MG29 A60, vol. 84, East Selkirk: Purchase 1898–99).

1032. James Yule to Van Horne, November 16, 1909 (MG29 A60, vol. 84, East Selkirk: James Yule (part 1), 1900–09).

1033. Janet Maclellan Toole, "A Viking Saga of the Twentieth Century" (*Our Stories: Heritage 94*, Fredericton: The Province of New Brunswick, 1994), 96.

1034. Francis McColl to Van Horne, July 29, 1912 (MG29 A60, vol. 70, Canadian Sardine Company, finances 1912), 18.

1035. Van Horne to Francis McColl, November 29, 1912 (MG29 A60, vol. 70, Canadian Sardine Company finances 1912), 18.

1036. Circular letter, July 25, 1913 (MG29 A60, vol. 70, Canadian Sardine Company Ltd. Gen. Corr., 1913–14).

1037. Duncan McDowall, "William Maxwell Aitken, 1st Baron Beaverbrook" (*The Canadian Encyclopedia*, 2nd ed., vol. 1), 47.

1038. Gregory Marchildon, "Max Aitken and the Great Laurier Boom" (*Canada, Confederation to Present*, Edmonton: Chinook Multimedia, 2001), screen 20.

1039. Sir Joseph Pope, *The Tour of Their Royal Highnesses The Duke and Duchess of Cornwall and York Through the Dominion of Canada in the Year 1901* (Ottawa: S.E. Dawson, the King's Printer, 1903), 29-31; The *Gazette* (Montreal, September 19, 1901), 1; and McDonald, 448.

1040. Arthur Cecil Bell, Diary of the Visit of the Duke and Duchess of York to Canada, September-October 1901, file 2, MG30, E536.

1041. Pope, *The Tour of Their Royal Highnesses*, 29–31; Mary Van Horne, daily journal, MG29 A60, vol. 96; McDonald, 448.

1042. Van Horne personal papers, Microfilm M 7494, 82.5.490.

1043. Ibid.

1044. Van Horne to Beckles Willson, September 7, 1914 (MG30 D5, file Beckles Willson, corr., gen. Strathcona, 1897–1915).

1045. Doug Mackey, "Ship Canal Planned for North Bay Area Came Close to Realization a Century Ago" (*Community Voices*, May 31, 2002, reproduced on the Internet); and D.J. Hall, *Clifford Sifton*, vol. 2, 327.

1046. Van Horne to Wilfrid Laurier, July 17, 1907 (MG26G, vol. 467, Microfilm C849), 126364.

1047. Vaughan, *The Life and Work of Sir William Van Horne*, 332.

1048. The *Gazette* (Montreal, April 26, 1910).

1049. R.W. Prittle to Van Horne, September 3, 1912 (MG29 A60, vol. 75, miscell., 1909–12).

1050. Van Horne to Wilfrid Laurier, July 20, 1903 (the Laurier papers, Microfilm C802), 75263–64.

1051. Kalman, 651.

1052. France Vanlaethem, "Beautification Versus Modernization" in *Montreal Metropolis 1880–1930*, edited by Isabelle Gournay and France Vanlaethem, Canadian Centre for Architecture (Toronto: Stoddart Publishing, 1998), 137, 140.

1053. Van Horne to W.D. Lighthall, July 30, 1910 (MG29 A60, vol. 56, Van Horne personal letterbook, No. 11), 1206.

1054. Jenkins, 436.

1055. Van Horne to W.D. Lighthall, July 30, 1910 (MG29 A60, vol. 56, Van Horne personal letterbook no. 11), 1206–07.

1056. Ibid.

1057. Vaughan, *The Life and Work of Sir William Van Horne*, 344.

1058. *National Encyclopedia of Canadian Biography* (Toronto: Dominion Publishing Company, 1935), 83.

1059. Margaret W. Westley, *Remembrance of Grandeur: The Anglo-Protestant Elite in Montreal*, 73; and Westley, *A Retrospect* (Montreal: Old Girls' Association of Miss Edgar's and Miss Cramp's School, 1984), 17.

1060. Van Horne to Cecil Carsley, August 28, 1909 (MG29 A60, vol. 56, Van Horne personal letterbook, No. 11 (1909–10)), 31.

1061. Van Horne's wife to Van Horne, February 1, 1913 (MG29 A60, vol. 86, file Lady Van Horne, 1913–15).

1062. Van Horne to Bennie Van Horne, January 24, 1913 (MG29 A60, vol. 94, file Sir William Van Horne, 1898–1913).

1063. Van Horne daily journal (McCord Museum, Montreal).

1064. G.M. Fairchild to Van Horne, April 1900 (MG29 A60, vol. 60, business corr. F, 1898–1900).

1065. Richard Harlan to Van Horne, October 4, 1912 (MG29 A60, vol. 73).

1066. Vaughan, *The Life and Work of Sir William Van Horne*, 380.

1067. Bennie Van Horne to his mother, July 24, 1891 (MG29 A60, vol. 88., file Richard Benedict Van Horne (pt. 1), n.d., 1882–92).

1068. Van Horne to his wife, March 12, 1906 (MG29 A60, vol. 87, file 1905–09, part 3).

1069. "May [sic] Humphry Ward," The National Archives Learning Curve, www.spartacus.schoolnet.co.uk.Wward.htm

1070. Bennie Van Horne to father, March 6, 1901 (MG29 A60, vol. 60, Van Horne business corr., 1898–1901).

1071. MG29 A60, vol. 102, biographical sketches, n.d. 1915.

1072. Ibid.

1073. *The Joliet News*, July 6, 1912, 6.

1074. *Joliet Evening Herald*, July 5, 1912, 3.

1075. Vaughan, *The Life and Work of Sir William Van Horne*, 354.

1076. Brown and Cook, 180.

1077. *The Gazette*, Montreal, 1 February 1911, 1.

1078. MG29 A60, vol. 102, Sir William Van Horne, Reciprocity Speech.

1079. Vaughan, *The Life and Work of Sir William Van Horne*, 347.

1080. Van Horne to his wife, March 27, 1911 (MG29 A60, vol. 88, Sir William Van Horne (pt. 4) 1910–1913).

1081. Joseph Gilder, "Recollections of the late Sir William Van Horne" (The *New York Times*, September 19, 1915), 20.

1082.   J.F. Tufts to Robert Borden, October 5, 1911 (Microfilm C4422, Borden papers, vol. 253), 142686.

1083.   MG29 A60, vol. 102, Sir William Van Horne Reciprocity Speech.

1084.   C.L. Sibley to (?) Dewar, February 24, 1911 (MG29 A60, vol. 76).

1085.   Robert Borden to Van Horne, September 23, 1911 (MG29 A60, vol. 76)

1086.   Gilder, 20.

1087.   Van Horne to Robert Borden, September 24, 1911 (Microfilm C4199, Borden papers, vol. 6), 630.

1088.   Ibid.

1089.   Ibid, 632-35.

1090.   Van Horne to Robert Borden, February 6, 1912 (Borden papers, Microfilm C 4234, vol. 43), 19608.

1091.   J.F. Tufts to Robert Borden, October 5, 1911 (Microfilm C4422, Borden papers, vol. 253), 142686.

1092.   Van Horne to Robert Borden, February 7, 1914 (MG29 A60, vol. 71, file Family Desertion & Non-Support Law).

1093.   MG29 A60, vol. 102, biographical sketches, n.d., 1915.

1094.   C.M. Keys, "American Builders in Canada"(*The World's Work*, January 1910, vol. XIX, # 3), 12476.

1095.   Van Horne to Beckles Willson (MG29 A60, vol. 58, personal letterbook), 532.

1096.   Van Horne to the editor of the *Daily Mail & Empire*, August 21, 1900 (MG29 A60, vol. 52, personal letterbook), 56.

1097.   Van Horne to Warren Hilton, October 2, 1913 (Van Horne personal corr., Microfilm M7494, 82.5.708).

1098.   MG29 A60, vol. 102, biographical sketches, n.d., 1915.

1099.   Sam Hughes to Van Horne, September 29, 1911 (MG29 A60, vol. 72, H: miscell., 1909–12).

1100.   Sam Hughes to Van Horne, April 30, 1913 (MG29 A60, vol. 69, H: miscell., 1909–1912).

1101.   Vaughan, *The Life and Work of Sir William Van Horne*, 357.

1102.   "Ormath (Ormazd) to Zarathustra" (MG29 A60, vol. 102, file Sir William Van Horne, "Zarathustra.")

1103.   Van Horne to Lord Strathcona, February 7, 1899 (MG29 A60, vol. 52, letterbook 1898–99), 150.

1104.   Van Horne to Otto Meysenburg (MG29 A60, vol. 52, personal letterbook, 1897–98), 336.

1105.   Van Horne to Sir Robert Borden, June 30 1915 (Borden papers, Microfilm C4308, vol. 60, 29660-61).

1106   Vaughan, *The Life and Work of Sir William Van Horne*, 358.

1107.   Van Horne to E.C. Smith, December 23, 1913 (MG29 A60, vol. 78, file E.C. Smith, 1909–14).

1108.   Van Horne to George Whigham, December 26, 1913 (MG29 A60, vol. 34, file 348, George Whigham, 1911–14).

1109.   Van Horne to W.M. Noble, 31 January 1914, MG29 A60, vol. 70, Canadian Sardine Co., General 1913-14.

1110.   Vaughan, *The Life and Work of Sir William Van Horne*, 360.

1111.   Van Horne to his wife, 4 June 1914, MG29 A60, vol. 88, file Sir William Van Horne (pt. 5), 1914-15.

1112.   Van Horne to his grandson, 21 June 1914, MG29 A60, vol. 95, file WCC Van Horne family corr. 1909, 14.

1113.   Augustus Bridle, "Sir William Van Horne," *Sons of Canada* (Toronto: J.M. Dent & Sons, 1916), 201.

1114.   Bridle, "Sir William Van Horne," 201.

1115.   Van Horne to Samuel McClure, January 31, 1910 (MG29 A60, vol. 74, S.S. McClure, 1909–14).

1116.   J. Klechzkowski to Van Horne, July 26, 1913 (MG29 A60, vol, 87, file 1905–09, pt. 3).

1117.   Van Horne to Beckles Willson, September 7, 1914 (MG30 D5, file Beckles Willson corr., gen. Strathcona, 1897–1915).

1118.   Macbeth, 231.

1119.   MG29 A60m vol. 96, file Sir William Van Horne: Illness 1914.

1120.   Van Horne to his wife, May 13, 1915 (MG29 A60, vol. 88, file Sir William Van Horne (pt. 5), 1914–15.

1121.   Van Horne to Donald Macmaster, July 22, 1915 (MG29 A30, vol. 74, file Donald Macmaster 1909–15).

1122.   Van Horne to Robert Borden, June 30, 1915 (Borden papers, Microfilm C4308, vol. 60, 29660).

1123.   Van Horne to Robert Borden, July 9, 1915 (Borden papers, Microfilm C4308, vol. 60, 29671).

1124.   Richard Van Horne to his wife (n.d., MG29 A60, vol. 95, file R.B. Van Horne 1915–16).

1125.   Van Horne's private secretary to Percival Farquhar, August 26, 1915 (MG29 A60, vol 71, file Percival Farquhar, 1909–15).

1126.   Vaughan, *The Life and Work of Sir William Van Horne*, 368.

1127.   Vaughan, *The Life and Work of Sir William Van Horne*, 378.

1128.   The *Gazette* (Montreal, September 15, 1915), 9.

1129.   "The Death of Sir William Van Horne" (*Canadian Railway and Marine World*, October 1915), 377; and John Whiteside,

"Queen knighted railroad tycoon from Joliet" (*The Herald News,* on the Internet).

1130. Vaughan, *The Life and Work of Sir William Van Horne,* 381.

1131. Iris Origo, *Images & Shadows: Part of a Life* (Boston: David R. Godine, 1999), 256.

1132. The *Gazette* (Montreal, January 25, 1929).

1133. Walker, 163.

1134. Walker, 163–64.

1135. A.J. Belanger to Louis A. Cormier, December 21, 1979 (MG29 A60, vol. 101, Adeline Van Horne estate, 1940–84).

1136. From typewritten notes in a dossier on the Van Horne mansion compiled by Michael Fish and presented to the author.

1137. Oscar Zanetti and Alejandro Garcia, *Sugar & Railroads: A Cuban History, 1837–1959* (Chapel Hill: the University of North Carolina Press, 1998), 292–94.

1138. Zanetti and Garcia, 384.

Index